P9-CEQ-759

THE ROUGH GUIDE TO
NEW YORK
CITY

**ROUGH
GUIDES**

This sixteenth edition updated by
Sarah Hull, Stephen Keeling and Andrew Rosenberg

Contents

OPPOSITE MANHATTAN BRIDGE FROM DUMBO PREVIOUS PAGE THE CHRYSLER BUILDING

Introduction to
New York City

For dynamism, cultural impact and sheer diversity, New York City is unbeatable. High finance, art, architecture, music, food... it's all here, in plenitude and peak form. You can eat or drink your way through the cuisines of the world, drape yourself in fast fashion or couture, gape at old masters in the Met or subversive art on the street, stumble across a Midtown film set or catch a forgotten movie at a repertory theatre. Icons familiar to the big screen – and popular imagination – are often staring you in the face, whether that's the raised torch of the Statue of Liberty, the bright lights of Times Square, the illustrious Empire State Building or the waterfront promenade at Brooklyn Heights.

Saying that, the city demands more than just a scratch at a familiar surface. Dig deeper – stay a week or two; move past Central Park and the famous museums on the Upper East and West sides, past the historical highlights of downtown and Midtown, and on to lesser-known neighbourhoods, buildings, green spaces and art collections; let yourself be diverted by a tree-lined street or stray path, a glimpse of an Art Deco detail, a hole-in-the-wall serving soul food or fried dumplings – and you'll start to feel a new rhythm. New York bristles with energy, for certain, but it also emits a slow-burning charm. Find it in hidden gardens next to postmodern skyscrapers; priceless art tucked away in unassuming lobbies, robber barons' homes and mock medieval cloisters; a riverside where you can bike, kayak or just stroll along to take in the view; or the late-night vibe in a Harlem jazz joint, underground Brooklyn rock club, even around a street-food cart in Jackson Heights, Queens. Essential to the experience is a sense of adventure – exploring is one of the great joys of the city, and every borough has its pleasures. Feel free to linger over individual sights, but when in doubt, get on the move for views of the twinkling cityscape from the Staten Island Ferry, a perfect espresso in a shabby chic Williamsburg café or a celebratory taco after riding the "A" to the Rockaways.

ABOVE CENTRAL PARK

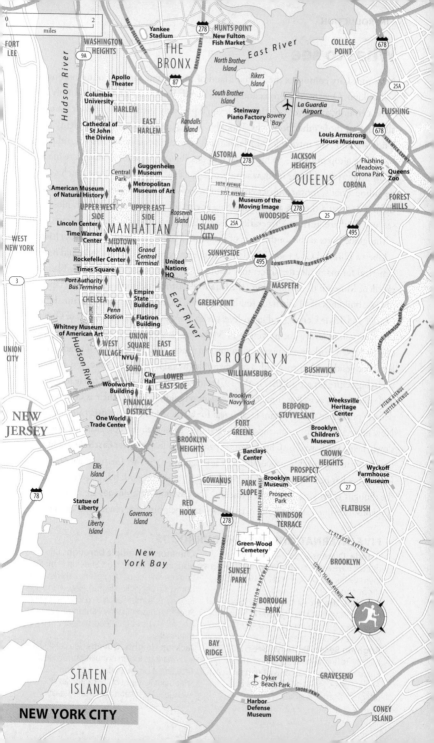

NEW YORK CITY

What to see

New York City comprises the central island of Manhattan and four outer boroughs – Brooklyn, Queens, the Bronx and Staten Island. For some, **Manhattan** simply is New York; certainly, whatever your interests, you'll probably spend most of your time here, although those other boroughs, Brooklyn and Queens especially have plenty going on. Understanding the intricacies of Manhattan's layout, especially beyond its grid pattern, should be a top priority – to hit as much as possible, you'll want to make use of the city's many subways and buses (and, when necessary, cabs). New York is very much a city of neighbourhoods, most compact enough to be explored on foot, and wandering through them is as great a thrill as any single sight. For an overview of each district, plus what to see and do there, turn to "Itineraries" (see p.18) and to the introduction of each chapter.

This guide starts at the southern tip of the island and moves north. The **Harbor Islands** – Liberty, Ellis and Governors islands – were the first glimpses of New York (and indeed America) for many nineteenth-century immigrants, a legacy celebrated in Ellis Island's excellent Museum of Immigration. The **Financial District** encompasses the skyscrapers and historic buildings of Manhattan's southern reaches, including the tallest structure in town, One World Trade Center (and its tri-level observatory), rising from the ashes of Ground Zero; at ground level is the moving 9/11 Memorial & Museum. Immediately east of here is **City Hall**, New York's well-appointed municipal centre, while to the west is swanky **Tribeca**, a loft-filled residential district with a number of high-end restaurants. **Soho**, just to the north, was a big centre for art galleries in the 1970s and 80s; it's better known today for its shops and street scene, as well as some historic cast-iron buildings. East of here is **Chinatown**, densely populated and a vibrant locale great for Chinese food and unstructured exploration. Now more a haven for pasta-and-red-sauce tourist traps than Italians, **Little Italy** next door is slowly being swallowed by Chinatown's expansion; while the **Lower East Side**, traditionally the city's gateway neighbourhood for new immigrants – whether German, Jewish or Hispanic – has been almost totally gentrified by a younger crowd, but preserves its history in the thought-provoking Tenement Museum. The **East and West villages** are known for their gorgeous, tree-lined streets, bohemian history and their hip bars, restaurants and shops.

FIVE INTERNATIONAL NEIGHBOURHOODS

Astoria, Queens (see p.246) All sorts of groups have settled here, but it's most famous for its Greek population and the Hellenic shops and tavernas.

Belmont, the Bronx (see p.258) Home to far more Italians than touristy Little Italy; the main drag, Arthur Avenue, hops with *salumerias* and bakeries.

Brighton Beach, Brooklyn (see p.241) Since the 1970s, Brighton Beach has been a strong Russian enclave; a walk down Brighton Beach Avenue takes you by food emporia and discount electronic stores.

Chinatown, multiple boroughs Busy restaurants pepper Mott Street in Manhattan's Chinatown (see p.70); grocers, bakeries and dumpling shops line Eighth Avenue in Brooklyn's Sunset Park (see p.239); and Main Street in predominantly Cantonese Flushing (see p.251) has street-food stalls and mini-malls.

Jackson Heights, Queens (see p.248) Best known for its Indian population, focused on 74th Street between Roosevelt and 37th Street, but just east of there, Roosevelt Avenue is like a Latin American bazaar.

Chelsea has established gay venues, a happening gallery scene and outdoor gems in the High Line and Hudson River Park developments; just below it, the **Meatpacking District** holds the Whitney Museum of American Art and plenty of high-fashion boutiques. The areas around **Union Square** and **Gramercy Park** feature some lovely skyscrapers, including the Flatiron Building, that nicely complement the green spaces, as well as an exciting eating scene. This is where the avenues begin their march north through the busy, regimented blocks of **Midtown**. In its eastern portion, it's dotted with some of the city's most impressive sights, including the Empire State Building, Grand Central Terminal and the Museum of Modern Art (MoMA). Modern and postmodern skyscrapers punctuate this business district. To the west, **Times Square** and the **Theater District** provide a commercialized look at the popular image of New York City, while **Hell's Kitchen**, along Ninth and Tenth avenues, at least vaguely harks back to a slightly grittier day.

Beyond the high-rise blocks of Midtown, the character of the city changes quite rapidly. The neck-cricking architecture and flagship stores along Fifth Avenue run into 59th Street, where the classic Manhattan vistas are broken by the broad expanse of **Central Park**, a supreme piece of nineteenth-century landscaping. Flanking the park, the **Upper East Side** is wealthy and grandiose, with many of its nineteenth-century millionaires' mansions now transformed into a string of magnificent museums known as **"Museum Mile"**; the most prominent of these is the vast Metropolitan Museum of Art. The residential neighbourhood boasts some of the swankiest addresses in Manhattan, as well as a nest of designer shops along Madison Avenue in the seventies.

On the other side of the park, the largely residential, less patrician enclave of the **Upper West Side** is worth a visit, mostly for Lincoln Center, the American Museum of Natural History and Riverside Park along the Hudson River; studenty Morningside Heights, home to Columbia University, tops off the neighbourhood. Immediately north of Central Park, **Harlem**, the historic black city-within-a-city, numbers elegant brownstones, Baptist churches, jazz landmarks and a strong sense of community among its high points. Still farther north, past residential Hamilton Heights and Washington Heights, a largely Hispanic enclave that few visitors ever venture to visit, stands Inwood at the tip of the island. It's here you'll find The Cloisters, a twentieth-century reconstruction of a medieval

---

TOP 5 ARCHITECTURAL NEIGHBOURHOODS

Fort Greene (see p.222) This well-preserved Brooklyn district has kept its look through gentrification, not least because it holds some of the borough's nicest nineteenth-century brownstones.

Harlem (see p.197) Some of the most beautiful residential architecture in the city, exemplified by blocks of brownstones and other styles south of 125th Street, and developments farther north like Strivers' Row and Hamilton Heights.

Midtown Manhattan (see p.123) A smorgasbord of twentieth-century architectural styles, including some of the city's greatest skyscrapers (the Empire State and GE buildings) and Modernist masterpieces (the Seagram Building and Lever House).

Soho (see p.67) The largest collection of cast-iron buildings in the world, with incredibly ornate, Neoclassical facades.

West Village (see p.94) Still home to the city's best and oldest residential architecture, with quiet mews and handsome Federal row houses from the 1830s.

monastery, packed with great European Romanesque and Gothic art and (transplanted) architecture – in short, one of Manhattan's must-sees.

It's a good thing that, more and more, visitors (even those on a short trip) venture from Manhattan to one or more of the outer boroughs: **Brooklyn**, **Queens**, **The Bronx** and **Staten Island**. In addition to the points of historical and contemporary interest in each, some of the city's most vibrant international neighbourhoods (and consequently best food) can be found out here: the Greek restaurants of the Astoria district in Queens, for example, or the Italian bakeries and trattorias of the Bronx's Belmont section. Individual sights like the New York Botanical Garden in the Bronx and Museum of the Moving Image in Queens have plenty of pull, too, and a ride on the Staten Island Ferry is a free thrill that's hard to beat. Brooklyn, however, tends to steal the show and is more or less Manhattan's equal – or at least rival. You can sample locally made food and buy snappy duds in hip Williamsburg and Greenpoint, wander the brownstone-lined streets of Cobble Hill and Brooklyn Heights, view cutting-edge exhibits at the Brooklyn Museum, ride a rickety roller coaster and soak up the old-world charm of Coney Island or hit Central Park's counterpart, activity-filled Prospect Park.

When to go

New York City's climate ranges from sticky, hot and humid in midsummer to very cold in January and February: be prepared to freeze or boil accordingly if you decide to visit during these periods. **Spring** is gentle, if unpredictable and often wet, while **autumn** is perhaps the most beguiling season, with crisp, clear days and warmish nights – either period is a great time to schedule a visit. Whenever you're visiting, plan to dress in layers, as it's the only way to combat overheated buildings in winter and overactive, icy air-conditioning come summertime.

ABOVE SOHO FIRE ESCAPES

19

things not to miss

It's not possible to see everything that New York City has to offer in one trip – and we don't suggest you try. What follows, in no particular order, is a selective taste of highlights: mind-blowing feats of engineering and design, waterfront amusements, hallowed art collections and, of course, plenty of eating, shopping and nightlife. All entries have a page reference to take you straight into the Guide, where you can find out more. Coloured numbers refer to chapters in the Guide section.

1 STATUE OF LIBERTY
Page 37
There's no greater symbol of the American dream than the magnificent statue that graces New York Harbor.

2 EMPIRE STATE BUILDING
Page 123
Still the most original and elegant skyscraper of them all.

3 METROPOLITAN MUSEUM OF ART
Page 158
You could easily spend a whole day (or week or month) at the Met, exploring everything from Egyptian artefacts to modern masters.

4 9/11 MEMORIAL & MUSEUM
Page 49
The pools in the buildings' footprints and museum artefacts including the "Last Column" can't help but stir emotion.

5 GRAND CENTRAL TERMINAL

Hit up the shops, throw back some oysters and gawk at the celestial ceiling above the majestic concourse.

6 BASEBALL

A summertime treat: enjoy a hot dog, a cold beer and America's pastime in the Yankees' or Mets' homes – or for a more intimate experience, see a Cyclones game in Coney Island.

7 MUSEUM OF MODERN ART

Simply put, MoMA holds the most comprehensive collection of modern art in the world, curated in a breathtaking setting of glass atriums and statuary.

8 PIZZA

Whether you go nouveau (like at *Roberta's*, see p.320), Neapolitan or classic New York-style, you can't leave without sampling the city's signature dish.

9 ROCKEFELLER CENTER
If anywhere can truly claim to be the centre of New York, this stylish piece of twentieth-century urban planning is it.

10 LIVE JAZZ
New York's jazz scene is vibrant, but Harlem is first choice for interesting venues and late-night jam sessions.

11 BAR-HOPPING IN WILLIAMSBURG
Haute food, house-made bitters, vintage arcade games, a beer or three at a beloved local brewery – it all adds up to a night of good fun.

12 THE FRICK COLLECTION
He may have been a ruthless coal baron, but Henry Frick's eye for art and the elegance of his collection's setting make this one of the city's best galleries.

13 BROOKLYN BRIDGE
Take the less-than-a-mile walk across the bridge to see beautiful views of the downtown skyline, Brooklyn waterfront and Harbor Islands.

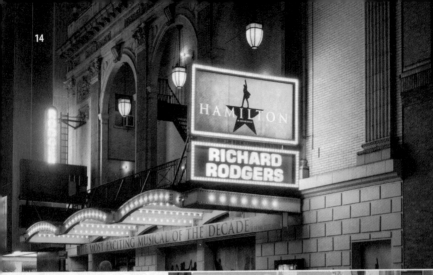

Itineraries

These themed itineraries are not meant to be followed exactingly; instead, let them lead you to unusual city sights, flavours and corners. Choose a few that interest you and you'll see a side of New York well away from the typical big-ticket attractions.

A HARLEM TOUR

This bastion of African American culture has pretty streets to explore – and in East Harlem you'll find plenty of street art, including Eva Cockroft's *Homage to Seurat: La Grande Jatte in Harlem* (see p.207).

❶ Schomburg Center for Research in Black Culture There's always a worthwhile exhibit or event going on at this research library. **See p.205**

❷ The churches of Harlem Some are distinguished for their architecture, others for their lively gospel services. **See p.204**

❸ A walk on 125th Street The Apollo Theater is the cultural lodestar, but there's plenty more here: sneaker stores, jazz clubs, museums and historic architecture included. **See p.201**

❹ Red Rooster Marcus Samuelsson's celebrated restaurant is upstairs; downstairs, find *Ginny's Supper Club*, for a musical nightcap. **See p.315 & p.340**

❺ Minton's Playhouse This historic bebop birthplace has been reborn for the twenty-first century. **See p.349**

A DAY IN THE VILLAGE

Take a day to explore historic Greenwich Village (aka the West Village), the artistic, bohemian heart of New York since the 1920s and now one of its wealthiest, most sought after neighbourhoods.

❶ Wander along historic Bedford Street One of the most beautiful streets in Manhattan drips with history, from the thinnest house to the oldest house (and that one from *Friends*). **See p.103**

❷ Coffee in Caffe Reggio Take in the Italian antiques, paintings and sculptures at this 1927 coffee shop, where Tennessee Williams once sipped espresso. **See p.296**

❸ Bleecker Street snacking Sample the prosciutto balls at *Faicco's*, cannoli at *Rocco's*, finest *fromage* at *Murray's Cheese*, cheap slices at *Joe's Pizza* and cupcakes from *Magnolia Bakery*. **See p.102**

❹ The 4th Street Courts Witness some high-quality street basketball at "The Cage", a magnet for NBA wannabes from all over the city. **See p.102**

❺ Sunset on the Hudson Stroll along the Hudson River Park as the sun sets behind New Jersey. **See p.104**

❻ Pints at the White Horse Grab a beer in this classic 1880 watering hole, the haunt of Kerouac, Mailer and Hunter S. Thompson, and the pub where Dylan Thomas reputedly supped his last drink. **See p.335**

❼ Live jazz Check out the dynamic West Village jazz scene at underground venue *Bar Next Door* or cosy dive *Smalls Jazz Club*. **See p.349**

ABOVE *SPIRIT OF HARLEM* MURAL, HARLEM **OPPOSITE** ROCKAWAY BEACH

EAT NEW YORK CITY

Something New York does better than pretty much anywhere else? Food, in all tastes and varieties. Eat your way around the city by visiting some of its top marketplaces and street-food centres.

❶ **Eataly (Flatiron District)** Celebrity-chef-run spot for immaculate produce, fresh breads and Italian groceries, plus places for meals, quick bites, coffee and gelato. There's also a branch in the Financial District. **See p.392**

❷ **Smorgasburg (Williamsburg)** This offshoot of the Brooklyn Flea, full of inventive food vendors, also spends time in Prospect Park and Soho. **See p.392**

❸ **Chelsea Market (Chelsea)** Lots of deliciousness under one roof: gooey brownies and just-from-the-ocean lobster are among the highlights. **See p.109**

❹ **Essex Street Market (Lower East Side)** Dominican fruit and veg stalls rub shoulders with New York classics (*Shopsin's*) and hip newcomers (*Saxelby Cheesemongers* and *Beurre & Sel*). **See p.83**

❺ **Le District (Battery Park City)** This international market in the old World Financial Center brings a bit of France (croissants, *fromage*, pâté) to NYC. *C'est magnifique.* **See p.281**

OFF THE BEATEN TRACK

Getting out to these stops is part of the adventure. Once there, you're likely to be surrounded by locals enjoying some of the city's less-advertised highlights.

❶ **Hamilton Grange, Hamilton Heights** The former home of founding father Alexander Hamilton is one of the more evocative stops on a northern Manhattan "Hamilton" tour. **See p.208**

❷ **The Rockaways, Queens** Over by Jamaica Bay and the Atlantic, the Rockaways have plenty of surf, art, food, free concerts and local flavour – take a bus, train or ferry. **See p.253**

❸ **Governors Island** This bucolic retreat sits in the harbour a short ferry ride from Wall Street, though its leafy parks and stately buildings are more New England than New York. **See p.40**

❹ **Greenpoint, Brooklyn** It doesn't get quite as much press as neighbouring Williamsburg, but the Polish restaurants and cool cafés make it just as worthwhile. **See p.226**

❺ **Flushing Meadows–Corona Park, Queens** Science and art museums, a skating rink and other sports facilities, and proximity to Flushing's Chinatown… what's not to like? **See p.250**

❻ **Green-Wood Cemetery, Brooklyn** The final resting place of many local notables, Greenwood adds a rural flair to the urban landscape, and its hills afford great views of Manhattan. **See p.239**

NEW YORK GRAFFITI

Basics

Getting there

Getting to New York is easy. There are three international airports (Ⓦ**panynj .gov**) that serve the city: John F. Kennedy (JFK), LaGuardia (LGA) and Newark (EWR). The city is on every major airline's itinerary, and is also a regional hub for train and bus travel. Expressways surround Manhattan, making driving another viable option.

Visas and red tape

Under the Visa Waiver Program, citizens of Australia, Ireland, New Zealand and the UK do **not** require visas for visits to the US of ninety days or less. You will, however, need to obtain **Electronic System for Travel Authorization (ESTA)** online before you fly, which involves completing a basic immigration form in advance, on the computer. Do this only on the **official US Customs and Border Protection website**: at the time of research the website was Ⓦesta.cbp.dhs.gov/esta, but note that similar sites that might seem official will charge you more and are a scam. There is an official processing fee of $4, and a further $10 authorization fee once the ESTA has been approved (all paid via credit card online). Once given, authorizations are valid for multiple entries into the US for around two years – it's recommended that you submit an ESTA application as soon as you begin making travel plans (in most cases the ESTA will be granted immediately, but it can sometimes take up to 72 hours to get a response). You'll need to present a machine-readable passport to Immigration upon arrival. Note that ESTA currently only applies to visitors arriving by air or cruise ship: crossing the **land border from Canada or Mexico**, those qualifying for the Visa Waiver Program do not need to apply for ESTA – instead you must fill in an I-94W form, though this may change in future. Canadians now require a passport to cross the border, but can travel in the US for up to a year without a visa or visa waiver.

CONSULATES IN NEW YORK CITY

Australia 34/F, 150 E 42nd St ☎ 212 351 6500, Ⓦ newyork.usa .embassy.gov.au
Canada 1251 Sixth Ave, at W 50th St ☎ 212 596 1628, Ⓦ can-am .gc.ca/new-york
Ireland 17/F, 345 Park Ave, between E 51st and E 52nd sts ☎ 212 319 2555, Ⓦ dfa.ie/irish-consulate/newyork
South Africa 333 E 38th St, between First and Second aves ☎ 212 213 4880, Ⓦ southafrica-newyork.net/consulate
UK 845 Third Ave, between E 51st and E 52nd sts ☎ 212 745 0200, Ⓦ gov.uk/government/world/usa

Flights from the US and Canada

From most places in North America, flying is the most convenient way to reach New York. Airfares to New York depend on the season and can fluctuate wildly. The highest prices are generally between May and September; you'll get the best prices by booking months in advance or flying during the low season, November to February (excluding late Nov until early Jan, the holiday season). The lowest round-trip fares (nonstop) from the West Coast tend to average around $350–450; from Chicago or Miami it's about $200–250. Nonstop flights from Canada are generally more expensive; reckon on paying Can$250–300 from Toronto or Montréal and at least Can$600–700 from Vancouver.

Flights from the UK and Ireland

Flying to New York from the UK takes about seven hours; flights tend to leave in the morning or afternoon and arrive in New York in the afternoon or evening, though the odd flight does leave as late as 8pm. Coming back, most flights depart in the evening and arrive in the UK early next morning; flying time, due to the prevailing winds, is usually a little shorter.

As far as **scheduled flights** go, Virgin Atlantic (Ⓦvirgin-atlantic.com) and British Airways (Ⓦbritish airways.com) offer the most direct services each day from London Heathrow to JFK and Newark. American Airlines (Ⓦaa.com), Delta (Ⓦdelta.com) and United (Ⓦunited.com) also fly direct on a daily basis; there is

A BETTER KIND OF TRAVEL

At Rough Guides we are passionately committed to travel. We believe it helps us understand the world we live in and the people we share it with – and of course tourism is vital to many developing economies. But the scale of modern tourism has also damaged some places irreparably, and climate change is accelerated by most forms of transport, especially flying. All Rough Guides' flights are carbon-offset, and every year we donate money to a variety of environmental charities.

not much difference in the prices between the major airlines. Round-trip fares (nonstop) also fluctuate wildly, averaging £450–550 for off-peak tickets bought in advance, to £900 and up in the summer. Norwegian Air Shuttle (Ⓦ norwegian.com) now offers budget nonstop flights between London Gatwick and JFK – round-trip tickets can be as low as £300. United also flies nonstop to Newark from Birmingham, Manchester and Glasgow. Aer Lingus (Ⓦ aerlingus.com; JFK/Newark), Delta (JFK) and United (Newark) all fly nonstop services to New York from Dublin – expect to pay at least €900 in the summer. United also flies nonstop from Shannon Airport to Newark.

Flights from Australia, New Zealand and South Africa

It's not yet possible to take a nonstop flight between New York and Australia or New Zealand, though Qantas (Ⓦ qantas.com.au) offers a direct service from Sydney, with a two-and-a-half-hour layover in Los Angeles (meaning you won't have to change planes). Most Aussies and Kiwis reach the eastern United States by way of LA and San Francisco (flying time is approximately ten hours to the West Coast, with another five-hour flight to New York). The best connections tend to be with United, Delta, Air New Zealand (Ⓦ airnewzealand .com) and Qantas; from Auckland, Air New Zealand connects with United flights in LA.

Fares from eastern Australian state capitals are generally the same: return flights for most of the year start at around Aus$1800 but can go up to more than Aus$2800 in December, when most Australians tend to visit; fares from Perth and Darwin can be up to Aus$500 more all year, and it's usually about the same from New Zealand (NZ$2500). If you intend to take in New York as part of a world trip, a **round-the-world** ticket offers the best value for money, working out just a little more than an all-in ticket.

South African Airways (Ⓦ flysaa.com) flies nonstop from Johannesburg to JFK (15hr 40min) from around R10,600; you might get cheaper rates by shopping around for indirect flights via Qatar (Qatar Airways; Ⓦ qatarairways.com), Dubai (Emirates; Ⓦ emirates.com), or Amsterdam and London.

Trains

New York is connected to the rest of the continent by several **Amtrak train lines** (Ⓣ 800 872 7245, Ⓦ amtrak.com). The most frequent services are

along the Boston–Washington, DC corridor; there is also one daily train between Montréal and New York (10hr 30min). Fares from Boston and DC start at around $140 round-trip, or $250 for the Acela Express, which saves 30–35 minutes on either route. Fares from Canada usually start around Can$190. Like planes, train fares are often based on availability; with the exception of peak travel times (ie Christmas), seats are much cheaper months in advance. Although it's possible to haul yourself long-distance from the West Coast, the Midwest or the South, it's an exhausting trip (three days-plus from California) and fares are expensive.

Buses

Going by bus is usually the cheapest, but also the most time-consuming and least comfortable, mode of travel. Unlike most parts of the country, where Greyhound is the only game in town, in the busy northeast corridor there is fierce competition between bus operators. One-way from either DC or Boston to New York can go for as little as $20 on one of the major lines. **Peter Pan Bus Lines** often has $15 one-way fares from New York to Boston and DC. Buses arrive in New York at the Port Authority Bus Terminal, Eighth Avenue and West 42nd Street.

For the best bargains along the East Coast check **Bolt Bus** and **Mega Bus**, which sometimes offer tickets for $1 (Mega Bus also runs buses to/from Toronto from around $39). Other cheap options (with the oldest buses) include **Lucky Star**, which runs nonstop between the Chinatowns of Boston and New York for $25 each way.

AGENTS AND OPERATORS

Amtrak Vacations US Ⓣ 800 654 5748, Ⓦ amtrakvacations.com. Rail, accommodation and sightseeing packages.

Contiki US Ⓣ 888 266 8454, Ⓦ contiki.com. 18-to-35-year-olds-only tour operator. Runs highly social sightseeing trips to New York that focus on major tourist attractions.

Delta Vacations US Ⓣ 800 654 6559, Ⓦ delta.com. Offers packages to New York that include mid-range to upscale accommodation, plus optional sightseeing and airport transfers.

International Gay and Lesbian Travel Association US Ⓣ 800 448 8550, Ⓦ iglta.org. Trade group with lists of LGBT-owned or LGBT-friendly travel agents, accommodation and other travel businesses.

New York City Vacation Packages US Ⓣ 888 692 8701, Ⓦ nycvp.com. All sorts of short, reasonably priced New York vacations, from spa weekends to Broadway shows.

North South Travel UK Ⓣ 01245 608 291, Ⓦ northsouthtravel .co.uk. Friendly, competitive travel agency, offering discounted fares worldwide. Profits are used to support projects in the developing world, especially the promotion of sustainable tourism.

STA Travel US ☎ 800 781 4040, UK ☎ 0871 2300 040; ⓦ statravel
.com. Worldwide specialists in independent travel; also student IDs, travel
insurance, car rental, rail passes and more. Good discounts for students
and under-26s.

Trailfinders UK ☎ 0845 058 5858, Republic of Ireland ☎ 01 677
7888; ⓦ trailfinders.com. One of the best-informed and most efficient
agents for independent travellers.

Viator US ☎ 866 648 5873, ⓦ viator.com. Books local tours and
sightseeing trips within New York.

BUS AND RAIL CONTACTS

Amtrak ☎ 800 872 7245, ⓦ amtrak.com
Bolt Bus ☎ 877 265 8287, ⓦ boltbus.com
Greyhound ☎ 800 231 2222, Canada ☎ 800 661 8747;
ⓦ greyhound.com
Lucky Star ☎ 617 426 8802, ⓦ luckystarbus.com
Mega Bus ☎ 877 462 6342, ⓦ megabus.com
Peter Pan ☎ 800 343 9999, ⓦ peterpanbus.com

Arrival

**Most visitors to New York arrive at one of
the three major international airports that
serve the city: John F. Kennedy, LaGuardia
and Newark. All three share a website at
ⓦ panynj.gov where you can find general
information about getting to and from the
airports (or call ☎ 800 247 7433). Amtrak
trains arrive at Penn Station, and most
buses at the Port Authority Bus Terminal,
both of which are in Midtown Manhattan.**

By plane

Whichever airport you arrive at, one of the simplest
ways into the city is by **bus**. All airport bus services
operate from one of two terminals in Manhattan:
Grand Central Terminal (at Park Ave and 42nd St)
and the **Port Authority Bus Terminal** (Eighth Ave at
34th St ☎ 212 564 8484). Grand Central is more
convenient for the east side of the island. The Port
Authority Bus Terminal isn't as good a bet for
Manhattan (as it entails carrying luggage from bus to
street level), though you'll find it handy if you're
heading for the west side of the city or out to New
Jersey (by bus). Some airport buses also stop at **Penn
Station** at West 32nd Street between Seventh and
Eighth avenues, where you can catch the Long Island
Railroad (LIRR), as well as Amtrak long-distance trains
to other parts of America. More convenient than the
bus but cheaper than a taxi, the **GO Airport Shuttle**
is a minibus that offers a drop-off service anywhere in
the city (shared with other riders).

Taxis are the most convenient option if you are
travelling in a group or are arriving at an antisocial
hour. Ignore the individual touts vying for attention
as you exit the baggage claim; these "gypsy cab"
operators are notorious for ripping off tourists. Any
airport official can direct you to the taxi stand,
where you can get an official New York City yellow
taxi. Remember to add a fifteen- to twenty-percent
tip for the driver. **Uber** (ⓦ uber.com) is safe and
popular in New York and offers similar rates to
conventional taxis from the airports, but you'll need
a working smartphone to use the service.

If you're not so pressed for time and want to save
some money, it is also possible to take the **train**,
commuter or subway, from Newark or JFK, and a
city bus from LaGuardia.

JFK

JFK International Airport (international and
domestic flights) is located in Queens, some fourteen
miles southeast of Times Square in Manhattan and
twelve miles east of Downtown Brooklyn. The **NYC
Airporter** (☎ 718 777 5111, ⓦ nycairporter.com) runs
airport buses between JFK and Grand Central
Terminal, Port Authority Bus Terminal, Penn Station
and Bryant Park (where there are free transfer shuttles
to Midtown hotels) every twenty to thirty minutes
between 6am and 11.30pm. Journeys take 45 to sixty
minutes, depending on time of day and traffic conditions. The fare is $18 one-way, $27 round-trip
(depending on current discount deals online). **Go
Airport Shuttle** (ⓦ goairportshuttle.com) offers
shared minibus services to your hotel door ($24 to
Midtown Manhattan), but you need to reserve this in
advance and be a little flexible on times.

The **AirTrain** (ⓦ panynj.gov/airtrain) runs every few
minutes, 24 hours daily, between all JFK terminals and
the Jamaica and Howard Beach stations in Queens.
You pay $5 when you exit, which can be debited from
your MetroCard (see p.25). The fastest onward
connection into Manhattan is to take the **LIRR** (Long
Island Rail Road) from Jamaica to Penn Station ($7.50
off-peak, $10.25 peak; 19–21min); buy tickets at the
station, as fares are almost double if purchased on
board. You can also take the **subway** (E, J, Z from
Jamaica, and A from Howard Beach) for just $2.75 on
MetroCard ($3 single-ride ticket), anywhere in the city.
In the daytime or early evening this is a cheap, viable
option, although late at night it isn't the best choice –
trains run infrequently and can be deserted. Travel
time to Manhattan is usually a little under an hour.

Taxis charge a flat rate of $52 to anywhere in
Manhattan from JFK (plus the state tax surcharge of
50¢ or a $4.50 surcharge Mon–Fri 4–8 pm). Tolls are

payable however, and some drivers will try to increase the $52 rate by claiming you must take a toll route. Insist on $52; there are no toll roads between JFK and Manhattan, and all the bridges are **free**. The only toll is payable on the **Midtown Tunnel** ($8.50 or just $5.76 if your taxi has an electronic E-Z Pass; toll payable in both directions), but unless you are in a real hurry (if you are heading to Midtown the tunnel is slightly faster), you can insist on taking one of the bridges instead. All non-Manhattan trips should be on the meter, which starts at $2.50; expect to pay $59–65 for Downtown Brooklyn.

LaGuardia

LaGuardia Airport (domestic and some Canadian flights) is located in northern Queens, around eight miles northeast of Times Square (Manhattan) and ten miles northeast of Downtown Brooklyn. The **NYC Airporter** (☎718 777 5111, ⓦnycairporter .com) runs express buses between LaGuardia and Grand Central Station, Port Authority Bus Terminal and Penn Station every twenty to thirty minutes between 6am and 11.30pm. Journey time is 45 to sixty minutes, depending on traffic. The fare is $15 one-way, $24 round-trip (depending on current discount deals online). **Go Airport Shuttle** (ⓦgoairportshuttle.com) offers shared minibus services to your hotel door (around $21.56 to Midtown Manhattan), but you need to reserve this in advance and be a little flexible on times.

You can also travel from the airport by **city bus**. The #Q70 LaGuardia Link runs every ten minutes (24hr) to subway stations at Jackson Heights (#7, E, F, M, R) and Woodside (#7 plus LIRR services) in Queens, while the #M60 bus takes you into Manhattan (every 7–30min, 24hr), along 125th Street (for #2, #3, #4, #5, #6, A, B, C, D subway lines) and down Broadway to West 106th Street. Alternatively, you can get off the #M60 bus at Hoyt Avenue South and 31st St. There you can transfer to the N or Q subway lines (the station is Astoria Blvd), which run through Manhattan and south to Brooklyn. Note that both of the bus routes are "Select Bus Services", which means you must buy tickets from the kerbside machines before boarding ($2.75 by MetroCard or coins, exact change only).

Taxis from LaGuardia use the meter (which starts at $2.50); reckon on $30–40 into Manhattan plus tip and surcharges (Mon–Fri 4–8pm $1; nightly surcharge 8pm–6am $0.50; NY state tax of $0.50 added to all trips within New York). Tolls are also extra, but you can insist on avoiding the Midtown Tunnel (see p.27).

Newark

Newark Liberty International Airport (inter-national and domestic flights) is located in New Jersey, 3.5 miles south of Newark and around fourteen miles southwest of Times Square (Manhattan), on the other side of the Hudson River – it's the only New York airport on mainland North America (the other two are on Long Island). **Newark Airport Express** (☎877 863 9275, ⓦnewarkairport express.com) runs buses to Grand Central Station, Port Authority Bus Terminal and Penn Station every thirty minutes daily between 4am and 1am (every 15min 6.45am–11.15pm). In the other direction, buses run from the same locations just as frequently between 4.45am and 1.45am. In either direction, the journey takes thirty to 45 minutes depending on the traffic. The fare is $16 one-way, $28 round-trip (plus $1 admin fee). **Go Airport Shuttle** (ⓦgoairport shuttle.com) offers shared minibus services to your hotel door (around $23 to Midtown Manhattan), but you need to reserve this in advance and be a little flexible on times.

From any of the terminals you can also take the short **AirTrain** ride to Newark Liberty International Airport Train Station and connect with frequent NJ Transit or Amtrak trains heading into Manhattan. The AirTrain runs 24 hours (every 3–15min) and nominally costs $5.50, but this is included when you buy an NJ Transit or Amtrak ticket from machines in the AirTrain terminals or at the main station – there's no need to pay separately for the AirTrain.

Heading into Manhattan (Penn Station; 30min) the fare for NJ Transit is $13 (Amtrak trains are more expensive). If you want to save $1.75 (or are heading to Lower Manhattan), take an NJ Transit train ($8.50) to Newark Penn Station (not to be confused with Penn Station in Manhattan) and transfer to the PATH system (☎800 234 7284, ⓦpanynj.gov/path) with connections to Downtown Manhattan (30–40min) for $2.75. The PATH train runs 24 hours, but service is limited between midnight and 7am.

Taxis from Newark into Manhattan charge according to an **expensive** fixed schedule of rates, clearly listed at terminal taxi ranks – the dispatcher will confirm the rate before you get in. For points south of Central Park the rate is $50–55 ($60–70 further north), plus $5 for locations on the east side of the island and a $5 peak-time surcharge (Mon–Fri 6–9am & 4–7pm, Sat & Sun noon–8pm). On top of that you need to add $1 per suitcase, a tip, $5.50 to use a credit card and any tolls incurred; you can ask the driver to avoid toll roads in New Jersey, but to get to Manhattan you'll need to take the Lincoln or Holland toll tunnels ($15 or $10.50–12.50 if your driver has an electronic E-Z Pass). Note, though, that this toll is only paid going into Manhattan, so even though you are obliged to pay "round-trip" tolls, the charge should only be a maximum $15. Figure on spending a total $85–100 to most hotels in Midtown Manhattan.

By car, train and bus

Though Grand Central Terminal is New York's original train station, it only handles commuter services today, and long-distance **rail** travellers are more likely to arrive at Penn Station. If you're coming from the East Coast (or if you don't mind long journeys), **driving** is an option, but note that you probably won't need (or want) a car once you're in the city. Major highways come in from most directions (I-87 and -95 from the north; I-95 from the south; and I-80 from the west). In terms of tolls, crossing the Hudson River costs $15, while bridges over the East River are free; the Midtown Tunnel is $8.50.

Penn Station

Amtrak, **Long Island Rail Road** and **New Jersey Transit trains** arrive at **Penn Station**, at West 32nd Street between Seventh and Eighth avenues (Midtown Manhattan), which is connected to the subway system and has plenty of taxis outside. Don't expect much – Penn is one of the city's ugliest structures (it's entirely underground, beneath Madison Square Garden) and is confusing to navigate, though if you follow the signs you'll eventually find the exit.

Port Authority Bus Terminal

If you come to New York by Greyhound or any other long-distance **bus** line (with the exception of the Chinatown buses, which arrive in Chinatown, and Mega Bus and Bolt Bus, which drop you off on Midtown streets), you arrive at the **Port Authority Bus Terminal** at West 42nd Street and Eighth Avenue (Midtown Manhattan) – this is also connected to the subway system (follow the signs) and it's fairly easy to catch a taxi outside.

City transport

Public transport in New York is excellent, extremely cheap and covers most conceivable corners of the city, whether by subway or bus. Don't be afraid to ask someone for help if you're confused. You'll no doubt find the need for a taxi from time to time, especially if you feel uncomfortable in an area at night; you will rarely have trouble tracking one down in Manhattan or on major Brooklyn avenues – the ubiquitous yellow cabs are always on the prowl for passengers. And don't forget your feet – New Yorkers walk everywhere.

By subway

The New York subway (☎ 718 330 1234, ⊕ mta.info) is initially incomprehensible, but it's also the fastest and most efficient way to get from place to place in Manhattan and to the outer boroughs. Put aside your qualms: it's much safer and user-friendly than it once was, and it's definitely not as difficult to navigate as it seems. Nonetheless, it pays to familiarize yourself with the subway system before you set out. Study the map in this book, or get a free map at any information kiosk. Though the subway runs daily 24 hours, some routes operate at certain times of day only; read any service advisories carefully. Most trains will be packed (the L train notoriously so) during rush hours (roughly 7–9am and 5–7pm). Official etiquette is to stand on the right on escalators, to allow people to pass on the left.

SUBWAY ESSENTIALS

Tickets The subway costs $2.75 per ride anywhere on the system if you purchase a stored-value MetroCard (new card $1) from a vending machine (in the subway station) or a subway teller, available in denominations between $5.50 and $80; a $20 purchase gives you $21 on your card. Vending machines accept all credit and debit cards, but keep some fresh bills on hand in case you have a problem. Single-ride tickets are also sold at vending machines, but cost $3 and are not really worth it if you intend to use the subway more than once. Unlimited-ride MetroCards – almost always the best deal if you intend to be on the go – allow unlimited travel for a certain period of time: a seven-day card for $32 and thirty-day card for $121 (there is no one-day card). Note that fares tend to be raised every two years.

Trains and routes Trains run uptown or downtown in Manhattan, following the great avenues. Crosstown routes are few. Trains and their routes are identified by a number or letter (not by their colour). There are two types of train: the express, which stops only at major stations, and the local, stopping at every station. Be aware that service changes due to track repairs and other maintenance work are frequent (especially after midnight and on weekends) and confusing.

Safety By day the whole train is safe, but don't go into empty cars if you can help it. Some trains have doors that connect between cars, but do not use them other than in an emergency, because this is dangerous and illegal. Keep an eye on bags (and especially smartphones and electronic devices, which can get snatched) at all times, especially when sitting or standing near the doors. With all the jostling in the crowds near the doors, this is a favourite spot for pickpockets. At night, always try to use the centre cars, because they tend to be more crowded. Yellow signs on

THE L TRAIN "APOCALYPSE"

Ever since Hurricane Sandy devastated New York in 2012, the busy L subway tunnels under the East River have required urgent repair. After much handwringing, the authorities have decided to **suspend the L train** completely between Brooklyn and Manhattan for 15 months, beginning April 2019, in order to complete the work.

the platform saying "During off hours train stops here" indicate where the conductor's car will stop. If you are lost, go to the subway teller or phone ☎ 718 330 1234. State your location and destination; the teller or operator will tell you the most direct route.

By bus

The **bus system** (☎ 718 330 1234, ⓦ mta.info) is simpler than the subway, as you can see where you're going and hop off at anything interesting. There are many crosstown routes and most services run 24 hours. The major disadvantage is that buses can be extremely slow due to traffic – in peak hours almost down to walking pace, despite the use of dedicated bus lanes.

Anywhere in the city the fare is $2.75, payable on entry with a MetroCard (the most convenient way) or with the correct change – coins only (no pennies). Bus maps can be obtained at the main concourse of Grand Central Terminal or at visitor information centres. There are routes on almost all the avenues and major streets. Most buses with an M designation before the route number travel exclusively in Manhattan; others may show a B for Brooklyn, Q for Queens, Bx for the Bronx or S for Staten Island. The crosstown routes are the most useful, especially the ones through Central Park. Also good are the buses that take you to east Manhattan where subway coverage is sparse. Most crosstown buses take their route number from the street they traverse, so the #M14 will travel along 14th Street. Buses display their number, origin and destination up front.

There are three main types of bus: **local**, which stop every two or three blocks at five- to ten-minute intervals; **limited stop**, which travel the same routes but stop at only about a quarter of the local stops; and **express**, which cost extra ($6.50) and stop hardly anywhere, shuttling commuters in and out of the outer boroughs and suburbs.

Note also that for any bus with an SBS or "**Select Bus Service**" designation in addition to the number, you must buy tickets at the kerbside machines at bus stops in advance (same fares) – you cannot buy tickets on these buses.

Bus stops are marked by a tall, round sign with a bus emblem and route number. Once you're on board, to signal that you want to get off a bus, press the yellow strip between the windows or one of the "stop" buttons on the grab bars; the driver will stop at the next official bus stop. Between 10pm and 5am you can ask to get off on any block along the route, whether or not it's a regular stop (not available on limited routes).

Transfers

A **transfer** allows a single fare to take you, one-way, anywhere in Manhattan, within two hours of your first ride. Pay by MetroCard and the transfer will apply automatically on the next bus/subway (no need to ask for it). If you pay with coins, ask your driver for a transfer (free) – you'll get a single-use MetroCard to use on your connecting bus/subway. Because few buses go up and down and across, you can transfer from any bus to almost any other that continues your trip. (You can't use transfers for return trips.) If you're unsure where to get off to transfer, consult the map on the panel behind the driver, or ask the driver for help.

By taxi

Taxis are always worth considering, especially if you're in a hurry or it's late at night. In Manhattan, you'll generally be using conventional **medallion cabs**, recognizable by their classic **yellow** paintwork and medallion up top. Before you hail a cab, work out exactly where you're going and if possible the quickest route there – a surprising number of cabbies are new to the job and speak poor English. If you feel the driver doesn't seem to know your destination, point it out on a map. An illuminated sign atop the taxi indicates its availability. If the words Off Duty are lit, the driver won't pick you up.

Boro taxis

Introduced in 2013, apple-green **Boro taxis** operate in areas of New York not commonly served by yellow cabs: north of West 110th Street and East 96th Street in Manhattan, the Bronx, Queens (excluding the airports), Brooklyn and Staten Island. They can drop you off anywhere in the city, but are not allowed to pick up passengers in Manhattan below 110th/96th streets. Otherwise Boro taxis follow the same rules and fare structure (see above) as yellow cabs (and you can hail them on the street).

Fares

Up to four people can travel in an ordinary medallion cab. Fares start at $2.50 for the first fifth of a mile plus New York state tax surcharge of 50¢ per ride and a 30¢ Improvement Surcharge (so a minimum of $3.30); it's 50¢ for each fifth of a mile thereafter or for each minute in stopped or slow traffic. An additional **surcharge** of 50¢ is payable every night between 8pm and 6am, and $1 Monday to Friday 4 to 8pm. When you take a cab outside the city limits you must agree on a flat fare with the driver before the trip begins (metered fare rules only apply to New York City; drivers can set prices to other destinations as they see fit). Note that this does not apply to trips to Westchester and Nassau counties, for which there are previously determined fare rules. Trips to Newark Airport are on the meter plus $17.50 and tolls. Note also that all trips from Manhattan to JFK should be a flat $52 (plus the state tax surcharge of 50¢), though drivers sometimes try and use the meter. Taxis do not charge for baggage.

Trips outside Manhattan can incur **toll fees** (which the driver will usually pay through E-Z Pass and which will be added to your fare); the only river crossings into Manhattan that cost money both ways are the Hugh L. Carey Tunnel and Queens Midtown Tunnel ($8.50 each; $5.76 with E-Z Pass). Tolls for the Holland Tunnel, Lincoln Tunnel and George Washington Bridge (all $15; $10.50–12.50 with E-Z Pass) are paid coming into Manhattan only. All the other bridges are free.

The **tip** should be fifteen to twenty percent of the fare; you'll get a dirty look if you offer less. Drivers don't like splitting anything bigger than a $20 bill, and are within their rights to refuse a bill over $20. Drivers are required to accept American Express, MasterCard, Visa and Discover for all fares. If they refuse, you may call ❶311 and report the medallion number.

Rules

Certain regulations govern yellow and Boro taxi operators. A driver can ask your destination only when you're seated (this is often breached) – and must transport you (within the five boroughs), however undesirable your destination may be. You may face some problems, though, if it's late and you want to go to an outer borough. Also, if you request it, a driver must pick up or drop off other passengers, turn on the air conditioning, and turn the radio down or off. Many drivers use a mobile (cell) phone while driving; this is common but prohibited, and while you can ask him or her to stop, don't expect compliance. If you lose something in a taxi, or you have a problem with a driver, get the licence number from the right-

hand side of the dashboard, or the medallion number from the rooftop sign or from the print-out receipt for the fare, and file a complaint at ❶311 or ⓦ1.nyc.gov.

Uber and "gypsy cabs"

Since 2015 there have been more **Uber** (ⓦuber.com) cars than yellow cabs in New York City. Ride-sharing service Uber connects riders with generally part-time drivers through a mobile app (so you need a smartphone to use it). Its introduction in New York has caused a backlash from yellow cab drivers, with calls for greater regulation, but at the time of writing the service remained popular and is generally safe. The cheapest base fare is $2.55 (uberX), followed by $1.75 per mile (there's usually a minimum payment of $8, making short trips uneconomical). Lyft (ⓦlyft.com) and Gett (ⓦgett.com) offer similar services and rates (also via apps). None of these services can be hailed on the street – you must reserve them through the apps.

Cars working for ride-sharing companies have started to replace the **"gypsy cab"** (which also looks like a regular car), traditionally divided into two types: licensed livery cabs (identified by a "T" on the number plate), only permitted to pick up passengers on call by telephone, but which often illegally seek passengers on the street; and completely unlicensed, uninsured operators who tout for business wherever tourists arrive. Avoid these drivers like the plague – they will rip you off (and can be unsafe). Their main hunting grounds are outside tourist arrival points like Penn Station and the Port Authority Bus Terminal. The main advantage of licensed livery cabs over ride-sharing services is that you can call them (you don't need to use an app). Always check the fare in advance, before getting in the car or when booking on the phone.

By ferry

Manhattan is connected to New Jersey, Staten Island, Queens and Brooklyn by a web of **ferry services**. These generally serve commuters, but some routes are worth checking out for a relatively cheap opportunity to get onto the water.

Beginning in 2017, the city's ferry system has been undergoing a major overhaul. A new city-supported ferry service dubbed **NYC Ferry** (ⓦferry.nyc) is gradually connecting dozens of neighbourhoods for a single $2.75 fare per ride. The initial system will comprise four core ferry routes: Rockaways to Lower Manhattan; South Brooklyn to Lower Manhattan; Astoria to Wall Street via 34th Street; and the existing East River Ferry Service (ⓦeastriverferry.com), which connects Midtown at 34th Street with various destinations in Brooklyn, Queens, Wall Street and Governors Island (in summer). In the meantime, separately managed **New York Water Taxi** (Wny watertaxi.com) is expected to continue to run a daily hop-on hop-off ferry service (April–Oct 9am–6.15pm; Nov–March 9am–5.30pm) around south Manhattan, linking Pier 79 (W 39th St) with World Financial Center, Pier 11 (near Wall St) and Dumbo in Brooklyn (day-pass $31, kids age 3–12 $19). Water Taxi is also expected to continue its daily shuttle from Wall Street's Pier 11 in Manhattan to Brooklyn's Ikea superstore in Red Hook (Mon–Fri 2–7.15pm, Sat & Sun 11.30am–8.40pm), an efficient way to reach this neighbourhood. The service is free on weekends, and $5 weekdays (if you spend over $10 in Ikea the ferry is free). In the summer (May–Sept) ferries from Pier 11 also zip across to Rockaway Beach (see p.253) and Sandy Hook on the Jersey Shore (W seastreak.com).

None of these options beats the bargain of the free Staten Island Ferry (☎718 727 2508, W siferry.com), which leaves from its own terminal in Lower Manhattan's Battery Park and provides stunning views of New York Harbor around the clock. It's also a commuter boat, so avoid crowded rush hours if you can. Departures are every fifteen to twenty minutes during rush hours (7–9am and 5–7pm), every thirty minutes during the day, and every sixty minutes late at night (the ferry runs 24hr) – weekends less frequently. Few visitors spend much time on Staten Island; it's easy to just turn around and get back on the ferry (you must disembark first), although there's plenty to see if you stay (see p.263).

By bike

Cycling is becoming a viable form of transport around New York, most enjoyable if you stick to the city's two hundred miles of **bike lanes** (W nycbike maps.com) as well as the cycle paths along the waterfront and in parks. Wear all possible safety equipment including pads and a helmet (required by law). When you park, double-chain and lock your bike (including wheels) to an immovable object if you'd like it to be there when you return.

In 2013 New York started a **bike share scheme** dubbed **Citi Bike** (W citibikenyc.com), with thousands of bikes and hundreds of stations all over the city. There are three payment options: 24-Hour Pass ($12; unlimited 30min rides), 3-Day Pass ($24; unlimited 30min rides) or annual membership ($163; unlimited 45min rides). Pay at any Citi Bike station kiosk with a credit card; you'll be given a code that will unlock a bike so you can begin your

trip – end at another station and relock the bike. Trips of over thirty minutes (or 45min with the annual pass) incur overtime fees of $4 for each additional fifteen minutes ($2.50 with annual pass).

Traditional **bike rentals** start at about $15–16 per hour or $45–55 per day – which means opening to closing (9.30am–6.30pm for instance). Bicycles can be rented all over the city (see p.400).

The media

Generally acknowledged as the media capital of the world, New York is the headquarters of just about all the country's major television news organizations and book and magazine publishers. This means that there is a newsstand on nearly every corner selling a wonderful variety of newspapers and magazines, as well as frequent opportunities to take part in television-show tapings (see box, p.360).

Newspapers and magazines

The New York Times ($2.50; W nytimes.com), an American institution (it was founded in 1851), prides itself on being the "paper of record" – America's quality national paper (it has the second-largest circulation in the US). "The Gray Lady" has solid international coverage, and places much emphasis on its news analysis.

It takes serious coordination to read the sizeable *Times* on the subway, one reason many turn to the *Daily News* and the *Post*. Tabloids in format and style, these rivals concentrate on local news. The *Daily News* ($1; W nydailynews.com) is a "picture newspaper" with many racy headlines. The *New York Post* ($1; W nypost .com), the city's oldest newspaper, started in 1801 by Alexander Hamilton, has been in decline for many years. Known for its solid city news and consistent conservative-slanted sermonizing, it also takes a fairly sensationalist approach to headlines.

The other New York-based daily newspaper is *The Wall Street Journal* ($3; W wsj.com); in fact a national paper (with the largest circulation in the US) that also has strong, conservative national and international news coverage – despite an old-fashioned design that eschews the use of photographs.

Weeklies and monthlies

The *Village Voice* (W villagevoice.com) stopped publishing its weekly print edition in 2017, but its website still offers opinionated stories that often focus on the media, LGBT issues and civil rights. It's also one of the best pointers to what's on around town (including the most interesting, inexpensive cuisine and shopping).

Other leading publications include the biweekly *New York* magazine ($5.99; Ⓦ nymag.com), which has reasonably good listings and is more of a society and entertainment journal, and weekly *Time Out New York* (Ⓦ timeoutny.com), a clone of its London original, combining the city's most comprehensive "what's on" listings with New York-slanted stories and features. Started in 1925, venerable weekly The *New Yorker* ($5.99; Ⓦ newyorker.com) has good highbrow listings, and features poetry and short fiction alongside its much-loved cartoons. The wackiest, and perhaps best, alternative to the *Voice* is *Paper* (Ⓦ papermag.com), a monthly that carries witty and well-written rundowns on city nightlife and restaurants as well as current news and gossip. If you want a weekly with more of a political edge, there's the ironic *New York Observer* (part-owned by Jared Kushner, President Trump's son-in-law), which ended its print run in 2016 and is now solely online (Ⓦ observer.com), and the *Forward* ($1; Ⓦ forward .com), a Jewish publication founded in 1897 that's also published in Russian and Yiddish editions.

Television

Any American will find on TV in New York mostly what they find at home, plus several multilingual stations. Channels 13 and 21 are given over to **PBS** (Public Broadcasting Service), which has earned the nickname "Purely British Station" for its fondness for British drama series (think *Downton Abbey*), although it excels at documentaries by the likes of Ken Burns and educational children's shows. The seventy-plus stations available on cable in most hotel rooms may be a bit more fascinating for foreign travellers; most cable channels are no better than the major networks (**ABC**, **CBS**, **NBC** and **Fox**), although a few of the specialized channels can be fairly interesting. Most of the national morning shows are taped live in New York, so you might recognize the backdrops and can even stop by (see box, p.360). NY1 is the city's 24-hour local news channel, available exclusively on cable.

Tourist information

The central **NYC Information Center** is at Times Square, Broadway Plaza (between W 43rd and W 44th sts; daily 9am–6pm; ☎ 212 484 1222, Ⓦ nycgo .com), with another inside Macy's at Herald Square,

151 W 34th St (between Seventh Ave and Broadway; Mon–Fri 9am–7pm, Sat 10am–7pm, Sun 11am–7pm). Both have bus and subway maps, information on hotels and accommodation (including discounts), and up-to-date leaflets on what's going on in the arts and elsewhere. You'll find other small tourist information centres and kiosks all over the city, starting with the airports, Grand Central and Penn stations, and Port Authority Bus Terminal.

INFORMATION CENTRES

Bronx Tourism Council 851 Grand Concourse, The Bronx ☎ 718 590 3518, Ⓦ ilovethebronx.com. Mon–Fri 9am–5pm.

Brooklyn Tourism and Visitors Center Brooklyn Borough Hall, 209 Joralemon St ☎ 718 802 3846, Ⓦ explorebk.com. Mon–Fri 9am–5pm.

Dairy Visitor Center & Gift Shop Central Park (mid-park at 65th St) ☎ 212 794 6564, Ⓦ centralparknyc.org. Daily 10am–5pm. Check also Ⓦ nycparks.org, the official word on all of the obscure, famous and thrilling events in the city's parks.

Downtown Alliance (Ⓦ downtownny.com) operates three visitor information kiosks (stocked with brochures and pamphlets): 7 World Trade Center (daily 9am–5pm); Bowling Green (daily 8am–6pm); Pier A Harbor House (daily 8am–6pm).

Federal Hall Information Center Federal Hall National Memorial, 26 Wall St. Mon–Fri 9am–5pm; closed federal holidays.

Official NYC Information Center–City Hall Southern end of City Hall Park, Broadway at Park Row ☎ 212 484 1222. Mon–Fri 9am–6pm, Sat & Sun 10am–5pm, holidays 9am–3pm.

Official NYC Information Center–South Street Seaport Hornblower Cruises, East River Waterfront Esplanade at Pier 15 ☎ 212 484 1222. Daily: May–Aug 9am–7pm; Sept–April 9am–5pm.

Tours and walks

First-time visitors may be interested in taking a tour – they come in all kinds of lengths, themes and modes of transport.

Bus tours

Bus tours can provide a good way to orient yourself. Gray Line New York, Port Authority Terminal at 42nd Street and Eighth Avenue (☎ 800 669 0051 or ☎ 212 445 0848, Ⓦ newyorksightseeing.com), runs a large number of popular **hop-on, hop-off bus tours** that range from $44 for just the Downtown Loop to two-day passes that cover all loops ($59). Discounts are available for children under 12. Call or look at the website for more information and to book a tour.

Helicopter tours

A more exciting option is to view the city by helicopter. This is very expensive, but you won't easily forget the experience. **Liberty Helicopter**

Tours (☎ 800 542 9933, ⓦ libertyhelicopter.com), at the Downtown Heliport at Pier 6 (near the Staten Island Ferry), offers tours from around $214 per person for twelve to fifteen minutes, to $299 per person for eighteen to twenty minutes (you also have to pay a $40 per person "heliport fee"). Helicopters take off regularly between 9am and 6pm every day unless winds and visibility are bad. Reservations are required; times vary on Sundays and holidays. **New York Helicopter** offers slightly cheaper rates from the same location (around $199 for a 12–15min tour, plus $30 "heliport fee"; ☎ 212 361 6060, ⓦ newyorkhelicopter.com).

Boat tours

A great way to see the island of Manhattan is to take one of many **harbour cruises** on offer. The **Circle Line** (☎ 212 563 3200, ⓦ circleline42.com) sails from Pier 83 at West 42nd Street and Twelfth Avenue, circumnavigating Manhattan and taking in everything from the Statue of Liberty to Harlem, complete with a live commentary; the three-hour tour runs year-round ($42, seniors $40, under-12s $34). The evening two-hour **Harbor Lights Cruise** (March–Sept; $38, seniors $36, under-12s $30) offers dramatic views of the skyline. Cruises also depart from Downtown Manhattan's South Street Seaport (see p.57). Alternatively, check the **NY Waterway** website (☎ 800 533 3779, ⓦ nywaterway.com).

SPECIALIST TOUR COMPANIES

★ **Big Apple Jazz Tours** ☎ 917 863 7854, ⓦ bigapplejazz.com. Insiders Gordon Polatnick and Amanda Humes offer a fabulous introduction to the Harlem jazz scene, with walking and bus tours that typically take in some of the lesser-known clubs and plenty of jazz history. Highlights include the Harlem Juke Joint Tours ($99; 4hr, two sets), and the Greenwich Village Jazz Crawl ($99; 4hr, three clubs). Both run every day but Tuesday.

★ **Big Onion Walking Tours** ☎ 212 439 1090, ⓦ bigonion.com. Guided by local history grad students, venerable Big Onion specializes in tours with an ethnic and historical focus. Almost every neighbourhood is

covered, from Harlem and the East Village, to Brooklyn Heights, Fort Greene and Chinatown. Cost is $25; the food-included "Multi-Ethnic Eating Tour" costs $32. Tours last about 2hr.

Greenwich Village Literary Pub Crawl ☎ 212 613 5796, ⓦ literarypubcrawl.com. Local actors lead you to several of the most prominent bars in literary history and read from associated works. Tours (3hr) run every Fri–Sun at 1pm beginning at the *White Horse Tavern* (see p.335). Reservations are required: $30; students and seniors $25. They also do literary tours of Brooklyn (Sat & Sun 1pm; 3hr), Times Square (Fri & Sat 2pm; 2hr 30min) and the High Line (Fri–Sun 11am; 2hr), all for the same price.

★ **Harlem Heritage Tours** ☎ 212 280 7888, ⓦ harlem heritage.com. Harlem native Neal Shoemaker runs cultural tours of this historic neighbourhood, ranging from Harlem Gospel (3hr; $39) to Harlem Renaissance-themed walking tours (2hr; $25). The tours sometimes include food, a cultural performance, film clips and/or bus service.

★ **Hush Hip Hop Tours** ☎ 212 714 3544, ⓦ hushtours.com. Illuminating 2–4hr bus and walking tours of the home of hip-hop, given by actual legends such as GrandMaster Caz, Rahiem, Kurtis Blow and DJ Kool Herc, from the South Bronx to Harlem and Brooklyn ($35–75).

Municipal Art Society of New York ☎ 212 935 3960, ⓦ mas .org/tours. Incredibly detailed historical and architectural tours in Manhattan, Brooklyn, Queens and the Bronx ($30), including daily tours of Grand Central Terminal (12.30pm; 1hr 15min; $25).

NoshWalks ☎ 212 222 2243, ⓦ noshwalks.com. Weekend ethnic culinary tours of neighbourhoods in Manhattan, Queens, Brooklyn and especially the Bronx, incorporating local history and culture, by the author of two NYC food guidebooks. Prices range $54–60 (Sat & Sun noon or 1pm; 3–4hr). Reservations recommended.

Scott's Pizza Tours ☎ 212 209 3370, ⓦ scottspizzatours.com. Yes, New York really does boast specialized pizza tours, and this is one of the best; Scott Wiener (and his team) knows his slices and leads gut-busting bus tours (Sun 11am only; $65; 4.5hr) or various walks (daily 11.15am or noon; $45; 3hr) of the best pizza joints all over the city – slices included.

Wall Street Experience ☎ 212 608 0130, ⓦ thewallstreetexperience.com. Edifying tours (1hr 15min–2hr) of the Financial District from Wall Street insiders (founder Andrew Luan was a trader at Deutsche Bank). Local history is enhanced with easy-to-understand segments on the 2008 financial crisis, 9/11 Memorial and the Wall Street Crash. Most tours range $35–50.

BIG APPLE GREETER

If you're nervous about exploring New York, or would just like to meet a local, contact **Big Apple Greeter**, 1 Centre St, Suite 2035 (☎ 212 669 8159, ⓦ bigapplegreeter.org), one of the best – and certainly cheapest – ways to see the city. This not-for-profit organization matches visitors with their active corps of trained volunteer "greeters". Specify the part of the city you'd like to see, indicate an aspect of New York life you'd like to explore, or plead for general orientation – whatever your interests, chances are they will find someone to take you around. Visits have a friendly, informal feel, and generally last a few hours. The service is free. You can call once you're in New York, but it's better to contact the organization as far in advance as possible.

Travel essentials

Costs

On a moderate budget, expect to spend at least $250 per night on accommodation in a mid-range, centrally located hotel in high season, plus $40–50 per person for a moderate sit-down dinner each night and about $20 more per person per day for takeaway and grocery meals. Getting around will cost $32 per person per week for unlimited public transport, plus $7–10 for the occasional cab ride. Sightseeing, drinking, clubbing, eating haute cuisine and going to the theatre can add exponentially to these costs. The combined New York City and State sales **tax** is 8.875 percent, payable on just about everything (the main exceptions are items of clothing or footwear that cost less than $110). Hotel rooms are subject to an additional 5.875 percent tax (for a total of 14.75 percent) and a $3.50 per night "occupancy tax" for rooms over $40 per night.

You're expected to **tip** in restaurants, bars, taxicabs, hotels (both the bellboy and the cleaning staff) and even some posh restrooms. In restaurants in particular, it's unthinkable not to leave the minimum (15 percent of the bill) – even if you hated the service.

Crime and personal safety

In two words: don't worry. New York has come a long way since the early 1990s. While the city can sometimes feel dangerous, the reality is somewhat different. As far as per capita crime rates go, New York is America's safest city with a population over one million; in 2016, the city recorded its lowest crime rate ever (since 1963, at least; statistics before then are unreliable). Areas such as Brownsville or East New York in Brooklyn remain sketchy, but you are highly unlikely to end up in either place. Take the normal **precautions** and you should be fine; carry bags closed and across your body, don't let cameras dangle, keep wallets in front – not back – pockets, and don't flash money around. You should also keep a firm grip on your phone/iPod/tablet on the subway (these are occasionally snatched just as the doors close). Mugging can and does happen, but rarely during the day. Avoid wandering empty streets or the subway late at night (especially alone). If you are unlucky enough to be mugged, try to stay calm and hand over the money. File the theft at the nearest police station and take the incident report to claim on your insurance back home.

Each area of New York has its own police precinct; to find the nearest station, call ☎ 646 610 5000 (during business hours only) or ☎ 311. In emergencies, phone ☎ 911 or use one of the outdoor posts that give you a direct line to the emergency services. This information, plus crime stats, is available at ⓦ nyc.gov/nypd.

Drugs

Possession of any "controlled substance" is still **illegal** in New York City, despite Mayor Bill De Blasio ordering the NYPD to stop arresting people for marijuana possession in 2014, and instead issue civil citations. That means that should you be found in possession of a very small amount of marijuana (up to 25g or just under one ounce), you won't go to jail – but you may be fined ($100 for a first offence) and, for foreigners, be threatened with deportation. Anyone caught smoking marijuana in public will be arrested however ($250 fine plus up to 90 days in jail), and if you have more than 25g (or try to sell any amount), you will likely go to jail (three months to fifteen years). Needless to say, being caught in possession of any amount of cocaine, heroin, crack or virtually any other drug will land you in serious trouble and will definitely lead to jail time.

Electricity

US electricity is **110V AC** and most plugs are two-pronged. Unless they're dual voltage (most mobile phones, cameras, MP3 players and laptops are), all Australian, British, European, Irish, New Zealand and South African appliances will need a voltage transformer as well as a plug adapter (older hair dryers are a common problem for travellers).

Health

There are few health issues specific to New York City, short of the common cold. Pharmacies can be found every few blocks – CVS and Duane Reade are the city's major chains, many open 24hr (such as the Duane Reade at 1470 Broadway, near Times Square). If you do get sick or have an accident, things can get incredibly **expensive**; organize **insurance** before your trip, just in case. It will cost upwards of $125 simply to see a doctor or dentist (plus extra for any treatment you receive), and prescription drugs can be very pricey – if you don't have US medical insurance (as opposed to normal overseas travel insurance), you'll have to cough up the money and make a claim when you get home.

Should you find yourself requiring a doctor or dentist, ask if your hotel has links to a local practice, or search online. Doctors in New York (especially Manhattan) often have long waiting lists however, and will be reluctant to see a new patient at short notice – if you have a minor ailment or injury a good option is to visit one of a growing number of **walk-in clinics** (no appointment required); CityMD (Ⓦcitymd.com) has several branches in the city including 216 E 14th St, 345 W 42nd St and 315 W 57th St. Most are open daily 8am to 10pm (with shorter hours Sat & Sun) and charge a basic fee of $125. If you have an accident or need urgent attention head to the **24-hour emergency rooms** at these and other Manhattan hospitals: New York Presbyterian (Cornell), E 70th St at York Ave (☎212 746 5050, Ⓦnyp.org); and Mount Sinai, 1468 Madison Ave at E 100th St (☎212 241 6500, Ⓦmountsinaihealth.org). Should you be in a serious accident don't worry, a medical service (ambulance) will pick you up and charge later (at least $1500).

Treatment is generally excellent, but note that even basic care at a hospital emergency room can rise from $300 to $15,000 incredibly quickly (fees for drugs, appliances, supplies and the attendant physician are all charged separately) – only go if you are very sick. Treatment for a simple leg break, for example, will total around $3000 – but if it requires surgery your final bill could range $20,000–35,000.

Insurance

You will want to invest in **travel insurance**. A typical travel-insurance policy usually provides cover for the loss of baggage, tickets, and – up to a certain limit – cash or cheques, as well as cancellation or curtailment of your journey. Many policies can be chopped and changed to exclude coverage you don't need – for example, sickness and accident benefits can often be excluded or included at will. Before you take out a new policy, however, it's worth checking whether you are already covered: some all-risks home-insurance

policies may cover your possessions when overseas, and many private medical schemes include cover when abroad.

Internet

Wireless is king in New York, with free wi-fi hotspots in places like Times Square and Bryant Park, most subway stations, complimentary connections at cafés like *Starbucks* and most hotels offering it for no charge. The new Link NYC scheme (Ⓦlink.nyc) is gradually replacing over 7500 payphones on New York streets with new structures called "Links", each providing superfast free wi-fi, phone calls (free to anywhere in the US), device charging and access to city services, maps and directions. If you're travelling without your own device, another alternative is to stop by a branch of the New York City Public Library, where free wi-fi (network "NYPL") and free computer internet access are available. To use the computers you first need to get a guest pass at the Stephen A. Schwarzman Building (the main library building; Mon & Thurs–Sat 10am–6pm, Tues & Wed 10am–8pm, Sun 1–5pm), at 42nd St and Fifth Ave; or Mid-Manhattan Library, 455 Fifth Ave (at 40th St; Mon–Thurs 8am–11am, Fri 8am–8pm, Sat & Sun 10am–6pm). Bring ID and proof of your home address. With the pass, you can reserve time slots at computers at any branch in person or via Ⓦnypl.org.

Laundry

Hotels do it but charge a lot. You're much better off going to an ordinary **laundromat** or dry cleaner, of which you'll find plenty listed in the *Yellow Pages* under "Laundries" or online. Most laundromats also offer a very affordable drop service, where, for about $1 per 1lb (0.45kg) or less, you can have your laundry washed, dried and tidily folded – often the same day (there's usually an $18–25 minimum though). Some budget hotels, YMCAs and hostels also have coin-operated washers and dryers.

ROUGH GUIDES TRAVEL INSURANCE

Rough Guides has teamed up with WorldNomads.com to offer great travel insurance deals. Policies are available to residents of over 150 countries, with cover for a wide range of adventure sports, 24hr emergency assistance, high levels of medical and evacuation cover and a stream of travel safety information. Roughguides.com users can take advantage of their policies online 24/7, from anywhere in the world – even if you're already travelling. And since plans often change when you're on the road, you can extend your policy and even claim online. Roughguides.com users who buy travel insurance with WorldNomads.com can also leave a positive footprint and donate to a community development project. For more information, go to Ⓦroughguides.com/travel-insurance.

Living and working in New York

It's not easy to live and work in New York, even for US residents. For anyone looking for **short-term** work, the typical urban employment options are available – temporary office work, waiting tables, babysitting, etc. For ideas and positions, check the employment ads in *The New York Times*, Craigslist NYC (Ⓦnewyork .craigslist.org) and the free neighbourhood tabloids available throughout the city.

If you're a foreigner, you start at a disadvantage. Unless you already have family in the US (in which case special rules may apply), you need a **work visa**, and these can be extremely difficult to get. The US visa system is one of the world's most complex, with a bewildering range of visa types to suit every circumstance (a "green card" refers to permanent resident status, meaning you can work without a visa, but this is hard to obtain without working or living here first) – most people hire a lawyer to do the paperwork ($2500 and up). Essentially, you'll need a firm offer of work from a US company; however, unless you have a special skill, few companies will want to go through the hassle of sponsoring you. Since tourists are not supposed to seek work, legally you'll have to apply for jobs from overseas. Plenty of foreigners do manage to work for short periods illegally in New York (typically cash-in-hand jobs, bar work or freelancing); be warned however that the penalties for doing so can be harsh (deportation and being barred from the US for up to ten years), and that if you repeatedly enter the country on a visa waiver, you are likely to be severely questioned at Immigration. For further visa information, go to Ⓦtravel.state.gov.

Finding a place to **stay** is tricky for everyone. A studio apartment – a single room with bathroom and kitchen – in a popular neighbourhood in Manhattan can go for upwards of $3000 per month (the more desirable Brooklyn neighbourhoods are not much cheaper). Many newcomers share studios and one-bedrooms among far too many people; it makes more sense to look in the outer boroughs or the nearby New Jersey towns of Jersey City and Hoboken. However, even some of these neighbourhoods are becoming expensive, and to find a real deal you must hunt hard and check out even the most unlikely possibilities. It frequently takes up to a month or two to find a place.

Most people employ the services of an agent, though they usually work for a fee based on a percentage of the first month's rent. Citi Habitats is one of the biggest agencies (Ⓦciti-habitats.com). Check also the ads in the *The New York Times* and on websites such as Ⓦstreeteasy.com/rentals. Try commercial and campus bulletin boards too, where you might secure a temporary apartment or sublet while the regular tenant is away.

Left luggage

The best place to leave luggage is with your **hotel concierge**, but you can also use Schwartz Luggage Storage ($10/day per item; ☎212 290 2626, Ⓦschwartztravel.com) at 357 W 37th St, near Penn Station (daily 8am–11pm), and 34 W 46th St, between Fifth and Sixth avenues near Grand Central (daily 9am–6pm).

Lost property

For things lost on **buses** or on the **subway**: NYC Transit Authority, at the West 34th Street/Eighth Avenue Station on the lower level-subway mezzanine (Mon, Tues & Fri 8am–3.30pm, Wed & Thurs 11am–6.30pm; ☎212 712 4500). See also Ⓦlostfound.mtanyct.info/lostfound. For things lost in a cab call ☎311; try to get the cab's medallion number (printed on your receipt).

Mail

Post offices in New York City are generally open Monday to Friday 9am to 5pm (though some open earlier) and Saturday from 9am to noon or later. The main post office in Midtown is at 421 Eighth Ave, at W 33rd St (☎212 967 8585) and is open Mon–Fri 7am–10pm, Sat 9am–9pm and Sun 11am–7pm. **Ordinary mail** within the US costs 49¢ for letters weighing up to an ounce, and 34¢ for postcards; addresses must include a **zip code** (postal code) and a return address in the upper left corner of the envelope. International letters and postcards will usually take about a week to reach their destination; rates are currently $1.15 for letters and postcards to all other countries. To find a post office or check up-to-date rates, see Ⓦusps.com or call ☎800 275 8777.

Maps

Other than our maps, the best maps of New York City are the free bus maps (ask any subway teller for one), as well as the huge, minutely detailed neighbourhood maps found fixed to the wall near the teller booth of subway stations. There's also a great selection at Ⓦrandmcnally.com. Street atlases of all five boroughs cost around $10–15; if you're after a map of one of the individual outer boroughs, try those produced by Geographia (**W**geographia-maps.com), on sale online and in bookshops for $5–15.

Money

US currency comes in bills of $1, $5, $10, $20, $50 and $100, plus various larger (and rarer) denominations. The dollar is made up of 100 cents (¢) in coins of one cent (usually called a penny), five cents (a nickel), ten cents (a dime), 25 cents (a quarter) and, rarely, fifty cents (a half-dollar) and one dollar. Change – especially quarters – is needed for buses, vending machines and telephones, so always carry plenty.

Most people on holiday in New York withdraw cash as needed from **ATMs**, which are at any bank branch and at many convenience stores and delis in the city, though the latter can charge fees of up to $3 for the service (in addition to bank charges). If you're visiting from abroad, make sure you have a personal identification number (PIN) that's designed to work overseas. A credit card is a must; American Express, MasterCard and Visa are widely accepted, and are almost always required for deposits at hotels. Most banks are open Monday to Friday 8.30am to 5pm, and a few have limited Saturday hours (major Citibank branches tend to open Sat 9am–3pm).

The value of the US dollar tends to vary considerably against other currencies. The dollar rose dramatically against the pound after the Brexit vote, and at press time one dollar was worth 0.78 British pounds (£), and 0.91 euros (€), 1.37 Canadian dollars (Can$), 1.35 Australian dollars (Aus$), 1.45 New Zealand dollars (NZ$) and 13.37 South African Rand (R). For current exchange rates, check **W**xe.com.

Opening hours

The opening hours of specific attractions are given throughout the Guide. As a general rule, most **museums** are open Tuesday to Sunday, 10am to 5/6pm, though most have one night per week where they stay open at least a few hours later. **Government offices** are open during regular business hours, usually 9am to 5pm. **Shop** hours vary widely, depending on the kind of shop and what part of town you're in, though you can generally count on their being open Monday to Saturday from around 10am to 6pm, with limited Sunday hours. Many of the larger chain or department stores will stay open to 9pm or later, and you generally don't have to walk more than a few blocks

anywhere in Manhattan to find a 24-hour deli. On national public holidays (see box below), banks and offices are likely to be closed all day, and most shops will be closed or have reduced hours.

Phones

International visitors who want to use their mobile (cell) phones in New York will need to check with their phone provider to make sure it will work, and what the call charges will be. Unless you have a tri-band phone, it is unlikely that a mobile bought for use outside the US or Canada will work inside the States (all iPhones should be OK). Even if your phone does work you'll need to be extra careful about **roaming charges**, especially for data, which can be extortionate; even checking voicemail can result in hefty charges. Many travellers turn off voicemail and data roaming before they travel. If you have a compatible (and **unlocked**) GSM phone and intend to use it a lot, it can be much cheaper to **buy a US SIM card** ($10 or less) to use during your stay (you can also buy a nano-SIM for iPhone 5 to 7). AT&T (**W**att.com) is your best bet. Some networks also sell basic flip phones (with minutes) for as little as $25 (no paperwork or ID required).

Public telephones are becoming harder to find due to the popularity of mobile phones; the new Link NYC scheme (p.32) is gradually replacing payphones in the city with internet stations, though these will also offer free phone calls to anywhere within the US. Assuming you can still find a payphone, the cost of a local call (within New York) is 25¢ for three or four minutes, depending on the

PUBLIC HOLIDAYS

The traditional **summer holiday period** runs between the weekends of Memorial Day, the last Monday in May, and Labor Day, the first Monday in September; when we denote "summer" hours in the Guide, this is what we mean.
New Year's Day Jan 1
Martin Luther King, Jr's Birthday Third Mon in Jan
Presidents' Day Third Mon in Feb
Memorial Day Last Mon in May
Independence Day July 4
Labor Day First Mon in Sept
Columbus Day Second Mon in Oct
Veterans' Day Nov 11
Thanksgiving Day Fourth Thurs in Nov
Christmas Day Dec 25

CALLING HOME FROM THE US

To make an international call, dial the international access code (in the US it's ☎011), then the destination's country code, before the rest of the number. Note that the initial zero is omitted from the area code when dialling the UK, Ireland, Australia and New Zealand from abroad.
Australia ☎011 + 61 + city code + local number.
Canada city code + local number.
New Zealand ☎011 + 64 + city code + local number.
UK ☎011 + 44 + city code + local number.
Republic of Ireland ☎011 + 353 + city code + local number.

---

carrier (each phone company runs its own booths). Calls elsewhere within the US are usually 25¢ for one minute; overseas long-distance rates are pricier, and you're better off using a prepaid calling card ($5, $10 and $20), which you can buy at most grocery stores and newsstands.

There are seven area codes in use in New York: ☎212, ☎332 and ☎646 for Manhattan, ☎718, ☎929 and ☎347 for the outer boroughs and ☎917 for (mostly) mobile phones city-wide. You must dial the area code, even if you're calling within the same area. For directory assistance, call ☎411.

Smoking

Since 2003 smoking has been banned in virtually all indoor public areas (including malls, bars, restaurants and most work places) in New York – fines start at around $100 for breaking this law. In 2011, smoking was also prohibited at all parks, beaches and pedestrian plazas.

Time

New York City is on Eastern Standard Time (EST), which is five hours behind Greenwich Mean Time (GMT), three hours ahead of Pacific Standard Time, fourteen to sixteen hours behind East Coast Australia (variations for Daylight Savings) and sixteen to eighteen hours behind New Zealand (variations for Daylight Savings).

Toilets

There are a variety of public restrooms scattered around the city, usually free (see ⓦ m3.mappler.net/nyrestroom).

Travellers with disabilities

In terms of sightseeing and entertainment, most New York ferries or cruise boats are accessible, as are Broadway theatres; top sights such as American Museum of Natural History, MoMA, Lincoln Center, 9/11 Museum, Empire State Building, Macy's, the Met and The Whitney are generally accessible, but many smaller museums and galleries are not.

For wheelchair users, getting around on the **subway** is next to impossible without someone to help you, and even then is extremely difficult at most stations. Several, but not all, lines are equipped with elevators, but this doesn't make much of a difference. The Transit Authority is working to make stations accessible, but at the rate they're going it won't happen soon. **Buses** are another story, and are the first choice of many disabled New Yorkers. All MTA buses are equipped with wheelchair lifts and locks. To get on a bus, wait at the bus stop to signal the driver you need to board; when he or she has seen you, move to the back door, where he or she will assist you. For travellers with other mobility difficulties, the driver will lower a special ramp to allow you easier access.

For wheelchair users, **taxis** are less of a possibility unless you have a collapsible chair, in which case drivers are required to store it and assist you; the unfortunate reality is that most drivers won't stop if they see you waiting. If you're refused, try to get the cab's medallion number and report the driver at ☎311. Most major hotels in New York have wheelchair-accessible rooms, including roll-in showers.

SERVICES

Big Apple Greeter (see box, p.30).
Lighthouse Guild 15 W 65th St ☎ 800 284 4422, ⓦ lighthouse guild.org. General services for the visually impaired.
The Mayor's Office for People with Disabilities 100 Gold St, 2nd floor ☎ 212 788 2830, ⓦ nyc.gov/html/mopd/home.html. General information and resources.
Traveler's Aid ☎ 202 546 1127, ⓦ travelersaid.org. Nonprofit organization with professional and volunteer staff who provide emergency assistance to disabled or elderly travellers at JFK Airport: you can find volunteers at the Ground Transportation Counters in each terminal or via their main office in retail area of Terminal 4 (daily 10am–6pm; ☎ 718 656 4870). They also operate at Newark Airport (Terminal B; ☎ 973 623 5052), daily 11am–9pm.

The Harbor Islands

The southern tip of Manhattan, together with the shores of New Jersey, Staten Island and Brooklyn, encloses the broad expanse of New York Harbor. When the Dutch arrived in 1624, it was teeming with fish, seals, whales and half of the world's oysters. With the water heavily polluted, the last oyster bed was closed in 1927, and though things are much improved (the harbour is officially clean enough to swim and fish), it will take many generations to recover its former glory. For now, the main attractions lie above water, where ferries provide dazzling views of New York's celebrated skyline. Take a boat to Liberty, Ellis or Governors islands (the only way to get to any of the Harbor Islands is by ferry) or catch the Staten Island Ferry, which traverses the harbour for free.

ARRIVAL AND DEPARTURE

Ferries to Liberty and Ellis islands Take the #1 train to South Ferry, R, W to Whitehall or the #4 or #5 trains to Bowling Green, then walk to Castle Clinton in Battery Park where you can buy tickets (round-trip $18.50, seniors $14, ages 4–12 $9). The best way to avoid the long wait (you must line up to buy tickets, and then again to clear security before boarding the ferry) is to buy tickets in advance online, preferably reserving the 9am slot, and have them emailed to you; you can then go straight to the security queue. From the nearby pier, Statue Cruises goes to Liberty, then on to Ellis Island (daily, every 30–45min; Nov–March 9.30am–5pm; March–Oct 8.30am–5pm; last departure from Battery Park 3.30pm; ☎ 201 604 2800, ⊛ statue cruises.com). You must be at security 30min before departure.

Ferries to Governors Island Ferries run from the Battery Maritime Building at Slip 7 (10 South St) just northeast of the Staten Island Ferry Terminal (May–Sept Mon–Fri 10am–4.15pm, hourly, last ferry back 6pm; Sat &

Sun 10am, 11am, then every 30min till 5.30pm, last ferry back 7pm; $2 return; free Sat & Sun 10am, 11am & 11.30am). Access is on a first-come, first-served basis, and limited to 400 people/trip. Call ahead or check the websites (☎ 212 825 3045, ⊛ nps.gov/gois and ⊛ govisland.com) for the up-to-date schedule. Ferries also run from Brooklyn Bridge Park's Pier 6 (end of Atlantic Ave) on weekends May to Sept (11am–5.30pm, hourly from 11.30am; last ferry back 7pm; $2 return; 11am & 11.30am free), and the new NYC Ferry service (see p.27) connects Pier 102 on the eastern side of the island with Wall St/Pier 11, Brooklyn Bridge Park, Red Hook and other locations along the East River on Sat and Sun in season ($2.75 per ride).

Ferries to Staten Island The Staten Island Ferry (free; ⊛ siferry.com) departs every 30min and shuttles between Manhattan and the "forgotten borough" (see p.263). While it provides a beautiful panorama of the harbour and downtown skyline, it doesn't actually stop at any of the Harbor Islands.

INFORMATION

Tickets The basic ferry ticket to Liberty and Ellis islands allows entry to Ellis Island (including the museum) and Liberty Island grounds only. If you want to visit the museum at the base of the Statue of Liberty and the pedestal observation deck (168 steps up), you need a "pedestal access" ticket (no extra charge; includes audio guide). To enjoy the cramped but spectacular views from the crown of the statue, buy a special "crown ticket" ($21.50, seniors $17, ages 4–12 $12; includes round-trip ferry) in advance and climb another 162 steps from the

pedestal – note that you must go through another security screening before entry to the statue and museum.

Timing your visit Give yourself at least half a day to see both Liberty and Ellis islands. Liberty Island needs at least one hour (that's only if you're walking around the island, and not going inside the statue), and Ellis requires at least two hours to do its museum justice. Start out as early as possible: keep in mind that if you take the last ferry of the day to Liberty Island, you won't be able to get over to Ellis. Allow at least two hours for a leisurely amble around Governors Island.

The Statue of Liberty

Liberty Island · Daily 9.30am–5pm · Free with ferry ticket (extra $3 for "crown ticket"); ranger-guided tours of Liberty Island are offered throughout the day (free) · ☎ 212 363 3200, ⊛ nps.gov/stli and ⊛ libertyellisfoundation.org

Of all America's symbols, none has proved more enduring than the **Statue of Liberty**, looming over the harbour from its pedestal on tiny **Liberty Island**. Indeed, there is probably no more immediately recognizable profile in existence than that of Lady

---

A BEACON TO THE WORLD

These days, an immigrant's first view of the US is more likely to be the customs check at JFK Airport, but the Statue of Liberty nevertheless remains a stirring sight. **The New Colossus** by American Jewish poet Emma Lazarus, inspired by the new immigrant experience and inscribed on a tablet on the pedestal, is no less quotable now than when it was written in 1883:

Give me your tired, your poor,
Your huddled masses yearning to breathe free,
The wretched refuse of your teeming shore.
Send these, the homeless, tempest-tost to me,
I lift my lamp beside the golden door!"

Liberty, who stands with torch in hand, clutching a stone tablet. Measuring some 305ft from her pedestal base, she has acted as the figurehead of the American Dream for more than a century. When the first waves of European refugees arrived in the mid-nineteenth century, it was she who greeted them – the symbolic beginning of a new life.

The **statue** itself, which depicts Liberty throwing off her shackles and holding a beacon to light the world, is the creation of French sculptor **Frédéric Auguste Bartholdi**, who crafted it a hundred years after the American Revolution, supposedly to commemorate the solidarity between France and America. (Actually, he originally intended the statue for Alexandria, Egypt.) Bartholdi built Liberty in Paris between 1874 and 1884, starting with a terracotta model and enlarging it through four successive versions to its present size of 151ft. The final product is a construction of thin copper sheets bolted together and supported by an iron framework designed by **Gustave Eiffel**. The statue had to be taken apart into hundreds of pieces in order to ship it to New York, where it was finally reassembled, although it was another two years before it could be properly unveiled. Only through the efforts of newspaper magnate Joseph Pulitzer, a keen supporter of the statue, were the necessary funds raised and Liberty was formally dedicated by President Cleveland on October 28, 1886, amid a

THE HARBOR ISLANDS

1

patriotic outpouring that has never really stopped. Indeed, fifteen million people descended on Manhattan for the statue's centennial celebrations, and some three million people make the pilgrimage here each year.

The **Liberty Island Museum** at the base of the **pedestal** (designed by famed architect Richard Morris Hunt) is definitely worth a visit, though you must get a crown or pedestal ticket in advance to enter (see p.37). The downstairs lobby contains the original torch and flame (completed first and used to raise funds for the rest of the statue), and the small exhibition upstairs tells the story of Lady Liberty with prints, photographs, posters and replicas. At the top you can look up into the centre of the statue's skirts – make sure you get a glance of her riveted and bolted interior, and her fire-hazard staircase. After you've perused the statue's interior offerings, take a turn around the balcony outside – the views are predictably superb. Many visitors pay the extra $3 (in advance; see p.37) to climb to the **crown** from here, though there's not much else to see (and the view is quite limited). Note that a brand-new **Statue of Liberty Museum** is due to open sometime in 2019.

Ellis Island National Museum of Immigration

Daily 9.30am–5.15pm • Free • Hourly 40min ranger-guided tours (free); audio tours (free); 90min "hard hat" tours ($53.50) • ☎ 212 363 3200, ⓦ nps.gov/elis and ⓦ libertyellisfoundation.org

Just across the water from Liberty Island, and fifteen minutes farther from Manhattan by ferry, sits **Ellis Island**, the former arrival point for over twelve million immigrants to the US. After $162 million was donated for its restoration, the main complex reopened in 1990 as the impressive **Ellis Island National Museum of Immigration**, which eloquently recaptures the spirit of the place with artefacts, photographs, maps and personal accounts that tell the story of the immigrants who passed through here on their way to a new life in America – some 100 million Americans can trace their roots to those who arrived on the island.

On the first floor, the excellent "**Peopling of America**" galleries chronicle four centuries of immigration, offering a statistical portrait of those who disembarked here – who they were, where they came from and why they came. After a major expansion, completed in 2015, you enter through the historic **Baggage Room** where a giant, glowing globe highlights migration patterns through history and the "**American Flag of Faces**" allows families to upload photos of their ancestors as part of a huge video installation. "**Journeys: New Eras of Immigration**" explores post-World War II and contemporary migration trends, while the huge, vaulted **Registry Room** on the second floor, scene of so much immigrant trepidation, elation and despair, has been left imposingly bare, with just a couple of inspectors' desks and American flags. The "**Through America's Gate**" exhibits in the west wing re-create the process that immigrants went through on their way to naturalization; the white-tiled chambers are soberingly bureaucratic. Exhibits in the east wing explore immigration from 1880 to 1924. Each gallery is augmented by recorded voices of those who passed through Ellis Island, recalling their experiences. On the third floor, "**Treasures From Home**" displays the photographs and small mementoes – train timetables, toiletries and toys – brought in by the immigrants.

The museum's **American Family Immigration History Center** (same times as museum) holds a database of over 22 million immigrants who passed through New York between 1892 and 1924. Outside, the names of over 700,000 of these immigrants are engraved in copper; while the "Wall of Honor" is always accepting new submissions, it controversially requires families to pay $150 to be included on the list.

You can also opt for a fascinating guided ninety-minute "**hard hat" tour** of the ruined Ellis Island Immigrant Hospital (reserve through Statue Cruises, p.37), on the other side of the island.

1

ELLIS ISLAND: THE IMMIGRANT EXPERIENCE

Up until the 1850s, there was no official **immigration process** in New York, but a surge of Irish, German and Scandinavian immigrants forced authorities to open an immigration centre at Castle Clinton in Battery Park. By the 1880s, millions of desperate immigrants (mostly southern and eastern Europeans) were leaving their homelands in search of a new life in America. The Battery Park facilities proved totally inadequate, and in 1892 Ellis Island became the new immigration station.

The immigrants who arrived on Ellis Island were all **steerage-class passengers**; richer immigrants were processed at their leisure on-board ship. Though the processing centre had been designed to accommodate 500,000 immigrants per year, double that number arrived during the early part of the twentieth century; as many as 11,747 immigrants passed through the centre on a single day in 1907. Once inside, each family was split up – men sent to one area, women and children to another – while a series of checks weeded out the undesirables and the infirm. The latter were taken to the second floor, where doctors would check for "loathsome and contagious diseases" as well as signs of insanity. Those who failed medical tests were marked with a white cross on their backs and either sent to the hospital or put back on the boat; only two percent of all immigrants were ever rejected, and of those, many jumped into the sea and tried to swim to Manhattan, or committed suicide. Eighty percent of immigrants were processed in less than eight hours, after which they headed either to New Jersey and trains to the West, or into New York City. After 1924, Ellis Island became primarily a **detention facility** (during World War II, some seven thousand German, Italian and Japanese people were detained here), which finally closed in 1954.

Governors Island

May–Sept Mon–Fri 10am–6pm, Sat & Sun 10am–7pm • Free • 1hr 30min guided tours Wed–Sun 2.30pm (free; see website for details) • ☎ 212 825 3045, ⓦ nps.gov/gois and ⓦ govisland.com

"Nowhere in New York is more pastoral," wrote travel writer Jan Morris of **Governors Island**, a 172-acre tract of land across from Brooklyn with unobstructed views of the Financial District and New York Harbor. With its village greens and colonial architecture reminiscent of a New England college campus, a visit here makes for an intriguingly offbeat and bucolic day-trip, offering a dramatic contrast to the skyscrapers across the water. The main ferry arrives at Soissons Landing, where you'll find the **visitors' centre** (with maps and information about the island) and a bookshop. You can explore on foot or by bike (Blazing Saddles, at Liggett Terrace; $25/day; ☎ 917 440 9094, ⓦ blazingsaddles.com), while two **food courts** (Liggett Terrace) provide a wide range of eating options.

When the Dutch arrived in 1624, they actually made camp here first before cautiously occupying Manhattan, and "purchased" what they called Noten Island from the Native Americans in 1637 (only to lose it to the British in the 1660s). Set aside for the "benefit and accommodation of His Majesty's Governors", Governors Island formally received its current name in 1784. Between 1794 and 1966, the US Army occupied the island, and for the following thirty years it was the US Coast Guard's largest and most extensive installation. In 2003, 22 acres of the island were sold to the National Park Service as the Governors Island National Monument.

Fort Jay and Colonels' Row

Fort Jay Mon & Tues 10am–4pm (grounds only), Wed–Sun 10am–5.30pm

It's a short stroll from the dock up to **Fort Jay**, completed in 1796. Rebuilt in 1806–09, its dense stone walls helped to deter the British from attacking the city in 1812, though its colonial-style interior buildings seem more in tune with the sleepy college campus vibe outside. To the south of the fort lies the grassy expanse of the **Parade Ground**, the grey stone Episcopalian **Chapel of St Cornelius the Centurion**, completed in 1906, and the humble white-clapboard **Our Lady Star of the Sea Chapel**, which served as the Roman Catholic house of worship from 1942. Lining the west side of the Parade

Ground is **Colonels' Row**, a collection of historic redbrick housing built between 1893 and 1917 (and used by officers). The row is backed by the impressive bulk of **Liggett Hall**, a barracks completed in 1929.

Nolan Park

On the east side of the Parade Ground the shady lanes of **Nolan Park** are home to some beautifully preserved, bright yellow Neoclassical and Federal-style mansions dating from 1854 to 1902 (occupied by officers during the army period), notably the **Governor's House** (built around 1813) and handsome **Admiral's House** (built in 1843 and the site of the Reagan–Gorbachev Summit in 1988). Many of these are gradually being opened, or converted into seasonal art galleries, studios and stores such as **Holocenter House** (#4B; Fri 2–4pm, Sat & Sun 11am–4pm), which specializes in light-based installations.

Castle Williams

Wed–Sun 10am–5.30pm • Tours Wed–Sun 11.30am–4.30pm every 30min; ticket required, 1hr in advance; free

Completed in 1811 on the northwest corner of the island, **Castle Williams** is a circular brick and sandstone fort built to complement the near-identical Castle Clinton in Battery Park. Used as a prison until 1966, the tiny cells inside held as many as a thousand Confederate soldiers during the Civil War. Renovated in 2012, the first floor is surrounded by small exhibits charting its varied history, while **tours** take in all three levels and the roof.

Hammock Grove and The Hills

The island also has plenty of green spaces in which to lounge in the sun, as well as a breezy promenade with stellar views of Manhattan – you can stroll or cycle right down to the southern tip, dubbed **Picnic Point**, via four man-made **hills**, rising 80ft above the harbour. En route, **Hammock Grove** is an enticing space just south of Liggett Terrace, studded with comfy red hammocks (first come, first served).

NEW YORK STOCK EXCHANGE

The Financial District

With its dizzying assemblage of skyscrapers, the Financial District has long been synonymous with the New York of popular imagination. This is where New Amsterdam was founded in the 1620s, and today the heart of the world's financial markets is still home to some of the city's most historic streets and sights. Over time, the area has seen more than its fair share of destruction and renewal; indeed, thanks to landfill, today's Financial District is double the size of that first Dutch colony, and many of the early colonial buildings burned down in either the Revolutionary War or the Great Fire of 1835. In September 2001, the character of the Financial District was altered radically once again after the attack on the Twin Towers, while Hurricane Sandy wreaked further devastation in 2012.

Yet the regeneration of the area is startling: the new One World Trade Center now towers above the city, and a spate of ambitious projects from parks and offices to transport hubs and new hotels peppers the area. Though some banks still maintain headquarters here, the most dramatic change is in the increase of residential development, as new condos and luxury conversions (many from former bank buildings) prove that the Financial District is once again in the process of integrating its present and future into its past.

Wall Street and around

2

Subway #2, #3, #4, #5 to Wall St

Associated with money since the eighteenth century, **Wall Street** takes its name from the wooden stockade built by the Dutch in 1653 to protect themselves from the British colonies further north (the wall was dismantled in 1699). Though it remains the apex of the global financial system thanks to the New York Stock Exchange, most of the street was closed to traffic after 9/11, and fitness studios and condos have replaced almost all the banks that were once based here.

Trinity Church

79 Broadway, at Wall St • Daily 7am–6pm • Free • ☎ 212 602 0800, ⓦ trinitywallstreet.org • Subway #4, #5 to Wall St

Perched at Wall Street's western end on Broadway is **Trinity Church**, a stoic onlooker of the street's dealings. The church held its first service in 1698, but this stern Gothic Revival structure – the third model – went up in 1846. It was the city's tallest building for fifty years, a reminder of how relatively recently high-rise Manhattan has sprung up. Despite now being surrounded by skyscrapers, Trinity has the air of an English country church – hardly surprising, given that its architect, Richard Upjohn, was English. As you enter the church itself, note the ornate bronze doors designed by Richard Morris Hunt in the 1890s, a memorial to John Jacob Astor III. Trinity's colonial **graveyard** also sees a steady stream of visitors, mainly thanks to blockbuster musical *Hamilton*; in

---

GREED IS GOOD: THE RISE AND FALL OF WALL STREET

Admired, feared and generally despised by most Americans at the time, **J.P. Morgan** is considered the godfather of US merchant banking (that is, banking for governments and big companies rather than individuals), presiding over New York's gradual replacement of London (largely bailed out by Morgan-led banks during World War I) as the world's biggest financial market from his base on **Wall Street** between 1858 and 1913. Wall Street and its merchant banks (also "investment banks") boomed in the 1920s, survived the Great Depression and regulation of the 1930s and led the world with innovative products such as "junk bonds" and derivatives into the 1990s. Yet today, all the big investment banks have gone and most of Wall Street has been converted into condos – so where did it all go wrong?

A series of crashes, starting with the dot-com bust and 9/11 attacks in 2001, battered the markets and began the physical move away from the Financial District and Wall Street (as much for security as high rental costs). The **2008–09 financial crisis** proved the hardest blow. Investment banks had arranged hundreds of CDOs (Collateralized Debt Obligations), essentially bonds secured by subprime mortgages, since 1987; when overextended borrowers began to default on their mortgages all over the US, the money dried up. Insurer AIG was bailed out by the US government to the tune of $186 billion, and one by one the investment banks failed, unable to cope with mind-boggling losses. Lehman Brothers, founded in 1850, collapsed with debts of over $700 billion (the largest bankruptcy in US history), and Bear Stearns and Merrill Lynch were sold to JPMorgan Chase and Bank of America respectively. Finally, Goldman Sachs and Morgan Stanley (the last heir to JP's empire) converted to traditional bank holding companies (thus allowing them access to federal funds), ending the era of merchant banks on Wall Street.

The financial sector remains a huge part of the New York economy, but these days hedge funds, not banks, tend to manage the biggest portfolios, and trading rooms are as likely to be based in Connecticut and Jersey City (aka "Wall Street West") as Manhattan.

the south churchyard, flowers often cover the tombs of **Eliza** and **Alexander Hamilton** (see box, p.208), while Revolutionary War spy **Hercules Mulligan** (another character in the musical) lies nearby. Eliza's sister, **Angelica Schuyler Church** (another beloved character from the musical), is buried at the back of the north churchyard.

1 and 14 Wall Street

1 and 14 Wall Street • Closed to the public • Subway #2, #3, #4, #5 to Wall St

Opposite Trinity Church, the soaring former Bank of New York building at **1 Wall Street** is an Art Deco wonder, topping out at 654ft in 1931. From the outside, you can

THE FINANCIAL DISTRICT

0   200
yards

■ ACCOMMODATION	
AKA Wall Street	3
Andaz Wall Street	5
The Beekman	1
Gild Hall	2
Riff Downtown	4

● EATING	
Acqua at Peck Slip	4
Adrienne's Pizzabar	14
Augustine	1
Black Fox Coffee	9
Blue Smoke	3
Bluestone Lane	10
Delmonico's	12
Eataly NYC Downtown	8
Fowler & Wells	2
Harry's Café & Steak	13
Le District	7
Leo's Bagels	11
Nobu Downtown	5
The Paris Café	6

■ SHOPPING	
Century 21	1

■ DRINKING	
BARS	
Clinton Hall	3
Dead Rabbit	4
Jeremy's Alehouse	2
Loopy Doopy Bar	1
Pier A Harbor House	6
The Porterhouse at Fraunces Tavern	5

FINANCIAL DISTRICT HIGHLIGHTS

African Burial Ground Visitor Center Rare and fascinating insight into the lives of African slaves in colonial New York. See p.61

Alfresco dining on Stone Street Historic street lined with bars and restaurants that spill outside in summer. See p.47

National September 11 Memorial & Museum Monumental and moving homage to those killed on 9/11. See p.49

One World Trade Center Observatory Visit the loftiest perch in America for sensational views of the city. See p.48

Pier A Harbor House Elegant nineteenth-century pier with oyster bar and restaurant overlooking the harbour. See p.52

Wall Street The heart of the world's financial system is lined with historic statues, skyscrapers and museums. See p.43

2

just about make out the shimmering mosaic lobby interior – when a Whole Foods supermarket opens here sometime in 2018 you might be able to get a closer look (the rest of the building is being converted into condos). On the other side of the street, the old Bankers Trust Building at **14 Wall Street** (539ft) was completed in 1912 and is best known for its ostentatious step-pyramid top, modelled on the Greek Mausoleum at Halicarnassus – wander down Broad Street for the best views.

New York Stock Exchange

11 Wall St and 18 Broad St • Closed to the public • ⓦ nyse.com • Subway #2, #3, #4, #5 to Wall St

The purse strings of the capitalist world are controlled behind the Neoclassical facade of the **New York Stock Exchange** at the corner of Wall and Broad streets, where billions of dollars change hands on an average trading day (Mon–Fri 9.30am–4pm). The stock exchange's public viewing galleries were closed indefinitely after 9/11, so it can only be admired from the outside. The main building at 18 Broad St, with its six mammoth Corinthian columns and monumental statues representing Integrity surrounded by Agriculture, Mining, Science, Industry and Invention, dates from 1903 and was designed by George B. Post (the statuary was created by John Quincy Adams Ward and Paul Wayland Bartlett).

The origins of the exchange lie in the aftermath of the Revolutionary War, when Secretary of the Treasury Alexander Hamilton offered $80 million worth of government bonds for sale. Not only did the public snap them up, but merchants also started trading the bonds, along with bills of exchange, promissory notes, and other commercial paper. Trading became so popular that in 1792 a group of 22 stockbrokers and merchants gathered beneath a buttonwood tree on Wall Street, signing the "**Buttonwood Agreement**" and forming the initial trading group that would go on to be renamed the New York Stock Exchange in 1817. The event is commemorated by a tiny **buttonwood tree** on the sidewalk in front of 18 Broad St (it's not the original).

Federal Hall

26 Wall St, at Nassau St • Summer Mon–Sat 9am–5pm; rest of year Mon–Fri 9am–5pm • Free; free 30min tours 10am, 1pm, 2pm & 3pm • ⓣ 212 825 6990, ⓦ nps.gov/feha • Subway #2, #3, #4, #5 to Wall St

One of the city's finest examples of Greek Revival architecture, **Federal Hall** was completed in 1842 as the US Customs House, but is best known today for John Quincy Adams Ward's monumental 1883 **statue of George Washington** outside. The statue recalls the heady days of 1789, when Washington was sworn in as America's first president on a second-floor balcony here – back then, this site was occupied by New York's second City Hall (demolished in 1812). Elements of the US Constitution and Bill of Rights were also hammered out by Congress inside between 1785 and 1790, when New York was the de facto capital of the nation.

The documents and exhibits inside are worth a look, as is the main hall itself, with its elegant marble rotunda, Corinthian columns and Cretan maidens worked into the decorative railings. Displays cover the history of the building and pay tribute to the Washington connection (the Bible he used in the 1789 ceremony is usually on display), as well as the landmark libel case of German immigrant John Peter Zenger (1697–1746), who was arrested for exposing government corruption in 1734, and was defended successfully by Scottish lawyer Andrew Hamilton. It's also worth checking out the well-stocked **Discover New York Harbor Visitor Information Center** at the back of the building.

2

23 Wall Street

23 Wall St • Closed to the public • Subway #2, #3, #4, #5 to Wall St

Opposite Federal Hall at **23 Wall Street** is the unassuming building that once lay at the heart of the global financial system. In 1912, financier **J.P. Morgan** had his marble-clad headquarters built here; the extravagant use of what was then the most expensive real estate in the world (the building is only four storeys tall) epitomized the patrician aloofness of the period – the bank didn't even bother adding its name to the facade. J.P. Morgan had been based on this spot since 1873, taking his father's words to heart – "always be a bull on America". In 1920, a horse-drawn cart blew up out front, killing 38 and wounding over a hundred. The bombing has never been explained, though the most popular theory holds that the blast was planned by Italian anarchists taking revenge for the arrest of Sacco and Vanzetti. The shrapnel marks on the building's wall have never been repaired, out of respect for the victims. In 2003, J.P. Morgan sold the building for $100 million and it's remained inexplicably empty ever since – at the time of research, Japanese clothing chain Uniqlo was considering leasing the space.

Trump Building

40 Wall St • Closed to the public • Subway #2, #3, #4, #5 to Wall St

Further along Wall Street, the former Bank of Manhattan Trust building was briefly the world's tallest skyscraper in 1930 (at 927ft), before being topped by the Chrysler Building (whose designers secretly increased the height of their tower after no. 40 was completed). Today, it's known as the **Trump Building** (as distinct from Trump Tower in Midtown; see p.131) after the flamboyant tycoon (and US president) who bought it for just $1 million in 1995 (he has claimed it is worth at least $600 million since then).

Museum of American Finance

48 Wall St • Tues–Sat 10am–4pm • $8 • ☎ 212 908 4110, ⓦ moaf.org • Subway #2, #3, #4, #5 to Wall St

Across William Street from the Trump Building, the former Bank of New York & Trust building is now home to the **Museum of American Finance**. Housed in the fittingly opulent former main banking hall completed in 1929, this illuminating museum is the best place to gain an understanding of what Wall Street is all about: stocks, bonds and futures trading are demystified through multimedia presentations and a stack of rare artefacts that include a 1792 bond signed by George Washington, an 1850s gold ingot and a stretch of ticker tape from the opening moments of 1929's Great Crash. Financial pioneer Alexander Hamilton (see box, p.208) is commemorated with his own room, while documentaries on Wall Street are shown throughout the day.

20 Exchange Place

20 Exchange Place • Closed to the public • Subway #2, #3 to Wall St

One block south of Wall Street on William Street, **20 Exchange Place** is a truly stupendous Art Deco tower (741ft), built for City Bank-Farmers Trust in 1931 and now a series of luxury apartments. The main entrance is adorned by eleven stone impressions of coins from the countries where the bank had offices, while the nineteenth floor is circled by fourteen "Giants of Finance", helmeted figures that look like classical Greek warriors.

Delmonico's

56 Beaver St, at William St • Mon–Fri 11.30am–10pm, Sat 5–10pm • ☎ 212 509 1144, ⓦ delmonicosrestaurant.com • Subway #2, #3 to Wall St

Venerable **Delmonico's** is technically the oldest restaurant in the country (see p.280), although it's been closed for prolonged periods and has changed owners several times over the years. The Swiss-born Delmonico brothers opened their first café on William Street in 1827, and moved here ten years later when eating options in New York were generally restricted to British-style taverns; in addition to the usual array of Astors and Morgans, Charles Dickens, French exile Louis-Napoléon and generals Grant and Sherman all dined here. The current building (completed in 1891) is a bastion of opulence, with its grand portico supported by columns brought from the ruins of Pompeii and a menu that still features many of the restaurant's culinary inventions.

Queen Elizabeth II September 11th Garden

Hanover Square, Pearl St and Stone St • 24hr • Free • ☎ 212 682 7945, ⓦ queenelizabethgarden.org • Subway #2, #3 to Wall St

Just to the south of *Delmonico's*, the **Queen Elizabeth II September 11th Garden** is dedicated to the 67 British and other Commonwealth citizens killed on 9/11 (Australia lost 11, Canada lost 24). Queen Elizabeth II paid her respects here in 2010 – the rounded "Braemar" stone and cairn at the south end of the garden comes from her Balmoral estate, inscribed with the distance from here to Aberdeen (3281 miles). Overlooking the garden is the majestic **India House**, completed in 1853 for Hanover Bank and subsequently used by the New York Cotton Exchange (1870–85). It's now an exclusive club for financial types, and houses the more accessible *Harry's Café* (see p.280).

70 Pine Street

70 Pine St • Subway #2, #3 to Wall St

One block north of Wall Street on Pearl Street, **70 Pine Street** (952ft) was completed in 1932 for Cities Service Company (the precursor of Venezuelan oil and gas conglomerate CITGO). It is one of New York's most graceful and iconic Art Deco towers, though it can be frustratingly hard to get a decent view – head down Cedar Street for the best glimpse. Insurance giant AIG bought the building in 1976, but as a consequence of the 2008 financial crisis sold it for around $150 million – it was converted to luxury condos in 2015. Since then the basement has been transformed into a **City Acres Market** food hall (ⓦ cityacresmarket.com), while the *Q&A Hotel* occupies another portion of the building. The gorgeous Art Deco lobby is open to the public (it's home to Aussie coffee shop *Black Fox*), while the former observation deck may be eventually turned into a restaurant.

Federal Reserve Bank

33 Liberty St (enter at 44 Maiden Lane) • ☎ 212 720 6130, ⓦ newyorkfed.org • Subway A, C, #2, #3 to Fulton St

Three blocks north of Wall Street lies the **Federal Reserve Bank of New York**. Completed in 1924 and the largest of America's twelve reserve banks, there's good reason for the building's fortress-like exterior (based on Florentine palazzi): stashed 80ft below street

---

FROM FIRE TO FINE DINING ON STONE STREET

The best-preserved block of nineteenth-century architecture in the Financial District is narrow, cobblestone **Stone Street**, between Hanover Square and Coenties Alley – also the Financial District's best place to eat and drink. It's a vast open-air beer garden packed with a party-hardy Wall Street crowd on summer nights, when places like *Adrienne's Pizzabar* (see p.281) cover the street with picnic tables. Many of the Greek Revival-style counting houses here were built in the wake of the Great Fire of 1835, which destroyed much of the area.

2

FEDERAL RESERVE BANK TOURS

Museum & Gold Vault Tours (45min–1hr; free) are normally given Monday to Friday (1pm & 2pm), but you must reserve these online at least one week in advance (try to make a booking when slots become available, thirty days in advance, as tours fill up fast). Tours begin with a look around the museum level and an explanation of the history and role of the reserve, followed by an elevator ride down to the vault itself; note that you'll only get close to one gleaming heap of gold bricks. You'll need to arrive thirty minutes early with your e-ticket and photo ID, such as a driving licence or passport; taking pictures or videos is not allowed.

---

level is ten percent of the world's gold reserves – seven thousand tonnes of it (worth around $255 billion in 2017). Yet as impressive as this sounds, gold has played a minor part in global finance since 1971 (when President Nixon ended trading gold at the fixed price of $35/ounce), and today the reserve is used primarily by foreign governments for bookkeeping and reporting purposes. The only way inside is by guided tour (see box above).

World Trade Center and around

ⓦ wtc.com • Subway A, C, #2, #3, #4, #5 to Fulton St; E to World Trade Center; R, W to Cortlandt St; #1 to Rector St

The former location of the Twin Towers and Ground Zero after the 9/11 attacks, the new **World Trade Center** complex is once again the centrepiece of Lower Manhattan. Anchored by **One World Trade Center**, the whole multibillion-dollar site (which includes five towers, transport hub and performing arts centre) is unlikely to be completed before 2021, though Fumihiko Maki's **4 World Trade Center** (978ft) opened in 2013 (containing a branch of **Eataly**; p.281) and **3 World Trade Center** (1079ft), designed by Richard Rogers, topped out in 2016. Construction of the potentially stunning **2 World Trade Center** (1270ft) by Bjarke Ingels is currently on hold (anchor tenants 21st Century Fox and News Corp backed out of the project in 2016). Santiago Calatrava's **St Nicholas Greek Orthodox National Shrine** (ⓦ stnicholaswtc.org), on the corner of elevated **Liberty Park**, should be open sometime in 2018. The park itself contains **The Sphere**, a large metallic sculpture by German sculptor Fritz Koenig, which survived the 9/11 attacks and was transferred here from Battery Park in 2017.

One World Trade Center

285 Fulton St (enter on West St, at Vesey St) • Daily: early May to early Sept 9am–10pm (last entry 9.15pm); early Sept to early May 9am–8pm (last entry 7.15pm) • $34, ages 6–12 $28 (reserve tickets online) • ☎ 844 696 1776, ⓦ oneworldobservatory.com • Subway A, C, #2, #3, #4, #5 to Fulton St; E to World Trade Center; R, W to Cortlandt St; #1 to Rector St

The tallest skyscraper in the US (if the spire is included), **One World Trade Center** (1776ft) finally topped out in 2012, a gleaming pinnacle of glass and steel that has garnered a fair degree of criticism for the design's apparent lack of imagination – UK graffiti artist Banksy called it a "shyscraper" in 2013. The tower opened to the public in 2015, with pricey visits to the **observatory** on floors 100, 101 and 102 (1250ft). Five high-speed elevators called Sky Pods whisk you to the top in just sixty seconds (as you rise, a virtual time-lapse image re-creates the development of New York's skyline from the 1500s to the present day), where sensational views of Manhattan, the harbour, Staten Island and beyond await. The entertainment begins before you even enter the lifts however, with a multimedia show dubbed "Voices", which tells the personal stories of the men and women who built the tower, and the Foundations exhibit, which displays the bedrock on which the building stands. The **See Forever Theater** on the 102nd floor shows a two-minute video of bird's-eye and abstract New York images on loop, while the **Main Observatory** on the 100th floor features interactive viewing screens and "Sky Portal", a 14ft-wide circular disc allowing spine-tingling views of the drop below. There are also three dining options up here, but you must have an Observatory ticket to visit them.

National September 11 Memorial & Museum

180 Greenwich St, between Fulton and Liberty sts • ☎ 212 266 5211, ⓦ 911memorial.org • Subway A, C, #2, #3, #4, #5 to Fulton St; E to World Trade Center; R, W to Cortlandt St; #1 to Rector St

The incredibly moving **National September 11 Memorial & Museum** was dedicated on September 11, 2011, to commemorate the ten-year anniversary of the 9/11 attacks. The memorial itself is free and easily accessible, while tickets to the museum can be purchased six months in advance (advised if you have limited time in the city) – though you can usually just turn up on the day and line up. **Guided tours** (45min) of the memorial (not the museum) by staff usually run hourly 10am to 2pm ($15; reserve on the website), while tours by people directly affected by 9/11 are provided by the 9/11 Tribute Center (see p.51).

2

9/11 Memorial

Daily 7.30am–9pm • Free

The two pools of the **9/11 Memorial**, representing the footprints of the original towers, are each around one acre in size, with 30ft waterfalls tumbling down their sides. The names of the 9/11 victims – some women listed with their unborn children – are inscribed on bronze parapets surrounding the pools, while the contemplative eight-acre Memorial Plaza is filled with nearly four hundred oak trees.

SEPTEMBER 11 AND ITS AFTERMATH

At 8.46am on September 11, 2001, a hijacked plane slammed into the north tower of the **World Trade Center**; seventeen minutes later another hijacked plane struck the south tower. As thousands looked on in horror – in addition to hundreds of millions more viewing on TV – the south tower collapsed at 9.50am, its twin at 10.30am. All seven buildings of the World Trade Center complex eventually collapsed, and the centre was reduced to a mountain of steel, concrete and glass rubble. As black clouds billowed above, the whole area was covered in a blanket of concrete dust many inches thick; debris reached several hundred feet into the air. The devastation was staggering. While most of the fifty thousand civilians working in the towers had been evacuated before the towers fell, many never made it out of the building; hundreds of firemen, policemen and rescue workers who arrived on the scene when the planes struck were crushed when the buildings collapsed. In all, **2977 people perished** at the WTC and the simultaneous attack on the Pentagon in Washington, DC, in what was, in terms of casualties, the largest foreign attack on American soil in history. Radical Muslim Osama bin Laden's terrorist network, al-Qaeda, claimed responsibility for the attacks.

Dominating Lower Manhattan's landscape from nearly any angle, the 110-storey **Twin Towers** always loomed over their surroundings. The first tower went up in 1972 and the second a year later, and while becoming integral parts of the New York skyline, they also evolved into emblems of American power in the eyes of Islamic extremists.

In the days after the attack, downtown was basically shut down, and the seven-square-block area immediately around the WTC was the focus of an intense rescue effort. New Yorkers lined up to give blood and volunteered to help the rescue workers; vigils were held throughout the city, most notably in Union Square, which was peppered with candles and makeshift shrines. Then-Mayor **Rudy Giuliani** cut a highly composed and reassuring figure as New Yorkers struggled to come to terms with the assault on their city. In 2011, hundreds gathered again at Ground Zero to celebrate the killing of Osama bin Laden, though most New Yorkers greeted the news more soberly, remembering those who were lost ten years earlier.

MOVING FORWARD

In 2003, Polish-born architect **Daniel Libeskind** was named the winner of a competition held to determine the overall design for the new World Trade Center, though his plans were initially plagued with controversy and he had little subsequent involvement with the project. In 2006, a modified design, still incorporating Libeskind's original 1776ft-high Tower of Freedom (now **One World Trade Center**), was finally accepted, supervised by architect David Childs and topping out in 2012, eleven years after the 9/11 attacks.

2

THE "GROUND ZERO MOSQUE"

In 2010, New York developer Sharif El-Gamal ignited a fiery debate over religious freedoms after proposing to build an Islamic cultural centre at 51 Park Place, two blocks north of the World Trade Center. The plan was dubbed pejoratively the "**Ground Zero mosque**" by anti-Islamic protestors who felt the site would be an insult to 9/11 victims (though actual relations of those killed were divided on the issue). El-Gamal eventually modified his plans, and the site is now slated to become a three-storey **Islamic museum** designed by "starchitect" Jean Nouvel (due to open in late 2018).

9/11 Memorial Museum

Mon–Thurs & Sun 9am–8pm, last entry 6pm, Fri & Sat 9am–9pm, last entry 7pm • $24, ages 7–17 $15; free Tues from 5pm (timed reservations available online); tours every 30min (1hr) $20

The underground **9/11 Memorial Museum** (which you have to pay to enter, and go through airport-like security), in between the two memorial pools, opened in 2014. The poignant exhibits inside, a blend of artefacts recovered from the site, personal testimonies and video presentations, are very comprehensive, covering not only the events of 9/11 but also the build-up to them and the aftermath. Ramps lead down to the spacious exhibitions level, where the **Foundation Hall** contains remnants of the original Twin Towers, a monumental section of the vast slurry wall protecting the site from the Hudson River, a half-crushed FDNY fire truck and the heavily inscribed "Last Column", the last piece of structural steel to be removed from Ground Zero in 2002. There's also **In Memoriam**, a contemplative space displaying photos of all 2983 people killed in 2001 (and the 1993 attack on the Twin Towers), while the artsy *Rebirth at Ground Zero* video (11min) is shown on loop, using time-lapse footage to show the recovery of the once devastated site. The heart of the museum is the **September 11, 2001 Historical Exhibition** (this section is oddly cramped compared to the big spaces outside), an extremely moving blend of images, recordings and videos covering the 9/11 attacks minute by minute: there are chilling radio recordings of firemen in the towers just before the collapse, heart-breaking phone calls made by passengers on doomed Flight 93 (which crashed in Pennsylvania), and harrowing photos of people jumping to their deaths from the burning buildings. Otherwise mundane items recovered from the rubble are displayed: mobile phones, watches and even the wallet of a British man on a business trip, still containing a twenty-pound note. Unlike previous memorials, the exhibit also includes a major section on **al-Qaeda** and the men who hijacked the planes on 9/11, though the motivation for their actions (other than a brief video about Osama bin Laden's experiences in Afghanistan and Islamic radicalism in general) is notably absent.

The Oculus

185 Greenwich St (also 50 Church St) • Mall open Mon–Sat 10am–9pm, Sun 11am–7pm • 212 284 9982 • Subway A, C, #2, #3, #4, #5 to Fulton St; E to World Trade Center; R, W to Cortlandt St; #1 to Rector St

A striking, bone-white, 160ft-tall edifice by Santiago Calatrava, **The Oculus** opened next to 3 World Trade Center in 2016, its two spiky steel ribs resembling a giant porcupine. Below it lies the World Trade Center Transportation Hub and the posh Westfield shopping mall. It's worth admiring the futuristic interior, with its soaring curves and arching skylight evoking the spirit of a great Gothic cathedral.

St Paul's Chapel

209 Broadway, at Fulton St • Mon–Sat 10am–6pm, Sun 7am–6pm • Free • 212 602 0800 • Subway A, C, #4, #5 to Fulton St; E to World Trade Center

Both the oldest church and the oldest building in continuous use in Manhattan, **St Paul's Chapel** dates from 1766, making it almost prehistoric by New York standards. The main attraction inside is **Unwavering Spirit**, a moving exhibition on September 11. For eight months after the 9/11 attacks, St Paul's Chapel served as a sanctuary for the rescue workers at Ground Zero, providing food, a place to nap and spiritual support.

The exhibit chronicles the church's role in these recovery efforts, with a touching ensemble of photos, artefacts and testimonies from those involved. The church itself was based on London's St Martin-in-the-Fields, with a handsome interior of narrow Corinthian columns and ornate chandeliers, though even **George Washington's pew**, preserved shrine-like from 1789–90 (when New York was the US capital), forms part of the September 11 exhibition (it served as a foot treatment chair for firefighters). Outside, the historic cemetery is worth a wander, sprinkled with colonial headstones and the **Bell of Hope**, a gift from London in 2002; the bell is rung every September 11.

2

9/11 Tribute Center

92 Greenwich St, at Rector St • Mon–Sat 10am–6pm, Sun 10am–5pm (last ticket sold 30min before closing) • $15; tours daily 11am, noon, 1pm, 2pm & 3pm ($10) • ☎ 866 737 1184, ⓦ tributewtc.org • Subway R, #1 to Rector St

The **9/11 Tribute Center** (which is separate from the official 9/11 memorial and museum site, three blocks north) houses several galleries that commemorate the attacks of September 11, beginning with a model of the Twin Towers and a section about that chilling day, embellished with video and taped accounts of real-life survivors. A handful of items found on the site – a pair of singed high-heel shoes, pieces of twisted metal – make heart-rending symbols of the tragedy. The centre also offers daily walking **tours** (1hr 15min) of the National September 11 Memorial by family members, survivors, rescue and recovery workers, civilian volunteers and Lower Manhattan residents (museum entry not included).

Battery Park City

Between West Side Hwy and the Hudson River, from Battery Park to Chambers St • ☎ 212 417 2000, ⓦ bpca.ny.gov • Subway R, W, #1 to Rector St

The hole dug for the foundations of the former World Trade Center threw up a million cubic yards of earth and rock, which was then dumped into the Hudson River to the west to form the 23-acre base of **Battery Park City**. This self-sufficient development of office blocks, apartments, chain boutiques and landscaped esplanade feels a far cry from the rest of Manhattan. Battery Park City's southern end is anchored by **Robert F. Wagner Jr Park**, a refuge from the ferry crowds – you can follow the **Esplanade** up the Hudson from here as far as Chelsea and Midtown.

Brookfield Place (World Financial Center)

230 Vesey St • Mon–Sat 10am–9pm, Sun 11am–7pm • ☎ 212 417 2445, ⓦ brookfieldplaceny.com

The centrepiece of the Battery Park City development is **Brookfield Place** (formerly World Financial Center), a rather grand and imposing fourteen-acre business, shopping and dining complex that looks down onto the new World Trade Center from just across West Street. Originally designed by César Pelli in the 1980s, an ambitious $250 million renovation of the whole complex was completed in 2014. Inside, the **Winter Garden**, a ten-storey, glass-ceilinged public plaza, brings light and life into a mall full of shops and two enticing food halls: French-themed **Le District** and **Hudson Eats** upstairs. Decorated by sixteen 45ft-high Washingtonia palms from Florida, the plaza is a veritable oasis, and connects with the **North Cove** yacht harbour on the Hudson River side. Don't miss the small chunk of the **Berlin Wall** tucked away on the south side of the cove, donated by the German Consulate in 2004.

The Irish Hunger Memorial

290 Vesey St • Daily: May–Oct 8am–9pm; Nov–April 8am–6.45pm • Free • Subway A, C, #1, #2, #3 to Chambers St; E to World Trade Center

Just north of Brookfield Place, facing the Hudson at the end of Vesey Street, the **Irish Hunger Memorial** is a sobering monument to the more than one million Irish people who starved to death during the Great Famine of 1845–52. The tragedy sparked a flood of Irish immigration to the US, mostly through New York. An authentic famine-era stone cottage, one of many abandoned in the west of Ireland, was transported from County

Mayo by artist Brian Tolle and set on a raised embankment overlooking the water. The passageway underneath echoes with haunting Irish folk songs, and you can follow the meandering path through the grassy garden and stones 25ft to the top.

Poets House

10 River Terrace, at Murray St • Tues–Fri 11am–7pm, Sat 11am–6pm • Free • ☎ 212 431 7920, ⓦ poetshouse.org • Subway A, C, #1, #2, #3 to Chambers St; E to World Trade Center

2

To the north of the Irish Hunger Memorial, the **Poets House** contains a fabulous 60,000-volume reference library, reading room and audio collection dedicated to poets of every nationality. Historic recordings include readings from W.H. Auden, e.e. cummings, T.S. Eliot, Allen Ginsberg and Ezra Pound – it's a relaxing place to end an afternoon (and it has free wi-fi).

Battery Park and around

Battery Place and State and Whitehall sts • Daily sunrise–1am • Free • ☎ 212 344 3491, ⓦ thebattery.org • Subway R, W to Whitehall St; #1 to South Ferry; #4, #5 to Bowling Green

Lower Manhattan lets out its breath in **Battery Park**, a breezy, 25-acre swathe of grass and gardens littered with monuments and fine views of the Statue of Liberty across the harbour. Dating back to 1693, the park is named after the gun batteries that once protected the city, and has been transformed by a mammoth renovation completed in 2015 that includes berms (barriers) and earthworks designed to withstand storm surges. New attractions include the **SeaGlass Carousel** (March–Oct daily 10am–10pm; Nov–Feb Sat & Sun 11am–7pm; $5 per ride; ⓦ seaglasscarousel.nyc) a whimsical, aquatic-themed merry-go-round, and **Battery Farm**, a section of vegetable, fruit and herb plots that promotes sustainable farming techniques.

Castle Clinton

Daily 7.45am–5pm • Free; free tours daily 10am, noon, 2pm & 4pm (20min) • ☎ 212 344 7220, ⓦ nps.gov/cacl • Subway R, W to Whitehall St; #1 to South Ferry; #4, #5 to Bowling Green

Before landfill closed the gap in the 1850s, **Castle Clinton**, the sandstone fort at the southern tip of Battery Park, was an island. Built in 1811, it was ceded to the city in 1823, finding new life as a prestigious concert venue known as Castle Garden before doing service (pre-Ellis Island) as the drop-off point for arriving immigrants; from 1855 to 1890, eight million people passed through its doors. After serving as an aquarium, the squat fortress is now the place to buy **tickets for the Statue of Liberty and Ellis Island** (see p.37); it also contains a small exhibit on the history of the site, and a section of the original "Battery Wall" constructed between 1730 and 1766. South of Castle Clinton stands the **East Coast Memorial**, a series of granite slabs inscribed with the names of all the American seamen who were killed in World War II.

Pier A Harbor House

22 Battery Place • Mon–Wed 11am–2am, Thurs–Sat 11am–4am, Sun 11am–midnight • ☎ 212 785 0153, ⓦ piera.com • Subway R, W to Whitehall St; #1 to South Ferry; #4, #5 to Bowling Green

Jutting into the harbour on the western side of Battery Park, **Pier A Harbor House** is a lavish nineteenth-century relic dating from 1886, originally the headquarters of the New York Harbor Police. A mammoth renovation was finally completed in 2014, filling the old wooden structure with a restaurant and an oyster bar (see p.330), and surrounding it with outdoor seating.

Bowling Green

Broadway • 24hr • Free • Subway R, W to Whitehall St; #1 to South Ferry; #4, #5 to Bowling Green

The southern end of Broadway meets tiny but momentous **Bowling Green** just before Battery Park. The city's oldest public garden, this is supposedly the location of the most famous real-estate deal in history, when Peter Minuit, the newly arrived director-general of the Dutch colony of New Amsterdam, bought the whole island from the Native Americans for a bucket of trade goods worth sixty guilders in 1626 (the figure of $24 was calculated in the 1840s). Though we don't know for sure who "sold" the island to Minuit (it was probably a northern branch of the Lenni Lenape), the other side of the story (and the part you never hear) was that the concept of owning land was utterly alien to Native Americans – they had merely agreed to support Dutch claims to use the land, as they did. The green was formally established in 1733, when it was used for lawn bowling by colonial Brits, on a lease of "one peppercorn per year". The encircling iron fence is the original from 1771, though the crowns that once topped the stakes were removed during the Revolutionary War, as was a statue of George III. The statue was melted into musket balls – little bits of the monarch that were then fired at his troops.

2

National Museum of the American Indian

1 Bowling Green • Daily 10am–5pm, Thurs until 8pm • Free • ☎ 212 514 3700, ⓦ nmai.si.edu • **National Archives** Mon–Fri 10am–5pm, first Sat of the month 10am–4pm • Free • ☎ 212 401 1620, ⓦ archives.gov/nyc • Subway R, W to Whitehall St; #1 to South Ferry; #4, #5 to Bowling Green

Bowling Green sees plenty of office folk picnicking in the shadow of Cass Gilbert's stately US Customs House, the former site of Fort Amsterdam and now (not without some irony) the only part of Manhattan dedicated to Native Americans, the Smithsonian **National Museum of the American Indian**. The main galleries lie on the second floor, where temporary exhibits focus on various aspects of Native American culture as well as shows by contemporary artists. Most exhibits last at least six months, though **Infinity of Nations: Art and History in the Collections of the National Museum of the American Indian** is expected to be permanent, highlighting artefacts from the Smithsonian's vast collection representing almost every Native American tribe from Patagonia to the Arctic; it was largely assembled by one man, George Gustav Heye (1874–1957), who travelled through the Americas picking up such works for over fifty years. **The National Archives at New York City** on the third floor contains a small exhibition featuring a changing selection of original documents from the National Archives (based in Washington, DC).

Completed in 1907 and in use until 1973, the Beaux Arts **Customs House** is itself part of the attraction; the facade is adorned with elaborate statuary representing the major continents (carved by Daniel Chester French), while the spectacular marble-clad Great Hall and Rotunda inside are beautifully decorated; the sixteen murals covering the 135ft dome were painted by Reginald Marsh in 1937.

THE CHARGING BULL (AND FEARLESS GIRL)

Just north of Bowling Green on the Broadway partition is a sculpture of a **Charging Bull** – not originally envisioned as a symbol of a "bull market" for Wall Street stocks, though that's how it is perceived by New Yorkers today. As the story goes, on December 15, 1989, Arturo Di Modica installed his sculpture in the middle of Broad Street, without a permit. The city removed the sculpture the next day, but was forced to put it here when public support for the statue was surprisingly vocal. Today hordes of tourists line up to take pictures under the bull, astride the bull and rubbing its huge bronze testicles, for "good luck". In 2017 another permit-less bronze sculpture dubbed the **Fearless Girl** appeared in front of the bull – designed by Kristen Visbal, the plucky figure seemed to be defiantly staring down the animal. The statue quickly became a feminist icon (despite being commissioned as part of a marketing campaign for a gender-diverse index fund), much to the irritation of Di Modica, who, apparently without irony, took legal action to have it removed. Mayor De Blasio agreed that Fearless Girl could stay for eleven months, but its future beyond 2018 was uncertain at the time of writing.

2

CROSSING THE HARBOUR

The **Staten Island ferry** (☎ 718 727 2508, ⊕ siferry.com) sails from the modern Whitehall Ferry Terminal on the east side of Battery Park, built directly above the equally well-designed South Ferry subway station (at the end of the #1 line and accessible via R and W trains to Whitehall Street). The #4 and #5 trains to Bowling Green also let you off within easy walking distance. The 25-minute ride is truly New York's best bargain: it's absolutely free, with wide-angle views of the city and the Statue of Liberty becoming more spectacular as you retreat (see p.37).

Skyscraper Museum

39 Battery Place • Wed–Sun noon–6pm • $5 • ☎ 212 968 1961, ⊕ skyscraper.org • Subway R, W to Whitehall St; #4, #5 to Bowling Green

Given the Financial District's love affair with soaring towers of steel and limestone, it's fitting that the **Skyscraper Museum** should be located down here, just behind the *Ritz-Carlton Hotel* on the northern edge of Battery Park. The core display area is usually taken up with temporary exhibits, but always with skyscraper focus. Permanent exhibits are dedicated to "Supertall" (over 380m) towers, the "history of height", One World Trade Center and the Twin Towers, and hand-carved miniature wooden models of Downtown and Midtown Manhattan created by Michael Chesko.

Museum of Jewish Heritage

36 Battery Place • Mon, Tues, Thurs & Sun 10am–5.45pm, Wed 10am–8pm, Fri 10am–5pm; Nov–March museum closes at 3pm on Fri; closed Jewish holidays • $12 (includes free audio guide); free Wed 4–8pm • Tours (free) Tues 3pm • ☎ 646 437 4202, ⊕ mjhnyc.org • Subway R, W to Whitehall St; #4, #5 to Bowling Green

Jewish culture remains a key component of New York's identity, and on the north side of Battery Park the **Museum of Jewish Heritage** stands as a memorial to the Holocaust; its six sides represent both the six million dead and the Star of David. The moving and informative collection, which covers three floors of permanent exhibits and multimedia installations, begins with the rituals and practical accoutrements of everyday Eastern European Jewish life pre-1930, before moving on to the horrors of the Holocaust and ending with the establishment of Israel and subsequent Jewish achievements. Some of the more memorable installations include a fine hand-painted Sukkah cover from 1930s Hungary, and a heart-rending display commemorating the children murdered by the Nazis. The Zen-like "Garden of Stones" stands on the second-floor terrace, while the innovative **Keeping History Center** and "Voices of Liberty" exhibit on the third floor features testimony from Holocaust survivors and immigrants via iPod-like audio guides (the main museum audio guides are worth picking up at the entrance, narrated by actress Meryl Streep and violinist Itzhak Perlman).

Shrine of St Elizabeth Ann Seton

7 State St • Daily 7am–5pm • ☎ 212 269 6865, ⊕ spcolr.org/st-seton-shrine-1 • Subway R, W to Whitehall St; #1 to South Ferry #4; #5 to Bowling Green

A rounded, redbrick facade on the east side of Battery Park identifies the **Shrine of St Elizabeth Ann Seton**, honouring the first native-born American to be canonized. The shrine comprises a working Catholic chapel, the Church of Our Lady of the Rosary, built in 1965 in Georgian style with a small room at the front containing a statue of the saint and rather pious illustrations of her life. Before moving to Maryland to found a religious community, St Elizabeth lived briefly (1801–03) in a small house on this site. You enter through the adjacent porticoed building, completed in 1793 and known as **Watson House**, one of only a few old buildings in the area to have survived the modern onslaught. Seton (1774–1821) was canonized in 1975, principally in recognition of her work establishing the Sisters of Charity and schools for poor women and children.

CLOCKWISE FROM TOP LEFT TRINITY CHURCH (P.43); GEORGE WASHINGTON STATUE (P.45); ONE WORLD TRADE CENTER (P.48); WALL STREET (P.43) >

Fraunces Tavern Museum

54 Pearl St, at Broad St · Mon–Fri noon–5pm, Sat & Sun 11am–5pm · $7 · ☎ 212 425 1778, Ⓦ frauncestavernmuseum.org · Subway R, W to Whitehall St; #1 to South Ferry; #4, #5 to Bowling Green

For a window into eighteenth-century Manhattan, check out the **Fraunces Tavern Museum**. The ochre-and-red-brick building was constructed in 1719 and became the Queen's Head Inn after Samuel Fraunces purchased the property in 1762; having survived extensive modifications, several fires and a brief stint as a hotel in the nineteenth century, the three-storey Georgian house was almost totally reconstructed by the Sons of the Revolution in the early part of the twentieth century to mimic how it appeared on December 4, 1783. It was then that a weeping George Washington took leave of his assembled officers, intent on returning to rural life in Virginia: "I am not only retiring from all public employments," he wrote, "but am retiring within myself." With hindsight, it was a hasty statement – six years later he was to return as the new nation's president. The **Long Room** where the speech was made has been faithfully decked out in the style of the time, while the adjacent Federal-style **Clinton Room** is smothered in rare and florid French wallpaper from 1838. The tavern's upper floors contain a permanent exhibit tracing the site's history, a room with over two hundred flags and an expansive collection of Revolutionary War artefacts; look out for a lock of Washington's hair, preserved like a holy relic. Fascinating temporary exhibits are also held here, usually on related themes (such as the influence of the Magna Carta on the Revolution). The *Porterhouse* restaurant and pub (see p.330) occupies the lower floors, where you can have a peek at the historic murals in the **Bissell Room** (at the back), and the plaque commemorating the bomb that killed four people here in 1975 (the Puerto Rican nationalist group FALN claimed responsibility).

The old Stadt Huys

85 Broad St · 24hr · Free · Subway R, W to Whitehall St; #1 to South Ferry; #4, #5 to Bowling Green

In the shadow of 85 Broad St (Goldman Sachs' old headquarters) are the oldest remnants of colonial New York. This was the site of the city's first tavern, transformed into the **Stadt Huys** or City Hall in 1653 when New Amsterdam was officially incorporated – the city government still dates its foundation from this year. Nothing remains from that period, but archeologists have uncovered the foundations of **Governor Lovelace's Tavern**, a British pub dating from the 1670s, preserved under glass panels just off the street; the outlines of where both buildings once stood are marked by coloured bricks. At nearby Coenties Slip you can turn left to reach historic **Stone Street** (see box, p.47), or turn right to the **Vietnam Veterans Memorial**, a modern assembly of glass blocks etched with troops' letters home. The mementoes are sad and often haunting, but the place is a peaceful spot for contemplation.

Seaport District NYC

Fulton St and South St · Ⓦ seaportdistrict.nyc · Subway A, C, J, #2, #3, #4, #5 to Fulton St

New York's original dockyards were located on Manhattan's southern tip between Battery Park and Fulton Street, and today a tiny part of this heritage is preserved as the touristy **Seaport District NYC**. This area was devastated by **Hurricane Sandy** in 2012, prompting a $1.7 billion redevelopment of the site by the Howard Hughes Corporation. The old **Fulton Market Building** now contains several ritzy boutiques and a branch of posh cinema chain **iPic Theaters** (daily 10am–2am; Ⓦ ipictheaters.com), while the new **Pier 17**, designed by lauded SHoP Architects, will include stores, restaurants and a concert venue (the pier is

---

CHEAP TICKETS

One of the best-kept tourist secrets is located in the Seaport District NYC: a **TKTS box office** (190 Front St, at John St; Mon–Sat 11am–6pm, Sun 11am–4pm; Ⓦ tdf.org). Like its counterpart in Times Square (see p.354), it sells same-day half-price tickets to **Broadway shows**, but the queues here are usually a fraction of those in Midtown.

expected to open in summer 2018). Next door, the refurbished 1904 **Tin Building** will host a Jean-Georges Vongerichten food market.

Created by the Dutch in the 1620s, the seaport boomed in the nineteenth century, favoured by sea captains for providing shelter from the westerly winds and the ice that floated down the Hudson River during winter. **Robert Fulton** started a ferry service from here to Brooklyn in 1814, leaving his name for the street and then its market, New York's largest (the fish market moved to the Bronx in 2006). After World War II, containers came to dominate shipping, and Manhattan effectively ceased being a port in the 1970s; ships were handled in New Jersey and Staten Island, and the docks were left as rotting eyesores. Beginning in 1966, a private initiative rescued some of the remaining warehouses, creating the historical seaport you see today.

The South Street Seaport Museum

12 Fulton St • Wed–Sun 11am–5pm • $12 • ☎ 212 748 8600, ⊕ southstreetseaportmuseum.org • Subway A, C, J, #2, #3, #4, #5 to Fulton St

Housed in a series of painstakingly restored warehouses, the **South Street Seaport Museum** owns a collection of maritime art and several refitted ships. The main ticket office and galleries lie on Fulton Street, in **Schermerhorn Row**, a unique ensemble of Federal-style warehouses dating to about 1812, badly damaged by Hurricane Sandy. In 2016 the museum restarted its exhibition programme with the permanent "Street of Ships: The Port and Its People", providing a history of the area and the restoration of the tall ship *Wavertree* (museum admission includes guided tours on both the *Wavertree* and the *Ambrose*; below). The museum's historic stores and workshops around the corner on **Water Street** include **Bowne Printers** at no. 209 (daily 11am–7pm) and **Bowne & Co Stationers** at no. 211 (daily 11am–7pm).

Pier 16 and 15

The South Street Seaport Museum owns a fleet of five historic ships, in varying states of restoration on nearby **Pier 16**. At the time of writing, two ships were open April to September Wednesday–Sunday 11am to 5pm ($12; includes museum entry): the **Ambrose**, a 1908 lightship that remained in service until 1964, having spent much of its working life in New York Harbor; and the artfully restored **Wavertree**, a graceful tall ship built in Southampton (UK) in 1885. Docked on adjacent **Pier 15** (but currently off limits), lies the 1930 wooden tugboat **W.O. Decker** (available for charter). The museum also owns the 1893 fishing schooner **Lettie G. Howard** and the schooner **Pioneer**, which cruises the harbour in the summer (see box below). The upper deck of Pier 15 is a great place to soak up harbour views (daily 8am–dusk), while *Watermark* restaurant and bar is strategically placed at the tip of the pier.

City Hall Park and around

City Hall Park has been the seat of New York's municipal government since 1812, but in the seventeenth century it was just communal pasture. An almshouse for the poor stood

---

SEAPORT CRUISING

During the summer months, the South Street Seaport Museum runs a programme of leisurely **cruises** around New York Harbor on its handsome 1885 schooner, the *Pioneer*. Two-hour cruises usually run May to October Wednesday and Thursday 7pm, Friday 3 & 7pm, Saturday 1pm, 4pm & 7pm, and Sunday 4pm & 7pm. Tickets are $32 (ages 2–11 $28). Call in advance for the latest information: ☎ 212 748 8600.

Meanwhile, Circle Line Downtown (☎ 866 925 4631, ⊕ circlelinedowntown.com) runs speedboat rides on *Shark* from May to September (daily noon–5pm every hr; 30min; $29, children $24). At Pier 15, Hornblower Cruises (⊕ hornblowernewyork.com) offers various boat trips, including its "Rock the Yacht!" series most Thursday, Friday and Saturdays nights 9pm–midnight (from $32).

on this site from 1736 to 1797, and during the Revolutionary War (1775–83) the British used the nearby debtors' prison to hold prisoners, hanging 250 of them. Today the park contains stately City Hall, with Tweed Courthouse just to the north, while from here the **Brooklyn Bridge**, a magnificent feat of engineering, soars over the East River (see p.216).

City Hall

City Hall Park • Free tours Thurs 10am (must reserve in advance at ☎ 212 788 2656, ⓦ nyc.gov/html/artcom) & Wed noon (sign up at the NYC information kiosk, opposite the Woolworth Building; Mon–Fri 9am–6pm, Sat & Sun 10am–5pm) • Subway J, Z to Chambers St; R, W to City Hall; #2, #3 to Park Place; #4, #5, #6 to Brooklyn Bridge-City Hall

Towards the northern end of City Hall Park sits **City Hall** itself, a gleaming white marble palace with Neoclassical columns, arches and furnishings virtually unchanged since it was completed in 1812. It's the oldest city hall in the US to retain its original government function; the **mayor's office** and the chambers of the New York City Council are inside. Increased security means the building is fenced off from the rest of the park, and the only way you can admire the magnificent interior is to take a **free guided tour** offered by Art Commission experts, well worth your time (tours take just over an hour).

Tours begin in the elegant triple-arcaded lobby, which opens up to the **rotunda**, one of the most sensational pieces of architecture in the city; the all-white coffered dome (topped with a skylight and invisible from the outside) is ringed by ten Corinthian columns and a floating marble staircase that spirals up to the second floor. Up here you'll see the **Council Chamber**, where the city council meets once a month; the ceiling is covered in a giant allegorical mural representing New York. Most of the decor dates back to1898, when the chamber was redesigned to take in the newly expanded city boroughs. An 1825 portrait of the Marquis de Lafayette by Samuel Morse (later of Morse Code fame) hangs on the wall.

More nineteenth-century portraits by John Trumbull adorn the **Governor's Room**, an immaculate French Regency-style reception room containing George Washington's writing desk and a rare mahogany table from 1814. The room hosted President-elect Abraham Lincoln in 1861 (who shook hands for eight hours straight), and served as the backdrop in 1865 when Lincoln's body lay in state for 120,000 sorrowful New Yorkers to file past.

Tweed Courthouse

52 Chambers St • Check ⓦ nyc.gov/html/artcom for tour information • Subway #4, #5, #6 to Brooklyn Bridge-City Hall

If City Hall is the acceptable face of New York's municipal bureaucracy, the spectacular **Tweed Courthouse**, just to the north, is a reminder of the city government's infamous corruption in the nineteenth century. The man behind this former county courthouse, **William Marcy "Boss" Tweed**, worked his way up from nowhere to become chairman of the Democratic Central Committee in 1856. Tweed embezzled the city's revenues (even the courthouse's budget, which rolled up from $3 million to $12 million during its construction between 1861 and 1881), until political cartoonist Thomas Nast and the editor of *The New York Times* (who'd refused a $500,000 bribe to keep quiet) turned public opinion against him in the early 1870s. Fittingly, Tweed was finally tried in an unfinished courtroom in his own building in 1873, and died in 1878 in Ludlow Street Jail – a prison he'd had built while he was Commissioner of Public Works.

Tweed's monument to greed, which now houses the Department of Education and a kindergarten, looks more like a mansion than a municipal building, especially after the lavish $85 million restoration completed in 2001. To get a look at its fabulous interior, you need to take a **free guided tour**, arranged by the Public Design Commission, though these had been suspended at the time of research – check the commission website for the latest.

Park Row

Between Broadway and Frankfort St • Subway J, Z to Chambers St; R, W to City Hall; #2, #3 to Park Place; #4, #5, #6 to Brooklyn Bridge-City Hall

City Hall Park is flanked on either side by impressive early twentieth-century skyscrapers. **Park Row**, the eastern edge of the park, was once known as "Newspaper Row". From the

1830s to the 1920s, the city's most influential publishers, news services and trade publications had their offices on this street or surrounding blocks. *The New York Times* operated from no. 41, a handsome Romanesque-Revival structure that grew from twelve storeys in 1889 to sixteen in 1904 (Pace University moved here in 1951). The wildly ornamented **Potter Building** at no. 38 dates from 1886, when it was a pioneer in fireproofing, thanks to its iron-clad lower floors and durable terracotta trim. Today, as with much of downtown, it's been converted into high-end apartments (with a *Starbucks* on the first floor). The **Park Row Building**, at no. 15, was completed in 1899; at 391ft, it was the tallest office building in the world. Behind the elaborate limestone-and-brick facade were the offices of the Associated Press as well as the headquarters of the IRT subway. The building towered over its surroundings until 1908, when the Singer Building, at 165 Broadway (now demolished), surpassed it – it's now primarily filled with expensive apartments and is being developed (with the whole lower row) into the "**Retail at Park Row**" shopping mall. It's worth taking a peek (or grabbing a pricey drink) inside the grand **Beekman Hotel** just behind the row at 123 Nassau St, just to see its spectacular atrium – the landmarked office building, built in 1883, reopened as a posh hotel in 2016.

Contrast this Gilded Age opulence with Frank Gehry's contemporary masterpiece, looming over Park Row at 8 Spruce St; his 77-storey **New York by Gehry** (870ft) topped out in 2009, its rippling stainless-steel curtain wall containing nine hundred luxury rentals and a new public elementary (primary) school at its base.

The Woolworth Building

233 Broadway • Tours (30min Sat 1pm; 1hr Tues, Thurs 2pm & Sat 11.30am; 1hr 30min Mon, Wed, Fri, Sat & Sun 2pm) • Tours $20 (30min), $30 (1hr), $45 (1hr 30min) • ☎ 203 966 9663, Ⓦ woolworthtours.com • Subway J, Z to Chambers St; R, W to City Hall; #2, #3 to Park Place; #4, #5, #6 to Brooklyn Bridge-City Hall

In 1913, the tallest building in the world was on the opposite side of City Hall Park: the **Woolworth Building** (792ft) held the title until the Chrysler Building topped it in 1929. Cass Gilbert's "Cathedral of Commerce" oozes money and prestige. The soaring, graceful lines are covered in white terracotta tiles and fringed with Gothic-style gargoyles and decorations that are more whimsical than portentous. Frank Woolworth made his fortune from his "five and dime" stores – everything cost either 5¢ or 10¢, strictly no credit. True to his philosophy, he paid cash for the construction of his skyscraper, and reliefs at each corner of the ornate lobby show him doing just that: counting out the money in nickels and dimes. After many years of being off limits, **guided tours** resumed in 2014 (you must book these online in advance): the basic tour includes all three areas of the lobby, while one-hour visits also include the lower level and the longest tour adds exclusive access to the mezzanine level.

The Municipal Building

1 Centre St • Mon–Fri 10am–5pm (City Store) • Free • Ⓦ nyc.gov • Subway J, Z to Chambers St; R, W to City Hall; #2, #3 to Park Place; #4, #5, #6 to Brooklyn Bridge-City Hall

At the east end of Chambers Street, across Centre Street, stands the imposing 580ft bulk of the **Municipal Building**, looking a bit like an oversized chest of drawers. Built between 1909 and 1914, it was the first skyscraper constructed by the well-known architectural firm McKim, Mead, and White, although it was actually designed by one of the firm's younger partners, William Mitchell Kendall. At its top, an extravagant "wedding cake" tower of columns and pinnacles, including Adolph Weinman's frivolous 25ft gilt sculpture *Civic Fame*, attempts to dress up the no-nonsense home of the Manhattan Borough President and much of the city government's offices. The shields decorating the moulding above the colonnade represent the various phases of New York as colony, city and state: the triple-X insignia is the Amsterdam city seal, and the combination of windmill, beavers and flour barrels represents New Amsterdam and its first trading products, images used on the city seal today. There's little to see inside, but the City Store at the base sells New York City maps, books and souvenirs.

New York Court District

Subway J, Z to Chambers St

To the north of City Hall Park lies New York's court district, familiar to fans of *Law &
Order* and countless other crime shows and dominated by the grandiose 590ft tower of the
Thurgood Marshall US Courthouse. Designed by Cass Gilbert and completed in 1936 at 40
Centre St, the building now serves as the US Court of Appeals for the Second Circuit. The
adjacent building, at 60 Centre St, is the **New York County Courthouse** (daily 9am–5pm),
now one of the state's supreme courts. A massive hexagonal Neoclassical structure
completed in 1927, it merits a quick peek inside to see its elaborate rotunda, decorated by
Attilio Pusterla in the 1930s with storybook murals illustrating the history of justice (you'll
have to pass through security to get a good look, but as it's a public building you are
allowed to go in).

Foley Square

The columned facades of the courthouses look onto **Foley Square**, named for the sheriff
and saloonkeeper Thomas "Big Tom" Foley, one of the few admirable figures in the
Tammany Hall era. The focal point of the wide concrete plaza is Lorenzo Pace's three-
hundred-tonne black granite sculpture, *The Triumph of the Human Spirit*, a tribute to the
many thousands of enslaved Africans who died on American soil – particularly those whose
bodies were discovered in the African Burial Ground just off the west side of the square.

Surrogate's Court

32 Chambers St, at Centre St • Library and exhibit Mon–Wed & Fri 9am–4.30pm, Thurs 9am–7pm • Free • ☎ 646 386 5000 • Subway #4,
#5, #6 to Brooklyn Bridge-City Hall

Completed in 1907 to serve as the city Hall of Records, the **Surrogate's Court** (a
surrogate is a type of elected judge) is a grand Beaux Arts pile with an ornate columned
facade of white Maine granite, the portico topped with statues of famous New Yorkers;
today the court still hears cases involving wills, the administration of estates and

---

THE NOTORIOUS FIVE POINTS

East of Foley Square is the area once known as **Five Points**, named for the intersection of
Mulberry, Worth, Park, Baxter and Little Water streets, the last of which no longer exists. A
former pond here, known as the Collect, was filled in as part of a public-works project by 1811,
but the fetid, damp location soon became a massive slum as a relentless influx of immigrants,
sailors and criminals sought refuge here, and toxic industries were shunted to this unlovely
side of town. In 1829, the local press started using the Five Points moniker, and by 1855, when
immigrants formed 72 percent of the population, its muddy streets – called Bone Alley,
Ragpickers' Row and other similarly inviting names – were lined with flimsy tenements.
Diseases such as cholera skipped easily from room to overcrowded room.

The neighbourhood was further marred by vicious pitched battles among the district's
numerous **Irish gangs**, including the Roach Guards, the Plug Uglies and the Dead Rabbits
(depicted with flair in Martin Scorsese's *The Gangs of New York*).

Upper-class sightseers like Charles Dickens (who came here in 1842 and describes it in
American Notes), both fascinated and repelled by Five Points, invented the concept of
"slumming" in their tours of the neighbourhood. They made lurid note of the crime, filth and
other markers of obvious moral depravity, and as a result most of Five Points was cleared by
the late 1860s. Yet some of the slums lingered until 1890, when Danish-born journalist and
photographer Jacob A. Riis published *How the Other Half Lives*, a report on the city's poor (he
calls "Mulberry Bend", the last remnant of Five Points, a "vast human pig-sty"). In particular, his
gripping images, which retained his subjects' dignity while graphically showing the squalor all
around them, helped convince readers that these people were not poor simply due to moral
laxity. The book was remarkably successful in its mission to evoke sympathy for the plight of
this troubled community, and it's in large part thanks to Riis that the Bend was razed in the
1890s, replaced by Columbus Park (p.72) and the current court district.

adoptions. It's worth going through security to see the stunning ceiling mosaics in the main hall by muralist William DeLeftwich Dodge, featuring the signs of the zodiac. From here, follow the signs to the New York Municipal Library and Archives, where a room contains the "Windows on the Archives" exhibit, a small collection of quirky historic artefacts such as the 1957 Ebbets Field home plate.

African Burial Ground National Monument

Duane St, at Elk St • Mon–Sat 9am–4pm; closed Nov–March • Free • ☎ 212 637 2019, ⓦ nps.gov/afbg • Subway A, C, J, Z to Chambers St; R, W to City Hall

In 1991, construction of a federal office building at 290 Broadway uncovered one of the most important US archeological finds of the twentieth century – the remains of 419 skeletons in what was once a vast African burial ground. Today, the **African Burial Ground National Monument** occupies a tiny portion of a cemetery that covered five blocks between the 1690s and 1794. Then outside the city boundary, this was the only place Africans could be buried. After being examined at Howard University (Washington, DC), the skeletons, along with artefacts (such as beads) buried with them, were reinterred at this site in 2003, marked by seven grassy mounds and a highly polished, black granite monument. The soaring **Ancestral Chamber** in the centre is a symbolic counterpoint to the infamous "Gate of No Return" on Gorée Island in Senegal, through which slaves would leave Africa for the New World. Instead of captivity and departure, this gateway represents spiritual freedom and return, facing east towards Africa.

The spiral path into the **Ancestral Libation Court**, 4ft below street level, is engraved with signs and symbols of the African diaspora, inspired by the discovery of what might be one symbol, the *sankofa*, on the coffin of a former slave – heart-rending evidence that despite their situation, slaves maintained spiritual links with their homeland (the *sankofa* symbolized "returning to your roots"). Despite its relatively small size, the curving walls and mystical symbols create a meditative, temple-like atmosphere, in utter contrast to its skyscraper-bound surroundings.

African Burial Ground Visitor Center

290 Broadway • Tues–Sat 10am–4pm, closed federal holidays • Free • ☎ 212 637 2019, ⓦ nps.gov/afbg • Subway A, C, J, Z to Chambers St; R, W to City Hall

To learn more about the African Burial Ground on Duane Street, walk around the corner to the **African Burial Ground Visitor Center**; look for the dedicated doorway just along from the main 290 Broadway entrance. A twenty-minute video (played throughout the day) introduces the site, while an interactive exhibition with touch-screen computers and replicas of the artefacts found here traces not just the history of the cemetery but of slavery in New York. Experts believe as many as fifteen thousand free and enslaved blacks were buried here, and examination of the bones revealed a cycle of back-breaking toil that began in childhood. One of the reasons the site is considered so significant is that slavery (and the cruelty that went with it) is something many people associate with the Deep South. In reality, the size of New York's enslaved population was second only to Charleston in South Carolina in 1776, and slave labour built much of the colonial city. Maya Angelou alluded to this misconception at the emotional reinterment ceremony: "You may bury me in the bottom of Manhattan. I will rise. My people will get me. I will rise out of the huts of history's shame." Slavery was abolished in New York State in 1827.

From here, if you retrace your steps to Foley Square and down Centre Street, you'll see the footpath that runs over the **Brooklyn Bridge** (see p.216).

LINGERIE SHOP, SOHO

Tribeca and Soho

The adjoining neighbourhoods of Tribeca and Soho, north of the Financial District, are home to wealthy New Yorkers with a taste for retro-industrial cool and the stores that cater to them. Nineteenth-century warehouses have been converted into vast lofts, and the area's cast-iron buildings (and their enormous ground-floor windows) make it a perfect spot for purveyors of fine art, fashion and luxury goods. The art scenes that flourished here in the 1970s and 1980s have generally moved on to Chelsea and the outer boroughs, and today Tribeca feels more residential, its streets populated by stylish mums and their hip kids. Soho is also the haunt of fashionable Hollywood types, though the focus here is on dining and, especially, shopping.

Tribeca

Tribeca (try-BECK-a), the Triangle below Canal Street, is a former wholesale-food district that has become an enclave of urban style, its old industrial buildings housing spacious loft apartments. Less a triangle than a crumpled rectangle, the neighbourhood is bounded by Canal and Murray streets to the north and south, and Broadway and the Hudson River to the east and west. The name is a mid-1970s invention of real-estate brokers who thought it better suited to the neighbourhood's increasing trendiness; Jay-Z, Taylor Swift and Gwyneth Paltrow are among a long list of celebrities who own apartments here. Another big name in the neighbourhood is Robert de Niro, who helped found both the **Tribeca Film Center**, a state-of-the-art building catering to producers, directors and editors, and the **Tribeca Film Festival** in 2002. The **Children's Museum of the Arts** is also located in the area (see p.411). It can be an intriguing neighbourhood to explore, but most visitors who trek to Tribeca do so for its **restaurants** (see p.281).

Chambers Street to the Hudson River

Subway A, C, #1, #2, #3 to Chambers St

3

Heading west from City Hall Park, you'll get a taste of Tribeca's historic roots at the triangular intersection between Chambers Street and West Broadway, known as the Bogardus Triangle. Here, the **James Bogardus Viewing Garden** is dedicated to James Bogardus (1800–74), an architect and inventor who put up the city's first cast-iron building in 1849. You can see one of his few remaining creations at **85 Leonard Street** between Church Street and Broadway, a graceful structure completed in 1868.

Head up Hudson Street from the Bogardus Triangle to equally compact **Duane Park**, a sliver of green between Duane, Hudson and Greenwich streets. Established in 1797 and the second-oldest park in New York City (after Bowling Green), it was also once the site of the city's egg, butter and cheese markets – the original depots (mostly posh restaurants and shops today), alternating with new residential buildings, form a picturesque perimeter around the little triangle.

From here you can continue up Greenwich Street to the thoroughly incongruous **Harrison Street Row**, such a contrast to the surrounding concrete that its nine Federal-style houses seem like reproductions. Though three of these late eighteenth-century homes were moved here in the 1970s, all are original, rare reminders of the area's preindustrial past. Immediately to the west lies the traffic-choked West Side Highway (aka West St) and the eminently more appealing **Hudson River Park** beyond, a landscaped promenade that stretches north towards Chelsea and Midtown; you can also wander south to the tip of the island along the shady **Battery Park City Esplanade**.

56 Leonard

56 Leonard St, at Church St • ⓦ 56leonardtribeca.com • Subway #1 to Franklin St

Tribeca's tallest building is a real stunner, with **56 Leonard** a shimmering stack of cantilevered glass blocks dubbed the "Jenga Building" by local media. The 821ft condo

---

TRIBECA AND SOHO HIGHLIGHTS

Balthazar Grab a bite at one of Soho's most iconic restaurants. See p.283

Cronuts at Dominique Ansel Bakery Sample the justifiably hyped donut/croissant hybrid. See p.284

Ear Inn Grab a pint at one of New York's oldest pubs. See p.330

Grand Banks Soak up the Hudson views as you slurp oysters on the deck of this old sailboat. See p.331

Housing Works Bookstore Cafe Enticing secondhand bookshop loaded with bargains and a popular café. See p.388

New York Earth Room Check out Walter de Maria's mind-bending installation of earth in a Soho loft. See p.68

TRIBECA AND SOHO

was designed by Herzog & de Meuron and completed in 2016, with penthouses selling for a mere $47 million. You can't go inside, but check out the giant, highly polished installation at its base by celebrated British sculptor **Anish Kapoor**.

Hook and Ladder Company #8

14 N Moore St, at Varick St • Subway #1 to Franklin St

Movie buffs may recognize the New York City Fire Department's **Hook and Ladder Company #8**, a handsome 1903 Beaux Arts fire station; it featured in the *Ghostbusters* films of the 1980s, and the 2016 remake (note the murals on the pavement outside). It also played a key role in the rescue efforts of September 11, and as it remains a working fire station, you can't do more than admire it from the outside.

New York City Fire Museum

278 Spring St, between Varick and Hudson sts • Daily 10am–5pm • $8; seniors, students and 12 and under $5 • ☎ 212 691 1303, Ⓦ nycfiremuseum.org • Subway C, E to Spring St; #1 to Houston St

Housed in a 1904 Beaux Arts fire station in the area north of Tribeca known as **Hudson Square**, the **New York City Fire Museum** displays old fire trucks dating back to the 1840s and plenty of art and NYFD memorabilia, but also acts as a touching memorial to the 343 firefighters who died on September 11. The NYFD lost 778 men in the line of duty between 1865 and September 10, 2001, but the devastating losses of the following day drew worldwide sympathy. Photos, videos and artefacts found at the site record the disaster, and tiles commemorate those lost.

Soho

Like Tribeca, **Soho** (short for *So*uth of *Ho*uston) has also undergone a series of transformations in the past few decades. In the 1970s and 1980s, Soho was the centre of New York's art scene, but today a mostly non-resident crowd uses the area between Houston and Canal streets and Sixth Avenue and Lafayette Street as an enormous outdoor shopping mall. By day a place to buy trendy labels, at night the neighbourhood becomes a playground for well-groomed bistro- and bar-goers.

Despite the commercialism, Soho's artistic legacy hasn't been completely eradicated. Check out **The Wall** (1973) by Forrest Myers, a giant installation of 42 aluminium bars, painted turquoise and bolted to a periwinkle blue wall at Houston and Broadway, or just cruise the visionary **Prada boutique** (Mon–Sat 10am–7pm, Thurs till 8pm, Sun 11am–6pm), designed by Dutch architect Rem Koolhaas. The store, 575 Broadway at Prince Street, acts as a sort of gatekeeper to the area's myriad shopfronts, which showcase everything from avant-garde home decor to conceptual fashion.

NEW YORK'S MR CHOCOLATE

Small-batch chocolate-making has become something of a trend in New York, but one name stands above all. Born in the small Provençal town of Bandol, France, chocolatier **Jacques Torres** came to New York in 1988, opening his first chocolate factory in 2000. In 2017 he opened the city's first ever chocolate museum, grandly dubbed **Chocolate Museum and Experience with Jacques Torres** (Wed–Sun 10am–5pm; $15, seniors and students $12, kids 4–12 $10; ☎ 212 414 2450, Ⓦ choco-storyny.com) at 350 Hudson St (entrance on King St), next to one of his well-established cafés and chocolate shops (Mon–Fri 8.30am–7pm, Sat 9am–7pm, Sun 10.30am–5pm). At the time of research the museum was a rather amateurish affair, with mildly interesting exhibits tracing the history of chocolate from its Mesoamerican and Mayan roots, but the excellent bonbon-making demonstrations held throughout the day (and plenty of free samples) are certainly a treat for chocoholics. The museum also runs chocolate-making classes.

> ### JACKIE ROBINSON MUSEUM
> Note that the long-anticipated **Jackie Robinson Museum**, commemorating the famous African American baseball player, will open at One Hudson Square, 75 Varick St, at Canal St, pending funds being raised; see ⓦjackierobinson.org for the latest progress.

Broadway
Subway B, D, F, M to Broadway-Lafayette St; N, R , W to Prince St

Any exploration of Soho's streets entails crisscrossing and doubling back, but an easy enough starting point is the intersection of Houston Street and Broadway. **Broadway** reigns supreme as downtown's busiest drag, and numerous storefronts, most of them jazzed-up chain shops trying to compete with Soho's pricey designer boutiques, make it easy to get swept up in the commercial frenzy. Broadway is also the place to start a tour of Soho's distinctive **cast-iron architecture**, best appreciated from the outside – many are now shops, and the interiors have usually been substantially remodelled.

Little Singer Building
561 Broadway, at Prince St • Mango store Mon–Sat 10am–8.30pm, Sun 11am–7.30pm • Subway B, D, F, M to Broadway-Lafayette St; N, R, W to Prince St

One of the later examples of Soho's cast-iron architecture is the **Little Singer Building**, which is actually an L-shaped structure with a second front at 88 Prince St. The twelve-storey terracotta-tiled office and warehouse of the sewing-machine company was erected in 1904 by architect Ernest Flagg, who went on to build the record-breaking Singer Tower in the Financial District in 1908, thus rendering this earlier creation "little" in comparison. Here, Flagg used wide plate-glass windows set in delicate iron frames, a technique that pointed the way to the glass curtain wall of the 1950s. Today, the first floor is a Mango fashion store while the rest is a posh residential co-op.

Haughwout Building
488–492 Broadway, at Broome St • Subway N, R, W to Prince St; #6 to Spring St

The magnificent 1857 **Haughwout Building** is the oldest cast-iron structure in the city, as well as the first building of any kind to boast a passenger elevator – the lift, designed by Elisha Otis, was steam-powered. Despite its dreary grey colour, the facade of the former housewares emporium is still mesmerizing; 92 colonnaded arches are framed behind taller columns and the whole building looks more like an elaborate sculpture.

Broome Street Building
451 Broome St, at Broadway • Subway N, R, W to Prince St; #6 to Spring St

Diagonally opposite the Haughwout Building and equally impossible to ignore, the ostentatious wedding-cake exterior of the **Broome Street Building** was completed in 1896. By the turn of the twentieth century, this was known as the Silk Exchange, but the building is mostly residential today – Britney Spears owned the penthouse before selling it in 2006.

Greene Street
Subway A, C, E, N, Q, R, W to Canal St

Greene Street, in the heart of Soho, boasts a couple of architectural beauties worth seeking out. Just south of Grand Street, **no. 28–30** is known as the "**Queen of Greene Street**". Architect Isaac Duckworth's five-storey French Second Empire extravagance dates from 1873 and was tastefully renovated in 2010 by trendy Swiss-based USM

Modular Furniture. Head north across Broome Street to see more of Duckworth's artistry at **72–76 Greene St**. Thanks to its mass of columns and peaked cornice, this palatial creation, completed just prior to no. 28–30, has naturally been given the title "**King of Greene Street**". The building was sold for a cool $41.5 million in 2012 (a Joseph fashion boutique occupies the retail space).

Drawing Center

35 Wooster St, between Grand and Broome sts • Wed & Fri–Sun noon–6pm, Thurs noon–8pm • $5 • ☎ 212, ⓦ drawingcenter.org • Subway A, C, E, N, Q, R, W to Canal St

The expertly curated **Drawing Center** focuses solely on the exhibition of historical and contemporary drawings, with changing exhibits taking in masters such as Marcel Duchamp and Richard Tuttle, as well as emerging and unknown artists. One block south lies the **Leslie-Lohman Museum of Gay and Lesbian Art** (see p.369).

The Wild Horses of Sable Island Gallery

64 Grand St, between West Broadway and Wooster St • Daily noon–6pm • Free • ☎ 212 219 9622, ⓦ dutescoart.com

Around the corner from the Drawing Center, **The Wild Horses of Sable Island Gallery** displays Roberto Dutesco's celebrated photographs of Canada's 43rd national park and its equine inhabitants. Remote Sable Island lies some one hundred miles off the coast of Nova Scotia (and 750 miles northeast of New York), its four hundred feral horses the descendants of shipwreck survivors.

Cast-Iron Historic District

Subway N, R, W to Prince St; #6 to Spring St

North of Spring Street lies the heart of the **Cast-Iron Historic District**, where you'll see vivacious facades, as well as curlicue bishop's-crook cast-iron lampposts. None quite as splendid as Duckworth's, but all are beautifully preserved and make excellent display cases for the high-end retail offerings inside. The busiest shop in this area is one of the few not devoted to fashion, cosmetics or high-end art (and is not cast iron): the landmark **Apple Store** (see p.390), occupying the former post office on the corner of Greene and Prince streets. Look out also for the **City Walls** (1975) trompe l'oeil mural at 112 Prince St (at Greene St) by Richard Haas, a solid wall craftily made to look like windows.

SOHO'S CAST-IRON ARCHITECTURE

In vogue from around 1860 to the turn of the twentieth century, the **cast-iron architecture** that is visible all over Soho initiated the age of prefabricated buildings. With mix-and-match components moulded from iron, which was cheaper than brick or stone, a building of four storeys could go up in as many months. The heavy iron crossbeams could carry the weight of the floors, allowing greater space for windows.

The label can be confusing at first, as you won't see any obvious sign of metal (other than fire escapes); another major appeal for architects was that it was easy to disguise the iron with remarkably **decorative facades**. Almost any style or whim could be cast in iron, painted or plastered and pinned to the front of an otherwise dreary building to resemble marble: instant face-lifts for Soho's existing structures, and the birth of a whole new generation of beauties. Glorifying Soho's sweatshops, architects indulged themselves in Baroque balustrades and forests of Renaissance columns. But as quickly as the trend took off, it fell out of favour. Stricter building codes were passed in 1899, when it was discovered that iron beams, initially thought to be fireproof, could easily buckle at high temperatures. At the same time, steel proved an even cheaper building material.

With nearly 150 structures still standing, Soho contains one of the largest collections of cast-iron buildings in the world, and the **Soho Cast-Iron Historic District** helps preserve the finest examples.

BROOKLYN COMES TO SOHO

Celebrated artisan market the **Brooklyn Flea** (ⓦ brooklynflea.com) crossed the East River in 2017, opening at 100 Sixth Ave in Soho (Sat & Sun 10am-6pm), two blocks north of Canal Street. The market is slated to remain here until at least the end of 2018 (see p.387). Smorgasburg has also opened in Soho (p.392).

The New York Earth Room

141 Wooster St, between Prince and W Houston sts • Wed–Sun noon–3pm & 3.30–6pm; closed mid-June to mid-Sept • Free • ⓦ diaart.org • Subway B, D, F, M to Broadway-Lafayette St; N, R, W to Prince St

Debuting in 1980, **The New York Earth Room** is one of the most startling permanent installations by local artist Walter de Maria (who died in 2013). This second-floor loft is covered in almost two feet of moist brown earth, all of which weighs some 140 tonnes. Commissioned and maintained by the Dia Art Foundation, the dirt is periodically aerated and cleaned, to keep mushrooms and bugs from flourishing. The grey-door entrance is easy to miss; press the buzzer for 2B and walk up to the second floor. You're not allowed to take photographs.

West Broadway and the South Village

Subway C, E to Spring St; N, R, W to Prince St

The north–south avenue of **West Broadway**, lined on either side with stately buildings, is the edge of the cast-iron district and was once the traditional boundary of Soho, though these days the blocks to the west are usually considered part of the area. Smaller and more residential, this section was once known as the **South Village**, its primarily Italian residents an extension of the Greenwich Village community until Robert Moses' brutal widening of Houston Street in 1940 effectively split them in two. The change in architecture is obvious, as the high-rise cast-iron warehouses give way to older Federal and Greek Revival row houses and cafés. At the top of Sullivan Street, **St Anthony of Padua Church** (daily 9am–4pm; ⓦ stanthonynyc.org) was built in 1888 by the oldest Italian congregation in the US. The church hosted the 2005 funeral of local resident and mafioso Vincent Gigante, better known as "The Oddfather" because he feigned mental illness for years to avoid prison (fittingly, it also featured in the movie *The Godfather II*). Walk back down to **116 Sullivan Street**, an elegant Federal-style townhouse completed in 1832 and particularly noted for its carved wooden doorway. Further south, below Spring Street, **83** and **85 Sullivan Street** are the oldest homes in the neighbourhood, completed in 1819.

The Broken Kilometer

393 West Broadway, between Broome and Spring sts • Wed–Sun noon–3pm & 3.30–6pm, closed mid-June to mid-Sept • Free • ⓦ diaart.org • Subway C, E to Spring St; N, R, W to Prince St

Just south of Spring Street on West Broadway you can find **The Broken Kilometer**, another mind-bending installation by Walter de Maria, dating from 1979. This collection of five hundred carefully arranged brass rods, each 2m long, is a slightly disorienting study in scale and perspective, as well as a testament to the sturdiness of cast-iron buildings – the collected rods weigh more than seventeen tonnes.

SHOPPING IN CHINATOWN

Chinatown, Little Italy and Nolita

Chinese immigrants have been coming to New York – and prospering – since at least the 1850s, making this Chinatown one of the oldest and biggest in the Western hemisphere. Indeed, with around five hundred restaurants and over one hundred thousand residents, Chinatown is Manhattan's most densely populated ethnic neighbourhood. Since the 1980s it has pushed into the smaller enclave of Little Italy, and has begun to sprawl east across Division Street and East Broadway. Little Italy itself, now squeezed into a narrow strip along Mulberry Street, is far more touristy than Chinatown, but both neighbourhoods are fun places to eat. Just to the north, the quarter known as Nolita is home to a number of chic restaurants, bars and boutiques.

Chinatown

Subway J, N, Q, R, W, Z, #6 to Canal St

Walk through the crowded streets of **Chinatown** at any time of day and you'll find packed restaurants; storefronts displaying heaps of shiny squid, clawing crabs and fresh lobsters; and street markets overflowing with piles of exotic fruits, vegetables and ginger root.

Lined with tacky shops and frequently a pedestrian traffic jam, the unappealing east–west thoroughfare of **Canal Street** is unfortunately often all visitors ever see of the neighbourhood – perhaps along with the inside of a *dim sum* palace on **Mott Street**. Explore the narrow side streets, though, and you will be rewarded with a taste of a Chinatown that functions more for its residents than for tourists and retains many of its older traditions. Mott Street is the main north–south avenue, although the streets around it – Pell, Bayard, Doyers and the Bowery – also host a glut of restaurants, tea-and-rice shops and grocery stores that are fun to browse. Nowhere in this city can you eat so well, and so much, for so little.

Brief history

The first known **Cantonese** immigrant to New York arrived in 1858, and settled on Mott Street. He was not joined by significant numbers of his countrymen – and they were virtually all men – until the 1870s. By 1890, the census recorded about twelve thousand Chinese. Most of these men had previously worked out West on the transcontinental railroad or in gold mines, and few intended to stay in the US. Their idea was simply to make a nest egg, then return to their families and (hopefully) a far easier life in China; as a result, the neighbourhood around the intersection of Mott and Pell streets became known as the "bachelor society". Inevitably, money took rather longer to accumulate than expected, and, though some did go back, Chinatown soon became a permanent settlement. Residents made their livings as cooks, cigar vendors, sailors and operators of fan-tan parlours and opium dens.

By the end of the nineteenth century, the quarter was notoriously violent, in large part due to its Triad-like "tongs". These Chinese organized-crime operations doubled as municipal-aid societies and thrived on prostitution, gambling and the opium trade. Beginning in the waning years of the nineteenth century, the **Tong Wars** raged well into the 1930s in the form of intermittent assassinations.

Growing resentment led to the Chinese Exclusion Act of 1882, which completely forbade entry to Chinese workers for ten years, and in the early twentieth century additional **immigration quotas**, particularly the 1924 National Origins Provision (NOP), further restricted the flow of Asians to America. In 1965, the Immigration Act did away with the NOP, and some twenty thousand new Chinese immigrants, many of them women, began to arrive in Chinatown. Local businessmen took advantage of the declining Midtown garment business and made use of the new, unskilled female workforce to open garment factories of their own.

The early 1990s saw another major shift, as large numbers of illegal immigrants from the Fujian province of China arrived. Unlike the established Cantonese, the **Fujianese**

CHINATOWN, LITTLE ITALY AND NOLITA HIGHLIGHTS

Di Palo's Fine Foods Charming old-world Italian deli since 1925, selling the best ricotta, olive oils and home-made pastas. See p.391

Eileen's Special Cheesecake Sample a classic New York treat at this venerable cake shop. See p.288

Museum of Chinese in America Explore Chinese American history in Maya Lin's artfully designed museum. See p.75

New Museum of Contemporary Art Fittingly creative premises for avant-garde art. See p.79

Prince Street Pizza Crazy-good pizza slices. See p.287

Ten Ren's Tea Exceptional Chinese teas sold in the heart of Chinatown. See p.286

CHINATOWN, LITTLE ITALY & NOLITA

DRINKING

BARS

Apothéke	7
Baby Grand	5
Black Lodge	1
Goldbar	3
Mulberry Street Bar	4
Pulquería	6
Sweet & Vicious	2

SHOPPING

Aesop	1
Aji Ichiban	9
Alleva Dairy	6
Di Palo's Fine Foods	7
Downtown Music Gallery	10
John Fluevog	3
McNally Jackson	2
Opening Ceremony	8
Posteritati	5
Resurrection	4

ACCOMMODATION

Bowery House	1
Hotel Mulberry	4
NobleDEN Hotel	2
Wyndham Garden Chinatown	3

EATING

Angelo's	19	Laoshan Shandong Dumplings	38
Black Seed Bagels	12	Le Coucou	21
Bo Ky	27	Lombardi's	11
Café Habana	3	Mac Bar	4
Chefs Club Counter	10	Nom Wah Tea Parlor	35
Chinatown Ice Cream Factory	28	Nyonya	18
Eileen's Special Cheesecake	13	Parm	5
Emilio's Ballato	1	Pasquale Jones	14
Famous Sichuan	31	Peasant	7
Fay Da Bakery	24	Peking Duck House	34
Ferrara Café	17	Pho Bang	16
Great N.Y. Noodletown	30	Ping's Seafood	36
Hop Shing Restaurant	39	Prince Street Pizza	2
Joe's Shanghai	32	Red Egg	20
		Rice to Riches	8
		Rubirosa	6
		Saigon Vietnamese Sandwich	15
		Sanur	33
		Tasty Hand-Pulled Noodles	37
		Ten Ren's Tea Time	26
		Uncle Boons	9
		Vincent's Clam Bar	22
		West New Malaysia	25
		Xi'an Famous Foods	29
		Zia Esterina Sorbillo	23

were largely uneducated labourers who spoke their own dialects along with Mandarin. Today, Cantonese is still the lingua franca of Chinatown; though many well-off Cantonese have moved to the outer boroughs, they remain the district's most important customers, and businesses remain largely Cantonese-owned. This, combined with high rents, has led many Mandarin-speaking "mainlanders" (immigrants from mainland China) to settle in Brooklyn's **Sunset Park** (p.239), though the southern half of **East Broadway** remains a Fujianese enclave.

Columbus Park

Baxter St, Mulberry St, Bayard St and Worth St · Daily 24hr · Free · ☎ 212 639 9675, ⓦ nycgovparks.org · Subway J, N, Q, R, W, Z, #6 to Canal St; J, Z to Chambers St

The southern limits of Chinatown begin just a few blocks north of City Hall Park at the intersection of Worth and Baxter streets. From here, **Columbus Park** stretches north, a green sward away from Chinatown's hectic consumerism. It's favoured by the neighbourhood's elderly, who congregate for morning *t'ai chi* and marathon games of *xiangqi* (Chinese chess). The park was laid out by Calvert Vaux, of Central Park fame, and opened in 1897 (replacing a slum known as Mulberry Bend, made infamous by Jacob A. Riis in *How the Other Half Lives*), but little of his original plan remains – ball fields take up one end, while craggy rock gardens are the backdrop on the north side.

Chatham Square

Bowery, Park Row and Worth St · Subway J, N, Q, R, W, Z, #6 to Canal St; J, Z to Chambers St

Southeast of Columbus Park, Worth Street ends at **Chatham Square**, really a concrete triangle hemmed in by traffic, where Fujianese civic organizations have erected a statue of **Lin Zexu**, a Qing-dynasty official who is revered in China for cracking down on the opium trade. Lin arrested thousands of Chinese opium dealers, destroyed 1180 tonnes of the drug and kicked out the British opium merchants in 1839, thereby precipitating the Opium Wars. The Fujianese have cast their hero as a

BEFORE CHINATOWN WAS CHINATOWN

As is true for many of the neighbourhoods in New York City, the area that is now known as Chinatown has undergone several transformations. The first trace of another culture is the **cemetery of Congregation Shearith Israel**, just south of Chatham Square on St James Place. The oldest Jewish congregation in North America, Shearith Israel was established in New York in 1654 by a small group of Sephardim from Brazil, descendants of Jews who had fled the Spanish Inquisition. This small graveyard was in use from 1683 to 1833, but all that remains today is a collection of seventeenth- and eighteenth-century headstones. The cemetery is opened every year around Memorial Day, when a special ceremony pays tribute to those Jews interred here who died in the Revolutionary War; at other times you can just peer through the iron railings.

Just around the corner at 32 James St, **St James Church** marks the arrival of the Irish in the mid-nineteenth century. A big Greek Revival brownstone, the Roman Catholic church was the gathering place of the first American division of the Ancient Order of Hibernians, an Irish-Catholic brotherhood, in 1836. True to the cultural mixing that is characteristic of Manhattan's slums, St James Church was founded with the help of a Cuban priest, Félix Varela, who was also instrumental in the early Catholic period of the Church of the Transfiguration on Mott Street. If you walk around the corner from St James Church to Oliver Street, you'll see the former church rectory in a row of tenement-style homes, as well as the much-worse-for-wear **Mariners' Temple**, completed in 1845 and the oldest Baptist church in Manhattan (both churches tend to open only for services).

Perhaps the most overlooked anachronism is the **Edward Mooney House**, a tiny Georgian-style brick building at 3 Pell St, on the corner of the Bowery, that looks very out of step with its plastic-facade neighbours. Built around 1785, it's the oldest surviving row house in New York City, erected by Edward Mooney, a wealthy butcher, who saw this neighbourhood's future as a centre for business (it contains private apartments and commercial spaces today).

"pioneer in the war against drugs", according to the inscription. Also in Chatham Square, the **Kimlau Memorial Arch** pays tribute to Chinese Americans killed in World War II. Just to the north looms **Confucius Plaza**, a 1970s housing complex that's still considered some of the best living quarters in Chinatown; a statue of the Chinese philosopher was erected outside in 1976.

Little Fuzhou

East Broadway • Subway F to East Broadway; J, N, Q, R, W, Z, #6 to Canal St

East from Chatham Square is the "new" Chinatown – the district expanded by the Fujianese and other mainland immigrants in the past few decades. East Broadway, often dubbed **Little Fuzhou**, is the main commercial avenue, an earthy, authentic blend of bakeries, restaurants and markets.

Grace Gratitude Buddhist Temple

48 East Broadway • Daily 10am–5pm • Free • ☎ 212 925 1335 • Subway F to East Broadway; J, N, Q, R, W, Z, #6 to Canal St

Founded in 1974 by revered Chinese monk Master Fayun, the **Grace Gratitude Buddhist Temple** is one of the oldest Chan (Zen) Buddhist temples in the city, a serious place of worship maintained by resident monks. The architecture is typically modern, but there's a shrine to Buddhist bodhisattva Guanyin (known as the "Goddess of Mercy") in the lobby, and the main hall is dominated by gold statues representing three incarnations of the Buddha.

Pell and Doyers streets

Subway J, N, Q, R, W, Z, #6 to Canal St

4

Just to the north of Chatham Square, on the corner of **Pell Street** and the Bowery, you'll find the **Huang Daxian Temple** (daily 9am–6pm; free; ☎ 212 349 6221), one of Chinatown's few Taoist temples and, like most of them, a converted shopfront. This one is dedicated to Huang Daxian, a quasi-historical figure who is said to have lived in China in the fourth century, worshipped today for his supposed powers of healing. Better known as Wong Tai Sin in Cantonese, he remains one of the most popular Taoist deities in Hong Kong. On the other side of Pell Street stands the venerable **Edward Mooney House** (see box opposite).

Further along Pell Street itself, no. 16 is the headquarters of the United in Victory Association, also called the **Hip Sing Tong**, where some seventy people were killed when the rival On Leong group raided the building in 1924 (the doorway is next to the "Foot Rub" place). Halfway along Pell is crooked **Doyers Street**. Once known as the "Bloody Angle" for its role as a battleground during the Tong Wars, there's little more malicious than barber shops operating here now.

Mott Street

Subway J, N, Q, R, W, Z, #6 to Canal St

At first glance, **Mott Street**, the "dragon's spine" of Chinatown, is a strip of tacky gift shops and countless modern teashops. Look past the kitsch, though, and you'll also find authentic herbal-medicine vendors and barely renovated tenements – this is the oldest section of Chinatown.

Church of the Transfiguration

29 Mott St, at Mosco St • Sat 2–5pm, otherwise services only • Free • ☎ 212 962 5157, ⓦ transfigurationnyc.org • Subway J, N, Q, R, W, Z, #6 to Canal St

The green-domed **Church of the Transfiguration** is an elegant Georgian building known as the "church of immigrants" for good reason. Established here in 1801 as a Lutheran parish, it was sold to Irish Catholics fifty years later; the plaque honouring those killed in World War I lists primarily Italian names, while today, Mass is said daily in Cantonese, English and Mandarin.

Eastern States Buddhist Temple

64 Mott St • Daily 8.30am–6pm • Free • ☎ 212 966 6229 • Subway J, N, Q, R, W, Z, #6 to Canal St

The oldest existing Chinese temple on the East Coast, the **Eastern States Buddhist Temple** was established in 1962 by the Ying family (originally from Ningbo, China), its linoleum floors and dropped ceiling making it more functional than fancy. The main deity here is the Sakyamuni Buddha, but note also the glass-encased gold statue of the "four-faced Buddha", a replica of the revered image in Bangkok's Erawan Shrine.

Ten Ren's Tea

75 Mott St • Daily 10am–8pm • Free • ☎ 212 349 2286, ⓦ tenrenusa.com • Subway J, N, Q, R, W, Z, #6 to Canal St

Tea lovers should visit **Ten Ren's Tea**, the lauded Taiwanese tea merchant established in the 1950s, which sells everything from cheap green tea to expensive oolongs (semi-fermented tea); try the delicious "Oriental Beauty". Head next door to *Ten Ren's Tea Time* (p.286) to sample a full range of bubble teas.

Canal and Grand streets

Subway J, N, Q, R, W, Z, #6 to Canal St

Say "Canal Street" to most New Yorkers, and they'll think not of a real canal (which this busy thoroughfare was until 1820) but of counterfeit handbags, watches and designer sunglasses, which you'll see on sale in nearly every shop you pass. A casual stroll here is impossible; the streets are lined with fruit vendors, souvenir stalls and hawkers talking up their knock-off bargains – foot traffic often grinds to a halt. One of the newer offerings is **Canal Street Market** at 265 Canal St (Mon–Wed 11am–7pm, Thurs–Sat 11am–8pm, Sun 11am–6pm; ⓦcanalstreet.market), a more fashionable indie shopping mall and food court. Canal Street channels its eastbound traffic onto the **Manhattan Bridge**, completed in 1909, which crosses the East River to Brooklyn via the grand Beaux Arts arch over the centre lanes (modelled on the Porte St-Denis in Paris).

Citizens Savings Bank

58 Bowery, at Canal St • Mon–Fri 8.30am–5pm, Sat 9am–1pm • ☎ 800 975 4722 • Subway J, N, Q, R, W, Z, #6 to Canal St

The former **Citizens Savings Bank** is something of a local landmark, its neo-Byzantine bronze dome looming majestically above the chaotic streets of Chinatown. Completed in 1924, it now functions as a branch of HSBC. Enter on Canal Street to take a peek at the interior of the dome and its four surviving murals: Thrift, Success, Safety and Wisdom (no photography allowed).

Mahayana Buddhist Temple

133 Canal St, at the Bowery • Daily 8.30am–6pm • Free • ☎ 212 925 8787, ⓦ mahayana.us • Subway J, N, Q, R, Z, #6 to Canal St

Chinese influence is obvious at the gilded **Mahayana Buddhist Temple**, which is much more opulent than its counterpart on Mott Street (it was converted from an old theatre in 1997 by the same family). Candlelight and blue neon glow around the giant gold Buddha on the main altar, while along the walls are 32 plaques that tell the story of the Buddha's life. Despite the assault of red and gold, it's a surprisingly peaceful place. The entrance hall contains a smaller shrine to Guanyin (see p.73) and the small shop upstairs sells books and statues.

Bowery Savings Bank

130 Bowery, at Grand St • Closed to the public • ☎ 212 334 5500, ⓦ capitaleny.com • Subway N, Q, R, W, #6 to Canal St; J, Z to Bowery

This lavish Roman Classical-style structure lies two blocks north of Canal Street, at the corner of Grand Street (the city's main east–west avenue in the 1800s). Designed by celebrated architect Stanford White in 1894, today the building is a posh location for private dinners and functions known as **Capitale**, and sadly off limits to visitors.

Museum of Chinese in America

215 Centre St, at Grand St • Tues, Wed & Fri–Sun 11am–6pm, Thurs 11am–9pm • $10, free first Thurs of the month • ☎ 212 619 4785, ⓦ mocanyc.org • Subway J, N, Q, R, W, Z, #6 to Canal St

Designed by Maya Lin (best known for her Vietnam Memorial in Washington, DC), the slickly presented **Museum of Chinese in America** provides a historical overview of the Chinese American experience from 1784 to the present, through an evocative blend of multimedia displays, artefacts and filmed interviews with real people. Some of the issues tackled are the Chinese Exclusion Act of 1882, the emergence of "Chop-Suey" restaurants and bigoted "Yellowface" movies in the 1930s, and the identity of second-generation Chinese Americans since the 1960s. Galleries are arranged around a sunlit courtyard reminiscent of a traditional Chinese house, and also include temporary exhibitions of Chinese and Chinese American art.

Museum

4 Cortlandt Alley, between Franklin and White sts • Sat & Sun noon–6pm • Free, $5 donation • No phone, ⓦ mmuseumm.com • Subway J, N, Q, R, W, Z, #6 to Canal St

Technically in Tribeca but just a short walk south of Canal Street, the creatively named **Museum** is a quirky New York sight not to be missed. Tucked away down a scruffy alley, it occupies just a single old warehouse elevator. Exhibits rotate (think New York City tip jars and fake vomit from around the world), but the permanent collection includes what claims to be one of the shoes thrown at George Bush in Iraq in 2008 (the US military said it destroyed both shoes). Check the website for current opening times; even if it's closed you can see most of the goofy treasures inside through the windows. In 2015 the curators opened a second space next door, hosting exhibitions such as the touching "Future Aleppo".

4

Little Italy

Subway J, N, Q, R, W, Z, #6 to Canal St

North of Canal Street, **Little Italy** is light years away from the solid ethnic enclave of old. Indeed, the red, green and white tinsel decorations along Mulberry Street and the suited hosts who aggressively lure out-of-town visitors to their restaurants are undeniable signs that the neighbourhood is little more than a tourist trap. Few Italians still live here, though a number still visit for a dose of nostalgia, some Frank Sinatra and a plate of fully *Americano* spaghetti with red sauce. For a more vibrant, if workaday, Italian American experience, you'll want to head to Belmont in the Bronx (see p.258).

This is not to advise missing out on Little Italy altogether. Some original bakeries and *salumerias* (Italian speciality food stores) do survive, and here, amid the imported cheeses, sausages and salamis hanging from the ceiling, you can buy sandwiches made with slabs of mozzarella or eat slices of fresh focaccia – **Alleva** on Mulberry Street (p.391) is an excellent example. In addition, you'll still find plenty of places to indulge with an espresso and a pastry, not least of which is *Ferrara's*, at 195 Grand St (p.288), the oldest and most popular café. Another establishment of note is the belt-defying *Lombardi's*, at 32 Spring St (p.286), the city's oldest pizzeria.

Brief history

The area was settled in the latter half of the nineteenth century by a huge influx of Italian immigrants, who supplanted the district's earlier Irish inhabitants and, like their Chinese and Jewish counterparts, clannishly cut themselves off to re-create the Old Country; even streets were claimed by different regions, with settlers from Campania and Naples on Mulberry, Sicilians on Elizabeth, and Mott Street divided between Calabrians (south end) and immigrants from Puglia (north end). After World War II, the Italians started moving out of the city (though Martin Scorsese and Robert de Niro roamed the area in the 1950s), and the neighbourhood is much smaller and more commercial than it once was, with Chinatown encroaching on three sides – Mulberry Street is the only Italian territory south of Broome Street.

Mulberry Street

Subway J, N, Q, R, W, Z, #6 to Canal St

Little Italy's main strip, **Mulberry Street** is an almost solid row of touristy restaurants and cafés. The street is particularly lively, if a bit like a theme park, at night, when the lights come on and the streets fill with restaurant hosts who shout menu specials at passers-by. If you're here in mid-September, the eleven-day **Festa di San Gennaro** (see p.408) is a wild and tacky celebration of the patron saint of Naples, held here since 1926. Italians from all over the city converge on Mulberry Street, and the area is filled with street stalls and numerous Italian fast-food and snack vendors.

Church of the Most Precious Blood

109 Mulberry St (main entrance at 113 Baxter St) • Daily 8am–8pm • Free • Ⓦ oldcathedral.org

The Festa di San Gennaro centres on the **Church of the Most Precious Blood**, a small Roman Catholic shrine completed in 1892. The peaceful but bright interior is home to a chapel containing the venerated statue of San Gennaro ("St Januarius" in English), and the intricately detailed *Nativity of Mercy* sculpture (a representation of the story of the birth of Jesus), created in Naples by famed crafts workshop La Scarabattola.

Italian American Museum

155 Mulberry St, at Grand St • Fri–Sun noon–6pm • Donation $5 • ☎ 212 965 9000, Ⓦ italianamericanmuseum.org • Subway J, N, Q, R, W, Z, #6 to Canal St; B, D to Grand St

To learn more about the historic roots of the area, stop by the **Italian American Museum** housed in the former Banca Stabile. The bank opened in 1885 and offered services to immigrants, including translation, letter writing, wire transfers and travel booking. The building still contains the old vault and banking machines, enhanced by small but enlightening exhibits on the old neighbourhood and Stabile family business – though the bank closed in 1932, the family maintained their other businesses here until the 1960s. Look out for a brutal extortion note from 1914,

---

THE MAFIA IN LITTLE ITALY

Little Italy has proved a rich backdrop for gangster movies, notably parts of the *Godfather* trilogy (especially *Godfather II*), *Donnie Brasco* and *Mean Streets* (the back room of the *Mulberry Street Bar*, at 176 Mulberry St, has been the setting for numerous Mob movies and episodes of *The Sopranos*). The neighbourhood has plenty of real-life Mafia history, however. Sicilian-born Giuseppe "the Clutch Hand" Morello ran his Black Hand extortion rackets from 8 Prince St in the early twentieth century (his mob would evolve into the Genovese crime family, New York's oldest). After Morello's conviction in 1909, Salvatore "Toto" D'Aquila ruled Little Italy from his apartment at 91 Elizabeth St (he founded what would become the Gambino crime family), while Giuseppe "Joe the Boss" Masseria ran open-air liquor markets in defiance of Prohibition on Kenmare, Broome and Grand streets in the 1920s (with the help of Lucky Luciano). The former site of *Umberto's Clam House* (now relocated to the other side of the street), at 129 Mulberry St, was also quite notorious in its time: in 1972, it was the scene of a vicious gangland murder when "Crazy Joey" Gallo was shot dead while celebrating his birthday with his wife and stepdaughter. Gallo, a big talker and ruthless businessman, was keen to protect his interests in Brooklyn; he was alleged to have offended a rival family and so paid the price. Today, the space is occupied by run-of-the-mill *Da Gennaro* restaurant. In later years the Gambino crime family ran operations from the **Ravenite Social Club**, at 247 Mulberry St, between Prince and Spring (now a posh shoe shop); boss John Gotti died in jail in 2002 (his son, John Gotti Jr, claims to have renounced crime). Today you are more likely to see tourists and hipsters than wise guys in Little Italy.

written by a member of the "Black Hand" to a local business owner, and the display about Giuseppe Petrosino, one of the first Italian American NYPD officers, who was murdered working a case in Sicily in 1909.

Nolita

Subway N, R, W to Prince St; #6 to Spring St

The blocks surrounding St Patrick's Old Cathedral, particularly north to Houston Street and east to the Bowery, were rechristened **Nolita** ("North of Little Italy") by savvy real-estate developers in the late 1990s. Stylish shop-owners are the newest variety of immigrant here, as numerous tiny boutiques have taken over former Italian haunts. Most are above Spring Street, but the trendiness has spread south too. Although this district is not cheap by any means, it is a bit more personal and less status-mad than much of neighbouring Soho. The shops showcase handmade shoes, custom swimwear and items with vintage flair, often sold by the designers themselves, or at least by obsessive buyers who have strong affection for the goodies they've collected from elsewhere.

If you're not interested in shopping, you should definitely check out the **New Museum of Contemporary Art** on the Bowery, a stylish showcase for the latest trends in multimedia art. Nolita is also an appealing place to put your feet up after a long walking tour. Choose from any of the numerous restaurants (see p.286), or head to the café inside the **McNally Jackson** bookstore, at 52 Prince St, or the **Housing Works Bookstore Café**, at 126 Crosby St.

Basilica of St Patrick's Old Cathedral

263 Mulberry St, at Prince St · Daily except Wed 8am–6pm · Free · ☎ 212 226 8075, ⓦ oldcathedral.org · Subway N, R, W to Prince St; #6 to Spring St

The **Basilica of St Patrick's Old Cathedral** was once the spiritual heart of Little Italy and is the oldest Catholic cathedral in the city. When it was consecrated in 1815, it actually served the Irish community and hosted the Roman Catholic archdiocese in New York. Catholic leadership has moved uptown to the newer St Patrick's Cathedral on Fifth Avenue (see p.128), and "old St Pat's" now serves local English-, Spanish- and Chinese-speaking worshippers. Designed by Joseph-François Mangin, the architect behind City Hall, the building is grand Gothic Revival, with an 85ft vault, a gleaming gilt altar and a massive pipe organ that was installed in 1868, when the church was restored following a terrible fire. The Vatican awarded Basilica status to the old cathedral in 2010, a title that confers increased ceremonial privileges.

Equally notable is the **cemetery** behind the church, which is ringed with a brick wall that the Ancient Order of Hibernians used as a defence in 1835, when anti-Irish rioters threatened to burn down the church. The cemetery is almost always locked, but try to peek through one of the gates – you may recognize the view from a scene in Martin Scorsese's *Mean Streets* (one of the few parts of the movie actually shot here, even though the film was set in Little Italy).

The Bowery

Subway B, D to Grand St; J to Bowery

Forming the boundary between Nolita and the Lower East Side, **the Bowery** was until relatively recently a byword for poverty and destitution, America's original **skid row**. At its peak in 1949, around fourteen thousand homeless people could be found here, most dossing down in hostels known as flophouses. Today, only a few flophouses remain, and these mostly cater to newly arrived Chinese labourers at the southern end of the Bowery. The street runs north from Chatham Square in Chinatown to Cooper Square in the East Village (see p.90), where it is increasingly lined with elegant, contemporary buildings.

CHANGING TIMES ON THE BOWERY

The current gentrification of this wide thoroughfare is just the latest of many changes over the years: the street takes its name from *bouwerie*, the Dutch word for farm, when it was the city's main agricultural outlet through the centre of Manhattan. In the nineteenth century, it was flanked by music halls, opera houses, vaudeville theatres, hotels and middle-market restaurants, drawing people from all parts of Manhattan – including opera lover **Walt Whitman**. The good times did not last, and by the early twentieth century the street was becoming associated with crime, prostitution and poverty, attracting religious and social welfare institutions like the **Bowery Mission**, which opened in 1880. The Bowery's notoriety immortalized it in literature, with many writers making use of its less than stellar reputation. Stephen Crane's 1893 novella *Maggie: A Girl of the Streets* is set here, while Theodore Dreiser closed his 1900 tragedy Sister Carrie with a suicide in a Bowery flophouse. Fifty years later William S. Burroughs alluded to the area in a story that complained of undesirables waiting to "waylay one in the Bowery" (Burroughs lived here between 1974 and 1981). The Great Depression signalled a low point in the Bowery's fortunes, and between the 1940s and 1980s the whole strip was synonymous with alcoholics and the homeless (though Blondie also lived for a time at 266 Bowery in the 1970s, when punk club *CBGB* was in its heyday). Those days are largely gone, and wine stores, galleries and high-end apartments are becoming far more prevalent, though the catering trade stores that have been here since the 1920s still remain.

New Museum of Contemporary Art

235 Bowery, opposite Prince St • Wed & Fri–Sun 11am–6pm, Thurs 11am–9pm • $18 (Thurs 7–9pm pay-what-you-wish) • Free guided tours (45min) Wed & Fri 12.30pm, Thurs, Sat & Sun 12.30pm & 3pm • ☎ 212 219 1222, ⓦ newmuseum.org • Subway N, R, W to Prince St; #6 to Spring St; F to Second Ave-Lower East Side

4

Opened here in 2007, the **New Museum of Contemporary Art** is a powerful symbol of the Bowery's rebirth. The building itself is as much the attraction as the avant-garde work inside, a stack of seven shimmering aluminium boxes designed by Tokyo-based architects Kazuyo Sejima and Ryue Nishizawa.

An industrial elevator glides between the four main floors, each holding one exhibition space. The warehouse-like galleries, all brilliant white with shiny concrete floors, are spacious but still small enough to digest without overdosing on the often thought-provoking and diverse range of temporary exhibits. The **shop** in the lobby has a fabulous book section and café, while the **Sky Room** on the seventh floor opens at weekends for fine views across the Lower East Side and Nolita.

International Center of Photography Museum

250 Bowery, opposite Stanton St • Tues, Wed, Fri–Sun 10am–6pm, Thurs 10am–9pm • $14 (Thurs 6–9pm pay-what-you-wish) • ☎ 212 857 0000, ⓦ icp.org • Subway F to Second Ave-Lower East Side

The **International Center of Photography Museum** was founded in 1974 by Cornell Capa (brother of war photographer Robert). This exceptional museum sponsors around twenty exhibits a year dedicated to "concerned photography", avant-garde works and retrospectives of modern masters. Many of the shows focus on holdings from the extensive permanent collection, which contains basically all of Robert Capa's photography, as well as that of New York sensationalist Weegee. The museum moved into its current premises in 2016.

KATZ'S DELI

Lower East Side

Historically the epitome of the American ethnic melting pot, the Lower East Side – bordered to the north by Houston Street, the south by East Broadway, the east by the East River and the west by the Bowery – is one of Manhattan's most enthralling downtown neighbourhoods. Today, a fair proportion of its inhabitants are Dominicans and Chinese, but among them you're also likely to find small Jewish communities, students, moneyed artsy types and hipster refugees from the more gentrified areas of Soho and the East Village. Many visitors come for the shopping; some of the city's best vintage-clothing and furniture stores are here, which has in turn attracted a number of emerging designers as well. The plethora of drinking, dancing and food options also draws large crowds every night of the week.

5

INFORMATION

Tourist information The Lower East Side Partnership website (Ⓦ lowereastside.org) offers lots of neighbourhood info, plus a comprehensive map of local art galleries.
Local tours For tours of the neighbourhood's Jewish heritage (and to gain entrance into some of the otherwise private synagogues), contact the Lower East Side Jewish Conservancy at 235 East Broadway (☎ 212 374 4100, Ⓦ nycjewishtours.org).

Brief history

Most of this area was owned by the pro-British DeLancey family until 1787, when it was confiscated and sold off by the new American government. The first tenement buildings in the city were constructed here in 1833, and the development of **Kleindeutschland** (Little Germany) followed closely behind. By 1860, Irish immigrants had started to dominate the neighbourhood, and by the end of the nineteenth century it was attracting international humanitarian attention as an insular slum for over half a million **Jews**. Mainly from Eastern Europe, these refugees came to America in search of a better life, but instead found themselves scratching out a living. By the 1880s, the area had also become America's **garment capital** – today, there are still over one hundred small garment factories in the Lower East Side. For many Jews, the entertainment industry was the only way out; comedian George Burns, composer George Gershwin, and William Fox, founder of the Fox Film Corporation, all grew up here.

Low standards of hygiene and abysmal housing made disease rife and life expectancy low: in 1875, the infant mortality rate was forty percent, mainly due to cholera. It was conditions like these that spurred reformers like Jacob Riis and Stephen Crane to record the plight of the city's immigrants in writing and photographs in the 1890s.

The **Chinese** and **Dominicans** moved into the area in the 1980s, but it wasn't until the 1990s that retro clubs, chic bars, gourmet restaurants and unique boutiques sprouted up all over. Despite the changes, about forty percent of the people living here were born in another country, with a quarter of residents Spanish-speaking, and around twenty percent from China and other parts of East Asia.

Houston Street to Grand Street

Jewish immigrants indelibly stamped their character on the Lower East Side with their shops, delis, restaurants and synagogues. Even now, with Chinatown overflowing into the neighbourhood, the area exhibits remnants of its Jewish past: on Houston itself, you'll find *Katz's Deli* (see p.290); *Russ & Daughters* (see p.290); and venerable knish-maker *Yonah Schimmel* (see p.289). South of Houston, **Orchard Street** is centre of the so-called **Bargain District**. This area is at its best on Sundays, when the street is closed to traffic between Houston and Delancey, and it's filled with stalls and storefronts hawking discounted designer clothes and accessories. South of Delancey, Orchard Street is gradually being colonized by hip, independent **art galleries** (see p.371).

LOWER EAST SIDE HIGHLIGHTS

Breakfast at Shopsin's Grab a hearty breakfast at this classic New York diner. See p.288
Doughnut Plant Scrumptious sweet snacks in a variety of creative flavours. See p.290
Katz's Delicatessen Legendary deli since 1888, serving gargantuan pastrami sandwiches. See p.290
Live music at Arlene's Grocery Iconic band venue, especially for punk and hard rock. See p.344
Lower East Side Tenement Museum Illuminating tours of this old tenement building shed light on New York's rich history of immigrant life. See p.82
Museum at Eldridge Street Beautifully restored synagogue with tours that pay tribute to the neighbourhood's Jewish heritage. See p.84

5

Lower East Side Tenement Museum

97 Orchard St • Tours every 15–30min, Mon, Tues & Fri 10.15am–5.15pm, Wed & Thurs 10.15am–6.30pm, Sat & Sun 10.30am–5pm; 1hr; $25; tours start at the visitor centre, 103 Orchard St (Fri–Wed 10am–6.30pm, Thurs 10am–8.30pm) • ☏ 212 431 0233, ⓦ tenement.org • Subway B, D to Grand St; F to Delancey St; J, M, Z to Essex St

Even if you don't have the time to tour the Lower East Side extensively, make sure you visit the **Lower East Side Tenement Museum**, an 1863 tenement building restored by the

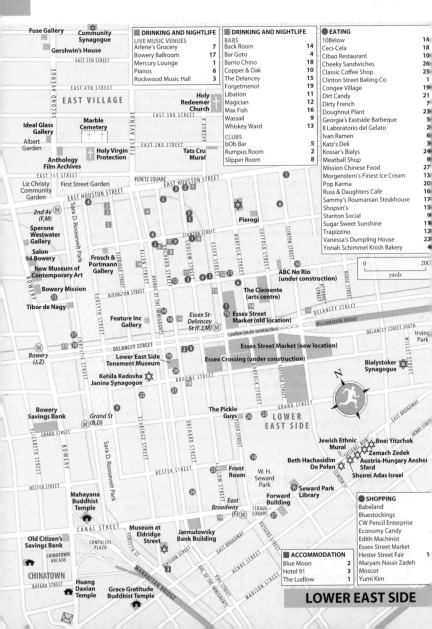

LOWER EAST SIDE

museum founders in the 1990s (it had been abandoned since 1935). If you've visited Ellis Island (see p.39), this museum continues the immigrant story: guides do a brilliant job bringing to life the building's (and the neighbourhood's) past and present, aided by documents, photographs and artefacts found on site, concentrating on the area's multiple ethnic heritages. This will probably be your only chance to see the claustrophobic, crumbling interior of a tenement, with its deceptively elegant, though ghostly, entry hall and two communal toilets for every four families. Various apartments inside have been renovated with period furnishings to reflect the lives of its tenants, from the mid-nineteenth century when there was no plumbing (or indoor toilets), electricity or heat, to the mid-twentieth century when many families ran cottage industries out of their apartments.

The tenement is accessible only by various themed **guided tours**. Start at the nearby **visitor centre**, where you can buy tour tickets, watch a couple of introductory videos (20min, on permanent loop), peruse the excellent bookshop, visit the demonstration kitchen for culinary programmes and view art exhibitions. **Tours** include "Hard Times", which focuses on a German-Jewish family and an Italian family in the depression years of 1863 and 1935; "Irish Outsiders", which examines the grim life of an Irish family 1868–69; and "Sweatshop Workers", which highlights the Jewish Levine family's garment workshop and the Rogarshevskys' Sabbath table in the early twentieth century. "Shop Life" explores a restored nineteenth-century German saloon at street level, and discusses other businesses located in that space. There are also excellent one-hour "Meet the Residents" encounters with costumed interpreters, such as 14-year-old Victoria Confino, who lived in the tenement in 1916, and series of **walking tours** of the neighbourhood (1hr 30min–2hr; $25–45), designed to complement the tenement tours.

Kehila Kedosha Janina Synagogue and Museum

280 Broome St, at Allen St • Sun 11am–4pm • Free • ☎ 212 431 1619, ⓦ kkjsm.org • Subway B, D to Grand St; F to Delancey St; J, M, Z to Essex St

Two blocks east of the tenement museum along Broome Street, the beautifully preserved **Kehila Kedosha Janina Synagogue and Museum** has been the home of the region's Romaniote Jews since 1927, an obscure branch of Judaism with roots in Roman-era Greece. Enthusiastic volunteers are on hand to provide background and introduce Jewish art and various exhibits, including costumes from Janina (the Romaniote capital of Greece), *alephs* (hand-painted birth certificates), and the first Holocaust Memorial to Greek Jews.

Essex Street Market

Delancey St, at Essex St • Mon–Sat 8am–7pm, Sun 10am–6pm • ⓦ essexstreetmarket.com • Subway F to Delancey St; J, M, Z to Essex St

The indoor **Essex Street Market** was erected under the aegis of Mayor La Guardia in 1939, when pushcarts were made illegal. Here you'll find all sorts of fresh fruit, fish and vegetables, along with artisan chocolates, cheese and *Shopsin's* restaurant (see p.288). The market should be merged into the new **Market Line** across the street sometime in 2018. Two blocks south, 357 Grand St (at Essex St) is home to **The Pickle Guys** (Mon–Thurs & Sun 9am–6pm, Fri 9am–4pm; ☎ 212 656 9739, ⓦ pickleguys.com), where people queue up outside the store to buy fresh home-made pickles, olives and other yummy picnic staples from huge barrels of garlicky brine.

Angel Orensanz Center

172 Norfolk St • Mon–Fri 10am–5pm by appointment • Free • ☎ 212 529 7194, ⓦ orensanz.org • Subway F to Delancey St; J, M, Z to Essex St

The **Angel Orensanz Center** was originally the Gothic Revival-style **Anshe Chesed Synagogue**, built in 1849 for the German Jewish community and the oldest surviving synagogue building in New York. The property was abandoned in the 1970s, but purchased in 1986 by Spanish sculptor and painter **Angel Orensanz** who converted it into an art gallery and performance space. Today the third and fourth floors serve as a museum displaying the work of Orensanz (who still maintains a studio here) while the Shul of New York, a liberal Reform synagogue, uses the main space for services. Sarah

5

Jessica Parker and Matthew Broderick, both half Jewish, were married here in super-secret in 1997 (though in a Christian service). To see the gorgeous interior you must make an appointment or check the website for upcoming events.

Canal Street and around

Though the southern part of the Lower East Side has largely been absorbed by Chinatown, the area used to be an important hub for the Jewish community. To get a feel for the old quarter, start on **Canal Street** at Eldridge Street, two blocks west of Orchard Street.

Museum at Eldridge Street

12 Eldridge St, between Canal and Division sts • Mon–Thurs & Sun 10am–5pm, Fri 10am–3pm • $14, free Mon; hourly guided tours only (last tour 4pm; 1hr) • ☎ 212 219 0888, ⓦ eldridgestreet.org • Subway B, D to Grand St; F to East Broadway

Completed in 1887 as the first **synagogue** constructed by Eastern European Orthodox Jews in the US, this painstakingly restored site opened as a museum in 2007. It's still one of the neighbourhood jewels: the facade is a grand brick and terracotta hybrid of Romanesque, Moorish and Gothic influences, but the real highlight is the **main sanctuary** upstairs, a gasp-inducing space with rich woodwork, painted ceiling, giant chandelier and original stained-glass windows, including the west-wing rose window – a spectacular Star of David roundel. The **women's balcony** offers a closer view of the artwork, while displays show just how dilapidated the synagogue had become by the early 1970s. The synagogue is a functioning house of worship, but you can visit the interior on **guided tours**, which provide plenty of entertaining stories about the neighbourhood. Tours begin at the lower level, where the **Bes Medrash** or "House of Study" also serves as a synagogue, and there's a shop and the Limud Center; the interactive computer displays here offer further insights into the history of the building.

Jarmulowsky Bank Building

54 Canal St, at Orchard St • Closed to the public • Subway B, D to Grand St; F to East Broadway

Above a row of food and electrical stores is the ornate Beaux Arts facade of the **Jarmulowsky Bank Building**, dwarfing the buildings around it. Founded in 1873 by a Russian-Jewish peddler who made his fortune reselling ship tickets, the bank catered to the financial needs of the area's non-English-speaking immigrants. Sender Jarmulowsky, who was dubbed the "East Side J.P. Morgan" and became the first president and key benefactor of the Eldridge Street Synagogue (see above), died less than a month after the current building was completed in 1912. As the threat of war in Europe grew, the bank was plagued by runs and riots, and in 1917 it finally collapsed; on its closure, thousands lost what little savings they had accumulated. The building has been in development limbo for several years, most recently undergoing renovation as retail and office space.

THE NEW LOWER EAST SIDE

New York's current construction boom has not spared the Lower East Side, and you'll see swish modern towers sprouting up between the old tenements all over the neighbourhood. Some of the more ambitious projects include **Essex Crossing** (ⓦ essexcrossingnyc.com), a massive, mixed-use development at the intersection of Delancey and Essex streets, which will involve updating and expanding Essex Street Market (p.83) as part of a new shopping mall, The Market Line (completion expected 2021–24). There's also the **Lowline** (ⓦ thelowline.org), a historic trolley terminal converted to a spectacular High Line-style park, albeit underground and lit by solar technology (opening very optimistically slated for 2021). To the south, the neighbourhood dubbed **Two Bridges** (roughly the area along the East River between the Brooklyn and Manhattan bridges) is to be the home of several eye-popping skyscrapers, beginning with Extell's 850ft **One Manhattan Square** at 252 South St, topping out in 2017.

A NEW HOME FOR ABC NO RIO?

Since 1980, **ABC No Rio** (famous for its weekly hardcore punk matinees) has been a vibrant arts presence on Rivington Street (one block north of Delancey St), originally occupying a squat and resisting eviction for decades. In 2006 the city finally sold 156 Rivington St to ABC No Rio for $1, but with the proviso it raise funds for a safer, new building. In 2017 the old premises were demolished and for now the arts collective is without a home. A new building at 156 Rivington St – designed by local architect Paul Castrucci – will offer larger exhibition and performance spaces, though at the time of writing funds were still being raised. See Ⓦ abcnorio.org for the latest.

East Broadway and Shtiebel Row

Subway F to East Broadway

Canal Street ends at **East Broadway**, now almost exclusively a Fujianese enclave but once a thriving Jewish neighbourhood. At the junction between the two streets, the handsome **Forward Building** at 175 East Broadway became the headquarters of the influential Jewish daily *The Forward* in 1912, with adjacent Straus Square a hangout for radicals and activists (the building features carved bas-relief portraits of Karl Marx and Friedrich Engels).

The section of East Broadway between Clinton and Montgomery streets is known as **Shtiebel Row**, once home to dozens of storefront *shtieblach* (small Jewish congregations) but now lined by ugly housing projects on the north side. Several remain in the historic row houses on the south side of the street, however, often marked by small signs in Hebrew; the **Congregation Beth Hachasidim De Polen**, a branch of Agudath Israel of America, a leading Orthodox organization, is at 233 East Broadway. The best way to see inside any of the *shtieblach* is to contact the Lower East Side Conservancy (see p.81). Look out also for the huge **Jewish Ethnic Mural** (1973) by Susan Caruso-Green, peeling but still visible on the east side of 232 East Broadway.

Bialystoker Synagogue

7 Willett St, near the junction of Grand St and East Broadway • Mon–Thurs 7–10am (to visit you must call in advance) • Free • ☎ 212 475 0165, Ⓦ bialystoker.org • Subway F to Delancey St; J, M, Z to Essex St

The incongruously located **Bialystoker Synagogue** was built in 1826 as a Methodist church and purchased by the Beth Haknesseth Anshe Bialystok Congregation in 1905. Sombre grey stone on the outside, hemmed in by grim housing projects, the synagogue's sanctuary is a trove of stained glass, gold leaf and exuberant murals of zodiac signs, all beautifully restored. There's a hidden door leading from the balcony to the attic, where runaway slaves being moved along the "underground railway" were hidden, and a memorial plaque to the gangster **Bugsy Siegel** (aka Benjamin Siegel), who worshipped here as a child.

THE EAST VILLAGE

The East Village

The East Village, which extends east from Broadway to the East River and north from Houston Street to 14th Street, is one of New York's most fashionable neighbourhoods, home to some of the best bars, restaurants and independent theatres in the city. Once a working-class refuge for immigrants, New York's nonconformist intelligentsia were sent scurrying here when rents began to rise in Greenwich Village, and by the 1960s the East Village was at the height of its creative and often lawless period. Since the 1990s, the area's flourishing culinary and bar scene (and its proximity to NYU) has ensured that rents here are almost as high as in neighbouring West Village. Thoughtful resistance to the status quo can still be found, however, through a smattering of independent boutiques, thrift stores, record shops and alternative performance spaces.

ARRIVAL

Public transport The East Village can be reached by taking the #6 train to Astor Place, the L train to Third or First Ave, or the N, R and W trains to 8th St.

Noho

Squashed between Astor Place, the Bowery, Broadway and Houston Street, **Noho** (north of Houston) was considered part of the East Village until the name was invented by a group of local activists in the 1970s. Most of the old warehouses here have been transformed into trendy galleries, condos and offices (Facebook's New York headquarters is at 770 Broadway). To view some of Noho's most cutting-edge contemporary architecture, wander along **Bond Street** between Broadway and the Bowery, with the condos at no. 22 and no. 40 standouts (Ian Schrager and Herzog & de Meuron collaborated on the latter).

6

Public Theater

425 Lafayette St, between Astor Place and E 4th St • Box office Mon & Sun 2–6pm, Tues–Sat 2–7.30pm • ☎ 212 967 7555, ⓦ publictheater.org• Subway N, R, W to 8th St; #6 to Astor Place

Just south of Astor Place lies the **Public Theater** (see p.355), a beautifully restored brownstone-and-brick building that was once the **Astor Library**. Built with a bequest from John Jacob Astor between 1853 and 1881 (in a belated gesture of *noblesse oblige*), it was the first public library in New York. It became the Public Theater in 1967; pop into the lobby to see Ben Rubin's *Shakespeare Machine*, a chandelier installation with 37 fan-like LED screens displaying text from the Bard's work.

Merchant's House Museum

29 E 4th St, between Lafayette St and the Bowery • Mon & Fri–Sun noon–5pm, Thurs noon–8pm; tours (free) daily 2pm, Thurs 6.30pm • $15 • ☎ 212 777 1089, ⓦ merchantshouse.com • Subway N, R, W to 8th St; #6 to Astor Place

Constructed in 1832, the **Merchant's House Museum** offers a rare and intimate glimpse of domestic life in New York during the 1850s. The elegant, Federal-style row house was purchased by Seabury Tredwell, a successful metal merchant, in 1835. Remarkably, much of the mid-nineteenth-century interior remains in pristine condition, largely thanks to Seabury's daughter Gertrude, who lived here until 1933 – it was preserved as a museum three years later. Folders loaded with information provide ample material for a self-guided tour of the house, providing fascinating background, anecdotes and quotes from the family, their servants and neighbours. Highlights include furniture fashioned by New York's best cabinet-makers, the mahogany four-poster beds upstairs (where both Gertrude and Seabury passed away) and the tiny brass bells in the basement, used to summon the servants.

THE EAST VILLAGE HIGHLIGHTS

Big Gay Ice Cream Shop Subtly named purveyor of sensational ice creams and sundaes. See p.294

East Village community gardens Tour some of these remarkable green spaces scattered across the neighbourhood. See p.93

McSorley's Old Ale House America's oldest pub is an atmospheric throwback to the nineteenth century. See p.334

Momofuku Noodle Bar David Chang's flagship restaurant remains one of the most popular joints in New York. See p.291

Nuyorican Poets Café Showcase for up-and-coming poets and artists. See p.364

St Mark's Comics This venerable comic store has been in business since 1984. See p.90

THE EAST VILLAGE

CBGB

315 Bowery, between E 1st and E 2nd sts • John Varvatos store open Mon–Fri noon–8pm, Sat 11am–8pm, Sun noon–6pm • ☎ 212 358 0315, ⓦ johnvarvatos.com • Subway N, R, W to 8th St; #6 to Bleecker St

The New York **punk-rock** scene emerged at the legendary underground music club **CBGB** in the 1970s, which famously hosted bands such as **The Ramones**, **Blondie**, **Patti Smith** and **Talking Heads**. In 2003, the city renamed the corner of East 2nd Street and the Bowery "Joey Ramone Place", in honour of the late punk legend. The club finally closed in 2006, and in a sign of the times has become a John Varvatos fashion boutique; designer clothes and vinyl records (which you can buy) are displayed in the original, dimly lit interior, with walls plastered with punk memorabilia. The store also hosts occasional live rock music, known as the **Bowery Live** concert series.

6

Astor Place

Subway N, R, W to 8th St; #6 to Astor Place

Between Broadway and Third Avenue lies **Astor Place**, a short street that forms a busy crossroads as it intersects with the Bowery, Third and Fourth avenues and St Mark's Place/East 8th Street, where students, tourists and teenagers mill around, wolfing pizza, drinking cheap beer or skateboarding. It's named for real-estate tycoon John Jacob Astor, the wealthiest person in the US at the time of his death in 1848 (worth $115 billion in modern terms). The balancing black steel cube in the centre of the intersection is the *Alamo* (1967) by Tony Rosenthal.

EAST VILLAGE REBELS: FROM REDS TO RENT

Over the years, the East Village has been home to its share of **radical artists**, **politicos** and **literati**. In 1916, the short-lived Communist journal *Novy Mir* operated from the basement at 77 St Mark's Place, numbering among its contributors **Leon Trotsky**, who lived in New York for three months (1916–17) – **W.H. Auden** lived in the same building between 1953 and 1972. At 208 E 13th St historical markers commemorate **Emma Goldman**, who lived here from 1903 to 1913 while publishing her anarchist paper *Mother Earth* (she was deported to the Soviet Union in 1919). In the 1950s, the East Village became one of the main New York haunts of the **Beat poets** such as Kerouac, Burroughs and Ginsberg – the last wrote *Kaddish* at 170 E 2nd St in 1961, as tribute to his mother, Naomi. The Yippies antiwar group was founded by Abbie Hoffman and Jerry Rubin here in 1967, and was based at 9 Bleecker St until being evicted – finally – in 2014. **Andy Warhol** debuted the Velvet Underground at the Fillmore East (105 Second Ave at E 6th St), which played host to just about every band you've ever heard of between 1968 and 1971, before becoming The Saint (also now defunct), a gay disco famous for its three-day parties (1980–90). In 1973, Puerto Rican artists established the **Nuyorican Poets Café** on East 3rd Street (see p.364), a haven for up-and-coming New York poets and writers. Live venue **CBGB** also opened in 1973, launching the careers of punk bands like the Ramones as well as Blondie and the Talking Heads (punk pioneer **Richard Hell** still lives on East 12th Street).

By the 1980s, the East Village was best known for its **radical visual artists**, including Keith Haring, Jeff Koons and **Jean-Michel Basquiat** – the last lived in a converted stable owned by Andy Warhol at 57 Great Jones St from 1983 to his death in 1988, commemorated by another plaque. Gay icon **Quentin Crisp** lived nearby at 46 E 3rd St from 1981 until his death in 1999. In the early 1980s **Madonna** lived at 230 E 4th St, while Chinese artist and activist **Ai Weiwei** lived on East 7th and East 3rd streets between 1983 and 1993, his apartments becoming a hub for other Chinese artists and intellectuals (Chen Kaige and Tan Dun among them). In 2001 and 2002 the East Village was the epicentre of the garage rock revival scene, led by groups such as The Strokes, Interpol and the Yeah Yeah Yeahs.

Towards the end of the 1980s, the neighbourhood was the centre of a different kind of attention: the city evicted the homeless from Tompkins Square Park, and the neighbourhood's many dead-broke squatter artists were forced out, a story memorialized in the hit Broadway musical **Rent**. With suitable irony, the show has made millions of dollars since its debut in 1996, and was successfully adapted for the big screen in 2005 – its Broadway run finally ended in 2008.

Cooper Union

7 E 7th St, between Third and Fourth aves • Mon–Thurs 7.30am–2am, Fri & Sat 7.30am–midnight, Sun noon–2am (limited hours during school holidays) • ☎ 212 353 4100, ⓦ cooper.edu

Just south of Astor Place, between the Bowery and Third Avenue, is **Cooper Square**, dominated by the brownstone mass of the Foundation Building of the **Cooper Union for the Advancement of Science and Art**, a college for the poor established in 1859 by the wealthy entrepreneur Peter Cooper (1791–1883). Today, Cooper Union is a prestigious art, engineering and architecture school, whose nineteenth-century glory is evoked with a statue of the benevolent Cooper by Augustus Saint-Gaudens just in front. Inside (lower level), the **Great Hall** is not particularly exciting, though it's where, in 1860, Abraham Lincoln wowed an audience of New Yorkers with his "right makes might" speech, criticizing the pro-slavery policies of the Southern states – before going to *McSorley's* on East 7th Street (see p.334) to quench his thirst. The art exhibitions in the second-floor **Arthur A. Houghton Jr. Gallery** (Tues–Fri 2–7pm, Sat & Sun noon–7pm; free) are also worth viewing.

You should also check out the gleaming **New Academic Building** at 41 Cooper Square across the street on Third Avenue, completed in 2009 with a contemporary, environmentally friendly design by LA-based Thom Mayne; it's usually closed to the public unless there's a public art exhibition on in the **41 Cooper Gallery**.

St Mark's Place

East from Cooper Square, between Third Avenue and Avenue A, East 8th Street is known as **St Mark's Place**, lined with souvenir stalls, punk and hippie-chic clothiers and newly installed chain restaurants, signalling the end of the gritty atmosphere that had dominated this thoroughfare for years. Indeed, the sections closest to Third Avenue have a discernable Asian/Japanese vibe these days, with noodle bars and fashions more akin to parts of Tokyo than 1970s New York.

LANDMARKS OF ST MARK'S

St Mark's Place isn't just a cool place to eat and drink. Check out these notable landmarks, walking east from Third Avenue. As you stroll along the street, note the mosaic-encrusted lampposts, part of the **Mosaic Trail** created by Jim Power, aka "Mosaic Man" (ⓦ mosaicmannyc .com), though several have now been relocated to Astor Place.

Hamilton-Holly House 4 St Mark's Place, at Third Ave. This 1831 Federal-style townhouse has become a minor pilgrimage site for fans of the musical *Hamilton* thanks to its association with Eliza Schuyler Hamilton, the widow of Alexander, who lived here with her children from 1833 to 1842.

St Mark's Comics 11 St Mark's Place, between Third and Second aves. One of the few iconic stores to have survived since the street's punk heyday in the early 1980s. Mon & Tues 10am–11pm, Wed 9am–1am, Thurs–Sat 10am–1am, Sun 11am–11pm.

German-American Shooting Society Clubhouse (Deutsch-Amerikanische Schuetzen Gesselschaft) 12 St Mark's Place. A rare German Renaissance-style beauty, built in 1889 when St Mark's was the heart of Kleindeutschland, or Little Germany (it's now a yoga studio and vegan restaurant).

Gem Spa 36 St Mark's Place, at Second Ave. This tiny newspaper/magazine shop dates back to 1900 (the current incarnation opened in 1957), but is best known as the birthplace of the authentic New York City-style egg cream (chocolate or vanilla syrup, milk and seltzer water; no eggs; $3) and its classic Zoltar Fortune Teller Machine. It also featured on the back of the New York Dolls' eponymous debut album in 1973. Open 24hr.

Physical Graffitea 96 St Mark's Place, between First Ave and Ave A. A teashop housed in the tenement that featured on the cover of the 1975 Led Zeppelin album *Physical Graffiti*. Daily 11am–10.30pm.

Museum of the American Gangster

80 St Mark's Place (go through the gate and up the stairs of no. 78), at First Ave • Daily 1–6pm • $20 (includes guided tours at 1pm, 2.30pm & 4pm) • ☎ 212 228 5736, ⓦ museumoftheamericangangster.org • **William Barnacle Tavern** Mon–Thurs 6pm–2am, Fri 6pm–4am, Sat 1pm–4am, Sun 1pm–2am • ☎ 212 388 0388 • Subway #6 to Astor Place

The **Museum of the American Gangster** is one of the oddest attractions on St Mark's, housed above what used to be an illegal speakeasy run by gangster Walter Scheib in the 1920s (now the **William Barnacle Tavern**, owned by the museum). Though the two exhibition rooms contain a handful of rare gangster-related curios (a John Dillinger death mask, and the bullet that killed Pretty Boy Floyd for example), there's not much to see, and it's the **guided tours** by enthusiastic owner Lorcan Otway (or his employees) that make this worth considering. After you've watched a video, they'll lead you into the bar and then the basement (where the illicit boozers once hid), regaling you with tales of prohibition, Cosa Nostra and Frank Sinatra, though again, you won't see anything especially exciting.

6

Little Ukraine

Just behind Cooper Square is an area long inhabited by New York's Ukrainian community, most evidenced by the lavishly adorned exterior of **St George Ukrainian Catholic Church** at 30 E 7th St (rebuilt in the 1970s), and the **Ukrainian Museum**. You can also grab a bite nearby at *Streecha Ukrainian Kitchen*, at 33 E 7th St, where most of the food is cooked up by elderly members of St George's (Wed–Fri 11am–5pm, Sat & Sun 9am–5pm; ☎ 212 674 1615), or *Veselka* (see p.294).

Ukrainian Museum

222 E 6th St, between Second and Third aves • Wed–Sun 11.30am–5pm • $8 • ☎ 212 228 0110, ⓦ ukrainianmuseum.org • Subway #6 to Astor Place

The small but beautifully maintained **Ukrainian Museum** is primarily a collection of Ukrainian folk costumes and textiles, as well as modern art from respected Ukrainian artists such as Nikifor (1896–1960) and Vasyl Krychevsky (1873–1952). You'll also see examples of the country's famous painted Easter eggs, known as *pysanky*.

Yiddish Theater District

On Second Avenue, between East 5th and 6th streets, the apartment on the second floor of no. 91 was the childhood home of the **Gershwin** brothers, one of the greatest musical partnerships in history. George and Ira grew up in the heart of the **Yiddish Theater District**, centred on Second Avenue, which by World War I rivalled Broadway in scale and quality. The Immigration Act of 1924 signalled the end, however, and today all that remains to commemorate this once exuberant art form is the **Yiddish Walk of Fame**, like the stars on Hollywood Boulevard, at the corner of East 10th Street.

St Mark's Church-in-the-Bowery

131 E 10th St, at Second Ave • Office hours Mon–Fri 10am–4pm • Free • ☎ 212 674 6377, ⓦ stmarksbowery.org • Subway L to Third Ave; #6 to Astor Place

Opposite the Yiddish Walk of Fame is **St Mark's Church-in-the-Bowery**, the second-oldest church in the city. **Peter Stuyvesant**, the last Dutch Director-General of the New Netherlands, who arrived in what was then New Amsterdam in 1647 and surrendered the city to the English in 1664, built a small chapel here in 1660. The chapel was close to his farm, and he was laid to rest inside twelve years later. The box-like Episcopalian house of worship that currently occupies this space was completed in 1799 – Stuyvesant's tombstone is now set into the outer walls. Nearby is a bust of the

Director-General donated by the Dutch in 1915, looking far nobler than the crude, early English caricatures of "Peg-leg Pete" suggest.

The church is normally locked – walk up to the office on the second floor (via a side door on the right side) and someone will let you in to see the vivid stained-glass windows inside. In 1966, the **St Mark's Poetry Project** (☎212 674 0910, ⓦpoetry project.org) was founded here by Paul Blackburn and friends (hosting the likes of Allen Ginsberg, Patti Smith and many others), to ignite artistic and social change. Today, the church remains an important cultural rendezvous, with poetry readings Monday, Wednesday and Friday at 8pm (all $8) and dance performances by the **Danspace Project** (ⓦdanspaceproject.org).

Tompkins Square Park

Aves A to B, and E 7th to E 10th sts • Daily 6am–midnight • Free • ☎212 674 6377, ⓦnycgovparks.org; • Subway L to First Ave; #6 to Astor Place

A great green square in the heart of the East Village, **Tompkins Square Park** has long been a focus for the local community as well as one of New York's great centres for political protest (see box below). In recent years the park has evolved like the rest of the Village, and is now a desirable outdoor space that appeals to everyone, from local families to drag queens. The cleaned-up park features handball courts, a dog run and free concerts in the summer. Near the centre of the park is the **Prabhupada elm tree** (aka Hare Krishna Tree), the site of the **Hare Krishna** movement's first ceremony outside of India, held in 1966, and named after the founder Swami Prabhupada (Allen Ginsberg was in attendance that day). Jazz legend **Charlie Parker** lived at 151 Ave B (closed to the public) on the east side of the park from 1950 until his death in 1954; the free **Charlie Parker Jazz Festival** features concerts in the park on the last weekend in August (see ⓦcityparksfoundation.org).

Russian and Turkish Baths

268 E 10th St, between First Ave and Ave A • Mon, Tues, Thurs & Fri noon–10pm, Wed 10am–10pm, Sat 9am–10pm, Sun 8am–10pm; men only Thurs noon–5pm, Sun 8am–2pm; women only Wed 10am–2pm; mixed otherwise (shorts are mandatory) • $45 • ☎212 473 8806, ⓦrussianturkishbaths.com • Subway L to First Ave; #6 to Astor Place

The old steam rooms at the redbrick **Russian and Turkish Baths** have been active since 1892; you can enjoy the no-frills steam baths, sauna and an ice-cold pool all day for $45 (includes soap, towel, robe, razor and slippers), though it's extra to get beaten with a *platza* oak-leaf broom ($40) or chow down on some *borscht* ($4) in the on-site restaurant. Don't expect a posh spa – this is a grungy, old-school experience.

THE TOMPKINS SQUARE RIOTS

Until 1991, Tompkins Square Park was more or less a shantytown (known locally as "Tent City" or "Needle Park"). Hundreds of homeless people slept on benches or under makeshift shelters between the paths. In the winter, only the really hardy or truly desperate lived here, but when the weather got warmer the numbers swelled, as activists, anarchists and all manner of statement-makers descended on the park. Things came to a head in the 1988 **Tompkins Square Riots**, when massive demonstrations against a 1am curfew for the previously 24-hour park led the police, badges covered and batons drawn, to attempt to clear the square of people. In the ensuing battle, 44 demonstrators and bystanders were hurt; the investigation that followed heavily criticized the police for the violence. It wasn't the first disturbance here – a far larger riot occurred in **1874**, when police crushed a demonstration involving thousands of unemployed. In 1991 the park was temporarily closed and dozens of homeless people who had been living here were relocated. The park was subsequently overhauled, its winding pathways and playground restored; the changes are enforced by a midnight lock-up and police surveillance.

THE EAST VILLAGE GARDENS

In the 1970s, huge parts of the East Village burned to the ground after cuts in the city's firefighting budget closed many of the local fire stations. Since then, **Green Thumb** (Ⓦgreenthumbnyc.org), founded in 1978 on the back of work by local (mostly female) activists, has helped the community transform these neglected and empty lots from rubble-filled messes into some of the prettiest and most verdant spaces in lower Manhattan. In 1995, NYC Parks & Recreation began managing the programme, but a dramatic reversal in city policy in 1998 – to convert garden land into real estate – almost scuppered the whole project. Despite a last-minute agreement that ensured the safety of 114 of the neighbourhood's 600-plus gardens in 1999, the battle reached fever pitch in February 2000, when **El Jardin de la Esperanza** (Hope Garden) on East 7th Street between avenues B and C was bulldozed to make way for market-priced housing. Around thirty local residents were arrested while protesting the action; the city began to bulldoze the garden while the last resister was being removed – a mere forty minutes before an injunction was issued to prevent the city from destroying any further community gardens. The final 2002 agreement guaranteed the preservation of an additional two hundred community gardens.

The fight seems to have been well worth it. There is no nicer way to spend a summer afternoon than by picnicking among the lush trees and carefully planted foliage of these spaces, though sadly, many gardens were badly damaged by **Hurricane Sandy** in 2012. Of particular note is the **6th & B Garden** (April–Oct Sat & Sun 1–6pm; Ⓦ6bgarden.org), which lost its willow tree but remains overgrown with wildflowers, vegetables and roses. The garden also provides a space for yoga classes in the morning and performance art in the evening during the summer, as well as a forum for bake sales, sing-alongs and other community events. Other gardens include the very serene and lush **6 B/C Botanical Garden** (April–Oct Mon–Fri 6pm–dusk, Sat & Sun noon–6pm; Ⓦ6bcgarden.org) on East 6th Street between B and C; and the willow-framed **La Plaza Cultural** (April–Oct Sat & Sun 10am–7pm; Ⓦlaplazacultural.com) on East 9th Street at Avenue C, with a fence rimmed by home-made pinwheels. Note that alcohol is not permitted inside any of the gardens.

Alphabet City

East of Tompkins Square Park and north of Houston Street is **Alphabet City**, one of the most dramatically revitalized areas of Manhattan. Deriving its name from the grid of avenues lettered A–D, Alphabet City is also known to its remaining Puerto Rican residents as **Loisaida** (a Spanglish rendering of "Lower East Side"). Like Tompkins Square Park, this used to be a notoriously unsafe corner of town run by drug pushers and gangsters; today, the crime rate is way down, many of the old buildings have been renovated, and the streets are increasingly the haunt of 20-somethings and edgier tourist youth. Restaurants and bars aside, it's worth wandering around this part of town just to see some of the **murals** by the likes of Antonio "Chico" Garcia, as well as the numerous **community gardens** (see box above). One definite cultural highlight is the **Nuyorican Poets Café**, at 236 E 3rd St (☎212 505 8183, Ⓦnuyorican.org), where you can catch some of the biggest stars of the spoken-word scene.

Museum of Reclaimed Urban Space

155 Ave C, at E 10th St • Tues & Thurs–Sun 11am–7pm • Free, suggested donation $5; tours $20 • ☎973 818 8495, Ⓦmorusnyc.org • Subway L to Third Ave

Alphabet City's tradition of resistance is commemorated at the tiny **Museum of Reclaimed Urban Space**, housed in a nineteenth-century tenement that has been a punk squat since 1986 (aka "C-Squat"). Inside you'll find photographs, posters, exhibits, a bicycle activism timeline and articles chronicling the history of social activism, community gardens and squatting in the East Village. Check the website for details of guided tours (usually Sun at 3pm).

WASHINGTON SQUARE PARK

The West Village

Greenwich Village (now commonly called the West Village or just "the Village") has been the artistic, bohemian heart of New York since the 1920s, and though still one of the more progressive neighbourhoods in the city, it has attained a moneyed status over the last four decades and is definitely the place for those who have "arrived". Celebrities seem to snap up properties left, right and centre – the likes of Julia Roberts, Leonardo DiCaprio and Sarah Jessica Parker – attracted for the same reasons as the intelligentsia a century ago: quaint side streets, charming brownstones and brick townhouses unrivalled elsewhere in Manhattan. It's quiet and residential, but with a busy streetlife that keeps humming later into the night than in many other parts of the city.

Washington Square Park

Fifth Ave, Waverly Place, W 4th St and MacDougal St • Daily 6am–midnight • Free • ☎ 212 998 6780, ⓦ nycgovparks.org • Subway A, B, C, D, E, F, M to W 4th St

The best way to see the Village is to walk, and by far the best place to start is its natural centre, **Washington Square Park**. Memorialized in Henry James's 1880 novel *Washington Square*, the city completed an extensive renovation of the park in 2011.

The park was established in 1827 on the site of a former cemetery and execution ground (up to ten thousand bodies are reputed to be buried here and the **Hangman's Elm** continues to grow in the park today). For years, the square was something of an open-air drug bazaar, but in the 1990s a heavy undercover police presence put an end to most of that activity. During the spring and summer months, the square becomes a combination of performance venue, giant chess tournament and social club, boiling over with life as skateboards flip, dogs run and guitar notes crash through the urgent cries of performers calling for the crowd's attention.

The most imposing monument in the park itself is Stanford White's **Washington Memorial Arch**, built in 1892 to commemorate the centenary of George Washington's presidential inauguration. On the northern side of the park, only the row of elegant Greek Revival mansions – the "solid, honourable dwellings" that James described – reminds visitors of the area's more illustrious past. The author based much of the novel on his grandmother's house at **no. 19**, while James himself was born around the corner on Washington Place (the house had already been torn down when he returned to the city in 1906, much to his disgust). Further along Washington Square North, **no. 11** served as Will Smith's home in the 2007 movie *I am Legend* (much of it shot in the area), while Edith Wharton lived at **no. 7** in 1882. Later, **no. 3** became known as the "studio building", home to artists such as William Glackens, Guy Pène du Bois and Edward Hopper, who lived here from 1913 until his death in 1967. Today, all these buildings, like most of the property around the square, belong to New York University (NYU) – unless you charm your way past the guard, the reverently preserved **Hopper Studio** (at no. 3) is usually open only in October on Open House weekend (see ⓦ ohny.org).

NYU and south of Washington Square

Subway A, B, C, D, E, F, M to W 4th St; N, R, W to 8th St

The south and east sides of the square are lined with bulky **New York University** buildings, including the university's innovative Grey Art Gallery. The university dates back to 1831, and is one of the largest (and wealthiest) private institutions of higher education in the US.

THE WEST VILLAGE HIGHLIGHTS

Bedford Street Stroll along one of New York's most attractive streets, lined with historic buildings. See p.103

Caffe Reggio This old-school Italian-American café has barely changed since it opened in 1927. See p.296

Comedy Cellar One of the nation's most respected comedy clubs features top talent every night. See p.359

Murray's Cheese Shop Hundreds of quality cheeses but also sandwiches, olive oil, artisanal chocolate and much more. See p.392

Washington Square Park Celebrated by Henry James and still a wonderful blend of gardens, fountains, street performers and historic monuments. See above

Village Vanguard Perhaps New York's most venerated jazz club since opening in 1935, home to Sonny Rollins and many others. See p.350

MEATPACKING DISTRICT

Apple Store

Soho House

The Standard Hotel

High Line

Whitney Museum of American Art

James Baldwin plaque

White Columns Gallery

Seravalli Playground

LGBT Community Center

NY City AIDS Memorial

St. Vincent's Hospital Park

Willa Cather plaque

Village Vanguard

WEST VILLAGE

Stonewall National Monument

Abingdon Square Park

Abingdon Square

Bleecker Playground

Charles Street Synagogue

Carrie's Stoop

Westbeth Artists Housing

New School Drama

Gay Liberation Monument

Christopher St-Sheridan Square (1)

Sheridan Square

Barrow St Theatre

Lucille Lortel Theatre

Twin Peaks no.17

Friends House

PATH Station (to NJ)

Grove Court

Isaacs-Hendricks House

no. 75½

Murray's Cheese Shop

Our of Po

St Luke's-in-the-Fields

Cherry Lane Theatre

Cosby House

Jimmy Walker House

Library

Tony Dapolito Recreation Center

James J. Walker Park

Carmine Swimming Pool & Keith Harding Mural

Gavin Brown's Enterprise Gallery

Hudson River Park

Hous St (

New York Cit Fire Museum

Pier 51

Pier 46

Christopher Street Pier (Pier 45)

Hudson River

Pier 40

14th St (A,C,E,L)

14th St (1,2,3)

Jackson Square

Hudson River Park

0   200
yards

THE WEST VILLAGE

Map labels:

6th Av–4th St (F,L,M)
New School Arnold Hall
New School Welcome Center
New School University Center
Regal Cinemas 14
WEST 13TH STREET
EAST 13TH STREET
13th Street Repertory Theatre
Quad Cinema
Parsons (Sheila C. Johnson Design Center)
Cardozo School of Law
Strand Bookstore
WEST 12TH STREET
EAST 12TH STREET
New School Kaplan Hall
First Presbyterian Church
Salmagundi Club
Cinema Village
WEST 11TH STREET
no.18
Eleanor Roosevelt's House
Church of the Ascension
Grace Church
WEST 10TH STREET
Lockwood DeForest House
Dawn Powell House
EAST 10TH STREET
Marianne Moore house
Mark Twain's House
WEST 9TH STREET
EAST 9TH STREET
C.O. Bigelow Pharmacy
Astor Place (6)
WEST 8TH STREET
EAST 8TH STREET
8th St-NYU (N,R,W)
Cooper Union Building
MACDOUGAL ALLEY
WASHINGTON MEWS
ASTOR PLACE
WASHINGTON SQUARE NORTH
Grey Art Gallery
Blue Man Group
Colonnade Row
Public Theater
Washington Arch
WAVERLY PLACE
Triangle Shirtwaist Fire Memorial
Tisch School of the Arts
NYU Bookstore
WEST WASHINGTON PLACE
Richard Wright plaque
Washington Square Park
WASHINGTON PL
Provincetown Playhouse
Catholic Center at NYU
Fred Lowe Theater
Merchant's House Museum
WASHINGTON SQUARE SOUTH
W 4th St-Washington Sq (A,B,C,D, E,F,M)
Vanderbilt Hall
Judson Memorial Church
Bobst Library
NYU Welcome Center
Stern Business School
WEST 3RD STREET
Kimmel Center
GREAT JONES STREET
Village Underground
Players Theatre
Café Wha?
LaGuardia Park
New York University
MINETTA LANE
OTHER DEMO SQUARE
Center for Architecture
Renee and Chaim Gross Foundation
BLEECKER STREET
SILVER TOWERS (NYU)
Time Landscape
WEST HOUSTON STREET
St Anthony of Padua
New York Earth Room
PRINCE STREET
Louis K. Meisel Gallery
Spring St (C,E)
SPRING STREET
no.116
Trump Soho

THE TRIANGLE SHIRTWAIST FIRE

One of New York's most infamous tragedies occurred on March 25, 1911, at the corner of Washington Place and Greene Street, when a fire started on the eighth floor of the **Triangle Shirtwaist garment factory**, one of the city's notorious sweatshops. A terrible combination of flammable fabrics, locked doors, collapsing fire escapes and the inability of fire-truck ladders to reach higher than the sixth floor resulted in the deaths of 146 workers – almost all women, primarily immigrants, and some only 13 years old – in less than fifteen minutes. The fire led to legislation requiring improved safety standards, and helped spur the growth of the International Ladies' Garment Workers' Union. The site is now known as the Brown Building and forms part of NYU, with flowers left in front of the plaque commemorating the disaster on March 25 each year.

Grey Art Gallery

100 Washington Square East • Tues, Thurs & Fri 11am–6pm, Wed 11am–8pm, Sat 11am–5pm • Suggested admission $5 • ☎ 212 998 6780, ⓦ greyartgallery.nyu.edu • Subway A, C, E, F, M to W 4th St; N, R, W to 8th St

The **Grey Art Gallery** hosts top-notch travelling exhibitions, which rotate every three months and feature a wide range of media, including sculpture, painting, photography and provocative video art. Temporary exhibits are also assembled from the university's permanent collection, especially strong in American painting from the 1940s to the present. The gallery is usually closed between exhibitions – check the website before you go.

Judson Memorial Church

55 Washington Square South • Only open before and after services Sun 10.30am–2pm; also Arts Wednesdays 7–10pm • ☎ 212 477 0351, ⓦ judson.org • Subway A, B, C, D, E, F, M to W 4th St; N, R, W to 8th St

Elegant **Judson Memorial Church**, one of Stanford White's most beautiful Italianate creations, stands out amid a messy blend of modern architecture on Washington Square South. Built as a Baptist church in 1892, the Judson is a hub of local activism today, particularly in the areas of immigration, Fair Trade and antiwar protest, but it's also worth a look inside for its seventeen gorgeous stained-glass windows by John La Farge and a small baptistry designed by Augustus Saint-Gaudens.

Center for Architecture

536 LaGuardia Place • Mon–Fri 9am–8pm, Sat 11am–5pm • Free • ☎ 212 683 0023, ⓦ aiany.org • Subway A, B, C, D, E, F, M to W 4th St

Two blocks south of Washington Square Park, the innovative **Center for Architecture** hosts temporary exhibitions highlighting every aspect of architectural design, from Modernism to specific shows on New York themes (such as the 1964 World's Fair). The centre itself, operated by the American Institute of Architects, is a bright and stylish hub for conferences, lectures, film screenings and off-site tours (check the website for details).

Renee & Chaim Gross Foundation

526 LaGuardia Place • Open for guided tours Thurs & Fri 1 & 3pm (closed July & Aug) • $15 • ☎ 212 529 4906, ⓦ rcgrossfoundation.org • Subway A, B, C, D, E, F, M to W 4th St

Lauded Jewish sculptor **Chaim Gross** lived next door to the Center for Architecture between 1963 and his death in 1991, his home now preserved as the Renee & Chaim Gross Foundation. Illuminating tours (the only way to get inside) take in Gross's first-floor sculpture studio, the "Building Identity" exhibition and the artist's living and dining quarters upstairs, featuring work from his personal art collection (Hartleys and de Koonings among them).

MacDougal Street

Subway A, B, C, D, E, F, M to W 4th St; N, R, W to 8th St

From the southwest corner of the Washington Square Park, **MacDougal Street** cuts south towards Soho; from the 1920s to the 1970s, this was the dynamic heart of

Village cultural life (see box below), and though it remains clogged with bars and cafés, its patrons these days are more likely to be NYU students looking for cheap drinks, than aspiring artists. No. 133–139 was once the home of the **Provincetown Playhouse** established here by the Provincetown Players in 1918; Eugene O'Neill, Edna St. Vincent Millay and Djuna Barnes were all key members. Despite vociferous local opposition, NYU demolished most of the building in 2009, retaining a portion of the facade for a new university theatre.

Continuing south brings you to venerable *Caffe Reggio* at 119 MacDougal St, one of the first and most atmospheric Village coffee houses, dating back to 1927 (see p.296). The brick row house opposite at no. 130–132 is where **Louisa May Alcott** lived between 1867 and 1870; it's thought she wrote most of *Little Women* (1868) here.

Washington Mews
Subway A, B, C, D, E, F, M to W 4th St; N, R, W to 8th St

Running between University Place and Fifth Avenue just north of the park, the small cobblestone street and old pastel buildings of **Washington Mews** seem out of place amid the grand brownstones that abut the square. This alley was used to stable horses until it was redesigned in 1916 to stable humans, and most recently NYU professors.

7

Fifth Avenue and around
Subway A, B, C, D, E, F, M to W 4th St; N, R, W to 8th St

Fifth Avenue begins its long journey uptown from the Washington Memorial Arch, and along the side streets just north of here you'll find some of the best-preserved, early nineteenth-century townhouses in the Village, rich in literary heritage. Pulitzer prize-winning poet **Marianne Moore** moved to 35 W 9th St in 1965, her last home in the city, commemorated by a plaque that describes her as "baseball enthusiast and lifelong New Yorker". Perhaps the most picturesque home is the exotic-looking **Lockwood de Forest house**, at 7 E 10th St (now the NYU Jewish student centre) – the

---

FROM BEBOP TO GAGA: MUSIC IN THE WEST VILLAGE

The West Village has been a breeding ground for innovative musicians since the 1930s, when jazz club **Village Vanguard** opened at 178 Seventh Ave – **Sonny Rollins** made a legendary recording here in 1957 and **John Coltrane** followed in 1961 (see p.350). In the early 1940s the **Almanac Singers** (which included Pete Seeger and Woody Guthrie) held "hootenannies" at 130 W 10th St ("Almanac House"), and in 1961, **Bob Dylan** played his first professional gig at legendary **Gerde's Folk City**, at 11 W 4th St (long ago absorbed by NYU buildings), while supporting John Lee Hooker. In 1970 Gerde's moved to 130 W 3rd St before finally closing in 1987 – the space is currently occupied by live venue *Village Underground*.

The infamous **Gaslight Café** opened in 1958 in the basement of 116 MacDougal St, closing in 1971. Next door at no. 114, the *Kettle of Fish* pub opened in 1950 and was where many performers hung out between sets – it later moved to Christopher Street (see p.335), where you can still see the original neon "Bar" sign inside, with which a drunken Jack Kerouac was famously photographed in 1957. At the corner of Bleecker Street, 93 MacDougal St was the site of the raucous **San Remo Café**, which Jack Kerouac turned into The Masque in his novel *The Subterraneans* (these days, it's a branch of *Denino's Pizzeria*). The original **Fat Black Pussycat** around the corner on Minetta Street – where Dylan allegedly wrote *Blowin' in the Wind* in 1962 – is *Panchito's* today. **Jimi Hendrix** began his career at **Café Wha?**, at 115 MacDougal St, one of the few MacDougal venues still open. Hendrix lived for a time at 59 W 12th St, while Dylan had digs at 161 W 4th St and later at 92–94 MacDougal St. By the 1970s, new musical genres such as disco, punk, salsa and hip-hop were emerging elsewhere in New York, though there are still several **jazz clubs** in the Village (see p.350), and venues such as the **Bitter End** at 147 Bleecker St (see p.347) occasionally nurture future stars: **Lady Gaga** was a struggling regular here in 2007.

ornate oriel window of intricate filigree is made from teak carved in India in the 1880s. Comic writer **Dawn Powell**, whose New York novels centred on the Village, lived next door at 9 E 10th St from 1931 to 1942, where a plaque declares "all but forgotten after her death, her work enjoyed an extraordinary revival in the 1990s". In stark contrast, **Mark Twain** lived the life of a national celebrity at 14 W 10th St between 1900 and 1902, while poet **Emma Lazarus** lived at no. 18 from 1883 until her untimely death here just four years later. **Eleanor Roosevelt** kept an apartment at 20 E 11th St between 1933 and 1942, but since this period coincided with her husband's presidency, it's probable that she spent more time talking domestic and foreign policies than playing bridge with her West Village neighbours.

Church of the Ascension

36–38 Fifth Ave, at 10th St • Mon–Fri noon–3pm • Free • ☎ 212 254 8620, ⓦ ascensionnyc.org • Subway L, N, Q, R, W, #4, #5, #6 to Union Square/14th St

Heading north up Fifth Avenue from Washington Square Park, you'll pass a couple of imposing churches. On the corner of West 10th Street stands the Episcopal **Church of the Ascension**, built in 1841 by Richard Upjohn (the Trinity Church architect), where a vast but gracefully toned La Farge altar painting and some fine stained glass dominate an interior designed by Stanford White in the 1880s. In 2011 the magnificent **Manton Memorial Organ**, built in France, was installed in the church to honour ex-parishioner and patron Jim Manton, a British expat who was knighted in 1994. For organ recitals and concerts given by the **Voices of Ascension** choral ensemble, see the website ⓦ voicesofascension.org.

First Presbyterian Church

12 W 12th St • Mon, Wed & Fri noon–12.30pm, Sun 11am service only • Free • ☎ 212 675 6150, ⓦ fpcnyc.org • Subway L, N, Q, R, W, #4, #5, #6 to Union Square/14th St

Continuing the Gothic theme, Joseph Wells's bulky, chocolate-brown **First Presbyterian Church**, just across 11th Street from the Church of the Ascension, was completed in 1845 with a crenellated tower modelled on the one at Magdalen College in Oxford, England. Inside, you'll find carved black-walnut pews, a soaring altarpiece and a fabulous Tiffany rose window.

Salmagundi Club

47 Fifth Ave, between E 11th and E 12th sts • Mon–Fri 1–6pm, Sat & Sun 1–5pm • Free • ☎ 212 255 7740, ⓦ salmagundi.org • Subway L, N, Q, R, W #4, #5, #6 to Union Square/14th St

Housed in a graceful 1852 Italianate brownstone, the members-only **Salmagundi Club** was founded in 1871 as one of the nation's foremost art associations – members have included William Merritt Chase, Childe Hassam, John LaFarge, Augustus Saint-Gaudens, Louis Comfort Tiffany and Stanford White. Take a peek inside the public galleries to view rotating exhibitions from contemporary members and items from the permanent collection, which include maritime paintings from John Noble (p.266) and John Stobart.

Parsons The New School for Design

Sheila C. Johnson Design Center 66 Fifth Ave, between W 12th and W 13th sts • Daily noon–6pm, Thurs till 8pm • Free • ☎ 212 229 8919, ⓦ newschool.edu/parsons • Subway L, N, Q, R, W, #4, #5, #6 to Union Square/14th St

One of the most prestigious art and design colleges in the world, **Parsons The New School for Design** was founded by American Impressionist William Merritt Chase in 1896, and now forms part of the New School, a private university. Like NYU, its campus is spread around the West Village, but you can visit the two public art galleries in the **Sheila C. Johnson Design Center** on Fifth Avenue – expect an eclectic programme of high-quality contemporary exhibitions.

Sixth Avenue

Subway A, B, C, D, E, F, M to W 4th St; #1 to Christopher St

Although **Sixth Avenue** is for the most part lined with mediocre stores, restaurants and modern buildings, there are some exceptions, like the unmistakeable clock tower of the nineteenth-century **Jefferson Market Courthouse**.

Across the street from the courthouse and opening onto West 10th Street, **Patchin Place** is a tiny mews constructed in 1848 (you can only peer through the gate). The row houses were home to the reclusive author Djuna Barnes for more than forty years beginning in 1941; supposedly, Barnes's long-time neighbour e.e. cummings (who lived here from 1923 until his death in 1962) used to call her "just to see if she was still alive". Patchin Place has also been home to Marlon Brando, Ezra Pound and Eugene O'Neill.

Heading south, look out for **C.O. Bigelow Pharmacy**, at 414 Sixth Ave, just north of West 8th Street, founded in 1838 and probably the city's oldest drugstore, and a few blocks further on (at Sixth Ave and 3rd St), the **West 4th Street Courts**. Known as "The Cage" for the physical style of basketball typically on display here, the courts attract amateur players from all over the city and regularly host high-quality street tournaments.

Jefferson Market Library

425 Sixth Ave, at W 10th St • Mon–Thurs 10am–8pm, Fri & Sat 10am–5pm, Sun 1–5pm • Free • Subway L, N, Q, R, W, #4, #5, #6 to Union Square/14th St

Completed in 1877 by Central Park co-designer Calvert Vaux and English-born Frederick Clarke Withers on the site of a former market, this imposing Victorian Gothic edifice served as a district courthouse until 1945; the murderer of architect Stanford White (see box, p.120) was tried here in 1906, as was Mae West, arrested for appearing in an "immoral" play (*Sex*) in 1927. It's been a public library since 1967, and is worth a quick peek inside; stroll up to the second floor via the spiral stone staircase to see the original ceiling and stained-glass windows, reminiscent of a Gothic church despite the rows of books.

Bleecker Street and around

Subway A, B, C, D, E, F, M to W 4th St; #1 to Christopher St

Off Sixth Avenue's west side are some of the Village's prettiest residential streets, where you can easily spend a couple of hours strolling and soaking up the neighbourhood's charms. To start exploring, cross Father Demo Square on Sixth Avenue and walk up **Bleecker Street**, past the Italian Renaissance-style **Our Lady of Pompeii Church** (Mon,

---

THE WEATHERMEN

In 1969, disillusioned by the failure of peaceful protest to stop the Vietnam War, a militant faction of pressure group Students for a Democratic Society set up a bomb factory in the basement of the Henry Brevoort-designed house at 18 W 11th St. Known as the **Weathermen** (after the Bob Dylan lyrics, "You don't need a weatherman to know which way the wind blows"), the group aimed to bomb a military ball to be held at Fort Dix, New Jersey, but the plan backfired disastrously. On March 6, 1970, the house's arsenal exploded, killing three of the group (two escaped). The organization went into hiding soon after, becoming the **Weather Underground** and evading capture by the FBI, despite being on their Most Wanted List. While the group was responsible for several bombings in the 1970s, the loss of life was studiously avoided – though buildings in New York and Washington, DC, were damaged, the group's most notorious exploit was busting counterculture guru Timothy Leary out of prison in 1970. By 1980, most of the group had surrendered to the authorities, though few were ever charged; the FBI had broken so many laws trying to catch them, most evidence was inadmissible.

Incidentally, the Weathermen's neighbour at the time of the 11th Street bomb was actor Dustin Hoffman, whose home at no. 16 suffered extensive damage from the blast.

KEITH HARING'S CARMINE STREET MURAL

New York-based Pop artist Keith Haring (1958–90) painted several murals in the city, with one of the most magnificent examples overlooking the public swimming pool at the back of the Tony Dapolito Recreation Center (at Clarkson and Seventh Ave). You can get a decent view of the iconic work, painted in 1987, from the street. Check out, too, the *Crack is Wack* mural (see box, p.201).

Tues, Thurs & Fri 7am–5.30pm, Wed & Sun 7am–7pm, Sat 7am–6pm; free), built in 1929 – check out the florid interior, replete with marble columns, stained glass and murals that evoke the spirit, if not quite the artistry, of classical Italy. Until the 1970s there was an Italian open-air marketplace on this stretch, and it's still lined by a few Italian stores and cafés, notably **Faicco's** (see p.297) and **Rocco's** (best known for its nut-sprinkled cannoli), as well as celebrated deli **Murray's Cheese Shop** (see p.392). If folk music is your thing, **Bob Dylan** lived for a time at 161 W 4th St, and the iconic cover of his 1963 *Freewheelin'* album was shot a few paces away on Jones Street, just off Bleecker, a scene faithfully re-created in the Cameron Crowe movie *Vanilla Sky*.

Bedford Street

Subway A, B, C, D, E, F, M to W 4th St; #1 to Christopher St

Bedford Street runs west off Seventh Avenue to become one of the quietest and most desirable Village addresses. Edna St. Vincent Millay, the young poet and playwright, lived at no. 75 1/2 in the 1920s; at only 9ft wide, it is one of the narrowest houses in the city. In 1924 Millay was one of the founders of the **Cherry Lane Theater**, just around the corner at 38 Commerce St, still going strong today. The brick and clapboard structure at 77 Bedford St is the **Isaacs-Hendricks House**, built in 1799 and the oldest house in the Village. The quirky home known as "**Twin Peaks**" (with its two distinctive steep gables) at no. 102 (next to 17 Grove St, below), dates back to 1830, but was rebuilt in a style dubbed "pure Hansel and Gretel" in 1926 by architect Clifford Daily to house artists, writers and actors.

Grove Street

Subway A, B, C, D, E, F, M to W 4th St; #1 to Christopher St

The building at 90 Bedford St, right on the corner of **Grove Street** (above the *Little Owl*), served as the exterior for Monica's apartment in *Friends*, though the TV series was shot entirely in L.A. studios. Opposite is **17 Grove St**, built in 1822 and one of the most complete wood-frame houses in the city. Turn left here down Grove Street and you'll find **Grove Court** just off the road, one of the neighbourhood's most attractive and exclusive little mews (you have to peer through the gate), dating from the 1850s.

Heading back to Seventh Avenue on Grove Street, *Marie's Crisis* café at no. 59 was the site of the rented rooms where English revolutionary writer and philosopher **Thomas Paine** died in 1809. Paine, who was reviled in England for his support of both the American and French revolutions, was the author of the eighteenth century's three bestselling pamphlets, his *Common Sense* of 1776 generally credited for turning public opinion in favour of US independence. Cantankerous and conceited to the end, Paine made plenty of enemies, and after the publication of the *Age of Reason*, many Americans assumed he was an atheist (he was actually a deist). By the time he died here, he was poverty stricken and abandoned by his former friends. The current building dates from 1839, the café named in part after Paine's masterful essay *The American Crisis*.

NY City AIDS Memorial

St. Vincent's Hospital Park (W 12th St and Greenwich Ave) • Ⓦ nycaidsmemorial.org • Subway L to Eighth Ave; #1, #2, #3 to 14th St

Inaugurated in 2016, the **NY City AIDS Memorial** is a moving tribute to the more than 100,000 New Yorkers who have died from AIDS since the 1970s. The memorial

STONEWALL RIOTS

On June 27, 1969, police raided the **Stonewall Inn gay bar** (see p.368) and started arresting its occupants – for the local gay community, simply the latest occurrence in a long history of harassment. Spontaneously, word got around to other bars in the area, and before long the *Stonewall* was surrounded by hundreds of angry protestors, resulting in a siege that lasted the better part of the night and ended with several arrests and a number of injured policemen. Though hardly a victory for their rights, it was the first time that gay men had stood up en masse to police persecution and, as such, formally inaugurated the gay-rights movement. The event is honoured by the annual **Pride March** (see p.406). In 2016, the *Stonewall Inn* and surrounding area (officially the "**Stonewall National Monument**") became America's first National Monument dedicated to the LGBTQ-rights movement. Funds are currently being raised for a visitor centre and ranger station.

7

comprises a giant steel canopy, with granite paving stones underneath designed by visual artist Jenny Holzer, featuring lines from Walt Whitman's poem *Song of Myself*.

Christopher Street

Subway A, B, C, D, E, F, M to W 4th St; #1 to Christopher St

Christopher Street runs west from Jefferson Market Courthouse past **Christopher Park**, the traditional centre of the city's LGBT community. Confusingly, the park contains a pompous-looking statue of Civil War cavalry commander General Sheridan, though Sheridan Square is actually the next space down, where West 4th Street meets Washington Place. Historically, the area is better known as the scene of one of the worst and bloodiest of New York's **Draft Riots** (see p.419), when a marauding mob assembled here in 1863 and attacked members of the black community, several of whom were lynched. Violence also erupted in 1969, when the **gay community** wasn't as readily accepted as it is now (see box above). The riots are commemorated by George Segal's **Gay Liberation Monument** in the park, four life-size white-painted figures (two males, two females), unveiled in 1992.

The Far West Village

Subway L to Eighth Ave; #1 to Christopher St; #1, #2, #3 to 14th St

The area northwest of Sixth Avenue, dubbed the **Far West Village** by those ever-creative estate agents, contains some of the most appealing and expensive residential streets in the city. Most of the gorgeous townhouses here are owned, not rented, and a bevy of unique stores, coffee bars and restaurants caters to its upwardly mobile and moneyed residential community – including plenty of Hollywood stars. Much to the chagrin of locals, you'll probably see small groups of excited fans taking photos at **66 Perry St**, between Bleecker and West 4th Street, used as the exterior of Carrie's apartment in *Sex and the City* ("Carrie's Stoop"), even though the show ended in 2004, while almost constant queues form outside lauded **Magnolia Bakery** at Bleecker and West 11th Street (see p.298). The historic **White Horse Tavern** (see p.335), over at West 11th Street and Hudson, was frequented by Norman Mailer and Hunter S. Thompson among others, and is where **Dylan Thomas** had his last drink – you'll see a portrait of the poet and various memorabilia in the wood-panelled room named after him. The area has its rock connections, too; between 1971 and 1973, John Lennon and Yoko Ono lived in relative obscurity at **105 Bank St**, a block from the *White Horse* at Greenwich Street, before moving uptown (see p.189). And in 1979, a 21-year-old Sid Vicious took a lethal dose of heroin at **63 Bank St**, between Bleecker and West 4th streets.

These days, a stroll along leafy **Hudson River Park** is more likely to reveal joggers and pushchairs than punks, though **Pier 45** (aka the Christopher Street Pier) remains a lively hangout for LGBT youth, especially at night.

WHITNEY MUSEUM OF AMERICAN ART

Chelsea and the Meatpacking District

A grid full of renovated tenements, row houses, warehouses and new developments, Chelsea lies west of Broadway between 14th and 30th streets. The arrival of a large gay community in the late 1980s and early 1990s, the decamping of the art scene from Soho to Chelsea's western reaches and, finally, the transformation of the High Line park – which starts in the now-fashionable Meatpacking District, the transplanted Whitney Museum as its anchor – have helped to make the neighbourhood a desirable one. The result: affluent townhouses, daring condo conversions, cutting-edge galleries, public parks and shops of every variety pepper the scene.

Brief history

The neighbourhood, developed on former farmland, began to take shape in 1830 thanks to **Clement Clarke Moore**, famous as the author of the surprise poetic hit *A Visit from St Nick* (popularly known as *'Twas the Night Before Christmas*), whose estate comprised most of what is now Chelsea. That year, Moore, anticipating Manhattan's movement uptown, laid out his land for sale in broad lots. However, stuck as it was between the ritziness of Fifth Avenue, the hipness of Greenwich Village and the poverty of Hell's Kitchen, the area never quite made it onto the shortlist of desirable places to live. Manhattan's chic residents bypassed Chelsea in favour of the East 40s and 50s, and the arrival of the slaughterhouses, an elevated railroad and working-class poor sealed Chelsea's reputation as a rough-and-tumble no-go area for decades.

The last few decades have seen a new Chelsea emerge. New York's drifting art scene has aided the neighbourhood's transformation. In the early 1990s, a number of respected **galleries** began making use of the large spaces available in the low-rise warehouses in far west Chelsea, securing the area's cultural standing. This influx has been counterbalanced by the presence of retail superstores on **Sixth Avenue**; the building of the **Chelsea Piers** mega-sized sports complex; and high-rise apartments and hotels springing up north of 23rd Street (and west of Eighth Avenue). Now crowded with shoppers, restaurant-goers and art seekers (especially those bent on exploring the Whitney), the lively neighbourhood shows no signs of quietening down.

Meatpacking District

8

Creating a buffer between the West Village and Chelsea proper, the **Meatpacking District** between Gansevoort Street and West 15th Street, west of Ninth Avenue, has seen the majority of its working slaughterhouses converted to French bistros, late-night (and hard-to-breach) clubs, wine bars and fancy galleries. Though a few wholesale meat companies remain, the area is now very much designer territory, with Diane Von Furstenberg, Tory Burch and Helmut Lang among the fashion boutiques lining the cobblestone streets. The High Line has added much to the area's appeal, providing a tranquil greenway right into the heart of Chelsea.

Whitney Museum of American Art

99 Gansevoort St, between Tenth and Eleventh aves • Mon, Wed, Thurs & Sun 10.30am–6pm, Fri & Sat 10.30am–10pm, free tours daily roughly on the hour from noon • $22, after 7pm on Fri free • ☎ 212 570 3600, ⓦ whitney.org • Subway A, C, E to 14th St; L to Eighth Ave

Transplanted from its home for 50 years on the Upper East Side (and much closer to where it began back in the 1930s, in Greenwich Village), the **Whitney Museum of American Art** debuted its Renzo Piano-designed building at the foot of the High Line in May 2015. The architecture attracts as much attention as the art: parts of the building look stacked or bolted together; it protrudes yet fits neatly into place; there are large windows, external stairs and roomy terraces that help the structure fit in with its surroundings.

As for what's on display, a much larger chunk of the permanent collection (generally spread across the sixth and seventh floors) now has space to shine. Though the Whitney

---

CHELSEA HIGHLIGHTS

Viewing Spur, High Line Be the subject of this quasi-billboard on the elevated walkway. See p.109

Whitney Museum of American Art In a stunning asymmetrical building. See p.106

Picnic lunch Grab a bite from the *Lobster Place* or *Rocket Pig* to picnic on the High Line. See p.298 & p.300

Museum at the FIT Catch up on the latest fashion-centric exhibition. See p.112

Atmospheric drinks Sip a drink on a rescued boat or in a fashionable tapas bar. See box, p.333 & p.336

CHELSEA AND THE MEATPACKING DISTRICT

0   yards   200

Map labels

FIFTH AVENUE

28th St (R, W)
BROADWAY
Eataly
Flatiron Building
West 25th Street Market
Edith Wharton Birthplace
Flatiron District

28th St (1)
WEST 28TH STREET
WEST 27TH STREET
WEST 26TH STREET
WEST 25TH STREET

FLOWER MARKET

23rd St (F, M)
23rd St (1)
WEST 23RD STREET
WEST 22ND STREET
WEST 21ST STREET
WEST 20TH STREET
WEST 19TH STREET
WEST 18TH STREET
WEST 17TH STREET

SIXTH AVENUE

6th Av–14th St (F, L, M)
Forbes Galleries
Quad Cinema
First Presbyterian Church
Church of the Ascension

Rubin Museum of Art

14th St (1, 2, 3)
WEST 16TH STREET
WEST 15TH STREET
WEST 14TH STREET
WEST 13TH STREET
WEST 12TH STREET
WEST 11TH STREET

SEVENTH AVENUE

FIT Museum
The Chelsea Hotel
18th St (1)

Joyce Theater

EIGHTH AVENUE

8th Av (M)
14th St (A, C, E, L)
8th Av (L)
White Columns Gallery

CHELSEA

Chelsea Park
London Terrace

CHELSEA HISTORIC DISTRICT
General Theological Seminary
Cushman Row
Oldest House in Chelsea

CHELSEA GALLERY DISTRICT
Greene Naftali
The Pace Gallery
Marianne Boesky Gallery
Gladstone Gallery
Mary Boone Gallery
Gagosian
Luhring Augustine
Sikkema Jenkins & Co
Tanya Bonakdar Gallery
David Zwirner
180 Tenth Avenue
Lehmann Maupin
Hauser & Wirth
303 Gallery
Paula Cooper Gallery
100 Eleventh Avenue
IAC Building
HL 23
200 Eleventh Avenue

Edward Thorp
High Line

Chelsea Waterside Park

NINTH AVENUE
TENTH AVENUE
ELEVENTH AVENUE
TWELFTH AVENUE

Chelsea Market
Apple Store

METPACKING DISTRICT
Soho House
The Standard Hotel
High Line
Whitney Museum of American Art

Pier 66
Pier 64
Pier 63
Pier 62
Pier 61
Pier 60
Pier 59
Chelsea Piers
Hudson River
Hudson River Bike Path

GREENWICH AVENUE
BANK STREET
WEST 4TH STREET
WEST 12TH STREET
WEST 13TH STREET
LITTLE WEST 12TH STREET
WASHINGTON STREET
GANSEVOORT STREET
GREENWICH STREET

● EATING
Amy's Bread	14
Billy's Bakery	8
Bottino	1
Cafeteria	11
Co.	5
Cookshop	9
El Quijote	7
Empire Cake	12
Lobster Place	13
The Old Homestead	15
Red Cat	6
Rocking Horse	10
Sullivan Street Bakery	3
Txikito	2

■ DRINKING AND NIGHTLIFE
BARS
Bar B	13
Bathtub Gin	10
El Quinto Pino	5
Peter McManus Café	8
Pier 66 Maritime	3
Smithfield Hall	4
Tia Pol	6

CLUBS
Le Bain	14
Marquee	2

LIVE MUSIC VENUES
High Line Ballroom	12

LGBT BARS & CLUBS
Barracuda	9
Big Apple Ranch	7
The Eagle NYC	1

GYM
	11

● SHOPPING
Annex Markets	3
The Bureau	12
Center for Book Arts	1
Chelsea Market	9
Comme des Garçons	4
Diane Von Furstenberg (DVF)	11
Harmon Face Values	5
Housing Works	8
Jazz Record Center	10
Jeffrey	3
Michaels	9
Nasty Pig	11

■ ACCOMMODATION
Chelsea Pines Inn	7
Chelsea International	4
Colonial House Inn	6
Dream Downtown	5
Gansevoort	9
Meatpacking NYC	3
The High Line Hotel	1
Leo House	10
Maritime Hotel	6
The Standard, High Line	7

is still a place for rotating exhibitions, you can hope to see favourites like Alexander Calder's *Circus*, a set of wire figures, nettings and more in glass, full of energy despite being encased; moody works by Mark Rothko and Edward Hopper; and Jacob Lawrence's moving *War Series*. Other well-known pieces include Jasper Johns' 3D *Three Flags*, video installations by Nam June Paik, Warhol's *Green Coca-Cola* and the colourful, jazzy works of Stuart Davis. Rotating displays are mostly on the fifth and eighth floors, though there's also a small gallery on the ground floor. Make sure to spend some time on the couches facing the Hudson River or out on the decks, which provide excellent views of the city, especially the Empire State Building (one good idea is to start on the top floor and work your way down the outdoor stairs at each level). The third floor is given over to a theatre; you'll find food and drink at the Danny Meyer-sponsored (*Gramercy Tavern*, *Shake Shack*) *Untitled* restaurant near the entrance and the *Studio Café* on the top floor.

Above all, the Whitney is most famous for its Biennial, which was initially held in 1932 and had its first go-round in its new digs in spring 2017. Designed to give a provocative overview of what's happening in contemporary American art, it's frequently panned by critics, but it's always a huge draw; the latest was no different, engendering controversy thanks to a painting of Emmett Till by artist Dana Schutz.

Brief history

Gertrude Vanderbilt Whitney (1875–1942), a sculptor and champion of American art, founded the Whitney Studio in 1914 to exhibit the work of living American artists who could not find support in established art circles – she was the first to exhibit Edward Hopper, in 1920. As her collection grew, she offered it, with a generous endowment, to the Met; having been turned down, Whitney set up her own museum in Greenwich Village in 1930, with her collection as its core exhibit, eventually relocating to the Breuer building on the Upper East Side in 1966. That Brutalist structure was initially a controversial addition to the neat townhouses it neighboured, but it became beloved, and plans to add on to it were frequently shouted down. Unable to expand, the Whitney voted in 2010 to move downtown to the base of the High Line, commissioning Piano to design the new museum. Its former digs, meanwhile, have become the Met Breuer (see p.175).

The High Line

Gansevoort St to 34th St, between Tenth and Eleventh aves; entrances at Gansevoort, 14th, 16th, 18th, 20th, 23rd, 26th, 28th and 30th sts • Daily: June–Sept 7am–11pm; April, May, Oct & Nov 7am–10pm; Dec–March 7am–7pm; Tues at dusk April–early Sept stargazing nights, weather permitting • Free, though some organized tours $15 • ☎ 212 500 6035, ⓦ thehighline.org • Subway A, C, E to 14th St; L to Eighth Ave; C, E to 23rd St ; #7 to 34th St-Hudson Yards

An ambitious renewal project that spans – and unites – the Meatpacking District, West Chelsea and a burgeoning area near the West Side rail yards, the **High Line** asserts itself as a new form of urban park. It's a stunning transformation of a disused railway that was built between 1929 and 1934, once moving goods and produce around lower Manhattan, then going on to spend a number of years rusted, overgrown and threatened with demolition. Concerned activists fought to stave off what seemed inevitable, but it wasn't until two locals formed the **Friends of the High Line** in 1999 that the tide began to turn. A deal with the city ensued, construction began in 2006, and the first phase opened in summer 2009 to big crowds and rave reviews; a second section debuted in June 2011; and what seemed to be the final one in autumn 2014 – though additional flourishes continue.

Much more than an elevated promenade-cum-public-park some 30ft in the air, the High Line forges a balance between the West Side's industrial tradition and its design-focused present. It pays proper homage to its history – steel rails peek out from the ground; smooth pavement and wood echo the lines of train tracks and sometimes slope right up onto the benches; like the old line did, it cleverly cuts through the middle of buildings and blocks – for example, the *Standard Hotel* (p.271) and the structure that holds the Chelsea Market (see below) – and many wild growth patches have been left as is. At various intervals on the line are art installations and some select food vendors (most of the latter congregate at West 15th Street).

The park

The initial completed stretch runs from Gansevoort to 20th Street. It's at its most untamed at the southernmost end, becoming a bit more elegant and organized above 14th Street. A subtle water feature between 14th and 15th streets is followed a block north by a spur that overlooks a horticultural preserve and an amphitheatre that offers a cinematic view up Tenth Avenue. The views shift just as the path does: move your gaze from the Hudson to the eclectic architecture of a neighbourhood in transition, some of its old factories and warehouses giving way to quite daring Modernist residences.

The second phase, between 20th and 30th streets, moves off Tenth Avenue to cut a swathe through the middle of the block, about 100ft west of the road. It's more intimate in feel; a walk here at times seems like you're tracing a narrow path along Chelsea's rooftop gardens. At 22nd Street, a grassy lawn beneath a faded brick facade is one of the few places you can divert from the path. Further on, the walkway rises and falls, at one point elevating about 8ft up on a metal catwalk to put you right up in the trees. A neat feature at 26th Street, the "viewing spur", places you as the subject in an advertising sign, for street onlookers – and also frames the neighbourhood for your benefit. As you approach 30th Street you'll pass the "cutout", which lets you see the inner workings of the old line below, before winding up face to face with the rail yards – a part of the city few previously ventured to (or wished to venture to, for that matter).

Thus begins the third segment, the so-called High Line at the Rail Yards, a stretch that heads out toward the river and curves around the rail terminus. It has a much more open feel than the previous segment – though it's already changing. For one, a spur is being added at West 30th Street, providing a piazza and a large space for public art, known as "the plinth." In addition, the yards themselves are undergoing a massive redevelopment to become almost a "city within a city", with new apartment towers and an extension of the #7 train that connects them to the rest of Manhattan. The supposed highlight of this Hudson Yards area is to be the Vessel, a honeycomb-like stairway structure that runs 150 feet tall and will be in the outdoor plaza below 33rd Street. Due sometime in 2018, it appears designed to work largely as an Instagram and selfie magnet.

West Chelsea

The far west of Chelsea, from **Ninth Avenue** over to the waterfront, holds many of the more scenic blocks, best galleries and most intriguing merchants the district has to offer. It's a part of the city in rapid development, thanks in large part to the effect of the High Line: cutting-edge residential architecture, a varied restaurant-and-bar scene, and a few hotels have sprung up to complement the sturdy old warehouses.

Chelsea Market

75 Ninth Ave, between 15th and 16th sts • Mon–Sat 7am–9pm, Sun 8am–8pm • ⓦ chelseamarket.com • Subway A, C, E to 14th St; L to Eighth Ave

A high-class food temple, the redbrick **Chelsea Market** is housed in the old National Biscuit Company (aka "Nabisco") factory, where legend has it the Oreo cookie was created. Many of the factory's features remain, including pieces of rail track used to transport provisions. The forty or so retailers inside sell fresh fruit, fish, bread, tacos, pasture-raised meats and flowers (see p.391). The building serves as home to the Food

Network (though there's no access to the studios) and to some offices for Google, which also occupies (and owns) the block-long 111 Eighth Avenue across the street.

Chelsea Historic District

West 20th, 21st and 22nd sts between Ninth and Tenth aves • Subway C, E to 23rd St

A few blocks north of Chelsea Market, the **Chelsea Historic District** boasts a picturesque variety of predominantly Italianate and Greek Revival row houses. Dating from the 1830s to the 1890s, they demonstrate the faith some early developers had in Chelsea as an up-and-coming New York neighbourhood. The **oldest house** in the area, at 404 West 20th St (just off Ninth Ave), stands out with its 1829 wood siding, predating as it does the all-brick constructions of James Wells, Chelsea's first real-estate developer. The ornate iron fencing heading west along this block, known as **Cushman Row**, is original and quite impressive. Closer to Tenth Avenue, Jack Kerouac lived at 454 20th St in 1951 with his wife Joan Haverty, while he wrote *On the Road*.

General Theological Seminary

440 W 21st St, bounded by Ninth and Tenth aves and 20th and 21st sts • Mon–Fri 11am–5pm • Free • ☎ 212 243 5150, ⓦ gts.edu • Subway C, E to 23rd St

The 1817 **General Theological Seminary** is one of Chelsea's secrets. Clement Clarke Moore, author of *'Twas the Night Before Christmas*, donated this island of land to the institute, and today the harmonious assembly of ivy-clad Gothic structures surrounding a green feels like part of a college campus. You can get in to explore the site as long as you sign in and keep quiet.

London Terrace

The block bounded by 23rd and 24th sts, and Ninth and Tenth aves • Subway C, E to 23rd St

Just north of the historic district is one of New York's premier residences for those who believe in understated opulence. **London Terrace**, two rows of apartment buildings a city block long, surrounds a private interior garden (the corner Towers and interior Gardens units are managed separately). The buildings had the misfortune of being completed in 1930 at the height of the Great Depression, and despite a swimming pool and other posh amenities, many of the 1665 apartments stood empty for several years. The first management, wanting to evoke thoughts of Britain, made the doormen wear London-style police uniforms, thereby giving the building its name. The apartments were later nicknamed "The Fashion Projects" because of their residents (the likes of Isaac Mizrahi and Annie Leibovitz).

Chelsea's gallery district

Tenth Avenue serves as a dividing line between Chelsea's more historic and quainter side to the east and its industrial past to the west. For years there was not much to see or do along this stretch – that is, until the galleries started swarming in. Along 22nd Street between Tenth and Eleventh avenues, as well as farther north up to West 29th, lie the few hundred **galleries and warehouse spaces** that house one of New York's most vibrant art scenes (see p.373). Even the ovular entryway to **Comme des Garçons** – the store is just west of Tenth Avenue at 520 West 22nd St – masquerades as art in this part of town.

Chelsea Piers

West 17th to West 23rd sts, on the West Side Highway • ☎ 212 336 6666, ⓦ chelseapiers.com • Subway C, E to 23rd St

Chelsea Piers, a glitzy, family-friendly, and somewhat incongruous entertainment development, stretches along the West Side Highway from piers 59 to 62. Its first incarnation opened in 1910, as the place where passengers would disembark from the great transatlantic liners (it was en route to the Chelsea Piers that the *Titanic* sank in 1912). By the 1960s, however, the piers had fallen into decay through disuse, and as

EIGHTH AVENUE **CHELSEA AND THE MEATPACKING DISTRICT** | 111

late as the mid-1980s an official report condemned them as "shabby, pathetic reminders of a glorious past". Reopened in 1995, the new Chelsea Piers is primarily a huge sports complex, with ice rinks and open-air roller rinks, as well as a bowling alley and a landscaped golf driving range (see p.401).

Around the piers

Just north of Chelsea Piers are the latest instalments in the continuation of **Hudson River Park** (see p.63), which have added large green spaces, a carousel, art displays and a skate park to piers 62, 63 and 64.

Across from the piers, at the end of 19th Street, warehouses and car parks have given way to the billowing, fluid walls of Frank Gehry's **IAC Building**, one of New York's most fanciful examples of contemporary architecture. It's right next to Jean Nouvel's similarly striking **100 Eleventh Avenue**, a glittering patchwork of glass that holds luxury condos. More new buildings with a strong design focus have followed: **515 West 23rd Street**, or **HL23**, an extremely close neighbour of the High Line (it hangs right over it, close enough to touch), is a slick steel-and-glass work by cutting-edge architect Neil Denari; and **200 Eleventh Avenue**, at the corner of 24th Street, is designed in keeping with the area's industrial past. Each condo in this stainless-steel mini-skyscraper has its own en-suite parking garage (reached by internal car elevator).

Eighth Avenue

Chelsea's main drag, **Eighth Avenue**, is full of vibrant retail energy, if nothing of particular note. Along here, dozens of trendy bars, restaurants, health-food stores, gyms, bookstores and clothes shops cater to Chelsea's large, out and proud gay population.

8

Hotel Chelsea

222 E 23rd St, between Seventh and Eighth aves • Subway C, E to 23rd St

One of the neighbourhood's major claims to fame is the **Hotel Chelsea**. Originally built as a luxury co-operative apartment building in 1884 and partially converted to a hotel in 1903, the building has served as the undisputed residence of the city's harder-up literati and its musical vagabonds. Mark Twain, Tennessee Williams, Dylan Thomas and Thomas Wolfe all spent time here, and in 1951 Jack Kerouac, armed with a specially adapted typewriter (and a lot of Benzedrine), supposedly typed the first draft of *On the Road* nonstop onto a 120ft roll of paper… though it more likely happened at his house nearby (see opposite). William Burroughs (in a presumably more relaxed state) completed *Naked Lunch* at the *Chelsea*, and Arthur C. Clarke wrote *2001: A Space Odyssey* while in residence.

In the 1960s, the *Chelsea* entered a wilder phase. Andy Warhol and his doomed protégées Edie Sedgwick and Candy Darling holed up here and made the film *Chelsea Girls*. In probably the hotel's most infamous moment, Sid Vicious stabbed Nancy Spungen to death in 1978 in their suite, a few months before he fatally overdosed on heroin. The photographer Robert Mapplethorpe and Patti Smith also lived here in the late 1960s and early 1970s, and the hotel inspired Joni Mitchell's song *Chelsea Morning* and Leonard Cohen's *Chelsea Hotel No.2*.

With a pedigree like this it's easy to forget the hotel itself, which has a down-at-heel Edwardian grandeur all its own – it will be revealed soon just how much of the interior charm is kept. After declaring bankruptcy in late 2010, the hotel was sold in the summer of 2011 to a developer, who closed it up and began renovations; these stalled and it's changed hands two more times since. Things remain up in the air, with a nominal plan for it becoming a hotel-condo combo sometime in 2018. Stop by for a pilgrimage, but don't count on seeing past the doors or being able to stay.

East Chelsea

Sandwiched between infinitely more interesting blocks, the eastern edge of Chelsea has become a buzzing strip of commerce, concentrated mostly along **Sixth Avenue** between West 17th and 23rd streets. A crush of discount emporiums like Best Buy and TJ Maxx, along with mediocre chain restaurants, has done its best to drive out the independent mom-and-pop businesses, and, on weekends especially, Sixth Avenue teems with bargain hunters lugging oversized bags from places like Bed, Bath and Beyond, the Container Store and Modell's Sporting Goods. Fortunately a few indoor flea markets remain.

Rubin Museum of Art

150 W 17th St, between Sixth and Seventh aves • Mon & Thurs 11am–5pm, Wed 11am–9pm, Fri 11am–10pm, Sat & Sun 11am–6pm • $15, free on Fri 6–10pm • ☎ 212 620 5000, ⓦ rubinmuseum.org • Subway F, M, #1, #2, #3 to 14th St; #1 to 18th St

For a brief escape from Chelsea's commercialism, visit the **Rubin Museum of Art**. The serene museum is one of the city's lesser-visited gems, a collection of two thousand paintings, sculptures and textiles from the Himalayas and surrounding regions. The permanent exhibits on the second and third floors are organized and labelled with great care and thought, essential for a subject that will be familiar to few. While some pieces manage to stand out – don't miss the small room on the third floor devoted to the fascinating, colourful Lukhang murals, taken from the Dalai Lama's temple – the thrust is less about individual artists and objects and more about understanding how and why art is created. The stylish ground-floor *Café Serai* serves Himalayan food and, on Friday nights, becomes the *K2 Lounge*, which hosts regular performances.

Flower Market

The area around West 28th Street is Manhattan's **Flower Market** – not really a market as such, more the warehouses and storefronts where potted plants and cut flowers are stored before brightening offices and atriums across the city. The district, which has atrophied against a tide of gentrifications, still manages to surprise, its greenery bursting out of the drab blocks in a welcome touch of life.

West 28th Street's historical background couldn't be more at odds with its present incarnation: from the mid-1880s until the 1950s, the short block between Sixth Avenue and Broadway was the original **Tin Pan Alley**, where music publishers would peddle songs by the likes of Irving Berlin and George Gershwin to artists and producers from vaudeville and Broadway. The name came from the piano-playing racket coming out of the publishing houses here at any time of the day, a sound that one journalist compared to banging on tin pans.

Museum at the Fashion Institute of Technology (FIT)

Seventh Ave at 27th St • Tues–Fri noon–8pm, Sat 10am–5pm • Free • ⓦ fitnyc.edu • Subway #1 to 28th St

A block west of the Flower Market, the **Museum at the Fashion Institute of Technology (FIT)** covers two levels; you'll find rotating exhibits on contemporary design and fashion history, often pulled from their extensive permanent collection. The buildings that make up the campus have some architectural interest too: take a quick walk along 27th Street to admire – or sniff at – the cold Modernist facades.

UNION SQUARE

Union Square, Gramercy Park and the Flatiron District

This knot of close-knit neighbourhoods east of Fifth Avenue has some of the city's best restaurants and shops, and several of New York's most historically significant buildings and landmarks. Chief among the latter is Union Square, between 14th and 17th streets, a bustling space that breaks up Broadway's pell-mell dash north. To the northeast is the posh neighbourhood of Gramercy Park, which surrounds the members-only square of the same name. Straddling Broadway northwest of Union Square and running up to 23rd Street, the Flatiron District was once Manhattan's shopping hub and still has an elegance and energy; from there, so-called "NoMad" (north of Madison Square Park) takes over, with its hip hotels and exclusive places to eat.

9

Union Square and around

Located at the confluence of Broadway, Fourth and Park avenues between 14th and 17th streets, **Union Square** is an inviting public space. Among the statues here are Gandhi; an equestrian of George Washington; a Lafayette by Bartholdi (more famous for the Statue of Liberty); and, at the centre of the green, a massive flagstaff base whose bas-reliefs symbolize the forces of Good and Evil in the American Revolution. Opened as a park in 1839, the square is surrounded by a crush of commerce and serves as a welcome respite from crazed taxi drivers and rushed pedestrians on 14th Street. Mostly, however, Union Square is beloved for its **farmers' market** (one in a citywide network known as Greenmarket) that sells all sorts of seasonal produce, wine, meats, hand-spun wools and flowers (see box, p.391).

The square is flanked by a range of excellent restaurants, as well as by buildings in a mismatched hotchpotch of architectural styles, not least of which is the old **American Savings Bank** at 20 Union Square East – now the **Daryl Roth Theatre** – of which only the grandiose columned exterior survives, completed in 1923 and designed by Henry Bacon. The pedimented **Union Square Theatre** just north of here at 17th Street became the second Tammany Hall in 1929, once headquarters of the Democratic Party and a fine example of Colonial-Revival architecture. A gaze across 14th Street reveals the **Metronome**, a moving sequence of fifteen numbers that show the time of day from left to right and the time remaining in the day from right to left, in military style. The middle three numbers move into tenths and hundredths of seconds, so fast you'll scarcely be able to make them out.

Decker Building

33 Union Square West • Subway L, N, Q, R, W, #4, #5, #6 to 14th St-Union Square

The narrow **Decker Building**, on the west side of the square, was where Andy Warhol moved his **Factory** in 1968, occupying the sixth floor until 1973; the artist was shot by Valerie Solanas here shortly after the move (the previous Factory was at 231 E 47th St; the one established post-Decker Building was at 860 Broadway). The building itself, completed in 1893, is a lavish, Moorish-inspired skyscraper.

Tibet House

22 W 15th St, between Fifth and Sixth aves • Mon–Fri 11am–6pm; guided tours by appointment • $5 suggested donation • ⓦ tibethouse. us • Subway F, M to 14th St

A nice complement to Chelsea's Rubin Museum of Art (see p.112), the **Tibet House** is dedicated to preserving Tibetan culture. Besides hosting classes and talks on yoga, meditation and religion, the institute has a gallery that houses exhibitions of Tibetan art.

Irving Place

East of Union Square, the six graceful blocks of **Irving Place** head north towards Gramercy Park. Irving Place was named for Washington Irving, the early nineteenth-century writer best known for his creepy tale of the Headless Horseman, *The Legend of Sleepy Hollow*, and also for supposedly being the first American to earn a living from his

---

SQUARE ROOTS ACTIVISM

Like the generally more rambunctious Washington Square in the West Village and Tompkins Square in the East Village, Union Square is also often the site of **civil demonstrations**. After 9/11, hundreds of vigils were held here, and the entire square became a makeshift memorial to the victims until it was finally ordered dismantled by then-Mayor Rudy Giuliani. The park's southern boundary serves as the informal centre of Manhattan protests against miscellaneous causes, everything from the wars in the Middle East to legalized marijuana to police shootings of African American men.

writing. The claims that he lived for a short time at no. 49 (trumpeted in a plaque outside the quaint house) are spurious; he did, at the least, frequently visit his nephew's house on East 21st Street, and a bust of Irving stands in front of the early nineteenth-century Washington Irving High School at East 17th Street.

Another celebrated author, Pulitzer Prize-winning short-story writer O. Henry, did live at no. 55 between 1902 and 1910. He reputedly dreamed up and wrote *The Gift of the Magi* at **Pete's Tavern** (see p.338), at 18th Street and Irving Place, one of New York's oldest bars. The legend serves the place and its atmosphere well.

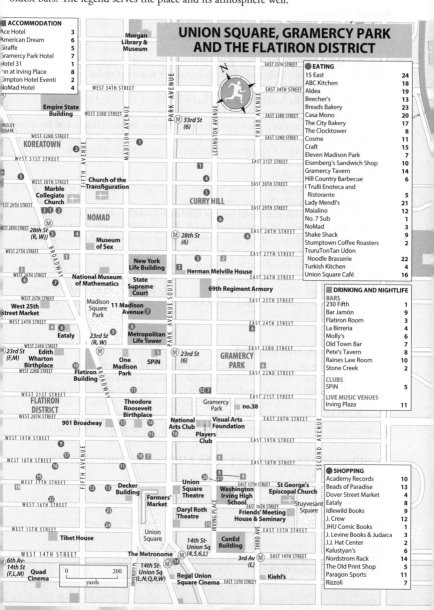

9

ConEd building

4 Irving Place • Subway L, N, Q, R, W, #4, #5, #6 to 14th St–Union Square

The **Consolidated Edison** (or **ConEd**) building, which anchors the southern end of Irving Place, is home to the company responsible for providing the city with both energy and steaming manholes. The majestic Warren & Wetmore-designed tower, completed in 1929, is topped by a 38ft-high bronze lantern (itself atop a colonnaded mini-temple and pyramid roof), a memorial to employees killed in World War I.

Stuyvesant Square

The land that makes up **Stuyvesant Square**, between East 15th and 17th streets, was gifted to the city in 1836 by **Peter Gerard Stuyvesant**, a descendant of the last Director-General of New Amsterdam (see p.418). The park contains Gertrude Vanderbilt Whitney's bronze statue of the Director-General (replete with peg leg), unveiled in 1941, and a sculpture of Czech composer **Antonín Dvořák**, who lived nearby on East 17th Street in the 1890s.

Though framed by the buildings of Beth Israel Medical Center and bisected by bustling Second Avenue, the park still retains something of its secluded quality, especially on the western side. Here you'll find the **Friends' Meeting House and Seminary** (1860), whose austere Greek Revival facade contrasts with the grand Romanesque brownstone of St George's Episcopal Church next door, completed in 1856.

St George's Episcopal Church

4 Rutherford Place, between Second and Third aves • Normally open for services only (Sun 8.30 & 10am), but you can schedule a weekday tour with the parish office • ☎ 646 723 4178 • Subway L to First or Third aves

The most famous member of the **St George Episcopal Church** congregation was J.P. Morgan, who lived just up the road (see p.132). Remembered as the most powerful and ruthless banker of the Gilded Age, Pierpont, as he was commonly known, was also a devout Episcopalian; in St George's, says Morgan biographer Ron Chernow, "he seemed mesmerized by ritual and lapsed into reveries of mystic depth". His funeral, held here in 1913, was more akin to that of a head of state. The interior is worth a peek for its soaring wood-beam roof, monument to Henry Bacon – designer of the Lincoln Memorial in Washington, DC, and of the American Savings Bank (see p.114) – and the carved pulpit, dedicated to J.P.

Gramercy Park and around

Irving Place comes to an end at the ordered open space of **Gramercy Park**. This former "little crooked swamp" (which is what the Dutch called it before the name was Anglicized) between East 20th and 21st streets is one of the city's prettiest squares. It is beautifully manicured and, most noticeably, completely empty for much of the day – principally because it is the city's last private park, and the only people who can gain access are those rich or fortunate enough to live here. Famous past key-holders have

---

UNION SQUARE, GRAMERCY PARK AND THE FLATIRON DISTRICT HIGHLIGHTS

Church of the Transfiguration Quiet contemplation in the church garden. See p.121

Eataly Prosciutto and mozzarella panini, seafood, perfect espressos, beer on the roof – this Italian market has it all. See p.392

Flatiron Building Get the best photos of this iconic building from across the street in Worth Square. See p.118

Molly's Grab a pint of Guinness at this traditional pub. See p.336

National Arts Club Free art exhibitions at an otherwise private club. See opposite

Union Square Greenmarket Flowers, freshly baked goods and from-the-farm fruits. See p.114

included Mark Twain, Uma Thurman and Julia Roberts, as well as a host of Kennedys and Roosevelts. Despite the park's exclusivity, it's well worth a walk around the edge for a glimpse of the trim, historic area that was once the city's main theatre district.

Inside the park gates stands a statue of the actor **Edwin Booth** (brother of Lincoln's assassin, John Wilkes Booth) in the guise of Hamlet, one of his most famous roles. (Ironically, Edwin rescued Lincoln's son, Robert, from a train accident years before John's fatal action.)

The Players Club

16 Gramercy Park South • ☎ 212 475 6116, Ⓦ theplayersnyc.org • Subway #6 to 23rd St

In 1888, aided by architect (and Gramercy Park resident) Stanford White, Edwin Booth turned his home into the private club **The Players**. The porch railings on this rather forbidding building are decorated with distinctive figures representing Comedy and Tragedy. In the nineteenth century, actors and theatre types were not accepted in general society, so Booth created the club for play and socializing – neglecting, however, to admit women, who were not allowed in until 1989. Later members included the Barrymores, Frank Sinatra and (oddly) Sir Winston Churchill, while more recent inductees are Morgan Freeman, Edie Falco, Jimmy Fallon and Martha Plimpton.

National Arts Club

15 Gramercy Park South • Mon–Fri 10am–5pm • ☎ 212 475 3424, Ⓦ nationalartsclub.org • Subway #6 to 23rd St

The patrician **National Arts Club** is fittingly located in the rather grand Tilden Mansion. Built in 1840, the mansion was Victorianized in the 1870s by Central Park co-designer Calvert Vaux at the request of owner Governor Samuel Tilden, and is studded with terracotta busts of Shakespeare, Milton and Franklin, among others. Charles de Kay, a *New York Times* art critic, founded the club in 1898 to create a meeting place for artists, patrons and audiences of all the arts; it moved here in 1906. Nonmembers are permitted to visit the temporary art exhibitions inside, free of charge.

The rest of the park perimeter

On the other side of The Players at no. 17 is the **Visual Arts Foundation**, occupying the former home of Joseph Pulitzer, while at no. 38 on the northeast corner of the square is the mock-Tudor building in which John Steinbeck, then a struggling reporter for the now-defunct *New York World*, lived from 1925 to 1926 (it took getting fired from that job to plunge him into fiction). The brick-red structure at no. 34 was one of the city's very **first building co-operatives**.

At 2 Lexington Ave and Gramercy Park North is the imposing 1920s bulk of the **Gramercy Park Hotel** (see p.272), whose elite early residents included Mary McCarthy, a very young John F. Kennedy and Humphrey Bogart. Lastly, lining Gramercy Park West is a splendid row of brick **Greek Revival townhouses** from the 1840s with ornate wrought-iron work; James Harper, of the publishing house Harper & Row, lived at no. 4 until his death in 1869.

The Flatiron District

The small district north and northwest of Union Square, between Fifth and Park avenues up to 23rd Street, is generally known as the **Flatiron District**, taking its name from the distinctive early skyscraper on the southwest corner of Madison Square Park (see p.118). The area is a nice enough place to stroll around in, though there's little to see. This stretch of Broadway was once the heart of the so-called "**Ladies' Mile**" which, from the mid-nineteenth century to the early twentieth century, was lined with fancy stores and boutiques. It started losing its lustre around the end of that timeframe, and by World War I, Ladies' Mile had all but disintegrated due to the department stores' uptown migration. However, a few sculpted facades and curvy lintels remain as

9

mementoes of that gilded age, including Lord & Taylor's Victorian wedding cake of a building at 901 Broadway at 20th Street, now converted into pricey apartments (the current store, itself a hundred-year-old landmark, is at 424 Fifth Ave, at 38th St).

Theodore Roosevelt's Birthplace

28 E 20th St • Tues–Sat 9am–5pm, tours on the hour (except at noon) 10am–4pm • Free • ☎ 212 260 1616, ⓦ nps.gov/thrb • Subway R, W to 23rd St

Standing apart from its rather commercial surroundings is **Theodore Roosevelt's Birthplace**, or at least a reconstruction of it, viewable on an obligatory guided tour. In 1923, the house was rebuilt as it would have been when Roosevelt was born there in 1858, the rooms restored to reflect their appearance between 1865 and 1872. The rather sombre (despite recent renovations over the past five years) mansion contains mostly original furnishings: a brilliant chandelier in the parlour, obelisks from a family trip to Egypt, young "Teedie's" crib and more. A room at the top of the house holds some of TR's hunting trophies; a gallery on the ground floor (there's an upper gallery as well) displays photos and documents from the life of the 26th president – before Donald Trump, the only one born in New York City.

The Flatiron Building

Broadway, Fifth Avenue and 23rd St • Subway R, W to 23rd St

The lofty, elegant and decidedly anorexic **Flatiron Building** (originally the Fuller Construction Company, later renamed in honour of its distinctive shape) is set on a narrow, triangular plot of land at a manic intersection. It is one of the city's most famous buildings, evoking images of Edwardian New York. There's much debate over whether it was NYC's first true skyscraper; certainly the Daniel Burnham-designed work signalled a new direction in the modern city: hung on a steel frame in 1902, its full twenty storeys dwarfed all the other buildings around. The uncommonly thin, tapered structure creates unusual wind currents at ground level; according to lore, the cry "23 Skidoo!" came from policemen warning off voyeurs gathering to watch the wind raise the skirts of women passing by – a story that seems fanciful, despite guidebooks perpetuating the notion. Such behaviour would presumably have horrified novelist **Edith Wharton**, who was born in 1862 at 14 W 23rd St, just around the corner. Her parents' townhouse has been altered many times since then, and is currently occupied (on its ground floor, that is) by a *Starbucks*.

Madison Square Park and NoMad

Just northeast of the Flatiron Building, between Park and Fifth avenues, lies **Madison Square Park**. Though enveloped by a maelstrom of cars, cabs, buses and dodging pedestrians, because of the stateliness of the surrounding buildings and its peaceful green spaces it possesses a grandiosity and neat seclusion that Union Square has long since lost. Surrounding the park are a few monumental buildings; north of it, the trendy neighbourhood of **NoMad** takes over, with a few unusual museums and lots of fashionable places to eat, drink and stay.

Around Madison Square Park

On Madison Square Park's east side, at 5 Madison Ave, stands the tiered, stately **Metropolitan Life Tower**, which at 700ft was the world's tallest building between 1909 and 1913, when it was surpassed by the Woolworth Building (see p.59). It was sold to a developer in 2007 for $200 million, and, following an area trend, is being converted into high-end residential apartments – and has been rechristened Madison Avenue Clocktower. Of course, **One Madison Park**, the new mirrored-glass condo across the way, at 23 E 22nd St, nearly foreclosed before it was finished (Tom Brady and Rupert Murdoch are among the tenants), so nothing in the way of real-estate development is guaranteed.

9

MetLife also once owned **11 Madison Avenue**, across East 24th Street (it now houses Credit Suisse), connected to the tower building by a sky-bridge. Completed in 1929, the onset of the Great Depression quashed MetLife's plans to make this section a mind-blowing hundred storeys high – viewed from the park, you can see how it was designed to be the base for something much bigger.

On the other side of 25th Street, at 27 Madison Ave, the Appellate Division of the **New York State Supreme Court** boasts a marble facade, resolutely righteous with its statues of Justice, Wisdom and Peace. The chamber inside where arguments are heard (open to the public Tues–Thurs 2pm; free) is almost Rococo in its detail.

The grand structure opposite is the **New York Life Building**, the work of Cass Gilbert, creator of the Woolworth Building downtown. It went up in 1928 on the site of the original **Madison Square Garden** (see box below), renowned scene of drunken and debauched revels of high and Broadway society. Some believe that the junction nearby, at Madison and West 27th Street, is the birthplace of baseball, as the members of the country's first ball club, the New York Knickerbockers, started playing here in 1842.

Over on the west side, a few lanes of traffic and a small pedestrianized triangle – known as **Worth Square**, home to the interred remains of a general from the Seminole and Mexican-American Wars – separate the park from the celebrity-chef-owned Italian market **Eataly** at 200 Fifth Ave (see p.392). It's full of high-quality, pricey gourmet goods, with cafés, restaurants, rooftop brewpub and cooking classes, and also offers walking tours (Wed 10.30am; $35).

National Museum of Mathematics

11 E 26th St, between Fifth and Madison aves • Daily 10am–5pm • $15, 12 and under $9 • ☎ 212 542 0566, Ⓦ momath.org • Subway R, W, #6 to 23rd St or 28th St

Somewhere between a high-minded institution and an interactive romper room, the **Museum of Mathematics** debuted in late 2012 with the goal of making maths fun and accessible to kids – and adults. Featuring roughly thirty permanent exhibits, plus a space for rotating ones, on two floors (one, the multiplication-oriented String Product, extends over both via a spiral staircase), the gallery puts a focus on experience and engagement over understanding, with the idea that the latter will naturally follow. Whimsical details abound – the pi-shaped door handles, the numbering of the floors ("0" and "–1"), the geometric sinks in the bathrooms – evidence that the museum's directors are not "museum people". There's the occasional lack of context or explanatory aid, but the overall effect is refreshing. Posing in front of the Human Tree, the most popular exhibit (though tucked away in a far corner of the lower level), throws up dazzling special effects projected on screen; taking a smooth ride on the Square-Wheeled Trike or Coaster Rollers will get you wondering about catenaries (even if you didn't know that was the name for the curves in the roadway); while

STANFORD WHITE AND THE OLD MADISON SQUARE GARDEN

Stanford White, a partner in the illustrious architectural team of McKim, Mead, and White, which designed many of the city's great Beaux Arts buildings, including the General Post Office and the old Penn Station, as well as the second incarnation of Madison Square Garden (at 26th St and Madison; now demolished), was by all accounts something of a rake. His dalliance with millionaire Harry Thaw's future wife, Evelyn Nesbit, a Broadway showgirl (who was unattached at the time), had been well publicized – even to the extent that the naked statue of the goddess Diana on the top of the Madison Square Garden building was said to have been modelled on her. Violent and possessive, Thaw could never accept his wife's past, and one night in 1906 he burst into the roof garden of White's Madison Square Garden tower apartment, found the architect surrounded, as usual, by doting women and admirers, and shot him in the head. Thaw was carted away after trial to a mental institution, which he was subsequently in and out of for around a third of his remaining years, while his wife's show business career took a tumble: she resorted to drugs and prostitution, dying in 1967 in Los Angeles.

Hoop Curves provides a basketball-launching robotic device to help with the arc of your free-throw shooting. After you've seen how fractals relate to the real world, take a breather in the Enigma Café – for sustenance, there are puzzles rather than coffee and baked goods.

Museum of Sex

233 Fifth Ave, at 27th St • Mon–Thurs & Sun 10am–8pm, Fri & Sat 11am–10pm • $17.50–20.50 depending on day and time, ages 18 and over only • ☎ 212 689 6337, ⓦ museumofsex.com • Subway R, W, #6 to 28th St

One of the city's more provocative institutions, the **Museum of Sex** attempts to bring serious study to its subject but is more of interest for its singularity than any new light it might shed. The first floor has temporary exhibitions on subjects like pornography and the sex lives of animals, while upstairs features a mishmash of items from the permanent collection (much of which has been donated), such as early vibrators, sex dolls and so forth, which look anything but titillating in this setting – presumably part of the point.

Church of the Transfiguration

1 E 29th St, just off Fifth Ave • Chapel open daily 8.30am–6pm, Tues lunchtime music performances, $5 suggested donation • ⓦ littlechurch.org • Subway R, W, #6 to 28th St

The lone reminder of the time when this area was New York's theatreland is the **Church of the Transfiguration**. Built in 1849, this dinky, rusticated church, made of brown brick, topped with copper roofs, and set back from the street, has long been a traditional place of worship for showbiz people and various social misfits. In 1870 the place was tagged with the name "The Little Church Around the Corner" after a devout priest from a larger, stuffier church had refused to officiate at the funeral of an actor named George Holland, sending the bereaved here instead. Since then, the church has been a haven for members of the theatre profession, and there is even an Episcopal Actors' Guild. The chapel itself is an intimate little building in a gloriously leafy garden, providing comfort and solace away from the skyscrapers on Fifth Avenue.

Marble Collegiate Church

1 W 29th St • Jazz Revelation services every first and third Fri at 7pm at 274 Fifth Ave • ⓦ marblechurch.org • Subway R, W, #6 to 28th St

Across Fifth Avenue from the Church of the Transfiguration is another house of worship, the 150-year-old **Marble Collegiate Church** which, in addition to having two Tiffany stained-glass windows in its sanctuary (plus a number of later knock-offs), was where preacher-cum-pop-psychologist Norman Vincent Peale held the pulpit for years.

Lexington Avenue

Two blocks east of Madison, **Lexington Avenue**, which begins its long journey north at Gramercy Park, passes the lumbering **69th Regiment Armory** at 26th Street (ⓦ sixtyninth .net). The site of the famous Armory Show of 1913, which brought modern art to New York, and a very early home to the Knicks basketball team, it retains its original function as the headquarters of the National Guard's "Fighting Sixty-Ninth", though its drill hall is still used for events and exhibitions. The modern-day Armory Show, the highlight of early March's **Armory Week** (ⓦ thearmoryshow.com), takes place at piers 92 and 94 on the Hudson River, with major art auctions and events elsewhere around town.

Just west of the Armory, on the corner of Park Avenue, 104 E 26th St was once the brownstone home of **Herman Melville**; it has long since been replaced with a modern office building but is remembered with a small plaque. The author moved here in 1863, and lived in the spot for nearly thirty years, toiling at the New York Custom House and, later, working on the unfinished *Billy Budd* before his death in 1891. The nearby intersection is named **Herman Melville Square** in his honour.

North of the Armory lies what is sometimes dubbed **Curry Hill**, a collection of Indian restaurants, snack shops and stores along Lexington Avenue between East 27th and 30th streets – blink and you might miss it. Most of New York's Indian population lives in Queens, but the cluster of businesses here just about warrants the moniker.

CHRYSLER BUILDING

Midtown East

The largely corporate and commercial area known as Midtown East rolls
north from the 30s to the 50s, and east to the river from Sixth Avenue. Some
of the city's most determinedly modish boutiques, richest Art Deco facades
and most sophisticated Modernist skyscrapers are in this district, primarily
scattered along Fifth, Madison and Park avenues. You'll find the Empire State
Building, the soaring symbol of New York City; the grand Neoclassicism of
the New York Public Library's main branch; the Art Deco, automobile-
inspired Chrysler Building; the rambling, geometric bulk of the United
Nations complex; and the peerless Museum of Modern Art. Affordable places
to eat and good nightlife spots may be relatively thin on the ground, but you
can spend plenty of worthwhile daylight hours here.

ARRIVAL AND DEPARTURE

By train and subway Grand Central is probably the best spot to emerge in this neighbourhood: it's not just a subway (the #4, #5, #6, #7 and S all stop here) and commuter rail hub, but also an elegant introduction to Midtown architecture. Fifth Avenue is just a stone's throw away.

Fifth Avenue

10

For the last two centuries, an address on **Fifth Avenue** has signified prosperity, respectability and high social standing. Whether around Washington Square or far uptown around the Harlem River, the boulevard has traditionally been the home to Manhattan's finest mansions, hotels, churches and stores. Thanks to its show of wealth and opulence, Fifth Avenue has always drawn crowds, nowhere more than on the stretch between 34th and 59th streets, home to grand institutions like **Rockefeller Center** and the **New York Public Library**. The streets nearly reach a standstill at Christmas, with shoppers stalled at elaborate window displays; at other times, it plays host to some of the city's biggest processions (see p.404).

The Empire State Building

350 Fifth Ave, between 33rd and 34th sts • **Observatory** Daily 8am–2am, last trip 1.15am • $34; you can buy tickets online or, for an extra $26, buy an Express Pass to skip queues • ☎ 212 736 3100, Ⓦ esbnyc.com • ☎ 212 279 9777 or ☎ 1 888 759 7433, Ⓦ skyride.com • Subway B, D, F, M, N, Q, R to 34th St-Herald Square; #6 to 33rd St

For two different eras the city's tallest skyscraper, the **Empire State Building** has easily been the most potent and evocative symbol of New York since its completion in 1931. The building occupies what has always been a prime piece of real estate, originally the site of the first *Waldorf-Astoria Hotel*, built by William Waldorf Astor and opened in 1893; its current Art Deco home lies on Park Avenue.

Wall Street visionary John Jacob Raskob and his partner Alfred E. Smith, a former governor, began accumulating funds in October 1929, just three weeks before the stock market crash. Despite the ensuing Depression, the Empire State Building proceeded full steam ahead and came in well under budget after just fourteen months. Since the opening, the building has seen its share of celebrity and tragedy: King Kong clung to it while grabbing at passing aircraft; in 1945, a B-25 bomber negotiating its way through heavy fog crashed into the building's 79th storey, killing fourteen people; and in 1979,

---

SKYSCRAPERS

New York is one of the best places in the world to see **skyscrapers**. There are only two main clusters – Midtown and the Financial District – but the concentration is high: the iconic skyline traces over forty buildings higher than 200m (roughly 650ft), a number of them more than eighty years old. In a small grid, Art Deco giants such as the Chrysler Building and Rockefeller Center rub shoulders with Modernist masterpieces like the Seagram Building and Lever House.

NEW YORK'S TALLEST BUILDINGS 1846–PRESENT

1846–1890 Trinity Church – Financial District (284ft/87m)
1890–1899 World Building – demolished 1955 (348ft/106m)
1899–1908 Park Row Building – City Hall Park (391ft/119m)
1908–1909 Singer Building – demolished 1968 (612ft/187m)
1909–1913 MetLife Tower – Madison Square Park (700ft/213m)
1913–1930 Woolworth Building – Financial District (792ft/241m)
1930 Bank of Manhattan Trust – Financial District (927ft/283m)
1930–1931 Chrysler Building – Midtown (1046ft/319m)
1931–1972 Empire State Building – Midtown (1250ft/381m)
1972–2001 World Trade Center – destroyed 2001 (1368ft/417m)
2001–2012 Empire State Building – Midtown (1250ft/381m)
2012–present One World Trade Center – Financial District (1776ft/541m)

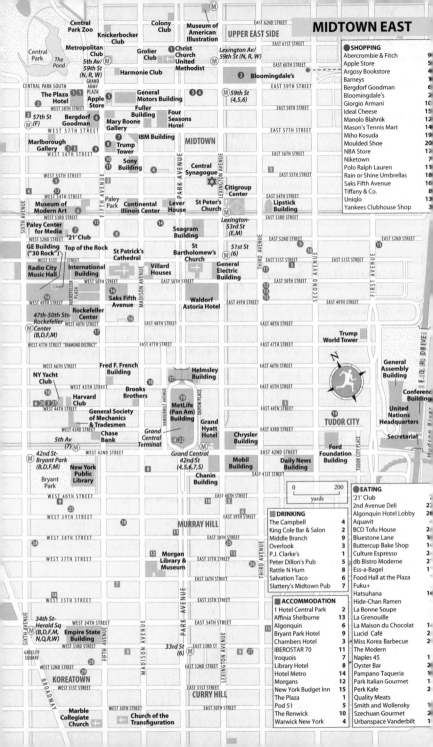

two Englishmen parachuted from its summit to the ground, only to be carted off by the NYPD for disturbing the peace. The darkest moment in the building's history came in February 1997, when a man opened fire on the observation deck, killing one tourist and injuring seven others; that's but one reason there is tight security upon entrance, with metal detectors, package scanners and the like (though in 2010, a Yale student still managed to scale a barrier on the main observation deck and jump to his death).

The building

From toe to TV mast including antennas, the building is 102 storeys and 1454ft tall, but its height is deceptive, rising in stately tiers with steady panache. Indeed, standing on Fifth Avenue below, it's quite easy to walk right by without even noticing it's there. From elsewhere in the city, it can seem ubiquitous, especially at night, when lit in various colours until the wee hours of morning (view the lighting schedule online at Ⓦesbnyc.com/current_events_tower_lights.asp).

10

Retrofitted since 2009 to make it more energy efficient (for example, all 6514 windows were taken out and reused after being turned into super-insulating windows on-site), the Empire State uses 38 percent less energy than it did a decade ago; a second-floor exhibit showcases all the sustainability achievements. The building is filled with Art Deco touches: the restored grand ceiling in the lobby with its cosmic gold murals; the elevator doors; the chandeliers in the *State Grill and Bar*, which is in the space that once held a post office.

Getting to the top

A first set of elevators takes you to the 80th floor, where a display covers the construction of the building. You then transfer to get up to the main observatory on the **86th floor**. The views from the outdoor walkways here are as stunning as you'd expect; on a clear day, visibility can be up to eighty miles, but given the city's air pollution, it's more likely to be between ten and twenty. You get a great vantage point over the Chrysler Building, completed not long before the Empire State, and over the surprisingly elegant Queensboro Bridge beyond that. For an additional $20, a manually operated elevator will take you to the glassed-in **102nd-floor observatory**, the base of the radio and TV antennas; all things considered, it's an unnecessary trip, unless you want to be able to say you've been as far up as you can go.

New York Public Library

Fifth Ave and 42nd St • Mon & Thurs–Sat 10am–6pm, Tues & Wed 10am–8pm, Sun 1–5pm (closed Sun in summer) • Tours start at the information desk in Astor Hall, the main lobby (1hr; Mon–Sat 11am & 2pm, Sun 2pm, with occasional other times for docent tours; free) • ☎ 212 930 0800 or ☎ 917 275 6975, Ⓦ nypl .org • Subway B, D, F, M to 42nd St-Bryant Park; #7 to Fifth Ave; #4, #5, #6, #7, S to Grand Central

Several unexceptional blocks north of the Empire State Building on Fifth Avenue is one of Midtown Manhattan's most striking buildings: the 105-year-old **New York Public Library** (more formally known as the Stephen A. Schwarzman Building), which stretches between 40th and 42nd streets. Beaux Arts in style and faced with white marble – restored for its centennial; approach from Library Way, or East 41st Street, for the most eye-catching introduction – it is the headquarters of the largest public-library system in the world.

To explore, either walk around yourself or take one of the **free tours**, which give a good all-round picture of the building, taking in the **Map Room** and evocative **Periodicals Room**, with its stunning faux-wood ceiling and paintings of old New York. The undisputed highlight of the library, however, is the large, coffered 636-seat **Reading Room** on the third floor – recently restored to better show off the plaster rosettes of the ceiling, among other features. Authors Norman Mailer and E.L. Doctorow worked here, as did Leon Trotsky during his brief sojourn in New York just prior to the 1917 Russian Revolution. It was also here that Chester Carlson came up with the idea for the Xerox copier and Norbert Pearlroth searched for strange facts for his "Ripley's Believe It or Not!" cartoon strip in the famed research library.

Bryant Park

Between 40th and 42nd streets, bordered by the New York Public Library and Sixth Ave • **Park** Hours vary but roughly 7am–10pm, closes earlier in March & later May–Sept **Ice skating** Nov–Feb daily 8am–10pm, midnight on weekends • $20 for skate rental • ☎ 212 768 4242, ⓦ bryantpark.org • Subway B, D, F, M to 42nd St-Bryant Park; #7 to Fifth Ave

Bryant Park, just behind the library, is Midtown's busiest outdoor space. Transformed a few decades ago from seedy eyesore to beautiful, grassy block filled with trees, flowerbeds and inviting chairs, it's a welcoming place to relax with a coffee or book on a warm day – or engage in any number of more organized activities. A sandwich and coffee kiosk in the northwest corner and alfresco bar in the southwest provide on-site refreshments; a small farmers' market sets up in between the two from April to September (Wed & Fri).

In summertime, free activities abound: dance and yoga classes, Monday evening movies and table tennis to name a few (there are also areas to play chess and petanque or practice your putting). Lectures and rallies take place in the park; there's a carousel ($3) for children, and in winter the park's pond turns into an ice-skating rink (with an accompanying holiday market). Donning your blades in the shadow of the library and giant Christmas tree rivals the more popular scenes at Rockefeller Center and Central Park for atmosphere.

North to Rockefeller Center

The **Chase Bank**, on the southwest corner of West 43rd Street and Fifth Avenue, is an eye-catcher. An early glass'n'gloss box, it teasingly displays its vault (no longer in use) to passers-by. Around the next corner, West 44th Street contains several old-guard New York institutions. The Georgian-style **Harvard Club**, at no. 35 (☎ 212 840 6600, ⓦ hcny .com), has an interior so lavish that lesser mortals aren't even allowed to enter (you must be a Harvard alumnus/a). Built in 1894, it was the first of several elite associations in the neighbourhood.

The private **New York Yacht Club**, at 37 W 44th St (☎ 212 382 1000, ⓦ nyyc.org), chartered in 1844 and in its current location since 1901, is just next door. The playfully eccentric exterior of bay windows is moulded as ships' sterns; waves and dolphins complete the effect of tipsy Beaux Arts fun. For years, this has been the home of the America's Cup, a yachting trophy first won by the schooner *America* in 1851. Across the street at no. 20, the 230-year-old **General Society of Mechanics and Tradesmen** occupies a late nineteenth-century building; step inside to peruse the library (Mon–Thurs 11am–7pm, Fri 10am–5pm; free; ⓦ generalsociety.org) and to examine their amazing collection of locks (by appointment ☎ 212 840 1840; $10 admission).

"Dammit, it was the twenties and we had to be smarty," said Dorothy Parker of the sharp-tongued wits known as the Round Table (see box below), whose members lunched and drank regularly at the **Algonquin Hotel**, at 59 W 44th St (see p.272).

THE ROUND TABLE

All across the globe, the period between World War I and World War II saw an incredible outpouring of creative energy. In America, one of the groups involved in this burst of productivity was the so-called **Round Table**, which originated at the *Algonquin Hotel*. Several writers, many of whom had worked together for the Army newspaper *Stars and Stripes*, met in June 1919 at the hotel to roast *New York Times* drama critic Alexander Woollcott. They had so much fun that they decided to return the following afternoon; it wasn't long before their meeting became a ritual. At the heart of the group were Dorothy Parker, Robert Benchley, Robert Sherwood, Irving Berlin, Harold Ross (founder of *The New Yorker* magazine), George Bernard Shaw and George S. Kaufman, among others. Outspoken and unafraid to comment on the state of the postwar world, they wielded an increasing influence on social issues throughout the 1920s; when the Round Table spoke, the country listened. Then the Great Depression arrived, and a decade after its inception, it finally faded from the scene.

FIVE UNIQUE CITY VIEWS

Top of the Rock and the Empire State Building are obvious places to go for panoramic **views** of New York, but you can find interesting angles on the city at any of the following:
Brooklyn Bridge See p.216
Brooklyn Bridge Park's Main Street Lot See p.219
Cantor Rooftop Garden See box, p.167
The High Line See p.108
The Panorama of the City of New York See p.251

10

Recent refurbishments have shut the hotel's legendary *Oak Room*, but the lobby's lounge and *Round Table Room* both offer excuses to pop in for a tea or just a look round.

It's worth ducking into the **Fred F. French Building** at 551 Fifth Ave. The colourful mosaics near the top of the building's exterior are a mere prelude to the combination of Art Deco and Middle Eastern imagery on the vaulted ceiling and bronze doors of the lobby.

Diamond District

West 47th Street, or the **Diamond District** (marked by the diamond-shaped lamps mounted on pylons at the Fifth- and Sixth-Avenue ends of the street), is a diverting side-trip from Fifth Avenue, a strip of wholesale and retail shops chock-full of gems and jewellery first established in the 1920s. These shops are largely managed by Hasidic Jews, who impart much of the street's workaday vibe, making the row feel less like something just off ritzy Fifth Avenue and more like the Garment District, by way of the Middle East. Come here to get jewellery fixed at reasonable prices.

Rockefeller Center

Taking up the blocks between Fifth and Sixth aves and 48th and 51st sts • Leaflets for self-guided tours available from GE Building lobby desk or online • ☎ 212 332 6868 or ☎ 212 632 3975, ⊛ rockefellercenter.com • Subway B, D, F, M to 47-50th sts-Rockefeller Center

Rockefeller Center is one of the finest examples of urban planning in New York. Built between 1930 and 1939 by John D. Rockefeller Jr, son of the oil magnate, its offices, cafés, theatre, underground concourse and rooftop gardens work together with an intelligence and grace rarely seen. The main part of the Center is along the block between 49th and 50th streets, though it extends down to 48th Street in the south and also includes, just across 50th Street on the corner of Sixth Avenue, the Art Deco-style **Radio City Music Hall** – arguably the most famous theatre in the United States.

GE Building ("30 Rock")

30 Rockefeller Plaza • **Ice rink** Daily 8.30am–midnight, with 90min sessions followed by 30min breaks • $25 (more around Christmas), $12 skate rental • ☎ 212 332 7654, ⊛ therinkatrockcenter.com • Subway B, D, F, M to 47-50th sts-Rockefeller Center

From Fifth Avenue, the gentle slope of the **Channel Gardens** leads to the focus of the Center – the **GE Building** (formerly the RCA Building), nicknamed "30 Rock". Rising 850ft, its monumental lines echo the scale of Manhattan, though they are softened by symmetrical setbacks to prevent an overpowering expanse of wall. At the foot of the building, the Lower Plaza holds a sunken restaurant in the summer months – a great place for afternoon cocktails – linked visually to the downward flow of the building by **Paul Manship**'s sparkling sculpture *Prometheus*. In winter this recessed area becomes an **ice rink** and, following a New York tradition that dates to 1931, a huge tree is displayed at Christmas time, drawing hordes of gawkers, especially the night it's initially lit (first week of Dec).

Inside, the GE Building is no less impressive. **José Maria Sert**'s lobby murals, *American Progress* and *Time*, are faded but still in tune with the 1930s ambience – presumably more so than the original paintings by Diego Rivera, which were removed by John D.'s son Nelson Rockefeller when the artist refused to scrap a panel glorifying Lenin.

10

NBC Studios

30 Rockefeller Plaza • Behind-the-scenes studio tours Mon–Fri 8.20am–2pm, Sat & Sun 8.20am–5pm • $33 • ☎ 212 664 3700,
ⓦ thetouratnbcstudios.com • For information on show tapings, visit ⓦ nbc.com/tickets-and-nbc-studio-tour or call the ticket line on
☎ 212 664 3056 (see p.360) • Subway B, D, F, M to 47-50th sts-Rockefeller Center

Among the GE Building's many offices is **NBC Studios** on 49th Street between Fifth
and Sixth avenues, which produces, among other things, the long-running sketch-
comedy hit *Saturday Night Live* and the popular morning programme the *Today* show.
Hour-long tours of the studios begin at the Shop at NBC Studios roughly every twenty
minutes; you'll get to see some sets and memorabilia and have an interactive moment
as part of your own show at the conclusion. To become part of the throng that appears
(and waves frantically) when the anchors step outside, all one has to do is show up
– the earlier the better. This is especially true on summer Fridays when the *Today* show
hosts concerts, which begin at 7am.

Top of the Rock

30 Rockefeller Plaza • Daily 8am–midnight, last elevator at 11.15pm • $34; "Sun & Stars" $49 • ☎ 212 698 2000, ⓦ topoftherocknyc.com •
Subway B, D, F, M to 47-50th sts-Rockefeller Center

The observation deck on the top of Rockefeller Center, first opened in 1933, fell into
disuse and was closed in the 1980s. The owners returned to John D.'s original vision by
restoring the platform on the structure's seventieth storey in November 2005. In
contrast to the Empire State Building, **Top of the Rock** offers completely unobstructed
views, and the timed-entry scheme, multiple observation decks and decent square-
footage of the viewing platforms make a visit seem less like a cattle call. The panorama
allows you to examine the layout of Central Park, how built-up Downtown Manhattan
is compared to the north and offers a vertiginous look at St Patrick's Cathedral below
– not to mention the Empire State Building nearby. A "Sun & Stars" ticket option
allows particularly dedicated visitors to scale the building twice in one day and
experience the city in two different veils of light.

Radio City Music Hall

1260 Sixth Ave • "Stage Door" walking tours (1hr) daily 9.30am–5pm every 30min • $26.95, 12 and under $19.95 • For tickets, call ☎ 212
307 7171, tour info ☎ 212 247 4777, ⓦ radiocity.com • Subway B, D, F, M to 47-50th sts-Rockefeller Center

On the northeast corner of Sixth Avenue and 50th Street is **Radio City Music Hall** (see
p.345), a sweeping and dramatic Art Deco jewel box that represents the last word in 1930s
luxury. The staircase is positively regal, the chandeliers are the world's largest and the
auditorium looks like an extravagant scalloped shell. You're unlikely to be taking in a show
here – with a couple of exceptions, the venue rarely books the type of cool acts that once
made it such a hot ticket – so to explore, take a tour. In addition to the behind-the-scenes
look at the building, the tour includes a brief meeting with a Rockette (the "house"
dancers that are part of the Christmas Spectacular, the big annual event at RCMH).

North to Central Park: St Patrick's Cathedral

Fifth Avenue has another sumptuous Art Deco component in the Rockefeller Center,
the **International Building**. The lobby looks out on **Lee Lawrie**'s bronze *Atlas*, which
rules the space; the muscleman gazes towards freshly renovated **St Patrick's Cathedral**
(ⓦ saintpatrickscathedral.org; Mass multiple times daily, frequent recitals and guest
choirs; free 10am tours 2–3 times weekly) across the avenue. Designed by James
Renwick and completed in 1888, St Patrick's sits on the corner of 50th Street amid the
glitz like a misplaced bit of moral imperative, painstakingly detailed yet –
notwithstanding the mysticism of **Lady Chapel** to the rear – spiritually lifeless. Despite
its shortcomings, St Patrick's is still an essential part of the Midtown landscape, a foil
for Rockefeller Center and one of the most important Catholic churches in America.

Across the street from St Patrick's are the striped awnings of **Saks Fifth Avenue** at no.
611, one of the last of New York's premier department stores to relocate to Midtown

from Herald Square. With its columns on the ground floor and graceful pathways through high-end fashion collections, Saks is every bit as glamorous today as it was when it opened in 1924.

Paley Center for Media

25 W 52nd St, between Fifth and Sixth aves • Wed & Fri–Sun noon–6pm, Thurs noon–8pm • Suggested donation $10 • ☎ 212 621 6600 or 6800, ⓦ paleycenter.org • Subway B, D, F, M to 47-50th sts-Rockefeller Center

If your body needs the kind of rejuvenation only an hour in front of a television can offer, visit the **Paley Center for Media**. Formerly known as the Museum of Television & Radio, the space was renamed in 2007 with a nod to the eventual inclusion of digital media. In a building designed by Philip Johnson, the organization preserves an archive of 160,000, mostly American, TV shows, radio broadcasts and commercials, accessible via an excellent computerized reference system. Occasional screenings (family friendly on Saturdays, more cultured on Sundays) and panel discussions take place in the downstairs theatre.

10

The '21' Club

21 W 52nd St • ☎ 212 582 7200, ⓦ 21club.com • Subway B, D, F, M to 47-50th sts-Rockefeller Center

Right next door to the Paley Center is the **'21' Club**, which has been providing food (and drink) since the days of Prohibition, and remains an Old Boys' institution. Founded by Jack Kriendler and Charlie Berns, the club quickly became one of the most exclusive establishments in town, a place where young socialites and local celebrities could spend wild nights dancing the Charleston and enjoying wines and spirits of the finest quality. Although '21' was raided more than once, federal agents were never able to pin anything on Jack and Charlie. At the first sign of a raid, they would activate an ingenious system of pulleys and levers, which would sweep bottles from the bar shelves and hurl the smashed remains down a chute into the New York sewer system.

Museum of Modern Art (MoMA)

11 W 53rd St, just off Fifth Ave • Daily 10.30am–5.30pm, Fri till 8pm • $25, free Fri 4–8pm • ☎ 212 708 9400, ⓦ moma.org • Subway E, M to 5th Ave-53rd St; B, D, F, M to 47-50th sts-Rockefeller Center

New York City's **Museum of Modern Art – MoMA** to its friends – offers the finest and most complete collection of late nineteenth- and twentieth-century art anywhere, with a permanent collection of more than 150,000 paintings, sculptures, drawings, prints and photographs, as well as a world-class film archive. Despite its high admission price, it's an essential stop for anyone even remotely interested in the world of modern art.

Founded in 1929 by three wealthy women, including Abby Aldrich Rockefeller (wife of John D., Jr), as the very first museum dedicated entirely to modern art, MoMA moved to its present home ten years later. Philip Johnson designed expansions in the 1950s and 1960s, and in 1984 a steel-pipe and glass renovation by Cesar Pelli doubled the gallery space. A renovation was completed in 2004 by Japanese architect Yoshio Taniguchi, doubling the exhibition space yet again and creating new and vibrant public areas; another rethinking and expansion is already in the works – with gallery space in a soaring new skyscraper next door that will be one of the city's tallest structures, as well as more public space, a two-storey lobby and additional street-level galleries.

Planning your visit

MoMA's building is quite clever: it's easy to navigate, but it also constantly and deliberately gives glimpses of other levels, like the sculpture garden, the lobby and the spacious second-floor landing where large canvases or installations are often displayed. The core collection – at least in the Painting and Sculpture galleries – has traditionally been arranged in more or less chronological order; that said, the museum intends to get away from dividing by discipline, and the fact that some new galleries have just been completed and more are in the works means that what's below should be taken more as a sampling of what might be on display rather than as a rule of thumb.

Despite all the space, the main galleries that hold the greatest hits can still feel very crowded, especially during weekends and free admission time on Friday evenings; queues can be long at the entrance, cloakroom, cafés and for audio guides. Try to avoid waiting in queue by booking tickets in advance on the website or by arriving either first thing or late in the afternoon. Note also that you must check-in large shopping bags and backpacks of any size – best to leave them at your hotel.

10

Painting and Sculpture I

The core of the collection is the Painting and Sculpture galleries, numbered from 1 to 25. Most visitors head directly for the fifth floor – to **Painting and Sculpture I**, which covers 1880 to the 1950s, although a few exceptions have been made lately. Gallery 1 opens with the **Post-Impressionists** of the late nineteenth century, with works by **Cézanne**, **Seurat**, **Van Gogh** (visitors always mill around his *Starry Night*) and **Gauguin** mixed in with vivid early paintings by **James Ensor** and **Henri Rousseau** that already hint at a more Modernist perspective. This is developed in the next gallery by **Picasso**, most notably with his seminal *Les Demoiselles d'Avignon*, as well as by some of his later, more Cubist pieces; you can also contrast his *Bather* with Cézanne's take on the same subject from the previous gallery. The big swirling colours of **Boccioni**, **Severini**, **Chagall** and the Futurists follow in Gallery 3, with Gallery 4 holding the works of **de Chirico** and his lonely, haunting explorations in perspective, best seen in *Gare Montparnasse*. Gallery 5 is given over to **Dada**; various pieces by Duchamp and Jean Arp punctuate the landscape. Gallery 6 is entirely devoted to **Matisse**. Featured are the flat, almost primitive *Dance I*; his *Red Studio*; and *The Moroccans*, at once still and rhythmic.

After Matisse is a so-called **"Crossroads" gallery** (Gallery 7), which houses some of the most recognizable pieces of the modern age – Picasso's *Three Women at the Spring*, the same artist's *Three Musicians* and Léger's *Three Women*, all painted in 1921, a smattering of works by the leading light of the Dutch De Stijl movement, Mondrian (hope that his exercise in colour, *Broadway Boogie-Woogie*, is somewhere on display). Gallery 14, which surrounds the staircase, is adjacent and typically holds some movement works – say, those of Russian constructivists like Alexander Rodchenko. After Monet's *Water Lilies* (Gallery 9), the adjoining room (Gallery 10) is devoted to Surrealists. Much of the artwork here will be familiar from popular reproductions: the vivid creations of **Miró**; **Magritte**'s *The Menaced Assassin*; Tanguy's *Furniture of Time*; the famously drooping clocks of **Dalí**'s *Persistence of Memory*, astonishingly detailed for its compact size – the last of these is often on loan to other galleries. Gallery 11 holds the Mexican modernists: Frida Kahlo, José Clemente Orozco and, grandest of all, Diego Rivera's heroic rendition of *Agrarian Leader Zapata*. You may find the Abstract Expressionists in Gallery 12, with large-scale compositions by Rothko, Barnett Newman and Jackson Pollock. Tiny Gallery 13 might hold **Jacob Lawrence**'s *Migration Series*, a shorthand history of the African American shift from the rural south to the urban north, or some mid-century modern theme. On long-term loan to the museum is *Glenn*, by Jean-Michel Basquiat, at either the beginning or end of your circuit of the floor, by the staircase; amazingly, the museum owns not a single painting of the artist.

THE MOMA SHUFFLE

While a number of the pieces and painters that we cover will (almost) always be on display, don't bank on the order, selections or even that every room mentioned will be open; recent trends have included more mixing of eras and artists in Painting and Sculpture I, a stronger emphasis on recent Conceptual Art in Painting and Sculpture II (and mixing media too), and an ongoing dedication to rethinking the canon and its sacred cows. As well, pieces go out on loan or become part of featured exhibitions at the museum (in recent years these have included Jacob Lawrence's *Migration Series* and Andy Warhol's *Campbell Soup Cans*).

Painting and Sculpture II

Painting and Sculpture II, the next floor down, displays works from the 1950s to 1980 and inevitably has a more American feel. Gallery 15 features a few artists influenced by New York in the 1940s, namely **Louise Bourgeois** and **Yves Tanguy**; the latter's surrealist canvases capture the confusion of the times. There's also an early Rothko, quite exuberant compared to his better-known works. In Gallery 16, the large canvases of Abstract Expressionist giants hold sway, most prominently the splatterings of **Pollock**. **De Kooning**'s fierce *Woman I* is also on hand. The "zips" of **Barnett Newman** and the "multiforms" of **Rothko** fill Gallery 17, while **Jasper Johns**' *Flag* and **Robert Rauschenberg**'s mixed-media paintings, including the barely-constrained bald eagle of *Canyon*, highlight Gallery 18. The remaining galleries survey Pop Art (**Warhol**'s soup cans and *Marilyn Monroe*), Minimalism (Sol LeWitt, Frank Stella) and various subsequent movements – including sculptures that begin to challenge just what art is.

10

Photography, Architecture and Design, Drawings

The other sections of the museum's collection are just as impressive and shouldn't be missed, though what will be on display will remain in flux until the renovations are done. **Photography** displays are typically devoted to a rotating selection of exceptional work from visiting artists and the museum's permanent collection – everything from the candid street photos of Paris by **Cartier-Bresson** and **Richard Avedon**'s penetrating portraits of well-known figures to **Helen Levitt**'s colourful shots of unwitting New York characters.

In terms of **Architecture and Design,** you might find illustrations of buildings, works of interior design, lots of glass and ceramics, high-backed chairs and early electronics, album covers and music posters, and a series of neat large-scale objects like vintage cars, bikes, surfboards, even helicopters.

There's usually material from the **Drawings** holdings, including works by twentieth-century notables such as **Pollock, Rauschenberg, de Kooning, Warhol, Jasper Johns** and **Roy Lichtenstein**.

The second-floor galleries give MoMA the chance to show its **contemporary art** in all media, and usually display works from the 1980s onward, focusing on single-artist installations in each of three spaces. You might see something by photographer **Nan Goldin** or conceptual artist **Dan Graham**.

Abby Aldrich Rockefeller Sculpture Garden

Outside the lobby on the 54th Street side, the **Sculpture Garden** (free 9–10.15am) is a serene space to take a break. There's plenty to gaze at: some Matisse and Giacometti works, *The River* by Aristide Maillol, various plantings and water features. It also serves as the setting for July's Summergarden classical music series.

53rd Street to Grand Army Plaza

Northward from MoMA, Fifth Avenue's ground floors shift from mundane offices to an elegant stretch of exclusive shops and art galleries. Taking ostentatious wealth to the extreme is **Trump Tower** (not to be confused with Trump World Tower over by the UN, or any other number of "Trump" city properties), at no. 725 at 56th Street. Perfumed air, polished marble panelling and a five-storey waterfall are calculated to knock you senseless with expensive "good taste". The building itself is clever: a neat little outdoor garden is squeezed high in a corner, and each of the 230 apartments above the atrium provides views in three directions. Another atrium, complete with piped-in sounds, connects the tower to the IBM Building (see p.133).

The stores on these blocks are as much sights as shops, with **Gucci, Tiffany & Co** and **Bergdorf** among the gilt-edged names (see p.378). At 59th Street, Fifth Avenue reaches **Grand Army Plaza** and the fringes of Central Park, where a golden statue of William Tecumseh Sherman stands guard amid all the highbrow shopping, and the copper-edged 1907 **Plaza Hotel** (see p.273) lords it over the square's western border.

Madison Avenue

Madison Avenue parallels Fifth with some of the grandeur but less of the excitement. In the East 30s, the avenue runs through the heart of the mundane and residential **Murray Hill** neighbourhood, an area distinguished mostly by the presence of the **Morgan Library & Museum**. Heading north to the East 40s and the Upper East Side, you encounter the Madison Avenue of legend, the centre of the international advertising industry in the 1960s and 1970s. Today, this section of town is a major high-end shopping boulevard.

10

Murray Hill

Madison Avenue is the main artery of **Murray Hill**, a tenuously tagged residential area (no commercial building was allowed until the 1920s) of statuesque, canopy-fronted buildings bounded by East 34th and 40th streets, and lacking any real centre or sense of community. Indeed, you're likely to pass through without even realizing it.

When Madison Avenue was on a par with Fifth as the place to live, Murray Hill was dominated by the Morgan family, including the crusty old financier J.P. and his offspring, who at one time owned a clutch of properties here. Morgan Junior lived in the brownstone house on the corner of 37th Street and Madison (after his death, it became headquarters of the American Lutheran Church, but the Morgan Library eventually bought it back), his father in a house that was later pulled down to make way for an extension to his library next door.

Morgan Library & Museum

225 Madison Ave at East 36th St • Tues–Thurs 10.30am–5pm, Fri 10.30am–9pm, Sat 10am–6pm, Sun 11am–6pm • $20, free Fri 7–9pm • ☎ 212 685 0008, ⓦ themorgan.org • Subway #6 to 33rd St

The uplifting **Morgan Library & Museum**, housed across multiple buildings on properties of industrial magnate J.P. Morgan, is dedicated largely to artefacts of the written and printed word. Morgan would often come to his library, a mock-Roman villa, to luxuriate among the art treasures he had acquired on his trips to Europe: manuscripts, paintings, prints and furniture. A stunning piazza-style gathering space, created by Pritzker Prize-winner Renzo Piano, brings together the building in which Morgan stored his collection, designed by noted architects McKim, Mead, and White, an annexe designed in somewhat similar fashion (that replaced Morgan's old townhouse) and Morgan Junior's brownstone. Piano's renovation, completed in 2006, also doubled the exhibition space and added several new features to the building, including a main entrance on Madison Avenue (you should still head around the corner on East 36th Street to get the best exterior perspective), a subterranean performance hall and a naturally lit reading room.

The collection of some ten thousand drawings and prints by such greats as Da Vinci, Degas and Dürer is augmented by rare literary manuscripts by Dickens, Austen and Thoreau as well as handwritten correspondence between Ernest Hemingway and George Plimpton, letters from Virginia Woolf and J.R.R. Tolkien, and musical scribblings by everyone from Haydn to Dylan. The museum also typically displays a copy of the Gutenberg Bible (it owns three out of the eleven that survive). Morgan's personal library and study, the crucial pieces of the McKim building, were recently restored; poke around them to see Morgan's extensive personal book archive, various paintings and exquisite

---

FIVE MIDTOWN RETREATS

With the crush of skyscrapers and street traffic in Midtown, it's nice to find a quiet nook to have a coffee and snack, read or just take a contemplative break from the hustle and bustle.
Ford Foundation Building atrium See p.138
IBM Building atrium See opposite
MoMA Sculpture Garden See p.131
Paley Park See opposite
Sutton Place Park See p.139

office furniture, and take note of the North Room, which showcases the museum's ancient and medieval holdings. Peek into the vault within his private study – the prizes of his manuscript collection were once held behind the combination-locked door.

North of Murray Hill

Leaving behind the relative quiet of Murray Hill, Madison Avenue becomes progressively more commercial the further north one goes. Several stores – some specializing in men's haberdashery, shoes and cigars – still cater to the needs of the more aristocratic consumer. **Brooks Brothers**, traditional clothiers of the Ivy League and inventors of the button-down collar, occupies a corner of East 44th Street. Between 50th and 51st streets the **Villard Houses**, a replica collection of Italian palazzi (ones that didn't quite make it to Fifth Ave) by McKim, Mead, and White, merit more than a passing glance. The houses have been surgically incorporated into the *New York Palace Hotel*, and the interiors polished up to their original splendour.

Madison's most interesting sight comes in a four-block strip above 53rd Street. The tiny, vest-pocket-sized **Paley Park** is on the north side of East 53rd between Madison and Fifth avenues, and has a soothing mini-waterfall and transparent water tunnel. Previously, a nearby plaza displayed a haunting five-panel section of the former Berlin Wall, though that curious relic was removed for its own protection from water damage and graffiti and placed in the lobby at 520 Madison Ave. Around the corner, the **Continental Illinois Center** looks like a cross between a space rocket and a grain silo.

A few streets up at East 57th Street, at no. 41–45, is the eye-catching **Fuller Building**. Black-and-white Art Deco, it has a fine entrance and tiled floor. Cut east on 57th Street to no. 57 to find the **Four Seasons Hotel**, notable for its sweeping marble and limestone design by I.M. Pei.

Sony Building

550 Madison Ave, between 55th and 56th sts • Daily 7am–11pm • Subway E, M to Fifth Ave-53rd St

The **Sony Building** (formerly the AT&T Building) has grabbed headlines since its construction thirty-plus years ago; it sold for an astounding $1.1 billion in 2013, was meant to undergo a luxury condo conversion and then was just as quickly sold again (for $1.4 billion) when the high-end apartment market softened. A Johnson–Burgee collaboration, it follows the postmodernist theory of borrowing from historical styles: a Modernist skyscraper is sandwiched between a Chippendale top and a Renaissance base. The grand, oversized entrance makes you feel quite small indeed and around the corner you'll find a glass-roofed atrium dotted with trees and a café to relax in.

IBM Building

590 Madison Ave, between 56th and 57th sts • Daily 8am–10pm • Subway E, M to Fifth Ave-53rd St

The green-tinted faceted **IBM Building** has a far more user-friendly plaza than the Sony Building; note the unusual shape of the structure, too – a pentagonal wedge, with a street-level cutaway. In its calm, glass-enclosed atrium, tinkling music, tropical foliage, a coffee bar and comfortable seating make for an uplifting experience – it also links to the Trump Tower (see p.131).

Park Avenue

In 1929, author Collinson Owen wrote that **Park Avenue** is "where wealth is so swollen that it almost bursts". Things have changed little since. The focal point of the avenue is the hulking **Grand Central Terminal**, at 42nd Street. South of Grand Central, Park Avenue narrows in both width and interest, but to the north of the building it becomes an impressively broad boulevard. Built to accommodate elevated rail tracks, the area quickly became a battleground, as corporate headquarters and refined residences jostled for prominence. Whatever your feelings about conspicuous wealth, from the 40s north Park Avenue is one of the city's most awesome sights. Its sweeping expanse, genteel facades and sculpture-studded medians capture both the gracious and grand sides of New York in one fell swoop.

Grand Central Terminal

87 E 42nd St, between Lexington and Vanderbilt aves • Daily 5.30am–2am • ⓦ grandcentralterminal.com • Subway S, #4, #5, #6, #7 to Grand Central-42nd St

10 Park Avenue hits 42nd Street at Pershing Square, where it lifts off the ground to make room for the massive **Grand Central Terminal**. More than just a train station, the terminal is a full-blown destination in itself. The most spectacular aspect of the building is its size, though the MetLife Building (see p.136) dwarfs it in height. The station's main concourse is one of the world's finest and most imposing open spaces, 470ft long and 150ft high. The **barrel-vaulted ceiling** is speckled like a Baroque church with a painted representation of the winter night sky, its 2500 stars shown back to front – "as God would have seen them", the French painter Paul Helleu reputedly remarked. Stand in the middle and you realize that Grand Central represents a time when stations were seen as miniature cities. Walking around the marble corridors and feeling the subtle shifts in dynamics, mood and pace is an elegant and instructive experience you're unlikely to forget.

Brief history

When it was constructed in 1913 (on the site of the original station built by Cornelius Vanderbilt), the terminal was a masterly piece of urban planning. After the electrification of the railways made it possible to reroute trains underground, the rail lines behind the existing station were sold off to developers and the profits went towards the building of a new terminal – built around a basic iron frame but clothed with a Beaux Arts skin. While Grand Central soon took on an almost mythical significance, today its traffic consists mainly of commuters speeding out to Connecticut, Westchester County and upstate New York, and any claim to being a gateway to an undiscovered continent is purely symbolic.

Food and drink

In addition to its architectural and historical offerings, there are around seventy shops and restaurants here, including the kiosks in the tantalizing **Grand Central Market**, which sells every gourmet food imaginable, and the fast-casual dining spots on the terminal's lower concourse. Chief among the places to eat is the *Grand Central Oyster Bar* (see p.304), which is located in the vaulted bowels of the station. Don't miss the acoustic fluke just outside the restaurant: two people can stand on opposite sides of any of the vaulted spaces and hold a conversation just by whispering.

A Scandinavian food hall courtesy of noted *Noma* chef Claus Meyer makes for another fine place to grab a bite; look out for the Danish-style hot dogs – and the fancy full-service restaurant *Agern*. As well, the *Campbell* is an upscale bar located in the one-time office of railroad tycoon John W. Campbell. One other retail spot of note is

---

TOURS OF GRAND CENTRAL TERMINAL

You'll no doubt find plenty to please the eye just wandering around Grand Central by yourself, but for some context and the odd inside secret, opt for one of the excellent tours run by the **Municipal Arts Society** (daily 12.30pm; 1hr 15min; $25; ⓦ mas.org), meeting at the info booth on the main concourse, or the **Grand Central Partnership** (Fri 12.30pm; 1hr 30min–2hr; free, tips welcome; ⓦ grandcentralpartnership.nyc), which meets across 42nd Street in the atrium at 120 Park Ave. Both will clue you in on the building's architecture and history; the latter walk takes you to a few nearby spots outside Grand Central as well. A third option is a **self-guided audio tour**; pick it up at GCT Tour window on the main concourse (daily 9am–6pm; $9).

FROM TOP ST PATRICK'S CATHEDRAL (P.128); GRAND CENTRAL TERMINAL (ABOVE) >

the Transit Museum Gallery Annex & Store, which usually has a train-related exhibition in addition to its goods.

MetLife Building

200 Park Ave • Subway S, #4, #5, #6, #7 to Grand Central–42nd St

Just north of Grand Central stands the Bauhaus bulk of the **MetLife Building**, built in 1963 as the Pan Am Building and impressive more for its size than its grandeur. Bauhaus guru Walter Gropius had a hand in designing the structure; the critical consensus is that he could have done better. As the headquarters of the now-defunct international airline, the building, in profile, was meant to suggest an airplane wing. The blue-grey mass certainly adds drama to the cityscape, although it robs Park Avenue of its southern views, sealing off 44th Street and sapping much of the vigour of the surrounding buildings.

Helmsley Building

230 Park Ave, at 46th St • Subway S, #4, #5, #6, #7 to Grand Central–42nd St

The high altar of the New York Central Building (built in 1928 and years later rechristened the **Helmsley Building**), a delicate construction with a lewdly excessive Rococo lobby, rises up directly in the middle of Park Avenue; twin tunnels allow traffic to pass beneath it. In its mid-twentieth-century heyday it formed a punctuation mark to the avenue, but its thunder was stolen in 1963 by the completion of the MetLife Building, which looms above and behind it.

St Bartholomew's Church

325 Park Ave, at 51st St • ⓦ stbarts.org • Subway #6 to 51st St

Crouching just across from the *Waldorf* on 50th Street, **St Bartholomew's Church** is a low-slung Byzantine hybrid with portals designed by McKim, Mead, and White; it adds an immeasurable amount of character to the area, lending the lumbering skyscrapers a much-needed sense of scale. The church fought against developers for years, and ultimately became a test case for New York City's landmark preservation law. Today, its congregation thrives – services are held throughout the week and four times on Sundays – and its members sponsor many community-outreach programmes; the church also serves as a prime place to hear sacred music, with a summer festival dedicated to the genre (June & July), not to mention the largest pipe organ in the city. Nearby, on 50th Street between Park and Madison avenues, the new **50th Street Commons** is a tiny, public-access park with an engaging waterfall opened by none other than the MTA (it's actually part of a ventilation facility).

Seagram Building

375 Park Ave, between 52nd and 53rd sts • Subway E, M to Lexington Ave–53rd St

It may be difficult at first to see the originality of the **Seagram Building** among the architectural ostentation of its neighbours. Designed by Mies van der Rohe and Philip Johnson, and built in 1958, this was the seminal curtain-wall skyscraper: deceptively simple and cleverly detailed, with floors supported internally rather than by the building's walls, allowing a skin of smoky glass and whisky-bronze metal. Although the facade has now weathered to a dull black, it remains the supreme example of Modernist reason. The **plaza**, an open forecourt designed to set the building apart from its neighbours and display it to advantage, was such a success as a public space that the city revised the zoning laws to encourage other high-rise builders to supply similar plazas.

Lever House

390 Park Ave, between 53rd and 54th sts • Subway E, M to Lexington Ave–53rd St

Across Park Avenue between 53rd and 54th streets is **Lever House**, the building that set the Modernist ball rolling on Park Avenue when it was constructed in 1952. Back then, the two right-angled slabs that form a steel-and-glass bookend seemed revolutionary when compared with the surrounding buildings. Its vintage appeal helps to make *Casa Lever*, the Italian restaurant on the ground floor (and one with some funky design touches itself), a welcome spot for a drink or meal.

Lexington Avenue

One block east of Park Avenue, **Lexington Avenue** marks a sort of border between East Side elegance and the everyday avenues closer to the East River. It roars into life around 42nd Street and the Chrysler Building, and especially through the mid-40s, where commuters swarm around Grand Central Terminal. From there, Lexington lurches northward past 53rd Street and the towering aluminium-and-glass **Citigroup Center**, to the bulk of **Bloomingdale's** department store at 59th Street, which marks the end of the avenue's Midtown stretch of highlights.

10

Chrysler Building

405 Lexington Ave, at 42nd St • Lobby Mon–Fri 8am–6pm • Subway S, #4, #5, #6, #7 to Grand Central-42nd St

The **Chrysler Building** dates from 1930, a time when architects married prestige with grace and style. For a fleeting moment, this was the world's tallest building; it was surpassed by the Empire State Building in 1931, and is currently tied with the new Times building for third tallest in the city. However, since the rediscovery of Art Deco, it has become one of Manhattan's best-loved structures. The building's car-motif friezes, hood-ornament gargoyles, radiator-grille spire, and the fact that the entire building is almost completely fashioned from stainless steel, evokes the golden age of motoring. Its designer, William Van Alen, indulged in a feud with an erstwhile partner, H. Craig Severance, who was designing a building at 40 Wall St at the same time. Each was determined to have the higher skyscraper. Van Alen secretly built the stainless-steel spire inside the Chrysler's crown, and when 40 Wall St finally topped out a few feet higher than the Chrysler, Van Alen popped the 185ft spire out through the top of the building and won the day.

The Chrysler Corporation moved out decades ago, and for a while the building was allowed to decline by a company that didn't wholly appreciate its spirit; fortunately, buyers in the late 1990s took more care and began restoration, while also renovating the **Chrysler Building East** (666 Third Ave), to a plan by Philip Johnson. The lobby (of the main Chrysler Building, that is), once a car showroom, is all you can see, but that's enough in itself. The opulent walls are covered in African marble; the ceiling shows a realistic, if rather faded, study of airplanes, machines and brawny builders who worked on the tower; and the lift doors have magnificent inlaid-wood designs.

Chanin and Mobil buildings

On the south side of 42nd Street flanking Lexington Avenue are two more noteworthy buildings. The **Chanin Building**, at 122 E 42nd St, on the right, is another Art Deco monument, cut with terracotta carvings of leaves, tendrils and sea creatures. Also interesting is the design of the weighty **Mobil Building** at no. 150. Built in 1956, it was the first metal-clad office building in the world. Made with seven thousand panels of chromium-nickel stainless steel, it was designed to enable the wind to keep it clean.

General Electric Building

570 Lexington Ave, at 51st St • Subway #6 to 51st St

Directly behind St Bartholomew's Church (see opposite), the spiky-topped **General Electric Building** seems like a wild extension of the church, its slender shaft rising to a meshed crown of abstract sparks and lightning strokes that symbolize the radio waves used by its original owner, RCA. Not to be confused with the GE Building, better known as 30 Rock (see p.127), this is another Art Deco delight, with nickel-silver ornamentation, carved red marble and a lobby with a vaulted ceiling.

Citigroup Center

153 East 53rd St, between Lexington and Third aves • Subway E, M to Lexington Ave-53rd St

Just as the Chrysler Building dominates the lower stretches of Lexington Avenue, the chisel-topped **Citigroup Center** (better known by its former name of Citicorp Center) towers above northern Midtown. Opened in 1978, the building, now one of New York's most conspicuous landmarks, looks as if it is sheathed in shiny graph paper. Its slanted roof was designed to house solar panels and provide power, but the idea was ahead of the technology and Citicorp, as the company was previously called, had to satisfy itself by adopting the distinctive top as a corporate logo.

St Peter's Lutheran Church

619 Lexington Ave, at 54th St • Ⓦ saintpeters.org • Subway E, M to Lexington Ave-53rd St

Hiding under one corner of Citigroup Center is **St Peter's Lutheran Church**, known as "the Jazz Church" for being the venue of many a jazz musician's funeral. It's also host to a long-running jazz-tinged vespers service on Sundays at 5pm, and there are jazz performances lunchtime on Wednesdays, as well as on Thursdays through summer, plus the occasional evening concert. The tiny church was built to replace the one demolished to make way for Citicorp, and part of the deal was that the church had to stand out from the Center – which explains the granite material. The minimalist, thoroughly modern interior includes sculptor Louise Nevelson's white-walled **Erol Beker Chapel of the Good Shepherd**. Another Nevelson sculpture (*Night Presence IV*) can be seen at East 92nd Street, on the median running down Park Avenue.

Central Synagogue

652 Lexington Ave, at East 55th St • Tues & Wed noon–2pm, tours Wed 12.45pm, organ concert Tues 12.30pm • Free • ☎ 212 838 5122, Ⓦ centralsynagogue.org • Subway E, M to Lexington Ave-53rd St

Striking in its Moorish appearance, the landmark structure that's home to the Reformed **Central Synagogue** was built in 1870–72 by German immigrant Henry Fernbach. The oldest continually used Jewish house of worship in the city, it was nearly razed to the ground in a 1998 blaze; only the ark, a few pews and some of the floor tiles remained, give or take. After three years of extensive rebuilding it reopened, with remade stained-glass windows, a new organ and a markedly different interior design.

Third, Second and First avenues

The construction of the Citigroup Center spurred the development of **Third Avenue** in the late 1970s. One 1980s postmodern entry on that stretch, the so-called **Lipstick Building** at no. 885, is a tiered, oval-shaped steel tower created by Philip Johnson and John Burgee; it also holds the former offices of disgraced (and incarcerated) Ponzischeme broker Bernard Madoff. Nightlife, however, congregates on **Second Avenue**, which also has some architectural attractions lying on or around 42nd Street.

Daily News Building

220 E 42nd St • Closed Sat & Sun • Subway S, #4, #5, #6, #7 to Grand Central-42nd St

The stone facade of the sombre yet elegant former **Daily News Building** fronts a surprising Art Deco interior. The most impressive remnant of the original 1929 decor is a large globe encased in a lighted circular frame (with updated geography), made famous by the 1970s and '80s Superman movies when the Daily News Building appropriately housed the *Daily Planet*. The tabloid after which the building is named has since moved to 4 New York Plaza.

Ford Foundation Building

320 E 43rd St, between First and Second aves • Subway S, #4, #5, #6, #7 to Grand Central-42nd St

Just north and around the corner from the Daily News Building is one of the city's most peaceful (if surreal) spaces – the **Ford Foundation Building**. Built in 1967, the building featured the first of the atria that are now commonplace across Manhattan. Structurally, the atrium is a giant greenhouse, gracefully supported by soaring granite columns and edged with two walls of offices visible through the windows. This subtropical garden, which changes with the seasons, was one of the first attempts to create a "natural" environment inside a building, and it's astonishingly quiet. 42nd Street is no more than a murmur outside, and all you can hear is the burble of water, the echo of voices, and the clipped clack of feet on the brick walkways. The indoor/outdoor experience here is one of New York City's great architectural coups.

10

Tudor City

At the east end of 42nd Street, steps lead up to the 1925 **Tudor City**, which rises behind a tiny tree-filled park. With coats of arms, leaded glass and neat neighbourhood shops, this area is the very picture of self-contained residential respectability. It's an official historic district to boot.

United Nations Headquarters

First Ave, between 42nd and 48th sts, visitor centre at First Ave and 46th St • Guided tours Mon–Fri 9am–4.30pm; tours last 45min • $22, ages 5–12 $13, 5 and under not allowed; bring ID and call ahead to see if anything is off limits that day • ☎ 212 963 8687, ⓦ visit.un.org • Subway S, #4, #5, #6, #7 to Grand Central-42nd St

Some see the **United Nations Headquarters** – built after World War II, when John D. Rockefeller, Jr donated $8.5 million to buy the eighteen-acre East River site – as one of the major sights of New York. Others, often those who've been there, are not so complimentary.

The complex consists of three main sites – the thin, glass-curtained slab of the **Secretariat**; the sweeping curve of the **General Assembly Building**, whose renovated chambers can accommodate 193 national delegations; and the low-rise **Conference Wing**, which connects the other two structures. Construction on the complex began in 1949 and finished in 1963, the product of a suitably international team of architects that included Le Corbusier – though he pulled out before work was completed.

Council chambers visited on the tour include the **Security Council**, the **Economic and Social Council** and the **Trusteeship Council** – all of which are similarly retro (note the clunky machinery of the journalists' areas) and sport some intriguing Marxist murals. More revealing are some thoughtful exhibition spaces and artful country gifts on view, including an intricate ivory carving from China and a huge (12ft by 15ft) stained-glass window by artist Marc Chagall, commissioned in 1964 as a memorial to Dag Hammarskjold, the second Secretary-General of the United Nations. Where the UN HQ has real class is in its beautiful **gardens**, with their modern sculptures (note the *Knotted Gun*, a piece by Swedish sculptor Carl Fredrik Reuterswärd that honours John Lennon, in front of the visitors' entrance) and views of the East River.

Beekman Place and Sutton Place

Outside of the environs of the UN, **First Avenue** has a certain looseness that's a relief after the concrete claustrophobia of Midtown. **Beekman Place** (49th to 51st sts between First Ave and the East River) is quieter still, a beguiling enclave of garbled styles. Similar, though not quite as intimate, is **Sutton Place**, which stretches from 53rd to 59th streets between First Avenue and the East River. Originally built for the lordly Morgans and Vanderbilts in 1875, Sutton Place increases in elegance as you move north. The UN Secretary-General has an official residence at 3 Sutton Place – some 14,000 square feet of living space – and current and past residents include the likes of Sigourney Weaver and I.M. Pei. For the real *crème de la crème*, **Riverview Terrace**, off 58th Street at the river, is a (very) private block-long street filled with a handful of pricey townhouses, though you can sit in (the public) Sutton Place Park for a view of the houses and the river.

MACY'S

Midtown West

Between West 30th and 59th streets and west of Sixth Avenue, much of Midtown Manhattan is enthralling, noisy and garish, packed with attractions meant to entertain legions of tourists. The heart of Midtown West is Times Square, where jostling crowds and huge neon signs assault the senses, and New York City reaches its commercial zenith. South of Times Square is the business-oriented Garment District, while just north of the once "naughty, bawdy 42nd Street", the Theater District offers the most impressive concentration of live theatre in the world. West beyond Eighth Avenue, the buzzing forces of gentrification have shifted the nature of Hell's Kitchen; back over in the centre of the island, Sixth Avenue's blend of cultural and corporate New York is good for a stroll.

ARRIVAL AND DEPARTURE

By public transport Nearly every subway, save the East Side's #4/#5/#6, goes to Midtown West. Central stops include: the B, D, F, M, N, Q, R, W to 34th St-Herald Square; the N, Q, R, S, W, #1, #2, #3, #7 to Times Square-42nd St; and, at the northern end, the A, B, C, D, #1 to 59th St-Columbus Circle. And, of course, this is the spot for arrivals and departures to and from Penn Station (trains) and Port Authority (buses).

The Garment District

Squeezing in between Sixth and Eighth avenues from West 30th to 42nd streets, the **Garment District** (sometimes referred to as the Fashion District), home to the twin modern monsters of Penn Station and Madison Square Garden, offers little of interest to the casual visitor.

With the rise in foreign production, fewer and fewer garments are put together in this tiny (and ever-diminishing) quarter, though a strong "made in America" revival keeps around seven thousand workers employed in the district. Walking around, you might just think nothing at all is going on: outlets are almost entirely wholesale and don't bother to woo customers, and the only visible evidence of the industry is the racks of clothes shunted around on the street and occasional bins of off-cuts that give the area the look of an open-air rummage sale. If you want a look behind the scenes, consider signing up for a free Garment District walking tour (Ⓦmikesnyctours.com).

One of the benefits of walking through this part of town is taking advantage of the designers' sample sales, where floor samples and models' castoffs are sold to the public at cheap prices (see box, p.385).

11

Greeley Square

Sixth Avenue collides with Broadway just below West 34th Street, making an unremarkable triangle with the somewhat overblown title of **Greeley Square**, in honour of Horace Greeley, founder of the *New York Tribune* newspaper. One could make the case that Greeley deserves better: known for his rallying call to the youth of the nineteenth century ("Go West, young man!"), he also supported the rights of women and trade unions, denounced slavery and capital punishment, and commissioned a weekly column from Karl Marx.

Herald Square

Herald Square opposes Greeley Square across 34th Street, in a continuation of the once fierce rivalry between the *New York Herald* newspaper and Horace Greeley's *Tribune*. (The two papers merged in 1924 to form the *New York Herald Tribune*, which was published until 1967.) During the 1890s, this was the Tenderloin area, with dance halls, brothels and rough bars like *Satan's Circus* and the *Burnt Rag* thriving beside the elevated railway that ran up Sixth Avenue. These days its streets are congested with consumers, many heading for the massive Macy's department store adjacent to the square.

MIDTOWN WEST HIGHLIGHTS

Broadway Theatre TKTS has half-price seats for many of the area's restored theatres. See p.354
Drama Book Shop Browse scripts and theatre books at this Tony Award-winning store. See p.390
Public art Admire modern works by Sol LeWitt and Roy Lichtenstein at AXA Equitable Center and Maya Lin at Penn Station. See p.148 & p.144
Ramen Heaven in a bowl of noodles at *Ippudo, Ivan Ramen* or *Totto Ramen*. See p.292, p.289 & p.307
Rudy's A lively bar for cheap pints and free hot dogs. See p.339

EATING

Ariana Afghan Kebab	5
Aureole	25
Becco	16
The Burger Joint	4
Chez Napoleon	12
Churrascaria Plataforma	8
City Kitchen	22
City Sandwich	19
Danji	7
Don Antonio by Starita	13
Esca	24
Gazala's Place	14
Gloria	4
Go! Go! Curry	26
Gotham West Market	1
Joe Allen	17
Le Bernardin	10
Larb Ubol	27
Little Pie Company	23
Margon	18
NY Pizza Suprema	28
Poseidon Greek Bakery	20
Pure Thai Cookhouse	9
Russian Tea Room	1
Samovar	
Totto Ramen	6
Vynl	11
Yakitori Totto	3

DRINKING AND NIGHTLIFE

BARS

Ardesia	5
Hellcat Annie's	13
Jimmy's Corner	17
Kashkaval	1
North River Lobster Company	20
Press Lounge	10
Rudy's	14
Rum House	11
Russian Vodka Room	4

CLUBS

Bowlmor	16
Lucky Strike Lanes	19
Swing 46	12

LIVE MUSIC VENUES

B.B. King Blues Club & Grill	18
Birdland	15
Hammerstein Ballroom	21
Iridium	8

LGBT BARS & CLUBS

Atlas Social Club	7
Boxers	9
Flaming Saddles	2
Industry	3
Therapy	6

ACCOMMODATION

414 Hotel	9
Ameritania at Times Square	2
Casablanca Hotel	13
citizenM New York Times Square	4
Distrikt	18
Edison	8
The French Quarters	10
Hilton Times Square	17
Kimpton Ink48 Hotel	6
Kimpton Muse Hotel	11
Knickerbocker	14
Mayfair	5
Night Times Square	7
Novotel	3
The Out NYC	15
The Quin	1
Refinery Hotel	19
Room Mate Grace	12
Stewart Hotel	20
Yotel	16

SHOPPING

Annex Markets	5
B&H Photo Video	8
Drama Bookshop	4
Forever 21	2
H&M	7
Kinokuniya Bookstore	3
Macy's	6
M&M's World	1

MIDTOWN WEST

Macy's

151 W 34th St • Mon & Thurs–Sat 10am–10pm, Tues & Wed 10am–11pm, Sun 10am–9pm • ☎ 212 695 4400, ⓦ macys.com • Subway B, D, F, M, N, Q, R, W to 34th St-Herald Square

Macy's bills itself as "the world's largest store", which is only somewhat hyperbolic, considering the building takes up an entire city block and offers well over one million square feet of selling space (the South Korean flagship of Shinsegae actually holds the title). Founded in 1858, the store moved to its current location in 1902, although it wasn't until the 1980s that Macy's went fashionably upmarket, with designers – such as Tommy Hilfiger – building their own shops in-store. Macy's fortunes declined dramatically, however, when the economy went into a tailspin in 1990, but scrambled out of its 1992 bankruptcy in the nick of time, complete with a debt-restructuring plan that allowed it to continue financing its famed annual Thanksgiving Day Parade (see p.409). That nadir seems a far cry from the $400 million renovation that was completed in 2015, which added the "world's largest shoe floor", a panoply of places to eat, an official NYC visitor center (Mon–Fri 9am–7pm, Sat 10am–7pm, Sun 11am–7pm) and a new Santaland for the holidays.

11

Penn Station and Madison Square Garden

The blocks between Seventh and Eighth aves, and West 31st and West 33rd sts • Subway A, C, E, #1, #2, #3 to 34th St-Penn Station

The most prominent landmark in the Garment District, the **Penn Station and Madison Square Garden** complex is a combined box-and-drum structure. At the same time as its train-station belly swallows up millions of commuters, its above-ground facilities, expensively refurbished in the past three years, house Knicks' basketball and Rangers' hockey games, as well as professional wrestling and boxing matches (see p.395).

There's nothing memorable about Penn Station (or Pennsylvania Station, as it is formally known); its grimy **subterranean levels** are an example of just about everything that's wrong with the subway. The original 1910 train station, which brought an air of dignity to the neighbourhood and set the stage for the ornate General Post Office and other elaborate belle-époque structures, was demolished in 1963 to make way for this monstrous structure (see box below). One of McKim, Mead, and White's greatest designs, the station's original edifice reworked the ideas of the Roman Baths of Caracalla to awesome effect: the floors of the grand arcade were pink marble, the walls pink granite. Glass floor tiles in the main waiting room allowed light from the glass roof to flow through to the trains and platforms below. Architectural historian Vincent Scully lamented the differences in the two structures in the 1960s, saying, "Through it one entered the city like a god... One scuttles in now like a rat." Some of Penn Station's

---

OLD PENN STATION AND THE LANDMARKS PRESERVATION LAW

When the old **Penn Station** was demolished in 1963 to expand the Madison Square Garden sports complex, the notion of conservation was only a gleam in the eye of its middle-class supporters, at the time few and far between, but ten years later a broad-based power group. Despite the vocal opposition of a few, "modernization" was the theme of the day – so much so that almost nothing of the original building was saved. A number of the carefully crafted statues and decorations actually became landfill for New Jersey's Meadowlands complex just across the Hudson River.

At around the same time, the Singer Building, an early, graceful skyscraper in the Financial District, was demolished to make way for the hulking US Steel Building. In the end, it was public disgust with the wanton destruction of these two buildings that brought about the passing of the **Landmarks Preservation Law**. This act ensures that buildings granted landmark status – a designation based on aesthetic value or historical importance – cannot be destroyed or even altered. The law goes beyond protecting buildings, and also applies to districts, such as Fort Greene and Soho, as well as "scenic" landmarks, including Verdi Square at Broadway and West 73rd Street.

lost lustre may be restored when – or rather, if – an expanded station opens in the General Post Office building (see below); in the meantime, there are major sections of the existing station undergoing work due to structural problems.

Glimpses of the **original structure** are visible in photos hanging in the Amtrak waiting area of today's Penn Station, as well as in the four-faced clock on display in the main Long Island Railroad (LIRR) ticket area (downstairs, near the Seventh Avenue entrance at West 32nd Street). Andrew Leicester's 1994 *Ghost Series* lines the walls: five terracotta murals saluting the Corinthian and Ionic columns of the old Penn Station. Also look for a rendering of Adolph A. Weinman's sculpture *Day & Night*, an ornate statue surrounding a clock that welcomed passengers at the old station's entrance. Be sure to look above your head in the LIRR ticket area for Maya Lin's *Eclipsed Time*, a sculpture of glass, aluminium and fibre optics that alludes to the immeasurability of time with random number patterns.

General Post Office

11

421 Eighth Ave, between 31st and 33rd sts • Mon–Fri 7am–10pm, Sat 9am–9pm, Sun 11am–7pm • Subway A, C, E, #1, #2, #3 to 34th St-Penn Station

Immediately behind Penn Station, the **General Post Office** (aka the James A. Farley Post Office) is a 1913 McKim, Mead, and White structure that survived the push for modernization, and stands as a relic from an era when municipal pride was all about making statements – the block-and-a-half-long building is fronted by twenty Corinthian columns and steps spanning the length of the colonnade. There's still a working post-office branch here – one where you'll find plenty of taxpayers filing up until midnight on April 15 – although the main sorting stations have moved into more modern spaces farther west. That said, the building is no architectural dinosaur: a new concourse for the Long Island Railroad was recently completed and plans to refit the interior for a new Amtrak station, keeping the original exterior preserved, are in the works (though these and other redevelopment plans have moved forward in fits and starts). If all goes well, the **Moynihan Train Hall** (after the late New York State Senator Daniel Patrick Moynihan) is due for completion by 2020.

Port Authority Bus Terminal

625 Eighth Ave, from West 40th to West 42nd sts • Subway A, C, E to 42nd St-Port Authority Bus Terminal

One of Midtown's more reviled landmarks, the **Port Authority Bus Terminal Building** crouches on Eighth Avenue for a few city blocks. Not long ago, it served as a magnet for down-and-outs, but it is remarkably safe now – if in need of upgrading, which is reportedly on the table. There's bowling (see p.400), a statue honouring Ralph Kramden (Jackie Gleason's character in *The Honeymooners*) and not much reason to hang around; Greyhound buses leave from here, as do several other regional services.

Times Square

42nd Street meets Broadway at the southern outskirts of **Times Square**, the fulcrum for the Theater District, where the constantly pulsating neon conjures up the notion of a beating heart for Manhattan. The area is certainly always alive with activity. Traditionally a melting pot of debauchery, depravity and fun, for decades the quarter was a place where out-of-towners provided easy pickings for petty criminals, drug dealers and prostitutes. Most of Times Square's legendary pornography and crime are long gone, replaced by sanitized superstores, high-rise office buildings and boutique hotels that have killed off the square's historically greasy appeal. More corporate big-ticket attractions have arrived or are on the way, like **National Geographic Encounter: Ocean Odyssey** and the **NFL Experience Times Square** (both opening after this guide goes to press). This doesn't mean, though, that the area is without charm, and hundreds of thousands of people still mass here every New Year's Eve, when a giant sparkling ball drops from the top of Times Tower on the stroke of midnight. If you have never seen Times Square, plan your first visit for after dark. Without passing through the square, take a taxi to 57th and Broadway (or the subway to, say, Columbus Circle) and start walking south. The spectacle will open out before your eyes, slowly at first, and then with a rush of energy and animation.

Orientation

Not actually a square at all, Times Square is formed by the intersection between arrow-straight Seventh Avenue and left-leaning Broadway; the latter more or less follows true north through much of the island, which tilts to the northeast. So narrow is the angle between these two thoroughfares that Broadway, which meets Seventh Avenue at 43rd Street, does not begin to strike off on its own again until 48th Street, just above the traffic island of Duffy Square. That stretch has been made into a pedestrianized plaza in an effort to improve traffic flow; there's seating along the way as well. On and off the street are the theatres that host big plays and musicals.

Brief history

Like nearby Greeley and Herald squares, Times Square took its name from a newspaper – *The New York Times* built its offices here in 1904. While the *Herald* and *Tribune* fought each other in ever more vicious circulation battles, the *Times* stood on more restrained ground under the banner "All the news that's fit to print", a policy that has enabled both its survival and its current status as the most powerful newspaper in the country. The newspaper's old headquarters, Times Tower, is at the southernmost end of the square on a small block between 42nd and 43rd streets. Originally an elegant building modelled on Giotto's campanile in Florence, the famous zipper sign displaying the news of the world was added in 1928. In 1965, the building was "skinned" and covered with the lifeless marble slabs visible today. The paper's offices have long since moved, and are now in a 52-storey Renzo Piano tower across from the Port Authority, with most of the printing done in College Point, Queens.

Gulliver's Gate

216 W 44th St • Daily: May–Sept 9am–10pm; Oct–April 10am–8pm • Tickets ⓦ gulliversgate.com • Subway N, Q, R, W, S, #1, #2, #3, #7 to Times Square-42nd St; A, C, E to 42nd St-Times Square

One of the newer – and more unusual, which is saying something – sights in Times Square, **Gulliver's Gate** attempts to render the world's regions and landmarks in miniature, much of it through the magic of 3D printing. The tiny models are not to scale nor do they follow traditional geography (or time; note Zeus on Olympus and NYC's West Village looking like something from Wild West times), but they are decent fun to investigate; there's even running water in the Panama Canal and lots of bits that move around with the turn of a key. Those with money to burn can get a scan of themselves done in the enormous 3D printer and be placed in miniature in the exhibit (for a mere $44).

The Theater District

Though many of the theatres hosting big-budget musicals and dramas considered to be "Broadway shows" are not technically on the eponymous avenue, they are, for the most part, located within a couple of blocks of it in the West 40s (concentrated on 44th and 45th sts), the heart of New York's **Theater District**. The majority of the great venues have been destroyed to make way for office buildings; however, some of the old grandeur still survives in the forty or so that remain (see box, p.146).

FIVE DISTINCTIVE BROADWAY THEATRES

When choosing a **Broadway show**, you won't necessarily be doing it by virtue of the venue; nevertheless, these theatres all stand out in various ways – regardless of what's on. The Lyceum, Music Box and Shubert are among the 25 Broadway theatres that are designated landmarks.

Helen Hayes Theatre 240 W 44th St, between Seventh and Eighth aves. This modest 1912 theatre is the smallest of the Broadway houses – recent renovations inside and out have modernized the simple Federal-style structure.

Lyceum Theatre 149 W 45th St, between Broadway and Seventh Ave. Original facade intact, the Lyceum is one of the area's few theatres whose lobby you can poke around without having bought a ticket.

Music Box Theatre 239 W 45th St between Seventh and Eighth aves. The exterior looks like it forms a stage, and the box office marquee is a cool, Art Deco touch.

New Victory Theater 209 W 42nd St, between Seventh and Eighth aves. First of the historic theatres to be refurbished – and sanitized – (by Disney) for the new-look Times Square more than twenty years ago; its programming is family oriented (see p.415).

Shubert Theatre 225 W 44th St, between Seventh and Eighth aves. This playhouse, which hosted *A Chorus Line* during its fifteen-year run (the longest-running show when it closed, though that record has since been surpassed multiple times), has a magnificent interior that belies its simple outward appearance.

Duffy Square

Bordered by Broadway and Seventh Ave, 45th and 47th sts • Subway N, Q, R, S, W, #1, #2, #3, #7 to Times Square-42nd St

Not much to look at itself, **Duffy Square** offers an excellent view of Times Square's lights, mega-hotels, theme stores and restaurants. A glass "stairway to nowhere", modest in comparison, is balanced on the renovated **TKTS booth**, which sells half-price, same-day tickets for Broadway shows, whose exorbitant prices these days make a visit to TKTS a necessity (see p.354). A lifelike statue of Broadway's doyen George M. Cohan looks on, while at eye level you can find enough gifts in the souvenir shops for your five hundred closest friends.

Brill Building

1619 Broadway; at 49th St • Subway #1 to 50th St; N, R, W to 49th St

For years a crucial hub in New York's entertainment business, the **Brill Building** is synonymous with the pop music sound of the 1960s. Here (and at a few nearby offices), songwriters such as Burt Bacharach and Hal David, Carole King, Barry Mann and Phil Spector cranked out hit after hit that your parents loved, like *You've Lost That Lovin' Feelin'* and *Walk on By*. Unfortunately, running those songs through your head is about all you can do here, save for admire the fine entrance. Note, however, that the block on 48th Street, between Sixth and Seventh avenues, was the city's nominal music row – not that any stores remain from the glory days.

Ed Sullivan Theater

1697 Broadway, between 53rd and 54th sts • Subway B, D, E to Seventh Ave

Past 50th Street, it's the **Ed Sullivan Theater** that attracts the most people on this stretch of Broadway. This is host to the *Late Show* recordings (see box, p.360), now with Stephen Colbert presiding rather than David Letterman – and, fifty-odd years ago, where the *Ed Sullivan Show* was held. You'll frequently see a line of folks waiting to get in, or just rubbernecking while taking pictures in front of the marquee.

Hell's Kitchen

Sprawling across the blocks west of Times Square to the Hudson River, between 30th and 59th streets, lies Clinton (named for nineteenth-century Governor Dewitt Clinton), more famously known as **Hell's Kitchen**, an area centred on the restaurants, bars and ethnic delis of Ninth Avenue – the staging set for the excellent Ninth Avenue International Food Festival (ⓦninthavenuefoodfestival.com) each May. The southern end of the neighbourhood is now the northern terminus for the High Line (see p.108).

From Eighth Avenue, walk west on 46th Street, so-called Restaurant Row – the area's preferred haunt for pre- and post-theatre dining, even though most of the strip's places to eat are mediocre at best – to arrive in the neighbourhood. The Gothic, red **St Clement's Episcopal Church**, at 423 W 46th St (ⓦstclementsnyc.org), doubles as a community theatre, very much in keeping with the local vibe.

Brief history

Among New York's most violent and lurid neighbourhoods at one time, Hell's Kitchen was purportedly named for a tenement at 54th Street and Tenth Avenue. More commonly, the term has been attributed to a veteran policeman who went by the sobriquet "**Dutch Fred the Cop**". In response to his young partner's comment – while watching a riot – that the place was hell, Fred reportedly replied, "Hell's a mild climate. This is Hell's kitchen." The area originally contained slaughterhouses and factories that made soap and glue, with sections named "Misery Lane" and "Poverty Row". Irish immigrants were the first inhabitants; Greeks, Puerto Ricans and African Americans soon joined them. Amid the overcrowding, tensions rapidly developed between (and within) ethnic groups – the rough-and-tumble neighbourhood was popularized in the musical *West Side Story* (1957). A violent Irish gang, the Westies, claimed the streets in the 1970s and early 1980s, but the area has since been cleaned up – even gentrified. Trim residential streets counter the odd tatty block, and construction and renovation of luxury apartments and hotels occur at sometimes breakneck speed. Along with other gentrifiers, there's now a substantial gay community, with as many gay bars and nightspots as in Chelsea or the East Village.

11

Intrepid Sea, Air & Space Museum

West 46th St and Twelfth Ave at Pier 86 • April–Oct Mon–Fri 10am–5pm, Sat & Sun 10am–6pm; Nov–March daily 10am–5pm • $33 • ❶ 212 245 0072, ⓦ intrepidmuseum.org • Subway A, C, E to 42nd St-Port Authority; C, E to 50th St

If you continue west to the river from Times Square, you'll reach the **Intrepid Sea, Air & Space Museum**. This huge (900ft-long) old aircraft carrier has a distinguished history: it picked up capsules from the Mercury and Gemini space missions and made several tours to Vietnam. It holds an array of modern and vintage air- and sea-craft, including the A-12 *Blackbird*, the world's fastest spy plane, and the USS *Growler*, the only guided-missile submarine open to the public. Interactive exhibits and simulators dominate the interior, but make sure to explore further into the bowels of the carrier,

---

WHERE THE STREETS HAVE TWO NAMES

Throughout Midtown (and all the city, really), you'll find **secondary street names** of all stripes: some descriptive, like **Little Brazil** (W 45th between Fifth and Sixth aves) and **Diamond and Jewelry Way** (47th St between Fifth and Sixth aves); some honorary, say, **Jerry Orbach Way** (W 53rd St, at Eighth Ave) or **W.C. Handy Place** (52nd St between Sixth and Seventh aves); and some a bit nonsensical. Take **Sixth-and-a-Half Avenue**, a pedestrianized passageway that cuts through buildings from 51st Street up to 57th Street, in between Sixth and Seventh avenues (though take note: you can keep cutting through buildings mid-block down to 48th Street; on that last part, there's a short glass tunnel enveloped by a waterfall – quite a nice touch). It was officially created in 2012 for the benefit of walkers, but the space had of course existed for years – this just put the secret to light. No traffic lights, middle-of-the-street crosswalks… and, of course, easier access to the commercial establishments tucked along the way.

where you can see the crew's dining and sleeping quarters, the anchor room and a lot of navigational gadgets. A retired *Concorde*, formerly operated by British Airways, is also at the pier, though the stats about the aircraft are more remarkable than an inspection of the craft itself. It shares pride of place with the space shuttle *Enterprise*; built in 1976 as a test orbiter, it was never space-ready and has spent the last 25-plus years as property of the Smithsonian Institution. If you're visiting at the end of May, **Fleet Week** (the week leading up to Memorial Day) is a big deal here, and deservedly so, with ships visiting from all corners of the globe, as well as military demonstrations and competitions. In early September (Labor Day weekend), an annual **tugboat festival** is held at the pier next door.

Sixth Avenue

East of Times Square, **Sixth Avenue** is officially named Avenue of the Americas but no New Yorker ever calls it that. While there's little of the ground-floor glitter of Fifth or the razzmatazz of Broadway, the street does more or less separate the business side of Midtown East from the theatre side of Midtown West (even though Fifth Avenue is where the east–west addresses switch).

Rockefeller Center Extension

1211–1271 Sixth Ave, between 47th and 51st sts • Subway B, D, F, M to 47-50th sts-Rockefeller Center

The **Rockefeller Center Extension** defines the Sixth Avenue stretch from 47th to 51st streets and gives it whatever visual excitement exists. Following the **Time-Life Building** at 50th Street, three near-identical buildings went up in the 1970s: **Exxon Building**, at no. 1251, **McGraw-Hill Building II**, at no. 1221, and **News Corp Building**, at no. 1211. Though they have none of the romance or style of their predecessor, they at least possess the monumentality. Backing onto Rockefeller Center proper (see p.127), the repeated statement of each building comes over with some power.

AXA Equitable Center

Occupying the block bordered by Sixth and Seventh aves and 51st and 52nd sts • Subway B, D, F, M to 47-50th sts-Rockefeller Center; B, D, E to Seventh Ave

The **AXA Equitable Center** has plenty for the eye in the form of its public art. The entrance to the UBS Building (one part of the Center), at 1285 Sixth Ave, has a small gallery that occasionally rotates exhibits; the mid-block galleria, connecting pedestrians to the Equitable Tower, is highlighted by a series of Sol LeWitt murals, while Roy Lichtenstein's *Mural with Blue Brushtroke* provides a rush of colour for the atrium at 787 Seventh Ave.

57th Street

The area just around **57th Street** from Broadway over to Fifth Avenue competes with Soho and Chelsea as a centre for upmarket art sales. **Galleries** here (see p.375) are noticeably snootier than their downtown relations, and some require appointments for viewings.

Hearst Tower

300 W 57th St, at Eighth Ave • Subway A, B, C, D, #1 to 59th St-Columbus Circle

If you head west from Carnegie Hall on 57th Street, at the intersection with Eighth Avenue you'll hit the **Hearst World Headquarters**, which had its 597ft, Norman Foster-designed **tower** completed in June 2006. The faceted steel-and-glass skyscraper, with its distinctive triangular pattern, is incongruously attached atop a multi-style six-storey base of precast limestone (built eighty years earlier). It is certified as one of the most environmentally friendly high-rise buildings ever constructed, employing technologies to reduce pollution and energy consumption, while fully utilizing renewable energy sources.

Art Students League of New York

215 W 57th St, between Broadway and Seventh Ave • Mon–Fri 9am–8pm, Sat 9am–4pm (Sept–Dec also Sun 9am–4pm) • ⓦ theartstudentsleague.org • Subway N, Q, R, W to 57th St

One gallery that provides something other than a quick, uncomfortable browse is the **Art Students League**, built in 1892 by Henry J. Hardenbergh (who later built the *Plaza Hotel*) to mimic Francis the First's hunting lodge at Fontainebleau. Its pedigree is impressive; Ben Shahn and Donald Judd are among the artists who trained here. Besides offering inexpensive art classes to the public, the League allows visitors the chance to observe the instructors and students in action.

Carnegie Hall

57th St at Seventh Ave (there are separate entrances for the box office, museum and Zankel Hall) • Tours Oct–May only, typically Mon–Fri 11.30am, 12.30pm, 2pm & 3pm, Sat 11.30am & 12.30pm, Sun 12.30pm, though call or check web for current schedule, as it can change with frequency; 1hr; $17 • Tours ☎ 212 903 9765, concert tickets ☎ 212 247 7800, ⓦ carnegiehall.org • Subway N, Q, R, W to 57th St

11

Stately **Carnegie Hall** is one of the world's greatest concert venues, revered by musicians and audiences alike. The Renaissance-inspired structure was built in the 1890s by steel magnate and self-styled "improver of mankind" Andrew Carnegie, and the still-superb acoustics ensure full houses most of the year. Tchaikovsky conducted the programme on opening night and Mahler, Rachmaninov, Toscanini, Frank Sinatra and Judy Garland have all performed here (not to mention Duke Ellington, Billie Holiday, the Beatles, Spinal Tap and Lady Gaga). If you're not here for a show, you can take a tour, which concludes in the small, second-floor gallery of memorabilia – a part that's actually open to the public for free.

North to Central Park

A few Carnegie Hall-vicinity apartment buildings are worth a gander on the way to Central Park. An absolute riot of terracotta embellishments cover the facade of **Alwyn Court**, at 180 W 58th St, though unfortunately you can't enter the building to see the mural and skylight in the courtyard. Around the corner is the **Gainsborough Studios** building, at 222 Central Park South, between Broadway and Seventh Avenue. Built in 1905, it became an official city landmark in 1988 and is notable for the Moravian tiles that dominate the top two floors, as well as the double-storey windows that peer onto Central Park. Note the bust of the building's eponym, English artist **Thomas Gainsborough**, which hovers above the entrance on the facade.

Central Park

"All radiant in the magic atmosphere of art and taste", raved *Harper's* magazine on the occasion of the opening of Central Park in 1876. A slight overstatement, perhaps, though it's fair to say that few people today could imagine New York City without this beloved green parcel. Devotedly used by locals and visited by nearly everyone who spends a few days here, it serves purposes as varied as the folks who take advantage of it: it's an environmental haven; a beach; a playground; a running track; and a venue for pop music, opera, theatre and street entertainers, for a start. The Reservoir divides Central Park in two. The larger southern park holds most of the attractions (and park goers), but the northern tract (above 86th Street) is well worth a visit for its wilder natural setting and dramatically quieter ambience.

Brief history

Poet and newspaper editor **William Cullen Bryant** is credited with first publicizing the idea for an open public space in Manhattan in 1844; seven years later, City Hall finally agreed to carry out his plan, paying $5 million for 840 acres north of the (then) city limits at 38th Street, a desolate swampy area occupied at the time by scattered shantytowns whose residents were evicted as planning began to pick up speed.

After a fierce design contest, **Frederick Law Olmsted and Calvert Vaux** were chosen to create the rural paradise they called "Greensward", an illusion of the countryside smack in the heart of Manhattan. They designed 36 elegant bridges, each unique, and planned an ingenious system of four sunken transverse roads to segregate different kinds of traffic.

It took sixteen years and $14 million ($300 million in today's money) to construct the entire park, though the sapling trees planted here didn't reach their full height for five decades. Central Park opened to the public in 1876. At its opening, the powers that be emphasized that Central Park was a "**people's park**", available to all; initially, many had neither the time nor the money to travel up to 59th Street from their downtown slums and enjoy it, but people eventually started flooding in as the city grew in size and wealth.

The park hit rock bottom in 1973, by which point it had degenerated into a vandalized, crime-infested eyesore on which the bankrupt city had no money to spare. It was only the suggestion that the park be turned over to the National Park Service that mobilized both politicians and local citizens to find funds to refit it, beginning around 1980. The ongoing effort is now overseen by a feisty nonprofit group called the **Central Park Conservancy** (see p.152), which works in conjunction with the city government to maintain the park.

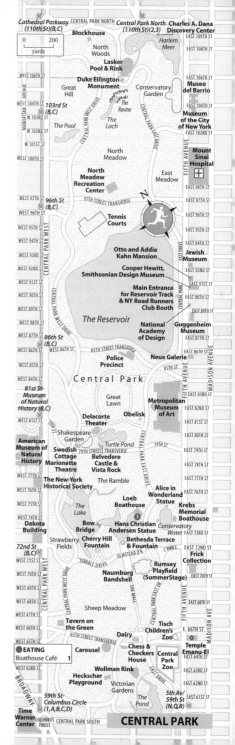

ARRIVAL AND DEPARTURE

By subway The park can be accessed from the east or west sides roughly every six or seven blocks; to see the greatest concentration of sights, your most logical starting places include the A, B, C, D and #1 stop at 59th St-Columbus Circle; the N, Q, R, W at Fifth Ave-59th St; and the B, C stop at 72nd St.

INFORMATION

Visitor centres The nonprofit Central Park Conservancy (☎ 212 310 6600, ⓦ centralparknyc.org), founded in 1980, is dedicated to preserving and managing the park. It runs five visitor centres, which have free maps and other helpful literature. The centres are: the Chess & Checkers House (64th St at mid-park; 10am–5pm; April–March Wed–Sun; ☎ 212 794 4064); the Dairy (65th St at mid-park; daily 10am–5pm; ☎ 212 794 6564); Belvedere Castle (79th St at mid-park; daily 10am–5pm; ☎ 212 772 0288); the North Meadow Recreation Center (mid-park at 97th St; April–June, Sept & Oct Tues–Fri 10am–6pm, Sat & Sun 10am–5pm; July & Aug Mon–Thurs, Sat & Sun 10am–5pm, Fri 10am–6pm; Nov–March Tues–Sun 10am–5pm; ☎ 212 348 4867); and the Charles A. Dana Discovery Center (110th St off Fifth Ave; daily 10am–5pm; ☎ 212 860 1374).

Restrooms Heckscher Playground (61st St at mid-park), Arsenal (64th St at Fifth Ave), *Tavern on the Green* (67th St near Central Park West), Ramble Shed (mid-park at 79th St), the Boat Pond (Conservatory Water), Mineral Springs House (northwest end of Sheep's Meadow), Bethesda Terrace, Loeb Boathouse, the Delacorte Theater, the East 85th Street Playground (aka the Ancient Playground, near Fifth Ave), the Tennis House (94th St at mid-park), the North Meadow Recreation Center, the Conservatory Garden, the Robert Bendheim Playground (East 100th St at Fifth Ave), the Great Hill and the Charles A. Dana Discovery Center.

Urban Park Rangers ☎ 212 628 2345, ⓦ nycgovparks .org. Rangers lead walking tours, give directions, provide necessary first-aid and even organize camping trips.

Safety You should be fine during the day, though always be alert to your surroundings and try to avoid being alone in an isolated part of the park. After dark, stick to busy areas. If you're there for a public event in the evening, make sure to leave when the crowds do. Emergency phone boxes can be found throughout the park and along the four transverses; they connect to the Central Park Precinct.

NAVIGATING THE PARK

Central Park is so enormous that it's nearly impossible to miss entirely and as impossible to cover in one visit. The intricate **footpaths** that meander through the park are some of its greatest successes. If you've lost your way among them, though, there are several tricks to finding it again. Every feature has a name in order that a rendezvous can be precise. Even the bodies of water are differentiated (a loch, a pool, a lake and even a meer) so that there can never be confusion. But if you do need **to figure out where you are**, find the nearest lamppost. The first two digits on the post indicate the number of the nearest cross street, while the last two show where you're nearer the east side (odd numbers) or west side (even). You can pick up free maps at any of the visitor centres (see above) or two dozen freestanding unmanned kiosks throughout the park. Organized walking tours (see p.29) are available from a number of sources, including the Urban Park Rangers and the visitor centres, but almost any stroll, formal or informal, will invariably lead to something interesting.

CYCLING

To make their way around from place to place, people typically either walk (there are no bus routes within the park) or don rollerblades and glide there. Other options include **renting a bike** – West Drive, East Drive and the 72nd Street Cross Drive all have specified car-free hours, allowing you to create various loops around the park in relative freedom. All bicycle rental shops require a credit card or refundable cash deposit.

Danny's Cycles 1690 Second Ave, between 87th and 88th sts ☎ 212 722 2201, ⓦ dannyscycles.com. East of the park (and with an Upper West Side location too, among others), Danny's Cycles offer good hourly rates, at $10–15/hr ($40–60/day).

Master Bike Shop NYC 265 W 72nd St, between Broadway and West End Ave ☎ 212 580 2355, ⓦ masterbikeshop.com. Reputable spot (also well placed for Riverside Park) with very good rates – adult bikes start at $20/4hr and $40/day.

Must See Central Park 56 W 56th St ☎ 212 247 4859, ⓦ mustseecentralpark.com. This small, popular spot has cheap online deals. Regular rates $15/hr, $40/day.

The southern park: 59th to 86th streets

Many visitors enter the park at Grand Army Plaza (Fifth Ave and 59th St); the sights below are roughly organized as a tour from there up to 86th Street, though you can obviously dip in and out from neighbouring points along the Upper East and West sides. Highlights in this busier part of the park include Central Park Zoo and Strawberry Fields, a tribute to John Lennon.

Wollman Rink and Victorian Gardens

63rd at mid-park • **Ice-skating** Nov–March Mon & Tues 10am–2.30pm, Wed & Thurs 10am–10pm, Fri & Sat 10am–11pm, Sun 10am–9pm • Mon–Thurs $12, Fri–Sun $19; skate rentals $9 • ☎ 212 439 6900, ⓦ wollmanskatingrink.com • **Amusement park** Late May–early Sept; check website for opening hours as can vary, although generally Mon–Thurs 11am–7pm, Fri 11am–8pm, Sat 10am–9pm, Sun 10am–8pm • $8.50 weekdays, $9.50 weekends; rides extra ($4/ride, $16–18 unlimited) • ☎ 212 982 2229, ⓦ victoriangardensnyc.com • Subway N, Q, R to Fifth Ave-59th St

Just north of **The Pond**, with its tiny nature sanctuary in the far southeast corner of Central Park, is the Trump-run **Wollman Rink**. Don blades for some of the city's most atmospheric ice-skating; you're surrounded by onlookers, trees and, beyond that, a brilliant view of Central Park South's skyline. In summer, the rink becomes **Victorian Gardens**, a small amusement park with rides and carnival-style entertainment.

Central Park Zoo

64th St and Fifth Ave • April–Oct Mon–Fri 10am–5pm, Sat & Sun 10am–5.30pm; Nov–March daily 10am–4.30pm • $12, ages 3–12 $7, 2 and under free • ☎ 212 439 6500, ⓦ centralparkzoo.com • Subway N, Q, R to Fifth Ave-59th St

The small, welcoming **Central Park Zoo** has over a hundred species on view in mostly natural-looking homes. The animals are as close to the viewer as possible: the penguins, for example, swim around at eye level in Plexiglas pools. Other highlights include a humid tropical zone filled with exotic birds, and the sea lions, which cavort in a pool right by the zoo entrance. This complex also boasts the **Tisch Children's Zoo**: there's a petting area, interactive displays and a musical clock just outside the entrance that draws rapt children at the start of each hour. The zoo is a charming stop-off for an hour or two, though it pales compared with the Bronx Zoo (see p.258).

12

Dairy

65th St at mid-park • Daily 10am–5pm • Check ⓦ centralparknyc.org for weekend walking tour times and routes

Close to Central Park Zoo stands the **Dairy**, a cutesy yellow neo-Gothic chalet built in 1870 as a café. Despite local lore, there were never any cows here, though it did sell milk for children. It's now one of the park's visitor centres (see opposite): weekend walking tours often leave from it and you can also pick up pieces for games at **Chess & Checkers House** (itself another visitor centre), near the zoo as well.

Carousel

64th St at mid-park • Daily 10am–6pm, weather permitting (call in winter months) • $3 • ☎ 212 439 6900 • Subway A, B, C, D, #1 to 59th St-Columbus Circle

Just west of the Dairy, an octagonal brick building houses the **Carousel**. Built in 1908 and moved to the park from Coney Island in 1951, this is one of the park's little gems. Fewer than 150 such vintage handmade carousels remain in the country (others in New York City are in Prospect Park, Dumbo, Flushing Meadows–Corona Park and Forest Park). A ride on it is a magical experience: its wood-carved, colourfully painted jumping horses are accompanied by the music of a military-band organ.

Tavern on the Green

67th St at Central Park West • Mon–Fri 11am–4pm & 5–11pm, Sat & Sun 9am–4pm & 5–11pm • ☎ 212 439 6900, ⓦ tavernonthegreen.com • Subway B, C to 72nd St-Central Park West

What was once one of the country's top-grossing restaurants shut down around a decade ago but reopened in 2014, far less ornate than in its previous incarnation.

Whether or not you choose to go for a pricey meal, you'll likely get a kick out of seeing if you recognize the place from films like *Ghostbusters*, *Mr. Popper's Penguins* and *Unbreakable Kimmy Schmidt*.

The Mall

Heading north from the Dairy, you'll pass through the avenue of trees known as **The Mall**. The trees, whose branches tangle together to form a "roof" (hence its nickname, "The Cathedral"), are elms, a rarity in America. The statues that line the avenue are mostly literary and artistic greats: Shakespeare arrived first, and others from across the world soon followed, often privately funded by the appropriate immigrant groups – hence Italy's Mazzini and Germany's Beethoven. At the base of The Mall is one of only two acknowledgements to either park architect: a small memorial garden in Frederick Law Olmsted's name. Poor Calvert Vaux wasn't commemorated anywhere until April 2008, when the 72nd Street transverse was rechristened "Olmsted & Vaux Way".

Sheep Meadow

Between 66th and 69th sts • **Bowling and croquet** $30 • Permits are available from the Arsenal at Fifth Ave and 64th St • ☎ 212 408 0226 (permit info only) • **Volleyball courts** Free (although you'll need to bring your own ball) • Subway B, C to 72nd St

West of The Mall lies the **Sheep Meadow**, fifteen acres of commons where sheep grazed until 1934, when they were banished to Brooklyn's Prospect Park. In the summer, the meadow is crowded with picnickers, sunbathers and Frisbee players. Two grass bowling and croquet lawns are maintained on a hill near the Sheep Meadow's northwest corner; to the southeast are a number of very popular volleyball courts. On warm weekends, an area between the Sheep Meadow and the north end of The Mall is usually filled with rollerbladers dancing to funk, disco and hip-hop – one of the best free shows in town.

Bethesda Terrace and Fountain

72nd St at mid-park • Subway B, C to 72nd St

At the northernmost point of The Mall lie the **Bandshell** and **Rumsey Playfield**, the sites of many free SummerStage performance series (see box, p.157). There's also the **Bethesda Terrace and Fountain**, one of the few formal elements planned by Olmsted and Vaux. The crowning centrepiece of the fountain is the nineteenth-century *Angel of the Waters* sculpture, the only statue included in the original park design (and reputedly the first public art commission in New York by a woman, sculptor Emma Stebbins). Its earnest puritanical angels have been featured in all kinds of books, plays and films – everything from *Angels in America* to *Elf*. The subterranean arcade boasts a series of intricate, multihued Minton tiles on its ceiling, a star turn of the park's original design.

Cherry Hill Fountain

West of Bethesda Terrace, along 72nd St at mid-park • Subway B, C to 72nd St

Originally a turnaround point for carriages, the **Cherry Hill Fountain** was designed to have excellent views of the Lake, The Mall and the Ramble. One of the pretty areas paved by city planner Robert Moses in the 1930s for use as a car park, it was restored to its natural state in the early 1980s.

Strawberry Fields

72nd St and Central Park West • Subway B, C to 72nd St

Strawberry Fields is a peaceful area dedicated to John Lennon, who was murdered in 1980 in front of his home at the Dakota Building, across the street on Central Park West (see p.189). Strawberry Fields is typically crowded with those here to remember Lennon, at no time more so than on December 8, the anniversary of his murder. Near the West 72nd Street entrance to the park is a round Italianate mosaic with the word "Imagine" at its centre, donated by Lennon's widow, Yoko Ono, and frequently covered with flowers. This is also a favourite spot for picnickers.

12

Lake

72nd to 77th sts at mid-park • **Boat rental** April–Nov daily 10am–dusk, weather permitting • Rowboats $15 for the first hr, $4 each 15min thereafter, $20 refundable cash deposit • **Gondola rides** $45 per 30min (up to six people per boat), reservation required • ☎ 212 517 2233, ⓦ thecentralparkboathouse.com • Subway B, C to 72nd St

Bethesda Fountain overlooks the **Lake**, where you can go for a Venetian-style gondola ride or rent a rowboat from the **Loeb Boathouse** on the eastern bank. The narrowest point on the lake is crossed by the elegant cast-iron-and-wood **Bow Bridge**.

Conservatory Water

72nd to 75th sts and Fifth Ave • Subway #6 to 77th St • **Model-boat races** April to early Nov Sat mornings (roughly 10am–1pm; ⓦ cpmyc.org); participate by showing up at the green boat-rental kiosk near the Kerbs Memorial Boat House, where you can also rent boats later in the day and the rest of the week (generally Mon–Thurs 11am–5pm, Fri 11am–7pm, Sat 1–7pm & Sun 10am–6pm) • $11.95 for 30min • ☎ 917 522 0054, ⓦ sailthepark.com • **Storytelling** June–Sept Sat 11am–noon • Free

To the east of Bethesda Terrace is the **Conservatory Water**, where **model-boat races** are held every Saturday morning in the summer; you can show up to watch or participate then, or come another time of the week to test your skills. The fanciful *Alice in Wonderland* statue at the northern end of the pond was donated by publisher George Delacorte. In the summer, the Hans Christian Andersen Storytelling Center sponsors Saturday-morning **storytelling** sessions for children at the *Hans Christian Andersen* statue on the west side of the pond.

The Ramble

Take the Bow Bridge if you want to amble to **the Ramble** on the Lake's northern banks, a 37-acre area of unruly woodland, filled with narrow winding paths, rocky outcrops, streams and an array of native plant life. Once a favourite spot for drug dealers and anonymous sex, it is now a great place to watch for one of the park's two-hundred-plus species of bird (borrow a birding "discovery kit" from Belvedere Castle between 10am and 3pm, free of charge; there are also birding tours from time to time) or take a quiet daytime stroll. Clean-up notwithstanding, steer clear of this area at night.

Great Lawn

81st St at mid-park • Subway B, C to 81st St-Museum of Natural History

Behind the **Metropolitan Museum of Art** (see p.159) stands the **Obelisk**, the oldest structure in the park, which dates from 1450 BC. It was a gift to the city from Egypt in 1881 and, like its twin on the River Thames in London, is nicknamed "Cleopatra's Needle". Immediately west of the needle is the **Great Lawn**. It was the site of the park's original reservoir from 1842 until 1931, when the water was drained to create a playing field. Years later, the lawn became a popular site for free concerts and rallies (Simon and Garfunkel, Elton John, Garth Brooks, Sting, and the Pope, who celebrated Mass here in 1995, have all attracted crowds numbering over half a million), but it was badly overused and had serious drainage problems. Reopened in late 1997 after a massive two-year, $18million reconstruction, the lawn retains its integrity by hosting the more sedate, free New York Philharmonic and Metropolitan Opera concerts (see box, p.157). The lawn features eight softball fields and, at its northern end, basketball and volleyball courts and an eight-mile running track; a four-acre pine-tree stand is at the northwest corner.

PICNICKING IN THE PARK

Central Park has ample **picnicking opportunities**, the most obvious of which is the hectic, perpetually crowded expanse of the Sheep Meadow. For (a very little) more peace and quiet, you might try one of these other fine locations: the western shore of the Lake, near Hernshead; the lawn in front of Turtle Pond, which has a nice view of Belvedere Castle; the Conservatory Garden; the lawn immediately north of the Ramble; Strawberry Fields; the Arthur Ross Pinetum; Cherry Hill; and the areas around the Delacorte Theater.

12

Turtle Pond

Between 79th and 80th sts, mid-park

Turtle Pond is at the southern end of the Great Lawn, with a wooden dock and nature blind designed for views of the aquatic wildlife. Note the massive statue of fourteenth-century Polish king **Wladyslaw Jagiello** on the southeast corner of the pond, donated by the Polish government as a Holocaust memorial.

Belvedere Castle and Vista Rock

79th St at mid-park • Daily 10am–5pm

The grey stone pile of **Belvedere Castle**, a mock medieval citadel erected on top of **Vista Rock** in 1869 as a lookout on the highest point in the park, edges just south of Turtle Pond. It's still a splendid viewpoint – its terraces prime perches for birdwatchers – and houses the New York Meteorological Observatory's weather centre; there's also a handy visitor centre here (see p.152). Numerous ranger-led tours leave from here as well.

Delacorte Theater and Shakespeare Garden

80th St at mid-park

Southwest of the Great Lawn is the **Delacorte Theater**, the venue of the annual free Shakespeare in the Park summer festival (see box opposite). In another of the park's Shakespearean touches, the theatre features Milton Hebald's sculptures of Romeo and Juliet and *The Tempest*'s Prospero, while the tranquil **Shakespeare Garden** next door claims to hold every species of plant or flower mentioned in the Bard's plays.

Swedish Cottage Marionette Theatre

79th St at mid-park • Most of the year Tues–Fri 10.30am & noon, Sat & Sun 11am & 1pm • $12, 12 and under $8 • ☎ 212 988 9093 • Subway B, C to 81st-Museum of Natural History

For puppet shows, check out the wooden **Swedish Cottage Marionette Theatre** at the base of Vista Rock, which holds fun shows aimed at young kids. The structure was imported from Sweden in 1876 for a world's fair and placed in the park in 1877.

The northern park

There are fewer attractions – but more open spaces – above the Great Lawn. Much of the northern park is taken up by the **Reservoir** (86th–97th sts at mid-park, main entrance at 90th St and Fifth Ave), a billion-gallon reservoir originally designed in 1862 and no longer active. It's a favourite for sporty uptown residents: the raised 1.58-mile running track is a great place to get 360-degree views of the skyline. North of the reservoir are a tennis-court complex (see p.403) and the soccer and baseball fields of the **North Meadow Recreation Center** (97th St at mid-park; ☎ 212 348 4867 or, for a permit, ☎ 212 408 0209). The landscape north of here, in the aptly named North Woods, feels more like upstate New York than Manhattan: the ninety-acre area contains the **Loch**, which is now more of a stream, and the **Ravine**, which conceals five small waterfalls.

Conservatory Garden

East 104th–106th sts along Fifth Ave with entrance at 105th • Daily 8am–dusk • Check ⓦ centralparknyc.org for tours, which run (weather permitting) Sat and one Wed a month • Subway #6 to 103rd St

If you see nothing else in the park above 86th Street, don't miss the **Conservatory Garden**. Filled with flowering trees and shrubs, planted flowerbeds, fanciful fountains and shaded benches, the space actually houses three gardens, each landscaped in a distinct style. You'll first walk through the Italian garden, a reserved oasis with neat lawns and trimmed hedges. To the south is the English area, enhanced by the Burnett Fountain, which depicts two of the children from F.H. Burnett's classic book *The Secret Garden*. The French garden, the northernmost of the three, hosts sculptor Walter Schott's *Three Dancing Maidens* – as well as some twenty thousand tulips in spring.

TOP FIVE SUMMER PARK EVENTS

Central Park holds **events** throughout the year, but summer is undoubtedly the busiest and most popular time for such celebrations. Best of all, most of the events are free and open to anyone willing to brave a queue, the crowds, the heat or whatever else might get thrown your way.

Harlem Meer Performance Festival 110th St between Fifth and Lenox aves ☎ 212 860 1370. Offers fairly intimate and enjoyable free performances of jazz and salsa music outside the Charles A. Dana Discovery Center on Sundays (mid-June to early Sept 2–4pm).

Metropolitan Opera Summer Recital Series ☎ 212 362 6000, ⓦ metopera.org. This could be the least stuffy way to enjoy a night at the opera. Performances occur in city parks in June; here, it might be at SummerStage or on the Great Lawn.

New York Philharmonic Concerts in the Park ☎ 212 875 5709, ⓦ nyphil.org. The Philharmonic holds a few evenings of classical music in the summer, a 50-year-old tradition. Central Park's takes place in June on the Great Lawn, often with a booming fireworks display to usher the crowds home.

Shakespeare in the Park ☎ 212 539 8750, ⓦ shakespeareinthepark.org. This much-anticipated

annual happening takes place at the open-air Delacorte Theater (performances usually Tues–Sun at 8pm, approx late May–early Aug, with a break in between productions; see opposite). Pairs of free tickets are distributed daily at noon for that evening's performance, but you'll have to get in queue early, as a crowd often gathers by 7am. Alternatively, try for a ticket via the Public Theater's (see p.355) online draw – register on the website.

SummerStage Rumsey Playfield near 72nd St and Fifth Ave ☎ 212 360 2777, ⓦ cityparksfoundation .org/summerstage. SummerStage presented its inaugural Central Park concert in 1986, with Sun Ra performing to an audience of fifty people. When he returned with Sonic Youth six years later, the audience numbered ten thousand. Musical acts cover pretty much every genre during the festival's run (which begins May or June, runs through September, and also takes place in other city parks).

12

Harlem Meer

East 106th–110th sts, near Fifth Ave • Subway #2, #3 to Central Park North-110th St

At the top of the park is the **Charles A. Dana Discovery Center**, an environmental education centre and visitor centre (see p.152). Crowds of locals fish in the adjacent **Harlem Meer**, an eleven-acre pond stocked with more than fifty thousand fish. The Discovery Center provides free bamboo fishing poles and bait (April–Nov daily 10am–4pm, earlier on Sun).

Lasker Pool and Rink

North end of the park, near 110th St and Lenox Ave entrance • **Ice rink** Nov–March Mon–Thurs 10am–4pm, Fri 10am–4.50pm & 6–11pm, Sat 1–11pm, Sun 12.30–4.30pm • $8, 11 and under $4, skate rentals $7 • **Pool** July & Aug daily 11am–3pm & 4–7pm • Free

Just south of Harlem Meer, the **Lasker Rink** provides another place to ice-skate in the park – usually less crowded than the Wollman Memorial Rink save for the occasional school group. The pool opens during a few months in summer; bring a lock with you to store your stuff.

Duke Ellington monument

110th St and Fifth Ave

In the extreme northeast of the park is a 1997 monument to **Duke Ellington**, the esteemed musician and composer of such classics as *Mood Indigo*. On top of the three columns that summon the nine Muses, the Duke stands before his grand piano, symbolically looking toward Harlem for the next generation of musical vanguards.

Blockhouse

In the park's northwestern corner stands the **Blockhouse**, one of the few landmarks still awaiting renovation: several such houses were built as lookouts over pancake-flat Harlem during the War of 1812, and it's the only one which remains. Now a ruin perched atop a small hill, it's a picturesque but iffy place to visit even during the daytime – stick to seeing it on one of the park's scheduled tours.

The Metropolitan Museum of Art

One of the greatest collections of art treasures in the world, the Metropolitan Museum of Art, or the Met, as it's usually called, owns over two million artefacts spanning five thousand years of world culture – almost every civilization on Earth is represented. The range is staggering: enough gold, bronze and marble to sink an aircraft carrier, Persian daggers, Baroque arquebuses, Art Deco sofas, Old Masters by the tonne, whole interiors of homes, palaces and chapels, an entire Egyptian temple and Impressionists by the hundreds. Take your time: the Met is a real joy to explore, with plenty of sunlit courtyards and cafés strategically placed for rest and contemplation.

The main entrance to the museum leads to the **Great Hall**, a deftly lit Neoclassical cavern where you can consult floor plans, check tour times and pick up info on the Met's excellent lecture listings. Straight across from the entrance is the **Grand Staircase**, which leads to, for many visitors, the museum's single greatest attraction – the European Paintings galleries.

13

Brief history
The Met was created in 1870 by the New York State Legislature as a kind of civic education project, opening in a brownstone downtown two years later. It decamped to its present site in Central Park, a Gothic Revival building designed by Jacob Wrey Mould and Calvert Vaux, in 1880. Over time, various additions to the site have completely surrounded the original structure; the museum's familiar multicolumn, wide-stepped facade on Fifth Avenue was conceived by Richard Morris Hunt and completed in 1902, while the north and south wings were added by McKim, Mead, and White between 1911 and 1913.

ARRIVAL

By subway Take subway #4, #5 or #6 to 86th St-Lexington Ave, and walk three blocks west to Fifth Ave. The museum is at 1000 Fifth Ave, at E 82nd St, set into Central Park.

INFORMATION

Opening hours Mon–Thurs & Sun 10am–5.30pm, Fri & Sat 10am–9pm; ☎212 535 7710, ⊚metmuseum.org. Note that the Met is so big that some sections may be closed for renovation when you visit.

Tickets There is no set admission price, but the suggested donation is $25, $17 for senior citizens and $12 for students. Includes admission to The Cloisters (see p.211) and the Met Breuer (p.175). These suggested amounts are exactly that: whether you pay $1 or $100, the cashier won't flinch. If you can, spread out your exploration over several days. Audio guides are $7, or $5 after 5pm Fri & Sat.

Tours The museum runs free guided tours daily in ten different languages, every 15min throughout the day (10.15am–4pm) from the Great Hall. Call or check the website for schedules.

Internet You can connect to the Met's free wi-fi network to also access the official audio guide (also for free) during your visit, but only with a smartphone (it doesn't work for desktop or tablet computers).

European Paintings
The Met's **European Paintings galleries** (600–644), located on the second floor at the top of the Grand Staircase, are organized roughly by nationality and period (1240 to 1800).

Italian paintings
The galleries begin with a huge trove of **Italian paintings**, with three ceiling-to-floor canvases by Venetian master **Tiepolo** in Gallery 600, and lesser-known Baroque work by the likes of Guido Reni in Gallery 601. **Duccio**'s sublime *Madonna and Child* currently holds court in adjacent Gallery 625; described by the Met as "one of the great single

---

THE MET HIGHLIGHTS

Duccio's *Madonna and Child* One of the Met's most precious Italian masterpieces. See above
Pieter Bruegel the Elder's *Harvesters* This iconic image perfectly captures a rustic scene in late medieval Flanders. See p.162
The Impressionists The Met owns a tonne of sublime work from perennial crowd-pleasers Manet, Monet, Renoir, Cézanne and co. See p.162
The American Wing An incredible cache of American art, from *Washington Crossing the Delaware* to interiors designed by Frank Lloyd Wright. See p.164
The Temple of Dendur An ancient Egyptian shrine displayed in its own, magical space. See p.165
Cantor Roof Garden The Met's breezy roof deck offers views across the park, contemporary art and cocktails. See p.167

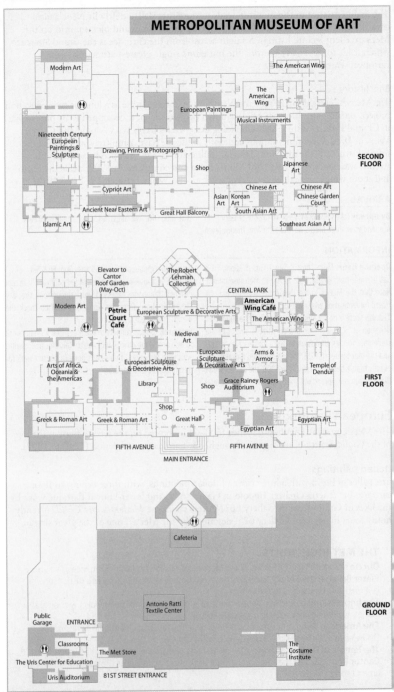

METROPOLITAN MUSEUM OF ART

SECOND FLOOR

Modern Art

The American Wing

European Paintings

The American Wing

Musical Instruments

Nineteenth Century European Paintings & Sculpture

Drawing, Prints & Photographs

Shop

Japanese Art

Cypriot Art

Chinese Art

Chinese Art

Chinese Garden Court

Ancient Near Eastern Art

Asian Art

Korean Art

Great Hall Balcony

South Asian Art

Islamic Art

Southeast Asian Art

FIRST FLOOR

Elevator to Cantor Roof Garden (May-Oct)

The Robert Lehman Collection

CENTRAL PARK

American Wing Café

Modern Art

Petrie Court Café

European Sculpture & Decorative Arts

The American Wing

Medieval Art

Arts of Africa, Oceania & the Americas

European Sculpture & Decorative Arts

European Sculpture & Decorative Arts

Arms & Armor

Temple of Dendur

Library

Shop

Grace Rainey Rogers Auditorium

Greek & Roman Art

Greek & Roman Art

Shop

Great Hall

Egyptian Art

Egyptian Art

FIFTH AVENUE

FIFTH AVENUE

MAIN ENTRANCE

GROUND FLOOR

Cafeteria

Antonio Ratti Textile Center

Public Garage

ENTRANCE

Classrooms

The Met Store

The Uris Center for Education

Uris Auditorium

81ST STREET ENTRANCE

The Costume Institute

acquisitions of the last half century", the delicately crafted painting is an extremely rare example of early Renaissance art, acquired by the Met in 2004 for around $45 million. The collection continues with Gothic altarpieces in Gallery 626 and work from northern Italian Gothic painters such as **Carlo Crivelli** in Gallery 627. Heading up a parallel route from Gallery 601, the medieval Italian theme is continued in gallery 602 with **Giotto**'s *Epiphany* and in 603 with **Botticelli**'s tiny *Last Communion of St Jerome*, along with work by Filippo Lippi, Perugino and Luca Signorelli. Gallery 606 is home to **Mantegna**'s *Adoration of the Shepherds*, as well as striking images by Venetian artists Vittore Carpaccio, and Jacopo and Giovanni Bellini. Gallery 607 features more Venetians, massive canvases by **Titian** and **Tintoretto**, though it's **Veronese**'s raunchy and artfully composed *Mars and Venus United by Love* that's especially appealing. Also here is the much-reproduced painting of **Christopher Columbus** attributed to Sebastiano del Piombo, though many scholars now doubt its authenticity. Neighbouring Gallery 608 contains work by Parma's **Correggio**; while 609 contains Mannerist master **Bronzino**'s dapper but haughty *Portrait of a Young Man* and a showy **Raphael**, *Madonna and Child Enthroned with Saints*, which features his signature, pin-up-pretty version of the Virgin Mary. Tiepolo's oil sketches feature in Gallery 622, while typical eighteenth-century Venetian scenes from **Canaletto** and **Francesco Guardi** are on show in Gallery 619.

French paintings

The Met's overhaul of this section has refocused attention on its **French collection**, for many years considered relatively unappealing to contemporary tastes. Baroque painter **Claude Lorrain** is highlighted in Gallery 618, with French seventeenth-century paintings from the likes of **Nicolas Poussin** (*Abduction of the Sabine Women*) and **Georges de la Tour** in Gallery 617 (the latter's enigmatic *Fortune Teller*, with its effete nobleman being gently relieved of his purse, is a classic). Adjacent galleries contain eighteenth-century French portraits by the likes of Elizabeth Vigée-Lebrun and Marie-Denise Villers, while lauded Neoclassical work by **Jacques-Louis David** includes *The Death of Socrates* (614). Look out for a renowned image of **Benjamin Franklin**, painted around 1778 in Paris by **Joseph-Siffred Duplessis** in Gallery 613.

Spanish paintings

The Met's small **Spanish** section includes **Goya**'s widely reproduced portrait of a toddler in a red jumpsuit, *Manuel Osorio Manrique de Zuniga*, in Gallery 612; **Velázquez**'s piercing and sombre *Portrait of Juan de Pareja* in Gallery 610; and a room of freaky, dazzling canvases by **El Greco** (Gallery 611), each of which underscores the jarring modernism of his approach. In solitary contrast is his wraith-like *View of Toledo*, one of the best of his works displayed anywhere in the world.

Northern European paintings

Galleries dedicated to Northern European schools open with a large collection from Flemish Baroque masters **Anthony van Dyck** and **Peter Paul Rubens** in galleries 628 and 630. **Vermeer** dominates Gallery 632, especially with his haunting *Study of a Young Woman*; she's an odd-looking creature with huge, doleful eyes and twinkly earrings, her enigmatic expression making her Vermeer's own *Mona Lisa*. While Vermeer's paintings focused on stillness and light, the portraits of **Hals** and **Rembrandt** burst with life. At first, galleries 634 and 637 simply seem full of men in jaunty hats and ruffles, but the personalities of the sitters emerge on closer inspection, from the heavy-lidded world-weariness of Rembrandt's *Portrait of a Man* (634) to his deeply reflective *Aristotle with a Bust of Homer* (637).

Other highlights include the paintings of **Jan van Eyck**, who is usually credited with beginning the tradition of North European realism. The freestanding panels of *The Crucifixion* and *The Last Judgement* in Gallery 641 were painted early in his career and are full of scurrying, startled figures, tightly composed with expressive and even horrific

13 detail. Another great Northern Gothic painter, **Gerard David**, used local settings for his religious scenes; the background of his exquisite *Virgin and Child with Four Angels* is medieval Bruges, and *The Rest on the Flight to Egypt* features a forest glade, again with the turrets of Bruges visible down below (both in Gallery 640). Head to Gallery 642 and **Pieter Bruegel the Elder**'s *Harvesters* to see how these innovations were assimilated. Made charming by its snapshot ordinariness (check the sprawling figure napping under a tree), this is one of the Met's most reproduced pictures.

The Met's collection of **English paintings**, back in Gallery 629, includes modest works from **Hogarth**, **Joshua Reynolds**, **Thomas Lawrence** and **Thomas Gainsborough**. **German paintings** are displayed in Gallery 643, with **Holbein** portraits, the haunting *Virgin and Child with Saint Anne* by **Dürer** and work from **Lucas Cranach the Elder** such as his influential image of the first black saint, *Saint Maurice*.

Photographs, Drawings and Prints

Most visitors to the Met head directly to the Nineteenth-Century European Paintings galleries (see below), following the left-hand corridor at the top of the Grand Staircase, but if you have time pause on the way to view **Drawings and Prints** (690) and **Photographs** (691–693, 851, 852), in galleries off the main corridor. Exhibitions here tend to revolve but treasures from the permanent collection include a rare album of photographs by William Henry Fox Talbot and fine examples of early French photography from the 1850s by Edouard Baldus, Charles Nègre and others. Modern work is represented by Cindy Sherman, László Moholy-Nagy, Man Ray and many others.

Nineteenth-Century European Paintings and Sculpture

The popular **Nineteenth-Century European Paintings and Sculpture galleries** (800–830) begin at Gallery 800, which is littered with stunning **Rodin** sculptures in white marble and bronze. Thirty rooms branch off from here, leading to an array of **Impressionist** and **Post-Impressionist** paintings. You'll find the **Neoclassicism** and **Romanticism** of painters such as **Delacroix**, **Gericault** and **Ingres** in galleries 801 to 803, while galleries 814 to 817 are devoted primarily to **Degas** (who actually hated the Impressionists), where fans will find studies in just about every medium, from pastels to sculpture.

Manet

Manet was the Impressionist movement's most influential predecessor, whose early style of contrasting light and shadow with modulated shades of black can be firmly linked to the traditions of Hals, Velázquez and Goya. *Boating* (Gallery 818) evokes a vividly fresh, spring morning, while the influential *Spanish Singer* is a vigorous and realistic portrayal of a guitar player (Gallery 810).

Monet

Monet was one of the Impressionist movement's most prolific painters, returning again and again to a single subject in order to produce a series of images capturing different nuances of light and atmosphere. The Met's hoard runs like Monet's greatest hits: the museum has a canvas from almost every major sequence by the artist, including *Water Lilies, Rouen Cathedral (The Portal)* and *Haystacks (Effect of Snow and Sun)*, all in Gallery 819.

Renoir

Though there's work here by every Impressionist from **Berthe Morisot** to **Pissarro**, it's **Renoir** who is perhaps the best represented. Sadly, most of his works are from after 1878, when he began to move away from the techniques he'd learned while working with Monet and toward the chocolate-boxy soft focus that plagued his later work. Of these, *The Daughters of Catulle Mendès* (Gallery 821) is a likeable enough piece, one whose affectionate tone manages to sidestep the sentimentality of this period.

Cézanne

Cézanne is regarded as bridging the gap between Impressionism and early twentieth-century art movements, and his technique was very different from Monet's – he laboured long to achieve a painstaking analysis of form and colour. Of his few portraits, the jarring, almost Cubist, angles and spaces of the rather plain *Mme Cézanne in a Red Dress* (Gallery 826) seem years ahead of their time: she looks clearly pained, as if she'd rather be anywhere than under her husband's gaze. Look out also for one of Cézanne's five famed portraits of the *Card Players* in the same gallery.

Post-Impressionists

One of the highlights of the **Post-Impressionists** collection is **Gauguin**'s masterly *Ia Orana Maria* in Gallery 825. This Annunciation-derived scene, a Renaissance staple, has been transferred to a different culture in an attempt to unfold the symbolism, and perhaps voice the artist's feeling for, the native South Sea islanders.

Also in Gallery 825 there are more than half a dozen canvases by **Van Gogh**, including his *Self-Portrait with Straw Hat* and famed *Irises*, and Pointillist work by the master of the technique, **Georges-Pierre Seurat** – the sparkling night-time scene *Circus Sideshow* was the first attempt to replicate artificial light using multicoloured dots. Gallery 829 features paintings by **Klimt** and **Munch**, while Gallery 830 contains work from **Picasso** and **Matisse**; look for one of Picasso's famed *Harlequin* paintings, just outside Gallery 830 in Gallery 917 (the upper entrance to Modern Art, see p.167).

Asian Art

Also on the second floor are the **Asian Art** galleries, an impressive, schizophrenic collection that includes works in various media from most major Asian civilizations.

Ancient Near Eastern Art

From the **Great Hall Balcony**, turning right leads to the **Ancient Near Eastern Art** galleries (400–406), with artefacts from Central Asia, Cyprus and the Near East, including some exceptional silver and gold pieces from Iran (Gallery 405) and an impressive hall (Gallery 401) of huge ninth-century-BC carvings from the palace of Assyrian king Ashurnasirpal II, in Nimrud.

Arts of Arab Lands (Islamic Art)

Beyond Near Eastern Art lies the **Arts of Arab Lands** and associated **Islamic Art** section (galleries 450–464), in an elegant series of galleries laced with rare Islamic texts, richly patterned carpets, Ottoman armour, ceramics and jewellery. Highlights include the vast Simonette Carpet (Gallery 459) from sixteenth-century Egypt, and the gorgeous reception room from Damascus (Gallery 461), dating from 1707 and saved after the French bombing of Syria in 1925.

Southeast Asian and Chinese Art

Turning left at the Great Hall Balcony takes you to the main **Southeast Asian and Chinese Art** galleries, beginning with the serene, 12ft-high *Stele with Buddha Dipankara* from the Northern Wei dynasty (386–495) and a 14ft-high Bodhisattva from China's Northern Qi dynasty (550–577) in Gallery 206. The focal point, however, is the enormous (and exquisite) mural, *The Pure Land of Bhaisajyaguru* (also known as the "Medicine Buddha"). This piece was carefully reconstructed after being severely damaged in an earthquake and is a study in calm reflection – it was created in China during the Yuan dynasty (c.1319).

13   Take the left fork here for more Chinese art and the real highlight of the Asian collection, the **Chinese Garden Court** (aka Astor Court, Gallery 217), a serene, minimalist retreat, and the adjacent **Ming Reception Room** (Gallery 218), a typical salon decorated in period style with wooden lattice doors. Assembled by experts from China, the naturally lit garden is representative of one found in wealthy Chinese homes of the Ming dynasty: a pagoda, small waterfall and stocked goldfish pond landscaped with limestone rocks, trees and shrubs conjure up a sense of peace.

Korean Art and South Asian Art

Take the right fork from Gallery 206 for **Korean Art** (Gallery 233) and **South Asian Art** (galleries 234–243). There's a vast, if rather monotonous, range of **statues** of Hindu and Buddhist deities here, alongside numerous pieces of friezes, many of which still possess exceptional detail despite years of exposure. *The Great Departure and the Temptation of the Buddha*, carved in the third century AD (Gallery 235), is particularly lively: Siddhartha sets out on his spiritual journey, chased by a harem of dancing girls and grasping cherubs.

Japanese Art

The **Japanese Art** galleries (223–232) contain objects from the prehistoric to the present, ordered not chronologically but thematically, with rotating exhibits divided by medium: ceramics, textiles, paintings and prints. The undeniable showstoppers here are the seventeenth- and eighteenth-century hand-painted **Kano screens**, often elaborate scenes of historical allusion and divine fervour. Since all the exhibited paintings, calligraphy and scrolls of Asian art are rotated every six months or so, the objects change, but their beauty remains constant.

Musical instruments

The Met's oft-ignored collection of **musical instruments** includes an astonishing 5000 examples from all over the world, from 300 BC to the present. Its second-floor galleries (680–684) reopened after a major restoration in 2017, its treasures including the oldest existing piano, by Bartolomeo Cristofori (1720); three priceless violins by Antonio Stradivari; the guitars of Spanish classical guitarist Andrés Segovia; a Ming-dynasty Chinese ivory *pipa*; and an ornate seventeenth-century Japanese *koto*.

The American Wing

Close to being a museum in its own right, the **American Wing** (galleries 700–774) is a thorough introduction to the development of fine art in America, with a vast collection of paintings, period furniture, glass, silverware and ceramics. The spectacular **Charles Engelhard Court** is studded with sculpture from the likes of Daniel Chester French and Augustus Saint-Gaudens – you can also grab a snack at the **American Wing Café** here (Mon–Thurs & Sun 10am–4.30pm, Fri & Sat 10am–8.15pm).

To view the Wing's **period rooms** in chronological order, begin on the third floor (Gallery 709) with the interior of a dark, low-beamed Jacobean beauty from Ipswich, Massachusetts, dating from 1680, and end with the Frank Lloyd Wright Room (Gallery 745), built in Minnesota (1912–14). Don't miss the collection of florid Tiffany glass in Gallery 743.

American Painting

The core **American Painting** galleries lie on the second floor, containing some real gems of New World artistry. Galleries 747 and 748 contain fine examples of colonial portraiture, featuring the work of **John Singleton Copley**, while Gallery 753 is primarily a homage to George Washington, with much-reproduced portraits by **John Trumbull**, **Charles Willson Peale** and **Gilbert Stuart** (Stuart's famed Athenaeum-type portrait of

13

America's first president resides in Gallery 774). Galleries 759 and 761 are dedicated to the **Hudson Valley School** (1825–75), who glorified the landscape in their vast lyrical canvases; English-born **Thomas Cole**, the school's doyen, is represented by *The Oxbow*, while his pupil **Frederic Edwin Church** also has work here and in Gallery 760, where the immense *Heart of the Andes* combines the grand sweep of the mountains with minutely depicted flora. Gallery 760 also contains **Albert Bierstadt**'s monumental *The Rocky Mountains, Lander's Peak*, but the real star here is *Washington Crossing the Delaware* by **Emanuel Leutze**, the celebrated image of Washington escaping across the river in the winter of 1776.

Post-Civil War painting

Winslow Homer is also well represented in the collection, from his early illustrations of the Civil War (Gallery 762) to his late, quasi-Impressionistic seascapes, of which *Northeaster* is one of the finest (Gallery 767). Look out, too, for the painters of the American West – **Frederic Remington**'s *On the Southern Plains* (Gallery 765) helped create the popular image of the swashbuckling Seventh Cavalry. Other highlights of the late nineteenth and early twentieth centuries include **Thomas Eakins**' subdued, almost ghostly *Max Schmitt in a Single Scull* (Gallery 767) and **William Merritt Chase**'s *For the Little One* (Gallery 769), an Impressionist study of his wife sewing. American Impressionism (1880–1920) is explored more fully in Gallery 769 with the work of **Childe Hassam**, and in Gallery 770 with **John Singer Sargent**, John H. Twachtman and J. Alden Weir.

Medieval Art

Behind the Great Hall staircase on the first floor lies **Medieval Art** (galleries 300–307), the initial corridor lined with sumptuous Byzantine metalwork and jewellery that financier **J.P. Morgan** donated to the museum in its early days. At the end of the corridor is the **Medieval Sculpture Hall** (Gallery 305), piled high with religious statuary and carvings; it's divided by a 52ft-high *reja* – a decorative open-work, iron altar screen – from Valladolid Cathedral in Spain. If you're here in December, you'll see a highlight of New York's Christmas season: a beautifully decorated, 20ft-high Christmas tree lit up in the centre of the hall. The **Medieval Treasury** (Gallery 306) to the right of the hall has an all-encompassing display of objects religious, liturgical and secular.

Egyptian Art

The Met hogs a collection of more than 35,000 objects from **ancient Egypt** (galleries 100–138). Brightly efficient corridors steer you through the treasures of the museum's own digs during the 1920s and 1930s, as well as other art and artefacts from 3000 BC to the Byzantine period of Egyptian culture.

THE TEMPLE OF DENDUR

At the end of the Egyptian section sits the **Temple of Dendur**, housed in the vast and airy Gallery 131, lined with photographs and placards about the temple's history and its original site on the banks of the Nile. Built by the Emperor Augustus in 15 BC for the goddess Isis of Philae, the temple was moved here as a gift from the Egyptian government during the construction of the Aswan High Dam in 1965 – otherwise, it would have drowned. Though you can't walk all the way inside, you can go in just far enough to get a glimpse of the interior rooms, their walls chock-full of hieroglyphs and the scrawls of nineteenth-century **graffiti** artists (though "J Livingston" is no relation to the famous explorer). The entire gallery is glassed-in on one side, and looks out onto Central Park; the most magical time to view the temple is when it's illuminated at night and the gallery seems to glow, lending it an air of mystery that's missing during the day.

13

Prepare to be awed as you enter from the Great Hall on the first floor: the large **statuary**, **tombs** and **sarcophagi** in the first few galleries are immediately striking. Don't miss the finely crafted models of ships, a brewery and a cattle stable in Gallery 105, offerings found in the **Tomb of Meketre**. Incredibly well preserved, they look as if they were made yesterday, not four thousand years ago, and offer a rare insight into everyday Egyptian life. Look, too, for the dazzling collection of **Princess Sithathoryunet jewellery** in Gallery 111, a pinnacle in Egyptian decorative art from around 1830 BC.

Greek and Roman Art

Thanks to a magnificent renovation completed in 2007, one of the largest collections of Greek and Roman art in the world occupies some of the most attractive wings of the museum (galleries 150–172). Enter from the southern end of the Great Hall, and you'll find yourself in the wonderfully bright **Greek Sculpture Court** (Gallery 153), a fittingly elegant setting for sixth- to fourth-century-BC marble sculptures. The adjacent galleries display Greek art from the prehistoric era through to the fourth century BC. Look out for the tiny but fanciful **Minoan vase** in the shape of a bull's head from around 1450 BC (Gallery 151) and the **Marble Statue of a Kouros** (Gallery 154) – one of the earliest examples of a funerary statue (*kouros* means "youth") to have survived intact. Dating from 580 BC and originally from Attica, it marked the grave of the son of a wealthy family, created to ensure he would be remembered.

Beyond here, the hefty **Sardis Column** from the Temple of Artemis marks the entrance into the stunning **Leon Levy and Shelby White Court** (Gallery 162), a soaring two-storey atrium of **Roman sculpture** from the first century BC to the second century AD, with mosaic floors, Doric columns and a glass ceiling – take a moment to soak up your surroundings at the fountain in the centre. Highlights include the incredibly detailed *Badminton Sarcophagus* towards the back, and beyond this a small but enigmatic bust of the Emperor Caracalla from the third century.

Arts of Africa, Oceania and the Americas

Michael C. Rockefeller, son of Governor Nelson Rockefeller, disappeared during a trip to West New Guinea in 1961. In 1969, Nelson donated the entire contents of his missing son's **Museum of Primitive Art** – over 3300 works, plus library and photographic material – to the Met. This wing, on the first floor past the Greek and Roman galleries, stands as a memorial to Michael. It includes many Asmat tribal objects, such as carved *mbis* (memorial poles), figures and a canoe from Irian Jaya, alongside the Met's comprehensive collection of art from **Africa**, **Oceania and the Americas**.

The **African galleries** (350–352) offer an overview of the major geographic regions and their cultures, though West Africa is better represented than the rest of the continent. Particularly awe-inspiring is the display of art from the Kingdom of Benin (in present-day Nigeria) – tiny carved ivory figures, created with astonishing detail (Gallery 352).

The **Pacific collection** (galleries 353–355) covers the islands of Melanesia, Micronesia, Polynesia and Australia, and contains a wide array of objects, including wild, somewhat frightening wooden masks with all-too-realistic eyes. Sadly, **Mexico, Central America and South America** (galleries 357–358) get somewhat short shrift, though there is a respectable collection of pre-Columbian jade, Mayan and Aztec pottery and Mexican ceramic sculpture; the best part by far, however, is the **Jan Mitchell Treasury** (Gallery 357), an entire room filled with South American gold jewellery and ornaments – particularly the exquisite hammered-gold nose ornaments and earrings from Peru and the richly carved, jewelled ornaments from Colombia.

Modern and Contemporary Art

13

The Met's **Modern and Contemporary Art** collection (galleries 900–926) is another fine hoard that includes several stunning individual works, from mid-century experimental and abstract canvases to contemporary sculpture.

First floor: 1900 to 1950

Work on the first floor is arranged thematically under the title **Re-imagining Modernism**. Picasso is particularly well represented, his work sprinkled throughout, from his Blue Period, through his Cubist Period, to more familiar skewed-perspective portraits. The first galleries are dedicated to "Retreat", opening with **Georgia O'Keeffe**'s *Cow's Skull: Red, White, and Blue* (Gallery 900), resembling a progressive-rock album cover, and various works by **Miró**, **Picasso** and **Chagall** in Gallery 901. In Gallery 902 ("The Metropolis") is work by **Edward Hopper** and the mural-like images of Broadway and Wall Street by **Florine Stettheimer**. European Modernism is presented in galleries 904 to 907, with highlights including a striking *Young Sailor II* by **Matisse** (904), *The Billiard Table* by **Braque** (905), *Thérèse Dreaming* by **Balthus** (907), the unsettling *Three Studies for a Self-Portrait* by **Francis Bacon** (907), and more from Miró in Gallery 906.

The "Avant-Garde" (908 and 910) is represented here by Braque, **Fernand Léger**, **Juan Gris** and more work from Picasso (*Woman in an Armchair* in 908), with the odd painting from **Kandinsky** and even Mexican legend **Diego Rivera** (*Café Terrace* in 910). The portrait of *Gertrude Stein* (Gallery 911) was the Met's first Picasso (donated by Stein herself in 1947). "Abstraction" (galleries 912 and 913) features the work of **Mondrian**, **Paul Klee**, **Modigliani**'s firm-breasted *Reclining Nude*, *Thérèse* by Balthus, **Dalí**'s *Crucifixion* and **Léger**'s *Woman with Cat*. Note that some of the most famous pieces in the collection are often moved around or on loan elsewhere.

Mezzanine and second floors: 1945 to the present

The **mezzanine level** (Gallery 915) displays paintings and sculpture from the 1970s on, including the work of Warhol, David Hockney and **Chuck Close**, whose *Lucas* has the characteristic intense stare of his giant portraits. The **second floor** is filled with giant, abstract canvases from postwar artists such as grumpy Abstract Expressionist **Clyfford Still** (Gallery 919), who once "repossessed" a picture by knifing it from its frame when he fell out with the owner. Gallery 920 features the New York School (Alexander Calder, Isamu Noguchi and Willem de Kooning), while Abstract Expressionism is the focus of galleries 921 and 922 with work from **Mark Rothko** and **Jackson Pollock**'s swirling *Autumn Rhythm (No. 30)*; if you stand up close, the painting seems to suck you in, and you'll spot far more colours than at first glance. American "Abstraction and Pop, 1950s–60s" holds court in galleries 923 to 925 (Warhol, Oldenburg and Lichtenstein), including the iconic *White Flag* by **Jasper Johns** in Gallery 924.

THE CANTOR ROOF GARDEN

From May to October, you can ascend to the **Cantor Roof Garden**, located on top of the Modern Art section. The leafy garden is an outdoor gallery, and each summer it's used to showcase contemporary sculpture; it's also a café and cocktail bar (Mon–Thurs & Sun 10am–4.30pm, Fri & Sat 10am–8pm), though the pricey snacks and drinks aren't the main reason to come here. The views are what draw most visitors – from this height, you can grasp how vast Central Park truly is. By far the best time to come for a cocktail is October, when the weather's cooler and the foliage has begun to turn.

To reach the garden, head for the southwest elevators on the first floor, just outside the Modern Art gallery – to get to the elevators, walk behind the main marble stairs in the Great Hall, into the main Medieval sculpture hall (Gallery 305), and turn left towards the Modern Art section.

13 European Sculpture and Decorative Arts

Most people pass right through the **European Sculpture and Decorative Arts** section (galleries 500–556) on their way between the Modern and Medieval art galleries, but there are a couple of reasons to pause. The **European Sculpture Court** (Gallery 548) is a gorgeous sunlit courtyard studded with grand marble statues, notably *Andromeda and the Sea Monster* by **Domenico Guidi** and the agonizing *Ugolino and his Sons* by **Carpeaux**, depicting the Pisan traitor from Dante's *Inferno*. There's also a cast of **Rodin**'s *Burghers of Calais*, an impressive bronze ensemble recalling the Hundred Years' War. The **Decorative Arts section** – furniture, ceramics, glassware and the like – is less appealing, but displayed in some opulent Baroque- and Rococo-style rooms reminiscent of a French palace.

Arms and Armor

Aficionados will enjoy the vast collection of ancient weaponry in the **Arms and Armor** galleries (370–380), the main court crammed with elaborate sixteenth- and seventeenth-century European armour fit for a royal joust – one of King Henry VIII's personal suits of armour is on display here (371). Gallery 377 features terrifying sets of Samurai armour.

The Robert Lehman Collection

The extraordinary **Robert Lehman Collection** (galleries 950–965) was tacked on to the rear of the museum in 1975 to house the holdings of Robert Lehman, a relentless collector and scion of the Lehman Brothers banking family. Lehman bequeathed his entire collection with the stipulation that the galleries retain the appearance of a private home, and parts of this extension – an octagonal building centred on a brilliantly lit atrium – do resemble rooms in his former mansion (Gallery 951 actually includes the stained-glass dome from the Lehman townhouse at 7 W 54th St, completed in 1905). The walls around the atrium (galleries 961 and 962) are lined with a mixed bag of **nineteenth-century** works from **Braque**, **Derain**, **Matisse**, **Renoir**, **Van Gogh** and **Sisley**, though **Balthus**'s creamy and disturbing *Nude before a Mirror* (at the entrance to the main galleries) is worth a longer look.

Italian Renaissance art

Lehman's artistic interests fill important gaps in the Met's collection, notably the **Italian Renaissance**. This period was his passion, with Gallery 950 containing one of the most celebrated collections of Italian **maiolica** (glazed ceramics) in the world. Extremely intricate and well-preserved fourteenth- and fifteenth-century Florentine and Sienese work features in Gallery 952, by masters such as **Simone Martini** and **Ugolino da Siena**. The red-velvet-walled Gallery 956 is home to more Sienese paintings, while standout Italian works in Gallery 959 include the tiny, easily missed *Annunciation* by **Botticelli** (in a display case). As impressive are the Venetian works, including a glassy *Madonna and Child* by **Giovanni Bellini** in which Mary looks like a 1920s screen goddess (also Gallery 959).

Northern European and Spanish art

Gallery 953 houses **Northern Renaissance art**, from the likes of **Petrus Christus** and **Gerard David** (look out also for **Holbein**'s emotive portrait of *Erasmus* in the display cabinet, painted around 1523), while eighteenth- and nineteenth-century paintings from France and England hold court in Gallery 957; Lehman evidently liked **Ingres**, whose languid, sculptural portrait of the *Princesse de Broglie* in her bright-blue dress sparkles on the wall. Similarly impressive is **El Greco**'s *Christ Carrying the Cross* (Gallery 958) and one of his *St Jerome* paintings, though one picture stands out from them all in this gallery: **Rembrandt**'s creepy *Portrait of Gerard de Lairesse*, his bug eyes and snout-like nose evidence of the ravages of congenital syphilis.

GUGGENHEIM MUSEUM

Upper East Side

The defining characteristic of Manhattan's Upper East Side – a two-square-mile grid that runs from 59th to 96th streets between Fifth Avenue and the East River – is wealth. This area has been an enclave of New York's upper class since the 1890s, when dynasties such as the Rockefellers, Whitneys and Astors built mansions here, and it remains a major tourist draw thanks to Museum Mile and the Met. Today, long-time resident Woody Allen and Madonna call the Upper East Side home, a world aptly portrayed in movies such as *Breakfast at Tiffany's*, and in TV shows *Sex and the City* and *Gossip Girl*. Shedding its stuffy image somewhat, an influx of young professionals has sparked a mini surge in gastropubs and cocktail bars in recent years – and it's become more accessible; the first phase of the Second Avenue Subway opened in 2017.

Upper East Side Historic District

Subway F to Lexington Ave/63rd St; #6 to 68th St or 77th St

Encompassing 59th to 78th streets, between Fifth and Lexington avenues, the **Upper East Side Historic District** has been the haughty patrician face of Manhattan since the late nineteenth century. Wealthy families built their fashionable residences on **Fifth Avenue** overlooking Central Park, lavish Neoclassical mansions cluttered with columns and classical statues.

Today, the area is jam-packed with museums: Henry Clay Frick's mansion at East 70th Street, marginally less ostentatious than its neighbours, is now the intimate and tranquil home of **The Frick Collection**, one of the city's must-see spots.

14

The Grolier Club

47 E 60th St, just off Park Ave • Mon–Sat 10am–5pm; closed Aug • Free • ☎ 212 838 6690, ⓦ grolierclub.org • Subway N, R, W to Fifth Ave/59th St; #4, #5, #6 to 59th St-Lexington Ave

North of **Grand Army Plaza**, Fifth Avenue and its opulent side streets are dotted with **private clubs** that served and still cater to the city's wealthy. One of the few open to the public (at least partly) is the relatively modest **Grolier Club**. There are four public art shows a year in the main ground-floor gallery, usually with a literary or artistic theme utilizing paintings, books and sculpture; recent exhibitions have focused on independent printers such as San Francisco's Grabhorn Press. Established in 1884 as a literary club (it's named after the sixteenth-century French bibliophile Jean Grolier), the Grolier's current premises date from 1917.

Christ Church United Methodist

524 Park Ave, at E 60th St • Mon–Fri 7am–6pm; Sun services only • Free • ☎ 212 838 3036, ⓦ christchurchnyc.org • Subway N, R, W to Fifth Ave/59th St; #4, #5, #6 to 59th St-Lexington Ave

Christ Church United Methodist looks relatively plain from the outside, but the interior is one of the most memorable in New York. Ralph Adams Cram started work on this Romanesque masterpiece in 1931, but the lavish Byzantine interior wasn't completed until 1949. The apse and vaulted ceiling are smothered in dazzling gold-leaf mosaics – parts of the choir screen date from 1660 and were once owned by Tsar Nicholas II of Russia. The altar itself is carved from Spanish marble, with the nave columns hewn from veined, purple Levanto marble.

Museum of American Illustration

128 E 63rd St, between Park and Lexington aves • Tues & Thurs 10am–8pm, Wed & Fri 10am–5pm, Sat 11am–5pm • $12, students $7, ages 10 and under free); free Tues 5–8pm • ☎ 212 838 2560, ⓦ societyillustrators.org • Subway F to Lexington Ave/63rd St

Fans of cartoon art should check out the **Museum of American Illustration**, New York's shrine to the genre. Rotating selections from the Society of Illustrators' permanent collection of more than two thousand items include everything from wartime propaganda to contemporary ads. Exhibitions are based on a theme or illustrator; designed primarily for aficionados, they are nonetheless accessible, well presented and topical. **Sketch Night** (Tues & Thurs 6.30–9.30pm; $20; $15 students) is lots of fun for budding artists, with live music and models to draw (supplies available for sale).

Park Avenue Armory

643 Park Ave • Guided tours (1hr 15min) on select Mon & Thurs 10am, Sat 2pm throughout the year (reservations required; check current times on website) • Tours $15 • ☎ 212 616 3930, ⓦ armoryonpark.org • Subway #6 to 68th St

The vast hulk of the **Park Avenue Armory** dominates the block of Park Avenue between East 66th and 67th streets. Completed in 1881 for the National Guard's Seventh Regiment, the exterior features pseudo-medieval crenellations, and the interior a grand double staircase and spidery wrought-iron chandeliers. The most reliable way to get a peek at the lavish rooms inside is to take a **guided tour** or to attend one of the frequent art and antique shows staged here (it's normally closed otherwise); you'll usually have to

UPPER EAST SIDE

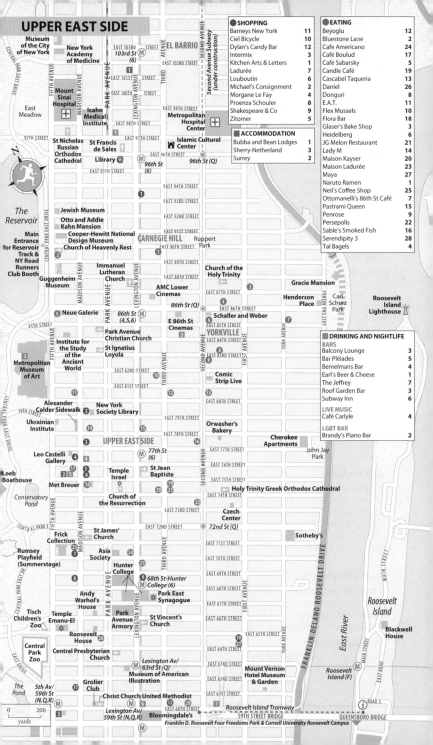

pay to attend the shows (which showcase the enormous **drill hall**), but the period rooms on the first floor will be open for **free self-guided tours**. Highlights include the incredibly opulent **Veterans Room** and **Library**, designed by Stanford White and decked out with Tiffany interiors and stained glass – the fireplace in the former is particularly fine, framed with blue glass tiles and murals. Check out also the portraits in the **Colonel's Reception Room**, where George Washington and compatriot Marquis de Lafayette would no doubt be mortified to find themselves on display with a very regal King George VI.

14

THE FIRST FAMILIES OF NEW YORK

The Upper East Side has long been associated with New York's richest and most influential families, though their opulent mansions only started to appear here in the late 1870s (an era memorialized in Edith Wharton's *The Age of Innocence*). Times have changed (with most mansions becoming museums), but the following families have retained a romantic grip on the city's collective imagination. Note that Scottish-born billionaire **Andrew Carnegie**, who lived at 2 E 91st St (p.177), gave most of his fortune away, and as he only had one daughter, there was no "Carnegie dynasty".

THE ASTORS

German-born **John Jacob Astor** (1763–1848) established the family fortune, principally through the fur trade, though it's his investments in Manhattan real estate that really made him America's first multimillionaire (he was worth at least $110 billion in modern terms when he died). Grandson William Backhouse Astor, Jr (1829–92) maintained the family legacy, marrying Caroline Schermerhorn (1830–1908). The **Schermerhorns** were New York's Dutch aristocracy – real "Old Money". Caroline's huge mansion at 840 Fifth Ave was designed by Richard Morris Hunt in 1893, but was demolished in 1927 (Temple Emanu-El occupies the space today). Her son, John Jacob Astor IV, died on the *Titanic* in 1912.

THE ROCKEFELLERS

John D. Rockefeller (1839–1937) still ranks as the wealthiest American of all time, worth around $360 billion in modern equivalent when he died (making Bill Gates a pauper in comparison). As head of Standard Oil, he essentially controlled the entire oil industry in North America. Though Rockefeller was originally based in Cleveland, the family eventually settled in New York, John D. Rockefeller, Jr moving into 740 Park Ave in 1937 (Jacqueline Kennedy Onassis grew up in the same posh building). His son Nelson Rockefeller (and New York governor) lived at 810 Fifth Ave.

THE ROOSEVELTS

New York's premier political family produced two US presidents (Teddy and FDR), descendants of a mid-seventeenth-century Dutch immigrant. FDR and **Eleanor Roosevelt** loved the Upper East Side. Eleanor was born at 56 W 37th St in 1884, but moved into 49 E 65th St with her husband in 1908 (a wedding gift from FDR's overbearing mother). The couple owned the property until 1941 (it's now the **Roosevelt House at Hunter College**); after a spell in the West Village, Eleanor (now a widow) moved to 211 E 62nd St in 1953 and then to 55 E 74th St in 1959 – she died there three years later.

THE VANDERBILTS

Commodore Cornelius Vanderbilt (1794–1877) made his millions through railways and shipping – he built the first Grand Central station. The family erected huge mansions on Fifth Avenue between 50th and 59th streets in the nineteenth century, with socialite Grace Vanderbilt later moving into 1048 Fifth Ave (now the Neue Galerie, p.176).

THE WHITNEYS

Descended from one **John Whitney** of London, who settled in Massachusetts in 1635, the Whitneys made their money through a vast web of industrial and financial concerns, settling in New York in the mid-nineteenth century. William C. Whitney built his mansion at 871 Fifth Ave, while his son Payne Whitney (1876–1927) commissioned Stanford White to build 972 Fifth Ave in 1902 (today it belongs to the French Embassy).

Temple Emanu-El

1 E 65th St, at Fifth Ave • Mon–Thurs & Sun 10am–4.30pm (museum closed Jewish holidays) • Free • ☎ 212 744 1400, ⓦ emanuelnyc.org • Subway F to Lexington Ave/63rd St; #6 to 68th St

Overlooking Central Park sits the awe-inspiring **Temple Emanu-El**, completed in 1929. Still America's largest Reform Jewish synagogue, this Romanesque-Byzantine cavern – a vast, moody and contemplative place – manages to feel even bigger inside than it looks from the outside. The entrance is on 65th Street, where there's also the **Herbert & Eileen Bernard Museum of Judaica** on the second floor (same hours; free); its three rooms hold both temporary exhibits on religious themes like the Kabbalah as well as an artefact-heavy history of the temple itself. Despite the official opening hours, both the temple and museum are often closed – **call ahead** to confirm times.

14

The Frick Collection

1 E 70th St, at Fifth Ave • Tues–Sat 10am–6pm, Sun 11am–5pm • $22 (includes free audio guide), pay what you wish Sun 11am–1pm and first Fri of the month 6–9pm • ☎ 212 288 0700, ⓦ frick.org • Subway #6 to 68th St

A spectacular feat of acquisitive good taste, the **Frick Collection** is one of New York's finest sights. The collection comprises the art treasures amassed by **Henry Clay Frick** (1849–1919), one of New York's most ruthless robber-barons, and is housed in the sumptuous mansion he had built in 1914. The legacy of his ill-gotten gains – he spent millions on the best of Europe's art – is a superb assembly of work.

Opened in 1935, for the most part the museum has been kept as it looked when the Fricks lived here. What sets it apart from most galleries is that it strives hard to be as unlike a museum as possible. There is no wall text describing the pictures, though you can dial up info on most pieces using the hand-held guides available in the lobby (included with the price of admission). There are few ropes, fresh flowers on every table, and chairs provided for weary visitors, even in the most lavishly decorated rooms. Make sure you pay a visit to the enclosed central **Garden Court**, where marble floors, fountains and greenery, all simply arranged, exude serenity.

Start your visit with the **introductory film** (22min) shown every hour in the Music Room, which provides background on Frick's coke and steel empire and his ravenous appetite for acquiring art, which really got going in the 1890s.

The South Hall to Fragonard Room

With its magnificent array of Old Masters, the collection rivals to a certain extent the much larger holdings of the Met, especially in the quality of Italian Renaissance pieces, an area in which the Met is comparatively weak. Don't rush; even the initial corridors beyond the entrance hold some exceptional pieces. The **South Hall** contains Renoir's beguiling *Mother and Children* (in the alcove under the stairs) and two fabulous Vermeers: *Girl at Her Muse* and *Officer and Laughing Girl*, the latter in particular a masterful play on light. Look out, too, for the elegant French Rococo furniture here – though paintings take the limelight, Frick also collected antique tables, chests and chairs, spread liberally throughout the mansion.

Keep an open mind as you enter the eighteenth-century **Boucher Room**. With its flowery walls and Boucher's Rococo representations of the Arts and Sciences in gilded frames, it is not to modern tastes. More reserved English paintings pack the **Dining Room**: giant portraits by Romney and Gainsborough, whose *St James's Park* is a study in social mores – there isn't a woman walking under the trees who isn't assessing the competition. The nearby **Fragonard Room** contains the French painter's typically florid *Progress of Love* series, painted for Louis XV's mistress Madame du Barry but discarded by her soon afterwards.

The Living Hall

The austere wood-panelled **Living Hall** houses one of the most impressive Renaissance pictures anywhere in America: Giovanni Bellini's sublime *St Francis in the Desert*. Stunningly well preserved, the picture suggests Francis's vision of Christ. This canvas unfairly overshadows the rest of the pieces in the room, although also notable are a couple of knockout portraits by Hans Holbein the Younger. His masterpieces *Thomas Cromwell* and *Sir Thomas More* are old adversaries who now seem to stare at each other – images that have helped to make the Tudor period one of Britain's most intriguing. More's world-weariness is graphically evidenced by the bags under his eyes and his five-o'clock shadow; recent fiction such as *Wolf Hall* has portrayed the saint more cynically, but look closely and you can see that Holbein clearly intended More to be viewed far more sympathetically than the shifty-eyed Cromwell. The two are separated by El Greco's restrained *St Jerome*.

14

Library and North Hall

Move into the oak-panelled **Library** to see more English paintings, such as Turner's early *Fishing Boats entering Calais Harbour*, Reynolds' *Lady Taylor*, who's dwarfed by her huge blue ribbon and feather hat, and one of Constable's *Salisbury Cathedral* series; there's also a portrait of Frick himself here, as a white-bearded old man, *Lady Peel* by Sir Thomas Lawrence, a lady adorned with flowing red plumage and one of Frick's rare American paintings, a portrait of George Washington by Gilbert Stuart. Across in the **North Hall**, look for the gorgeous but chill-inducing *Vétheuil in Winter* by Monet.

The West and East galleries

The **West Gallery** is a long, elegant room, decorated with dark-green walls and carpet, a concave glass ceiling and ornately carved wood trim. There's a clutch of snazzy Dutch pictures here, including Rembrandt's enigmatic *Polish Rider* and his most magnificent self-portrait, regal robes contrasting with his sorrowful, weary expression. Look out for a couple of uncharacteristically informal portraits of Frans Snyders and his wife by Anthony van Dyck, Frick's favourite artist, and Turner's vast canvases of Dieppe and Cologne. Also here is the last picture Frick himself bought before his death in 1919: Vermeer's seemingly unfinished *Mistress and Maid*, a tantalizing snapshot of an intimate moment.

At the far end of the West Gallery is the tiny **Enamel Room**, named for the exquisite set of mostly sixteenth-century Limoges enamels on display. There's also a collection of small altarpieces by Piero della Francesca; it's another sign of Frick's good taste that he snapped up work by this artist, who is now one of the acknowledged Italian masters but was little regarded in the nineteenth century. The **Oval Room** at the other end of the West Gallery is filled (unless there's a special exhibit on show) with a quartet of pretty portraits by James McNeill Whistler, the only US painter admired by Frick.

Like the Oval Room, the **East Gallery** and modern **Lower Level Galleries** are often used for temporary exhibits; accessible only by a steep spiral staircase just to the left beyond the entry hall, the lower floor is easy to miss unless you're looking for it.

St James' Church

865 Madison Ave, at E 71st St • Tues–Sun 8am–8pm • Free • ☎ 212 288 4100, ⓦ stjames.org • Subway #6 to 68th St

One block east of the Frick Collection is the stately and elaborate neo-Gothic facade of **St James' Church**. This Episcopal place of worship was first constructed in 1885, but what you see today dates mostly from the 1920s, including the graceful, gilded reredos above the marble altar, designed by Ralph Adams Cram.

Asia Society

725 Park Ave, at E 70th St • Tues–Sun 11am–6pm, Fri until 9pm mid-Sept to June • $12, free Fri 6–9pm • ☎ 212 517 2742, ⓦ asiasociety.org/new-york • Subway #6 to 68th St

A prominent educational resource founded by John D. Rockefeller III, the **Asia Society** offers two floors of small but nevertheless enthralling exhibition spaces dedicated to both traditional and contemporary art from all over Asia. In addition to the usually worthwhile temporary exhibits, ranging from Japanese lacquerware to ancient Buddhist sculpture, a variety of intriguing performances, political roundtables, lectures, films and free events are frequently held here.

Czech Center

321 E 73rd St • Mon–Fri 10am–6pm • Free • ☎ 646 422 3300, ⓦ bohemiannationalhall.com • Subway Q to 72nd St-Second Ave

The grand old Bohemian National Hall, completed in 1897, now functions as the **Czech Center**, home to the Czech Consulate and a series of public art galleries well worth checking out. Exhibits change every few months, featuring notable names in Czech contemporary art. **East 73rd Street** was once the heart of a flourishing **Czech community** in the late nineteenth century (memorably described by Jacob Riis in *How the Other Half Lives*).

Met Breuer

945 Madison Ave, at E 75th St • Tues–Thurs & Sun 10am–5.30pm, Fri & Sat 10am–9pm • Suggested admission $25 (includes same-day entry to the Met and the Cloisters • ☎ 212 517 2742, ⓦ metmuseum.org • Subway #6 to 77th St

The Whitney Museum relocated in 2015 (see p.106), its old home acquired by the Met and reopened as the **Met Breuer** in March 2016, a museum of revolving modern and contemporary art exhibitions. The site's annual $17 million operations bill has put a strain on the Met's finances, but the programming has been superb so far, with wonderfully curated exhibitions by Kerry James Marshall, Diane Arbus and Marsden Hartley among several others.

The Marcel Breuer-designed building originally opened in 1966; the Brutalist design was initially a controversial addition to the neat townhouses of the Upper East Side, but in a sign of how beloved the structure became, plans to wreck its integrity with a Neoclassical addition were shouted down in the late 1980s.

St Jean Baptiste Church

184 E 76th St, at Lexington Ave • Daily 7am–7pm • Free • ☎ 212 288 5082, ⓦ stjeanbaptisteny.org • Subway #6 to 68th St

Built in 1913 to serve the local French-Canadian community, **St Jean Baptiste Church** is an opulent Italian Baroque and Neoclassical confection with a magnificent 175ft dome and rare Chartres stained-glass windows. The church is also a **national shrine for St Anne** (Mary's mother), with a special chapel on the right side, and an important pilgrimage site for American Catholics.

Museum Mile and Carnegie Hill

Subway #4, #5 or #6 to 86th St; #6 to 96th St

Upper Fifth Avenue is nicknamed **Museum Mile**, home to New York's greatest concentration of museums, several of which are housed in the area's remaining mansions. North of the Met, the neighbourhood is known as **Carnegie Hill** after steel magnate Andrew Carnegie, who constructed his mansion on Fifth Avenue and 91st Street; it's now the Cooper Hewitt, Smithsonian Design Museum (see p.177). Note that the Museo del Barrio is covered in the Harlem chapter (see p.206).

Ukrainian Institute

2 E 79th St • Tues–Sun noon–6pm • $5 donation suggested • ☎ 212 288 8660, ⓦ ukrainianinstitute.org • Subway #4, #5, #6 to 86th St

Inevitably overshadowed by the Met just up the road, the **Ukrainian Institute** boasts a small but intriguing art collection. Temporary exhibits from modern Ukrainian artists take up the second floor, but the upper levels contain some real gems: still life from Sergei Belik, abstract work from sculptor Alexander Archipenko and paintings from David Burliuk, the one-eyed "father of Russian Futurism". The real highlights are the huge Soviet Socialist Realist canvases, saved from destruction in the 1990s by collector Jurii Maniichuk and on loan here till at least September 2018; think Khrushchev meeting Yuri Gagarin in *Motherland Greets a Hero*. The building itself is a gorgeous example of Fifth Avenue opulence, built for wealthy banker Isaac Fletcher by C.P.H. Gilbert in 1899 but more famous for being the home of scandal-prone oilman Harry Sinclair in the 1920s.

14

Institute for the Study of the Ancient World

15 E 84th St, near Madison Ave • Tues–Thurs, Sat & Sun 11am–6pm, Fri 11am–8pm • Free • ☎ 212 992 7843, ⓦ isaw.nyu.edu • Subway #4, #5, #6 to 86th St

Primarily a cutting-edge research facility, NYU's **Institute for the Study of the Ancient World** also hosts thought-provoking exhibitions on prehistory – anything from mysterious Central European objects dating back five thousand years to ancient grave goods from the Republic of Georgia. Exhibitions usually last five months, but sometimes there are gaps between shows, so check in advance.

Park Avenue Christian Church

1010 Park Ave, at E 85th St • Daily 8am–5pm • Free • ☎ 212 288 3246, ⓦ parkavenuechristian.com • Subway #4, #5, #6 to 86th St

The Upper East Side's surfeit of spectacular churches continues with Gothic **Park Avenue Christian Church**, completed in 1911 by the ubiquitous firm of Ralph Adams Cram to mimic La Sainte-Chapelle in Paris – an audacious comparison that, incredibly, it almost pulls off. The magnificent Tiffany windows are the showstoppers here, a blend of figurative and symbolic coloured panels.

One block south at 980 Park Ave lies the incredibly opulent **Church of St Ignatius Loyola** (same hours; ⓦ stignatiusloyola.org), a grand Italian Baroque masterpiece of marble and vibrant murals that successfully re-creates Italy's High Renaissance (despite being completed for the Jesuits in 1898).

Neue Galerie

1048 Fifth Ave, at E 86th St • Mon & Thurs–Sun 11am–6pm • $20, free first Fri of the month 6–8pm; premium admission $30 (guarantees entry at designated time slot; buy online) • ☎ 212 628 6200, ⓦ neuegalerie.org • Subway #4, #5, #6 to 86th St

Once frequented only by aficionados, long lines now regularly form outside the small but enchanting **Neue Galerie**, dedicated to early twentieth-century art from Austria and Germany. The increased popularity is largely thanks to the 2015 film *Woman in Gold*, starring Helen Mirren, which told the remarkable story of the museum's star painting, **Gustav Klimt**'s *Portrait of Adele Bloch-Bauer I*, a resplendent example of Klimt's "Golden Period". The Bloch-Bauers were one of Vienna's richest Jewish families; the painting was looted by the Nazis in 1938 but descendants sued the Austrian government and had the painting returned in 2006 – the gallery is said to have paid $135 million for it soon after. The portrait holds court on the wood-panelled second floor, dedicated to art from Vienna circa 1900, where you'll also find exceptional work by **Egon Schiele** and **Max Oppenheimer**. The third floor is usually reserved for rotating German work from various movements of the early twentieth century: look out for Paul Klee (of the Blaue Reiter and Bauhaus movements), Ernst Ludwig Kirchner (of Die Brücke) and Otto Dix (of the Neue Sachlichkeit). If you don't have much time, consider buying the "premium admission" tickets online, which guarantee that you'll jump the queue.

The gallery occupies an ornate Georgian-style mansion completed in 1914 by Carrère & Hastings for industrialist William Starr Miller, but became the residence of formidable New York socialite Grace Vanderbilt between 1944 and 1953, after the death of her millionaire husband, Cornelius Vanderbilt III. In 2001, it was transformed into the museum, thanks largely to the work of New York art collectors Serge Sabarsky and Ronald S. Lauder. At the Neue's *Café Sabarsky* (see p.309), you can pause for exquisite Viennese pastries before heading back to Museum Mile.

Guggenheim Museum

1071 Fifth Ave, at E 89th St • Mon–Wed, Fri & Sun 10am–5.45pm, Sat 10am–7.45pm • $25, pay what you wish Sat 5.45–7.45pm; multimedia tours free or free apps from iTunes or Google Play via free wi-fi; guided tours daily 2pm (free) • ☎ 212 423 3500, ⓦ guggenheim.org • Subway #4, #5, #6 to 86th St

Multistorey car park or upturned beehive? Whatever you may think of the collection, it's the **Guggenheim Museum** building that steals the show. The structure, designed by **Frank Lloyd Wright** specifically for the museum, caused a storm of controversy when it was unveiled in 1959, bearing, as it did, little relation to the statuesque apartment buildings of this most genteel part of Fifth Avenue. Reactions ranged from disgusted disbelief to critical acclaim – "one of the greatest rooms erected in the twentieth century", wrote Philip Johnson, himself no slouch in the architectural genius stakes. Time has been kinder than his contemporaries were – nearly half a century later, the museum is now a beloved New York landmark.

The institution's namesake, **Solomon R. Guggenheim** (1861–1949), was one of America's richest men, thanks to his silver and copper mines. Although abstract art was considered little more than a fad at the time, Guggenheim, always a man with an eye for a sound investment, began collecting modern paintings with fervour. He bought wholesale the canvases of **Kandinsky**, then added works by **Chagall**, **Klee** and **Léger**, among others, and exhibited them to a bemused American public in his suite of rooms in the *Plaza Hotel*. The Guggenheim Foundation was created in 1937; after exhibiting the collection in various rented spaces, it commissioned Wright to design a permanent home. The museum's holdings have been bolstered since Guggenheim's day via acquisitions and donations. A significant gift came in 1976 when collector **Justin K. Thannhauser** handed over more works by Cézanne, Degas, Gauguin, Manet, Toulouse-Lautrec, Van Gogh and Picasso, among others, greatly enhancing the museum's Impressionist and Post-Impressionist holdings.

The building

Collection of art aside, it's the **structure** that dominates – it's not hard to theorize that the egomaniacal Wright engineered it that way. Most visitors find it difficult not to be impressed (or sidetracked) by the tiers of cream concrete overhead, an uplifting interior space designed so that the public could experience the spiral of the central rotunda from top to bottom. The circular galleries rise upward at a not-so-gentle slope, so you may prefer to start at the top of the museum and work your way down; most of the temporary exhibits are designed to be seen that way.

The collection

Magnificent **temporary exhibitions** take up most of the museum, but you'll always see plenty of **Kandinsky**'s exuberant work (most temporary shows are linked, albeit tenuously, to pieces in the permanent collection). The Level 3 annexe normally houses the permanent **Kandinsky Gallery**, where you'll find some of the best pieces, including the jarring *Komposition 8*.

The Level 2 annexe (Thannhauser Gallery) also contains a small permanent display from the **Thannhauser Collection**: it's almost overwhelming to immediately see **Picasso**'s haunting *Woman Ironing* (on the right as you enter the annexe). Next in line are works by **Van Gogh** including his vivid *Roadway with Underpass* and *Landscape with Snow*. Further around the room you'll find a **Gauguin**, *In the Vanilla Grove*; **Monet**'s *The Palazzo Ducale Seen from San Giorgio*; and **Cézanne**'s hazy *Bibémus* and the wonderful *Man with Crossed Arms*. Note, though, that even the permanent displays get moved around, so you may not see all of the above.

Cooper Hewitt, Smithsonian Design Museum

2 E 91st St, at Fifth Ave • Daily 10am–6pm, Sat till 9pm • $18 ($16 online); pay what you wish Sat 6–9pm • ☎ 212 849 8400, ⓦ cooperhewitt.org • Subway #6 to 96th St

Housed in an elegant mansion completed for industrialist **Andrew Carnegie** in 1902, the **Cooper Hewitt, Smithsonian Design Museum** was established by the granddaughters of Peter Cooper (see p.90). The newest incarnation of the museum blends modern galleries with the original staircase, Scottish oak interiors and parquet floors – don't miss the first-floor Drawing Room (now housing changing exhibits), and the old Carnegie Library on the second floor, designed by Lockwood de Forest (see p.99) and adorned with intricate Indian-style teak carvings. Much of the museum comprises temporary or rotating exhibits with a design theme (such as how tools extend the human body), though some version of "**Making Design**" on the second floor, showcasing the permanent collection, should be on display; porcelain chess sets, rubber chairs, steel necklaces and digitally printed fruit, but also one of the largest collections of work from American artists Winslow Homer and Frederic Edwin Church. The "**Hewitt Sisters Collect**" galleries are housed in the former Carnegie bedrooms and display some of the original collection of founders Sarah and Eleanor Hewitt (prints, drawings, furniture and, oddly, birdcages).

14

On entry you'll be given a gimmicky but super cool "**Pen**" that you can use to interact with touchscreen tables inside and draw your own wallpaper designs in the **Immersion Room**. The pens are also able to "save" exhibits you like (through touch technology), accessible via a dedicated website later (the web address will be on your ticket).

Jewish Museum

1109 Fifth Ave, at E 92nd St • Mon, Tues, Sat & Sun 11am–5.45pm, Thurs 11am–8pm; also Fri 11am–5.45pm March–Nov • $15, Sat free, Thurs 5–8pm pay what you wish • ☎ 212 423 3200, ⓦ thejewishmuseum.org • Subway #6 to 96th St

Given how Jewish culture has flourished in New York, it is fitting that the **Jewish Museum** is the largest museum of Judaica outside Israel. Housed in the French Gothic **Felix Warburg Mansion** (built for the famous Jewish banker in 1908), the museum was given a huge makeover in 2017. In future most exhibitions are likely to be temporary (tackling subjects such as the work of Walter Benjamin), though the third-floor "**Scenes from the Collection**" is expected to be permanent; the 650 rare objects on display will include ancient pottery, ageing Hanukkah lamps, Roman burial stones and precious Torahs, through to contemporary Jewish art (individual items will revolve every six months to a year – the museum owns nearly 30,000 objects). As an added bonus, there's now a branch of lauded Jewish deli *Russ & Daughters* (p.290) in the basement.

It's a short walk from here north to the next museum, but make a detour along East 97th Street to see the **St Nicolas Russian Orthodox Cathedral**, its onion domes and crosses a wonderfully incongruous slice of Moscow amid the East Side mansions.

Museum of the City of New York

1220 Fifth Ave, at E 103rd St • Daily 10am–6pm • $18; free tours Wed, Fri & Sun 2pm • ☎ 212 534 1672, ⓦ mcny.org • Subway #6 to 96th St

Housed in a grand neo-Georgian building purpose-built in 1930 (that also served as the posh high school in the cult TV series *Gossip Girl*), the **Museum of the City of New York** has been transformed by major renovations in recent years and is well worth several hours of your time (it's rarely busy). Most of the stylish galleries feature temporary exhibits – subjects delve into all sorts of New York-themed topics, from affordable housing design and Currier & Ives prints (the museum has one of the world's largest collections) to World Fairs and hip-hop. The first-floor "**New York at Its Core**" is permanent, with two illuminating galleries tracing the city's history from 1609 to 2012, with a third room crammed with video and interactive programmes that help to imagine New York's future. Don't miss the excellent "**Timescapes**" audiovisual presentation in the basement (30min; every 40min), narrated by Stanley Tucci, which tackles the history of the city from the Lenape to the present day. The **Activist New York** gallery (second floor) should also be permanent, a thought-provoking journey through the city's most contentious protest movements, from fighting against slavery and for women's suffrage to ongoing debates on LGBT rights, park access and bike lanes. Also on the second floor is the museum's prized **Stettheimer Dollhouse**, a giant, intricate work of art created by Carrie Walter Stettheimer between 1916 and 1935.

North and east of here, the neighbourhood rather joltingly switches from blocks of quiet, moneyed apartment buildings to **El Barrio**, or **Spanish Harlem** (see p.205).

Yorkville and around

Subway Q, #4, #5 or #6 to 86th St

It's only in **Yorkville** that the Upper East Side displays minute traces of New York's European immigrant history: around 1900, this was a German–Hungarian neighbourhood that spilled out from East 79th to 96th streets between Lexington Avenue and the East River.

Hints of the old neighbourhood include sausage-maker **Schaller & Weber**, at 1654 Second Ave at East 86th Street (Mon–Sat 10am–7pm), established in 1937; and **Heidelberg**, next door (see p.310), which is one year older. **Orwasher's Bakery**, at 308 E 78th St near Second Avenue (Mon–Sat 7.30am–8pm, Sun 8am–6pm), was founded by Hungarian Jewish émigré Abraham Orwasher in 1916.

14

Gracie Mansion

East End Ave, at E 88th St • 1hr tours Tues 10am, 11am, 2pm & 3pm • Free, reservations required, online only • ☎ 212 676 3060, ⊛ 1.nyc.gov/site/gracie/index.page • Subway Q to 86th St

One of the reasons that riverside Carl Schurz Park, at the end of East 86th Street, is so exceptionally well maintained is the high-profile security that surrounds **Gracie Mansion**. Built in 1799 by Scottish-born merchant Archibald Gracie, it is one of the best-preserved Federal-style buildings in New York. Appropriated by the city in 1896 (in lieu of unpaid taxes), Gracie Mansion has been the official **residence of the mayor of New York City** since 1942, when Fiorello La Guardia set up house here; the name's a misnomer, since it's more a large wood-frame house than a grand residence. Current mayor **Bill de Blasio** (from 2014) and his photogenic family have opted to live at Gracie Mansion (at least until January 2018); a far cry from the **Michael Bloomberg** era (2002–13), when the billionaire and three-time incumbent chose to reside at his own (far more luxurious) digs.

Tours, reserved in advance, should be available on Tuesdays, but always check the website for the latest. The mansion was meticulously restored in 2002 (and the art given a makeover by the de Blasios in 2015), but other than a few antiques and the bold murals in the dining room, the house itself isn't particularly compelling; the tours are most interesting for the effusive guides and the stories associated with past mayors.

Mount Vernon Hotel Museum

421 E 61st St, between First and York aves • Tues–Sun 11am–4pm • $8; visits by guided tours only (provided on demand until 3.30pm) • ☎ 212 838 6878, ⊛ mvhm.org • Subway N, R, W, #4, #5, #6 to Lexington Ave/East 59th St

Close to the East River is the **Mount Vernon Hotel Museum and Garden**, a fine schist stone house squashed between modern tower blocks. Inside, you'll find a series of 1820s period rooms, meticulously restored since 1924 when the house was saved by the Colonial Dames of America (an association of women who can trace their ancestry back to colonial times). The Dames were attracted by a connection with **Abigail Adams Smith** (daughter of President John Adams), though recent research has revealed this to be rather tenuous; the property was indeed once part of an estate bought by Abigail and her husband in 1795 (when this area was lush countryside), but the family soon went bankrupt, and it was actually completed as a carriage house in 1799 by the new owner. It served as a hotel between 1826 and 1833 before reverting to a private residence.

Roosevelt Island

Roosevelt Island sits in the middle of the East River, an odd little corner of New York that's home to around thirteen thousand people. While the modern tower blocks and new town layout might seem a little soulless, there is a languid, small-community vibe on the island that can be appealing – it also has a breezy promenade with fabulous views of Midtown, and a scintillating (and bargain) **cable-car ride** across the river. The south half the island is to change dramatically in the next few years, however, as **Cornell University** builds its new, innovative technology campus here.

ARRIVAL AND INFORMATION

Public transport A scenic aerial tramway near the Queensboro Bridge (E 60th St and Second Ave) connects Manhattan with Roosevelt Island (3min) every 15min, 6am–2am, Fri & Sat until 3.30am; every 7.5min during rush hour; $2.75 one-way (with Metrocard); ☎ 212 832 4583. You can also take the F train here. The Roosevelt Island Red Bus (free) loops from Tramway Plaza north to the new Octagon development then down to Southpoint Park.

Information Head to the Roosevelt Island Historical Society kiosk, situated across from the tramway station (☎ 212 688 4836, ⓦ rihs.us); usually open Mon & Wed–Sun noon–5pm, though times vary.

14

Brief history

Only two miles long and no more than 800ft wide, the island was known as **Minnahannock** by the local Native Americans. In 1686, ownership passed to English farmer Robert Blackwell, who imaginatively renamed it **Blackwell Island**. In 1828, the city of New York snapped up the land for $32,000 and assigned it for use as a **quarantine site** for criminals, lunatics and smallpox victims; in 1843, Charles Dickens came to expose conditions of the chronically ill, insane and destitute who were crowded into the eight hospitals and asylums built here. By 1921, it was officially known as **Welfare Island**, but by the 1950s much of the island was deserted, forgotten and unloved. Forward-thinking city mayor John Lindsay enlisted architects John Burgee and Philip Johnson to demolish most of the old buildings and create a master plan for new residential living areas. Duly rechristened Roosevelt Island in 1973, the island received its first new inhabitants two years later. Today, locals are fiercely protective of their hidden enclave: to snag one of the cheap apartments here, you'll have to join the years-long official waiting list.

North island

Arriving via the tramway or subway, stroll north along Main Street to see the white clapboard **Blackwell House**, built between 1796 and 1804 by James Blackwell; the exterior has been lovingly restored, but you usually can't go inside. From here you can take the bus or wander up the west promenade soaking up the views of the Upper East Side. At the north end of the island, **Octagon Tower** was built in 1839 as the admin centre of New York's first municipal asylum (most of it was demolished in the 1970s) and is now incorporated into the Octagon Development; you can take a peek at the magnificent domed lobby and spiral staircase inside. At the northern tip of the island itself, **Lighthouse Park** affords excellent views of the upper reaches of the East River, and is also home to a 50ft-high neo-Gothic lighthouse, dating back to 1872.

South island

The southern end of the island is encompassed by **Southpoint Park** and the **Franklin D. Roosevelt Four Freedoms Park** (Mon & Wed–Sun: April–Sept 9am–7pm, Oct–March 9am–5pm; free; ⓦ fdrfourfreedomspark.org), designed by famed architect Louis Kahn in the 1970s but only completed in 2012. Lined with 120 linden trees, the tranquil park ends at the island's southern tip with a portrait bronze of the 32nd president and his "four freedoms", engraved in large slabs of granite. Adjacent Southpoint Park contains a ghostly reminder of the island's past: the ruins of the **Smallpox Hospital**, completed in 1856 by architect James Renwick. Nearby, the **Strecker Laboratory**, the city's premier laboratory for bacteriological research when it opened in 1892, was restored in the early 1990s and houses subway electrical infrastructure.

Upper West Side and Morningside Heights

While the Upper East Side has always been a privileged stronghold, the Upper West Side, its counterpart on the other side of Central Park, is the slightly younger, vaguely hipper, but nonetheless affluent rival. A decade or two ago, the Upper West Side was the neighbourhood of choice for upwardly mobile dot-commers, and though those days seem long gone, young professionals and families with school-age children still make up a sizeable part of the population. This isn't to say it lacks glamour; the lower stretches of Central Park West and Riverside Drive are quite fashionable, while the network of performing spaces at Lincoln Center makes the neighbourhood New York's de facto centre of culture.

As you move further north, gorgeous – and occasionally landmarked – blocks pop up in the 80s, 90s and 100s, especially off and along Riverside Drive and the West End. In general, though, the neighbourhood loses some of its lustre along the way, culminating in **Morningside Heights**, home to **Columbia University** at the edge of Harlem, as well as the monolithic **Cathedral of St John the Divine**.

ARRIVAL AND DEPARTURE

By subway The #1, #2 and #3 lines run up Broadway the length of the Upper West Side and Morningside Heights, with the #1 stopping locally every six or so blocks; the B and C trace the path up and down Central Park West.

Upper West Side

North of 59th Street, Midtown West morphs into the largely residential **Upper West Side**, though the area around Lincoln Center is quite commercial. The neighbourhood stretches alongside Central Park, running west from the park to the Hudson River, and north from Columbus Circle at 59th Street to 110th Street and the beginning of Morningside Heights. Its main artery is **Broadway** and its twin pinnacles of prosperity are the historic apartment houses of **Central Park West** and **Riverside Drive**. In between is a chequerboard of modern high-rise buildings, old brownstones, gourmet markets, flashy boutiques and family restaurants.

15

Brief history

Like practically every other neighbourhood in the city, the Upper West Side was once farmland. That began to change in 1879, when the opening of the Ninth Avenue elevated train made the open space west of Central Park more accessible to city residents, who mainly still lived downtown. Cheap tenements began to pop up, and the New York Central Railroad line, which transported livestock to the 60th Street stockyards, went in about a year later. Between 59th and 65th streets, the neighbourhood became home to more warehouses than anything else, and the district had the early makings of a soulless slum.

One diamond in the rough, though, was the **Dakota Building** on 72nd Street, built in 1884. Slowly, other townhouses and high-class living quarters rose around it, displacing some of the hulking warehouses. Ten years later, as Manhattan began to grow north in earnest, the confluence of Eighth Avenue, Broadway and 59th Street became a hotbed of excitement. Concerts were held at the Majestic Playhouse on Broadway and 60th Street, theatres showcased popular vaudeville acts and quality watering holes multiplied. By the 1920s, theatres for all types of entertainment (some more risqué than others) lined the Ninth Avenue train circuit. By 1929, shopping had taken over as the neighbourhood's main attraction, and the area has hardly looked back since.

Columbus Circle

Intersection of Broadway, Central Park West and 59th St • Subway A, B, C, D, #1 to 59th St-Columbus Circle

Columbus Circle is a roundabout, a rarity in Manhattan. It's also a pedestrian's worst navigation nightmare – be careful crossing the street. Amid the hum of traffic it's easy

---

UPPER WEST SIDE AND MORNINGSIDE HEIGHTS HIGHLIGHTS

American Museum of Natural History Best with kids, who'll love the dinosaur fossils on display. See p.190

Barney Greengrass Visit the sturgeon king for the best in smoked fish. See p.313

A night at the opera Dress up for a performance at the Lincoln Center's Metropolitan Opera. See p.186

Riverside Park Enjoy waterfront views and plenty of room to roam. See p.193

EATING

Absolute Bagels	2
Awash	3
Bar Boulud	23
Barney Greengrass	8
Boat Basin Café	17
Bouchon Bakery	25
Café Lalo	13
Café Luxembourg	22
Caffè Storico	19
Calle Ocho	15
Celeste	10
Dovetail	18
Flor de Mayo	5
Gennaro	7
Good Enough to Eat	9
Gray's Papaya	21
Jacob's Pickles	11
Jean-Georges	24
Kefi	12
Peacefood Café	14
Per Se	26
Saiguette	4
Salumeria Rosi Parmacotto	20
Tom's Restaurant	1
Turkuaz	6
Zabar's Café	16

SHOPPING

Apple Store	6
Barney Greengrass	2
Blades West	5
Book Culture	1
Microsoft Store	7
Town Shop	3
Zabar's	4

ACCOMMODATION

Beacon	5
Broadway Hotel & Hostel	
Hostelling International New York	1
Lucerne	3
NYLO	4

DRINKING AND NIGHTLIFE

BARS

Dead Poet	4
Dublin House Tap Room	5
E's Bar	3

LIVE MUSIC VENUES

Dizzy's Club Coca-Cola	6
Postcrypt Coffeehouse	1
Smoke	2

0 ___ 400
yards

UPPER WEST SIDE
& MORNINGSIDE HEIGHTS

to overlook Columbus himself, a **statue** of whom stands uncomfortably atop a lone column in the centre island. Sit on the steps below and you can check out some striking nearby architecture.

Time Warner Center

10 Columbus Circle • Mon–Sat 10am–9pm, Sun 11am–7pm, restaurant hours may vary from these • Subway A, B, C, D, #1 to 59th St-Columbus Circle

The glitzy **Time Warner Center**, a massive, multimillion-dollar home for companies like CNN and Warner Books, finally opened in February 2004 after a highly publicized and problematic construction that included worker deaths and an on-site fire. The business part of the complex squats on top of the Shops at Columbus Circle (ⓦ theshopsat columbuscircle.com), a multistorey mall where, aside from some 45 or so mostly high-end stores, you'll find a couple of the city's priciest restaurants, including *Per Se*, run by Thomas Keller (see p.312). If your budget doesn't allow for a few hundred per head for dinner, you can kill some time – and still try some of Keller's creations – at the casual, third-floor *Bouchon Bakery* (see p.313), which overlooks the shopping ruckus.

15

Museum of Arts and Design

2 Columbus Circle • Tues–Sun 10am–6pm, Thurs & Fri till 9pm • $16; pay what you wish Thurs after 6pm, free volunteer-led tours (with admission) at 11.30am & 3pm • ☎ 212 299 7777, ⓦ madmuseum.org • Subway A, B, C, D, #1 to 59th St-Columbus Circle

The oddball, vaguely Venetian building of white marble capped by lollipop columns and portholes that once loomed over Columbus Circle's southern side (at no. 2) was originally constructed as a museum showplace for Huntington Hartford's private art collection, opening its doors to the public in 1964. As a misjudged counter to his contemporaries' funding of Expressionist art, however, the museum lasted only five years, while the building itself was considered by some New York residents to be one of the city's grand follies, a sentiment that resonated for years afterwards.

Despite this, and after years of standing empty and falling into disrepair, preservationists were furious when the **Museum of Arts and Design** chose the site for the relocation of its collection. The battle was fought over whether or not the museum's practical needs should take precedence over the building's architectural importance to the city. In the end, with lawsuits flying all around, the museum won its case. The Museum of Arts and Design moved in after $90 million worth of renovations had converted the former gallery into a sleek tower with random cutaways that allow light to penetrate the building and which tripled the exhibition space. The eclectic collection, featuring everything from blown-glass objets d'art to contemporary jewellery, is now displayed to full effect across half the building's twelve floors, which also contain a small theatre and artist-in-residence studios. Changing exhibits cover a wide array of media (from paper to porcelain to metal to glass) and are often accompanied by lectures and workshops. A modern American restaurant, *Robert*, occupies the top floor and offers extravagant views.

Around Columbus Circle

Opposite Columbus Circle, on the park side, stands the **Maine Monument**, a large stone column with the prow of a ship jutting out from its base, erected in 1913 and dedicated to the 260 seamen who died when the battleship *Maine* inexplicably exploded in Havana Harbor in 1898, propelling forward the Spanish-American War. The boat was built over nearly a decade's time in the Brooklyn Navy Yard (see p.219). Across the street, at the junction of Broadway and Central Park West, is the **Trump International Hotel**, which is responsible for the **Unisphere** outside, though it's not a patch on the one out in Flushing Meadows (see p.251).

For aesthetic relief, go west a few blocks and contemplate the **Church of St Paul the Apostle**, at Columbus Avenue and 60th Street (☎ 212 265 3495, ⓦ stpaultheapostle.org), a beautiful Old Gothic structure housing Byzantine basilica features, including a high altar by Stanford White.

New York Society for Ethical Culture

2 W 64th St, at Central Park West • ☎ 212 874 5210, ⓦ nysec.org • Subway #1 to 66th St-Lincoln Center

A few steps north of Columbus Circle is the **New York Society for Ethical Culture**, "a haven for those who want to share the high adventure of integrating ethical ideals into daily life". Founded in 1876 (though the building itself wasn't built until 1902), this distinguished organization also helped to found the NAACP (National Association for the Advancement of Colored People) and the ACLU (American Civil Liberties Union). It holds regular Sunday meetings; organizes occasional recitals and lectures on social responsibility, politics and the like; and conducts film screenings and book discussions.

American Folk Art Museum

2 Lincoln Square, Columbus Ave, at 66th St • ☎ 212 595 9533, ⓦ folkartmuseum.org • Tues–Thurs & Sat 11.30am–7pm, Fri noon–7.30pm, Sun noon–6pm • Free • Subway #1 to 66th St-Lincoln Center

The **American Folk Art Museum**, once housed in an asymmetrical bronze building right next to MoMA (MoMA purchased the structure in 2011, after the Folk Art Museum went into default, and tore it down to build an addition – though is storing its beloved facade somewhere), occupies a smallish exhibit space across from Lincoln Center. What you'll see is somewhat unpredictable and rotates regularly, but the main holdings – which are lent out frequently for travelling exhibitions and to other spaces – include an array of quilts, photos, carvings and unusual portraits by self-taught, or outsider, artists. Free Music Fridays, at 5.30pm, is a draw.

Lincoln Center

Between 62nd and 66th sts, bordered by Amsterdam and Columbus aves and Broadway

Lincoln Center for the Performing Arts, an imposing group of six marble-and-glass buildings arranged around a large plaza, serves as the city's temple of high culture. Home to the world-class **Metropolitan Opera**, the **New York City Ballet** and the **New York Philharmonic**, as well as a host of other smaller companies, Lincoln Center is worth seeing even if you're not catching a performance; the best way is on an **organized tour** – otherwise you'll only be allowed to peek into the ornate lobbies of the buildings.

Not everything takes place in the concert halls; there's a sloped, grassy park atop the glassed-in *Lincoln Ristorante*; an "urban grove", full of trees and benches, sits next to the David H. Koch Theater; and the celebrated **fountain**, a popular meeting spot at the centre of it all, offers *Bellagio*-style effects – designed by the folks who were also responsible for the flamboyant waterworks at the renowned Vegas mega-hotel.

Brief history

The centre is not, as most assume, named for President Abraham Lincoln; rather, it honours the name of the surrounding area in Manhattan's early times, probably named Lincoln for a tenant farmer who tilled the land here. Robert Moses came up with the idea of creating a cultural centre here in the 1950s as a way of "encouraging" the area's gentrification, one of his rare exercises in urban renewal that has been extremely successful. A number of architects worked on the plans, and the complex was finally built in the mid-1960s on a site that formerly held some of the city's poorest slums. In a case of life imitating art imitating life, once the slums were emptied and their residents moved to ghettos farther uptown, the deserted area became a movie set: before construction began in 1960, the run-down buildings served as the open-air location for *West Side Story*, which was based on the stage musical set here.

INFORMATION AND TOURS   **LINCOLN CENTER**

Access The fountain, between 63rd and 64th sts, is a good meeting spot, and the David Rubenstein Atrium, 61 W 62nd St (see opposite), serves as the visitor centre (Mon–Fri 8am–10pm, Sat & Sun 9am–10pm).

Subway #1 to 66th St-Lincoln Center or A, B, C, D to 59th St-Columbus Circle.

Information and events Contact Lincoln Center Information (☎ 212 875 5000 or 5456, ⓦ lincolncenter.org)

for specifics on scheduled entertainment at the Lincoln Center, which is often free (for example, there are crafts festivals in June and September, folk and jazz bands at lunchtime, Thursday evening concerts in the Atrium and dazzling fountain and light displays every evening in the summer). In addition, Lincoln Center hosts a variety of affordable summertime events, including July's Midsummer Night Swing and August's multicultural Out of Doors festival.

Tours Tours leave from the airy, pleasant David Rubenstein Atrium, and take in the main part of the Center (2–5 tours daily 10.30am–4pm, 60–90min; $25; ☏ 212 875 5350). Be warned that they can get booked up and times vary each day (phone ahead to be sure of a place), and note that some focus more on art and architecture; whichever kind you take, you'll likely get to peek in on some rehearsals. The Atrium also hosts free music Thursdays (7.30pm). Backstage tours of the Met are available too: Sept–June Mon–Thurs 3pm, Sun 10.30am & 1.30pm; reservations required; $25; ☏ 212 769 7028.

The David H. Koch Theater

20 Lincoln Center Plaza, Lincoln Center • ☏ 212 496 0600 for ticket information • Subway #1 to 66th St-Lincoln Center

Philip Johnson's spare and elegant **David H. Koch Theater**, on the south side of Lincoln Center Plaza, is home to the New York City Ballet (including its famed annual performances of *The Nutcracker* in December). Its enormous foyer is ringed with balconies embellished with delicate bronze grilles and boasts an imposing, four-storey ceiling finished in gold leaf; the auditorium itself, a flashy jewel-box, feels fitting for the high-art performances. An enormous *Numbers* by Jasper Johns lords it over one of the landings and deserves a look. The ballet season is broken up into autumn, winter and spring, with a long summer off between early June and late September.

15

David Geffen Hall

10 Lincoln Center Plaza, Lincoln Center • ☏ 212 721 6500 • Subway #1 to 66th St-Lincoln Center

Opposite David H. Koch Theater on the north side of Lincoln Center Plaza, **David Geffen Hall** was the first of the three major buildings to be completed. Johnson had a hand in this one, too; he was called in to refashion the interior after its acoustics were found to be below par, and worked in collaboration with sound expert Cyril Harris on the project. Untouched during the renovations that marked the Center's fiftieth anniversary, the hall will be dramatically overhauled, most likely beginning in 2019. The Philharmonic performs here from late September into June, while **Mostly Mozart**, the country's first and most popular indoor summer chamber-music series, takes place in July and August.

WHAT'S IN A NAME?

Famous buildings and institutions, not to mention roads, bridges and more, undergo name changes for various reasons: company transformations (Citicorp to Citigroup), the choice to honour a public figure (the Queensboro Bridge – already also known as the 59th Street Bridge – has become the Ed Koch Queensboro Bridge, in honour of the ex-mayor) or, most commonly, money (note that Avery Fisher Hall has now become David Geffen Hall, thanks to the record exec's $100 million gift). A few of the more noteworthy instances:

OLD NAME	CURRENT NAME	WHY?
Museum of Radio & Television	Paley Center for Arts	William Paley, an early CEO of CBS, founded the museum
New York State Theater	David H. Koch Theater	Billionaire energy mogul who made $100 million donation to Lincoln Center
New York General Post Office	James Farley Building	Democratic politician who was also US Postmaster General
New York Public Library main building	Stephen A. Schwarzmann Building	Investment banker who donated $100 million for renovation and expansion
Triborough Bridge	Robert F. Kennedy Bridge	New York senator and US attorney general

The Metropolitan Opera House

30 Lincoln Center Plaza, Lincoln Center • Tickets available ⓦ metopera.org; see p.357 • Subway #1 to 66th St-Lincoln Center

In contrast to the surrounding Modernist starkness, Lincoln Center Plaza's focal point, the **Metropolitan Opera House** (aka "the Met"), is gushingly ornate and oozes opulence, with enormous crystal chandeliers – more sparkling than ever thanks to every stone being replaced in a 2008 refurbishment – and swooping, red-carpeted staircases, designed for grand entrances in evening wear. Behind two of the high arched windows hang **murals by Marc Chagall**. The artist wanted stained glass, but at the time it was felt that glass wouldn't last long in an area still less than reverential toward the arts, so paintings were hung behind square-paned glass to give a similar effect. These days, they're covered for part of the day to protect them from the sun; the rest of the time they're best viewed from the plaza outside. The mural on the left, *Le Triomphe de la Musique*, is cast with a variety of well-known performers, while *Les Sources de la Musique* is reminiscent of Chagall's renowned scenery for the Met production of *The Magic Flute*: the god of music strums a lyre while a Tree of Life, Verdi and Wagner all float down the Hudson River.

15

Lincoln Center plazas

Two piazzas flank the Met. To the south there is **Damrosch Park**, a large space facing the Guggenheim Bandshell, where chairs are set up in the summer so you can catch free lunchtime concerts and various performances, namely those that are part of the Out of Doors Festival. To the north you will find the lovely, smaller **Hearst Plaza**, which has an infinity pool, and the so-called **Illumination Lawn**, a grassy spot on the roof of a stylish café-restaurant. It also faces the **Vivian Beaumont Theater**, designed by Eero Saarinen in 1965 and home to the smaller **Mitzi E. Newhouse Theater** and **Claire Tow Theater**, allowing Broadway, off-Broadway and off-off-Broadway venues to coexist under the same roof.

New York Public Library for the Performing Arts

40 Lincoln Center Plaza, Lincoln Center • Mon & Thurs noon–8pm, Tues, Wed, Fri & Sat noon–6pm • Free • ☎ 917 275 6975 or ☎ 212 870 1630, ⓦ nypl.org/locations/lpa • Subway #1 to 66th St-Lincoln Center

The **New York Public Library for the Performing Arts** holds over eight million items (everything from performing-arts ephemera to scores and manuscripts), plus a museum that exhibits costumes, set designs and music scores; it hosts performances and screenings as well. In 2017 it acquired Lou Reed's archives, full of the singer's penned lyrics, recordings and all kinds of memorabilia.

Alice Tully Hall, Walter Reade Theater and Juilliard School of Music

Broadway, at 65th St

Off of Lincoln Center Plaza stand a few more related structures, including **Alice Tully Hall**, a recital hall that houses the Chamber Music Society of Lincoln Center, and the **Walter Reade Theater**, which features foreign films and retrospectives and, together with the David Geffen and Alice Tully halls, hosts the annual New York Film Festival in September (see p.409). The celebrated **Juilliard School of Music** is in an adjacent building (see p.357).

Dante Park

The smallish **Dante Park**, an island on Broadway across from the main Lincoln Center Plaza, features a statue of its namesake; the American branch of the Dante Alighieri Society put it up in 1921 to commemorate the 600th anniversary of the writer's death. But the park's *pièce de résistance* is a piece of art dating from 1999: *Time Sculpture*, a bronze and stone geometric slab featuring a series of large clocks, was designed by Philip Johnson and dedicated to the patrons of Lincoln Center.

Central Park West

Central Park West stretches north from Columbus Circle to 110th Street along the western edge of the park. Home to some of the city's most architecturally distinguished apartment buildings, like the **Dakota** and **Majestic**, as well as the enormous **American Museum of Natural History**, it bustles with taxis and tour buses. In contrast, the side streets between Central Park West and Columbus Avenue in the upper 60s and 70s are quiet, tree-lined and filled with beautifully renovated brownstones, many of which are single-family homes.

Most of the monolithic, mansion-inspired apartment complexes in this area date from the early twentieth century and rim the edge of the park, hogging the best views. The southernmost of these is the **Hotel des Artistes**, at 1 W 67th St on Central Park West. It was built in 1917 especially for artists (hence the name), and was once the Manhattan address for the likes of Noël Coward, Norman Rockwell, Isadora Duncan and Alexander Woollcott. The building now consists of expensive apartments.

Four blocks north, between 71st and 72nd streets, you'll find the fittingly named **Majestic**. This gigantic, pale yellow, Art Deco landmark was thrown up in 1930 and is best known for its twin towers and avant-garde brickwork.

15

Dakota Building

1 W 72nd St, at Central Park West • Subway B, C to 72nd St

One of New York's more illustrious residences, the **Dakota Building** was a very early exercise in large housing co-operatives. So the story goes, when construction finished in 1884, its uptown location was considered as remote as the Dakota Territory by Manhattanites (in truth, the builder had a thing for many of the new names in the West; he named a contemporary development in Midtown West the Wyoming – a replacement of that apartment, under the same name, still stands). Whatever the case, this grandiose hulk of German Renaissance masonry is undeniably impressive. Its turrets, gables and other odd details were all included for one reason: to persuade wealthy New Yorkers that life in an apartment could be just as luxurious as in a private house. For the most part, the developers succeeded: over the years, few of the residents here haven't had some sort of public renown, whether Lauren Bacall, Judy Garland or Leonard Bernstein; of course, it's best known as the home of the late John Lennon (see box below).

San Remo

145–146 Central Park West, at 74th St • Subway B, C to 72nd St

North of the Dakota Building is **San Remo**, another apartment complex, dating from 1930, which is one of the most significant components of the skyline here: its ornate twin

---

THE DEATH OF JOHN LENNON

The Dakota Building, at 1 W 72nd St, is most famous as the former home of **John Lennon** – and present home of his widow, **Yoko Ono**, who owns a number of the building's apartments. It was outside the Dakota, on the night of December 8, 1980, that the ex-Beatle was murdered – shot by a man who professed to be one of his greatest admirers.

His murderer, **Mark David Chapman**, had hung around outside the building all day, clutching a copy of his hero's latest album, *Double Fantasy*, and accosting Lennon for his autograph, which he received. When the couple returned from a late-night recording session, Chapman was still there, and he pumped five .38 bullets into Lennon as he walked through the Dakota's 72nd Street entrance. Lennon was rushed to hospital in a taxi, but he died on the way from blood loss. Chapman was given a sentence of twenty years to life in prison; he has since been denied parole on nine separate occasions – Ono has sent a letter opposing his release each time. (He's up again in 2018, but his chances of freedom seem unlikely.)

Fans of Lennon may want to light a stick of incense across the road in **Strawberry Fields** (see p.154), a section of Central Park that has been restored and maintained in his memory through an endowment by Ono.

towers, topped by columned, mock-Roman temples, are visible from most points in Central Park. Architecture aside, the residents' board is known for its snooty exclusiveness: they rejected Madonna as a buyer of a multimillion-dollar co-op, though her former boyfriend Warren Beatty did live here with Diane Keaton; Bono, Steve Martin and Steven Spielberg all have places too (Dustin Hoffman sold his triplex for $21 million a few years back; Demi Moore recently sold hers, a penthouse, for an astonishing $45 million).

Central Park West–76th Historic District

A block north from San Remo is the **Central Park West–76th Historic District**, from 75th to 77th streets on Central Park West, and on 76th Street toward Columbus Avenue. It's home to a number of small, late nineteenth-century row houses, as well as the **Kenilworth Apartments**, at 151 Central Park West, at 75th Street, notable for its mansard roof and carved limestone exterior.

The New-York Historical Society

15

170 Central Park West, at 77th St • Tues–Thurs & Sat 10am–6pm, Fri 10am–8pm, Sun 11am–5pm • $20, ages 5–13 $6; pay what you wish Fri 6–8pm; free tours 2pm & 3.30pm • ☎ 212 873 3400, ⓦ nyhistory.org • Subway B, C to 81st St-Museum of Natural History

The sometimes-overlooked **New-York Historical Society** greatly enhanced its appeal a few years ago with a renovation that added, among other enticements, a soaring entryway, full of city artefacts; a museum within a museum, down in the basement; and a cheery, upscale café-restaurant, *Caffè Storico*, that's open after museum hours for dinner (see p.314).

Start your visit off with a dramatic eighteen-minute film (narrated by Liev Schreiber) running through the history of the city, and then move on to the highlights of the permanent collection. Among the books, prints and portraits, as well as a research library with some two million manuscripts, are illustrations by **James Audubon**, the Harlem artist and naturalist who specialized in lovingly detailed paintings of birds: remarkably, the Historical Society holds all 433 existing original watercolours of Audubon's landmark *Birds of America*, though only a handful are shown at a time (except for a full exhibition in springtime) in order to preserve their condition. Elsewhere, a broad cross-section of **nineteenth-century American painting** holds lots of portraiture and Hudson River School landscapes, most notably Thomas Cole's metaphorical *Course of Empire* series, though the sharp realism of Asher Brown Durand is also worth pausing over. The **Henry Luce Center**, on the top floor, spotlights more than one hundred colourful Tiffany lamps in the Tiffany Gallery and a collection of Americana; meanwhile, a new multimedia Center for Women's History is the first museum space dedicated to its subject. Among its exhibits are pieces from tennis player Billie Jean King's career. In the **library** are the original Louisiana Purchase document and the correspondence between Aaron Burr and Alexander Hamilton that led up to their deadly duel (see box, p.208), though the space is mainly geared toward researchers.

The **DiMenna Children's History Museum**, on the lower level, is an unusual mini-museum. It takes a unique approach by teaching history to children through the history of children; kids (it will probably be of most interest to those 8 to 10) can learn about New Yorkers in the seventeenth to twentieth centuries, from famous folk to orphans and poor children who sold newspapers on the street, as well as thumb through books from an extensive library.

The American Museum of Natural History

Central Park West, between 77th and 81st sts, main entrance to museum on Central Park West at 79th St and to Rose Center on 81st St • Daily 10am–5.45pm, Rose Center open until 8.45pm on first Fri of month • Suggested admission $22, ages 2–12 $12.50, with additional cost for IMAX films, certain special exhibits and Hayden Planetarium shows ($35/$22 for an all-in pass), tours hourly 10.15am–3.15pm • ☎ 212 769 5100, ⓦ amnh.org • Subway B, C to 81st St-Museum of Natural History

The **American Museum of Natural History** is one of the best museums of its kind in the world, an enormous complex of buildings full of fossils, gems, taxidermy and other

THE BUTTERFLY CONSERVATORY

Half the year at the American Museum of Natural History (generally Dec to May), the **Butterfly Conservatory** provides a welcome change from taxidermy and fossils. For an extra $5 (well worth it; note that it's a timed admission ticket), you get to step inside a vivarium – a hothouse environment – and watch colourful butterflies, from all over the world, flit about on plants, walls and, on occasion, you or your neighbour (don't brush them off if they do land on you). It's humid and a bit smelly inside, but you soon forget any discomfort with the magic going on around you. You can even see pupae developing in a display case.

natural specimens. This elegant giant fills four blocks with a strange architectural melange of heavy Neoclassical and rustic Romanesque styles – it was built in several stages, the first of which was overseen by Central Park designer Calvert Vaux. Founded in 1869, it is one of the oldest natural-history museums in the world, with four floors of exhibition halls and some thirty million-plus items on display.

The entrance and second floor

The museum's vast marble front steps on Central Park West are a great place to read or soak up the sun. An appropriately haughty statue of museum co-founder Theodore Roosevelt looks out towards the park from his perch on horseback, flanked by a pair of Native Americans marching gamely alongside. This entrance (which opens onto the second floor) leaves you well positioned for a loop of the more interesting halls on that level: principally the **Hall of Asian Peoples** and **Hall of African Peoples**, both of which are filled with fascinating, often beautiful, art and artefacts, and backed up with informal commentary and indigenous music. The Hall of Asian Peoples begins with relics from Russia and Central Asia, moves on to pieces from Tibet – including a gorgeous re-creation of an ornate, gilded Tibetan Buddhist shrine – and then takes in China and Japan, with displays of some fantastic textiles, rugs, brass and jade ornaments; a Chinese bridal chair is topped with so many ornaments you wonder if it might just tip over when held aloft. The Hall of African Peoples displays ceremonial costumes, musical instruments and masks from all over the continent. Another highlight of this floor is the lower half of the **Hall of African Mammals**, a double-height room whose exhibits continue on to the third-floor balcony: don't miss the life-size family of elephants in the centre of the room (it's fairly difficult to do so).

The third and fourth floors

Once you're on the third floor, stop by the mildly creepy **Reptiles and Amphibians Hall**, filled with samples of almost any species in the category. A little less interesting is the **Eastern Woodlands and Plains Indians** exhibit, a rather pedestrian display of artefacts, clothing and the like.

The wildly popular **Dinosaur Exhibit**, the first stop for many, dominates the fourth floor. The museum houses the largest dinosaur collection in the world, with more than one hundred specimens on display. Here, you can touch fossils, watch robotic dinosaurs and walk on a transparent bridge over a 50ft-long Barosaurus spine. The museum has also added an example of what's known as a "titanosaur," measuring more than 120 feet in length – so long, in fact, the model pokes out into the hallway. Interactive computer programs supplement the multilevel exhibits. The rest of the floor is given over to early vertebrates and mammals, from miniature camels to the largest known specimen of turtle.

The first floor

Downstairs on the first floor is the **Hall of Gems and Minerals**, which includes some strikingly beautiful crystals – not least the Star of India, the largest blue sapphire ever found. The enormous, double-height gallery dedicated to **Ocean Life** includes a 94ft-long (life-size) blue whale disconcertingly suspended from the ceiling. The recently refreshed dark corridors, marble floors and illuminated diorama cases of the **Hall of North American Mammals** are filled with stuffed mammoths, stately caribou and flying squirrels, among other creatures big and small. Adjacent to this hall is the **Theodore Roosevelt Memorial Hall**, where you can sit on a bench next to another statue of the president. The greatest draw in this area, however, is the **Hall of Biodiversity**. It focuses on both the ecological and evolutionary aspects of biodiversity, with multimedia displays on everything from the changes humans have wrought on the environment (with examples of solutions brought about by local activists and community groups in all parts of the world) to a walkthrough of a simulated Central African rainforest. The **Lefrak Theater**, also located on this floor, presents some interesting nature-oriented IMAX films (there is an additional charge of $5).

The Rose Center for Earth and Space

Across from the Hall of Biodiversity is the **Rose Center for Earth and Space**, including the **Hall of Planet Earth**, a multimedia exploration of how the Earth works, with displays on a wide variety of subjects such as the formation of planets, underwater rock formation, plate tectonics and carbon dating. Items on display include a 2.7-billion-year-old specimen of a banded iron formation, volcanic ash from Mount Vesuvius and an earthquake monitoring system – a three-drum seismograph and colour screen work together to show real-time seismic activity from around the globe. The centrepiece of the room is the Dynamic Earth Globe, where visitors are able to watch the Earth go through its full rotation via satellite, getting as close as possible to the views astronauts see from outer space.

The Hall of Planet Earth links visitors to the rest of the Rose Center, which is made up of the **Hall of the Universe** and the **Hayden Planetarium**. The latter, an enormous sphere 87ft in diameter, appears to be floating inside a huge cube above the 81st Street entrance. Inside are research facilities, classrooms and two theatres.

The state-of-the-art **Space Theater** uses a Zeiss projector to create sky shows with sources like the Hubble telescope and NASA laboratories; showing roughly every half-hour is the *Dark Universe* ($5), a 25min look at the cosmos narrated by Neil deGrasse Tyson. On the planetarium's second floor, the **Big Bang Theater** offers a multisensory re-creation of the "birth" of the universe. Outside the globe, the **Cosmic Pathway** is a sloping spiral walkway that takes you through thirteen billion years of cosmic evolution via a computerized timeline. It leads to the Hall of the Universe, which offers exhibits and interactive displays on the formation and evolution of the universe, the galaxy, stars and planets, including a mini-theatre where visitors can journey inside a black hole through computerized effects. There is even a display here entitled "The Search for Life" – examining the planetary systems on which life could exist.

North on Broadway

Back on Broadway, at 72nd Street, tiny, triangular **Verdi Square** makes a fine place to take a break from the marvels of Lincoln Center. From the square, featuring a craggy statue in the likeness of the composer, you can fully appreciate the ornate balconies, round towers and cupolas of the **Ansonia Hotel** across the street (2109 Broadway, at West 73rd St). Never actually a hotel (it was planned as luxury apartments), the Ansonia was completed in 1904 and the dramatic Beaux Arts building is still the grande dame of the Upper West Side. It's been home to luminaries like Enrico Caruso, Arturo Toscanini, Lily Pons, Florenz Ziegfeld, Theodore Dreiser, Igor Stravinsky, Babe Ruth and, more recently, Angelina Jolie and Natalie Portman.

The enormous limestone **Apthorp Apartments** occupy an entire block from Broadway to West End Avenue, between 78th and 79th streets, and were built in 1908 by William Waldorf Astor. The ornate iron gates of the former carriage entrance lead into a central courtyard with a large fountain visible from Broadway, though you won't be allowed to stroll in. The building, recently converted to condos from its former rent-stabilized self, is in a fair enough state now, though its fortunes have hiccuped over the years – it was used as the location for the crack factory in the 1991 movie *New Jack City*. The Upper West Side above 79th Street has seen a lot of changes in the last fifteen years as the forces of gentrification have surged northward. One of the older establishments in the area is gourmet hub **Zabar's** (see p.393), at 2245 Broadway, at 80th Street, which has been selling baked goods, cheese, caviar, gourmet coffee and tea – as well as an exhaustive collection of cooking gadgets – since 1934.

Children's Museum of Manhattan

212 W 83rd St, between Broadway and Amsterdam Ave • Tues–Fri & Sun 10am–5pm, Sat 10am–7pm, first Fri of the month 10am–8pm • $12, free first Fri of month 5–8pm • ☏ 212 721 1223, ⓦ cmom.org • Subway #1 to 86th St

Just off Broadway, the **Children's Museum of Manhattan** holds five floors of interactive exhibits that stimulate learning in a fun, relaxed environment for kids (and babies) of all ages. Things rotate somewhat regularly, but a few permanent exhibits can be found: one centres on characters from *Dora the Explorer*, and the other is the floor-wide PlayWorks area, where the younger set can occupy themselves with a talking dragon, fire truck and sand box, among other diversions.

Riverside Park

At the western edge of 72nd Street begins the four-mile stretch of **Riverside Park**. The entrance is marked by Penelope Jencks' pensive **Eleanor Roosevelt Monument** on the corner of 72nd Street and Riverside Drive, dedicated in 1996 by then First Lady Hillary Clinton. A less appealing local landmark is the forest of skyscrapers overlooking the park from what used to be derelict shipping yards south of 72nd Street. This development, known as **Riverside South**, evolved – if that's the right word – from longtime plans to build something colloquially known as **Trump City** (who else but the billionaire developer and 45th president); at least the waterfront alongside has been preserved.

Riverside Park was conceived in the mid-nineteenth century as a way of attracting the middle class to the remote Upper West Side and covering the unappealing Hudson River Railway tracks that had been built along the Hudson in 1846. Though not as imposing or as spacious as Central Park, Riverside was designed by the same team: Frederick Law Olmsted and Calvert Vaux. Begun in 1873, the park took 25 years to finish; rock outcrops and informally arranged trees, shrubs and flowers surround its tree-lined main boulevards, and the overall effect is much the same today as it was then. The biggest changes to the park came in the 1960s, when Robert Moses widened it and added some of his usual concrete touches, including the rotunda at the **79th Street Boat Basin**. The basin is a delightful place for a break, with paths leading down to it located on either side of 79th Street at Riverside Drive (you'll hit Moses' rotunda first – keep going until you see water). Not on many visitors' itineraries, this is a small harbour and one of the city's most peaceful locations – and, once, a thriving location for houseboat dwellers, though hardly any remain. There are summertime **kayak launches** from here and from a bit farther south, at 72nd Street.

The park continues along the water, punctuated by tennis courts, ball fields and a community garden (between 90th and 91st streets) before terminating just north of the General Grant National Memorial (see p.196).

Riverside Drive

The main artery of the Riverside Park neighbourhood is **Riverside Drive**: starting at West 72nd Street, it winds north, flanked by palatial townhouses and multistorey apartment buildings, mostly thrown up in the early part of the twentieth century. In the 70s, especially, there is a concentration of lovely turn-of-the-twentieth-century townhouses, many with copper-trimmed mansard roofs and private terraces or roof

15

RIVERSIDE DRIVE MONUMENTS

Riverside Drive is dotted with notable monuments: at West 89th Street, look for the **Soldiers and Sailors Monument** (1902), a marble memorial to the Civil War dead. Then there's the **Joan of Arc Monument** at West 93rd Street, which sits on top of a 1.6-acre cobblestone-and-grass park named Joan of Arc Island and is located in the middle of the Drive; it dates from 1915. You'll hit the **Firemen's Memorial** at West 100th Street, a stately frieze designed in 1913 with the statues of Courage and Duty on its ends. The most famous of Riverside Drive's monuments is **Grant's Tomb** (see p.196), further north.

gardens. Between 80th and 81st streets you will find a row of historic **landmark townhouses**: classic brownstones, they have bowed exteriors, bay windows and gabled roofs. You'll find a number of architectural surprises in this area, as many of the residences in the 80s between Riverside and West End have stained-glass windows as well as stone gargoyle faces leering from their facades.

There are more historic apartment buildings on Riverside Drive as you head north between 105th and 106th streets. What is now the **Riverside Study Center** (used by the shadowy Catholic sect Opus Dei) at 330 Riverside is a glorious five-storey Beaux Arts house built in 1900 – note the copper mansard roof, stone balconies and delicate iron scrollwork. The current headquarters of the **New York Buddhist Church** is at 331 Riverside Drive, though it was formerly the home of Marion "Rosebud" Davies, a 1930s actress most famous for her role as William Randolph Hearst's mistress.

The odd little building next door to no. 331 is also part of the church; it showcases a larger-than-life bronze statue of **Shinran Shonin** (1173–1262), the Japanese founder of the Jodo-Shinsu sect of Buddhism. The statue originally stood in Hiroshima and somehow survived the atomic explosion of August 1945. In 1955 it was brought to New York as a symbol of "lasting hope for world peace" and has been in this spot ever since. When it arrived, local lore had it that the statue was still radioactive, so in the 1950s and 1960s children were told to hold their breath as they went by. The Beaux Arts **River Mansion**, as 337 Riverside Drive is called, was home to **Duke Ellington** – and the stretch of West 106th Street between here and Central Park has been tagged Duke Ellington Boulevard in his honour.

Nicholas Roerich Museum

319 West 107th St, off Riverside Drive • Tues–Fri noon–5pm, Sat & Sun 2–5pm • Free, donations welcome • ☎ 212 864 7752, ⓦ roerich.org • Subway #1 to Cathedral Parkway-110th St

Near to Riverside Drive, in a manicured brownstone house, is the overlooked but appealing **Nicholas Roerich Museum**. It contains a small, weird and virtually unknown collection of original paintings by Nicholas Roerich, a Russian artist who lived in India and was influenced by religious mysticism; there are also some pieces by his son on display.

Strauss Park

Broadway, 106th St and West End Ave • Subway #1 to Cathedral Parkway-110th St

At the terminus of West End Avenue – itself running more or less parallel to Riverside Drive – is the small, triangular **Strauss Park**. The statue by Augustus Lukeman of a reclining woman gazing over a water basin was dedicated by Macy's founder Nathan Strauss to his brother and business partner, Isidor, and Isidor's wife, Ida, both of whom went down with the *Titanic* in 1912.

Morningside Heights

North of the Upper West Side, **Morningside Heights** stretches from 110th Street to 123rd Street, west to the Hudson River and east to Morningside Park, a small and rather unspectacular green space. The neighbourhood has a somewhat cool, college-town aura, a diverse mix of academics, professionals and working-class families who have banded together in the name of community preservation. Excepting the massive **Cathedral of Saint John the Divine** and **Columbia University**, there are few sights here per se, but it's worth ambling up here to get a sense of a close-knit neighbourhood, a feeling that the Upper West Side lost some time ago.

The Cathedral Church of Saint John the Divine

1047 Amsterdam Ave, at 112th St · Daily 7.30am–6pm, services throughout the day · Free · ☎ 212 316 7540, ⓦ stjohndivine.org · Subway #1 to Cathedral Parkway-110th St

The **Cathedral Church of Saint John the Divine** rises out of its surroundings with a solid majesty – hardly surprising, since it claims to be the largest Gothic-style cathedral in the world, if yet unfinished. Indeed, its floor space – 600ft long by 320ft wide at the transepts – is big enough to swallow both the cathedrals of Notre Dame and Chartres whole. Still, that would only seem to place it second, behind the Seville Cathedral, in the Gothic race; it is, for certain, the biggest Anglican cathedral in the world.

This Episcopal church was conceived, in 1892, as a Romanesque monolith. When the architect in charge was replaced in 1911, the building's style shifted: it has ended up French neo-Gothic and is one of New York's most impressive sights. Work progressed well until the outbreak of war in 1939, and it wasn't until the late 1970s that it resumed. Though the structure appears finished at first glance, take a look up into one of its huge, incomplete towers, and you'll see how much there is left to do – financial difficulties in the late 1990s halted works, and a fire in 2001 did significant damage to the cathedral. Whether it ever gets completed or not doesn't change the church's activity: St John's is very much a **community church**. It houses a soup kitchen and shelter for the homeless; sponsors HIV testing and health outreach initiatives; and has a gymnasium.

15

The interior

The **Portal of Paradise** at the cathedral's main entrance was completed in 1997, and is dazzlingly carved from limestone and painted with metallic oxide. Keep an eye out for the 32 biblical figures depicted (both male and female) and such startling images as a mushroom cloud rising apocalyptically over Manhattan. The portal is evidence of just how slow progress here really is: the carving took ten years. Only after entering the church does its staggering size become clear; the space is awe-inspiring, and definitely adds to the building's spiritual power. The interior shows the melding of the two architectural styles, particularly in the choir, where a heavy arcade of Romanesque columns rises to a high, Gothic vaulting; it is hoped that the temporary dome will someday be replaced by a tall, delicate Gothic spire.

The open-minded, progressive nature of the church is readily visible throughout the cathedral building: note the intricately carved wood **Altar for Peace**, the **Poets Corner** (with the names of American poets carved into its stone-block floor), and an altar honouring AIDS victims. The amazing stained-glass windows include scenes from both the Bible and American history. All kinds of art, both religious and secular, grace the interior, from teak Siamese prayer chests to seventeenth-century tapestries, to a rare religious work by the late graffiti artist Keith Haring – his final finished piece.

CATHEDRAL TOURS

Public **tours** of the Cathedral Church of Saint John the Divine are given Monday 11am and 2pm, Tuesday to Saturday at 11am and 1pm, and Sunday at 1pm ($14) – meet at the Info Center, the blue booth right inside the main door. "Vertical tours" that allow you to clamber up spiral stone staircases to the roof, and be rewarded with a super view, take place Wednesday, Friday and Saturday at noon, with an additional Saturday tour at 2pm; call ☎ 212 932 7347 to make a reservation ($20). Consider, too, visiting on a Monday around 1pm for the free organ recital.

15

The gardens

Outdoors, the cathedral's south side features the **Bestiary Gates**, their grilles adorned with animal imagery (celebrating the annual Blessing of the Animals ceremony held here on the Feast of St Francis), and a **Children's Sculpture Garden**, showcasing small bronze animal sculptures created by local schoolchildren. Afterwards, take a stroll through the cathedral yard.

Columbia University and around

The seven blocks between Broadway and Morningside Drive from 114th to 121st sts, with its main entrance at Broadway and 116th St • Tours of the campus leave from the Visitor Center at the Low Memorial Library (Mon, Wed & Thurs 1pm, self-guided tours also available; free) • ☏ 212 854 1754, Ⓦ columbia.edu • Subway #1 to 116th St-Columbia University

Ivy League-affiliated **Columbia University** is one of the most prestigious academic institutions in the country. Established in 1754, Columbia has a long and venerable history – it is the country's fifth-oldest institution of higher learning, it awarded the first MD degree in America, and the university sponsored ground-breaking atomic research in the 1940s. The Morningside Heights campus, modelled after the Athenian *agora* (or town square), was laid out by McKim, Mead, and White after the university moved here from Midtown in 1897.

Amid the campus's Italian Renaissance-style structures, the domed and colonnaded **Low Memorial Library**, at 116th St at Broadway, is a real stunner. Built in 1902, the Neoclassical structure is on the New York City Register of Historic Places and is a commanding sight. St Paul's Chapel, with its dome, stained glass and Guastavino tiling, is also worth poking around. Across Broadway sits women's-only **Barnard College**, one of the Seven Sisters' institutions and a part of Columbia University.

Running alongside the campus, Broadway is characterized by a lively bustle, with numerous inexpensive restaurants, bars and cafés, and a few bookstores. The former *West End* bar (2911 Broadway, at 113th Street) was the hangout of Jack Kerouac, Allen Ginsberg and the Beats in the 1950s; it now serves as an events and catering facility under the management of local brewery Bernheim and Schwartz.

Riverside Church

490 Riverside Drive, at 120th St • Daily 9am–5pm, Sun service 10.45am, hour-long tours follow service at 12.15pm • Free • ☏ 212 870 6700, Ⓦ trnyc.org • Subway #1 to 116th St-Columbia University

Several blocks north and west of Columbia University, **Riverside Church** has a graceful French Gothic Revival tower, loosely modelled on the cathedral at Chartres. Like St John the Divine, it has become a community centre for the surrounding parish and puts on the odd musical and theatrical event. Twenty floors up, the **carillon** (the largest in the world, with 74 bells) has great views of Manhattan's skyline, New Jersey and beyond; however, tours up the tower have been suspended for a number of years – and that's unlikely to change soon (you can always call to be sure). Make sure to root around inside the body of the church, too: its open interior stands in stark contrast to the mystery of St John the Divine.

Grant's Tomb

Riverside Drive, at 122nd St • Wed–Sun 9am–5pm, mausoleum open every other hour from 10am; free talks at 11.15am, 1.15pm & 3.15pm • ☏ 212 666 1640, Ⓦ nps.gov/gegr • Subway #1 to 125th St-Columbia University

Up the block from Riverside Church is the General Grant National Memorial, better known as **Grant's Tomb**. This Greek-style memorial is the nation's largest mausoleum, home to the bodies of conquering Civil War hero (and blundering eighteenth US president) Ulysses S. Grant and his wife, in two black marble Napoleonic sarcophagi. The main floor has displays on the general's life and exploits.

Harlem and north Manhattan

The most famous black community in America, Harlem has been the bedrock of African American culture since the 1920s, when poets, activists and jazz blended in the Harlem Renaissance. Though it acquired a notoriety for street crime in the 1970s, it is now a neighbourhood on the rise, thanks to real estate and retail developments. Indeed, Harlem's streets are as safe as any other in New York, and the most pressing issue of the day is gentrification. Though most tourists still visit Harlem solely to see its wonderful gospel choirs on Sundays, you'll also find some fabulous West African and soul food restaurants, a vibrant local jazz scene and plenty of historic sights – some of the prettiest streets in the city are preserved here.

Further uptown is **Hamilton Heights**, a largely residential spot pepped up by Alexander Hamilton's Federal-style historic mansion and the campus of the City College of New York. Continuing north from there, you'll hit the Dominican stronghold of **Washington Heights**, while the northernmost tip of the island, known as **Inwood**, is home to **The Cloisters**, a museum-as-mock-medieval-monastery that holds the Met's superlative collection of medieval art. All the areas detailed below are generally safe for visitors, especially during the day when there are usually lots of people around – just take the usual precautions at night, and stick to the main thoroughfares. To get around at night by **taxi**, your best bet is to use Uber (see p.27) or grab one of the many livery cabs or Boro Taxis cruising the main avenues (see p.26) – negotiate the fare in advance (around $25–30 to Midtown).

ARRIVAL AND INFORMATION

Arrival Subway A, B, C, #1, #2 and #3 to 125th St (for central Harlem); it can be helpful to take a guided tour (see p.30) to get acquainted with the area.

Tourist information You'll find plenty of help at the Harlem Heritage Tourism and Cultural Center, at 104 Malcolm X Blvd, just south of W 116th St; ☏ 212 280 7888, ⓦ harlemheritage

.com); this is the office of local tour operator Neal Shoemaker (see p.30), who is a wealth of local knowledge. His office is nominally open daily 10am–6pm, though Neal is often out on tours. Of the websites that serve the neighbourhood, ⓦ harlemonestop.com and ⓦ exploreharlemnyc.com have excellent listings and local information.

Brief history

Although the Dutch founded the settlement of **Nieuw Haarlem** in 1658, naming it for a town in Holland, the area remained primarily farmland up until the mid-nineteenth century, when the New York and Harlem Railroad linked the area with Lower Manhattan. The suburb's new, fashionable brownstones attracted better-off immigrant families, mainly German Jews from the Lower East Side, but they failed to tempt the wealthy northwards. Black real-estate agents saw their chance: from the late 1890s they snapped up the empty houses for next to nothing, then rented them to the city's growing community of African Americans.

The 1920s saw an explosion of black culture in Harlem, with the musical and literary movement known as the **Harlem Renaissance** (see box, p.200). The Depression and postwar years were not kind to the area, however, and the Renaissance was followed by several decades of worsening economic conditions. Writer **James Baldwin**, who was born here in 1924, simply described his old stomping ground as "squalid"; in **Ralph Ellison**'s 1948 essay **Harlem is Nowhere**, the author of *Invisible Man* states "to live in Harlem is to dwell in the very bowels of the city. . . Harlem is a ruin." In the 1960s and 1970s, drug lords such as **Frank Lucas** and **Nicky Barnes** made millions selling heroin; in the late 1980s, crack-cocaine devastated the neighbourhood.

In the late 1990s, things began to turn around. A plethora of urban and community grants were put into effect for commercial and retail development, housing and general urban renewal. That initial investment is paying off: Harlem's historic areas are well maintained and there seems to be construction everywhere you turn. The questions facing the community now are how to manage and control the area's development (particularly as Columbia University expands into older neighbourhoods), as well as how to reconcile it with the long-term poverty and unemployment still very much in evidence.

Up to 116th Street

Subway B, C to Cathedral Parkway; #2, #3 to Central Park North for 110th St; B, C, #2, #3 to 116th St

Harlem lies north of 110th Street and Central Park, and it's from here along any of Harlem's main north–south arteries to **116th Street** and 125th Street that the neighbourhood's recent transformation is most in evidence. Sixth Avenue becomes Malcolm X Boulevard (though it's still known to many by its old name Lenox Ave), while Seventh Avenue becomes Adam Clayton Powell, Jr Boulevard (shortened to

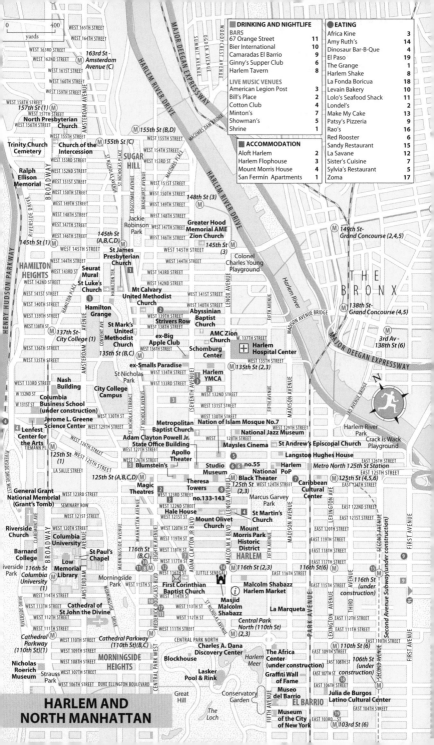

**HARLEM AND
NORTH MANHATTAN**

■ **DRINKING AND NIGHTLIFE**

BARS
67 Orange Street	11
Bier International	10
Camaradas El Barrio	9
Ginny's Supper Club	6
Harlem Tavern	8

LIVE MUSIC VENUES
American Legion Post	3
Bill's Place	2
Cotton Club	4
Minton's	7
Showman's	5
Shrine	1

● **EATING**
Africa Kine	3
Amy Ruth's	14
Dinosaur Bar-B-Que	4
El Paso	19
The Grange	1
Harlem Shake	8
La Fonda Boricua	18
Levain Bakery	10
Lolo's Seafood Shack	11
Londel's	2
Make My Cake	13
Patsy's Pizzeria	9
Rao's	16
Red Rooster	6
Sandy Restaurant	15
La Savane	12
Sister's Cuisine	7
Sylvia's Restaurant	5
Zoma	17

■ **ACCOMMODATION**
Aloft Harlem	2
Harlem Flophouse	3
Mount Morris House	4
San Fermín Apartments	1

THE HARLEM RENAISSANCE

The **Harlem Renaissance**, during which the talents of such icons as Billie Holiday, Paul Robeson and James Weldon Johnson took root and flowered, served as inspiration for generations of African American musicians, writers and performers. In the 1920s, Manhattan's white residents began to notice Harlem's cultural offerings: after downtown went to bed, the sophisticated set drove north, where **jazz musicians** such as Duke Ellington, Count Basie and Cab Calloway played in packed venues like the Cotton Club, Savoy Ballroom, Apollo Theater and Smalls Paradise, and the liquor flowed freely, despite Prohibition. But the Harlem Renaissance wasn't just about music. It was also characterized by the rich body of **literature** produced by Johnson, Langston Hughes, Jean Toomer and Zora Neale Hurston, among many others – Hughes declared the movement to be over in 1931 after the death of noted African American socialite and patron **A'Lelia Walker**.

Yet even before the Great Depression, it was hard to scrape out a living here, and the economic downturn of the 1930s drove out the middle class. It may be because evening revellers never stayed longer than the last drink that neither they, nor many histories of the period, recall the rampant **poverty** that went hand in hand with Harlem's raunchy, anything-goes nightlife.

One of the lasting legacies of this period, however, has been the neighbourhood's sense of **racial consciousness**. First evidenced during the 1920s and 1930s in the writings and speeches of men like Marcus Garvey, W.E.B. DuBois and Charles S. Johnson, the same spirit is still alive today in such larger-than-life firebrands as reverends Al Sharpton (whose National Action Network is based in Harlem) and Calvin Butts (influential minister of the Abyssinian Baptist Church).

16

Powell Blvd here), a primarily residential strip of graceful brownstones. From Cathedral Parkway subway station wander up **Frederick Douglass Boulevard** (Eighth Ave) between 110th and 125th streets to see the most obvious signs of change, with new cafés, stores and bars replacing vacant lots; the new condo buildings around here have been dubbed Harlem's "Gold Coast".

At 116th Street, turn right – the stretch between Frederick Douglass and Malcolm X boulevards has been a hub for West African immigrants since the 1980s and is unofficially known as **Little Senegal** ("Le Petit Sénégal"). It's estimated that at least 40,000 Senegalese have settled in New York in the last few years, as well as smaller groups from Nigeria, Ivory Coast, Guinea and Mali. They originally opened up shops, beauty parlours and restaurants here, though Harlem's gentrification and rising rents have also started to impact this area, with many African businesses moving to the outer boroughs.

Malcolm Shabazz Harlem Market

52 W 116th St, at Malcolm X Blvd • Daily 10am–8pm • Free • ☎ 212 987 8131 • Subway #2, #3 to 116th St

Just beyond Malcolm X Boulevard you'll see the bazaar-like **Malcolm Shabazz Harlem Market**, established in 1994 with help from the nearby mosque (see below), its entrance marked by colourful fake minarets. The market's offerings include T-shirts, jewellery, clothing and more, all with a distinctly Afro-centric flavour – it's worth stopping by, mostly since what's on sale here differs so much from the usual flea-market staples. Note that many stalls don't open until after lunch.

Masjid Malcolm Shabazz

102 W 116th St, at Malcolm X Blvd • Visits by appointment only • Free • ☎ 212 662 2200 • Subway #2, #3 to 116th St

At the junction of Malcolm X Boulevard and West 116th Street, look for the green onion dome of the **Masjid Malcolm Shabazz**, once the Nation of Islam's Temple No.7 and Malcolm X's base until his split with the Nation in 1964 (see box, p.211). After Malcolm's assassination in 1965, the mosque was firebombed, then rebuilt with the dome you see today. The Nation of Islam later moved to 106 W 127th St, and the Shabazz mosque now serves an Orthodox Sunni community of predominantly African American and Senegalese Muslims. Non-Muslims can **visit the mosque**, but you must email ✉ msmosque@aol.com in advance (name, reason to visit, preferred time) – do so and you'll get a rare insight into the American Muslim community.

Mount Morris Park Historic District

Subway #2, #3 to 125th St

The area around Malcolm X Boulevard between West 118th and 124th streets is known as the **Mount Morris Park Historic District**. Initially inhabited by white commuters, the area later became home to the city's second-largest neighbourhood of Eastern European Jewish immigrants (after the Lower East Side), and finally shifted to a primarily black neighbourhood in the 1920s. Today, it's an eminently desirable place to live – writer Maya Angelou lived on 120th Street until her death in 2014 – and the district has an active community-improvement association (☎212 369 4241, ⓦmmpcia.org) that runs events and talks. It also holds the **Morris Park Annual Historic House Tour Open Day** in June, the best time to see inside the area's elegant homes.

One of the district's most interesting buildings is **Mount Olivet Baptist Church**, at 201 Malcolm X Blvd, at West 120th Street, a Greco-Roman-style temple that was built as a synagogue in 1907 (the Baptists bought it in 1925). Compare its design with the sombre, bulky Romanesque Revival **St Martin's Episcopal Church**, at the southeast corner of Malcolm X Boulevard and West 122nd Street; completed in 1889, it's noted for the 42-bell carillon installed in the tower (rung on Sundays). Both buildings open only for services.

Marcus Garvey Park

W 120th and 124th sts, between Mount Morris Park West and Madison Ave • Daily 6am–dusk • Free • ⓦ nycgovparks.org • Subway #2, #3 to 125th St

Heading east along West 122nd Street from Malcolm X Boulevard brings you to **Marcus Garvey Park**, formerly Mount Morris Park; it takes its new name from the black leader of the 1920s. This is where the **Last Poets** arts collective was formed in 1968, at a celebration of Malcolm X's birthday. The park's most notable feature is an octagonal 47ft-high cast-iron **Mount Morris Fire Watchtower**, built in 1857 on a peak in the centre, a unique example of the early-warning devices once found throughout the city and in operation till 1909.

16

125th Street and around

Subway A, B, C, D, #2, #3, #4, #5, #6 to 125th St

The stretch of **125th Street** between Broadway and Park Avenue is Harlem's main commercial drag. It's here that recent investment in the area is most obvious – note the presence of numerous chains and fashion retailers like H&M, The Gap, Jimmy Jazz boutiques and even Whole Foods. Yet this was **Malcolm X**'s beat in the 1950s and 1960s, while jazz poet **Gil Scott-Heron** (who grew up in the Bronx) named his first album *Small Talk at 125th and Lenox* in 1970. Ex-President **Bill Clinton** – still much admired in Harlem – established his offices at 55 W 125th St just east of Malcolm X Boulevard in 2001, a move that in large part accelerated the current renaissance of the area.

Caribbean Cultural Center

120 E 125th St, between Park and Lexington aves • Tues, Wed & Fri 11am–3pm, Thurs 11am–8pm • $5 • ☎ 212 307 7420, ⓦ cccadi.org • Subway #4, #5, #6 to 125th St

The **Caribbean Cultural Center** opened in this former firehouse in 2016, offering a series

---

CRACK IS WACK

Keith Haring fans should make the pilgrimage to the subtly named **Crack is Wack Playground** (E 127th St and Second Ave), where the pop artist painted the now-famous *Crack Is Wack* mural in 1986 on both sides of the handball court walls. Featuring Haring's signature cartoonish style and bright colours, the mural made a serious anti-drug statement at the height of the Harlem crack epidemic. Note that it will be impossible to view the mural (as it's enclosed by a protective shelter) during reconstruction of Harlem River Drive (to be completed by the end of 2019).

of revolving art exhibitions (focused on the African diaspora in the Americas), and a rich programme of events and performances.

National Jazz Museum in Harlem

58 W 129th St • Mon & Thurs –Sun 11am–5pm • Free, $10 suggested donation • ⓦ jazzmuseuminharlem.org • Subway #2, #3 to 125th St

Harlem – along with New Orleans – is one of the cradles of **jazz**. Duke Ellington, Thelonious Monk, Charlie Parker, Count Basie, John Coltrane and Billie Holiday all got their start here, yet there is surprisingly little to show for this musical heritage. The **National Jazz Museum in Harlem** is a rare exception, though for now its main function is to arrange jazz-related programmes, classes and live events (check the website). Aficionados should check it out anyway, with one small gallery full of jazz memorabilia, much associated with **Duke Ellington** ("Ellingtonia") – his white 1920s piano is on display, plus a scarf he gave to his wife and other mementoes. There's also a copy of the now legendary "**Great Day in Harlem**" photo, taken by Art Kane in 1958 and a one-time ensemble of all the era's top jazz musicians (Count Basie, Sonny Rollins and 55 others). Fans can visit the stoop where the shoot took place at 17 E 126th St.

Langston Hughes House

20 E 127th St, between Fifth and Madison aves • Tues noon–5pm, Thurs noon–7pm, Sat noon–5pm • Free • ⓦ itooarts.com • Subway #4, #5, #6 to 125th St

The **Langston Hughes House** is the faded 1869 brownstone where the celebrated poet lived from 1948 till his death in 1967, writing classics such as *Montage of a Dream Deferred* – a plaque marks the connection. The local **I, Too, Arts Collective** leased the house at the end of 2016 – at the time of writing the parlour was open to visitors, with Hughes' typewriter and piano on display – the second and third floors may be open in future. Check the website for details of the group's poetry salons and "creative conversations" series.

Studio Museum in Harlem

144 W 125th St, at Malcolm X Blvd • Thurs & Fri noon–9pm, Sat 10am–6pm, Sun noon–6pm • $7, free Sun • ☎ 212 864 4500, ⓦ studiomuseum.org • Subway #2, #3 to 125th St

The absorbing **Studio Museum in Harlem** is dedicated to contemporary African American painting, photography and sculpture. The permanent collection is displayed on a rotating basis and includes works by Harlem Renaissance-era photographer James Van Der Zee, as well as paintings and sculptures by postwar artists. The museum should remain open during a major expansion over the next couple of years – designed by celebrated architect David Adjaye, the new five-storey facility will feature a glass-fronted lobby, café and a free rooftop terrace.

Adam Clayton Powell, Jr State Office Building

163 W 125th St, at Powell Blvd • Mon–Sat 10am–5pm • Free, photo ID required to enter • ☎ 212 961 4390 • Subway A, B, C, D, #2, #3 to 125th St

Looming over the middle of West 125th Street, the Brutalist **Adam Clayton Powell, Jr State Office Building** was commissioned in 1972 and built on the corner of Powell

---

REVEREND ADAM CLAYTON POWELL, JR

In the 1930s, the **Reverend Adam Clayton Powell, Jr** (1908–72) was instrumental in forcing Harlem's stores, most of which were white-owned and retained a white workforce, to begin employing the blacks whose patronage ensured the stores' survival. Later, he became the first African American on the city council, then New York's first black congressional representative, during which time he sponsored the country's first minimum-wage law. His distinguished career came to an embittered end in 1967 when, amid strong rumours of the misuse of public funds, he was excluded from Congress by majority vote. This failed to diminish his standing in Harlem, where voters re-elected him: he sat until the year before his death, and there's a fitting memorial on the boulevard that today bears his name.

Boulevard (it's still Harlem's tallest building). The building was named in honour of Harlem's first black congressman (see box opposite), and his 12ft-high bronze **statue** was unveiled here in 2005. The lobby contains a small art gallery that displays changing exhibits by local artists (before you go through security).

Apollo Theater and around

253 W 125th St, at Frederick Douglass Blvd • Gift shop daily 10am–6pm • ☎ 212 531 5300, ⓦ apollotheater.org • Subway A, B, C, D, #2, #3 to 125th St

Walk a little further west along 125th Street from the Powell Building and you reach the legendary **Apollo Theater**. Although it's not much to look at from the outside, from 1934 to the 1970s this venue was the centre of black entertainment in New York. Almost all the great figures of jazz and blues played here, along with singers, comedians and dancers; past winners of its famous **Amateur Night** (still running March–Oct Wed 7.30pm; tickets usually $21–33) have included Ella Fitzgerald, Billie Holiday, Luther Vandross, The Jackson Five, Sarah Vaughan and James Brown.

Yet the Apollo is not just a music venue; it's become the spiritual heart of black America, a place where locals and outsiders instinctively come together at important moments in history: when **James Brown**'s casket lay in state in the theatre in 2006, the queues to view it stretched for blocks, and when **Michael Jackson** died in 2009, fans gathered to celebrate his music outside – an official exhibit was arranged inside the theatre a few days later.

Manhattanville

W 125th St to 133rd St, between Broadway and Twelfth Ave • ⓦ manhattanville.columbia.edu

Columbia University's new **Manhattanville** campus opened in 2017, essentially a massive showcase for starchitect **Renzo Piano**. Piano designed the hyper-cool **Jerome L. Greene Science Center**, as well as the **Lenfest Center for the Arts**, which will host exhibitions, performances, readings and lectures, most open to the public. The **Nash Building**, 3280 Broadway at W 133rd St, contains the campus **historical interpretive exhibit** (with displays charting the history of the area) on the ground floor.

16

135th Street and around

Subway B, C, #2, #3 to 135th St

The blocks north of 125th Street contain little of interest until you reach **135th Street**, the historic heart of Harlem; though the commercial pulse of the neighbourhood has drifted south over the years, back in the 1920s and 1930s this was where most of the action took place (**Harry Belafonte** and **James Baldwin** grew up around here). The junction of Powell Boulevard and West 135th Street was particularly important: legendary **jazz** clubs Small's Paradise and Big Apple faced each other on 135th Street, on the west side of Powell (see box, p.206). The streets nearby were also the haunt of ragtime composer **Scott Joplin**, who moved to Harlem around 1916, while Billie Holiday got her start on West 133rd Street, known as "**Jungle Alley**" in the 1930s, when it was lined with speakeasies.

Equally famous is **West 136th Street**, a block of narrow faux brownstones (with plaster facades) between Powell and Douglass completed in 1896; no. 108–110 was the

---

TOURS OF THE APOLLO THEATER

You can tour the nation's temple of African American culture, but you'll need to call in advance. Prearranged one-hour **guided tours** of the Apollo Theater are available for groups of twenty or more on Monday, Tuesday, Thursday and Friday at 11am, 1pm and 3pm; Wednesday at 11am; weekends at 11am & 1pm ($16 Mon–Fri, $18 Sat & Sun). Individuals or smaller groups should call Billy Mitchell, the tour director (☎ 212 531 5337), and he will try to add you to the next scheduled group.

home of African American millionaire **A'Lelia Walker** (see box, p.200), where Harlem artists, writers and musicians gathered for all-night parties.

Abyssinian Baptist Church

132 Odell Clark Place (formerly 138th St), at Powell Blvd • Tourists welcome at the Sun 11.30am service only; 2hr 30min • Free • ☎ 212 862 7474, ⓦ abyssinian.org • Subway B, C, #2, #3 to 135th St

Thousands of tourists visit the **Abyssinian Baptist Church** each year just to see and hear the gut-busting **choir** on Sunday (see box below) – it's a magical experience, but remember that this is a religious service and not a show (no photos). The church was first incorporated in 1808 in what is now Tribeca (making it the second-oldest black church in the US). Its founders were a group of African Americans who were tired of segregated seating at Baptist churches (the church's name was inspired from the traditional name for Ethiopia). The Abyssinian started becoming the religious and political powerhouse that it is today in 1908, when the **Reverend Adam Clayton Powell, Sr** (1865–1953) was appointed pastor, moving the church to Harlem in 1920. Construction on the current Gothic and Tudor building was completed in 1923, and **Reverend Adam Clayton Powell, Jr** (see box, p.202) took over in 1937. He remained pastor until 1971, and for a while this was the largest Protestant congregation in the US.

Strivers' Row

W 138th and W 139th sts, between Powell Blvd and Frederick Douglass Blvd • Subway B, C, #2, #3 to 135th St

The three blocks known as **Strivers' Row** contain some of the finest row houses in Manhattan. A dignified Renaissance-derived strip that's an amalgam of simplicity and elegance – officially designated the **St Nicholas Historic District** – it was conceived during the 1890s housing boom by McKim, Mead, and White among others. Note the unusual rear service alleys of the houses, reached via iron-gated cross streets (replete with the original "Walk your Horse" signs). At the end of the nineteenth century, this came to be the desirable place for ambitious professionals within Harlem's burgeoning black community to reside – hence its nickname. It's regained its status in recent years; Bob Dylan owned 265 W 139th St between 1986 and 2000 – it's currently worth around US$4 million.

16

SUNDAY GOSPEL AND HIP-HOP CHURCH

Harlem's uplifting **gospel music** has long enticed visitors, and for good reason: both it and the entire revival-style Baptist experience can be mind-blowing. Gospel tours are big business; most are pricey, but they usually offer transport uptown and brunch after the service. If you don't feel like shelling out the cash, or if you're looking for a more authentic experience, you can also easily go it alone (services are always free). The choir at the **Abyssinian Baptist Church** (Sun 11.30am only; no services in Aug) is arguably the best in the city, but long queues of tourists (which can stretch around the block) make the experience, well, touristy (you'll need to get to the "Tourist Entry Point" on the southeast corner of W 138th St and Powell Blvd at least 30min early). Another fairly popular option is the **Metropolitan Baptist Church**, at 151 W 128th St, at Powell Blvd (Sun 11am; ☎ 212 663 8990, ⓦ mbcharlem.org). **Mount Neboh Baptist Church**, at 1883 Powell Blvd on W 114th St (Sun 8am & 11am; ☎ 212 866 7880, ⓦ mountneboh.org), is much less of a circus; worship here is taken seriously and services are not designed as tourist attractions, but the congregation is very welcoming to nonmembers (you can also catch the choir rehearsing at 6.30pm on Tues). Wherever you go, dress accordingly: those wearing vests, flip-flops or shorts will not be allowed to enter.

For a quite different experience, the **Hip-Hop Church** currently meets at the Greater Hood Memorial AME Zion Church, at 160 W 146th St (Thurs 6.30pm; ☎ 212 281 3130); once again, this is a serious place of worship, but with rappers and DJs supplying the music. Hip-hop pioneer **Kurtis Blow** is one of the founders.

Schomburg Center for Research in Black Culture

515 Malcolm X Blvd, at W 135th St • Exhibitions Mon & Thurs–Sat 10am–6pm, Tues & Wed 10am–9pm • Free • ☎ 212 491 2200, ⓦ nypl.org/locations/schomburg • Subway #2, #3 to 135th St

If you're interested in learning more about African American history and culture, visit the **Schomburg Center for Research in Black Culture**, a member of the New York Public Library system. Primarily a **research library**, the main reason for a visit is to explore the superb temporary **exhibitions** here, held in three small galleries and covering a range of related African American themes, such as the struggle to end segregation in US schools and Black Power. From the Latimer/Edison Gallery you can glimpse the main reading room below, and take in the four murals painted by Harlem Renaissance artist **Aaron Douglas** in 1934. The centre is also the site of the ashes of renowned poet **Langston Hughes**, known for works such as *The Negro Speaks of Rivers*. That poem inspired Houston Conwill's terrazzo and brass "cosmogram" in the atrium beyond the main entrance; it's a mosaic built over a tributary of the Harlem River. Seven of Hughes' lines radiate out from a circle, and the last line, "My soul has grown deep like the rivers", located in a fish at the centre, marks where he is interred.

Originally a lending branch, the Division of Negro Literature, History and Prints was created in 1925 after the community began rallying for a library of its own. The collection grew dramatically, thanks to **Arthur Schomburg**, a black Puerto Rican nicknamed "The Sherlock Holmes of Black History" for his obsessive efforts to document black culture. Schomburg acquired over ten thousand manuscripts, photos and artefacts, and he sold them all to the NYPL for $10,000; he then worked as curator for the collection, sometimes using his own funds for upkeep, from 1932 until his death six years later. Since that time, the amassing of over ten million items has made the centre the world's top research facility for the study of black history and culture.

16

El Barrio

Subway #6 to 103rd St, 110th St or 116th St

East Harlem (or Spanish Harlem) extends from the affluence of the Upper East Side to East 132nd Street, and from the Harlem River as far west as Park Avenue. The neighbourhood has been a centre of New York's large **Puerto Rican** community since the 1950s, and is better known by locals as **El Barrio** – which simply means "the neighbourhood". Before World War II, this was actually **Italian Harlem**, a major Sicilian enclave: actor Al Pacino was born here in 1940, while *Rao's* restaurant (see p.316) – established in 1896 – and *Patsy's Pizzeria*, which opened in 1933, still remain. Today the character of East Harlem is changing again, with a large Mexican population and a fast-growing Chinese community creating what some call Manhattan's second Chinatown.

Harlem's regeneration is gradually spilling over to El Barrio – optimistic estate agents have dubbed it "**SpaHa**" – and the southern and western sections, particularly along Lexington Avenue, can be fun to explore (especially for the street art and the food). Yet most of the neighbourhood remains characterized by blocks of low-rise, low-income housing, shabby bodegas and livery-cab services that give the area an intimidating atmosphere – it still has the highest violent crime rate in Manhattan and the highest jobless rate in the city. Until the 1970s, the hub of the area was **La Marqueta** (Mon–Wed 8am–5pm, Thurs–Sat 8am–6pm) under the elevated Metro North railway tracks on Park Avenue between East 111th and 116th streets (officially 1590 Park Ave, at 115th St); originally a street market of Hispanic products, a major revitalization effort was renewed in 2017. If you're looking for insight into New York's Latin culture, start at the **Museo del Barrio** (see p.206).

Taller Boricua

Julia de Burgos Latino Cultural Center, 1680 Lexington Ave, at E 106th St • Wed, Fri & Sat noon–6pm, Thurs 1–7pm • Free • ☎ 212 831 4333, ⓦ tallerboricua.org • Subway #6 to 103rd St

To check out the contemporary art scene, check out the revolving exhibitions at the

HARLEM'S HISTORIC JAZZ VENUES

Jazz remains a fundamental part of Harlem's appeal, though most clubs today are small, intimate affairs – between the 1920s and 1960s, Harlem was home to some of the biggest nightspots in the city, many of which attracted hordes of white patrons from downtown as well as middle-class blacks. The legendary **Renaissance Ballroom**, a tile-trimmed, square-and-diamond-shaped dance club at Powell Boulevard, at West 138th St, once hosted Duke Ellington and Chick Webb in the 1920s. Nicknamed the "Rennie", it was a haven for middle-class blacks but closed in 1979 – the dilapidated structure was finally demolished in 2015.

   Small's Paradise at 2294 Powell Blvd, at West 135th St, hosted a mixed black and white crowd from the beginning, when the club was known as "The Hottest Spot in Harlem"; Malcolm X worked here in 1943. Today, it's occupied by an *International House of Pancakes* and topped by the state-of-the-art Thurgood Marshall Academy High School, opened in 2004. On the other side of West 135th Street, at 2300 Powell Blvd (now *Popeye's Chicken*), was the **Big Apple Restaurant and Jazz Club**, which is rumoured to be the birthplace of New York City's nickname. It's said that when jazzmen met on the road in the 1930s, they would call to each other, "See you at the Big Apple" as a sort of shorthand reference to the city. The term duly entered the vernacular after local journalists started using it and the city's tourism authorities adopted it in the 1970s.

   Opened in 1938, **Minton's Playhouse**, at 206–210 W 118th St between St Nicholas and Powell, became the birthplace of **bebop**. In the 1940s, after finishing their sets at Harlem's clubs, Dizzy Gillespie, Charlie Parker, John Coltrane and other greats would gather at Minton's for late-night jam sessions that gave rise to the improvised jazz style – innovator **Thelonious Monk** was house pianist here for three years; Miles Davis called it "the black jazz capital of the world". Shuttered in 1974, *Minton's* reopened as a low-key jazz supper club in 2013 (see p.349).

   As for the **Cotton Club**, it was originally at West 142nd Street and Lenox Avenue in the 1920s, and was a segregated establishment – though most of the performers here were black, as was the staff, only whites were allowed to attend as guests. That building was demolished in 1958, but a new version reopened in Harlem in 1978 at 656 W 125th St, where it continues to put on a good jazz show at night as well as a Sunday gospel brunch.

Taller Boricua gallery inside the redbrick Julia de Burgos Latino Cultural Center. The centre is named for the lauded Puerto Rican poet who died poverty-stricken in Harlem in 1953, a striking mosaic **mural** of whom (created by Manny Vega in 2006) is on the opposite corner of East 106th Street, part of the ongoing Hope Community project. You'll see *Nuyorican Poets Café* founder Pedro Pietri commemorated at East 104th Street and Lexington (a mural completed by James de la Vega in 2004), as well as the awe-inspiring **Spirit of East Harlem** mural, initiated by Hank Prussing in 1973 and completed five years later (Manny Vega restored it in 1998).

Graffiti Wall of Fame

Park Ave and E 106th St • Subway #6 to 103rd St

Facing Park Avenue, the **Graffiti Wall of Fame** (on the west side of the railway viaduct) commemorates the exuberant street art that developed in New York in the 1970s. Featuring art from many of the city's best-known graffiti writers (it was founded in 1980 by street artist Ray Rodríguez), the inner side of the wall (with the best work) is actually located in the Junior High School 13 Jackie Robinson playground, so the gates are sometimes locked during term – you'll have to ask at the school further along 106th Street for a closer look.

Museo del Barrio

1230 Fifth Ave, at E 104th St • Wed–Sat 11am–6pm, Sun noon–5pm • Suggested donation $9, free every third Sat of month • ☎ 212 831 7272, ⓦ elmuseo.org • Subway #6 to 103rd St

Literally translated as "the neighbourhood museum", the **Museo del Barrio** has two sections, both hosting temporary exhibits on various aspects of Puerto Rican and

LA GRANDE JATTE IN HARLEM

Harlem is littered with great street art, but if you see just one mural make it Eva Cockcroft's *Homage to Seurat: La Grande Jatte in Harlem* (1986), on West 142nd Street, between Amsterdam Avenue and Hamilton Place. Beautifully restored in 2009, Cockcroft has replaced the French painter's demure Parisiens with African American figures.

Latino culture. The permanent collection galleries display everything from the museum's rare **Taíno** artefacts, a pre-Columbian civilization that flourished in Puerto Rico and other Caribbean islands, to modern and conceptual art, while the other section hosts high-quality travelling exhibitions.

The galleries are relatively small, but there's also a decent **café** on site (selling duck, cheese and guava *empanadas*, *tamales* and rice pudding for around $4–5), and the museum also hosts concerts, poetry readings and other events.

The Africa Center

1280 Fifth Ave, at E 110th St • ⓦ theafricacenter.org • Subway #2, #3 to Central Park North, #6 to 110th St

Its opening delayed for over a decade, **The Africa Center** (formerly the Museum for African Art) was still short of funding at the time of research. Check the website for the latest progress.

Hamilton Heights and Sugar Hill

Subway #1 to 137th St; #1, A, B, C, D to 145th St

16

Much of West Harlem, between West 125th and 155th streets, and from St Nicholas Avenue to the Hudson River, is taken up by the area known as **Hamilton Heights**. Like Morningside Heights to the south, there's a blend of campus buildings (in this case, belonging to the City College of New York) and residences here, lightened by a sprinkle of slender parks on a bluff above Harlem. One stretch, the **Hamilton Heights Historic District**, bounded by Amsterdam and St Nicholas avenues from West 140th to 145th streets, contains florid row houses in a variety of architectural styles, including Beaux Arts and Romanesque Revival. In the 1920s and 1930s, many affluent African Americans began to migrate to the neighbourhood – as a result, the area between West 145th and 155th streets and Edgecombe and Amsterdam avenues became known as **Sugar Hill**. Today, it's another area of gorgeous townhouses, well worth exploring. The bi-monthly **Sugar Hill Market** – of curated designer goods stalls – is also worth checking out (visit ⓦ sugarhillmarket.com for the latest location).

City College

160 Convent Ave, at W 138th St • Campus open daily 24hr • ☎ 212 650 7000, ⓦ ccny.cuny.edu • Subway #1 to 137th St

Visitors wandering up from 125th Street and St Nicholas Avenue B or C subway station will be pleasantly surprised by **Convent Avenue** and the nearby grounds of **City College**. The rustic-feeling campus of Collegiate Gothic halls mantled with white terracotta fripperies occupies 35 acres along Convent Avenue, from West 131st Street to 141st Street. The most impressive section is the **North Campus Quadrangle** just before 140th Street, designed by the noted architect George Browne Post and completed in 1908. Nearby **Shepard Hall** (home to the School of Architecture) is the tallest and most striking building, soaring over the campus like a Gothic cathedral.

Founded downtown in 1847 (as the Free Academy of the City of New York), the college didn't charge tuition, and thus became the seat of higher learning for many of New York's poor, including polio-vaccine pioneer Jonas Salk, writer Mario Puzo and soldier-turned-statesman Colin Powell. The college has also produced an astounding ten Nobel laureates. Even though free education here came to an end in 1976, three-quarters of the students still come from minority backgrounds.

ALEXANDER HAMILTON

Alexander Hamilton's life is much more fascinating than his house – indeed, the **musical** based on his biography became the hottest show on Broadway in 2015. Born around 1755 on the island of Nevis in the British West Indies, he came to the American colonies in 1772. He was an early supporter of the Revolution, and his intelligence and enthusiasm quickly brought him to the attention of George Washington. Hamilton became the general's aide-de-camp, and rose quickly through military ranks. When Washington was elected President in 1789, he named Hamilton as the first Secretary of the Treasury (a position he held until 1795). He established the First Bank of the United States, the US Mint, cut down on smuggling (creating the forerunner of the US Coast Guard), taxed whisky and boosted manufacturing, gradually becoming a leader of what was known as the Federalists, an early political party. Yet Hamilton, quick in both understanding and temper, tended to tackle problems head-on, a propensity that made him enemies as well as friends. He alienated both political ally John Adams and Republican Party leader Thomas Jefferson, and when Jefferson won the presidency in 1801, Hamilton was left out in the political cold. Temporarily abandoning politics, he moved away from the city to his grange (or farm) to tend his plantation and conduct a memorably sustained and vicious feud with **Aaron Burr**, who had beaten Hamilton's father-in-law in a Senate election.

Following a short tenure as Vice President under Jefferson, Burr ran for governor of New York; Hamilton strenuously opposed his candidacy and, after an exchange of extraordinarily bitter letters, the two men fought a **duel** in Weehawken, New Jersey (roughly where the Lincoln Tunnel now emerges), on July 11, 1804. When pistols were drawn, Hamilton honourably discharged his into the air, a happening possibly explained by the fact that his eldest son had been killed in a duel on the same field a few years earlier. Burr, evidently made of lesser stuff, Burr aimed carefully and fatally wounded Hamilton. One of two non-presidents to find his way onto US money, you'll find Hamilton's portrait on the $10 note.

16

Hamilton Grange National Memorial

414 W 141st St, between Convent and St Nicholas aves • Visitor Center Wed–Sun 9am–5pm; ranger-guided tours at 10am, 11am, 2pm and 4pm; self-guided tours 9–10am, noon–1pm and 3–4pm • Free • ⓦ nps.gov/hagr • Subway A, B, C, D to 145th St

Until Lin-Manuel Miranda's hit musical opened on Broadway in 2015, the **Hamilton Grange National Memorial**, last home of founding father Alexander Hamilton, saw just a trickle of visitors. Today, guided tours of the handsome Federal-style mansion (fifteen people maximum) are often full, so get here early (it's first come, first served). The lower floor contains an exhibit and brief film highlighting the major events in Hamilton's life (see box above), while the historically furnished floor upstairs (access limited to tour times) has been artfully restored – wall colours have been accurately reproduced and several items (books, chairs, pianoforte) are family originals. Completed in 1802, Hamilton was to spend just two years at the house, but his long-suffering wife Eliza was able to live here until 1833. Tours include a video of how the Grange ended up here; it stood at its original site on 143rd Street until 1889, then was moved to 287 Convent Ave, in the shadow of the fiercely Romanesque St Luke's Church to which it was originally donated (Hamilton's statue remains here). In 2008, the 298-tonne structure was lifted (in one piece, no less) up and over the church's entryway to begin the journey to its new home in the northwest corner of St Nicholas Park.

Washington Heights

Subway A, C, #1 to 168th St

The largely **Dominican** neighbourhood of **Washington Heights** encompasses most of the northern tip of Manhattan between West 155th and Dyckman streets (200th St).

From Sugar Hill, walk along St Nicolas Avenue, which eventually runs into Broadway some ten blocks north. This is the main drag of a once elegant, now mostly raggedy neighbourhood, though the gentrification of Harlem has also had an impact up here. The area is best known as the stomping ground of New York's pioneer **graffiti** artists:

TAKI 183 started tagging in 1969, while his inspiration was **Julio 204**, a Puerto Rican from 204th Street who had started a few years earlier.

Hispanic Society of America

613 W 155th St, at Broadway • Tues–Sat 10am–4.30pm, Sun 1–4pm, library closed Aug • Free, $10 donation suggested • ☎ 212 926 2234, ⓦ hispanicsociety.org • Subway C to 155th St; #1 to 157th St

One of the few sights worth visiting in Washington Heights is **Audubon Terrace**. Completed in 1908, this Acropolis of folly is what's left of a hopelessly optimistic attempt to beautify this area, when museums were dolled up as Beaux Arts temples. There is only one museum left here, the **Hispanic Society of America** (most of the complex is occupied by Boricua College), but it makes the trip worthwhile; note however that the museum will be closed for extensive renovations until the end of 2019.

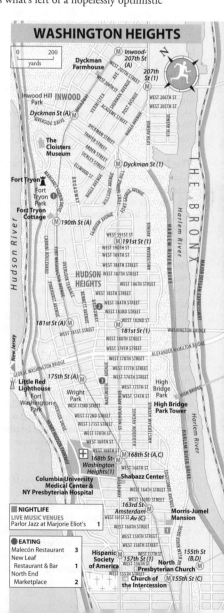

Founded in 1904 by wealthy railroad heir Archer Huntington, the Society owns one of the largest collections of Hispanic art outside Spain. The main, dimly lit gallery glows with the rosy hues of a Castilian palace, the first floor boasting Goya's *Duchess of Alba* in imperious pose as a Spanish *maja*. The adjacent Bancaja Gallery is a real treasure, containing fourteen giant murals by Joaquín Sorolla y Bastida (his *Vision of Spain* was commissioned specifically for the society in 1911). Upstairs there are galleries of painted tiles and ceramics, rare Spanish lustreware and Roman mosaics, but the paintings on the balcony above the main gallery take precedence: some classics from El Greco, including his *Holy Family*, and typically expressive portraits by Velázquez and Goya among them. Note also the equestrian statue of El Cid and limestone reliefs of Don Quixote in the courtyard outside, created by Huntington's wife Anna Hyatt in the 1920s.

Trinity Church Cemetery

West division entrance at 770 Riverside Drive, near W 153rd St; east division entrance W 155th St at Church of the Intercession • Daily 9am–5pm (closes 4pm Sept–May) • ☎ 212 368 1600, ⓦ trinitywallstreet.org • Subway C to 155th St; #1 to 157th St

Just across West 155th Street from Audubon Terrace lies the **Trinity Church Cemetery**, its large, placid grounds dotted with some fanciful mausoleums and divided into two sections by Broadway. The eastern division contains the Celtic-cross monument to naturalist John James

THE INVISIBLE MAN

"I am invisible, understand, simply because people refuse to see me."
Born in the segregated Deep South in 1913, **Ralph Ellison** moved to Harlem in 1936, spending most of his life here – he's still regarded as one of America's seminal African American authors. His pioneering novel, *Invisible Man* (1952) is a dark, semiautobiographical account of his struggles against racism (much of it set in Harlem), commemorated at the **Ralph Ellison Memorial**, W 150th St and Riverside Drive (Ellison lived nearby at 730 Riverside Drive from the early 1950s). Designed by Elizabeth Catlett and erected in 2003, the large slab of bronze features a cut-out male figure to symbolize "invisibility"; four engraved stone markers include information about Ellison and quotes from his work. In 1994 the writer was interred in the Trinity Church Cemetery mausoleum, near the Riverside Drive entrance.

Audubon (near the church entrance on 155th St), and the tomb of former mayor Ed Koch, who died in 2013. Robber-baron John Jacob Astor is buried in the western division (as is his great-grandson, John Jacob Astor IV, whose body was recovered from the *Titanic*), along with poet and Chelsea developer Clement Clark Moore, Alfred Tennyson Dickens, the son of Charles Dickens (who died suddenly on a visit to New York in 1912) and Eliza Jumel (see below).

The Morris–Jumel Mansion and around

65 Jumel Terrace, at W 160th St and Edgecombe Ave • Tues–Fri 10am–4pm, Sat & Sun 10am–5pm • $10 • ☎ 212 923 8008, ⓦ morrisjumel.org • Subway C to 163rd St

16

Within easy walking distance of Audubon Terrace and the Trinity Church Cemetery is the **Morris–Jumel Mansion**. Another uptown surprise, this creaky old house somehow survived the urban renewal (or better, destruction) that occurred all around it, and is now one of the city's more successful museums, its proud Georgian outlines faced with a later Palladian portico. Built as a rural retreat in 1765 by Loyalist Colonel Roger Morris, the house served briefly as Washington's headquarters in 1776 before falling into the hands of the British. Wealthy wine merchant Stephen Jumel bought the derelict house in 1810 and refurbished it for his wife (and ex-mistress) Eliza, formerly a prostitute. New York society didn't take to such a past, but when Jumel died in 1832, Eliza married ex-Vice President Aaron Burr, twenty years her senior (he was 77), in the front parlour: the marriage lasted for six months before old Burr left, having gone through her inheritance, only to die on the day of their divorce. Eliza battled on to the age of 91, and on the second floor of the house you'll find her portrait, bedroom and boudoir, restored to circa 1820s. You can also see Burr's and Washington's bedrooms, the kitchen in the basement and the gold wings above the downstairs foyer doors, allegedly given to Eliza by Napoleon.

Just opposite the entrance to the mansion's grounds is the gorgeous block of **Sylvan Terrace**, a tiny cobblestone mews lined with yellow and green wooden houses built in 1882 – and seeming impossibly out of place just barely off the wide-open intersection of Amsterdam and St Nicholas avenues.

The Shabazz Center

3940 Broadway, at W 165th St • Mon–Fri 10am–5pm • Free • ☎ 212 568 1341, ⓦ theshabazzcenter.net • Subway A, C, #1 to 168th St

Northwest of the Morris–Jumel Mansion is the **Audubon Ballroom**, scene of **Malcolm X**'s assassination in 1965 and now, after some controversy, a part of the huge Columbia-Presbyterian Hospital complex. Columbia restored a portion of the original ballroom facade during construction, and now the Malcolm X and Dr Betty Shabazz Memorial and Educational Center, or just **Shabazz Center**, commemorates the black leader with murals, events and film screenings. The first floor also contains illuminating touch-screen panels that highlight important phases of Malcolm's life, including interviews and videos of the man himself.

Little Red Lighthouse

Riverside Drive, at W 178th St • **Fort Washington Park** Daily sunrise–sunset • Free • ⓦ nycgovparks.org/parks/fortwashingtonpark • Subway A to 175th St

Blanketing much of the shoreline between Washington Heights and the Hudson River, **Fort Washington Park** is named after a Revolutionary War fort once located here (now long gone), but best known today for the George Washington suspension bridge and the 40ft-high **Little Red Lighthouse** beneath it. The lighthouse is an incongruous structure, immortalized in Hildegarde Swift's classic 1942 children's book of the same name – the **Little Red Lighthouse Festival** every September includes a special guest reading of the book (and this is usually the only time you can go inside the lighthouse). Originally named Jeffrey's Hook Lighthouse, the current structure was completed in 1889 in Sandy Hook, New Jersey, and moved here in 1921 where it operated for another 26 years.

Highbridge Park

W 155 St and Dyckman St, Edgecombe Ave and Amsterdam Ave • Daily sunrise–sunset • Free • ⓦ nycgovparks.org/parks/highbridgepark • Subway A to 175th St

Another New York green space given a makeover in recent years, **Highbridge Park** is best known for its iconic Romanesque High Bridge Water Tower (200ft), completed in 1872, and the **High Bridge** itself, a pedestrian-and-bicycle-only walkway reopened in 2015 to connect with parkland in the Bronx. Part of the Old Croton Aqueduct, the 1450ft-long granite bridge served the city from 1848 until 1958, carrying nearly one hundred million gallons of water a day at its peak.

The Cloisters Museum

16

99 Margaret Corbin Drive, Fort Tryon Park • Daily: March–Oct 10am–5.15pm; Nov–Feb 10am–4.45pm • Suggested donation $25, includes same-day admission to the Metropolitan Museum of Art and Met Breuer • ☎ 212 923 3700, ⓦ metmuseum.org • Subway A to 190th St-Fort Washington Ave (10min walk from the museum or one stop on #M4 bus); a taxi from Midtown will cost $27–35

The main reason visitors come this far uptown is to see **The Cloisters Museum**. It stands above the Hudson like some misplaced Renaissance palazzo-cum-monastery, and is home to the Met's collection of medieval tapestries, metalwork, paintings and

MALCOLM X

Born Malcolm Little in 1925, in Omaha, Nebraska, influential African American Muslim minister and political activist **Malcolm X** spent much of his later life in New York. He had a rough childhood and after moving to Harlem in 1943 became a small-time crook. In 1946, he ended up in jail; by the time he was released in 1952, he had become a committed follower of Elijah Muhammad's **Nation of Islam**. Despite the name, orthodox Muslims consider the Nation to be a separate religion, with many differences from Islam (members believe, for example, that Allah came to Earth in the person of one W. D. Fard, and that interracial marriage is forbidden). Malcolm rose quickly within the Nation, setting up temples in Boston and becoming minister of No. 7 Temple in Harlem in 1954. Tall, handsome and an enigmatic speaker, he soon became the public face of the group, speaking out against the inequalities and racism of the time. Yet by 1964, Malcolm had fallen out with the Nation's leaders, who were finding it difficult to control their star speaker; and Malcolm was becoming disillusioned with the Nation's unorthodox doctrine (not to mention Elijah Muhammad's alleged sex life). Malcolm converted to more orthodox Sunni Islam (adopting the name **El-Hajj Malik El-Shabazz**), and took a life-changing pilgrimage to Mecca in 1964 – seeing Muslims of all races praying together was especially enlightening.

Back in the US, he started two new organizations – Muslim Mosque Inc, and the Organization of Afro-American Unity – but by now he was receiving regular death threats. He was finally gunned down on February 21, 1965, at a meeting in the Audubon Ballroom (see opposite). Three members of the Nation of Islam were eventually imprisoned for the murder (all three were subsequently released). Today, Malcolm X is considered one of the greatest and most influential civil rights leaders; his autobiography (co-written by Alex Haley) is still widely read, and he was portrayed by Denzel Washington in the lauded Spike Lee movie *Malcolm X* (1992).

sculpture. The museum opened in 1938, largely thanks to donations from **George Grey Barnard** and **John D. Rockefeller, Jr**, and though it looks authentic, it was designed by modern architect Charles Collens (who also did Riverside Church; see p.196), with portions of five medieval cloisters cleverly incorporated into the structure.

The collection

Start from the entrance hall and work counterclockwise: the collection is laid out in roughly chronological order. First off is the simplicity of the **Romanesque Hall** and the frescoed Spanish **Fuentidueña Chapel**, dominated by a huge, domed twelfth-century apse from Segovia that immediately induces a reverential hush. The hall and chapel form a corner on one of the prettiest of the cloisters, **St Guilhem**, which is ringed by Corinthian-style columns topped by carved capitals from late twelfth-century southern France. At the centre of the museum is the **Cuxa Cloister**, from the twelfth-century Benedictine monastery of Saint-Michel-de-Cuxa near Perpignan in the French Pyrenees; its Romanesque marble capitals are brilliantly carved with monkeys, eagles and lions, whose open mouths reveal half-eaten human legs.

The nearby **Unicorn Tapestries** (c.1495–1505, Flanders) are even more spectacular – brilliantly alive with colour, observation and Christian symbolism. The most famous is the seventh and last, where the slain unicorn has miraculously returned to life and is trapped in a circular pen. It isn't just the creature's resurrection that's mystifying – the entire sequence is shrouded in mystery: aside from the fact that they were designed in France and probably made in Brussels, little else is known for certain, even who the intended original recipients were (the most plausible claim is Anne of Brittany, wife of King Louis XII). As for the tapestries' allegorical meaning, the unicorn is said to represent both a husband captured in marriage and Christ risen again.

Most of the Met's medieval paintings are to be found downtown (p.165), but one important exception is Dutch master **Robert Campin**'s *Mérode Triptych*. This fifteenth-century oil painting depicts the Annunciation scene in a typical bourgeois Flemish home of the day, and is housed in its own antechamber next to the Boppard Room, outfitted with a chair, cupboard and other household articles from that period (though from different countries of origin). On the left of the altarpiece, the artist's patron and his wife gaze timidly through an open door; to the right, St Joseph works in his carpenter's shop. St Joseph was mocked in the literature of the day, which might account for his rather ridiculous appearance – making a mousetrap, a symbol of the way the Devil traps souls.

The lower level

On the lower level, a large **Gothic chapel** boasts a high vaulted ceiling and mid- to late fourteenth-century Austrian stained-glass windows, along with the monumental **sarcophagus of Ermengol VII**, Count of Urgell (Urgell is now in Catalunya, Spain), with its whole phalanx of (now sadly decapitated) family members and clerics carved in stone to send him off.

Also on the lower floor are two further cloisters to explore (one with a small café), along with the **Treasury**, crammed with spellbinding objects. Try not to miss the *Belles Heures de Jean, Duc de Berry*, perhaps the greatest of all medieval Books of Hours; it was executed by the Limburg Brothers with dazzling miniatures of seasonal life and extensive border-work in gold leaf. Other highlights include the twelfth-century walrus tusk **Cloisters Cross**, believed to have been made by a craftsman known as Master Hugo for the now-ruined great abbey at Bury St Edmunds in England. It contains a mass of 92 tiny expressive characters from biblical stories, as well as what seem to be disturbing anti-Semitic inscriptions. The cross is one of the most controversial pieces in the collection; experts still debate its provenance and meaning, and the story of how one of England's greatest pieces of medieval art ended up here is equally hazy – the Met outbid the British Museum for the piece in 1963 (paying $600,000), but how the shady Croatian seller acquired it is unknown.

Brooklyn

"The Great Mistake". So ran local newspaper headlines when Brooklyn became a borough of New York in 1898. Then the fourth-largest city in the US, it began a century of labouring in the shadow of its taller but smaller brother across the East River, drawing hordes to the famous Coney Island beach – the closest white-sand strip to Manhattan – but not offering much in the way of high culture. No longer. Brooklyn has established itself as a fully fledged brand; its signature brownstone townhouses and tree-lined streets are complemented by top-rated restaurants, cool bars, pop-up flea markets, standout museums, and galleries and performance spaces that present more daring work than you'll generally find in Manhattan.

17

To start your trip in grand style, walk or cycle here from Lower Manhattan over the **Brooklyn Bridge**, and try to be on the Dumbo waterfront or the Brooklyn Heights promenade at sunset – the light is magical. **Dumbo** is worth a visit, holding Brooklyn Bridge Park, some cobblestone streets and warehouses that have been converted to expensive apartments, furniture stores and art spaces; it's flanked by **Fulton Ferry** and **Vinegar Hill**, home to the revived Brooklyn Navy Yard. The most accessible district in the borough is pretty, elite **Brooklyn Heights**, a clutch of old mansions and townhouses abutting the East River directly opposite Lower Manhattan. Inland from there, the civic squares of **Downtown Brooklyn** take over; while there's not too much of interest on those blocks, the neighbourhood does abut pretty **Fort Greene**, where you'll find

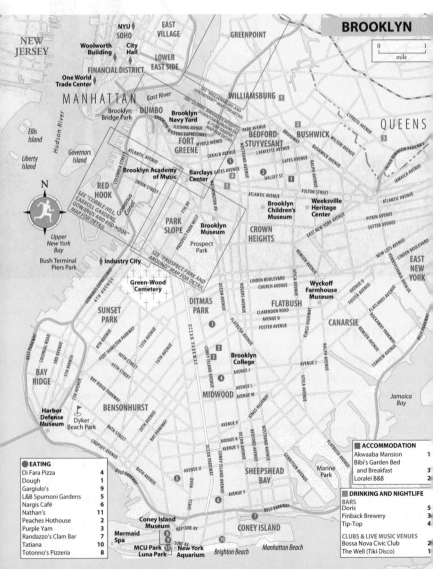

BROOKLYN

0 — 1
mile

NEW JERSEY

MANHATTAN

Ellis Island

Liberty Island

Hudson River

Governors Island

Upper New York Bay

Bush Terminal Piers Park

NYU SOHO
EAST VILLAGE
Woolworth Building
City Hall
LOWER EAST SIDE
FINANCIAL DISTRICT
One World Trade Center
East River
Brooklyn Bridge Park
DUMBO
Brooklyn Navy Yard
FORT GREENE
Brooklyn Academy of Music
Barclays Center
RED HOOK
Gowanus Canal
PARK SLOPE
Brooklyn Museum
Prospect Park
Green-Wood Cemetery
Industry City
DITMAS PARK
SUNSET PARK
BAY RIDGE
Harbor Defense Museum
Dyker Beach Park
BENSONHURST
MIDWOOD

GREENPOINT
WILLIAMSBURG
QUEENS
Park Avenue
BEDFORD-STUYVESANT
BUSHWICK
Broadway
DeKalb Avenue
Myrtle Avenue
Flushing Avenue
Atlantic Avenue
Gates Avenue
Halsey St.
Lafayette Avenue
Fulton Street
Brooklyn Children's Museum
Weeksville Heritage Center
CROWN HEIGHTS
Atlantic Avenue
Pitkin Avenue
Sutter Avenue
EAST NEW YORK
Linden Boulevard
Church Avenue
Wyckoff Farmhouse Museum
FLATBUSH
Clarendon Road
Avenue D
Foster Avenue
CANARSIE
Brooklyn College
Avenue J
Avenue L
Avenue M
Kings Highway
Avenue P
Jamaica Bay
Marine Park
SHEEPSHEAD BAY
Coney Island Museum
Mermaid Spa
MCU Park
Luna Park
New York Aquarium
CONEY ISLAND
Brighton Beach
Manhattan Beach

EATING

Di Fara Pizza	4
Dough	1
Gargiulo's	9
L&B Spumoni Gardens	5
Nargis Café	6
Nathan's	11
Peaches Hothouse	2
Purple Yam	3
Randazzo's Clam Bar	7
Tatiana	10
Totonno's Pizzeria	8

ACCOMMODATION

Akwaaba Mansion	1
Bibi's Garden Bed and Breakfast	3
Loralei B&B	2

DRINKING AND NIGHTLIFE

BARS

Doris	5
Finback Brewery	3
Tip-Top	4

CLUBS & LIVE MUSIC VENUES

Bossa Nova Civic Club	2
The Well (Tiki Disco)	1

BROOKLYN HIGHLIGHTS

17

Brooklyn Bridge Park Home to playgrounds, picnic spots and stunning views of Manhattan. See p.219

Brooklyn Academy of Music High culture hits its borough peak. See p.222

Brooklyn Botanic Garden Go for a peaceful stroll among the blooms. See p.233

Red Hook Lots of idiosyncratic bars and restaurants – and a real community feel. See p.237

Live music in Williamsburg You'll find it in bowling alleys, music shops and gritty rock clubs. See p.348

Pizza *Paulie Gee's* (see p.318), *Roberta's* (see p.320), *L&B Spumoni Gardens* (see p.323), *Totonno's* (see p.323) . . . take your pick of landmark pizza joints.

some of the most pristine residential blocks in the city along with the famous Brooklyn Academy of Music (BAM) performance complex.

Anyone visiting New York for contemporary art or music (or vintage clothes or nightclubs, for that matter) should head to gallery-dotted **Williamsburg**, just one stop on the L train from Manhattan's East Village and also a top choice for eating, drinking and general carousing. **Greenpoint**, north of Williamsburg on the border of Long Island City, houses the artsy overflow from Williamsburg and manages to balance the new incursions with the Polish old guard still prevalent. Further along the L train, struggling artists and hipsters have also moved out to **Bushwick**, where you'll find some truly innovative galleries.

Back where Fort Greene leaves off, **Bedford-Stuyvesant**, the largest African American community in New York, takes over. Bed-Stuy, as it's known, in turn links to **Crown Heights**, home to a large Hasidic Jewish population. Move west and you'll hit **Prospect Park**, designed by Central Park creators Frederick Law Olmsted and Calvert Vaux. It contains the usual ball fields and trails and is flanked by the first-rate Brooklyn Botanic Garden and Brooklyn Museum, plus the leafy **Park Slope** neighbourhood. The Gowanus Canal – and the increasingly transformed, former industrial namesake district on its banks – separates the Slope from a trio of plush neighbourhoods: **Boerum Hill**, **Cobble Hill** and **Carroll Gardens** (BoCoCa, as some, though not the locals, refer to them collectively), with no real attractions but block after block of historic brownstones and some of the borough's best restaurants and cafés. The most popular areas to visit here are Court and Smith streets, lined with some of Brooklyn's best boutiques and places to dine. The Brooklyn–Queens Expressway cuts them off from **Red Hook**, full of stone-block streets, warehouses-turned-artists'-studios and some limited waterfront attractions.

Then there's coastal Brooklyn: start in polyglot **Bay Ridge** for a scenic bike ride along the water, and then head to **Coney Island**, the venerable seaside amusement district known for its rattletrap roller coaster, the Cyclone, and the New York Aquarium. Grab some *borscht* (beetroot soup) at the nearby Russian enclave of **Brighton Beach** and, if there's time, make your way to the under-visited, marina-lined **Sheepshead Bay** for a plate of fresh-from-the-sea clams.

INFORMATION

Tourist information Your main sources for information on the borough are the Brooklyn Tourism Visitor Center, 209 Joralemon St (Mon–Fri 9am–5pm; ⓦ explorebk.com), in Downtown Brooklyn, and the Brooklyn Historical Society (see p.221) in Brooklyn Heights.

Brief history

In 1636, **Dutch colonists** bought farmland from the **Lenape Indians** amid the flat marshes in the southwestern corner of Long Island. The **Village of Breuckelen** received a charter from the Dutch West India Company in 1646. The town began to take on its present form in 1814 when Robert Fulton's steamship service linked

17

Long Island with Manhattan and Brooklyn Heights was established as a leafy retreat for wealthier Manhattanites.

Brooklyn's **incorporation** into the City of New York in 1898 was a bitterly fought political battle. In the end it was decided by just 277 votes – a tiny percentage of the total 129,000 cast. By the early 1900s, Brooklyn had more than one million residents, many of them Jewish and Italian; in 1910, 35 percent of its population was foreign born (the proportion is similar today).

Even with the population boom, Brooklyn suffered in the twentieth century: its strong manufacturing and shipping sectors dwindled, and unemployment climbed steadily. By the 1980s, "white flight", provoked first by racism, then by drug-related crime and violence, had left previously desirable residential neighbourhoods vacant and impoverished.

With a citywide drop in crime beginning in the mid-1990s, however, middle-class families began restoring townhouses in Park Slope, Cobble Hill, Prospect Heights and Fort Greene, and young artists and professionals flooded Williamsburg, trends that have continued and spread into Bushwick, Clinton Hill and whatever the next happening neighbourhood might be.

Brooklyn Bridge

Subway J, Z to Chambers St; R to City Hall; #2 or #3 to Park Place; #4, #5 or #6 to Brooklyn Bridge-City Hall

One of several spans across the East River, the **Brooklyn Bridge** is today dwarfed by lower Manhattan's skyscrapers, but in its day, the bridge was a technological quantum leap, its elegant gateways towering over the brick structures around it. For twenty years after its opening in 1883, it was the world's largest and longest suspension bridge, and – for many more years – the longest single-span structure.

The **view** from below (especially on the Brooklyn side) as well as from the top is undeniably spectacular. You can **walk across** its wooden planks from Centre Street, but resist the urge to look back until you're at the midpoint, when the Financial District's giants stand shoulder to shoulder behind the spidery latticework of cables. You can follow the pedestrian path straight to its end, at the corner of Adams and Tillary streets in **Downtown Brooklyn** (see p.221), behind the main post office. More convenient for sightseeing, however, is to exit the bridge at the first set of stairs: walk down and bear right to follow the path through the park at Cadman Plaza. If you cross onto Middagh Street, you'll be in the core of **Brooklyn Heights** (see

---

THE MAKING OF THE BROOKLYN BRIDGE

When the Brooklyn Bridge was completed in 1883, it was an object of awe – for New Yorkers, it was a concrete symbol of the Great American Dream. Italian immigrant painter Joseph Stella called it "a shrine containing all the efforts of the new civilization of America". Indeed, the bridge's meeting of art and function, of romantic Gothic and daring practicality, became a sort of spiritual model for the next generation's skyscrapers. On a practical level, it expanded the scope of New York City, paving the way for the incorporation of the outer boroughs and the creation of a true metropolis.

The bridge didn't go up without difficulties. Early in the project, in 1869, architect and engineer **John Augustus Roebling** crushed his foot taking measurements for the piers and died of tetanus less than three weeks later. His son Washington took over, only to be crippled by the bends after working in an insecure underwater caisson; he subsequently directed the work from his sickbed overlooking the site. Some twenty workers died during construction, and a week after the opening day, twelve people were crushed to death in a panicked rush on the bridge's footpath. Despite this tragic toll (as well as innumerable suicides over the years), New Yorkers still look to the bridge with affection, celebrating its milestone anniversaries with parades and respecting it as a civic symbol on a par with the Empire State Building.

p.220); or follow Cadman Plaza West down the hill to Old Fulton Street and the
Fulton Ferry District (see below).

17

Fulton Ferry District

Though you'd hardly guess it today, this small historic district, bounded by the East
River, Old Fulton Street, Front Street and Main Street, was at one time the busiest spot
on the Brooklyn waterfront. If you arrive **on foot** from the Brooklyn Bridge, take the
first set of stairs off the **bridge** and follow Cadman Plaza West down the hill to Old
Fulton Street on the west edge of the district. The A and C trains to High Street will
also let you off at Cadman Plaza West, and the **ferry** is a pleasant alternative in the
summer months (see p.27).

Named for **Robert Fulton**, the area was the hub of steamship traffic until the 1883
opening of the Brooklyn Bridge precipitated an economic slump only recently
remedied by the booming residential real-estate market. Check out the imposing **Eagle
Warehouse**, at 28 Old Fulton St; its penthouse, with a huge glass clock-window, is one
of Brooklyn's most coveted apartments (though no match for the $18 million
penthouse triplex in Dumbo's Clock Tower, at 1 Main St). The headquarters of *The
Brooklyn Eagle*, the newspaper edited for a time by **Walt Whitman**, previously stood on
this spot, and its old press room was integrated into the 1893 warehouse.

The landing is flanked by the area's two biggest tourist attractions: an old coffee barge
that hosts classical music concerts – so-called **BargeMusic** (see p.357) – and the ritzy
River Café, at 1 Water St, known as much for its views as for its food.

Dumbo

Just east of the Fulton Ferry District, **Dumbo** is short for Down Under the Manhattan
Bridge Overpass, a term coined in 1978 by residents of the neighbourhood – mostly
artists – who thought the awkward moniker would deter developers. No such luck:
many of Dumbo's handsome brick factories have been transformed into luxury
condominiums, joined by glass towers housing more of the same. In a way, it's
Brooklyn's answer to Tribeca, with its glossy mix of chichi design emporia, art galleries,
waterfront parks, high-priced apartments and cool restaurants. And then there's the
allure of its cobblestone streets and jaw-dropping views of the Manhattan and
Brooklyn bridges, forming one of New York's most dramatic, Gotham-esque cityscapes.

Dumbo's core – which was landmarked by the city in 2007 – lies between the
Brooklyn and Manhattan bridges, north of the Brooklyn–Queens Expressway. Water
and Front streets are the main thoroughfares, but any side street is equally evocative,
and the waterfront is the place to take your lunch or coffee and laze away a few hours.

THE DUMBO ART SCENE

The local galleries and venues – even bookstores and record shops, which also get in on the
act – populating Dumbo's lofts and warehouses provide an anchor and identity for the
neighbourhood. The second floor of the 111 Front St building is home to ten or so galleries,
most of which are open Wed–Sat/Sun noon–6pm; poke around to see lots of mixed-media
efforts. Nearby, SmackMellon, 92 Plymouth St (Ⓦsmackmellon.org), shows daring pieces by
emerging artists, and PowerHouse Arena, 28 Adams St (Ⓦpowerhousearena.com), an
art-publisher-cum-bookstore, holds readings and photography exhibitions. Meanwhile, the
Dumbo Improvement District (Ⓦdumbo.is) promotes events like Live at the Archway
(Thurs May–Oct), with musical performances at the Archway Plaza under the Manhattan
Bridge, and has collaborated with designers to create public artworks around the
neighbourhood. A monthly **Gallery Walk** (first Thurs 5.30–8.30pm; check Ⓦdumbo.is for
participating venues) is good for homing in on free receptions.

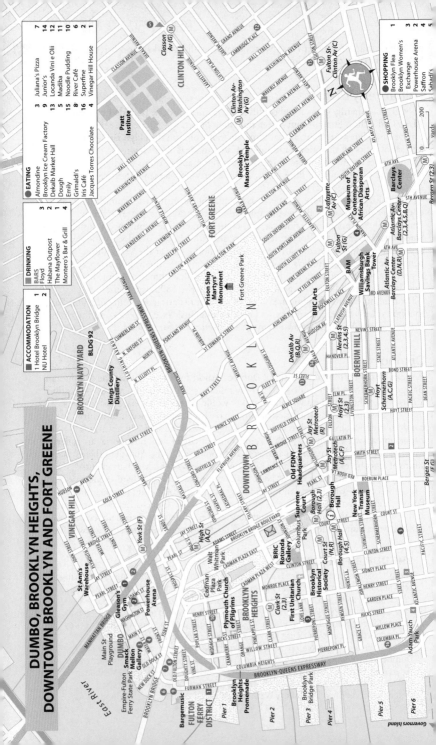

DUMBO, BROOKLYN HEIGHTS, DOWNTOWN BROOKLYN AND FORT GREENE

■ ACCOMMODATION
1 Hotel Brooklyn Bridge ... 1
NU Hotel ... 2

■ DRINKING
BARS
Floyd ... 3
Habana Outpost ... 1
The Mayflower ... 2
Montero's Bar & Grill ... 4

● EATING
Almondine ... 3
Brooklyn Ice Cream Factory ... 1
Dekalb Market Hall ... 13
Dough ... 7
Emily ... 15
Grimaldi's ... 2
Iris Café ... 8
Jacques Torres Chocolate ... 4

Juliana's Pizza ... 3
Junior's ... 9
Locanda Vini e Olii ... 12
Madiba ... 5
Noodle Pudding ... 10
River Café ... 6
Superfine ... 16
Vinegar Hill House ... 4

● SHOPPING
Brooklyn Flea ... 1
Brooklyn Women's Exchange ... 2
Powerhouse Arena ... 3
Saffron ... 4
Sahadi's ... 5

Gleason's Gym

17

130 Water St • Call ahead for details of Saturday-night boxing events (usually monthly; $20) • ☎ 718 797 2872, ⓦ gleasonsgym.net • Subway A, C to High St; F to York St

To savour what's left of Dumbo's old-fashioned grit, head to **Gleason's Gym**, where tomorrow's prizefighters work out. Everyone from Jake LaMotta to Muhammad Ali has trained at Gleason's, first established in Manhattan in 1937; drop by to see people punch heavy bags or, if you're lucky, spar with each other ($10 spectator fee).

Brooklyn Bridge Park

Brooklyn waterfront, from Manhattan Bridge to Atlantic Ave • ⓦ brooklynbridgepark.org • Subway A, C to High St; F to York St; #2, #3 to Clark St

The redeveloped waterfront along Dumbo and Brooklyn Heights goes by the umbrella name of **Brooklyn Bridge Park**; it's a series of playgrounds, scenic viewpoints and reclaimed quays, and plays host to a variety of events and activities. Just east of the Brooklyn Bridge, Empire Fulton Ferry State Park is the oldest section and boasts the restored Jane's Carousel (May–Sept daily except Tues 11am–7pm; Oct–April Thurs–Sun 11am–6pm; $2). Adjacent to this is Main Street Lot, with a playground, large lawn and giant steps for picnicking.

On the other side of Brooklyn Bridge, the piers beneath the Brooklyn Heights Esplanade hold all sorts of family fun. Pier One has a small play area and waterside promenade; in summertime, its "boathouse" offers free kayaking at weekends (sometimes available further up in Dumbo, too). Pier Two has been a big hit since its introduction, with shuffleboard courts, a roller rink and much more under its covered recreation space, while Pier Five is home to sports fields and a "picnic peninsula". Pier Six is also impressive, at least to the youngest visitors, with a popular water park, climbing area, giant slide and a ferry link to Governors Island. Elsewhere, there are green swathes, fishing spots, a bike path and, in summertime, a pop-up pool (between piers One and Two); an aggressive programming schedule features yoga, open-air movies, book readings and conservation tours, for a start.

Vinegar Hill

A few seemingly stray cobblestone blocks northeast from the heart of Dumbo make up **Vinegar Hill**, a historic district that took its name from Ireland's Battle of Vinegar Hill – it was developed in the early nineteenth century mainly to house Irish immigrants who worked at the Brooklyn Navy Yard. On a sunny day, don't miss dining outdoors at the *Vinegar Hill House* (see p.317).

Brooklyn Navy Yard

Brooklyn waterfront, from Manhattan Bridge to Williamsburg Bridge • **BLDG 92 Visitor Center** 63 Flushing Ave, at Carlton Ave • Wed–Sun noon–6pm • Free • ☎ 718 907 5992, ⓦ brooklynnavyyard.org • Turnstile Tours offers a variety of ways to see the yard, including regular "Past, Present and Future" hop-on, hop-off bus tours on Sat & Sun 2pm (2hr; $30) • Subway A, C to High St; F to York St

The industrial park of **Brooklyn Navy Yard** – nearly derelict save for some unglamorous city works usage since its decommissioning in the 1960s – has recently become not just a thriving business setting but an attraction in its own right. Anyone can visit **BLDG 92** to get acquainted with some Navy Yard history; a modular, energy-efficient glass structure is attached to an 1857 brick house originally built for the marine commandant and now a museum holding three floors' worth of exhibitions. Linger over models of well-known ships built at the yard, including the USS *Ohio, Maine* and *Missouri*, and hear oral history from the likes of historian Howard Zinn, who worked at the yards in his youth.

To appreciate what the place was, and what it's become, it's essential to take one of the fascinating tours. The most frequent of those, an overview called "Past, Present and Future" (others include World War II tours and kids' detective tours), goes into great detail on the yard's former military importance – an astonishing 71,000 people worked here during World War II – and its current redevelopment. Some three hundred businesses call

17 the grounds home these days; tenants include a body armour manufacturer, the **Kings County Distillery** (a bourbon maker holed up in the redbrick Paymaster Building; tours Sat every 30min 2–5pm, Tues–Fri & Sun 3pm & 5pm; $14; ⊚kingscountydistillery.com) and Steiner Studios, where *Girls*, *Gotham*, *Boardwalk Empire* and a whole host of movies are shot. One highlight is Dry Dock One, in which a visiting ship may or may not be docked; a viewing platform gives views out to the river and of various cranes hard at work.

Brooklyn Heights

Brooklyn Heights is one of New York City's most beautiful and historical neighbourhoods, and is the borough's most coveted place to live. Downtown bankers and financiers began building brownstone townhouses here in the early nineteenth century, while writers flocked to the Heights after the subway opened in 1908; W.H. Auden, Carson McCullers, Truman Capote, Tennessee Williams, Norman Mailer and Paul and Jane Bowles (pre-Morocco) all lived in the neighbourhood. Although many one-family brownstones were divided into apartments during the 1960s and 1970s and the streets now feel fairly cosmopolitan – if a bit frumpier than you'd expect, given what it costs to live here – Brooklyn Heights today is in many ways not much different from how it was a hundred years ago. The Court Street N, R stop and the Clark Street stop on the #2 and #3 put you in or on the edge of the Heights, though any of the Downtown Brooklyn stops suffice as well.

Henry, Middagh and Pierrepont streets

The north edge, along **Henry Street** and Columbia Heights, is the oldest part of the neighbourhood, where blocks are lined with Federal-style brick buildings. The unassuming, well-maintained wooden structure at **24 Middagh St** (at the corner of Willow), erected in 1824, is the area's longest-standing house, though other examples from around the era can be found along Middagh and Willow.

Continue south on Henry to **Pierrepont Street**, studded with fine brownstone townhouses; it's a scenic stretch by which to reach the **Promenade**. At the corner of

WALT WHITMAN: BROOKLYN BOY

Though only sporadically celebrated during his lifetime, poet **Walt Whitman** (1819–92) has moved to the pantheon of Great American Writers. And of the many places he lived, none was as influential as Brooklyn.

Born in Huntington, Long Island, Whitman moved to the borough at the age of 4, moving from place to place thanks to his family's precarious financial situation. His formal schooling ended at age 11, after which he began working as a typesetter's apprentice in what is now Downtown Brooklyn. Whitman went on to found his own paper, *The Long-Islander*, which he sold after only nine months, but it was enough experience to get him hired as editor of *The Brooklyn Eagle*.

During his two-year tenure at the *Eagle* – still published in Brooklyn Heights – he argued for the establishment of Fort Greene Park and fought for recognition of local artists. But most importantly, he gathered ideas for his magnum opus, *Leaves of Grass*, which he would begin to write in 1850. Whitman himself paid for the publication of the first edition in 1855, even helping with the typesetting to keep costs down. Predictably, he couldn't even sell the first run of 795 copies; when newspapers got around to reviewing it, many denounced it as obscene.

Undeterred, Whitman revised *Leaves* for the rest of his life, expanding the original twelve-poem booklet to a 400-page tome. These first lines of the penultimate poem, *Crossing Brooklyn Ferry*, capture Whitman's wide embrace of all humanity:

Crowds of men and women attired in the usual costumes, how curious you are to me!
On the ferry-boats the hundreds and hundreds that cross, returning home, are more curious to me than you suppose, And you that shall cross from shore to shore years hence are more to me, and more in my meditations, than you might suppose.

Pierrepont and Monroe Place, look in if you can on the neo-Gothic interior of the **First Unitarian Church**.

Plymouth Church of the Pilgrims

75 Hicks St, at Orange St • Mon–Fri 10am–4pm, services Sun 11am, tour follows (or by appointment) • Free • ☏ 718 624 4743, ⓦ plymouthchurch.org • Subway #2, #3 to Clark St, A, C to High St

The simple **Plymouth Church of the Pilgrims** (entrance on Orange St) went up in the mid-nineteenth century and became famous as the preaching base of **Henry Ward Beecher**, abolitionist and campaigner for women's rights. His fiery orations drew men like Horace Greeley and Abraham Lincoln, and Mark Twain based *Innocents Abroad* on travels with the church's social group. The building was also a stop on the Underground Railroad, where slaves were hidden on their way to freedom. Fitting, then, that in 1963, Martin Luther King, Jr delivered an early version of his "I Have a Dream" speech here. Tours of the church, focusing on the history and architecture, can be arranged by calling in advance; Sunday afternoons also see the appearance of an "underground thrift store" upstairs in the space.

Brooklyn Historical Society

128 Pierrepont St, at Clinton St • Wed–Sun noon–5pm; library Wed–Sat 1–5pm • $10, 12 and under free • ☏ 718 222 4111, ⓦ brooklynhistory.org • Subway R to Court St; #2, #3, #4, #5 to Borough Hall

The **Brooklyn Historical Society** explores the borough's neighbourhoods, architecture, ecology and subcultures with changing exhibits – though there is one long-term display, "In Pursuit of Freedom", that highlights the borough's role in the abolitionist movement. The second-floor library, with its local history collection, is an evocative highlight; there's a host of talks, tours, readings and screenings; and the Society publishes detailed neighbourhood guides to a handful of Brooklyn districts, for sale at the front desk.

The Promenade

Walk back west on any street between Clark and Remsen to reach the **Promenade** (more formally known as the Esplanade), a pedestrian path with terrific views of the Statue of Liberty, Downtown Manhattan's skyscrapers and the Brooklyn Bridge. Below is the still-developing Brooklyn Bridge Park (see p.219).

Downtown Brooklyn

Spilling out from the foot of the Brooklyn and Manhattan bridges between Atlantic and Flatbush avenues, Downtown Brooklyn is a somewhat motley district of office buildings and commuter colleges – albeit an area in the midst of rampant development. While it has touches of metropolitan grandeur and civic pride, for the most part it lacks Manhattan's sophistication; indeed, aside from the Brooklyn Tourism and Visitors Center in Borough Hall (see p.215), the subterranean New York Transit Museum and, perhaps, the historic turreted former headquarters of the NYC Fire Department, at 365–367 Jay St, there's surprisingly little to see here. The handiest stops for the business district in Downtown Brooklyn are Jay St-MetroTech on the A, C, F or R and Borough Hall via the #2, #3, #4 or #5.

Cadman Plaza, Borough Hall and Atlantic Avenue

The eastern edge of residential Brooklyn Heights is defined by **Cadman Plaza**, created after World War II when the city decided to move Brooklyn's elevated streetcars underground. Nowadays it hosts a farmers' market (Tues & Sat year-round, plus Thurs from April to mid-Dec; 8am–4pm). Just south of the plaza, at Court and Montague streets, stands the lovely, massive **State Supreme Court**, designed by the same architects responsible for the Empire State Building. Further south, the Greek-style **Borough Hall**, at 209 Joralemon St, looks tiny in comparison; it was erected in 1849, then topped

17

with its odd cupolated belfry near the end of the century. On the southern border, Atlantic Avenue (which is claimed by Boerum Hill and Brooklyn Heights as well to an extent) holds a number of antique shops and Middle Eastern food joints; it's also the site of September's boisterous Atlantic Antic street party.

New York Transit Museum

Two blocks south of Borough Hall, on Boerum Place, at Schermerhorn St • Tues–Fri 10am–4pm, Sat & Sun 11am–5pm • $7, ages 2–17 $5 • ☎ 718 694 1600, Ⓦ nytransitmuseum.org • Subway #2, #3, #4, #5 to Borough Hall; A, C, F, R to Jay St-MetroTech

The **New York Transit Museum** is housed underground in the refurbished Court Street shuttle station from the 1930s. Popular with kids (and school groups) for good reason, museum exhibits include maps, models and photographs that detail the evolution of the city's public transit system, along with antique turnstiles and some interactive displays of fuel technologies. The highlight for many is jumping on and off the various models of restored subway and tram cars in the lower level, though few parents will be able to resist the photo opportunity of placing their children in the driver's seat of one of the buses on the main floor. There's also a gallery annexe in Grand Central Terminal (see p.134).

Barclays Center

Atlantic Ave, at Flatbush Ave • ☎ 917 618 6100, Ⓦ barclayscenter.com • Subway B, D, N, Q, R, #2, #3, #4, #5 to Atlantic Ave-Barclays Center

The anchor of the Atlantic Yards development, Bruce Ratner's vision for turning a smallish parcel of land into an arena and a sixteen-skyscraper subdivision (drawn-out protests and lawsuits, followed by years of sluggish economy, curtailed much of the plans) opened its doors in late 2012. Home to the Brooklyn Nets, previously owned by Ratner and then sold to Russian billionaire Mikhail Prokhorov – with a tiny share (since divested) held by rapper Jay-Z – the stadium has brought the first professional major-league team to the borough since baseball's Dodgers left town nearly sixty years ago. The New York Islanders, a pro hockey team, joined the party for the 2015–16 season, and plenty of concerts are staged here as well. Though controversial, Barclays is less of an eyesore than one might imagine – the rust-coloured, low-lying stadium swooping almost gracefully towards the busy intersection at which it lies.

Fort Greene

Cross over chaotic Flatbush Avenue, and Fulton Street will bring you into the heart of **Fort Greene**, a historically African American neighbourhood that withstood the dark days of the 1970s and 80s better than many places in Brooklyn and is now quite prosperous, holding some of the city's most beautiful residential architecture. There are two main commercial drags – DeKalb and Lafayette avenues, which run roughly parallel to each other – but it's the blocks connecting them that hold the most historic and attractive buildings and townhouses.

Brooklyn Academy of Music (BAM)

30 Lafayette Ave • ☎ 718 636 4100, Ⓦ bam.org • Subway B, D, N, Q, R, #2, #3, #4, #5 to Atlantic Ave-Barclays Center; C to Lafayette Ave; G to Fulton St

The multipurpose **Brooklyn Academy of Music** marks the high-culture centre of the borough. At the corner of Ashland Place and Fulton Street is the BAM Harvey Theater, where most plays are staged, many with top-tier actors. The interior has been preserved in a state of glamorous pseudo-decay. Continue south on Ashland Place to reach BAM's main building – the 1908 opera house, which boasts a colourful terracotta cornice and undulating glass canopy. BAM also hosts dance, classical music and film; theatre and opera; the BAMkids film festival; and the adventurous Next Wave Festival. The swanky, glittering *BAMcafé*, on the second floor of the opera house, offers free live music – jazz, blues, R&B – Friday and Saturday nights from 9 or 9.30pm until late. The institution is adding other buildings, one of which will have a programming space shared by BAM and other local cultural organizations (including the Brooklyn Public Library and the Museum of Contemporary African Diasporan Arts; see below) along with an outdoor plaza.

17

Williamsburgh Savings Bank Tower

1 Hanson Place • Subway B, D, N, Q, R, #2, #3, #4, #5 to Atlantic Ave-Barclays Center; C to Lafayette Ave; G to Fulton St

Sharing the block with BAM is the **Williamsburgh Savings Bank Tower**, Brooklyn's second-tallest building and its most iconic. Built in 1927 but only recently turned into luxury condos, it stands 512ft (34 storeys) tall and sports one of the biggest four-sided clocks in the world, each face measuring 27ft in diameter.

Museum of Contemporary African Diasporan Arts

80 Hanson Place, at South Portland • Wed, Fri & Sat noon–7pm, Thurs noon–8pm, Sun noon–6pm • $8, under 12 free • ☎ 718 230 0492, Ⓦ mocada.org • Subway B, D, N, Q, R, #2, #3, #4, #5 to Atlantic Ave-Barclays Center; C to Lafayette Ave; G to Fulton St; D, N, R to Pacific St

At the intersection of Hanson Place and South Portland Avenue, the **Museum of Contemporary African Diasporan Arts** makes its home – though it is due to move sometime in 2018 to a mixed-use building shared by BAM (see opposite). The museum tends to mount provocative multimedia exhibits on issues like race, class and police violence.

South Portland Avenue

Heading north on **South Portland Avenue** from the Museum of Contemporary African Diasporan Arts, you'll soon come to one of the prettiest blocks in all of New York City – the stretch between Lafayette and DeKalb avenues, which is lined with stately townhouses with high stoops under a lush canopy of trees. The biannual Fort Greene House Tour in early May allows you to peek inside several residences, gardens and artists' studios ($25; ☎718 875 1855, Ⓦhistoricfortgreene.org); note that it alternates with an equally worthwhile Clinton Hill House Tour (Ⓦsocietyforclintonhill.org), which covers the adjacent neighbourhood, also full of brownstone houses, gardens and the like.

The next block down, South Elliott Place, is landmarked on its east side; Spike Lee's production offices, Forty Acres and a Mule, and the super-narrow home at no. 37 – just 13ft wide – can be found here.

BRIC House

647 Fulton St, at Rockwell Place • Daily 10am–6pm • Free • Enquiries ☎ 718 855 7882, tickets ☎ 866 811 4111, Ⓦ bricartsmedia.org • Subway #2, #3, #4, #5 to Nevins St

The multidisciplinary BRIC Arts group houses its extensive operations in a one-time theatre space, now known as the **BRIC House** and modernized to hold musical performances, art exhibitions and classrooms. The on-site gallery puts on contemporary art installations that rotate frequently, but also on the premises is the headquarters for **Urban Glass** (Mon–Fri noon–7.30pm, Sat 11am–7.30pm, Sun 11am–6pm; tours Sat 1pm; free; ☎718 625 3685, Ⓦurbanglass.org). You'll need to make an appointment to check out its studios, but you can peek around its gallery and store during all open

---

OUTER BOROUGHS ARCHITECTURE

Not all of New York's most dazzling residential architecture is in Manhattan; Brooklyn, in particular, has eye-catching blocks of Italianate and neo-Gothic townhouses built in the mid- to late 1800s sprinkled through its historic neighbourhoods. The following streets/areas in the outer boroughs are worth the trek to see:

23rd Street, Long Island City, Queens See p.245
45th Avenue between 21st and Bed-Stuy historic district, Brooklyn See p.228
Grand Concourse, the Bronx See p.256
Middagh Street, Brooklyn Heights See p.220
South Portland Avenue, Fort Greene, Brooklyn See above

17

PRATT INSTITUTE AND CLINTON HILL

In stately **Clinton Hill**, artsy Pratt Institute, 200 Willoughby Ave (☎718 636 3600, ⓦpratt.edu), sits on a 25-acre campus and, if not a must-see, is worth a wander to check out its sculpture park – roughly sixty pieces (including ones from such notables as Robert Indiana and Richard Serra), and changing each year – and verdant grounds. Artist Robert Mapplethorpe and designer Betsey Johnson are just a few of the well-known alumni. After touring, take a look around the houses of Clinton Hill, full of Italianate and Gothic Revival styles; some of the finest examples are along Clinton Avenue.

hours. What you'll find is a vast glass-blowing facility dedicated to artists who fire and use the material in their work. BRIC are also the folks behind the popular outdoor summer concert series Celebrate Brooklyn (see p.407).

Fort Greene Park

Myrtle Ave, Washington Park, Dekalb Ave and St Edwards St • Subway G to Fulton St; #2, #3, #4, #5 to Nevins St

South Portland Avenue comes to a dead end at **Fort Greene Park**, designed by Frederick Law Olmsted and Calvert Vaux in 1867, and named after Revolutionary War general Nathaniel Greene. Seventy years later, Walt Whitman, as editor of *The Brooklyn Eagle*, urged that the space be turned into parkland, a "lung" for the growing borough. At the park's summit, the 148ft **Prison Ship Martyrs Monument** (1908) commemorates the estimated 11,500 Americans who died in the floating prison camps maintained by the British during the Revolutionary War. Sixteen squalid ships, rife with smallpox, were moored in old Wallabout Bay (just offshore from the Brooklyn Navy Yard). The bones of the dead, collected as they washed ashore for decades after, are housed in a small crypt at the base of the tower.

Heading diagonally from the monument (due west), seek out the bench honouring novelist **Richard Wright**, who wrote *Native Son* here in Fort Greene Park in the 1930s. Installed in 2001, the modest but striking memorial is slyly camouflaged the park seating; you'll know you've found it when you spot the inscription, cleverly hidden on the side: "In the writing of scene after scene, I was guided by but one criterion: to tell the truth as I saw it."

Elsewhere, there are tennis courts, playgrounds, a weekend farmers' market and a nature path with labels for the wide variety of trees in the park.

Brooklyn Masonic Temple

317 Clermont St, at Lafayette Ave • Subway G to Clinton-Washington aves

The 1909 **Brooklyn Masonic Temple** rises like a fortress from its surroundings on Clermont Street. Masons no longer meet here, but hipsters do, with indie bands and DJs playing in the renovated theatre.

Williamsburg

Northeast of downtown and past Fort Greene is **Williamsburg**, which is mostly divided north–south: the so-called Northside is overrun by artsy refugees from Manhattan, would-be hipsters and folks with enough money to buy condos along the waterfront; in the south are sections that remain strongly Hasidic Jewish or Latino. South-side Williamsburg can seem frozen in time, especially in the vicinity of **Lee Avenue** and Bedford Avenue, which run parallel between Division Avenue and the Brooklyn– Queens Expressway. Here, kosher delicatessens line the streets and signs are written in Yiddish and Hebrew, thanks to the large population of **Hasidic Jews** in the area – a community presence since 1903, when the Williamsburg Bridge brought over many Jews from the cramped Lower East Side. The L train goes to Williamsburg, with Bedford Avenue and Lorimer Street the most convenient stops.

Bedford Avenue and around

Bedford Avenue is the heart of Williamsburg, where the blocks teem with a particular breed of self-consciously downmarket bohemian, decked out in vintage clothes and hopping from coffee shop to record store to nifty boutique.

While the densest concentration of activity is on Bedford, many of the more interesting spots are elsewhere, having gravitated towards cheaper rents. **Grand Street**, for one, is lined with some fine galleries and shops, and some of the formerly industrial spaces on **North 6th Street** between Bedford and Wythe avenues are now filled with bars and design stores. **Metropolitan Avenue** also has some good bars and restaurants.

A prime culinary attraction is **Smorgasburg** (ⓦsmorgasburg.com), a food market that's a spin-off of the Brooklyn Flea (see box, p.70); the Williamsburg version (April to

DRINKING AND NIGHTLIFE

BARS
Allswell	10
Barcade	15
The Commodore	16
Featherweight	5
Pete's Candy Store	9
Radegast Hall & Biergarten	13
Først	4

NIGHTLIFE
Baby's All Right	17
Brooklyn Bowl	7
Good Room	2
Knitting Factory	14
Music Hall of Williamsburg	11
Output	6
Saint Vitus	1
Schimanski	8

LIVE MUSIC
Warsaw	3

LGBT BAR
Metropolitan	12

EATING
Bamonte's	7
Blue Bottle	8
Cafe Grumpy	1
DeStefano's Steakhouse	6
Devoción	13
Diner	17
Egg	9
Enid's	4
Fette Sau	12
Gimme! Coffee	10
Paulie Gee's	2
Peter Luger Steak House	16
Peter Pan Donut	3
Pies and Thighs	15
Roberta's	5
Rye	14
Saltie	11

SHOPPING
Amarcord	9
Antoinette	11
Awoke Vintage	8
Beacon's Closet	3
Book Thug Nation	6
Domsey Express	12
Halcyon	13
Mast Brothers	10
Moore Street Market	4
Record Grouch	1
Smorgasburg	5
Spoonbill & Sugartown	7
WORD	2

ACCOMMODATION
Box House	1
Henry Norman Hotel	2
Le Jolie	6
McCarren Hotel & Pool	7
NY Moore Hostel	3
Pointe Plaza	8
The William Vale	4
Wythe Hotel	5

WILLIAMSBURG AND GREENPOINT

17

BROOKLYN BEER

In 1900 nearly fifty breweries operated in Brooklyn, but the last of these, Schaefer and Rheingold, closed in 1976. For years after its founding in 1987, the **Brooklyn Brewery**, at 79 N 11th St (☎718 486 7422, ⊕brooklynbrewery.com), was "Brooklyn" in name only – the founders had their beer produced upstate. But in 1996 the operation moved into its Williamsburg headquarters, reviving Brooklyn's brewing tradition and making Brooklyn Lager a very popular beverage citywide; it has gained borough rivals in recent years, namely Red Hook's SixPoint (see box, p.237), Greenpoint Beer and Ale Co., within the bar *Dirck the Norseman* (7 N 15th St, ⊕dirckthenorseman.com) and Fort Greene's Kelso (made by Greenpoint Beer Works); there are also growing scenes in the Bronx and Queens.

Hang out in the brewery's cafeteria-style beer hall or take a tour (Sat 1, 2, 3, 4 & 5pm; free; no reservations). It's $4 for a beer; offerings may include seasonal brews you can't always find in stores and restaurants.

---

mid-Nov Sat 11am–6pm) is held near the water at 90 Kent Ave, at North 7th Street. Scores of vendors sell everything from delectable *dosa*s and *banh mi* to BLTs and beef jerky, with an emphasis on local, fresh and sustainable.

Many of the city's best vintage clothing shops can be found in here (see p.381), as well as some solid art galleries. Next to the Williamsburg Bridge, the **Williamsburg Art and Historical Center (WAH)**, at 135 Broadway on Bedford (Thurs–Sun noon–6pm; ☎718 486 6012, ⊕wahcenter.net), displays local painting and sculpture in a vast gallery on the second floor of the imposing Kings County Savings Bank.

City Reliquary

370 Metropolitan Ave, at Havemeyer St • Thurs–Sun noon–6pm • $5 suggested donation • ☎718 782 4842, ⊕cityreliquary.org • Subway L to Lorimer St; G to Metropolitan Ave

A bit more history-oriented than any of the galleries but still in the same vein, the **City Reliquary** displays a mishmash of NYC-related ephemera such as vintage postcards, seltzer bottles and Jackie Robinson memorabilia; the fact that it grew from an apartment window display to a museum speaks volumes about the 'hood. But the cutting-edge feel of Williamsburg has substantially worn away: ultra-sleek high-rises have sprouted up, capitalizing on views like the one from tiny **Grand Ferry Park**; just south, the massive Domino's Sugar Factory is being converted into housing.

Greenpoint

Quiet **Greenpoint**, which hugs the northern border of the borough, has the distinction of being the childhood home of Mae West, the birthplace of the oft-ridiculed Brooklynese accent and home to the largest Polish community in New York City; there's also a substantial Puerto Rican contingent. The relaxed, low-rise area has absorbed much of the artsy feel of Williamsburg to the south – and the popularity of the TV show *Girls* has certainly helped bring the young, hip and curious to the neighbourhood – but the new generation hasn't totally erased the Polish character of the businesses along its tidy main strip, **Manhattan Avenue** (partly because they're establishing their own strip on **Franklin Street**, though to be fair there are a few cool spots mixed in on Manhattan).

While Greenpoint and neighbouring areas were originally known as Boswijck (later Bushwick), meaning "wooded district", the Industrial Revolution took the "green" out of Greenpoint, as the area became home to the "Black Arts" – printing, pottery, gas, glass and iron. In 1950, refineries caused a 17- to 30-million-gallon underground oil spill, larger than the Exxon Valdez disaster in Alaska, which spilled "only" eleven million gallons. It's not immediately visible except as an occasional slick on the surface of Newtown Creek, which separates Greenpoint from Queens, but it's very much on

17

the minds of residents who fear the toxic effects of the residue. Cleanup is ongoing, but still has years to finish – if that's even possible at this point.

The G train goes to Greenpoint, with Nassau Avenue the most convenient stop, though if you're already in Williamsburg, just walk across McCarren Park (see below) to get here.

McCarren Park

Greenpoint merits a quick visit for its blend of Polish and hipster cultures and their respective cuisines. If you're coming from Williamsburg, take Driggs Avenue north past the **Russian Orthodox Cathedral of the Transfiguration**, at North 12th Street on Driggs, a New York City landmark whose five green-copper onion domes hover above the trees of **McCarren Park**. The park itself forms the unofficial line between Greenpoint and Williamsburg; in addition to tennis courts, playgrounds and dog runs, it contains a historic pool and a seasonal ice-rink.

Manhattan Avenue and around

Turn left on Manhattan Avenue and continue straight to get to the heart of Greenpoint. Along the way you'll find an assortment of Polish delis and bakeries, which spill over onto Nassau Avenue. Keep moving north on Manhattan and an air of isolation takes over, though there are an increasing number of cool cafés and restaurants in these parts. Wander down the narrow side-streets of Manhattan and you'll get a feel for the tight-knit local community – and how it is changing. *Café Grumpy*, 193 Meserole Ave, at Diamond, is a neighbourhood landmark (not least for its starring role on the TV series *Girls*), while further towards the water, an assortment of bars and restaurants has sprouted up along Franklin Street and around Greenpoint Avenue.

Newtown Creek Nature Walk and Wastewater Treatment Plant

East end of Paidge Ave • Park daily sunrise–sunset • Subway G to Greenpoint Ave, then two blocks east to Provost St and about eight blocks north to Paidge Ave

On the banks of Newtown Creek, an unusual waterfront park offers splendid views and unmatched solitude. A walkway, formed like the hull of a ship (complete with portholes), snakes down to the water, along which are plantings, sculptures, benches and steps that go right down to creek level; look out and you'll see bridges to Queens, the occasional barge, giant mounds of trash – more mesmerizing than it sounds – and the Chrysler Building, among other skyline beauties. You can also catch sight of what's behind you: the bulbous silos (they call them "digester eggs") of the Newtown Creek Wastewater Treatment Plant, which has a visitor centre, 329 Greenpoint Ave (by appointment ☎718 595 5140; they also run free quarterly tours of the eggs, which last 90min, along with a variety of educational programmes in the centre). As you descend back to the parking lot on your way down the path, note how the walkway perfectly frames the Empire State Building.

Bushwick

Many of Brooklyn's arty types have decamped for Bushwick – whose borders blur with those of East Williamsburg; officially, it begins below Flushing Avenue and east of Broadway – or parts farther from the gentrified blocks of Williamsburg. One neighbourhood highlight is its collection of street art, but it does hold lots of offbeat music venues, cocktail dens, hip restaurants and small, gung-ho galleries. To be closest to the action, take the L train to Jefferson Street.

Bedford-Stuyvesant

Immediately east of Clinton Hill, **Bedford-Stuyvesant** is the nation's largest black community after Chicago's South Side, with more than 400,000 residents. It stretches north–south from Flushing to Atlantic avenues, and east as far as Saratoga; its main

17

arteries include Bedford and Nostrand avenues and Fulton Street. The C line runs along the neighbourhood's southern border; take it to Nostrand Avenue or Kingston–Throop Avenues (the A also runs to the former) to be near the historic district and latest eateries.

Originally two separate areas, the adjacent districts of Bedford and Stuyvesant were populated by both blacks and whites in the nineteenth century. During the Great Migration between 1910 and 1920, large numbers of southern African Americans moved north and settled in this area. In the 1940s the white population began to leave, taking funding for many important community services with it. Economic decline continued for several decades, reaching an all-time low in the 1980s.

The poverty and neglect had an unintended upside: because few of its brownstones were razed in the name of economic development, the neighbourhood has the densest collection of pre-1900 homes in New York, attracting a fervent crowd of young fixer-uppers – both white and black – over the past decade.

Gothic, Victorian and other classic brownstones abound, especially inside the **Stuyvesant Heights Historic District**, which includes parts of MacDonough, Macon, Decatur, Bainbridge and Chauncey streets, primarily between Tompkins and Stuyvesant avenues. Outside the main historic section, make sure to swing by the landmark **Boys' High School**, at 832 Marcy Ave, on any wanderings; the Romanesque Revival pile saw the likes of Norman Mailer pass through its halls. The couple of blocks of row houses on Jefferson and Hancock streets between Nostrand and Tompkins are as dignified and radiant as any in the city.

Crown Heights

South of Bedford-Stuyvesant and east of Prospect Heights is thrumming **Crown Heights**, bounded by Atlantic Avenue and Empire Boulevard to the north and south, and Ralph and Washington avenues to the east and west. This community is home to the largest **West Indian** community in New York as well as an active, established population of about ten thousand **Hasidic Jews**, most of them belonging to the Russian Lubavitcher sect (in the mid-twentieth-century, roughly 75,000 Jews called the neighbourhood home).

Eastern Parkway, the large throughway that runs past the Brooklyn Museum, is the main traffic artery of Crown Heights, and landscaped walkways on either side of the path provide much-needed green space.

WEEKSVILLE

In the shadow of a housing project on the eastern reaches of Crown Heights stands one of the most fascinating historical sights in Brooklyn – the remnants of the once-thriving town of **Weeksville**. Founded by African American James Weeks in 1838 just eleven years after New York abolished slavery, Weeksville soon became a refuge for both escaped slaves from the South and free blacks fleeing racial violence in the North (a similar if smaller village, Carrsville, existed adjacent to it). By the 1860s it had its own schools and businesses, and had begun turning out some of the city's first black professionals. Weeksville flourished until the 1930s; by the 1950s all but four wood-frame cottages from the town had been destroyed. In the late 1960s efforts headed by a Pratt Institute history professor, James Hurley, led to the (re)discovery of the so-called Hunterfly Road Houses (the name of the former alley that ran by the homes), and activists petitioned the city to preserve them. Call in at the brand-new headquarters of **Weeksville Heritage Center**, 158 Buffalo Ave, between Bergen St and St Marks Ave (Tues–Fri 9am–5pm, tours Tues–Fri at 3pm; $5; ☎718 756 5250, ⓦweeksvillesociety.org), to get oriented and join a tour of the three houses (one of which is a double house) that remain. They date back to the 1860s and are furnished in line with various periods of Weeksville's century-long existence. Tour guides do an admirable job of adding atmosphere with stories about Weeksville, gleaned from ongoing research, oral histories and archeological digs. It's a bit of a hike to get here; the closest subway is the A or C train to Utica Avenue, from where you'll walk four blocks south on Utica to Bergen, turn left and walk another couple of blocks.

17

Over Labor Day weekend, Crown Heights hosts the annual **West Indian–American Day Parade and Carnival**, during which almost two million revellers dance, eat and applaud colourful floats and steel-drum outfits. The parade, which organizers claim is the biggest in the nation, runs west along Eastern Parkway from Rochester Avenue in Crown Heights to Grand Army Plaza (see Chapter 30 for more information). To get a taste of West Indian culture and cuisine year-round, wander along Nostrand Avenue from the #3 train stop, where there's a string of dirt-cheap Caribbean snack joints – grab a "double" (fried bread wrapped around a chickpea mixture, topped off by pepper sauce) and take in the scene. Meanwhile, Franklin Avenue, to the west, has shown serious signs of gentrification in recent years, with some fancyish cafés, restaurants and shops lining the blocks between Lincoln Place and St Mark's Avenue.

Brooklyn Children's Museum

145 Brooklyn Ave, at St Mark's Ave • Tues–Sun 10am–5pm, Thurs till 6pm (free 3–6pm Thurs) • $11 • ☎ 718 735 4400, ⓦ brooklynkids .org • Subway #3 to Kingston Ave; C to Kingston–Throop Avenues

North of Eastern Parkway, the **Brooklyn Children's Museum** was the first museum of its kind, founded way back in 1899; a "green" renovation and expansion by Uruguayan architect Rafael Viñoly added solar panels and other energy-saving devices, doubled the space and gave the museum the chance to modernize its collection. Galleries hold hands-on exhibitions concentrating on science, the environment, local neighbourhood life – which highlights various ethnic districts around Brooklyn – and much more; the "Water Wonders" play area and the live animals on display downstairs should especially thrill the younger set.

Wyckoff Farmhouse Museum

5816 Clarendon Rd, at Ralph Ave • Fri & Sat tours every half-hour from 1–4pm; grounds open noon–4pm on tour days • $5, 10 and under $3 • ☎ 718 629 5400, ⓦ wyckoffmuseum.org • Getting there requires some work, either by subway on the A or #4 to Utica Ave then the #B46 bus, then a nine-block walk; the #2, #5 to Newkirk, then #B8 bus to Beverley Rd at 59th St; or the #3 train to Sutter Ave–Rutland Rd then the #B47 bus to Clarendon Rd and Ralph Ave

The oldest house in the city is by no means an essential stop for casual visitors, but for those interested in architectural, colonial or borough history, it may be worth the trek – especially if coupled with a visit to Weeksville (see box, p.229) and Prospect Park's Lefferts Homestead (see p.232). The wooden saltbox structure, built by Pieter Claesen Wyckoff, dates back to around 1652, though renovations and additions are circa mid-1800s. A guided tour takes in the cramped space – a family of thirteen resided in the original one-room house – and reimagines colonial times; docents do their best to evoke the customs and lifestyle.

Prospect Park and around

Where Brooklyn really surpasses itself is on Flatbush Avenue in the vicinity of **Grand Army Plaza** – an elegant, if congested, traffic circle around a stately memorial arch. The plaza faces the **Brooklyn Public Library** and the entrance to **Prospect Park**, and immediately east of it on Eastern Parkway, the **Brooklyn Museum** houses, among other things, an excellent ancient Egyptian trove and the **Brooklyn Botanic Garden**. The plaza also acts as a border to several very different neighbourhoods, including up-and-coming **Prospect Heights** and the serene, liberal bastion of **Park Slope**. South of the green are the Victorian-lined streets of **Ditmas Park**; continue in that general direction to hit **Brooklyn College**.

ARRIVAL AND DEPARTURE

By subway The #2 and #3 subway lines stop at Grand Army Plaza, while the Brooklyn Museum has its own stop just a few blocks further down the line. The B and Q trains to Prospect Park get you closest to the park's main attractions, and Park Slope's chief subway stops are the F to Seventh Ave/9th St and the R to Fourth Ave/Union St.

Grand Army Plaza

Central Park architects Frederick Law Olmsted and Calvert Vaux designed **Grand Army Plaza** in the 1860s and 1870s as an approach to Prospect Park, but it didn't take on its current grandeur until the end of that century. The 80ft-tall triumphal **Soldiers' and Sailors' Memorial Arch**, modelled on Paris's Arc de Triomphe and a tribute to the Union victory in the Civil War, was unveiled in 1892.

Saturday is by far the best day to visit, when dozens of farmers from New York and New Jersey set up stalls here at the city's second-largest **farmers' market** (Sat year-round 8am–4pm). At the height of summer, expect to find bounteous produce, meats, flowers, jams and pickles, along with occasional cooking demonstrations. The wintertime selection can be thin, but you can always get a crunchy apple, donut and steaming cup of cider. The plaza is also the site of a big New Year's firework display.

Brooklyn Public Library

10 Grand Army Plaza • ☏ 718 230 2100, Ⓦ bklynlibrary.org • Subway #2, #3 to Grand Army Plaza

On the east side of Grand Army Plaza, you'll find the central branch of the immense

PROSPECT PARK AND AROUND

17

Brooklyn Public Library, which was started in 1912 with the help of a $1.6 million donation from Andrew Carnegie and finally finished in 1941. Its entrance curves along with the roundabout; move up close to decipher the literary allusions of the gold figurines on the gate.

Prospect Park

718 965 8951, 🌐 prospectpark.org

Energized by their success with Central Park, Olmsted and Vaux landscaped **Prospect Park** in the early 1860s. Its 585 acres include a sixty-acre lake on the east side, a ninety-acre open meadow on the west, and a circular 3.35-mile park drive around the periphery, primarily reserved for runners, cyclists and rollerbladers (vehicular traffic is allowed during weekday rush hours only). Despite attractions that have sprung up over the years – the Lakeside recreational development (with a return to the original Olmsted and Vaux lake-area design), a seasonal Sunday **Smorgasburg** (see p.392), a tennis centre and the popular Celebrate Brooklyn outdoor music festival – Prospect Park remains for the most part remarkably bucolic.

For casual fun, head to the **Drummer's Grove** near the Parkside and Ocean Avenue entrance on the southeast corner of the park; the crowd that gathers on Sunday afternoons (April–Oct; 2pm) is no amateur circle – some very accomplished musicians have been jamming here for decades. The **Celebrate Brooklyn** concert series likewise draws top-notch musical and dance talent to its summer series of outdoor concerts, held at the **Bandshell**, just inside the 9th Street entrance at Prospect Park West ($3 donation requested; 718 683 5600, 🌐 bricartsmedia.org); they also hold a few shows at Brooklyn Bridge Park (see p.219). More active pursuits can be had at the **LeFrak Center at Lakeside**, with its seasonal ice-skating and roller-skating rinks (see p.402), not to mention free summertime water-splash park – great for cooling down on a hot day. It is also a prime place to rent bikes ($8–15/hr) and boats ($25–35/hr), available seasonally.

Audubon Center

In the Boathouse, close to the Lincoln Rd entrance at mid-park on the east side • April–Oct Thurs–Sun noon–5pm, also Pop-Up Audubon takes place April–Dec Sat & Sun noon–5pm, Nov & Dec Sat & Sun noon–4pm at various designated locations • Free • 718 287 3400, 🌐 prospectpark.org • Subway B, Q to Prospect Park

The **Audubon Center** serves as the park's main visitor centre, with a few nature exhibitions, as well as being the start of the park's four nature trails. Their programming has been cut back a bit due to budget constraints, but a "Pop-Up Audubon" has taken over some of the slack: nature tours, ecological exhibitions and other activities are all on offer. Check the park's website for details.

Prospect Park Zoo

450 Flatbush Ave, on the eastern side of the park • April–Oct Mon–Fri 10am–5pm, Sat & Sun 10am–5.30pm; Nov–March daily 10am–4.30pm • $8, ages 3–12 $5 • 718 399 7339, 🌐 prospectparkzoo.com • Subway B, Q to Prospect Park

The **Prospect Park Zoo**, run by the venerable Wildlife Conservation Society, showcases kangaroos, red pandas, venomous frogs, peacocks, baboons and much more in natural-looking habitats. It's a small-scale affair but likeable enough for those with kids in tow – little ones should especially enjoy milking cows in the Barn and Garden exhibit (mid-May to mid-Oct only), and watching the playful sea lions being fed (thrice daily).

Lefferts Historic House

Just south of Prospect Park Zoo, on the eastern side of the park • April, May, Oct & Nov Thurs–Sun noon–5pm; June & Sept Thurs–Sat noon–5pm; July & Aug Thurs–Sun noon–6pm; Dec, Feb & March Sat & Sun noon–4pm • $3 suggested donation • 718 789 2822 • Subway B, Q to Prospect Park

Tour guides at the **Lefferts Historic House**, an eighteenth-century Dutch farmhouse, use the place as a prop to talk (mostly to children) about what Brooklyn was like in the 1820s. Just south of the house stands a 1912 **carousel** (April, May, Sept & Oct

Thurs–Sun noon–5pm; July & Aug Thurs–Sun noon–6pm; $2) with 51 hand-carved horses and other animals; it was originally installed at Coney Island.

Brooklyn Museum

200 Eastern Parkway • Wed & Sun 11am–6pm, Thurs 11am–10pm, Fri & Sat 11am–8pm, first Sat of every month (save Sept) until 11pm • Suggested donation $16, free first Sat 5–11pm • ☎ 718 638 5000, ⓦ brooklynmuseum.org • Subway #2, #3 to Eastern Parkway

East of Grand Army Plaza and the Public Library stands the imposing **Brooklyn Museum**. Designed by McKim, Mead, and White, it's second only to the Metropolitan Museum of Art in terms of exhibit space in New York City, with five floors of galleries. The museum is best known for its distinguished store of Egyptian relics and a feminist art wing that includes Judy Chicago's ground-breaking 1970s installation, *The Dinner Party*. A regular schedule of talks, arts-and-crafts demonstrations and performances is best experienced via the free **First Saturdays** programme, held on the first Saturday evening of each month. On these nights, the museum stays open until 11pm (admission is free after 5pm), becoming a vast all-ages party with live music and dancing.

The collection

Just inside the front entrance stands a changing selection of a dozen bronze sculptures by Auguste Rodin. Elsewhere, exhibits are set up to showcase a cross-section of museum holdings, with some detailed African carvings and pencil drawings by artists such as Isamu Noguchi and Louise Nevelson.

The second floor is dedicated to the **Asian and Islamic galleries**, with pieces from China, Korea, India and Japan, as well as Ottoman Turkish and Qajar Persian textiles, mosaics, manuscripts and jewellery.

The carved-stone *Brooklyn Black Head* of the Ptolemaic period, arguably the museum's crown jewel, is one of 1200 objects in the authoritative **Ancient Egyptian Art** collection – one of the largest outside of Egypt – on the third floor. Sarcophagi and sculptures are nicely complemented by small galleries of Assyrian, Sumerian and other ancient Middle Eastern art; keep an eye out for the exquisite "Coffin for an Ibis", decorated in astonishing detail. Those who don't spook easily may also enjoy the "Mummy Chamber", which features four Egyptian mummies plus a mummified cat. On the same floor, **European Paintings** presents works by Monet and a few other big names, though none is particularly essential viewing.

One flight up, most of the **Decorative Arts collection** is in six evocative period rooms, including a nineteenth-century Moorish smoking room from John D. Rockefeller's estate. It shares the floor with the Elizabeth A. Sackler Center for Feminist Art, the centrepiece of which is **The Dinner Party**, a massive triangular dinner table with custom-made china place settings for 39 famous women. Constructed in 1974–79 by artist Judy Chicago and hundreds of volunteers, it's an impressive and moving display, even if the explanatory timeline – or "herstory" – in the adjoining gallery feels a bit dated.

On the fifth floor, Georgia O'Keeffe's sensual *Brooklyn Bridge* opens the "American Identities" permanent exhibition, which draws thematic connections among works in the museum's varied **Painting and Sculpture** collection. More interesting – in fact, one of the most diverting parts of the entire museum – is the **Visible Storage/Study Center** exhibit, which is basically a couple of thousand museum holdings not on display in the main museum. Besides paintings, more than a thousand objects of Americana are packed behind glass, including chairs, Tiffany lamps and a futuristic bicycle.

Brooklyn Botanic Garden

900 Washington Ave • March–Oct Tues–Fri 8am–6pm, Sat & Sun 10am–6pm; Nov Tues–Fri 8am–4.30pm, Sat & Sun 10am–4.30pm; Dec–Feb Tues–Sun 10am–4.30pm • $15, under 12 free, free Tues and Sat before noon, also free on weekdays Dec–Feb • ☎ 718 623 7200, ⓦ bbg.org • Subway #2, #3 to Eastern Parkway; #4, #5 to Franklin Ave

Located just behind the Brooklyn Museum, the **Brooklyn Botanic Garden** is one of the most enticing park spaces in the city. Plants from around the world occupy 22 gardens

17

and exhibits spread over 52 acres, all sumptuous but not over-manicured. What you'll see depends largely on the season. Late March brings colour to Daffodil Hill, while April and May see the cherry trees blooming in the Japanese Garden; designed in 1914, it is the oldest garden of its kind outside of Japan. The Rose Garden starts to flourish in the early summer, the elaborate water-lily ponds are at their best in mid- to late summer and early fall, and the fall colours in the Rock Garden are striking. A winter visit lets you enjoy the warmth of the Steinhardt Conservatory, filled with orchids, tropical plants, palms and one of the largest collections of bonsai trees in the West. One part that's not season-determinant is the Celebrity Path, a stone walkway that honours Brooklyn's famous sons and daughters. The new Discovery Garden gives young kids space to make some nature discoveries, with different habitats geared towards exploration and interactivity; a garden shop stocks a wide array of exotic plants, bulbs and seeds; and the pleasant *Yellow Magnolia Café* offers a farm-friendly array of mostly organic meals and snacks.

Park Slope
The western exits of Prospect Park leave you in **Park Slope**, a district of stately nineteenth-century brownstone townhouses inhabited since the 1970s by a notoriously liberal crew of urban pioneers; it's also in an eternal baby boom, and pushchairs jam the pavements.

The tree-lined blocks between Prospect Park West and Eighth Avenue from Union to 15th Street contain some of the finest Romanesque and Queen Anne residences in the US, helping this area earn the nickname "The Gold Coast of Brooklyn". Almost all the buildings were constructed in the 1880s and 1890s but they're hardly uniform, displaying a fine array of building materials (brick, brownstone and granite in various combinations) and details, from original gaslights to turrets and bay windows. Especially attractive blocks to seek out include Montgomery Place and 3rd Street, near the north end of the Slope, and, just beyond the southern borders, Webster Place, between Sixth and Seventh avenues. **Seventh Avenue** is the Slope's traditional main drag, lined with all the essentials – florists and wine shops, cafés and boutiques – but it can lack a bit of excitement. These days you'll find a younger crowd, along with trendier shops, bars and restaurants, on **Fifth Avenue**.

Long known as an LGBT-friendly neighbourhood, the Slope is home to the **Brooklyn Pride Festival & Parade**, a community-oriented, relatively uncommercial event that takes place every June; it includes a fun run, daylong entertainment and a night-time parade along Fifth Avenue.

Old Stone House
Between Fourth and Fifth aves, and 3rd and 5th sts • Fri 3–6pm, Sat & Sun 11am–4pm • $3 suggested donation • ☎ 718 768 3195, ⓦ theoldstonehouse.org • Subway R to Union St-Fourth Ave

You can learn about the Slope's history at the **Old Stone House** in J.J. Byrne Park, famous as the site of one of the most dramatic skirmishes of the Battle of Brooklyn and the first headquarters of the Brooklyn Dodgers baseball team. The reconstructed building contains changing exhibits and a diorama of the house as it looked in its early days – it is, however, frequently rented out for parties or other events.

Prospect Heights
Just north of Grand Army Plaza, **Prospect Heights** has handsome and varied late nineteenth-century residences that rival those of nearby Park Slope. You could spend a pleasant hour or so walking up and down its lovely side streets, but its main appeal will probably be its **food and drink** options, which are within easy walking distance of the Brooklyn Museum and the Brooklyn Botanic Garden; **Vanderbilt Avenue** is your best bet.

Ditmas Park and Midwood
South of Prospect Park, a few under-visited areas provide some fun exploration, assuming you have the time and aren't set on just seeing major parks and museums.

Ditmas Park has the city's most attractive collection of stand-alone Victorian mansions, on the plot bordered by Stratford, Cortelyou, Marlborough and Albemarle; it feels as far removed from the city as you can get. After wandering up and down, hit Cortelyou Road for its burgeoning collection of cool restaurants and cafés (the Q train will get you there). If you keep venturing east over to Flatbush, you'll be a block or two from the 3000-seat **Kings Theatre** (ⓦkingstheatre.com), a once-grand movie palace built in the 1920s that has, after closing in 1977, been restored to its former luxury (thanks to $95 million from a few sources, with the city on the hook for more than half).

DRINKING AND NIGHTLIFE

BARS

Black Mountain		Sunny's	12
Winehouse	5	Threes Brewing	3
Brooklyn Inn	1		
Brooklyn Social	7	NIGHTLIFE	
Clover Club	2	The Bell House	9
Gowanus Yacht Club	6	Jalopy Theatre &	
Fort Defiance	11	School of Music	8
Other Half Brewing	10	Littlefield	4

EATING

Baked	11	Mile End	1
Battersby	4	Petite Crevette	5
Buttermilk Channel	9	Pok Pok NY	3
Café Pedlar	2	Prime Meats	8
Frankies 457 Spuntino	7	Red Hook Lobster Pound	10
Good Fork	12	Steve's Authentic	
Hometown Bar-B-Que	14	Key Lime Pie	13
Lucali	6		

ACCOMMODATION

Le Bleu	1
NU Hotel	2

SHOPPING

Brooklyn Strategist	2
D'Amico Coffee	1

COBBLE HILL, CARROLL GARDENS, GOWANUS AND RED HOOK

17

A bit further south, **Brooklyn College** is the most attractive part of **Midwood**, and you're free to walk around the manicured green of the small campus; free tours are also held at 10am and 3pm. The area's other claim to fame is as the home to *Di Fara's* (see p.323), which many consider to be the best pizzeria in the whole of New York City.

Cobble Hill and Boerum Hill

Just south of Atlantic Avenue, the main east–west streets through **Cobble Hill** – Amity, Congress and Warren – are a mix of brownstones and redbrick row houses built between the 1840s and the 1880s. **Court Street** is the neighbourhood's main commercial artery, though the pickings here get a bit more interesting as you head further south towards Carroll Gardens; **Smith Street** caters to a slightly younger crowd, mostly because of its profusion of bars, skate shops and the like.

Over on Clinton Street, which runs parallel to Court, sits the idyllic little **Cobble Hill Park**. Along the park's southern border is a cobblestone alleyway – **Verandah Place**, a renovated mews built in the 1850s. Writer Thomas Wolfe lived in the basement at no. 40 in the 1930s and described the apartment in his novel *You Can't Go Home Again*: "Here, in winter, the walls… sweat continuously with clammy drops of water. Here, in summer, it is he who does the sweating." Living conditions weren't nearly so dismal in the nearby **Home Buildings**, a tidy row of redbrick cottages lining a pedestrian mews, Warren Place. Built in 1878 as utopian workers' housing, the 44 homes are each only 11ft wide.

Meanwhile, the neighbourhood's literary attachments continue; Martin Amis lives on the block-long Strong Place, and Jonathan Lethem, noted former denizen of **Boerum Hill**, has written about both areas in his novels. Beastie Boy Mike D also lives here and helped develop the new corner property at Pacific Street and Boerum Place. Boerum Hill, to Cobble Hill's east, is less architecturally impressive than its neighbour, though it has its share of sober Greek Revival and Italianate buildings, developed around the same period. The F or G to Bergen St deposits you on the border shared by Cobble Hill, Boerum Hill and Carroll Gardens.

Carroll Gardens

As you walk south along Court Street, Cobble Hill blends into **Carroll Gardens** around Degraw Street (alternatively, the F or G to Carroll St puts you right in the middle of Carroll Gardens). Built as a middle- and upper-class community between 1869 and 1884, this part of South Brooklyn has been an Italian enclave since dockworkers arrived here in the early 1900s; **Al Capone** is said to have been married in 1918 at the St Mary Star of the Sea Church on Court Street. The area was later named for Charles Carroll, the only Roman Catholic to sign the Declaration of Independence.

Many of the neighbourhood's older Italian residents have moved out to Staten Island and New Jersey, but you'll still find a few classic *salumerias* and pastry shops alongside the hipper places on Court and Smith streets, the area's arteries. Duck a few blocks south, turning on Fourth Place, to find one of the more unusual residential alleys in the city, Dennet Place, its shortened doorways evoking something out of the Brothers Grimm.

West of the main blocks, across the Brooklyn-Queens Expressway (BQE) overpass, greet the **Columbia Street Waterfront District**, a perpetually up-and-coming district of shops and restaurants that forms the gateway to grittier Red Hook further south. Don't expect Brooklyn Heights esplanade, however; the waterfront here is still an active loading and unloading area for deep-sea container ships and cruise ships, with very limited public access.

Gowanus

The southeast edge of Carroll Gardens is defined by the **Gowanus Canal**, a name that inspires a bit of a shudder in older Brooklynites. Originally a wetlands area famous for its oysters, it became a fetid stillwater around 1870, thanks to sewers from Park Slope that drained here and oil refineries that sat along its banks. In 1999, however, city engineers finally repaired the drain pump so water could flow freely through the canal and into Gowanus Bay, and the canal now supports a surprising amount of marine life, including shrimp and oysters; meanwhile, the neighbourhood on either side of the banks has become a thriving one for art, restaurants and nightlife.

The **Gowanus Dredgers Canoe Club** (☎718 243 0849, ⓦgowanuscanal.org) runs a canoeing programme from May to October, starting at Second Street at Bond, which allows experienced paddlers to get out on the canal; walking and bike trips along the banks are an option for anyone still wary of the water.

Red Hook

Though only a half-mile from the Columbia Street Waterfront District, **Red Hook** feels oddly like the outskirts of a city in the Deep South, a place where hulking redbrick warehouses crumble along the waterfront while, inland, two- and three-storey apartment buildings share cobblestone blocks with garden centres and car-repair shops. A handful of quirky stores, restaurants and cafés line the main strip, **Van Brunt Street**, where the service is almost universally relaxed and friendly – a community vibe that served Red Hook well when it was devastated by 2012's Hurricane Sandy; the look-out-for-one-another ethos helped immensely with the cleanup and with getting businesses back up and running.

ARRIVAL AND DEPARTURE

By subway The F or G to the Carroll St stop leaves you at the southern end of Carroll Gardens, a bus ride or longish walk to Red Hook.

By bus No subway line goes out to Red Hook, but it's easy enough to reach by bus. Take the #B61 bus from Columbia St on the western edge of Carroll Gardens and Cobble Hill.

By water taxi New York Water Taxi (☎212 742 1969, ⓦnywatertaxi.com) runs a free weekend ferry service from Pier 11 in Manhattan to Ikea, at the southern tip of Red Hook; boats leave and arrive every 40min (11.30am–8.40pm). During the week it's $5 (every 40min; 2–7.15pm).

Brief history

Settled by the Dutch in 1636, Red Hook got its name from the colour of the soil and the shape of the land, which forms a corner, or *hoek*, where the Upper New York Bay meets the Gowanus Bay. It eventually became one of the busiest and toughest shipping centres in the US, inspiring Hubert Selby's book *Last Exit to Brooklyn* and Arthur Miller's play *A View from the Bridge*. Some say that urban planner **Robert Moses** deliberately severed the notoriously crime-ridden neighbourhood from the rest of

---

SMALL-BATCH RED HOOK

In **Red Hook**, you can do a mini-trail of some of the more interesting local drink producers, who have taken advantage of the large industrial spaces to set up shop. The best-known, and oldest, such local maker is Six Point Brewery, 40 Van Dyke St (ⓦsixpoint.com; check the website to see if tours are running), which turns out some hop-heavy quaffs – look out for Sweet Action and Righteous Ale, two of their top sellers, in local bars and shops. Along the waterfront, the Red Hook Winery, Pier 41, Suite 325A (☎347 689 2432, ⓦredhookwinery.com; daily noon–6pm; tastings $15, free tours with [paid] tasting 1pm Sat and Sun; otherwise, call ahead for barrel tasting and tour, $35), has a tasting room fronting its winemaking facilities. They cultivate their grapes on the North Fork of Long Island, a region best known for its Merlots, Cabernet Francs and Sauvignon Blancs – all of which are featured here. A newer spot melds two great tastes: Cacao Prieto (☎347 225 0310, ⓦcacaoprieto.com; Sat & Sun 11am–7pm), a chocolatier that also distils whisky under the name Widow Jane (ⓦwidowjane .com) in a brick warehouse at 218 Conover St; tours available at noon, 2pm and 4pm ($20). Leave with a bar of dark chocolate ($8), a bottle of smooth rye ($40) and a smile.

17

Brooklyn when he routed the Brooklyn-Queens Expressway down Hicks Street in 1954. In any case, by the 1960s, the increasing automation of the docking industry left longshoremen out of work and sent most of the freighters from Red Hook to bigger ports in New Jersey.

The waterfront and piers

Red Hook's waterfront is now a curious assemblage of abandoned and repurposed warehouses and parkland. From the end of Pier 41 Governors Island appears almost within wading distance and Lady Liberty seems to raise her torch just for you. Nearby, the **Waterfront Museum** (Thurs 4–8pm, Sat 1–5pm; donation requested; ☎718 624 4719, ⊛waterfrontmuseum.org), at 290 Conover St at Pier 44, presents historical exhibits, art and occasional kid-friendly workshops and performances in a restored railroad barge moored off a small park at the end of Conover Street.

Adjacent **Fairway**, at 480–500 Van Brunt St, is Brooklyn's best mainstream supermarket; at the back is a waterfront café. In the warehouse across the street from Fairway, the **Brooklyn Waterfront Artists Coalition (BWAC)**, at 499 Van Brunt St, holds three main group shows per year, on weekends (1–6pm) from mid-May to mid-June, from late July to mid-August and from late September to late October, as well as October's two-day Red Hook Film Festival (☎718 596 2506, ⊛bwac.org). Another gallery of note in the area is the **Kentler International Drawing Space**, at 353 Van Brunt St, which, as its name suggests, displays fine works on paper (Thurs–Sun noon–5pm; ☎718 875 2098, ⊛kentlergallery.org); meanwhile, a large multipurpose art space, **Pioneer Works**, at 159 Pioneer St (Wed–Sun noon–7pm; ☎718 596 3001, ⊛pioneerworks.org), has settled in, with exhibitions, screenings and even the odd concert in its programme.

Red Hook Ball Fields

There are a couple of good dining options in the neighbourhood (see p.322), but if you're in Red Hook on a summer weekend it's a tradition to eat at the **Red Hook Recreational Area** (also called the **Red Hook Ball Fields**; May–Oct Sat & Sun 10am–early evening), at Clinton and Bay streets. Surrounding a soccer pitch, a dozen or so food-stands dole out delicious tacos, *ceviche*, *tamales*, *pupusas* and more. To reach the fields from Van Brunt, head east on Van Dyke Street.

INDUSTRY CITY

With all the focus in recent years on **waterfront redevelopment**, it's no surprise that a somewhat derelict group of buildings, cut off by the BQE, has managed to become a hotbed for small producers and artists. A series of uniform warehouses was built around the turn of the twentieth century – and had their own railroad. Bush Terminal, as it was once known, was a crucial manufacturing and shipping centre that was also commandeered by the government for military purposes in wartime. After years of postwar decline, it was renamed and eventually reborn as a site for creative types; there are galleries, artist studios, green businesses and a food hall. Two of the spots that may attract more than a passing glance are **Industry City Distillery** (33 35th St) and **Li-Lac Chocolates** (68 35th St). The former, the city's only vodka maker, has in a few years managed to build an energy- (and space-) efficient distillery for its beet-sugar-based beverage. You can't buy it on the premises, but you can take a tour (1hr 30min; Sat 3pm; $15) that gets into the mechanics and chemistry of the process. The latter is a much older business, located for years in Greenwich Village and now taking advantage of the lower rents to house its factory for hand-made confections. While you can't take a tour, you can peek in to see the product being made – and purchase some on-site.

After wandering through a few of the buildings, take a walk up to 43rd Street and First Avenue, where you'll find the entrance for peaceful **Bush Terminal Piers Park**. A walk out on the pier opens up wide views of the harbour, from Staten Island to the Statue of Liberty to One World Trade.

Sunset Park

The borders of the **Sunset Park** district are not always agreed upon, but suffice to say they take in a vast expanse, starting along the harbour and going inland to around Eighth Avenue, and running from around 25th to 60th streets. The main commercial strips, Fifth Avenue and Eighth Avenue, are strongholds of (respectively) Mexican and Chinese shops, markets and restaurants. The namesake park at the centre provides excellent views of the harbour and over to Manhattan, though head towards **Industry City** near the waterfront (see box opposite) for a better perspective. The D express train to 36th Street will get you here the quickest, though the R stops at multiple places.

Green-Wood Cemetery

500 25th St, at Fifth Ave; another entrance on Fourth Ave, at 35th St; and weekend entrances on Fort Hamilton Parkway and Prospect Park West • Daily: May–Aug 7am–7pm; March, April, & Sept & Oct 7.45am–6pm; Nov–Feb 8am–5pm • Guided tram tours May–Aug Wed & Sun 1pm; $20 • ⓦ green-wood.com • Subway R to 25th St

Southwest of Prospect Park – and a hardy walk from central Park Slope – is the famed **Green-Wood Cemetery**. Founded in 1838 and, at 478 acres, almost as large as Prospect Park, Green-Wood was very much *the* place to be buried in the nineteenth century. Interred here are politician and crusading newspaper editor Horace Greeley; famed preacher Henry Ward Beecher; William Marcy "Boss" Tweed, Democratic chief and scoundrel; glass-maker Louis Comfort Tiffany; composer Leonard Bernstein; a monument to the fallen of the Battle of Brooklyn, which was waged on this land (which also happens to be the highest point in the borough); and the entire Steinway clan of piano fame, at peace in a 119-room mausoleum. Guided explorations of the site are held regularly via weekly trolley tours and full-moon "flashlight tours".

Bay Ridge

In the farthest corner of southwest Brooklyn, this large, quiet neighbourhood is known for its ethnic mix (Chinese, Irish, Italians, Scandinavians and Lebanese) and good schools; senior citizens, many of them longtime residents, make up a large chunk of the population.

The main reason to visit Bay Ridge is to ride the **Shore Road Bike Path**, which offers a glorious ride along the bay, including views of the shimmering **Verrazano-Narrows Bridge** (built in 1964), which flashes its minimalist message across the entrance to New York Bay. At 4260ft, this slender, beautiful span was, until Britain's Humber Bridge opened in 1981, the world's longest. The bridge, which connects Brooklyn to Staten Island, is named for the first European explorer of New York Harbor, Giovanni da Verrazano. You can't pedal across it, unfortunately: urban planner Robert Moses vetoed the pedestrian/bicycle pathways that flanked the roadway in the original design for fear they'd lead to a rash of suicides.

To reach the bike path, get off the R train at Bay Ridge Avenue (locals know it as 69th St) and ride west toward the water (depending on where you're coming from, you can hop on various buses, including the #B1, #B4, #B9, #B63 and express #B27 and #B37). At the pier at the street's end, a path leads south right along the water's edge; however, to see some of Bay Ridge's nicest homes, turn left before the water on Shore Road. Wind through Shore, Narrows and River roads between 75th and 83rd streets, where you'll see some Greek and Gothic Revival houses. Most distinctive is the **Gingerbread House**, at 8220 Narrows Ave, at 83rd Street; the 1916 structure, done in a rare style known as Black Forest Art Nouveau, looks like a witch's backwoods lair, all piled-up stones and drooping eaves. It was put on the market several years ago for $12 million – and taken off after about twelve months, without being sold.

17

Coney Island

Accessible to anyone for the price of a subway ride, beachfront **Coney Island** has given working-class New Yorkers a holiday ever since a kerosene-lit carousel opened here in 1867. A series of fabulous amusement parks drew huge crowds on hot summer days over the years until the 1960s, when the area fell into slow decline, only to be adopted and repopularized by a hip crowd of historians and artists drawn to its retro charm in the 1990s. A lot of dollars have been spent with the intention of modernizing the site, but outside of some new or revamped rides, changes have been slow going (and were slowed further by the effects of Hurricane Sandy); something of a honky-tonk vibe remains firmly in place.

It's an enjoyable place to spend an afternoon or evening, despite – or perhaps because of – its seediness. Most rides and attractions are open daily from late May to early September, with weekend hours in the spring and autumn. If you can, visit Coney Island on a Friday night during the season, when the beach is lit up by an impressive **fireworks** display; a walk along the famous **boardwalk**, where hip-hop blares from boom boxes and loudspeakers, and the language of choice is Spanish or Russian as often as English, is essential whenever you go. The raucous annual **Mermaid Parade** (ⓦconeyisland.com) in mid- to late June ranks as one of the oddest, glitziest small-town festivals in the country, where participants dress (barely) as mermaids, King Neptune and other sea-dwellers.

Luna Park, Wonder Wheel, Cyclone and Thunderbolt

Coney Island Boardwalk • Luna Park $69 for unlimited rides (not including Cyclone or Thunderbolt), though you can purchase individual tickets • ☎ 718 373 5862, ⓦ lunaparknyc.com • Subway D, F, N, Q to Coney Island-Stillwell Ave

The amusement park area, inland of the boardwalk, centres on the modern **Luna Park**, which has a slightly incongruous look and feel. It does offer some unique, head-spinning (and stomach-churning) rides, like the Eclipse and the Air Race; time will tell if they gain classic status of the most thrilling attractions in the vicinity. It has managed to incorporate one of those, the venerable **Cyclone** roller coaster (late March–Oct hours vary, weekends-only early and late in the season; $10; ☎718 265 2100), into its fold. A creaky wooden contraption roughly ninety years old, it's not for the faint-hearted – as you wait in the snaking line, you can actually see the cars lose contact with the metal rails at one point. Sit up front for the most terrifying view or in the back for an extra-strong sense of vertigo.

Its shiny new coaster counterpart, the **Thunderbolt** ($10), offers some of the thrills – rising slowly and near vertically to a precipitous height and then speeding down almost before you've had time to scream – but little of the character.

Less scary but still good fun, the **Wonder Wheel** (late March to Oct hours vary; $8; ☎718 372 2592, ⓦdenoswonderwheel.com) is an official New York City landmark. From the top you get panoramic views of Coney Island and the ocean. It's the signature ride in **Deno's Wonder Wheel Amusement Park**, with its kiddie park ($4 per ride) and handful of adult thrills.

MCU Park

Surf Ave between W 17th and 19th sts • Subway D, F, N, Q to Coney Island-Stillwell Ave

Another great summer attraction in Coney Island is **MCU Park**, the scenic oceanside baseball stadium that has helped lend a more prosperous air to the neighbourhood. The park is home to the **Brooklyn Cyclones** (see p.396), a New York Mets-affiliated minor-league team that draws a dedicated crowd. Seating is intimate, beer flows freely and tickets usually run around $17.

Coney Island Museum

1208 Surf Ave • June–Aug Wed–Sat noon–7pm, Sun 2–7pm; Sept–May Sat noon–6pm, Sun 2–6pm • $5, 11 and under $3 • ☎718 372 5159, ⓦ coneyisland.com • Subway D, F, N, Q to Coney Island-Stillwell Ave

East of Stillwell Avenue, the nonprofit **Coney Island Museum** is one indoor destination you don't want to miss. You can tour relics of Coney Island past, hear a lecture on the beach's history or catch a night-time burlesque performance or film screening.

Sideshows by the Seashore

W 12th St, at Surf Ave • Early June to early Sept daily 1–8pm; May and second half of Sept Sat & Sun 1–8pm • $10, under 12 $5 • ⓦ coneyisland.com • Subway D, F, N, Q to Coney Island-Stillwell Ave

This 45-minute act, the modern incarnation of the long-running amusement park "freak show", features sword-swallowers, contortionists, fire-eaters and other masochists. If you love what you see, sign up for ongoing classes to learn the skills.

New York Aquarium

Surf Ave and W 8th St • Late May to Aug daily 10am–6pm; Sept to late May daily 10am–4.30pm • $11.95 • ☎ 718 265 3474, ⓦ nyaquarium.com • Subway F, Q to West 8th St-NY Aquarium

On the boardwalk, east of the amusement park and halfway to Brighton Beach, sits the seashell-shaped New York Aquarium, a top-of-the-line operation run by the Wildlife Conservation Society, which also administers New York's four excellent zoos. It's had its ups and downs recently – the benefits of a large expansion and the thrill over the acquisition of the baby walrus Mitik, which was originally rescued off the coast of Alaska, were tempered by the water damage from Hurricane Sandy, which shut the place for more than half a year.

Check out the indoor pools in Conservation Hall and Glovers Reef, where you'll see rays and piranha, and learn about coral and habitat protection. Outside folks crowd around the otter and penguin displays, and no doubt will too at the new shark exhibit, complete with glass tunnel – the better to see the creatures swim above you – meant to open by 2018. The sea-lion show at the "Aquatheater" is slickly produced and several steps beyond most feeding demonstrations – it's guaranteed to delight the kids.

Brighton Beach, Manhattan Beach and Sheepshead Bay

East along the boardwalk from Coney Island (and walkable from there), at Brooklyn's southernmost end, **Brighton Beach** was once an affluent seaside resort of its own. Often called Little Odessa, it is now home to the country's largest community of immigrants from Russia and the former Soviet states, who started relocating here in the 1970s. The eldest of them pack the boardwalk benches to soak up the sun and gossip.

Brighton Beach Avenue runs parallel to the boardwalk; the street is a bustling mixture of Russian souvenir shops and **food emporiums**. Sit-down food is also readily available at restaurants on the boardwalk, though you might want to wait until evening, when the **supper clubs** open up. These cavernous places offer a near-parody of a rowdy Russian night out, complete with lots of food, loud music, surreal floor shows and plenty of vodka.

Manhattan Beach, just east from Brighton Beach, offers a less-trammelled strip of sand and some pricey real estate to match. Just above Manhattan Beach is maritime **Sheepshead Bay** – worth visiting to walk along the marina and dine on clams at *Randazzo's* (see p.323). The B and Q lines run to Brighton Beach and Sheepshead Bay.

Queens

With its ever-shifting ethnic composition and frankly utilitarian housing stock, Queens represents the "new" New York – the city as an international crossroads, the melting pot on full boil. The largest (in terms of physical size) of the boroughs, Queens is, in fact, the most diverse county in the US, with nearly half the 2.3 million residents foreign-born, and these hailing from 150 different countries. Not surprisingly, it's something of a culinary hotspot. Take the elevated #7 train to Woodside, Jackson Heights and Flushing and you can eat unassailably authentic versions of Thai catfish salad, Indian *vindaloo* and Colombian *arepas*, respectively. In Astoria you'll find Bosnian *burek* and Greek *spanakopita*, Brazilian *feijoada* and Egyptian braised lamb cheeks.

Culturally, the richest spot in Queens is **Long Island City**, where a cluster of galleries has cropped up around the contemporary art centre MoMA PS1, an affiliate of Midtown's Museum of Modern Art. Farther out, **Flushing Meadows–Corona Park** draws sports fans for baseball and tennis; families come for the Queens Museum, Queens Zoo and New York Hall of Science. At the southeast end of the borough (accessible via the A train or, in some cases, by ferry), in **Jamaica Bay** and the **Rockaways**, lie parks and beaches that feel miles from the city.

INFORMATION

18

Tourist information For information on the borough, contact the Queens Economic Development Corporation (☎ 718 263 0546, ⊕ itsinqueens.com).

Long Island City and Astoria

Long Island City and **Astoria**, only a few minutes by subway from Midtown Manhattan, rank as the hippest neighbourhoods in Queens. It can be a little unclear which is which, given that the whole area is technically Long Island City, with Astoria a self-designated neighbourhood within it. Practically speaking, though, most people think of Astoria as the part of Long Island City north of 36th Avenue, and Long Island City as the area south of the Queensboro Bridge and north of the Long Island Expressway. Astoria is more residential and has more sights, like museums focusing on movie history or the sculptor Isamu Noguchi, but there are some charming pockets along Long Island City's largely industrial streets, and the area has cultural draws of its own.

ARRIVAL AND INFORMATION

By train/subway Edging the East River, Long Island City is a 5min ride on the #7 train from Grand Central Terminal. For Astoria, the N and W head north through the neighbourhood, and the R train stops at Steinway St.
By bus The #Q103 bus, which runs along Vernon Blvd, connects Long Island City with the Noguchi Museum and Socrates Sculpture Park in Astoria; the #Q104 and #66 buses connect major sights in the neighbourhoods as well.

There's also the free LIC Art Bus, which runs in summertime between the major cultural institutions of Long Island City.
By ferry The expanded East River ferry line stops at Hunters Point, in Long Island City.
Information The Greater Astoria Historical Society, at 35-20 Broadway (☎ 718 278 0700, ⊕ astorialic.org), organizes walking tours and screenings, and has books on the borough for sale.

Long Island City

If you've been to MoMA, your ticket stub from that institution gets you free entrance into Long Island City's main attraction, **MoMA PS1**, while **SculptureCenter** and the **Fisher Landau Center for Art** also put on first-rate shows, as do a number of small galleries. The other cultural claim to local fame is **Silvercup Studios**, the largest film and television production studio on the East Coast, which stretches out along 21st Street next to the Queensboro Bridge. *Sex and the City* (both movies included), *30 Rock*, *Girls* and *The Sopranos* were shot here; a handful of others still are.

NAVIGATING QUEENS

Queens' unsettling street-number system can leave you baffled – say, on the corner of 30th Road and 30th Street – but the so-called "Philadelphia method" of addressing, applied borough-wide in the 1920s, does have an underlying logic. Basically, **streets** run north–south, while **avenues**, **roads** and **drives** run east–west. Avenue numbers get higher as you head south, while street numbers get higher as you head east (First Street is on the East River, and 180th is in Jamaica). And in Queens, addresses let you know right where you are: the digits before the hyphen indicate the cross-street: 20-78 33rd Street, for instance, is between 20th and 21st avenues.

QUEENS

DRINKING AND NIGHTLIFE

BAR
SingleCut Beersmiths   1

LGBT BAR
Hombres   2

● **EATING**

Benfaremo	1
Empanadas Café	9
Jackson Diner	4
La Fusta	7
La Pequeña Colombia	3
Shaheen Sweets	10
Spicy and Tasty	2
SriPraPhai	5
Tacoway Beach	11
Tai Pan Bakery	1
Tortillería Nixtamal	6

Despite the construction of massive high-rise condo buildings on the waterfront, there's a keen sense of community, which you can feel in the eating and drinking establishments in the **Hunters Point** neighbourhood along **Vernon Boulevard** between 46th and 51st avenues. Stroll two blocks west to get some eye-grabbing views of the United Nations and the east side of Manhattan from sylvan **Gantry Plaza State Park**. Within the park sits a giant **Pepsi-Cola sign**, a preserved relic from a nearby bottling plant, along with the wacky new **Hunters Point Community Library** – the cutouts on the side of the building make a bold architectural statement. Continue along the waterfront and then along 46th Avenue to hit the **LIC Flea & Food** (no. 5-25; April–Oct Sat & Sun 11am–6pm; ⓦlicflea.com), the neighbourhood entry in an increasingly competitive field of outdoor forums for local food, drink and craft vendors; there's also a beer garden where you can hear live music or DJs.

18

MoMA PS1 Contemporary Art Center

22-25 Jackson Ave, at 46th Ave • Mon & Thurs–Sun noon–6pm • $10 suggested donation, free with MoMA ticket (14 days to use) • ☎718 784 2084, ⓦmomaps1.org • Subway #7 to 45th Road-Court Square, E; M to 23rd St-Ely Ave; G to Long Island City-Court Square

The renowned **MoMA PS1 Contemporary Art Center** occupies a hundred-room nineteenth-century brick schoolhouse. Founded in 1971, PS1 became affiliated with the **Museum of Modern Art** in 2000. It has no real permanent collection of its own, instead using its substantial space to mount sprawling thematic shows and retrospectives. However, the reinstallation of James Turrell's *Meeting* (closed in inclement weather) means that the museum's signature piece – and one of the city's best sitting spaces – will stick around. On summer Saturdays, the music-and-dance party Warm Up (noon–9pm; $22, includes museum admission) takes over the courtyard, with DJs and art projections. The schoolroom-themed *M. Wells Dinette*, on the ground floor (museum admission not required), marks the city's most daring museum café (see p.324).

Hunters Point Historic District and around

Near PS1, the **Hunters Point Historic District** centres on 45th Avenue between 21st and 23rd streets, with an immaculate string of late nineteenth-century row houses in the shadow of the **Citigroup Building**, which is the tallest building in the city outside of Manhattan. Past that tower and the Neoclassical **Long Island City Courthouse**, **SculptureCenter**, 44-19 Purves St (Mon & Thurs–Sun 11am–6pm; $5 suggested donation; ☎718 361 1750, ⓦsculpture-center.org), displays innovative work in a former trolley-repair shop that was cleverly renovated by architect Maya Lin and has a courtyard exhibition space and clean, modern lobby area.

Fisher Landau Center for Art

38-27 30th St, between 38th and 39th aves • Mon & Thurs–Sun noon–5pm • Free • ☎718 937 0727, ⓦflcart.org • N, W to 39th Ave-31st St

In a bit of a no-man's land between the hearts of Astoria and Long Island City, the **Fisher Landau Center for Art** occupies a surprising cultural oasis near a spider's web of elevated trains and congested roads. You'll almost certainly have this airy space to yourself as you contemplate works by Jenny Holzer, Jasper Johns, Donald Judd and Yinka Shonibare – or whatever other big names in contemporary art happen to be

---

QUEENS HIGHLIGHTS

Bohemian Hall and Beer Garden Share a pitcher with some friends in the expansive back yard. See p.343

Flushing restaurants Indulge in Chinese, Taiwanese, Korean and other Asian cuisines. See p.325

Museum of the Moving Image Find out why Queens was once the centre of the US film industry. See p.246

Rockaway Beach Discover the city's best beaches (and some of its best tacos). See p.253

Titan Foods Sample more Greek specialities than you'll find in any grocer near or far. See p.392

currently selected from real-estate heiress Emily Fisher Landau's thousand-item-plus personal collection.

Astoria

Northeast of Long Island City is **Astoria**, bounded on the north and west by the East River, to the south by 36th Avenue and to the east by 46th Street or thereabouts. The diverse neighbourhood is best known for being home to the largest concentration of Greeks outside Greece, though many other groups are in abundance as well, including Moroccans, Egyptians, Bangladeshis, Bosnians and Brazilians; plenty of young professionals live in the 1930s brick apartment buildings and vinyl-sided row houses. The N and W trains from Manhattan run north through the middle of the neighbourhood, stopping at all of the major avenues, each of which forms its own community: 30th Avenue and Broadway are liveliest, with Greek coffee joints and nightclubs, discount department stores, butchers, fishmongers and ethnic restaurants of every type; a few cafés and restaurants on 34th and 35th avenues cater to **Kaufman Astoria Studios'** workers and visitors. The **Astoria Boulevard** stop will get you closest to one of New York's biggest and best beer gardens, *Bohemian Hall* (see p.343), which hosts the Sunday **Astoria Market** (ⓦastoriamarket.com). Quieter Ditmars Boulevard is near **Astoria Park**, which has beautiful views of Manhattan and a mammoth public pool.

Alternatively, you can take the R to Steinway Street, which accesses the east side of the neighbourhood; between 28th Avenue and Astoria Boulevard, Steinway is a strip of Egyptian- and Moroccan-run businesses.

Museum of the Moving Image

36-01 35th Ave, between 36th and 37th sts • Wed & Thurs 10.30am–2pm, Fri 10.30am–8pm, Sat & Sun 11.30am–7pm • $15, free Fri 4–8pm • ⓣ 718 777 6888, ⓦ movingimage.us • Subway M, R to Steinway St; N, W to 36th Ave-31st St

Between 1920 and 1928, Astoria was the capital of America's **silent film industry**, and Paramount Pictures got its start at the present site of Kaufman Astoria Studios, drawing stars such as Rudolph Valentino and the Marx Brothers. Moviemakers were soon lured to Los Angeles by more reliable weather, but the business was rekindled in the 1970s and the studios are busy once again. Part of the Kaufman Astoria complex is dedicated to the **Museum of the Moving Image**, complete with a theatre, education centre and a

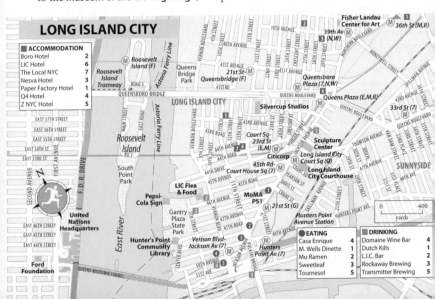

courtyard garden. The museum is the anchor of the nominal Kaufman Arts District (ⓦkaufmanartsdistrict.com).

As for the building itself, a mirrored glass facade gives way to a white, angular entryway that feels not unlike a spacecraft (or at least a spacecraft of the popular imagination). Upstairs, the museum's core collection, "Behind the Screen", is spread over two floors and contains old movie cameras and special-effects equipment; early televisions; all kinds of costumes and props, including the chariot from *Ben Hur*; fascinating detailed sketches and set design models from *The Silence of the Lambs*; fan magazines, posters and enough *Star Wars* action figures to make an obsessed fan drool with envy; and movie stills and (psychologically) revealing black-and-white photos of famous actors and directors. There's a real focus on interactivity, too, as you have the opportunity to create a short animated film, make a soundtrack and see how live television is edited.

Another permanent gallery holds "The Jim Henson Exhibition", filled with puppets from his years as the creative force behind *Sesame Street*, *The Muppet Show* (and Muppet films) and a handful of sci-fi/fantasy movies. On the ground floor, the main theatre shows all sorts of cool film series.

Noguchi Museum

9-01 33rd Rd • Wed–Fri 10am–5pm, Sat & Sun 11am–6pm • $10 • ☎ 718 204 7088, ⓦ noguchi.org • Subway N, W to Broadway (Queens) station; head west to Vernon Blvd, then south two blocks to 33rd Rd – about a 15min walk or a 5min ride on the #Q104 bus; #7 train to Vernon Blvd-Jackson Ave, then #Q103 bus

Off the beaten track but definitely worth the detour, the **Noguchi Museum** is devoted to the works of Japanese-American abstract sculptor Isamu Noguchi (1904–88), who worked in Long Island City for many years and designed this museum at his studio site shortly before his death. At its centre is a garden filled with his stone sculptures, while the surrounding galleries include a special section on his design work. It's a place for quiet contemplation of the artist's sublime exercises in simplicity.

Socrates Sculpture Park

32-01 Vernon Blvd, at Broadway • Daily 10am–sunset • ☎ 718 956 1819, ⓦ socratessculpturepark.org • Same directions as Noguchi Museum, which is one block south

While you're out at the Noguchi Museum, it would be crazy not to stop in at **Socrates Sculpture Park**. The park was an abandoned landfill until 1986, when sculptor Mark di Suvero transformed it into an outdoor studio, with space for artists to build on a massive scale. The resulting works range from ingenious kinetic installations to bizarre structures that appear to be growing out of the lawn. The site also hosts frequent events, including a spring kite festival, free yoga sessions, musical performances and, during warm weather, weekend kayak launches from the nearby beach at Hallets Cove (Sat or Sun 1–4pm).

STEINWAY & SONS PIANO FACTORY

Astoria has a reputation as an international crossroads, but it boasts few international exports, with one notable exception: **Steinway pianos**. Founded in 1853 in Manhattan by German immigrant Henry Steinway, the company moved its factory to Astoria in the late nineteenth century and has been turning out the finest pianos in the world ever since (though only 3 percent of pianos are Steinways, 98 percent of recording artists use them). About two thousand Steinway grand pianos are built in New York every year, retailing from $40,000 to well over $100,000. They are said to be the most complex object on Earth that's put together by hand, with twelve thousand parts assembled over the course of nine months. See this fascinating process yourself on a free **factory tour** (Sept–June Tues 9.30am, approx 2hr 30min; call at least a few months ahead for reservations; ☎ 718 721 2600, ⓦ steinway.com). Take the N or W to Ditmars Boulevard, walk seven blocks east to 38th Street and then go three blocks north to 1 Steinway Place at 19th Avenue.

Sunnyside and Woodside

After Astoria, the E and R trains run north of **Sunnyside** and **Woodside**, historically Irish enclaves but now also home to many Asian and Latino immigrants (Woodside, especially, has some authentic Thai restaurants). You're not missing too much if you skip these neighbourhoods on your way to the more interesting Jackson Heights, though planning enthusiasts may want to see the **Sunnyside Gardens** development, a utopian working-class "garden city" built in 1924 with support from Eleanor Roosevelt and Lewis Mumford.

ARRIVAL AND DEPARTURE

By train and subway For Sunnyside, take the #7 train to the 46th Street stop and walk north on 46th (the opposite direction from the Art Deco "Sunnyside" sign on Queens Boulevard). East of Sunnyside, the #7 train swings away from Queens Boulevard and heads up narrower Roosevelt Avenue.

Jackson Heights

Developed just after the construction of the elevated train in 1917, **Jackson Heights** was laid out as a unified district of tidy brick homes and apartment blocks with attractive garden courtyards (the term "**garden apartment**" was coined here), lending

ASTORIA

●EATING	
Arepas Café	9
Djerdan	4
Kabab Café	3
Loukoumi Taverna	2
Malagueta	8
Omonia Café	7
The Queens Kickshaw	6
Taverna Kyclades	1
Zenon Taverna	5

●SHOPPING	
Titan Foods	1

■DRINKING	
Bohemian Hall and Beer Garden	1
Cronin & Phelan's	2

the area a cohesiveness that's rare in Queens. Walking tours of the **historic district** – including its private gardens – are offered during Historic Jackson Heights Weekend each June (Ⓦjhbg.org). If you're not on a tour, take a stroll down 35th and 37th avenues between 78th and 88th streets to get a feel for the architecture; the Towers, the Chateau and Linden Court are but a few of the attractive co-ops.

The neighbourhood is the most diverse in the city, with especially large concentrations of Latin American immigrants. Amble up **Roosevelt Avenue** and you'll find Argentinian steakhouses, Colombian street vendors selling treats such as *arepas* (savoury corn cakes) and Mexican bakeries displaying stacks of bread and pastries.

18

ARRIVAL AND DEPARTURE

By train and subway Get off at 74th St or 82nd St (or take the E, F or R to Roosevelt Ave) and you'll find yourself in central Jackson Heights.

Little India

Little India, along 74th Street between Roosevelt and 37th Avenue, is something of a contrast. This is the largest Indian community in New York, and South Asians from all over come here to find colourful saris, elaborate gold jewellery for weddings, groceries and music, and perhaps a pungent betel leaf from a street cart. You may want to stop for a bite to eat as well: *Jackson Diner* (see p.325) is one of the older, more popular spots.

Corona and Flushing Meadows

East of Jackson Heights is gritty **Corona**, immortalized in Queens native Paul Simon's song *Me and Julio Down by the Schoolyard*. Once entirely Italian (*corona* is Italian for "crown"), the fast-growing neighbourhood is now mostly first- and second-generation immigrants from the Dominican Republic, Mexico, Ecuador and Colombia, and about a fifth of households live below the poverty line. It's also home to the New York Mets baseball team.

Louis Armstrong House Museum

34-56 107th St, between 34th and 37th avenues • Tues–Fri 10am–5pm, Sat & Sun noon–5pm • $10 • ☎ 718 478 8274, Ⓦ louisarmstronghouse.org • Subway #7 to 103rd St-Corona Plaza, walk north on 104th St, turn right on 37th Ave and then left on 107th St

Opened as a museum in 2003, the great jazz artist's home has been preserved just as he and his wife, Lucille, left it. Armstrong, who lived here from 1943 until his death in 1971, made audio recordings of the day-to-day goings-on in the house, and these play inside, creating a ghostly atmosphere. Guided tours, which show off Armstrong's trumpets, furnishings and various other artefacts, start every hour on the hour (the last

---

THE WORLD COMES TO QUEENS

In late April 1939, as the US emerged from the Great Depression and war loomed, 1200 acres of the new Flushing Meadows–Corona Park became the stage for America's love affair with modernity. Drawing visitors from across the nation (and delegates from 62 others), the **1939–40 World's Fair** featured displays of technologies yet to be realized, including robotics and fluorescent lights. General Motors sponsored a "Futurama" ride through a utopian modern city, and New Yorkers saw broadcast television for the first time. The fair was a great success, and brought attention to this little-known borough. In part due to the reputation established by the expo, the United Nations briefly operated from here following World War II.

The **1964–65 World's Fair**, held in the same location, in many ways book-ended the era of jubilant optimism that the 1939 fair had opened. While technological and engineering advances such as lasers and computers thrilled 52 million fair-goers, the fair's tone – in the wake of President Kennedy's assassination – was markedly different. Many of the temporary structures still stand around the park: some, like the Theaterama and the original portion of the New York Hall of Science, appropriated for other uses, and others left to decay.

one begins at 4pm); the visitors' centre across the street holds much more of Armstrong's personal archives. Queens actually has a substantial jazz history; in addition to Dizzy Gillespie and Cannonball Adderley, who lived near Armstrong, such notables as Ella Fitzgerald, Count Basie, Lena Horne, Fats Waller and, briefly, Charles Mingus called the borough home.

Flushing Meadows–Corona Park

18

Between the Van Wyck Expressway and Grand Central Parkway, east of 111th St • ⓦ nycgovparks.org • Subway #7 to Mets-Willets Point, then walk south past the tennis complex to the park; or head directly to the museums by getting off at the 111th St station and walking south on 111th St until you hit the park's northwest corner

Flushing Meadows–Corona Park is an enormous (though determined a few years back to be 897 acres, a downgrade from its purported 1255 acres) swathe of green first laid out in the 1930s, and its few key attractions – a couple of interesting museums, a zoo, and some relics of the two World's Fairs held here (see box, p.249) – make for a good afternoon out, especially if you have children who need space to run around. It's home to what was reputedly the first US playground for both able-bodied children and children with disabilities, and there are other spots for physical activity, including an 18-hole, par 54 golf course and the World Ice Arena (Mon–Thurs 9am–5.15pm, Fri 9am–5.15pm & 7–9.50pm, Sat noon–4.45pm & 8–9.50pm, Sun noon–4.45pm; ☎718 760 9001, ⓦworldice.com; $6 weekdays, $9 weekends, $5.50 skate rental), a large indoor skating facility; calmer amusement can be found at the Flushing Meadows Carousel (April to early Oct hours vary, usually 11am–7pm; $3.50), which is surrounded by a few other rides.

For refreshment after seeing the park, visit the *Lemon Ice King of Corona* (see p.325).

Citi Field

123-01 Roosevelt Ave • Subway #7 to Mets-Willets Point

Citi Field replaced decrepit Shea Stadium as the home field of the **New York Mets** (see p.396) baseball team in April 2009. The stadium seats 45,000 (10,000 fewer than Shea) and has an old-fashioned facade of brick, granite and cast stone, mimicking that of old Ebbets Field in Brooklyn, former home of the Brooklyn Dodgers, New York's previous National League franchise. Indeed, the Jackson Robinson Rotunda pays homage to a former Dodger, though there is a Mets Hall of Fame and Museum on the premises where you can check out World Series trophies and other great moments in team history. The Mets have a loyal fan base, if for no other reason than that many Queens and Brooklyn residents can't stand the Yankees.

Billie Jean King National Tennis Center

Flushing Meadows–Corona Park • Subway #7 to Mets-Willets Point

Due south of the Citi Field stadium stands the US Tennis Association's **Billie Jean King National Tennis Center**, the largest public tennis facility in the world, with more than thirty indoor and outdoor courts, a new dome for one of its existing stadiums and a new eight-thousand-seat grandstand. The main event, the US Open Tennis Championships (see p.399), takes place at the end of each summer. Tickets to the early matches are easy enough to come by; closer to the finals, you may have to buy from touts.

New York Hall of Science

47-01 111th St, at 46th Avenue • April–Aug Mon–Fri 9.30am–5pm, Sat & Sun 10am–6pm; Sept–March same hours except closed Mon • $16, ages 2–17 $13, free Sept–June Fri 2–5pm & Sun 10–11am, playground $5, mini-golf $6 • ☎718 699 0005, ⓦ nysci.org • Subway #7 to 111th St

A concrete and stained-glass structure retained from the 1964 World's Fair, the **New York Hall of Science** dazzles kids with interactive science exhibits. It's divided into around ten different sections, some of the best of which include "Mathematica" and "Seeing the Light" – puzzle at the Moebius Strip or how shadows are cast. Elsewhere, you can measure what percentage of your body is water and how fast you can throw a baseball; there's also a design lab for kids to experiment and build using different tools and scientific concepts. Outside are two more of the museum's highlights: a mini-golf course, under the shadow of two rockets; and a giant, fun Science Playground, with contraptions that function as both exhibits and playspaces. It's a must if you're there with children under the age of 10. The grounds of the hall serve as host to September's World Maker Faire, which anyone with a passing interest in invention should find their way to.

Queens Zoo

53-51 111th St • April–Oct Mon–Fri 10am–5pm, Sat & Sun 10am–5.30pm; Nov–March daily 10am–4.30pm • $8, ages 3–12 $5 • ☎ 718 271 1500, ⓦ queenszoo.com • Subway #7 to 111th

18

Adjacent to the New York Hall of Science, the **Queens Zoo** is not nearly as spectacular as those in Central Park and the Bronx, although it has transformed Buckminster Fuller's 1964 geodesic dome into a dizzying aviary, and some beautiful animals both big (bison, Shetland cattle) and small (coyote pups, pudú deer) roam the grounds.

Unisphere and New York Pavilion

East of the Queens Zoo, the **Unisphere** is a 140ft-high, stainless-steel globe that weighs 450 tonnes – probably the main reason why it was never moved after the 1964 fair. Robert Moses intended this park to be the "Versailles of America", but the severe, perfectly symmetrical pathways radiating out from the sphere, the anachronistic and often bizarrely ugly architecture, and the roaring Grand Central Parkway all feel more Eastern Bloc than French – particularly when you look south and see the rusting towers of Philip Johnson's 1964 **New York Pavilion**, now home to **Queens Theatre** (☎718 760 0064, ⓦqueenstheatre .org), which puts on music, dance, film and family-friendly programmes.

Queens Museum

New York City Building, Flushing Meadows–Corona Park • Wed–Sun 11am–5pm; guided tours Sun at 2, 3 & 4pm • Suggested donation $8 • ☎718 592 9700, ⓦ queensmuseum.org • Subway #7 to 111th St

Flushing Meadows–Corona Park's finest attraction is the **Queens Museum**, housed right next to the Unisphere in a building from the 1939 fair that served briefly as the first home of the United Nations. The must-see item in the museum is the **Panorama of the City of New York**, a product of the 1964 fair. With a scale of one inch to one hundred feet, the 9300-square-foot panorama is the world's largest architectural model, incorporating 895,000 buildings, each hand-carved out of wood, as well as rivers, harbours, bridges and even tiny planes drifting in and out of the airports. The two other permanent exhibits of note in the museum are the collection of glassworks by **Louis Comfort Tiffany**, who established his design studios in Corona in the 1890s, and the relief map of New York's water-supply system, a wood-and-plaster model that dates back to the time of the 1939 World's Fair.

Flushing

Originally an early Quaker community, **Flushing** is most notable as the city's second Chinatown: more than two-thirds of the neighbourhood is Asian or Asian-American, a far greater proportion than in Manhattan's Chinatown. While it's not as architecturally quaint as its counterpart, it feels more authentic, and its bustling **restaurants** (see p.325) and shops cater almost exclusively to locals rather than to tourists.

Main Street

Head north on **Main Street** from the subway station and you'll pass a couple of old Quaker landmarks, as well as a few other historical buildings. On the west side of Main Street between 39th and 38th avenues is **St George's Church**, an elegant 1854 Gothic landmark with a tall central tower. A few blocks north, Romanesque Revival **Flushing Town Hall**, at 137-35 Northern Blvd (box office Tues–Fri noon–5pm, gallery Tues–Sun noon–5pm; ☎718 463 7700, ⓦflushingtownhall.org), is now a cultural centre with a

18

THE QUAKER LEGACY

You may spot the occasional sign in the neighbourhood indicating your place on the Flushing Freedom Mile, which commemorates the neighbourhood's Quaker associations (along with a few other random historical events). Just across the street from the town hall is a shingle cottage, the **Flushing Quaker Meeting House**, at 137-16 Northern Blvd (☎929 251 4301, ⓦflushingfriends.org), which dates from 1694, making it the oldest surviving house of worship in the city and the second-oldest Quaker institution in the country. It is open Sundays at 11am for services and noon for 30min tours (free), on which you can also see the centuries-old cemetery (without headstones, as per Quaker tradition).

Flesh out the Quaker story with a quick visit to the **Kingsland Homestead**, at 145-35 37th Ave (Tues, Sat & Sun 2.30–4.30pm; $5; ☎718 939 0647, ⓦqueenshistoricalsociety.org), a small wooden farmhouse maintained by the Queens Historical Society. You can see the house from Bowne Street (which runs south from Northern Boulevard), where it is set back in **Weeping Beech Park**. South of the park on Bowne Street, the 1661 Quaker-style **Bowne House** (☎718 359 0528, ⓦbowne house.org) was the home of John Bowne, who helped Flushing acquire the tag "birthplace of religious freedom in America" by resisting discrimination at a time when the Dutch persecuted anyone who wasn't Calvinist; the gardens and parlour can be viewed on group tours.

---

sophisticated calendar of musical performances, including a springtime jazz festival (ⓦqueensjazz.org); there's also an art gallery inside ($5 suggested donation).

Alternatively, you might head south from the Main Street subway station; at the first intersection, with 40th Road, a pavement counter, *Corner 28 Restaurant and Caterers* (full restaurant inside), serves succulent Peking duck to go, either on the bone or in a bun. More treats can be had at the nearby **Golden Shopping Mall**, at 41-28 Main St, such as hand-pulled noodles, dumplings and cumin-flavoured lamb. Veer off on Kissena Boulevard and you'll pass the stately **Free Synagogue of Flushing**, at no. 41-60 (☎718 961 0030, ⓦfreesynagogue.org), on your right. The oldest surviving Reform Jewish synagogue in the US, it looks like a small-town courthouse, but with brick additions and blue stained-glass windows.

Sri Mahā Vallabha Ganapati Devasthānam

45-57 Bowne St • Mon–Fri 8am–9pm, Sat & Sun 7.30am–9pm • Free • ☎718 460 8484, ⓦnyganeshtemple.org • Subway #7 to Flushing-Main St, take the #Q65 bus south from the Free Synagogue

The **Sri Mahā Vallabha Ganapati Devasthānam** is the most visually arresting of a handful of Eastern-religion temples in the neighbourhood (though the Buddhist Nichiren Shoshu Temple, at 42-32 Parsons Blvd, gives it a good run for its money). Also known as the **Ganesh Temple**, this grey building honours the elephant-headed Hindu god.

Jamaica Bay

Make your way to **Jamaica Bay** – what looks on the map like it might be part of Brooklyn but largely takes up the extreme southern edge of Queens – if you're looking to get a bit of a nature break from urban life.

Jamaica Bay Wildlife Refuge

Gateway National Recreation Area • Trails daily sunrise to sunset, visitor centre Wed–Sun 10am–4.pm • ☎718 318 4340, ⓦnps.gov/gate • Subway A to Broad Channel and walk a half-mile north; bus #Q53 from Rockaway Park or Jackson Heights, #Q21 from Rockaway Park or Woodhaven

Jamaica Bay Wildlife Refuge is named for the Jameco Indians, whose territory this once was. Near Broad Channel on the largest of these islands, you can hike trails through the diverse habitats of more than 325 varieties of migrating **bird**; the main loop encircles the West Pond, home to flocks of ducks and geese. A unit of the 26,607-acre Gateway National Recreation Area, which extends through coastal areas of Queens, Brooklyn,

Staten Island and New Jersey, this is one of the most important urban wildlife areas in the United States – and an odd juxtaposition, where, in between glimpses of diving ibises and the like, you'll see giant jets taking off from JFK Airport, just minutes away.

The Rockaways

Subway A (rush hour) to Rockaway Park-Beach 116th St or the A to Broad Channel, where you transfer to the S (Rockaway Shuttle – all times of day), which also takes you to Rockaway Park-Beach 116th St; there are numerous other stops the length of the peninsula, depending on which part of the beach you wish to access; NYC Ferry from Wall St/Pier 11, via Sunset Park, one per hour

18

Partly enclosing Jamaica Bay, the spit of **Rockaway** stretches for ten miles southwest of Brooklyn and is home to the only places to surf in New York City. The eponymous beach, celebrated by the Ramones in song, runs along the shore from Beach 9th Street to Beach 149th Street. Unfortunately, few if any areas suffered more harm from October 2012's Hurricane Sandy (see box below), though the 5-mile-plus boardwalk has been entirely reconstructed and reopened. Meanwhile, hotspots like the hip *Playland Motel* and the *Rockaway Beach Surf Club* have popped up; there are places to rent boards and take surf lessons; and excellent coffee and meals can be enjoyed from *Cuisine by Claudette*. Alternatively, grab a snack from one of the pop-up concession stands close to the ocean (the highest concentration is at Boardwalk and Beach 97th Street, but you'll find others elsewhere) and make your way to the sands.

Jacob Riis Park and Breezy Point

No subway access, so unless you've got a bike to take you from the end of the A line, take the #Q22 bus from Beach 116th St, the #Q35 from Flatbush Ave in Brooklyn, the Rockaway NYC Ferry (a free shuttle takes you to from the landing to Riis Park) or the New York Beach Ferry (Sat & Sun; ⓦ newyorkbeachferry.com) from Pier 11 in Manhattan • ☎ 718 318 4300, ⓦ nyharborparks.org

The lovely sands of **Jacob Riis Park** on the western end of the Rockaway spit are quieter and more pristine (if certainly disturbed by Hurricane Sandy) than the rest of the shore, because it's part of the Gateway National Recreation Area. This is widely considered to be New York City's best beach, and it features an in-need-of-renovation Art Deco bathhouse and an outdoor clock that have been New York City Landmarks since the 1930s. Things get lively during the summertime **Riis Park Beach Bazaar**, 157 Rockaway Beach Blvd (ⓦ riisparkbeachbazaar.com). At the westernmost tip of the peninsula, also beyond the reach of public transport but an easy bicycle ride from the end of the train line, the heavily Irish cooperative community of **Breezy Point** feels like a beach town imported from another state – come here to truly escape New York City.

HURRICANE SANDY

In 2012, **Hurricane Sandy** brought the city to a temporary halt. Ravaging the East Coast (with damages estimated at around $75 billion), the storm touched down in the New York City area late evening on October 29 and proceeded to bring floods that surged nearly 14ft at their highest, near Downtown Manhattan's Battery; winds reached up to 80 miles per hour. Bridges and tunnels shut; the subways stopped running; power was lost in various areas, including lower Manhattan below 34th Street, where in many places it took days to come back – a wander through the empty, darkened city streets was a surreal adventure. Almost every street in Brooklyn's Red Hook flooded and parts of Staten Island's Midland Beach area were turned to rubble. The worst of the damage, however, may well have been in the Rockaways, where days of waiting for power and other amenities usually taken for granted turned into weeks, or longer. Residents here, as elsewhere in low-lying areas, were told to evacuate prior to the hurricane, but most remained to see the storm through. In addition to the wreckage caused by flooding and wind – strong enough to rip off roofs and take out the Rockaway Beach boardwalk – a fire destroyed more than one hundred homes in the close-knit community of Breezy Point. Photos made the places look like war-torn neighbourhoods, and folks were still digging out their homes months later. Despite all that, the beaches managed to open for the traditional start of the season, Memorial Day weekend, the following year, though the boardwalk was in need of being entirely rebuilt.

NEW YORK BOTANICAL GARDEN

The Bronx

"The Bronx?" wrote poet Ogden Nash in 1931. "No thonx!" Nash eventually recanted his two-line barb, but many New Yorkers hold similar feelings due to the borough's reputation for being tough and crime-ridden. Still, what has some truth in the South Bronx – which, despite a few signs of gentrification, remains one of the city's poorest areas – hardly applies to the whole of the Bronx, which harbours beautiful parks, posh neighbourhoods, a world-class botanic garden and zoo, and, of course, Yankee Stadium. The Bronx is New York's only mainland borough, its hilly geography more like neighbouring Westchester County than Long Island and Manhattan. Sights are mostly spread far apart, except near the Little Italy section of Belmont, which is within walking distance of the Bronx Zoo and the New York Botanical Garden.

INFORMATION

Tourist information Find out more about the borough from the Bronx Tourism Council (☎718 590 3518, ⓦilovethebronx.com) or the Bronx Council on the Arts

(☎718 931 9500, ⓦbronxarts.org). BCA sponsors all sorts of events and series, as well as a tram (see below) that hits some of the top area sights.

Brief history

First settled in the seventeenth century by a Swedish landowner named **Jonas Bronck**, the Bronx became part of New York City in the late nineteenth century. For half a century, it was solidly working class and middle class, only taking a turn into serious poverty in the 1950s, when urban planner Robert Moses sliced the borough in half with the **Cross Bronx Expressway**, severing the South Bronx from its wealthier neighbours to the north. The South Bronx was left to burn, literally, in the 1970s, taking the reputation of the whole borough down with it, but it has been making a slow recovery in the years since, with substantial residential development over the past decade.

The South Bronx

19

When most people hear the words "the Bronx", they think of the **South Bronx**, the mostly residential, impoverished area south of the Cross Bronx Expressway. It was here, on the streets of Hunts Point and other tough neighbourhoods of "the Boogie Down" – hip-hop's name for the borough – that rap, break-dancing and graffiti art were born in the 1970s. Anyone interested in street culture should do a lot of random strolling, preferably by day, or take a **Birthplace of Hip-Hop Bus Tour** (☎212 714 3544, ⓦhushtours.com; $75), led by well-known scene insiders.

The main reason most people visit the South Bronx, though, is to see the **New York Yankees** play on their home field, **Yankee Stadium**. The area southeast of the stadium – mostly in the neighbourhoods of **Hunts Point** and **Mott Haven** – is also a locus of culture for the Bronx, with a handful of community-oriented art galleries and boutiques, and some small performance spaces. Mott Haven, especially, has interesting corners to poke around, with a couple of designated historic districts full of elegant apartments and brownstones, fanciful churches and antique shops. Hunts Point, meanwhile, is the home of the **New Fulton Fish Market**, formerly down in the South Street Seaport; the action takes place weekdays very early in the morning (1am–9am; ⓦnewfultonfishmarket.com).

Every first Wednesday of the month (except in Jan & Sept), the Bronx Council on the Arts (see above) sponsors a free **culture tram**, known as The Bronx Trolley, which tours some of the arts-oriented sights, starting at the Longwood Art Gallery at Hostos Community College, 450 Grand Concourse on 149th Street; trolleys leave at 5.30pm, 6.30pm and 7.30pm.

Yankee Stadium

East 161st St, at River Ave • Game days and times vary, but take place April–Sept; tours 11am–1.40pm every 20min, depending on whether it's game day ($20 online, $25 in person) • ☎646 977 8687 for tours, ☎718 293 4000 box office, ⓦnewyork.yankees.mlb.com • Subway B, D, #4 to 161st St-Yankee Stadium

The 2009 **Yankee Stadium** is home to the legendary **New York Yankees** baseball team (see box, p.257) and – appropriately, perhaps, given the team's gigantic payroll – remains the most expensive stadium ever built in the US; estimates range from $1.5 billion up to $2 billion. The design of the 53,000-capacity, open-air park revived aspects of the 1923 stadium – "The House That (Babe) Ruth Built" – that were lost in subsequent renovations, such as the limestone and granite exterior facade, and includes a spot for Monument Park, where fans can find retired jersey numbers and plaques honouring famous Yankees.

The best way to see the stadium is, of course, to catch a game (see p.395), though die-hard fans may want to take a guided tour, which offers access to Monument Park, the field, dugouts, press box and clubhouse when available.

The Grand Concourse

The aptly named **Grand Concourse**, east of Yankee Stadium, runs through a rather low-income area, though you wouldn't guess it from much of the street's architecture. In its southern reaches, the concourse is a magnificent wide boulevard marked by tree-lined medians and opulent Art Deco buildings that now house apartments, social-service organizations and retirement homes. Head south to 149th Street to see thirteen murals painted by artist Ben Shahn and his wife, Bernarda, at the former **Bronx General Post Office**, now the Bronx Post Place – a mixed-use commercial space that has preserved the historic nature of the old lobby. Across from Yankee Stadium at 161st Street is the massive **Bronx County Courthouse and Borough Hall**, a 1933 construction that combines Neoclassical columns with Art Deco friezes and statuary. North of here stretches **Joyce Kilmer Park**, named for the woman who penned the lines "I think that I shall never see / A poem lovely as a tree…" A monument to Louis J. Heintz, who first proposed the Grand Concourse, and the white Lorelei Fountain (officially the Heinrich Heine Fountain, after the

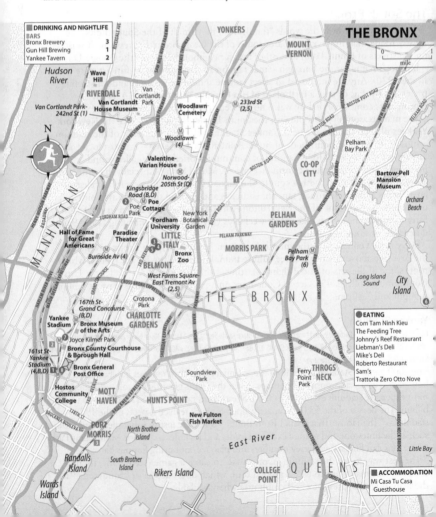

THE BRONX

DRINKING AND NIGHTLIFE
BARS
Bronx Brewery — 3
Gun Hill Brewing — 1
Yankee Tavern — 2

EATING
Com Tam Ninh Kieu
The Feeding Tree
Johnny's Reef Restaurant
Liebman's Deli
Mike's Deli
Roberto Restaurant
Sam's
Trattoria Zero Otto Nove

ACCOMMODATION
Mi Casa Tu Casa
Guesthouse

THE BRONX BOMBERS

The **Yankees**, who inspire love and loathing in New York (and mostly the latter outside the city), moved from north Manhattan to the Bronx in 1923. Leading the way was **George Herman "Babe" Ruth**, who had joined the team in 1920 (fleeced from the Boston Red Sox, still the team's arch-rivals). The original "Bronx Bomber", Ruth hit the stadium's first home run – and soon enough, Yankee Stadium was known as "**The House That Ruth Built**".

Playing alongside Ruth, **Lou Gehrig** earned the nickname "The Iron Horse" by playing in 2130 consecutive games (a record that stood for 56 years); the championships began to roll in, even more so when **Joe DiMaggio** joined Gehrig on the team after Ruth's retirement. **"Yogi" Berra**, **Mickey Mantle**, former single-season home run leader **Roger Maris**, **Reggie Jackson** and, more recently, **Mariano Rivera** were but a few other greats who also wore the famous Yankee pinstripes.

The Yankees won the World Series an amazing nineteen times between 1927 and 1962 and finished the twentieth century with three straight titles; after a nine-year gap, they returned to the top in 2009. With one of the highest payrolls in the major leagues – once routinely topping $200 million, though now in a new era of fiscal "restraint" as they develop promising youngsters – they're always a threat to do it again. For their devoted fans (and sworn enemies), they remain the team to beat.

19

German poet) form a gracious backdrop for residents, who come here to take in the sun on benches and stroll at sunset.

More Art Deco and Art Moderne architecture proliferates in the central and northern stretches of the Concourse, with particularly scenic blocks right around 175th Street and 181st Street. Further north, the 1929 **Paradise Theater**, at no. 2403 (Ⓦworldchangerschurchnewyork.org), hides an elaborate confection of chandeliers and filigree behind its landmarked facade; damaged by fire in late 2012, it's now been transformed into a mega-church.

The Bronx Museum of the Arts

1040 Grand Concourse, at East 165th St • Wed, Thurs, Sat & Sun 11am–6pm, Fri 11am–8pm • Free, though donations accepted • ☎718 681 6000, Ⓦbronxmuseum.org • Subway B, D to 167th St-Grand Concourse

The Bronx Museum of the Arts occupies a converted synagogue that was expanded and modernized by the renowned firm Arquitectonica in 2006; look for the jagged glass facade. Exhibits of contemporary art by Asian, Latino and African American artists lie within, and readings, performances and other events are held from time to time.

The Central Bronx

The **Central Bronx**, north of the Cross Bronx Expressway and south of Gun Hill Road, has neither the intense grit of the South Bronx nor the quiet ritz of the borough's extreme north. As in much of the Bronx, its inhabitants are working-class African Americans, Puerto Ricans and Dominicans, though its historic centre is prestigious (and predominantly white) **Fordham University**, founded by Jesuits in 1841 and set on lush green lawns. Other points of interest include **Belmont**, better known as the Bronx's Little Italy, and verdant **Bronx Park**, home to the city's prized **Bronx Zoo** and **New York Botanical Garden**. Serious sightseers can seek out the **Poe Cottage** and the **Hall of Fame for Great Americans**.

ARRIVAL AND DEPARTURE

By train/bus Take the B, D or #4 train to Fordham Rd, then transfer to the eastbound #Bx12 for the short ride to Arthur Ave, or take the #2 train to Pelham and transfer to the #Bx12 bus headed west. Almost everything you'll want to see in Belmont lies on Arthur between Crescent Ave and E 187th St; from there, it's not far to both the zoo (to the east) and the botanical garden (directly to the north). Special express buses run up Madison Ave (#BxM11), heading straight to these two sights.

19

FIVE FOOD STOPS ON ARTHUR AVENUE

There is no better part of the Bronx than Arthur Avenue to visit if you want to do a little eating tour. Venerable bakeries, family-friendly restaurants, gourmet delis that make their own sauces and sausages – all proliferate in this Italian food haven. Here are a few favourites:

Calandra Cheese 2314 Arthur Ave. They don't have prepared foods, but there's no denying the creamy richness of their home-made ricotta and mozzarella cheeses – good enough to eat on their own.

Cosenza's Fish Market 2354 Arthur Ave. The market runs a pavement stand outside the shop in warm weather – the perfect stop for fresh clams ($5 for 6) or oysters (as little as $1.50 a pop) on the half-shell.

DeLillo's Pasticceria 610 E 187th St, at Arthur Ave. This 90-year-old shop, which recently moved into sleek new digs, was once owned by author and native son

Don DeLillo's parents; the pastries, coffees and Italian ice cream are still spot-on.

Madonia Brothers Bakery 2348 Arthur Ave. Arguably the best Italian bakery in the city; the olive bread, thick and chewy and studded with whole salty olives, is a knockout, and toothsome cannoli are filled on the spot.

Mike's Deli Near the back of Arthur Avenue Retail Market, 2344 Arthur Ave. Try their enormous focaccia sandwiches, from offerings with spicy *soppressata* and fresh mozzarella to eggplant *parmigiana*.

Belmont

Smack in the middle of the Bronx, and within easy walking distance of the Fordham University campus, the New York Botanical Garden and the Bronx Zoo, **Belmont** is home to one of New York's largest Italian-American communities, with its main thoroughfare, **Arthur Avenue**, where you'll find shops and places to eat (see box above) offering a more authentic and low-key alternative to Little Italy in Manhattan.

The neighbourhood dates to the late nineteenth century, when Italian craftsmen building the Bronx Zoo settled here, and although Haitians, Mexicans and Albanians are just a few of the ethnic groups who also operate businesses on Arthur Avenue, the Italian community dominates.

Bronx Zoo

Bronx River Parkway, at Fordham Rd • April–Oct Mon–Fri 10am–5pm, Sat & Sun 10am–5.30pm; Nov–March daily 10am–4.30pm • $23.95, ages 3–12 $16.95; Wed by donation, additional charges for some rides and exhibits (or purchase "Total Experience" tickets) • ☎ 718 367 1010 or ☎ 718 220 5103, ⓦ bronxzoo.org • Subway #2, #5 to West Farms Square–East Tremont Ave, then three blocks north to Asia Gate entrance; bus #BxM11 express ($6.50, MetroCard or exact change) from Madison Ave to Bronx River Gate B

One of the Bronx's main attractions, the **Bronx Zoo** is the largest urban wildlife park in the country. Opened in 1899, the zoo has significantly expanded from its small cluster of original buildings to reach 265 wooded acres harbouring nearly eighteen thousand creatures in natural-looking habitats. Check the website for daily feeding times and educational events; naturally, spring is generally the season for newly born animals; and try to come on a weekday to avoid large crowds.

The forty-acre **Wild Asia** exhibit (May–Oct; $6), where tigers, elephants and gaur (big cows) roam relatively freely, is one of the zoo's highlights, though don't expect to linger; the only way to see it is on a narrated twenty-minute, all-inclusive ride on the Bengali Express Monorail train. You can also take a camel ride ($8) around the plaza. The revamped **Children's Zoo** (open only in warm weather; April–Oct; $6) allows kids to climb with lemurs, learn camouflage skills from tortoises and feed farm animals.

The innovative **Congo Gorilla Forest** ($6) houses more than four hundred African animals representing 55 species, including tiny colobus monkeys, mandrill baboons and the largest population of Western gorillas in the country; some are quite playful and will show off to the crowd. **Madagascar!**, which has taken up residence in the converted Lion House, a 1903 Beaux Arts beauty, showcases lemurs, crocodiles, hissing cockroaches and the plump, reddish-orange tomato frog, among other rare species. Look also at the **Sea Bird Colony**, **World of Reptiles** and the **Himalayan Highlands**, home to endangered species like the red panda and the snow leopard, and pass by the **Zoo Center** building to see three specimens of the rare Komodo dragon.

In winter, many animals are kept in indoor enclosures without viewing areas, but the endangered Siberian tigers love a snowy day; if you visit the three-acre **Tiger Mountain** habitat at that time, it may just be you and these enormous cats, separated by a thin plate of glass.

New York Botanical Garden

2900 Southern Blvd, at Fordham Rd and Bronx River Parkway • Tues–Sun 10am–6pm, until 5pm mid-Jan to Feb • $23–28 all-access, kids 2–12 $10–12; $15 grounds-only, free Wed and 9–10am Sat • ☎ 718 817 8700, ⓦ nybg.org • Subway B, D, #4 to Bedford Park, then a 20min walk; Metro-North Harlem Line to Botanical Garden Station

Adjacent to the zoo, just north of Fordham Road, is a quieter but equally worthwhile attraction: the lush, 250-acre **New York Botanical Garden** offers a lot of bang for the buck, especially in warm weather. The main entrance, the Conservatory Gate opposite Fordham University, is a short walk north from the zoo along Southern Boulevard; the gates will be on your right. Just inside the Mosholu Gate, a pedestrian entrance across from the commuter rail station, you'll find a seasonal farmer's market.

The glittering glass **Enid A. Haupt Conservatory**, built when the park opened in 1891, acts as a dramatic entrance, magnificently showcasing rainforest, aquatic and desert ecosystems. It also houses a palm court with towering old trees and a fern forest, and hosts special exhibits like the popular orchid show in March/April and the always-crowded **Holiday Train Show**, a twinkling winter wonderland of miniature structures and model trains, which opens close to Thanksgiving and runs until mid-January (for which you should get an advance ticket).

To explore the garden, hop aboard the tram near the entrance, which – if taken straight through – wends around the park in about thirty minutes. You can get off at any of the half-dozen stops, depending on what strikes your fancy: cherry and lilac collections; daffodil hill; conifers; peonies; crab apples... the list goes on. Most of these plantings edge a fifty-acre core of native **forest**.

What you'll see is seasonally dependent. Nearly four thousand plants make up the **Peggy Rockefeller Rose Garden**, in bloom in late May/June and early September. The **Azalea Garden** peaks in late April and early May, with a shower of pinks and purples covering a tree-filled slope; fortunately, other colours last on these hills through summer and into fall. The **Native Plant Garden** focuses on species from the Northeast and is meant to have different flowers and ferns, among other flora, flourishing each season; there are around a hundred thousand plantings here in total.

Kids can head to the **Everett Children's Adventure Garden**, twelve acres of plant and science exhibits and some mazes. Programmes let kids cook, taste and draw popular plants such as peppermint, chocolate and vanilla.

Poe Cottage

2640 Grand Concourse, at East Kingsbridge Rd • Thurs & Fri 10am–3pm, Sat 10am–4pm, Sun 1–5pm • $5 • ☎ 718 881 8900, ⓦ bronxhistoricalsociety.org • Subway B, D to Kingsbridge Rd

West of Fordham University is the **Edgar Allan Poe Cottage**, built in 1812. This white-clapboard anachronism on a twenty-first-century working-class Latino block was Edgar Allan Poe's rural home from 1846 to 1849, just before he died in Baltimore. It originally sat in a farmland setting on East Kingsbridge Road near East 192nd Street, but was moved to its current location, at the northern tip of **Poe Park**, when threatened with demolition. Never a particularly stable character and dogged by financial problems, Poe also had to contend with the death of his wife, Virginia, shortly after they moved in. In his gloom, he did manage to write the short, touching poem *Annabel Lee* (in homage to his wife) and other famous works, including *The Bells*, during his stay. The restored cottage displays several rooms as they were in Poe's time, as well as a small gallery of 1840s artwork; first stop before the actual house, though, is the **visitor**

19

centre in Poe Park, 2650 Grand Concourse at 192nd Street (Tues–Sat 8am–5pm; rotating exhibitions on display), with its sharply angled roof meant to conjure the image of a raven.

Valentine-Varian House

3266 Bainbridge Ave, at East 208th St • Sat 10am–4pm, Sun 1–5pm • $5 • ☎ 718 881 8900, ⓦ bronxhistoricalsociety.org • Subway D to Norwood–205th St

The Bronx Historical Society also runs the **Valentine-Varian House** (otherwise known as the Museum of Bronx History), an eighteenth-century Georgian stone farmhouse that was occupied by the British during the American Revolution. Only recommended for serious history buffs, the museum stands in a small park and contains numerous old photographs that show just how rapidly the Bronx shifted from an agrarian landscape to an urban one.

Hall of Fame for Great Americans

19

2155 University Ave • Mon–Fri 9am–5pm, Sat & Sun 10am–4pm • $5 suggested donation; tours ☎ 718 289 5160, ⓦ bcc.cuny.edu/halloffame • Subway #4 to Burnside Ave

On the picturesque campus of the Bronx Community College – formerly New York University's Bronx campus – stands the **Hall of Fame for Great Americans**, a 630ft-long open-air hilltop colonnade designed by the renowned architect Stanford White in 1900 and studded with bronze busts of the 98 honourees. Together they form a peculiar cast of characters, with world-famous figures like George Washington and Henry David Thoreau rubbing shoulders with virtual unknowns like steamboat builder James Buchanan Eads and dentist William Thomas Green Morton.

The North Bronx

The **North Bronx**, shorthand for the area above 225th Street in the west and Gun Hill Road in the east, is the northernmost area of the city; anyone who makes it up here usually wants to see the stately **Riverdale** neighbourhood and its incredible riverfront estate **Wave Hill**, the rolling hills of **Woodlawn Cemetery** and **Van Cortlandt Park**, or the ocean views from **City Island** and **Orchard Beach**.

ARRIVAL AND DEPARTURE

By train Getting up this way by public transport is not impossible – the Metro North Railroad is particularly useful in getting to Riverdale – but if you have access to a car, this is a good time to use it. Otherwise, it's best to visit particular groups of sights together, like Woodlawn Cemetery and Van Cortlandt Park, or City Island and Orchard Beach.

Woodlawn Cemetery

Entrances on Jerome Ave, at Bainbridge and on Webster Ave, at East 233rd St • Daily 8.30am–4.30pm; audio tours available $5, walking tours second Sun of month 2pm $15 • Call for availability and reservations ☎ 718 920 1469; otherwise ☎ 718 920 0500, ⓦ thewoodlawncemetery.org • Subway #4 to Woodlawn; #2, #5 to 233rd St; Metro North Harlem Line railroad to Woodlawn

The venerable **Woodlawn Cemetery** is a huge place and a bucolic joy to walk around. Like Green-Wood in Brooklyn, it boasts a number of tombs and mausoleums that are memorable mainly for their gaudiness, although a few monuments stand out: Oliver Belmont, financier and horse dealer, rests in a Gothic fantasy modelled on the resting place of Leonardo da Vinci in Amboise, France; F.W. Woolworth built himself an Egyptian palace guarded by sphinxes; John H. Harbeck is interred in a (not-so) mini-cathedral with heavy bronze doors; and sculptor Patricia Cronin's 2002 marble *Memorial to a Marriage* depicts the artist and her partner, Deborah Kass, locked in a sleepy embrace. You can pick up a self-guided walking tour map at the main gates and security booths to locate the many famous individuals buried here, including Herman Melville, Irving Berlin, Elizabeth Cady Stanton, Joseph Pulitzer, Fiorello La Guardia, Robert Moses, Celia Cruz, Miles Davis and Duke Ellington.

Van Cortlandt Park

Between Broadway and Jerome Ave • ⓦ vcpark.org • Subway #1 to 242nd St; #4 to Woodlawn

Immediately west of Woodlawn Cemetery across Jerome Avenue lies vast **Van Cortlandt Park**, a forested and hilly all-purpose recreation space. Apart from the pleasure of hiking and running through its woods or watching a cricket game on the parade ground, the park only holds a few scattered sights, like a nature centre, a house museum (see below) and also the country's oldest public golf course (see p.401).

Van Cortlandt House Museum

242nd St, at Broadway • Tues–Fri 10am–4pm, Sat & Sun 11am–4pm • $5, Wed free • ☎ 718 543 3344, ⓦ vchm.org • Subway #1 to 242nd St; #4 to Woodlawn

The **Van Cortlandt House Museum**, nestled in Van Cortlandt Park's southwestern corner, is the best thing in the grounds. This is the Bronx's oldest building, an authentically restored Georgian structure built in 1748, complete with a historically accurate herb garden. New York City's archives were buried for safekeeping on the hills above, and it was in this house that George Washington slept before marching to victory in Manhattan in 1783.

19

Wave Hill

249th St, at Independence Ave • Tues–Sun: mid-March to Oct 9am–5.30pm; Nov to mid-March 9am–4.30pm • $8, Sat 9am–noon & all day Tues free (May, June, Sept & Oct free 9am–noon); free garden/greenhouse tours from Perkins Visitor Center Sun at 2pm and some Tues at 11am • ☎ 718 549 3200, ⓦ wavehill.org • Metro North Hudson Line to Riverdale Station and take free shuttle (at 50min past the hour, 9.50am–3.50pm), or walk up 254th St three blocks, turn right on Independence Ave and proceed two blocks; a shuttle also runs from Van Cortland Park-242nd St stop on #1 subway at 10min past hour

The spectacular country estate of **Wave Hill**, in the moneyed district of Riverdale, offers one of the city's best escapes from the urban grind, with lush exotic gardens, greenhouses, an art gallery, several easy but varied nature trails and rolling lawns dotted with Adirondack chairs overlooking the Hudson River and dramatic Palisades.

At various times home to Teddy Roosevelt (as a child), Arturo Toscanini and Mark Twain, the Wave Hill house was built in 1843 by jurist William Lewis Morris, but credit for the site's astounding beauty goes to George W. Perkins, a partner at JP Morgan, who linked the house's property with that of the adjacent villa (now called the Glyndor House) in the early twentieth century and landscaped the grounds with an artistry rivalling that of Central Park creator Frederick Law Olmsted. The Perkins family donated the estate to the city in 1960; a recent restoration fixed up parts of the facade and interior stairs, among other upgrades. The busy events calendar includes everything from classical music concerts and family art classes to beekeeping workshops; check the website for details.

City Island

Take subway #6 to Pelham Bay Park (the end of the line), then transfer to the #Bx29 bus, which runs over a short causeway to and from the mainland. On the first Friday of the month, from 5.30pm to 8.30pm, a tram (free; ☎ 718 885 9100, ⓦ cityislandchamber.org) runs from the subway station around the island and back, via Pelham Bay Park

On the far east side of the Bronx, 230-acre **City Island** juts into Long Island Sound and has the feel of a seaside New England town (the population is around five thousand), albeit one with a bit of urban grit.

There are a few quirky shops along the main strip (City Island Avenue), and a quaint museum just off it, the **City Island Nautical Museum**, at 190 Fordham St (Sat & Sun 1–5pm or by appointment; $5; ☎ 718 885 0008, ⓦ cityislandmuseum.org), which touts all of the island's claims to fame – the yachts that won the America's Cup from 1958 to 1987 were built here, for instance – and often hosts interesting lectures by local historians. One of the most evocatively sited burial grounds you'll see anywhere, **Pelham Cemetery**, is a short walk away.

Most people come for the waterfront **restaurants** though: the food may not be particularly creative, but seaside dining is a treat. To avoid the crowds, come on a

THE BRONX'S PHANTOM THEME PARK

Pelham Bay Park looks to the west over **Co-op City**, a seemingly endless tract of middle-class housing that is one of the Bronx's bleaker icons. Few residents know that their homes stand on New York's great, lost amusement park: **Freedomland**.

Built in the shape of the United States, the 205-acre park opened in 1960 with entertainments based on American history: the Great Fire of 1871 raged in Chicago, gunfights blazed in the Old Southwest, and earthquakes rocked San Francisco. Reporters loved Freedomland because it inspired such headlines as "Stagecoach Wreck Injures 10 in the Bronx". But the public was not so enthralled. Park developers blamed competition from the 1964 World's Fair in Flushing, though the expo had barely begun when Freedomland declared bankruptcy late in the year. By 1965, Co-op City was in progress; Freedomland had vanished without a trace.

19

weekday, when the fish is also fresher. Try the venerable *Lobster Box*, at 34 City Island Ave, for old-school seafood, or, just down the road at the fishing piers, the charmingly downscale *Johnny's Reef Restaurant* (see p.326), at 2 City Island Avenue.

Pelham Bay Park and Orchard Beach

Subway #6 to Pelham Bay Park station • In summer, buses #Bx5 and #Bx12 run from the station to Orchard Beach; on the first Friday of the month, from 5.30 to 8.30pm, a tram (free; ☎ 718 885 9100, ⓦ cityislandchamber.org) runs from the station around the island and back, via Pelham Bay Park; parking is $7 summer weekdays, $9 weekends

The wide crescent of **Orchard Beach**, the easternmost part of expansive **Pelham Bay Park** (the city's largest green space), marks one of the few really pleasant additions to the "master builder" Robert Moses made to the city. Just turn right after the causeway, and then follow the path along the water. The beach and boardwalk pulse constantly during summertime; a once grand, and now decrepit, bathhouse pavilion offers some architectural interest; and a nature centre organizes walks, birdwatching and other events.

At the northern end of the boardwalk, a sign for the **Kazimiroff Nature Trail** points the way into a wildlife preserve named for Theodore Kazimiroff, co-founder of the Bronx County Historical Society and an amateur naturalist who helped stop these wetlands from being turned into landfill. The network of trails, which wind through 189 acres of meadow, forest and marsh, is serene and peaceful – a stark contrast to the rest of Pelham Bay Park, now crisscrossed by highways.

Bartow-Pell Mansion Museum

895 Shore Rd, Pelham Bay Park • Wed, Sat & Sun noon–4pm, guided tours hourly beginning 12.15pm, gardens daily 8.30am–dusk • $8 for museum, grounds free • ☎ 718 885 1461, ⓦ bartowpellmansionmuseum.org • Westchester Bee-Line bus #45 runs from Pelham Bay Park subway; on the first Friday of the month, from 5.30pm to 8.30pm, a free tram (☎ 718 885 9100, ⓦ cityislandchamber.org) runs from Pelham Bay Park subway station to the mansion

The Greek Revival **Bartow-Pell Mansion Museum** is a national landmark worth seeing for its beautifully furnished interior, which gives a glimpse of how the other half lived in the 1800s (Mayor La Guardia wisely commandeered the place for his summer office in 1936); the lavish gardens overlook Long Island Sound.

Staten Island

The free ride across the harbour to Staten Island is one of the highlights of New York, but is there any point in getting off the ferry? The island is almost fourteen miles long and 7.5 miles wide, making it more than twice the size of Manhattan. Primarily a collection of sleepy suburban communities, culturally it has more in common with New Jersey than with the other four boroughs – most tourists promptly hop on the next boat back to the big city. Yet it would be a mistake to dismiss the "forgotten borough" so readily; its leafy streets harbour some real gems, not least a fabulous Chinese garden, a Tibetan gallery and an authentic colonial village, as well as some excellent Sri Lankan restaurants, the city's only outlet mall and the biggest Ferris wheel in North America.

ARRIVAL AND INFORMATION

By ferry The free Staten Island Ferry (☎ 718 727 2508, ⓦ siferry.com) departs from the Whitehall Ferry Terminal (subway #1 to South Ferry; R, W to Whitehall St; #4, #5 to Bowling Green). Departures every 15–20min during rush hours (7–9am & 5–7pm), every 30min throughout the rest of the day and evenings, and every hour late at night (the ferry runs 24hr). On weekends, boats run every 30min from Manhattan, but slightly less frequently on the return trip.
By train The Staten Island Railway (SIR; 24hr; ⓦ mta.info) runs from the ferry terminal (St George) to Tottenville at the southern end of the island; you can use your MetroCard, but the fare ($2.75 with MetroCard; otherwise $3) is only payable at St George and Tompkinsville (free otherwise).

By bus Given the limited scope of the railway, you'll need to take a bus (ⓦ mta.info) to fully explore Staten Island; you can use your MetroCard to pay ($2.75; express bus $6.50). Bus maps are available at the ferry terminal in St George; the main bus station is just outside. Take #S40 for Snug Harbor; #S51 for Alice Austen House and Fort Wadsworth; #S74 for Historic Richmond Town and Jacques Marchais Museum of Tibetan Art. Most services operate every 20–30min Mon–Sat, and less frequently Sun.

Information For more information on Staten Island events and attractions, or to download free maps, visit ⓦ statenislandarts.org or ⓦ visitstatenisland.com.

St George and around

Passengers disembark the ferry on the northeast corner of the island, in the town of **St George**, Staten Island's "Downtown" district, home to most of the borough government offices and law courts. The arrival of the **New York Wheel** and **Empire Outlets** mall in 2018 (see box below) is expected to dramatically increase tourist traffic to this formerly sleepy backwater.

20

National Lighthouse Museum

200 The Promenade at Lighthouse Point (just off Bay St, south of the ferry dock) • Tues–Sun 11am–4pm • $5 • ☎ 718 390 0040, ⓦ lighthousemuseum.org • SIR to St George

Part of an ambitious project to transform the former General Depot for the US Lighthouse Service on the St George shorefront (dubbed **Lighthouse Point**), the **National Lighthouse Museum** is set to develop into an absorbing attraction in the next few years. Currently housed in the old foundry, the museum will eventually move next door into Lamp Shop No. 2, built in 1907. Exhibits include a display of over 160 miniature lighthouses, examples of Fresnel lenses and panels telling the stories of local lightkeepers over the years, many of whom were exceptional women. Docents are on hand to add local colour and background.

Borough Hall

10 Richmond Terrace • Mon–Fri 9am–5pm • Free • ☎ 718 816 2000 • SIR to St George

The 1906 French Renaissance **Borough Hall**, straight ahead as you walk out of the ferry terminal, has a marble lobby adorned with vivid WPA murals illustrating the island's history (enter at the back on Stuyvesant Place). Local artist Frederick Charles Stahr completed the thirteen murals in the late 1930s, beginning with Verrazano's "discovery" of Staten Island in 1524 and ending with the construction of the Bayonne Bridge (1928–31). The hall still houses the Borough President's Office and other civic offices, so you must pass through security to get inside.

STATEN ISLAND'S GIANT WHEEL AND OUTLET MALL

By the end of 2018, Staten Island's north shore will be transformed by two high-profile projects, conveniently located right next to the ferry dock. The most ambitious is a 630ft-high Ferris wheel, aka the **New York Wheel** (daily 10am–midnight; ⓦ newyorkwheel.com), the second largest in the world – it's expected to offer a similar experience to the London Eye, with revolutions every 38 minutes. Next door, lavish **Empire Outlets** (ⓦ empireoutletsnyc .com) will be the city's only outlet mall (for discounted goods and fashions), with a huge food court and hotel.

Snug Harbor Cultural Center

1000 Richmond Terrace • **Visitor Center** April–Sept Wed–Sun 10am–5pm; Oct–March Thurs–Sun 11am–4pm • Free • ☎ 718 448 2500, ⓦ snug-harbor.org • Bus #S40

In contrast to the more urban area around the ferry terminal, the atmosphere of the **Snug Harbor Cultural Center**, in nearby New Brighton, is one of bucolic calm, with museums, gardens and galleries spread over 83 rolling acres.

The campus functioned as an affluent retirement community for "aged, decrepit and worn-out sailors" from 1833 to 1976 (thanks to wealthy benefactor Robert Randall), before being renovated for public use, with its 28 remaining buildings ranging in style from grand Greek Revival halls to sophisticated Italianate buildings. The oldest structure is the beautifully restored Main Hall (Building C), which functions as the **Visitor Center**. Inside, you'll find temporary art exhibitions and a small display on the history of the site; you can also get a free map here. At the back of the visitor centre, you can walk through to the **Newhouse Center for Contemporary Art**, a showcase for local artists (same hours; $5). The campus also contains the **Staten Island Children's Museum** (p.413).

LITTLE SRI LANKA

New York's Little Sri Lanka lies in the Tompkinsville neighbourhood of Staten Island (centred along Victory Blvd), a short, stiff walk from the ferry terminal – it's one of the largest Sri Lankan communities outside of Sri Lanka itself. Try the cheap hoppers (noodles) and curries at *New Asha* (see p.327), or peruse the local grocery shops for Ceylon teas, chutneys, spices, sweets and other delicacies.

Staten Island Botanical Garden

Daily dawn–dusk • Free • ☎ 718 273 8200

Most of the Snug Harbor grounds are given over to the **Staten Island Botanical Garden**. This 53-acre sanctuary includes a section of flowers catering to butterflies and an antique rose garden, but the real gem is the **Chinese Scholar's Garden** (April–Sept Tues–Sun 10am–5pm; Oct–March Fri–Sun 11am–4pm; $5). This one-acre complex of Ming dynasty-style, pagoda-roofed halls, artfully planted courtyards, bamboo groves and goldfish ponds was completed in 1999 by artists from Suzhou, China.

Staten Island Museum

Building A • Mon–Fri 11am–5pm, Sat 10am–5pm, Sun noon–5pm • $8 (free audioguides) • ☎ 718 727 1135, ⓦ statenislandmuseum.org

The brand-new **Staten Island Museum** occupies buildings A and B on the Snug Harbor campus (to the right of the visitor centre), with bright, state-of-the art galleries displaying much of its renowned art collection from the Hudson River School, and its natural history, fossil and mineral collections. Permanent exhibits chronicle the history of the island, with rare Lenape artefacts.

Noble Maritime Collection

Building D • Thurs–Sun 1–5pm • Free, donation suggested • ☎ 718 447 6490, ⓦ noblemaritime.org

The building to the left of the visitor centre houses the **Noble Maritime Collection**, which displays the prints and paintings of nautical painter John Noble (1913–83), as well as his houseboat studio (Noble began to build the studio in New York Harbor in 1941, out of parts of boats he salvaged).

Alice Austen House

2 Hylan Blvd, at Edgewater St • March–Dec Tues–Sun 11am–5pm; suggested donation $3 • ☎ 718 816 4506, ⓦ aliceausten.org • Bus #S51 from the ferry dock to Hylan Blvd and Bay St (15min), then walk one block east down the hill toward the waterfront

Some 2.5 miles southeast of St George, the **Alice Austen House** is a tiny but enigmatic clapboard cottage facing the Verrazano-Narrows Bridge. Austen (1866–1952) was a pioneering amateur photographer whose work comprises one of the finest records of American daily life in the early twentieth century. Her photography was rediscovered only shortly before her death in 1952 (in 1950, bankrupt, she'd been admitted to the borough poorhouse). The house exhibits only a small selection of her photos, but they're fascinating, and the home's beautiful location is a sight in itself; built in 1690, it was bought and modified by Austen's grandfather in the nineteenth century.

Fort Wadsworth

210 New York Ave (Bay St) • Site open daily: April–Oct 5am–10pm; Nov–March 5am–8pm; office Sun 10am–2pm; Visitor Center Fri–Sun noon–4pm • Free • ☎ 718 354 4500, ⓦ nps.gov/gate/index.htm • Bus #S51 (or 15–20min walk from the Alice Austen House)

At the base of the Verrazano-Narrows Bridge, a critical position for the defence of New York Harbor, sits sprawling **Fort Wadsworth**. The site itself comprises **Fort Tompkins** (which was built between 1859 and 1876); the adjacent and ruined **Battery Duane** (1896); and far below, **Battery Weed**, built between 1847 and 1862 – this was the site of the original fort, which dates back to the colonial period and was originally known as Fort Richmond. You can't go inside any of these fortifications unless you take a tour (see website), and the real star is the view from the **overlook** above Battery Weed – the panorama of the harbour, Manhattan and the Verrazano Bridge is mesmerizing.

Jacques Marchais Museum of Tibetan Art

338 Lighthouse Ave • Wed–Sun 1–5pm (closed Jan) • $6 • ☎ 718 987 3500, ⊛ tibetanmuseum.org • Bus #S74 (ask to be let off at Lighthouse Ave after around 35–40min, then hike about 10min up the steep hill); a cab from the ferry terminal is $20–22

In the centre of Staten Island's residential heartland, the **Jacques Marchais Museum of Tibetan Art** is an unlikely treasure. Despite being christened Jacques, Marchais (1887–1948) was actually female. Starting in the 1920s, she became a successful art dealer, and used her income to indulge a passion for Tibetan art (though she never visited Tibet herself). Eventually, she assembled about three thousand pieces, and between 1943 and 1947 built this small fieldstone complex, which clutches onto the steep hillside much like monasteries in Tibet. One building houses the museum gift shop and a small gallery, and the other, designed to resemble a *gompa*, or temple, displays changing exhibits and a small fraction of the collection, including religious sculptures, *thangka* paintings, a rare Bhutanese sand *mandala* and a 250-year-old carved-wood *stupa*. In October, monks in maroon robes perform ritual ceremonies at the annual Tibetan Festival, and food and crafts are sold.

Historic Richmond Town

441 Clarke Ave • Wed–Sun 1–5pm • $8, ages 4–11 $5; free Fri 1–5pm • Free guided tours Wed–Fri 2.30pm, Sat & Sun 2pm & 3.30pm • ☎ 718 351 1611, ⊛ historicrichmondtown.org • Bus #S74

20

Spread out along Richmond Road, a half-mile west and south from the Tibetan museum, lies **Historic Richmond Town**. Home to the Staten Island Historical Society, it's an open-air museum of around 27 historic buildings; at its core is the old village of Richmond itself, centre of the island's government until 1898 (when St George started to take over), as well as clapboard houses transported from other parts of the island.

The **visitor centre**, housed in the stately courthouse and built in 1837, is home to a gift shop, maps and small exhibitions about the site. Opposite lies the **Historical Museum**, which contains exhibits about the history of Staten Island, while in the streets nearby there are around fifteen restored buildings you can go inside (including the 1696 Dutch-style **Voorlezer's House**, the nation's oldest existing school building) – at weekends and during peak months, these are often staffed by costumed volunteers who use traditional techniques to make wooden water buckets and weld tin, all carried off to surprisingly picturesque and un-gimmicky effect.

Conference House

298 Satterlee St, at Hylan Blvd • Guided 1hr tours roughly every 20min, April to mid-Dec Fri–Sun 1–4pm • Suggested donation $4 • ☎ 718 984 6046, ⊛ conferencehouse.org • SIR to Tottenville or bus #S74 from Historic Richmond Town

At the far southern end of the island, in the quiet seaside neighbourhood known as **Tottenville**, the **Conference House** is a fine rubble-stone manor built by English Captain Christopher Billopp around 1680. Other than its age (ancient by American standards), its claim to fame is acting as host to the failed **peace conference** in 1776 during the American Revolution; the American delegation was led by Benjamin Franklin and John Adams, the British by Admiral Richard Howe. The nearby **visitor centre** lays out the history of the site, while guided tours take you inside the house for a peek at period furnishings and the original kitchen, which has been restored to working order. The surrounding grounds are occupied by the lovely 267-acre **Conference House Park**.

THE ALGONQUIN

Accommodation

Accommodation in New York eats up the lion's share of travellers' budgets. Most hotels in the city charge more than $200 a night; $400–600 in high season can be common – and these are pre-tax rates (see opposite). It is certainly possible to get a safe, clean room for less than that, but it's almost always easier to find a place to splurge on than it is to find a real bargain. That said, the thrill of staying in a sleek, at-the-heart-of-it hotel or romantic hideaway is one of the joys (albeit a pricey one) of touring a major city. There are a handful of hostels – some quite noteworthy – with dorms for the young or budget-minded. Other moderately priced options include bed and breakfasts, which go for approximately $150–250 for a double.

One of the most enjoyable ways to save your pennies and get an in-depth look at New York is to sublet a local's apartment. Filling a much-needed demand for affordable accommodation, sites such as ⓦairbnb.com and ⓦcouchsurfing.com offer cut-rates on housing; in the case of the latter, there is no cost at all. As with hotels, it is best to contact potential hosts as far in advance as possible, and exercise common-sense caution: be thorough in checking reviews, speak to the subletter personally and only give credit card information to a trusted source.

Note also that since 2010, it has been **illegal** in New York to **rent out a whole apartment** on ⓦairbnb.com for fewer than thirty days (as of 2017 this law is being vigorously enforced by the city) – it is, however, permissible to rent out rooms or part of an apartment/house where the owner resides for shorter durations. With ⓦairbnb.com, prices for rooms range $60–180 a night for Manhattan, with rates as low as $40 in the outer boroughs. Couchsurfing – just what it sounds like – conjures roommates and air mattresses; the pay-off is a fun community vibe, an unbeatable price and excellent insider tips.

BOOKING AND INFORMATION

Reservations Make these as far in advance as you can: although it is possible to get good last-minute deals, you may also find a special rate for an advance purchase (usually at least two weeks). And, at certain times of the year (May, Sept and Oct as well as the weeks leading up to Christmas and New Year), you're likely to find everything chock-full if you wait until just before your trip. Months like January, February, July and August tend to have better deals.

Discount websites Tales of staying at a luxury Midtown hotel for $99/night are not an impossibility. Try ⓦpriceline.com, ⓦexpedia.com, ⓦhotwire.com, ⓦjetsetter.com and ⓦhoteltonight.com. Reservations here are slightly more adventurous: it helps if you're comfortable not knowing a hotel's name before booking, or with leaving things till the last minute. The last two sites work best with smartphones – their apps offer great same-day deals, and send offers based on your current location.

Taxes Hotels will nearly always quote you the price of a room before tax. Taxes will add 14.75 percent to your bill, plus $3.50 per night in "occupancy tax" and room fees.

Tipping Expected at hotels – tip the bellhop a few bucks if you're going to let him carry your bags to your room, and leave something for the cleaning staff too ($3–5/day, depending on the type of place).

HOTELS

While Midtown Manhattan, with its proximity to the main tourist sights, still dominates the **hotel** landscape, many of the hipper hotels to appear in recent years have done so in Chelsea and the Meatpacking District, Tribeca, the Financial District, Lower East Side and across the water in Brooklyn or Long Island City (Queens). The following selection of hotels runs the gamut from the city's cheapest to most luxurious. The prices quoted at the end of each listing represent the expected price of the hotel's cheapest double room, excluding all taxes, during the high season; note, though, that there's hardly such a thing as a fixed room price. "Published" rates may be quite different from advance online reservations, and figures quoted to you can change on a daily basis, depending on availability.

FINANCIAL DISTRICT

AKA Wall Street 84 William St, at Maiden Lane ☎212 252 9090, ⓦstayaka.com; subway #2, #3 to Wall St; map p.44. This 1907 landmark has been converted into sleek, luxurious studios and one- or two-bedroom suites in the heart of the Financial District (also targeted at long-stay travellers), decked out with rich hardwood floors and warm, refined furnishings made of natural materials. Kitchens included, plus there's a rooftop lounge and private cinema. $375

★**Andaz Wall Street** 75 Wall St, at Water St ☎212 590 1234, ⓦandaz.hyatt.com; subway #2, #3, #4, #5 to Wall St; map p.44. Spacious, stylish rooms right on Wall Street from the Hyatt stable, with a host of generous extras: 24hr tea and coffee (posh Italian espresso, no less) in the lobby, free wine daily 5–7pm and free snacks and soft drinks at any time. $525

★**The Beekman** 123 Nassau St, at Beekman St ☎212 233 2300, ⓦthebeekman.com; subway A, C, #2, #3 to Fulton St; map p.44. The grand Temple Court 1883 office building (modelled on the Royal Courts of Justice in London) was converted into a stunning hotel in 2016, with a gorgeous nine-storey atrium and pyramidal skylight, luxurious rooms (think vintage furnishings, aged oak floors and spacious marble baths with rain showers), plus restaurants by celebrity chefs Keith McNally and Tom Colicchio. $500

Gild Hall 15 Gold St, at Platt St ☎212 232 7700, ⓦthompsonhotels.com; subway #2, #3 to Fulton St; map p.44. Boutique featuring a striking "Aspen country house"

21

theme by famed designer Jim Walrod with big leather headboards, antique brass and antler chandeliers and an old country-club feel. The gourmet Dean & Deluca minibar adds a finishing touch. Free bikes in the lobby. **$368**

Riff Downtown 102 Greenwich St, between Carlisle and Rector sts ☎212 766 8888, ⓦriffdowntown.com; subway #1 to Rector St; map p.44. This quirky hotel (considered budget in this area), offers interiors inspired by the New York party scene of the 1980s (1980s music, free Atari and board games), with rooms ("lofts") featuring kitchenettes (some have balconies). **$269**

TRIBECA AND SOHO

The Mercer 147 Mercer St, at Prince St ☎212 966 6060, ⓦmercerhotel.com; subway N, R to Prince St; map p.64. Housed in a Romanesque Revival building in Soho, *Mercer* has been one of the top accommodation choices of visiting celebs such as Kanye West since it opened in 1998. The loft studios also have massive 90-square-foot bathrooms, with over-sized tubs and walk-in showers for splashing around, and the concierge can arrange private training or massage virtually around the clock. Free access to local gyms. **$543**

Roxy Hotel Tribeca 2 Sixth Ave, between White and Walker sts ☎212 519 6600, ⓦroxyhotelnyc.com; subway #1 to Franklin St; map p.64. The former *Tribeca Grand* has been reborn as an Art Deco tribute, anchored by a soaring atrium and the *Roxy Bar & Lounge*. Rooms are fashionably understated, though bathrooms boast phones and TVs, and the staff are extra-attentive. Off-season weekends can be several hundred dollars cheaper. **$517**

★**Smyth** 85 West Broadway, between Warren and Chambers sts ☎212 587 7000, ⓦthompsonhotels.com; subway A, C, #1, #2, #3 to Chambers St; map p.64. One of the best boutique hotels in this part of town, with plush, contemporary design and furnishings with Classical and Art Deco touches; iPod docking station, plasma TV and large bathroom (with Kiehl products) included. **$593**

CHINATOWN AND NOLITA

Hotel Mulberry 52 Mulberry St, between Mosco and Bayard sts ☎212 385 4633, ⓦhotelmulberry.com; subway J, Z, #6 to Canal St; map p.71. A relatively good deal in the heart of Chinatown, with small but comfy rooms, (some with balconies) and terrific views of the Financial District and Columbus Park (check out the roof terrace). Decent breakfast in nearby *Mama Eatery* included. **$249**

★**NobleDEN Hotel** 196 Grand St, between Mott and Mulberry sts ☎212 390 8988, ⓦnobleden.com; subway B, D to Grand St; map p.71. With an unbeatable location close to all the Chinatown and Little Italy action, this relative newcomer offers compact but stylish rooms, hardwood floors and large flatscreen TVs. Note that the Feast of San Gennaro (p.406) celebrations take place outside every September. **$309**

Wyndham Garden Chinatown 93 Bowery, at Hester St ☎646 329 3400, ⓦwyndhamgardenchinatownnyc.com; subway B, D to Grand St; map p.71. Another top Chinatown option, within strolling distance of some of the city's best cheap eats. Rooms are stylish and well equipped with contemporary furnishings, and most offer spectacular views – rates drop considerably in low season. **$359**

LOWER EAST SIDE AND EAST VILLAGE

Blue Moon 100 Orchard St, between Delancey and Broome sts ☎212 533 9080, ⓦbluemoon-nyc.com; subway F to Delancey St, J, M, Z to Essex St; map p.82. Lower East Side tenement transformed into a luxurious boutique, with rooms named after 1930s and 1940s starlets and decked out with period iron-frame beds and the odd antique – rooms on the sixth, seventh and eighth floors also come with fabulous views across the city. Continental breakfast, iPod docks included. **$299**

Bowery Hotel 335 Bowery, at E 3rd St ☎212 505 9100, ⓦtheboweryhotel.com; subway #6 to Bleecker St; map p.88. This fabulous boutique property oozes sophistication and tempts guests with countless amenities, including iPod docks, DVD players, floor-to-ceiling windows, marble tubs with a view and a cool lounge bar. **$575**

Hotel 91 91 E Broadway, at Forsyth St ☎646 438 6600, ⓦhotel91.com; subway F to East Broadway; map p.82. Funky Lower East Side boutique, with a slightly Asian theme – orchids grace every room, and a statue of the Buddha sits in the lobby. Rooms are compact but well equipped, with LCD TVs and plush marble bathrooms – this is a real bargain for the area, but ask for a room away from Manhattan Bridge if you're a light sleeper. **$180**

The Ludlow 180 Ludlow St, between E Houston and Stanton sts ☎212 432 1818, ⓦludlowhotel.com; subway F to Second Ave; map p.82. Chic boutique hotel on one of the city's trendiest streets, with compact single and double studios, plus larger rooms with gorgeous terraces and extremely cool lofts. The stylish decor includes black and cream silk rugs, white marble tables and round brass chandeliers from Morocco. Continental breakfast at *Dirty French* (p.289) included. **$375**

THE WEST VILLAGE

★**The Jane** 113 Jane St, at West St ☎212 924 6700, ⓦthejanenyc.com; subway A, C, E to 14th St, L to Eighth Ave; map p.96. Known for hip club/bar the *Jane Ballroom* (see p.335), this is a chic place to stay and an excellent deal in the West Village. Rooms are inspired by ship cabins (the building was completed in 1908 and originally served as a hotel for sailors), with the bunk-bed cabins for two people like a plush hostel, with shared bathrooms but flatscreen TV, DVD player and iPod dock. Captain's cabins are much bigger and have private bathrooms. **$120**

Larchmont 27 W 11th St, between Fifth and Sixth aves ☎ 212 989 9333, ⊛ larchmonthotel.com; subway F, L to 14th St; map p.96. A budget hotel, in a terrific location on a tree-lined street in Greenwich Village. Rooms are small but cosy and clean (with TV and a/c). A robe and slippers are thoughtfully provided so you can traipse down the hall to the shared bathroom. Includes continental breakfast. $119

Marlton Hotel 5 W 8th St, between Fifth and Sixth aves ☎ 212 321 0100, ⊛ marltonhotel.com; subway A, B, C, D, E, F, M to W 4th St; map p.96. This former flophouse (where Jack Kerouac once crashed) has been transformed into a lavish hotel with rooms blending contemporary design, ornate mouldings and early twentieth-century style (including Serge Mouille light fixtures), though the cheapest "petite" rooms are exceptionally small. $375

Walker Hotel 52 W 13th St, between Fifth and Sixth aves ☎ 212 375 1300, ⊛ walkerhotel.com; subway F, M to 14th St, L to Sixth Ave; map p.96. A gorgeous boutique hotel in the heart of the Village, with an eclectic theme blending nineteenth-century antiques, red-brick and pressed-tin ceilings with small Art Deco rooms, all-white subway-tiled bathrooms (some rooms just have showers) and modern amenities. $535

Washington Square 103 Waverly Place, at Washington Square Park ☎ 212 777 9515, ⊛ washingtonsquarehotel .com; subway A, B, C, D, E, F, M to W 4th St; map p.96. Right on the park since 1902, in the heart of Greenwich Village. Don't be deceived by the posh-looking lobby – the rooms are surprisingly plain for the price (though rates are significantly cut in August). The Art Deco "Deluxe" rooms have a bit more character and continental breakfast is included. $325

CHELSEA AND THE MEATPACKING DISTRICT

★ **Chelsea Pines Inn** 317 W 14th St, between Eighth and Ninth aves ☎ 212 929 1023 or ☎ 888 546 2700, ⊛ chelseapinesinn.com; subway A, C, E to 14th St; map p.107. Housed in an old brownstone on the Greenwich Village/Chelsea border, this extra-friendly hotel offers a personalized experience and has clean, comfortable, "shabby chic" rooms, all done with a movie motif and recently renovated. In warm weather, the superb breakfast (complimentary) is served in a lush, ivy-draped garden. Long popular with an LGBT clientele. Best to book in advance. $299

★ **Dream Downtown** 355 W 16th St, between Eighth and Ninth aves ☎ 212 229 2559, ⊛ dreamhotels.com; subway A, C, E, L to 14th St; map p.107. Visually stunning, this Miami-esque hotel has a lobby with cut-out "skylights" – the base of its swimming pool is lined in glass, so while you're checking in, you'll see guests gliding in the water overhead. Stylish all-white guest rooms have

porthole windows and pops of pink, and there's exceptional concierge service plus a rooftop bar with magnificent views up to Midtown. Keep the party going at the pool – one of Manhattan's best – it's decked out with chaise longues, a stocked bar and even a small sandy beach. $446

Gansevoort Meatpacking NYC 18 Ninth Ave, at W 13th St ☎ 212 206 6700, ⊛ gansevoorthotelgroup .com; subway A, C, E to 14th St, L to Eighth Ave; map p.107. When cobblestone streets in the Meatpacking District were torn up to make room for this sleek hotel in 2004, preservationists were horrified, but the *Gansevoort* has become a cornerstone of the fashionable neighbourhood scene. Rooms, in muted tones with pops of fuchsia, are stylish, with top-notch electronics, but you're really paying for the 360-degree views, the full spa, the heated rooftop pool (one of very few in the city) and the scene at its *Plunge Rooftop Bar & Lounge*. $348

The High Line Hotel 180 Tenth Ave, between W 20th and 21st sts ☎ 212 929 3888, ⊛ thehighlinehotel.com; subway C, E to 23rd St; map p.107. Set in the former dormitory of a nineteenth-century Episcopal seminary (of all things), this Gothic domicile, refashioned by the masterminds who designed the *Ace Hotel* (see p.272), has charming, old-timey details like wallpapered guest rooms with rotary phones, decorative fireplaces and muted Americana prints in gilded frames. There's also an excellent little coffee shop (*Intelligentsia*). $499

Leo House 332 W 23rd St, between Eighth and Ninth aves ☎ 646 868 3639 ext 219, ⊛ leohousenyc.com; subway #1, #2, to 23rd St; map p.107. This nonprofit German Catholic guesthouse (anyone can stay) has offered affordable lodging in the heart of Chelsea since 1926 (it's named after benefactor Pope Leo XII). Rooms are small and simple but bright and spotless, with TVs and a/c – most have bathrooms but the cheapest options have shared showers and private toilets. Buffet breakfast included. $180

Maritime Hotel 88 Ninth Ave, between W 16th and 17th sts ☎ 212 242 4300, ⊛ themaritimehotel.com; subway A, C, E, L to 14th St; map p.107. The nautical theme runs delightfully throughout at this contemporary hotel, glimpsed in the lobby's deep-sea-blue sofas and tiled walls and the cruise-ship-sized guest rooms (outfitted with porthole windows). Other fun perks include complimentary bike use, a top-of-the-range gym with tropical frond wallpaper and a gorgeous rooftop bar with dangling lamps and grand potted palms. $435

The Standard, High Line 848 Washington St, at W 13th St ☎ 212 645 4646, ⊛ standardhotels.com; subway A, C, E to 14th St, L to Eighth Ave; map p.107. With the High Line running under it, fabulous views from its floor-to-ceiling glass-walled rooms and a bevy of exclusive food and nightlife options nearby, André Balazs' *Standard* is just about too hip for its own good. There's a clean, Modernist feel to the decor. $503

21

UNION SQUARE, GRAMERCY AND THE FLATIRON DISTRICT

★**Ace Hotel** 20 W 29th St, at Broadway ☎212 679 2222, ⊕acehotel.com; subway N, R to 28th St; map p.115. Capturing the spirit of old New York yet fully modern, the *Ace Hotel* has set a new standard for bohemian chic (it was once the Breslin Hotel, built in 1904). A whole host of different room styles is on offer (including bunks), with muted tones, artwork and the odd retro-style fridge or guitar that can make it feel even more expensive than it is. In a short time, it's also established itself as a restaurant hotbed, with *The Breslin* gastropub, *Stumptown Coffee* (see p.302), *No. 7 Sub* (see p.302) and *The John Dory Oyster Bar* all on the premises. **$399**

Giraffe 365 Park Ave S, at E 26th St ☎212 685 7700, ⊕hotelgiraffe.com; subway #6 to 28th St; map p.115. The tall and slender *Hotel Giraffe* contains rooms that invoke the sleek Art Moderne style of the 1920s and 1930s. Prices include complimentary breakfast, afternoon wine and cheese, and a 24hr espresso bar. **$475**

Gramercy Park Hotel 2 Lexington Ave, at E 21st St ☎212 920 3300, ⊕gramercyparkhotel.com; subway #6 to 23rd St; map p.115. The Ian Schrager Group (enlisting the help of artist Julian Schnabel) renovated the once-bohemian *Gramercy Park* into a very different property: the grand entrance got a red carpet and a chandelier, but also reclaimed lumber, a stunning collection of modern art and lots of flickering candles. Rooms are similarly eclectic, bold and luxurious. It's in a lovely location – guests get a key to the adjacent private park (see p.116). President Obama had dinner here when he visited the city in 2014. **$579**

Hotel 31 120 E 31st St, between Park and Lexington aves ☎212 685 3060, ⊕hotel31.com; subway #6 to 28th St; map p.115. An affordable Murray Hill option, with sixty colourful, clean rooms (some share bathrooms), cable TV, a/c and a quiet location. **$134**

Kimpton Hotel Eventi 851 Sixth Ave, at W 30th St ☎212 564 4567, ⊕hoteleventi.com; subway N, R, #1 to 28th St; map p.115. On the eastern cusp of Chelsea, *Eventi* is handily situated with good proximity to the Empire State Building and Madison Square Park. Patronized by all stripes, rooms are stylish without being overdone, and there's a tempting Portuguese restaurant (*Lupulo*), knowledgeable staff and an excellent spa. **$551**

★**NoMad Hotel** 1170 Broadway, at W 28th St ☎212 796 1500, ⊕thenomadhotel.com; subway #6 to 28th St; map p.115. Housed in the 1900 Beaux-Arts Johnston Building, restored by French designer Jacques Garcia, with a celebrated on-site restaurant (see p.302). The welcoming *NoMad* offers stylish, spacious rooms with damask patterns, Iranian rugs, clawfoot tubs, king-size beds and a mishmash of tasteful art on the walls – different in each space. A definite cut above. **$615**

MIDTOWN EAST

★**1 Hotel Central Park** 1414 Sixth Ave, at W 58th St ☎212 369 1000, ⊕1hotels.com/central-park; subway N, R to Fifth Ave-59th St; map p.124. The ecofriendly hotel chain conceived by hotelier Barry Sternlich arrived here in 2015, with a three-storey living wall, reclaimed rustic-chic furniture and everything organic, plus an on-call Tesla car. Note the small details in the luxurious rooms; notepads are replaced by miniature chalkboards, the clothing hangers are cardboard and an hourglass timer suggests guests should leave the shower after five minutes. **$589**

Affinia Shelburne 303 Lexington Ave, between E 37th and 38th sts ☎212 689 5200, ⊕affinia.com/shelburne; subway #6 to 33rd St; map p.124. Luxurious hotel in the most elegant part of Murray Hill. Many of the freshly decorated rooms (mostly suites) have kitchenettes, and there's a separate restaurant downstairs, *Rare*, that specializes in gourmet burgers (and provides room service). There's also a buzzing bar scene – with the requisite great views – on the seasonal roof terrace. **$324**

★**Algonquin** 59 W 44th St, between Fifth and Sixth aves ☎212 840 6800, ⊕algonquinhotel.com; subway B, D, F, M, #7 to 42nd St-Bryant Park; map p.124. New York's oldest continuously operated hotel (it opened in 1902) and one of the city's famed literary hangouts (see p.126) has retained its old-club atmosphere and decor from the days of the Round Table, though the rooms have been refurbished to handsome effect (large flatscreens, refreshed carpets and bedding, bursts of colour). Ask about summer and weekend specials. **$499**

Bryant Park Hotel 40 W 40th St, between Fifth and Sixth aves ☎212 869 0100, ⊕bryantparkhotel.com; subway B, D, F, M, #7 to 42nd St-Bryant Park; map p.124. This hotel – in the old American Radiator Building, a striking black-and-gold mix of Gothic and Art Deco architecture built in 1924 – shows off its edgy attitude in its stylish contemporary rooms, luxurious seventy-seat film-screening room, and vaulted *Cellar Bar*, which is always filled with media types. **$545**

Chambers Hotel 15 W 56th St, between Fifth and Sixth aves ☎212 974 5656, ⊕chambershotel.com; subway F to 57th St; map p.124. Designed by architect David Rockwell, *Chambers* is well placed for Central Park and MoMA visits, though you can just sit and admire the five hundred original works of art in its gallery-sized hallways. The modern, tasteful rooms approximate a New York apartment, as do the mezzanine-level lounge spaces. A *Momofuku* offspring, *Má Pêche*, is the on-site restaurant. Good off-season deals. **$383**

Hotel Metro 45 W 35th St, between Fifth and Sixth aves ☎212 947 2500, ⊕hotelmetronyc.com; subway B, D, F, M to 34th St-Herald Square; map p.124. A stylish hotel, with some minimal Hollywood theming, a delightful seasonal rooftop, clean, understated rooms and free continental breakfast. There's also a fitness room and a nice restaurant, the *Metro Grill*. **$479**

IBEROSTAR 70 Park Avenue 70 Park Ave, at W 38th St ☎ 212 973 2400, ⓦ iberostar.com; subway #4, #5, #6, #7 to Grand Central-42nd St; map p.124. This snazzy and very popular chain hotel is adorned with original lighting and furnishing design featuring rich woods and pewter tones. Extras include 24hr fitness centre (and in-room spa services). Pet-friendly (U$10/night per pet). **$210**

Iroquois 49 W 44th St, between Fifth and Sixth aves ☎ 212 840 3080, ⓦ iroquoisny.com; subway B, D, F, M, #7 to 42nd St-Bryant Park; map p.124. Once a haven for rock bands, this elegant, reinvented boutique hotel has comfortable, tasteful rooms with Italian-marble baths and mahogany and suede headboards. The lounge is named for actor James Dean, resident at the hotel from 1951 to 1953 (room no. 803). **$499**

★ **Library Hotel** 299 Madison Ave, between E 41st and E 42nd sts (entry on E 41st St) ☎ 212 983 4500, ⓦ libraryhotel.com; subway #4, #5, #6, #7 to Grand Central-42nd St; map p.124. The *Library*'s concept, one of New York hostelry's quirkier, has each floor devoted to one of the ten major categories of the Dewey Decimal System. Coloured in shades of brown and cream, the rooms come in petite-size (can sleep two, but very snug) and deluxe (a bit more breathing room, though still average-size), but are nicely appointed with big bathrooms. There's a wine-and-cheese get-together every evening. **$550**

Morgans 237 Madison Ave, between E 37th and E 38th sts ☎ 212 686 0300, ⓦ morganshotelgroup.com; subway #6 to 33rd St; map p.124. Even though this 1920s hotel was converted to a posh boutique back in 1984, *Morgans* is still one of the chicest places to lay your head in town. Rooms, with maple panelling, neutral tones and checkerboard accents, are soothing, with specially commissioned black-and-white photos by the late Robert Mapplethorpe. **$310**

★ **The Plaza** 768 Fifth Ave at Central Park South ☎ 212 759 3000, ⓦ theplazany.com; subway N, R to Fifth Ave-59th St; map p.124. *The Plaza* has come back from its hiatus and transformation, which turned part of it into apartments, looking better than ever. The grand tradition of the hotel (it's been open since 1907) is still there in the Baccarat chandeliers (in the rooms too) and 24-carat-gold fixtures, but now there are flatscreen TVs and iPads, wireless control panels to dim the lights and summon the floor butler, along with every other amenity you can imagine. Needless to say, service is impeccable, the prices astronomical. **$1050**

★ **Pod 51** 230 E 51st St, between Second and Third aves ☎ 212 355 0300, ⓦ thepodhotel.com; subway #6 to 51st St; map p.124. This pleasant hotel is one of the best deals in Midtown. All 370 pods (solo, double, bunk, queen and

TOP 5 HOTEL ROOFTOP BARS 21

Dream Downtown See p.271
Gansevoort See p.271
Knickerbocker See p.274
McCarren Hotel & Pool See p.276
The William Vale See p.276

"double double", each reminiscent of a colourful ship's quarters) come with a/c, iPod docks and flatscreen TVs, though single and bunk rooms share bathrooms. The open-air roof-deck bar is a bonus, with stunning views. **$175**

The Renwick 118 E 40th St, between Park and Lexington aves ☎ 212 687 4875, ⓦ therenwickhotel newyork.com; subway S, #4, #5, #6, #7 to Grand Central-42nd St; map p.124. This literary-themed luxury hotel features loft-like rooms renovated from historic artists' studios and apartments originally designed by St Patrick's Cathedral architect James Renwick Jr in 1928 (F. Scott Fitzgerald, Thomas Mann and John Steinbeck all crashed here). The creatively styled rooms are equipped with easels and paint, writing paper and ink, artwork and books, in addition to the usual amenities. **$373**

Warwick New York 65 W 54th St, at Sixth Ave ☎ 212 247 2700, ⓦ warwickhotels.com/new-york; subway F to 57th St; map p.124. Legendary newspaperman William Randolph Hearst commissioned the hotel in 1926, and stars of the 1950s and 1960s – including Cary Grant, Elizabeth Taylor, the Beatles, Elvis Presley and Marilyn Monroe – stayed here as a matter of course. Although the hotel has lost its showbiz cachet, the elegant lobby, restaurant and cocktail lounge still make it a pleasant place to stay. Staff are helpful and quite friendly. **$449**

MIDTOWN WEST

★ **414 Hotel** 414 W 46th St, between Ninth and Tenth aves ☎ 212 399 0006, ⓦ 414hotel.com; subway C, E to 50th St; map p.142. Popular with Europeans but welcoming to all, this guesthouse, which has larger-than-ordinary rooms across two townhouses, makes a nice camp a bit removed from Times Square's bustle. The courtyard garden is a wonderful place to enjoy your morning coffee. **$309**

Ameritania at Times Square 230 W 54th St, at Broadway ☎ 212 247 5000, ⓦ ameritanyc.com; subway B, D, E to Seventh Ave; map p.142. With sleek, angular furnishings, soaring columns and a bold colour palette, this offbeat hotel is one of the cooler-looking options in the city. Rooms have ample though not extravagant amenities; deluxe rooms (only a little pricier than the standard ones) feature marble baths. **$240**

Casablanca Hotel 147 W 43rd St, between Sixth Ave and Broadway ☎ 212 869 1212, ⓦ casablancahotel .com; subway B, D, F, M, #1, #2, #3, #7 to 42nd St; map p.142. Geometric Moorish tiles, inlaid wood and *Rick's Café*

21

(free continental breakfasts and 24hr coffee) are all here in this small, themed hotel along with daily wine-and-cheese reception (5–8pm; free) and complimentary gym passes. While the decor is 1940s Morocco, the rooms all have up-to-date amenities (DVD, iPod dock, etc). **$360**

citizenM New York Times Square 218 W 50th St, between Broadway and Eighth Ave ❶ 212 461 3638, ⓦ citizenm.com; subway #1 to 50th St; map p.142. The first US outpost of this trendy Dutch chain, this stylish, limited-service hotel offers compact, minimalist rooms with Samsung tablet, plus a guests-only rooftop lounge and use of Apple computers in the library. Breakfast is $19 extra (booked online). **$349**

★ **Distrikt** 342 W 40th St, between Eighth and Ninth aves ❶ 212 706 6100, ⓦ distrikthotel.com; subway A, C, E to 42nd St-Port Authority; map p.142. With a city neighbourhood theme – subtle in the decor, more obvious in having floors named "Chelsea", "the Village", etc – the welcoming *Distrikt* has rooms done in classy muted browns and beiges, with black-and-white accents; choose one of the upper floors ("Harlem") for the best views. **$319**

Edison 228 W 47th St, between Broadway and Eighth Ave ❶ 212 840 5000, ⓦ edisonhotelnyc.com; subway N, Q, R to 49th St or #1 to 50th St; map p.142. The most striking thing about the one-thousand-room *Edison* is its beautifully restored Art Deco lobby (it opened in 1931). The rooms, while not fancy, are clean and the prices are reasonable for Midtown. If you want a big hotel right on Broadway, look no further. **$295**

The French Quarters 346 W 46th St, between Eighth and Ninth aves ❶ 212 359 6652, ⓦ frenchquartersny .com; subway C, E to 50th St; map p.142. These New Orleans-themed serviced apartments are a great deal and subsequently very popular – book months ahead. The elegant rooms feature kitchenettes, DVD players and separate sitting areas. Continental breakfast included. **$280**

Hilton Times Square 234 W 42nd St, between Seventh and Eighth aves ❶ 212 840 8222, ⓦ hilton.com; subway A, C, E to 42nd St-Port Authority or N, Q, R, S, #1, #2, #3, #7 to Times Square-42nd St; map p.142. This gorgeous property is housed in a 44-storey tower, with awesome views in all directions. The neutral-toned rooms are especially good size for a Manhattan hotel, freshly done up with attractive furnishings and rather large-screen TVs. **$339**

★ **Kimpton Ink48 Hotel** 653 Eleventh Ave, between 47th and 48th sts ❶ 212 757 0088, ⓦ ink48.com; subway C, E to 50th St; map p.142. On a strip of car-related businesses (petrol stations, dealers, repair shops), this old printing press has been remade into a dashing hotel; all the spacious rooms face out, many to the Hudson, for splendid views (try to get a corner room on one of the upper floors if possible), and have modern decor, (typically) king beds and lofty ceilings. The rooftop bar, *Press Lounge* (see p.339), is a real plus, as is the full-treatment spa. Dog-friendly. **$474**

Kimpton Muse Hotel 130 W 46th St, between Sixth and Seventh aves ❶ 212 485 2400, ⓦ themusehotel .com; subway B, D, F, M to 47–50th sts-Rockefeller Center; map p.142. A small hotel in the centre of the Times Square area from the Kimpton stable; the slightly dark and oddly decorated lobby contrasts with the airy rooms, done in bold black-and-white patterns. **$539**

Knickerbocker 6 Times Square (Broadway and W 42nd St) ❶ 212 204 4980, ⓦ theknickerbocker.com; subway N, Q, R, S, #1, #2, #3, #7 to Times Square-42nd St; map p.142. This fabulous luxury hotel lies smack in the heart of Times Square, an artful renovation of John Jacob Astor IV's 1906 Beaux-Arts original building. The sleek, modern rooms feature sound-proofed windows and automated black-out drapes to cut out the light, while spectacular views can be had from the rooftop bar, *St. Cloud*. **$518**

Mayfair 242 W 49th St, between Broadway and Eighth Ave ❶ 212 586 0300, ⓦ mayfairnewyork.com; subway C, E, #1 to 50th St or N, R to 49th St; map p.142. This boutique-style hotel, across the street from the St Malachy Actors' Chapel, has toile-papered rooms and a charming, old-fashioned feel. A nice touch is the preponderance of historic photographs on loan from the Museum of the City of New York (see p.178). **$265**

Night Times Square 157 W 47th St, between Sixth and Seventh aves ❶ 212 768 3700, ⓦ nighthotels.com; subway B, D, F, M to 47–50th sts-Rockefeller Center; map p.142. The colourful, funky lobby, filled with distinctive chandeliers and fish-filled aquariums, gives way to more restrained rooms that are relatively good value for the area. **$299**

Novotel 226 W 52nd St, at Broadway ❶ 212 315 0100, ⓦ accorhotels.com; subway #1 to 50th St; B, D, E to Seventh Ave, N, Q, R to 49th St; map p.142. This international chain hotel is large enough to offer a decent range of facilities while small enough (though not approaching boutique size) to cultivate some character. The look is casual but sleek, featuring uncluttered wood with blue accents. **$399**

The Quin 101 W 57th St, at Sixth Ave ❶ 212 245 7846, ⓦ thequinhotel.com; subway F, N, Q, R to 57th St; map p.142. Exceedingly posh landmark property choicely situated between Central Park, Carnegie Hall and Tiffany's. Rooms have a soothing palette of oatmeal, heather and cream; the lobby is punchier, with an exceptional contemporary art collection. If you're planning to visit at Thanksgiving, *The Quin* is a good one to know about – the gorgeous floats and massive balloons of the Macy's Day Parade will pass right in front of your door. **$499**

Refinery Hotel 63 W 38th St, between Fifth and Sixth aves ❶ 646 664 0310, ⓦ refineryhotelnewyork.com; subway B, D, F, M to 42nd St-Bryant Park; map p.142. Named for the distinguished ladies who once shopped for exquisite hats here – completed in 1912, this Gothic building was once a centrepiece of the millinery industry – the *Refinery* is a relaxed boutique hotel with a smart location right by Grand Central and Bryant Park. Rooms are turned out in hues of mahogany and have high ceilings, hardwood floors and desks that emulate sewing tables. **$489**

Room Mate Grace 125 W 45th St, between Sixth and Seventh aves ☎212 354 2323, ⓦroom-matehotels .com/en/grace; subway B, D, F, M to 42nd St-Bryant Park; map p.142. You won't find many hotels like this one, with a lobby that resembles a filigreed Easter basket; a tiny glassed-in pool overlooked by a louche loungey bar; different retro wallpaper on each floor; and ultra-modern rooms, with platform beds and, in some rooms, bunks (great if you've got a small group). **$311**

Stewart Hotel 371 Seventh Ave, at W 31st St ☎212 563 1800, ⓦstewarthotelnyc.com; subway #1, #2, #3 to 34th St-Penn Station; map p.142. This large hotel is housed in a 1929 building opposite Penn Station and Madison Square Garden; a redesign by the Rockwell Group brought a more artistic flair to the place, as well as added rooms – they still have numerous suites with kitchenettes but also petite queens. Though it's a bustling address, the elegant lobby, in-room spa service and a menu of pillow options all help foster relaxation. **$323**

Yotel 570 10th Ave, between W 41st and 41nd sts ☎646 449 7700, ⓦyotel.com; subway A, C, E to 42nd St-Port Authority; map p.142. Just a couple of blocks west of Times Square, this über-modern hotel is big on innovative design details (a massive robotic arm to deliver your luggage, swift check-in computers, beds that bend and fold with the touch of a switch) but still exudes plenty of warmth and humanity. Rooms are notably small, but there are a number of expansive common areas, including a huge outdoor terrace and workspaces with computers at the ready. **$313**

UPPER EAST SIDE

Sherry-Netherland 781 Fifth Ave, at E 59th St ☎212 355 2800, ⓦsherrynetherland.com; subway N, R to 59th St; map p.171. If a large sum of money ever comes your way, rent a whole floor here and live-in permanently (many of the guests do) – the stunning views of Central Park are worth it. Dating from 1927, the lobby is modelled after the Vatican Library and splendidly ornate; service is excellent and room service is by the in-house Harry Cipriani restaurant. **$530**

The Surrey 20 E 76th St, at Madison Ave ☎212 288 3700, ⓦthesurrey.com; subway #6 to 77th St; map p.171. Just steps from "Museum Mile", this plush hotel has hosted guests since 1926, but the interior is a showcase for contemporary design; standard "salons" (rooms) have been beautifully furnished with ornate carpets, hand-crafted wardrobes and modern desks. Has a spa and rooftop garden. **$555**

UPPER WEST SIDE AND MORNINGSIDE HEIGHTS

Beacon 2130 Broadway, at W 75th St ☎212 787 1100, ⓦbeaconhotel.com; subway #1, #2, #3 to 72nd St; map p.184. Perfectly situated for strolling the gourmet markets and museums of the Upper West Side. Rooms are comfortable and reasonably sized, with kitchenettes and plenty of suites, making them quite family friendly. **$359**

Lucerne 201 W 79th St, at Amsterdam Ave ☎212 875 1000, ⓦthelucernehotel.com; subway #1 to 79th St, B, C to 81st St; map p.184. This beautifully restored 1904 brownstone, with its extravagant Baroque terracotta entrance, charming rooms and accommodating staff, is just a block from the Museum of Natural History (see p.190) and close to the liveliest stretches of Broadway and Columbus Ave. **$378**

NYLO 2178 Broadway, at W 77th St ☎212 362 1100, ⓦnylohotels.com; subway #1 to 79th St; map p.184. This neighbourhood gem comes well stocked with two restaurants, an inviting bar and newly renovated guest rooms outfitted with azure drapes, pale wood fixtures and furniture, bright art and lots of sunlight. At the heart of the UWS, it rubs elbows with iconic cafés and shops, and it's a short walk from here to Central Park. **$359**

HARLEM AND NORTH MANHATTAN

★ **Aloft Harlem** 2296 Frederick Douglass Blvd ☎212 749 4000, ⓦaloftharlem.com; subway A, B, C, D to 125th St; map p.199. The first hotel to open in Harlem since the early 1960s, with a bright, stylish interior, high-tech amenities (a pair of iMacs for use), contemporary decor and airy, loft-inspired rooms with large showers and platform beds. **$249**

BROOKLYN

Note that the L subway line (which connects Manhattan to Brooklyn neighbourhoods such as Williamsburg and Bushwick) will be completely suspended for tunnel repairs for at least fifteen months beginning April 2019. Local hotels should have a clearer idea of public transport alternatives nearer the time.

1 Hotel Brooklyn Bridge 60 Furman St (Brooklyn Bridge Park) ☎877 803 1111, ⓦ1hotels.com/Brooklyn -Bridge; subway A, C to High St; map p.218. It's priced to compete with New York's most exclusive hotels for good reason – the second of Sternlich's eco-conscious hotels in the city (p.272), this one has all the green features and amenities, plus possibly the best view of the Manhattan skyline and the Brooklyn Bridge anywhere. **$720**

Box House 77 Box St, at McGuinness Blvd, Greenpoint ☎718 383 3800, ⓦtheboxhousehotel.com; subway #7 to Vernon Blvd-Jackson Ave; map p.225. Just across the Newtown Creek from Queens, this popular Brooklyn option offers industrial chic in the form of oak floors, antique furnishings, contemporary art by Brooklyn artist Kip

21

Jacobs, kitchenettes and modern amenities (iPod docks etc.). Free shuttle in classic 1970s checker cabs helps with the location. **$399**

Henry Norman Hotel 239 N Henry St, between Norman and Meserole aves, Greenpoint ☎ 212 277 8700, ⓦ henrynormanhotel.com; subway G to Nassau Ave; map p.225. Though it might seem a little out of the way in the eastern part of Greenpoint, this hotel (conceived by the *Box House* folks) offers bright, stylish rooms in a converted nineteenth-century warehouse, plus a wet and dry sauna. Free transport within a one-mile radius (enough for Williamsburg bars). **$379**

Le Bleu 370 Fourth Ave, between 4th and 5th sts, Gowanus ☎ 718 625 1500, ⓦ hotellebleu.com; subway F, G, R to Fourth Ave-9th St; map p.225. If you can ignore the disjunctive positioning of this modern glass stack right next to a Staples megastore, *Le Bleu* has a lot of things going for it: a boutique feel, with fewer than fifty rooms; bright, airy quarters, many with terraces and balconies; reasonable rates; and proximity to Carroll Gardens, Whole Foods and Prospect Park, as well as good views of Manhattan. **$280**

Le Jolie 235 Meeker Ave, at Withers St, Williamsburg ☎ 212 216 0000, ⓦ hotellejolie.com; subway G to Metropolitan Ave, L to Lorimer St; map p.225. Close to all the Billyburg action, rooms at this small boutique feature bright wallpaper designs and contemporary fittings, some with views of Manhattan. Decent continental breakfast included. **$289**

McCarren Hotel & Pool 160 N 12th St, between Bedford Ave and Berry St, Williamsburg ☎ 718 218 7500, ⓦ mccarrenhotel.com; subway L to Bedford Ave; map p.225. Just off the main Williamsburg strip and overlooking McCarren Park, this chic option features a seasonal outdoor pool (with lively party scene in the summer), compact but comfy rooms and a rooftop lounge with the requisite Manhattan views. **$315**

NU Hotel 85 Smith St, at Atlantic Ave, Boerum Hill ☎ 718 852 8585, ⓦ nuhotelbrooklyn.com; subway F, G to Bergen St, A, C, G to Hoyt-Schermerhorn sts; map p.218. Cool, bright rooms, some with hand-painted murals by local artists, in one of the few convenient Brooklyn hotels that's not a depressing chain. Though on a high-traffic thoroughfare, it's close to some of the nicest walking neighbourhoods around. **$278**

Pointe Plaza 2 Franklin Ave, at Wallabout St, Williamsburg ☎ 718 782 7000, ⓦ pointeplazahotel.com; subway G to Flushing Ave; map p.225. It's a bit out of the way, but these loft-style suites with full kitchens are a grand deal, right at the southern boundary of Williamsburg. Breakfast included, plus 24hr tea and coffee and a free shuttle to the subway station. **$152**

★**The William Vale** 111 N 12th St, between Wythe and Berry sts, Williamsburg ☎ 718 631 8400, ⓦ thewilliamvale.com; subway L to Bedford Ave; map

p.225. One of the newest hotels in Williamsburg, this posh boutique is known chiefly for its wacky architecture and spectacular rooftop bar and panoramas of Manhattan, but its stylish contemporary rooms are also a real treat, featuring floor-to-ceiling windows, open-air balconies and those stunning views. **$449**

★**Wythe** 80 Wythe Ave, at N 11th St, Williamsburg ☎ 718 460 8000, ⓦ wythehotel.com; subway L to Bedford Ave; map p.225. This old factory has been smartly converted into a chic boutique hotel; various industrial touches have been preserved and emphasized, whether exposed brick or floor-to-ceiling warehouse-style windows. "Baby Queens" offer a good deal, though you may want to pay extra for more space and the Brooklyn or Manhattan-side views from higher floors. **$382**

LONG ISLAND CITY (QUEENS)

Boro Hotel 38-28 27th St, at 39th Ave ☎ 718 433 1375, ⓦ borohotel.com; subway N, W to 39th Ave; map p.246. Leading the new wave of Long Island City hotels, this attractive, modern boutique offers stunning views of Manhattan from its rooftop as well as the floor-to-ceiling windows in its industrial-chic loft-like rooms, many with balconies. **$305**

LIC Hotel 44-04 21st St, at 44th Ave ☎ 718 406 9788, ⓦ lichotelny.com; subway E, M to Court Square-23rd St; map p.246. Modern, motel-like option with simple, small but spotless rooms with hardwood floors and flatscreen TVs. The roof deck is a great place to relax in warm weather. Basic quality but full cooked breakfast included (eggs, toast, sausage, etc). **$175**

Nesva Hotel 39-12 29th St, between 39th and 40th aves ☎ 917 745 1000, ⓦ nesvahotel.com; subway N, W to 39th Ave; map p.246. Spanking-new boutique just one subway stop from Manhattan, decorated with work from local artists and featuring minimalist rooms with walnut wood furniture and soothing earth tones. Good continental breakfast included (blueberry muffins, cereal, bagels, etc). **$143**

Paper Factory Hotel 37-06 36th St, at 37th Ave ☎ 718 392 7200, ⓦ paperfactoryhotel.com; subway E, M, R to 36th St; map p.246. Swish hotel in a former radio and paper factory dating to 1922, with eclectic decor (there's a red phone booth in the lobby), original polished concrete floors and reclaimed materials giving a slightly steampunk vibe. **$219**

Z NYC Hotel 11-01 43rd Ave, at 11th St ☎ 212 319 7000, ⓦ zhotelny.com; subway F to 21 St-Queensbridge; map p.246. A few blocks from the East River, this is another hip LIC option that offers good value – it's just two subway stops from Midtown. The slender hotel blends a Jazz Age theme with the contemporary industrial design so common in this part of the city – front desk constructed from classic steamer trunks, rooms with floor-to-ceiling windows, jazz wall murals, amazing views and all the usual electronic amenities. Free hourly shuttle to Lexington Ave in Manhattan. **$247**

HOSTELS

Hostels are generally a solid budget option when travelling in New York. In recent years, a number of hip, young hostels have popped up in Brooklyn and Long Island City (Queens), as the outer boroughs have grown into destinations themselves. Expect to pay $40–70 for a dorm bed, two to three times as much for a private double with bathroom; note that prices change seasonally (not always in line with the high seasons listed at the start of this chapter).

American Dream 168 E 24th St, between Third and Lexington aves ☎ 212 260 9779, ⓦ americandream hostel.com; map p.115. A great location, a pleasing design sense (there's an upbeat palette of white, lemon yellow and navy blue) and free continental breakfast all help make this clean, hospitable budget inn a good option for a short-term stay. All rooms come with bunk beds (up to three people per room), with TVs and shared bathrooms. No elevator; expect a three-storey walk up. Singles $94, doubles $148, triples $180

★**Bowery House** 220 Bowery, between Spring and Prince sts ☎ 212 837 2373, ⓦ theboweryhouse.com; subway J, Z to Bowery; map p.71. This 1927 Bowery flophouse has been transformed into a stylish hostel in a prime Nolita location, featuring original "cabins" (with single beds, latticework ceilings and shared bathrooms) as well as compact doubles (also shared bathrooms). Everything has been beautifully renovated, with Italian marble floors, posh sheets and bath products and local artwork. Singles $99, doubles $139

Broadway Hotel & Hostel 230 W 101st St, at Broadway ☎ 212 865 7710, ⓦ broadwayhotelnyc.com; subway #1 to 103rd St; map p.184. Comfy, modern hostel in a quiet section of the Upper West Side, with simple but elegant private double (with flatscreen TVs and iPod docks) and dorms with shared or private bathrooms. Dorms $55, doubles $135

Chelsea International 251 W 20th St, between Seventh and Eighth aves ☎ 212 647 0010, ⓦ chelsea hostel.com; subway C, E to 23rd St; map p.107. A basic choice located in the heart of Chelsea. The shared dorms (four single beds) are clean and rudimentary, or you can book a private single or double (add around $7–8 for private bathroom). All guests must leave a $10 key deposit. Breakfast included, and free pizza every Wednesday. Dorms $48, doubles $100

Hostelling International New York 891 Amsterdam Ave, between Broadway and Columbus aves ☎ 212 932 2300, ⓦ hinewyork.org; subway #1 to 103rd St; map p.184. Stellar hostel, way uptown, in a gorgeous

Gothic-style building with a state-of-the-art kitchen, café, bike rental, laundry and an enormous brick patio and garden. One block from the subway, two blocks from Central Park and very convenient for Columbia University. Dorms $50

The Local NYC 1302-44th Ave, between 11th and 21st sts, Long Island City, Queens ☎ 347 738 5251, ⓦ thelocalny.com; subway E, M to Court Square-23rd St; map p.246. Much closer to Manhattan than you might think (by subway, it's 10min to Grand Central), this Queens favourite has a chic, whitewashed look and a convivial bar. Solid hostelling perks like kitchen access, a laundry room, computer set-up (free) and daily breakfast. Dorms $40.50, doubles $159

New York Budget Inn 200 E 34th St, at Third Ave ☎ 212 689 6500, ⓦ hostelnewyorkny.com; subway #6 to 33rd St; map p.124. Centrally located bargain accommodation (it's an old brick apartment building), with 64 rooms ranging from modern, four-bed dorms (female, male and mixed) to simple doubles with private or shared bathrooms (prices double for en-suite rooms). It's all fairly basic and utilitarian, but clean and great value. Free donuts and coffee in the morning. Dorms $50, doubles $80

NY Moore 179 Moore St, between Bushwick and White, East Willamsburg, Brooklyn ☎ 347 227 8634, ⓦ nymoorehostel.com; subway L to Morgan Ave; map p.225. Arty loft space in the slightly scruffy (but definitely hip) neighbourhood of East Willamsburg. The decor is a funny mix of antique sofas and Modernist bed frames, but the rooms are spotless, the staff are friendly and knowledgeable and it's a quick subway ride into Manhattan. Dorms $45.60

★**Q4 Hotel** 29-09 Queens Plaza N, at 29th St, Long Island City, Queens ☎ 718 706 7700, ⓦ q4hotel.com; subway E, M, R to Queens Plaza; map p.246. Hip hostel in up-and-coming Long Island City, with some of the cheapest rates in New York. Neat, clean dorms, small but stylish doubles and spotless bathrooms, plus you get access to shared kitchen, TV lounge and pool and ping-pong tables. Dorms $33, doubles $120

BED AND BREAKFASTS AND APARTMENTS

Staying at a **bed and breakfast** is an enjoyable way of visiting New York, with better rates than you'll find at a hotel (guest rooms start at around $130 for a double), though airbnb has had a negative impact on traditional B&Bs, especially in Manhattan. B&Bs are a still good bet in the outer boroughs, especially in Brooklyn, where there are quite a few attractive townhouses to choose from. There are a number of official agencies keen to help with booking such as ⓦ citylightsbed andbreakfast.com and ⓦ bedandbreakfast.com.

21

MANHATTAN B&BS AND APARTMENTS

Bubba and Bean Lodges 1598 Lexington Ave, between E 101st and E 102nd sts ☎917 345 7914, ⓦbblodges.com; subway #6 to 103rd St; map p.171. Cool East Harlem guesthouse, close to the north end of Museum Mile, with modern rooms set in conjoined mid-nineteenth-century townhouses owned by Jonathan and Clement, all with their own kitchenettes (so you must make your own breakfast; tea and coffee provided). Bargain rates Jan & Feb. $190

Harlem Flophouse 242 W 123rd St, between Powell and Frederick Douglass blvds ☎212 662 0678, ⓦharlemflophouse.com; subway A, B, C, #2, #3 to 125th St; map p.199. This hip, beautiful, artist-owned 1890s brownstone has just four rooms each with sinks, and two shared bathrooms with antique clawfoot tubs. Charming, but it's an old building and dimly lit throughout; not to everyone's taste. $125

Inn at Irving Place 56 Irving Place, at E 17th St ☎212 533 4600, ⓦinnatirving.com; subway L, N, Q, R, #4, #5, #6 to 14th St-Union Square; map p.115. Frequented by celebrities, this handsome pair of 1834 brownstones rank as one of the most exclusive guesthouses in the city. The twelve rooms and "residences" are each named for a famous architect, designer or actor and all have different rates. The *Inn* also offers five-course high teas for $59/person (see p.303). $275

Jones Street Guesthouse 31 Jones St, between Bleecker and W 4th sts ☎212 242 1279, ⓦjonesstreetguesthouse.com; subway A, B, C, D, E, F, M to W 4th St, #1 to Christopher St; map p.96. Rare find in the heart of the West Village, just off Bleecker; two nicely renovated en-suite rooms, spotlessly clean, with friendly owners in the apartments above (which is sometimes available to rent) – it's the closest you'll get to "living like a local". Breakfast is courtesy of a $5 voucher at nearby café *Doma Na Rahu*. $250

★**Mount Morris House** 12 Mt Morris Park W, between W 121st and W 122nd sts ☎917 478 6214, ⓦmountmorrishousebandb.com; subway #2, #3 to 125th St; map p.199. This guesthouse is an elegant brownstone built in 1888, just across the street from Marcus Garvey Park in Harlem. The five sumptuous suites are loaded with period antiques and feature parquet floors, fireplaces and high ceilings. No breakfast, but shared kitchen comes with tea and coffee (and freshly baked cakes every day). $225

★**San Fermín Apartments** 195 Edgecombe Ave, between 142nd and 145th sts ☎917 940 2682, ⓦsanferminapartmentsny.com; subway A, B, C, D to 145th St; map p.199. Set in a lovely 1910 brownstone in Sugar Hill (Harlem), this guesthouse features three comfortable en-suite doubles, and three doubles with shared bath, all dressed in a cool contemporary style. Small kitchen included. $150

BROOKLYN B&BS AND APARTMENTS

Akwaaba Mansion 347 MacDonough St, at Stuyvesant Ave, Bedford-Stuyvesant ☎718 455 5958, ⓦakwaaba.com; subway A, C to Utica Ave; map p.214. A New York landmark, this 1860s Italianate mansion is one of a kind, featuring Afrocentric details like Daffodil rag dolls and Adinkra fabrics. A tearoom, sunny porch and Southern-style breakfast will make anyone feel right at home. If you were wondering, the Ghanaian name translates as "welcome". $205

★**At Home In Brooklyn** 15 Prospect Park W, between Carroll and President sts, Park Slope ☎718 622 5292, ⓦathomeinbrooklyn.com; subway #2, #3, #4 to Grand Army Plaza; map p.231. Right on Prospect Park in the heart of Park Slope, this handsome brownstone features four comfy bedrooms, all with fresh-cut flowers and DVD players (there's a huge library downstairs); three share a gorgeous 1930s glass tile Art Deco bathroom. The breakfast is delicious (local bagels included) and the views from the roof deck are sensational. $175

Bibi's Garden Bed and Breakfast 762 Westminster Rd, between Ave H and Glenwood Rd, Flatbush-Ditmas Park ☎718 434 3119, ⓦbibisgarden.net; subway Q to Ave H; map p.214. Set in a beautiful shingle-style 1904 home with a tranquil porch deck and five lovely rooms decorated with antiques. Includes a tasty continental breakfast spread. $125

Loralei B&B 667 Argyle Rd, between Foster Ave and Glenwood Rd, Flatbush-Ditmas Park ☎646 228 4656, ⓦloraleinyc.com; subway B, Q to Newkirk Plaza; map p.214. This three-storey clapboard beauty with an enticing wraparound porch dates from 1904, set in a leafy section of Ditmas Park (two blocks from the subway). The two rooms are dressed in a simple but elegant Victorian style, with TVs and private bathrooms. Continental breakfast included. $170

THE BRONX B&BS AND APARTMENTS

★**Mi Casa Tu Casa Guesthouse** 143 E 150th St, just off the Grand Concourse ☎718 402 9310, ⓦfacebook.com/Micasatucasa150; subway #2, #5, to 149th St-Grand Concourse; map p.256. "Bed and breakfast" might seem out of place in the South Bronx, but host Julio Pabón, friendly and knowledgeable long-time Bronx resident, offers four cosy rooms in a beautifully weathered nineteenth-century clapboard house just off the main drag. There are three shared bathrooms, a shared kitchen and a tranquil backyard garden. No website – look for it on sites such as ⓦairbnb.com or ⓦbedandbreakfast.com. $85

RUSS & DAUGHTERS CAFÉ

Eating

New York has long been a culinary powerhouse, a city where ambitious chefs study to become great chefs and bold experimentation is forged beside proudly maintained tradition. Exacting standards are the standard here, whether you're globe-trotting among the ever-evolving menus of Queens, eating at one of the world's most celebrated showcases of gourmet dining or simply biting into a fat, fresh-from-the-oven bagel or slice of pizza. As well as being an international centre and a creative hotbed, New York is exceptionally competitive. Bring these three elements together and you're in for a world-class feast.

22

Some of America's most iconic snacks were created (or at least perfected) in New York, from Patsy Lancieri's classic pizza slice to Dominique Ansel's contemporary cronut. Jewish immigrants refined the bagel in the nineteenth century (along with challah bread, knishes and egg creams), while Polish-Jewish entrepreneur Nathan Handwerker is largely responsible for Coney Island's hot dog, now sold from carts on practically every corner. The Oreo cookie was created in 1912 (at today's Chelsea Market) and Häagen-Dazs was founded here in 1961. Delis such as *Katz's* – open since 1888 – continue to knock out mountainous pastrami sandwiches, while German émigré Arnold Reuben is credited with inventing New York-style cheesecake (as well as the Reuben sandwich). The black-and-white cookie is another classic, introduced to New York by Bavarian immigrants John and Justine Glaser in 1902.

Though it's not traditionally known for its café culture, New York does boast a handful of historic coffee shops, especially in the West Village and Little Italy. And though coffee in New York was once epitomized by the drip-brewed swill served at local bodegas in those paper Anthora "Greek" cups, newer chains such as *Bluestone Lane* (see opposite) have raised the bar considerably, competing with West Coast imports like *Blue Bottle Coffee* and *Stumptown* (see p.302). Another recent trend has been the arrival of the gourmet food hall (see p.287).

THE FINANCIAL DISTRICT

With the neighbourhood becoming more residential, eating options in the Financial District have improved dramatically in recent years. Celebrity chefs and restaurateurs such as Keith McNally (opposite), Tom Colicchio (below), Wolfgang Puck and Mario Batali (*Eataly*, opposite) have all opened shop here, with Jean-Georges Vongerichten and David Chang slated to open new ventures in Seaport District NYC in 2018. The best areas for eating are Stone Street, Front Street and the newer places around Battery Park City; for cheap eats consider the cluster of halal kebab vans in Zuccotti Park.

AMERICAN

Blue Smoke 255 Vesey St, between West St and North End Ave ☎212 889 2005, ⓦbluesmoke.com; subway #2, #3 to Park Place, E to World Trade Center; map p.44. Authentic Southern barbecue courtesy of pitmaster Kenny Callaghan and the Danny Meyer empire, with juicy blue smoke burgers ($18) and classics like fried chicken and biscuits ($25). Mon–Thurs 11.30am–10pm, Fri 11.30am–11pm, Sat 11am–11pm, Sun 11am–10pm.

Delmonico's 56 Beaver St, at William St ☎212 509 1144, ⓦdelmonicosrestaurant.com; subway #2, #3 to Wall St; map p.44. Patrons tend to come to this 1837 landmark steakhouse for its historic charms, murals and classic dishes: the Delmonico steak (boneless ribeye; $51), lobster Newburg (created in 1876; market price) and Baked Alaska (created in 1867; $13). Cheaper dishes are available in the bar. Mon–Fri 11.30am–10pm, Sat 5–10pm.

TOP 5 CLASSIC NEW YORK

Sylvia's Harlem. See p.315
Katz's Deli Lower East Side. See p.290
Oyster Bar Midtown East. See p.304
Peter Luger Steak House Williamsburg, Brooklyn. See p.320
Shopsin's See p.288

Fowler & Wells Beekman Hotel, 5 Beekman St, between Broadway and Nassau St ☎212 685 1848, ⓦfowlerandwells.com; subway A, C to Fulton St; map p.44. Celebrity chef Tom Colicchio's gorgeous and pricey restaurant in the *Beekman* serves up quintessential Old New York with classics such as oysters Rockefeller ($25), Maine lobster and lamb Wellington, as well as prime steaks (dinner mains range $36–65). Sun–Wed 6.30am–10pm, Thurs–Sat 6.30am–11pm.

Harry's Café & Steak 1 Hanover Square, at Pearl St ☎212 785 9200, ⓦharrysnyc.com; subway #2, #3 to Wall St; map p.44. Housed in the basement of historic India House since 1972, and traditionally the haunt of Wall Street deal-makers. Order sandwiches ($17–28) or the lauded prime steaks (from $49) while soaking up the "Gilded Age" atmosphere, immortalized in novels such as Tom Wolfe's *Bonfire of the Vanities* and Brett Easton Ellis's *American Psycho*. The unlimited champagne brunch (Sat 11am–3pm) is a good deal (mains $18–46). Mon–Fri 11.30am–midnight (bar till 1am), Sat 11am–midnight (bar till 2am).

The Paris Café 119 South St ☎212 240 9797, ⓦpariscafenyc.com; subway A, C, J, Z, #2, #3, #4, #5 to Fulton St; map p.44. Established in 1873, this old-fashioned restaurant (more Irish pub than French bistro) has played host to a panoply of luminaries, but was completely renovated after Hurricane Sandy shut it down for almost a year. The decent draught Guinness, pub-food menu and sports on TV still pull in a lively crowd; try the shepherd's pie or fish and chips (mains $18–27). Daily 11am–4am.

BAGELS

Leo's Bagels 3 Hanover Square, at Stone St ☎ 212 785 7828, ⓦ leosbagels.com; subway #2, #3 to Wall St; map p.44. Get your bagel fix at this popular local joint, with the hand-rolled, chewy main event going for $1.25 (add $2.95 for huge dollops of cream cheese and various spreads). Also does salads, soups and sandwiches. Mon–Fri 6am–5pm, Sat & Sun 7am–5pm.

COFFEE

★ Black Fox Coffee Co 70 Pine St, between Pearl and William sts ☎ 212 945 0528, ⓦ blackfoxcoffee.com; subway #2, #3 to Wall St; map p.44. Housed in the lobby of an Art Deco icon, with an appropriately spacious and sophisticated interior, this Australian-influenced café offers a menu of gourmet roasts, including Melbourne's Small Batch Roasting Co (all served in jet-black mugs). Mon–Fri 6.30am–6pm, Sat 8am–2pm.

Bluestone Lane 30 Broad St (enter on New St, at Exchange Place) ☎ 646 684 3771, ⓦ bluestonelaneny .com; subway #4, #5 to Wall St; map p.44. Another Australian-influenced chain taking New York by storm; this branch of *Bluestone* occupies the Art Deco Continental Bank Building, with a circular wooden bench within a former revolving door adding character. Quality espresso drinks – including "flat whites", "long blacks" and hot Milo. Mon–Fri 7am–5.30pm, Sat & Sun 8am–5pm.

FRENCH

★ Augustine Beekman Hotel, Beekman St, at Nassau St ☎ 212 375 0010, ⓦ augustineny.com; subway #2, #3 to Wall St; map p.44. Famed NY restaurateur Keith McNally's *Beekman Hotel* outpost is one of his best so far, a fittingly elegant space with an enticing brasserie-type menu, blending French and American flavours; think posh burgers with Comté cheese and *frites* ($27), duck *à l'orange* ($33) and *porc calvados* ($27). Mon–Thurs 7.30am–11pm, Fri 7.30am–midnight, Sat 10am–midnight, Sun 10am–10pm.

★ Le District Brookfield Place, 225 Liberty St ☎ 212 981 8588, ⓦ ledistrict.com; subway R, W to Cortlandt St, #4, #5 to Fulton St; map p.44. Opened in 2015 inside Brookfield Place, this French-themed food court features four restaurants and three themed areas ("market", "café" and "garden") with counters selling cheese, seafood, fruit, pastries, cookies, sandwiches, crêpes, and even rotisserie chicken ($16 for half a bird). You can grab a stool inside, snack in the atrium or sit by North Cove, just outside. Mon–Fri 7.30am–11pm, Sat 8am–11pm, Sun 8am–10pm.

ITALIAN

Acqua at Peck Slip 21 Peck Slip, at Water St ☎ 212 349 4433, ⓦ acquarestaurantnyc.com; subway A, C, J, Z, #2, #3, #4, #5 to Fulton St; map p.44. Most authentic Italian food downtown, served in a bright, exposed-brick dining room; home-made, local and Italian ingredients make for excellent pastas ($15–28) and pizzas ($14–18). Close to Seaport District NYC, but not touristy. Daily noon–midnight.

Adrienne's Pizzabar 54 Stone St ☎ 212 248 3838, ⓦ adriennespizzabarnyc.com; subway #2, #3 to Wall St; map p.44. One of the better restaurants downtown, with outdoor seating in summer. The food is fantastic; "old-fashioned" square pizzas come with red ($25) or white ($26) sauces and a huge variety of add-your-own toppings ($2–6), from sun-dried tomatoes to sausage and meatballs (standard 12in round pizzas $15–23). Mon–Sat 11am–midnight, Sun 11am–10pm.

★ Eataly NYC Downtown 3/F, 4 World Trade Center, 101 Liberty St, at Church St ☎ 212 897 289, ⓦ eataly .com; subway R, W to Cortlandt St; map p.44. Downtown outpost of Mario Batali's posh Italian food court (p.392), with a variety of sit-down and takeaway options. *Osteria della Pace* serves southern Italian dishes (pastas $20–26; mains such as roasted lamb loin $34); there's an excellent bakery, *La Focacceria* (pizza slices from $2.90; peach bread $3.90); and *Caffè Lavazza* serves quality coffee, breakfasts and pastries. Daily 7am–11pm.

JAPANESE

Nobu Downtown 195 Broadway, between Dey and Fulton sts ☎ 212 219 0500, ⓦ noburestaurants.com; subway A, C, #4, #5 to Fulton St; map p.44. Nobu Matsuhisa's iconic restaurant moved to this luxurious space in the Financial District in 2017, but still serves superlative Japanese cuisine. Try the black cod with miso ($38) or rock shrimp tempura ($27). Mon–Wed 11.30am–2.15pm & 5.30–10.15pm, Thurs & Fri 11.30am–2.15pm & 5.30–11.15pm, Sat 5.30–11.15pm, Sun 5.30–10.15pm.

22

TRIBECA

AMERICAN

Bubby's 120 Hudson St, between Franklin and N Moore sts ☎ 212 219 0666, ⓦ bubbys.com; subway #1 to Franklin St; map p.64. A relaxed place serving American comfort food, like matzo-ball soup ($12) and shaved rare roast beef sandwich ($20). It's the pies, though, that really pull in the crowds – try a slice of the banana cream or local apple ($7). Mon–Thurs & Sun 8am–10pm, Fri & Sat 8am–11pm.

The Odeon 145 West Broadway, at Thomas St ☎ 212

TOP 5 BURGERS

Corner Bistro West Village. See p.295
Diner Williamsburg, Brooklyn. See p.318
Emily Clinton Hill. See p.320
Minetta Tavern West Village. See p.295
Shake Shack Flatiron District. See p.302

22

233 0507, ⓦ theodeonrestaurant.com; subway #1, #2, #3 to Chambers St; map p.64. Keith McNally's original restaurant was a 1980s icon – it featured in Jay McInerney's *Bright Lights, Big City*. It's having a renaissance mainly thanks to the Condé Nast crowd (who work nearby), but its French and American standards (from *moules frites* to steaks; $23–40) and Art Deco bar are definitely worth savouring. Mon & Tues 8am–11pm, Wed–Fri 8am–midnight, Sat 10am–midnight, Sun 10am–11pm.

★**Square Diner** 33 Leonard St, at Varick St ⓣ 212 925 7188, ⓦ squaredinernewyorkcity.com; subway #1 to Franklin St; map p.64. Opened in 1922, this is one of Manhattan's last remaining old-fashioned diners – eat here while you can. Set inside a vintage train car, with wood-panelled walls and reddish vinyl booths, the menu features Greek (lamb gyros; $9) and American classics (reuben sandwich $16; meat loaf $15.75). Cash only. Mon–Fri 6am–9pm, Sat & Sun 7.30am–4pm.

Tribeca Grill 375 Greenwich St, at Franklin St ⓣ 212 941 3900, ⓦ myriadrestaurantgroup.com; subway #1 to Franklin St; map p.64. The *Grill* is part-owned by Robert de Niro, but it's really the food – fine American cooking with Asian and Italian accents – that takes centre stage. The setting is attractive, too: an airy, brick-walled eating area in a 1905 warehouse, around a central Tiffany-designed bar. Main dishes range $24 to $42 (for the steak). Mon–Thurs 11.30am–10pm, Fri 11.30am–11.30pm, Sat 5.30–11.30pm, Sun 11am–10pm.

AUSTRIAN/GERMAN

Blaue Gans 139 Duane St, between Church St and W Broadway ⓣ 212 571 8880, ⓦ kurtgutenbrunner.com /restaurants/blaue-gans; subway A, C, #1, #2, #3 to

Chambers St; map p.64. Poster-filled walls and a long bar made of zinc add personality to this bright Austro-German restaurant, with tasty schnitzels, goulash and fresh trout (main dishes $18–30) the highlights of Chef Kurt Gutenbrunner's menu. The beer selection includes some unusual – and tasty – German draughts. Mon–Sat 11am–midnight.

COFFEE

Laughing Man Coffee 184 Duane St, between Hudson and Greenwich sts ⓣ 212 680 1111, ⓦ laughingman foundation.org; subway #1, #2, #3 to Chambers St; map p.64. Tiny takeaway counter (there are some chairs outside) established by actor Hugh Jackman and friends in 2011, serving gourmet espresso blends, all fair-trade certified (flat whites from $5). Though coffee giant Kuerig now owns the brand, a portion of the profits is still donated to Jackman's charitable foundation. Mon–Fri 6.30am–6pm, Sat & Sun 7am–6pm.

FRENCH

Maman 211 W Broadway, at Franklin St ⓣ 646 882 8682, ⓦ mamanyc.com; subway 1 to Franklin St; map p.64. Popular bakery and café inspired by the south of France (one of the founders is award-winning French chef Armand Arnal), with dishes such as freshly made chicken couscous ($16), quiche ($14), baskets of pastries ($10), croissants ($3.25) and coffee from Toby's Estate in Brooklyn. Leave room for the nutty chocolate chip cookie ($4.50). Mon–Fri 7am–6pm, Sat & Sun 8am–6pm.

ITALIAN

★**Locanda Verde** 377 Greenwich St, at N Moore St ⓣ 212 925 3797, ⓦ locandaverdenyc.com; subway #1 to Franklin St; map p.64. This casual Italian *taverna* is a showcase for star chef Andrew Carmellini's exceptional creations; try the *porchetta* sandwich (lunch only; $24), roast duck ($38), or his fabulous pastas ($25–28). Mon–Thurs 7–11am, 11.30am–3pm & 5.30–11pm, Fri 7–11am, 11.30am–3pm & 5.30–11.30pm, Sat 8am–3pm & 5.30–11.30pm, Sun 8am–3pm & 5.30–11pm.

SOHO

Soho's foodie scene is expected to get a major boost from the opening of **Smorgasburg SoHo**, an outpost of the celebrated Brooklyn food market (ⓦ smorgasburg.com; p.392), at 76 Varick St (at Canal St). Indoor and outdoor stalls should be open year-round (daily 11am–9pm) by 2018.

AMERICAN

Aquagrill 210 Spring St, at Sixth Ave ⓣ 212 274 0505, ⓦ aquagrill.com; subway C, E to Spring St; map p.64. The expensive seafood at this cosy Soho spot is incredibly fresh. Russian Osetra caviar chimes in at $185 per ounce, or try the grilled yellowfin tuna for a comparative bargain at $32. The excellent raw bar and weekend brunch dishes are

cheaper ($16–19.50). Mon–Thurs 11.30am–10pm, Fri 11.30am–11pm, Sat 11am–11pm, Sun 11am–10pm.

★**Black Tap** 529 Broome St, between Sullivan and Thompson sts ⓣ 917 639 3089, ⓦ blacktapnyc.com; subway C, E to Spring St; map p.64. The burgers here are fabulous ($14–19), but long lines form outside for the notorious "crazy milkshakes" – outlandish creations that would make Willy Wonka proud. The "Sweet N' Salty" is a concoction of chocolate gems, peanut butter cups, pretzel rods, chocolate-covered pretzels, whipped cream and chocolate drizzle. Sun–Wed 11am–midnight, Thurs–Sat 11am–1am.

Cupping Room Café 359 W Broadway, between Broome and Grand sts ☎ 212 925 2898, ⓦ cupping roomcafe.com; subway A, C, E to Canal St; map p.64. Snuggle in at this affordable American bistro for comfort food, but avoid visiting at weekends – the brunch queue can stretch around the block. Good bets are the vast choice of salads ($14–20) or the juicy Pat LaFreida burger ($14). Live music on Wed–Sat nights. Mon–Thurs & Sun 8am–10pm, Fri & Sat 8am–12.30am.

★ **The Dutch** 131 Sullivan St, at Prince St ☎ 212 677 6200, ⓦ thedutchnyc.com; subway C, E to Spring St; map p.64. Andrew Carmellini shook up the Soho scene with this American bistro, with locally sourced produce and seasonal salads accompanying steaks, shellfish, hefty sandwiches, flavourful chilli, wildly popular fried chicken and freshly baked pies (dinner mains $25–36). Mon–Thurs 11.30am–3pm & 5.30–11pm, Fri 11.30am–3pm & 5.30–11.30pm, Sat 10am–3pm & 5.30–11.30pm, Sun 10am–3pm & 5.30–11pm.

Lure Fishbar 142 Mercer St at Prince St ☎ 212 431 7676, ⓦ lurefishbar.com; subway N, R, W to Prince St; map p.64. Stylish seafood restaurant and sushi bar, with a posh nautical interior and everything from steamed red snapper ($36) and crispy calamari ($18), to sushi rolls ($8–22) and clam chowder ($16) on the menu. Mon–Thurs 11.30am–11pm, Fri & Sat 11.30am–midnight, Sun 11.30am–10pm.

Mercer Kitchen Mercer Hotel, 99 Prince St, at Mercer St ☎ 212 966 5454, ⓦ themercerkitchen.com; subway N, R, W to Prince St; map p.64. This café and dimly lit cellar restaurant entices hotel guests and scenesters alike with its casual modern American creations and wood-burning oven; think raw tuna and wasabi pizza, fine steaks, burgers and slow-cooked salmon. With most dishes ranging from $14 to $30, this is one of the cheaper members of the Jean-Georges (see p.313) stable, and a good choice for Sunday brunch. Mon–Thurs 7am–midnight, Fri & Sat 7am–1am, Sun 7am–4pm.

EAST ASIAN

★ **Blue Ribbon Sushi** 119 Sullivan St, between Prince and Spring sts ☎ 212 343 0404, ⓦ blueribbon restaurants.com; subway C, E to Spring St; map p.64. Widely considered one of the best sushi restaurants in New York, with fish flown in daily from Japan and sushi master Toshi Ueki at the helm. Sip cold sake and feast on the outstanding oysters at the raw bar. Sushi platters from $28. Daily noon–2am.

Kelley and Ping 127 Greene St, between Prince and Houston sts ☎ 212 228 1212, ⓦ kelleyandping.com;

subway N, R, W to Prince St; map p.64. Sleek pan-Asian tearoom and restaurant that serves tasty bowls of Thai and Malaysian curry ($16) and other dishes at moderate prices ($14.50–17). Dark wood cases filled with Thai herbs and cooking ingredients add to the informal, street market-esque ambience. Mon–Wed & Sun 11.30am–5pm & 5.30–10pm, Thurs–Sat 11.30am–5pm & 5.30–11pm.

Omen Azen 113 Thompson St, between Prince and Spring sts ☎ 212 925 8923, ⓦ omen-azen.com; subway C, E to Spring St; map p.64. Traditional Kyoto-style restaurant with beautiful crockery and menus made from rice paper. Though named for its famous udon noodle soup ($23.50), it also serves some of the best sashimi in the area (mixed sashimi platter; $36.50), with a rotating seasonal menu and an extensive sake list. Daily 6pm–midnight.

FRENCH

★ **Balthazar** 80 Spring St, between Crosby St and Broadway ☎ 212 965 1414, ⓦ balthazarny.com; subway #6 to Spring St; map p.64. Keith McNally's bistro is still one of the hottest restaurants in town. The tastefully ornate Parisian decor keeps your eyes busy until the food arrives; think fresh oysters ($24 half-dozen), duck shepherd's pie ($31) and *moules frites* ($28), as well as exquisite pastries. Main dishes $17–44. Mon–Thurs 7.30am–midnight, Fri 7.30am–1am, Sat 8am–1am, Sun 8am–midnight.

Raoul's 180 Prince St, between Sullivan and Thompson sts ☎ 212 966 3518, ⓦ raouls.com; subway C, E to Spring St; map p.64. Sexy French bistro seemingly lifted from Paris (the founders actually arrived from Alsace in the 1970s). The food, especially the steak *au poivre* with *frites* ($48), is wonderful, if pricey (mains $26–54) – the service is great too. Reservations recommended. Mon–Thurs 5.30pm–midnight, Fri 5.30pm–1am, Sat 11.30am–3.30pm & 5.30pm–1am, Sun 11.30am–3.30pm & 5.30pm–midnight.

INDIAN

★ **Hampton Chutney** 143 Grand St, between Crosby and Lafayette sts ☎ 212 226 9996, ⓦ hamptonchutney .com subway N, R, W to Prince St; map p.64. Don't let the name deceive you: this place is all about *dosas* and *uttapas* ($8.95–13.95), traditional South Indian food, albeit with plenty of American ingredients. Orders are spiced up with a choice of fresh, home-made chutneys: coriander, curry, mango, tomato or peanut. Mon–Sat 11am–8pm, Sun 11am–7pm.

MEXICAN

Dos Caminos 475 W Broadway, at Houston St ☎ 212 277 4300, ⓦ doscaminos.com; subway #1 to Houston St; map p.64. Real-deal Tex-Mex served with style – try the table-side guacamole ($14.50) or red snapper *ceviche* ($13). Brunch

22

22

TOP 5 COFFEE SHOPS

Coffee is big business in New York, and there are plenty of spots to find baristas elegantly swirling a leaf on the top of a latte. The following pour the best cups in the city:

Abraço East Village. See p.292
Blue Bottle Williamsburg, Brooklyn; also High Line, Chelsea and Midtown. See p.318
Café Grumpy Greenpoint, Brooklyn; also Park

Slope, Chelsea and Lower East Side. See p.318
Mud East Village. See p.292
Stumptown Coffee Roasters Flatiron District. See p.302

should cost you $16–21 per main dish, while dinner mains range between $19 and $29. Mon–Wed 11.30am–10pm, Thurs 11.30am–10.30pm, Fri 11.30am–11.30pm, Sat 11am–11.30pm, Sun 11am–10pm.

SWEET TREATS

Balthazar Bakery 80 Spring St, between Crosby St and Broadway ☎212 965 1785, ⓦbalthazarny.com /bakery; subway #6 to Spring St; map p.64. This bakery (attached to the popular French bistro, see p.283) has wonderful breads (including a walnut loaf for $8) and pastries of all sorts (from $2.50 for the madeleines). They also serve great home-made fizzy lemonade ($3.50), sandwiches ($10–11.25), and hefty slices of cake ($6.50). Mon–Fri 8am–7pm, Sat & Sun 8.30am–7pm.

Chobani SoHo 152 Prince St ☎212 364 3970, ⓦchobani.com/chobani-cafe; subway N, R, W to Prince St; map p.64. Hamdi Ulukaya's wildly popular Greek yogurt company opened a retail outlet in Soho in 2012, selling delectable combinations such as fig and walnut, and cucumber and olive oil ($5.75 for half-bowl; $6.75 for full). Mon–Fri 7.30am–7pm, Sat & Sun 8.30am–7pm.

★**Dominique Ansel Bakery** 189 Spring St, between Thompson and Sullivan sts ☎212 219 2773, ⓦdominiqueansel.com; subway C, E to Spring St; map p.64. The bakery responsible for the "Cronut" craze that

swept NYC in 2013; fans still line up two hours before opening to get their hands on the fried, flaky (and trademarked) delight that's a cross between a donut and a croissant ($5.75), though the buttery DKA ("Dominique's Kouign Amann") is just as addictive ($5.50). Mon–Sat 8am–7pm, Sun 9am–7pm.

Once Upon a Tart 135 Sullivan St, between Houston and Prince sts ☎212 387 8869, ⓦonceuponatart.com; subway C, E to Spring St; map p.64. A good place for a light lunch (sandwiches $12–15) or for real French-style tarts (pecan, chocolate and pumpkin among them, from $8.50). The interior is a bit cramped but intimate and oh-so-quaint. Also plenty of options for vegetarians. Mon–Fri 7am–7pm, Sat & Sun 8am–7pm.

UKRAINIAN

★**Korchma Taras Bulba** 357 West Broadway, between Broome and Grand Sts ☎212 510 7510, ⓦtarasbulba.us; subway N, Q, R, W, #1, #2 to Canal St; map p.64. New York outpost of the popular chain of Ukrainian restaurants founded in Moscow, with servers in traditional costume, live music and a menu that includes favourites such as hearty *borscht* ($12), *pierogis* ($15), home-made sausages ($25) and yes, even chicken Kiev ($24). Sun–Thurs noon–11pm, Fri & Sat noon–midnight.

CHINATOWN

If you're after authentic (not to mention cheap) Chinese or Southeast Asian food in Manhattan, head for Chinatown, where the chaotic streets are lined with dumpling houses and roast-duck window displays. Weekends are especially busy, as New Yorkers come to this neighbourhood for dim sum. Walk down Eldridge Street and you'll see authentic Fujianese fish-ball shops, while Vietnamese food dominates Baxter Street.

BAKERIES

Fay Da Bakery 83 Mott St, at Canal St ☎212 791 3884, ⓦfayda.com; subway J, N, Q, R, W, Z and #6 to Canal St; map p.71. Chinatown is littered with Hong Kong-style bakeries, but this is one of the best. Try the hot dog-like sausage or pork floss buns ($1.35), egg custard tarts (*dan tat* in Cantonese; $1.35) and the fresh mango or green-tea *mochi* rice balls ($1.50). Cash only. Daily 7am–8.30pm.

Hop Shing Restaurant 9 Chatham Square ☎212 267 0220; subway J, N, Q, R, W, Z and #6 to Canal St; map p.71. Offers bargain $2.30 dim sum, but it's their baked goods that

really set them apart from other Chinatown diners; try the pineapple buns (*bo lo bao*) and roast pork buns (*char siu bao*), only $1.10 per bun from the takeaway counter just inside. Sun–Thurs 7am–9.30pm, Fri & Sat 7am–10pm.

CHINESE

Famous Sichuan 10 Pell St ☎212 233 3888, ⓦfamous sichuanofnewyork.com; subway J, N, Q, R, Z and #6 to Canal St; map p.71. Specializing in spicy Sichuan food, with all the classics; fiery bean curd Sichuan style (*mapo doufu*), sautéed string beans, hotpot, fragrant tea-smoked duck and *dan dan* noodles. Most dishes range $16–28. Lunch special sets are just $8.95. Daily 11am–11pm.

Great N.Y. Noodletown 28 Bowery, at Bayard St ☎ 212 349 0923; subway J, N, Q, R, W, Z and #6 to Canal St; map p.71. *Noodletown* is best during soft-shell crab season (May–Aug), when the crustaceans are crispy, salty and delicious (priced seasonally). The Cantonese-style roast meats, *lo mein* (noodles; from $7.50) and soups (from $4.50) are good year-round (try the baby pig on rice for $8.95). Daily 9am–4am.

Joe's Shanghai 9 Pell St, between Bowery and Mott St ☎ 212 233 8888, ⊛ joeshanghairestaurants.com; subway J, N, Q, R, W, Z and #6 to Canal St; map p.71. Probably Chinatown's most famous restaurant, this is really a temple to American-Chinese cuisine (think General Tso's chicken) rather than explicitly Shanghai food, though the classic "soup dumplings" (*xiao long bao*) for $6.25 and seafood dishes ($15.25–30.25) are pretty authentic. Daily 11am–11pm.

★**Laoshan Shandong Fried Dumpling** 106 Mosco St, between Mulberry and Mott sts ☎ 212 693 1060; subway J, N, Q, R, W, Z and #6 to Canal St; map p.71. Identified simply by a "Fried Dumpling" sign in English, this hole-in-the-wall specializes in pan-fried pork dumplings characteristic of northern China, with the absolute bargain price of $1 for five. Squeeze onto a bench inside or take away. Daily 10am–9pm.

★**Nom Wah Tea Parlor** 13 Doyers St ☎ 212 962 6047, ⊛ nomwah.com; subway J, N, Q, R, W, Z and #6 to Canal St; map p.71. Dating back to 1920 but spruced up in 2010, this elegant and old-fashioned dim sum place offers a select menu of tasty snacks, from taro and shrimp dumplings ($4.75) to salt and pepper shrimp ($12.50) and their original egg roll ($7). Sun–Thurs 10.30am–9pm, Fri & Sat 10.30am–10pm.

Peking Duck House 28 Mott St, between Chatham Square and Pell St ☎ 212 227 1810, ⊛ pekingduckhousenyc.com; subway J, N, Q, R, W, Z and #6 to Canal St; map p.71. This chic and shiny-clean restaurant dishes up – you guessed it – duck; the crispy fried birds are carved tableside ($56). Slightly pricier than the competition, but worth it. Sun–Thurs 11.30am–10.30pm, Fri & Sat 11.45am–11pm.

Ping's Seafood 22 Mott St, between Chatham Square and Pell St ☎ 212 602 9988; subway J, N, Q, R, W, Z and #6 to Canal Street; map p.71. While this Hong Kong-style seafood restaurant is good any time, it's most enjoyable on weekends for dim sum, when carts of tasty, bite-sized delicacies ($4–5) whir by every thirty seconds. Offers superb bang for your buck (most mains average $11–20). Mon–Thurs 10.30am–11pm, Fri 10.30am–11.30pm, Sat 9am–11.30pm, Sun 9am–11pm.

Red Egg 202 Centre St at Hester St ☎ 212 966 1123, ⊛ redeggnyc.com; subway J, N, Q, R, Z and #6 to Canal St; map p.71. Modern restaurant serving high-quality American-Chinese favourites (think crispy garlic chicken, orange flavoured beef; mains $13–30) and excellent dim sum; the delicious snacks are made to order and served throughout the day ($2.75–4.75 per order). Don't miss the exquisite coconut pudding served in a coconut shell (serves two; $7). Mon–Fri 11am–11pm, Sat & Sun 10am–11pm.

Tasty Hand-Pulled Noodles 1 Doyers St, at Bowery ☎ 212 791 1817; subway J, N, Q, R, W, Z and #6 to Canal St; map p.71. Fresh, hand-pulled noodles made to order – choose from seven different types, then opt to have them pan-fried ($7–9.75) or in soup ($5.50–10) with pork, fish, beef, chicken, shrimp and several other combos. They also do excellent dumplings (from $4.75 for six). Daily 10.30am–10.30pm.

★**Xi'an Famous Foods** 45 Bayard St, between The Bowery and Elizabeth st ⊛ xianfoods.com; subway J, N, Q, R, W, Z and #6 to Canal St; map p.71. Delicious specialities from northwest China: hand-pulled noodles with chilli oil and cumin-spiked lamb ($10.61) or savoury cumin lamb burger ($5.65) – chunks of succulent lamb stuffed into pitta bread. Now has twelve other locations in the city (see website). Sun–Thurs 11.30am–9pm, Fri & Sat 11.30am–9.30pm.

SOUTHEAST ASIAN

Bo Ky 80 Bayard St, at Mott St ☎ 212 406 2292; subway J, N, Q, R, W, Z and #6 to Canal Street; map p.71. The inexpensive noodle soups ($5–7) are good value at this cramped Chinese–Vietnamese restaurant. The house speciality is a big bowl of rice noodles with shrimp, fish or duck. Daily 9am–10pm.

Sanur 18 Doyers St, at Pell St ☎ 212 233 2288; subway J, N, Q, R, W, Z and #6 to Canal St; map p.71. Don't be put off by the shabby exterior; this Indonesian hole-in-the-wall serves knockout curry with noodles from just $6.95, and breakfast *nasi lemak* for $3.50 (fragrant rice served with anchovies, peanuts, egg and curry). There's a larger restaurant in the basement. Tues–Sun 8am–10pm.

★**West New Malaysia** Chinatown Arcade #28, 48 Bowery, between Bayard and Canal sts ☎ 212 964 0284; subway J, N, Q, R, W, Z and #6 to Canal St; map 71. Tucked away in a dingy arcade, this is one of the best Malaysian restaurants in town, with perfect *roti canai* ($4.50), *laksa* ($8) and crunchy satay sauce. Main dishes $8–27.50. Daily 11am–10.30pm.

SWEET TREATS

Chinatown Ice Cream Factory 65 Bayard St, between Mott and Elizabeth sts ☎ 212 608 4170, ⊛ chinatownicecreamfactory.com; subway J, N, Q, R, W, Z and #6 to Canal St; map p.71. An essential after-dinner stop, though the wondrously unusual flavours are good any time. Specialities include black sesame, taro, green tea, ginger, almond cookie and lychee (from $4.95 for one scoop to $8.95 for three). Daily 11am–10pm.

TEA SHOP

Ten Ren's Tea Time 73 Mott St ☎212 732 7178, ⓦtenrenusa.com; subway J, N, Q, R, W, Z and #6 to Canal St; map p.71. Modern Chinese tea shop owned by the famous Taiwanese tea importers next door, serving all the classic varieties plus tapioca, pearl and bubble teas (from $3–5). Sun–Thurs 11am–11pm, Fri & Sat 11am–midnight.

LITTLE ITALY AND NOLITA

22

Mulberry Street is Little Italy's main drag, and though often crowded, the mostly Southern Italian restaurants and carnival-like atmosphere can make for an entertaining dinner or dessert excursion. It's best not to have high culinary hopes for the neighbourhood, however: Little Italy's many red-sauce restaurants are fair, but not great. In contrast, Nolita is notable for its popular cutting-edge restaurants, which are often packed to the gills with aspiring fashionistas and film-industry hipsters.

AMERICAN

★**Chefs Club Counter** 62 Spring St, at Lafayette St ☎646 438 9172, ⓦchefsclubcounter.com; subway #6 to Spring St; map p.71. Small restaurant with a simple but ingenious concept; it serves some of the world's most popular dishes (by a roster of famous chefs) to eat-in or take away, with each item only available in a limited quantity for a limited time. The rotating menu has featured dishes from the likes of Eric Kayser (ham and cheese baguettes; $9.50) and Jean-Georges Vongerichten (JB burger; $14). Mon–Fri 8am–10pm, Sat & Sun 9am–10pm.

Mac Bar 54 Prince St, between Lafayette and Mulberry sts ☎212 226 0211, ⓦmacbar.net; subway N, R, W to Prince St, #6 to Spring St; map p.71. Celebration of macaroni and cheese, with offerings starting at the classic ($6.99), moving on to the mac stroganoff ($8.25), mac lobsta' ($9.99) and the mac quack ($8.50, with duck confit). Sun–Thurs 11am–11pm, Fri & Sat 11am–midnight.

Parm 248 Mulberry St, between Prince and Spring sts ☎212 993 7189, ⓦparmnyc.com; subway N, R, W to Prince St; map p.71. Sensational Italian-American sandwiches from the dynamic team of Mario Carbone, Rich Torrisi and Jeff Zalaznick – try their Turkey Hero ($14) or Saratoga Club ($14). Dine in or take away. Credit cards only. Sun–Thurs 11.30am–10pm, Fri & Sat 11.30am–11pm.

BAGELS

Black Seed Bagels 170 Elizabeth St, between Delancey and Spring sts ☎212 730 1950, ⓦblackseed bagels.com; subway J, Z to Bowery; map p.71. This bagel specialist has garnered quite a following for hand-rolled, wood-fired creations ($1.50), blending the best of New York and Montréal bagel traditions; toppings range from house-made cream cheeses with beet-cured lox to egg salad and smoked trout. Stumptown coffee served. Mon–Fri 7am–3pm, Sat & Sun 7am–6pm.

CUBAN/LATIN AMERICAN

★**Café Habana** 17 Prince St, at Elizabeth St ☎212 625 2001, ⓦcafehabana.com; subway N, R, W to Prince St; map p.71. Small and always crowded, this Cuban–Mexican diner features some of the best Cuban sandwiches ($12.50) and grilled corn ($7.95) this side of Havana. They also have a takeaway counter next door (*Habana To Go*: daily 11am–11pm) that serves great *café con leche* and tacos/burritos ($6.95–12.95). Daily 9am–midnight.

FRENCH

★**Le Coucou** 138 Lafayette St, at Howard St ☎212 219 3300, ⓦlecoucou.com; subway N, Q, R, W, #6 to Canal St; map p.71. Wildly popular French restaurant from Stephen Starr and acclaimed chef Daniel Rose, a gorgeous space featuring oak tables, antique French doors and a huge mural. Enjoy smoked salmon for breakfast, duck leg confit for lunch (prix fixe of two courses for $48) or *tout le lapin* ("all the rabbit") for dinner (mains $22–52). Mon–Fri 7–10.30am, 11.30am–2pm & 5–11pm, Sat 7am–2pm & 5–11pm, Sun 7am–2pm & 5–10pm.

ITALIAN

Angelo's 146 Mulberry St, between Hester and Grand sts ☎212 966 1277, ⓦangelosofmulberryst.com; subway N, R, W, #6 to Canal St; map p.71. Little Italy's red-sauce restaurants cater firmly to tourists these days, but this 1902 Neapolitan classic is the best place to get a sense of the area's original style, flavours and home-made pastas ($22–26). Mains range $27–36. Tues–Thurs & Sun noon–11.30pm, Fri noon–midnight, Sat noon–12.30am.

★**Emilio's Ballato** 55 E Houston, between Mulberry and Mott sts ☎212 274 8881; subway B, D, F, M to Broadway-Lafayette St; map p.71. Serving some of the best Italian cuisine in the area, Emilio Vitolo's joint has a low-key, clubby atmosphere (popular with celebs like Rihanna and Lenny Kravitz, and ex-presidents – Obama ate here in 2017), a spicy *penne arrabbiata*, tasty spaghetti *vongole* and veal chops so tender they melt in your mouth. Dishes average $18–29. Mon–Fri noon–11pm, Sat 4pm–midnight, Sun 4–11pm.

Lombardi's 32 Spring St, at Mott St ☎212 941 7994, ⓦfirstpizza.com; subway #6 to Spring St; map p.71. The oldest pizzeria in Manhattan (since 1905), *Lombardi's* still serves some of the best pizzas in town, though price hikes have made this an expensive experience (margherita $21.50–24.50; 14in clam pizza $35); there are no slices, and it's often mobbed by tourists. There's open-air dining upstairs. Cash only (ATM on-site). Sun–Thurs 11.30am–11pm, Fri & Sat 11.30am–midnight.

★**Pasquale Jones** 187 Mulberry St, at Kenmare St No phone, ⓦpasqualejones.com; subway #6 to Spring St; map p.71. Laidback, modern Italian diner known for its wood-burning ovens and menu of pasta ($25–26), crispy pizzas ($21–28) and small plates of cuttlefish and white asparagus ($22–23). Larger dishes include the fabulous pork shank for two ($65). Mon–Thurs 5.30–11pm, Fri & Sat noon–3pm & 5.30–11pm, Sun noon–3pm & 5.30–10pm

★**Peasant** 194 Elizabeth St, between Prince and Spring sts ☎212 965 9511, ⓦpeasantnyc.com; subway N, R, W to Prince St, J, M, Z to Bowery, #6 to Spring St; map p.71. A bit of a hangout after hours for city chefs, paying homage to Frank De Carlo's beautifully crafted Italian food such as *agnello con polenta* (lamb chops with polenta; $39), sumptuous pastas ($26–32) and brick-oven-fired pizzas ($16). Tues–Thurs 6–11pm, Fri & Sat 6–11.30pm, Sun 6–10.30pm.

Prince Street Pizza 27 Prince St, between Mott and Elizabeth sts ☎212 966 4100; subway N, R, W to Prince St; map p.71. When the original Ray's closed on this site in 2012, this pizza joint took up the tradition, with its game-changing, utterly addictive SoHo Squares ($3.95), topped with mozzarella and "secret sauce". Sun–Thurs 11.30am–10pm, Fri & Sat 11.30am–11pm.

Rubirosa 235 Mulberry St, between Prince and Spring sts ☎212 965 0500, ⓦrubirosanyc.com; subway #6 to Spring St; map p.71. This contemporary take on Little Italy's classic red-sauce restaurants offers exceptional home-made pastas (black and white seafood tagliatelle; $18), and ultra thin-crust pizzas, from vodka sauce and mozzarella to sausage and broccoli incarnations ($18–28). Sun–Wed 11.30am–11pm, Thurs–Sat 11.30am–midnight.

Vincent's Clam Bar 119 Mott St, at Hester St ☎212 226 8133, ⓦoriginalvincents.nyc; subway J, N, Q, R, W, Z, #6 to Canal St; map p.71. Another Little Italy mainstay since 1904 that serves fresh, cheap and spicy seafood dishes – clams, mussels and squid – with its famous sweet, medium or hot pepper *marinara* sauces (lunch plates $10–15; dinner $12–30). Daily 11.30am–midnight.

★**Zia Esterina Sorbillo** 112 Mulberry St, between Canal and Hester sts. No phone, ⓦsorbillo.it/en; subway #6, J, N, R, Q, W, Z to Canal St; map p.71. Gino Sorbillo, the most celebrated pizza chef in Naples, comes to New York, opening this tiny *pizza fritta* (fried pizza; $11) and pizza (from $7) spot, with a few tables and chairs on the street (and a full pizzeria to follow on the Bowery in 2018). Daily 11.30am–9.30pm.

SOUTHEAST ASIAN

Nyonya 199 Grand St, between Mott and Mulberry sts ☎212 334 3669, ⓦilovenyonya.com; subway B, D to Grand St; map p.71. The food at this Malaysian restaurant is superb, and comes at wallet-friendly prices. Try the *roti canai* (crispy, light bread with curry; $3.95), mango chicken, *mee goreng* (fried noodles) and *nasi lemak*, a Malaysian favourite of coconut rice and curry chicken, or beef *rendang* (most main dishes range $8–15; lunch specials $7.95). Sun–Thurs 11am–11.30pm, Fri & Sat 11am–midnight.

★**Pho Bang** 157 Mott St, between Grand and Broome sts ☎212 966 3797; subway B, D to Grand St, J, Z, #6 to Canal St; map p.71. One of the most popular Vietnamese restaurants in the city, often packed with diners at weekends. The main event is *pho*, Vietnamese beef noodle soup (from $7.50), which comes in several varieties, though the crispy spring rolls ($5.25 for four) and chicken curry with French baguette ($8) are also excellent. Daily 10am–10pm.

Saigon Vietnamese Sandwich 369 Broome St, between Mott and Elizabeth sts ☎212 219 8341, ⓦbanhmi.nyc; subway #6 to Spring St; map p.71. One of the best makers of Vietnamese sandwiches (known as *bánh mi*) in the city. The classic is made with a large chunk of French bread, and stuffed with grilled pork, sausage and thinly sliced pickled vegetables, all for just $6–6.75. Daily 7am–7pm.

★**Uncle Boons** 7 Spring St, between Elizabeth St and the Bowery ☎646 370 6650, ⓦuncleboons.com; subway J, Z to Bowery; map p.71. Hip, contemporary Thai restaurant, with an innovative menu divided simply into small and large plates: from green curry snails with crispy

22

FOOD HALLS AND MARKETS

With the success of Mario Batali's Eataly, opened in 2010, and Smorgasburg, the Brooklyn food fair that debuted in 2011, gourmet food halls and markets are now all the rage in New York. Celebrity chef Anthony Bourdain is planning to open his own "Bourdain Market" (farmers' market, oyster bar, rooftop beer garden and Singaporean hawker-style food stalls) on Pier 57 (Chelsea) in 2018. Below is a list of some of the city's current crowd pleasers:

Chelsea Market See p.391
City Kitchen See p.306
Dekalb Market Hall See p.317
Eataly See p.392
Gotham West Market See p.307

Le District See p.281
The Plaza Food Hall See p.304
Smorgasburg See p.392
Urbanspace Vanderbilt See p.305

FAVOURITE PIZZERIAS

John's Pizzeria West Village. See p.297
Juliana's Dumbo, Brooklyn. See p.317
Lucali Carroll Gardens, Brooklyn. See p.322
Motorino East Village. See p.292
Paulie Gee's Greenpoint, Brooklyn. See p.318
Roberta's Brooklyn. See p.320
Totonno's Coney Island. See p.323

garlic ($13) and crispy dried squid ($14), to crab fried rice ($26) and golden curry with egg noodles ($21). Mon–Thurs 5.30–11pm, Fri & Sat 5.30pm–midnight, Sun 5.30–10pm.

SWEET TREATS

Eileen's Special Cheesecake 17 Cleveland Place, at Kenmare St ☎212 966 5585, ⓦeileenscheesecake.com; subway #6 to Spring St; map p.71. Eileen Avezzano has battled *Junior's* in Brooklyn (see p.317) for title of best cheesecake in the city since 1975; her heavenly version is light and fluffy (whipped) with a graham cracker base. Cheesecake tarts for $4.25, whole cakes from $32 (10in). Mon–Fri 9am–9pm, Sat & Sun 10am–7pm.

Ferrara Café 195 Grand St, at Mulberry St ☎212 226 6150, ⓦferraranyc.com; subway #6 to Spring St; map p.71. The best known and most traditional of Little Italy's coffee houses, this neighbourhood landmark has been around since 1892. Try the New York cheesecake, hand-dipped chocolate cannoli ($6.85) or the gelato served on the street ($5–7; cash only). Outdoor seating is available in warmer weather. Sun–Thurs 8am–midnight, Fri 8am–12.30am, Sat 8am–1am.

★**Rice to Riches** 37 Spring St, between Mott and Mulberry sts ☎212 274 0008, ⓦricetoriches.com; subway #6 to Spring St; map p.71. Rice pudding made hip and utterly irresistible, served up in a variety of sweet flavours, from peanut butter and choc chip to mango and cinnamon. Bowls start at $8.50. The trippy, space-age interior contains a few tables. Sun–Thurs 11am–11pm, Fri & Sat 11am–1am.

LOWER EAST SIDE

The trendy Lower East Side has turned into something of a culinary destination. You'll find some inviting gastronomic highlights here – such as *Mission Chinese Food* – which have garnered dedicated fans for their sophisticated and unusual menus. There are also some terrific little Latin *comedores*, along with some stalwart old-time joints selling Jewish and Eastern European delicacies.

AMERICAN

Cheeky Sandwiches 35 Orchard St, between Hester and Canal sts ☎212 555 5555, ⓦcheeky-sandwiches.com; subway B, D to Grand St, F to Delancey St, J, M, Z to Essex St; map p.82. Visit tiny *Cheeky's* (look for the blue shutters) for fried chicken and gravy between buttermilk scones ($6.50) – they also do a classic shrimp or oyster Po' Boy sandwich ($8.50). Mon–Thurs 7am–9pm, Fri 7am–midnight, Sat 8am–midnight, Sun 8am–9pm.

Classic Coffee Shop 59 Hester St, at Ludlow St ☎917 685 3306; subway F to East Broadway; map p.82. One of the last old-school diners on the east side, open since 1976 (though it was a coffee shop long before that), with seating restricted to the counter or two small tables. It offers a basic menu of sandwiches made by owner Carmine Morales, from grilled cheese to tuna melts ($4–6), plus beloved egg creams. Cash only. Mon–Fri 8am–4pm.

Clinton Street Baking Co 4 Clinton St, at E Houston St ☎646 602 6263, ⓦclintonstreetbaking.com; subway F to Delancey St, J, M, Z to Essex St; map p.82. This former bakery has become one of the city's most popular brunch spots (no reservations), especially noted for its delicious blueberry pancakes ($15). Dinner is just as good, however, and less crowded; try the buttermilk fried chicken and waffles ($19). Mon–Fri 8am–4pm & 5.30–11pm, Sat 9am–4pm & 5.30–11pm, Sun 9am–5pm.

★**Georgia's Eastside BBQ** 192 Orchard St, at Houston St ☎212 253 6280, ⓦgeorgiaseastsidebbq.com; subway F to Lower East Side-Second Ave; map p.82. Not smoked but equally mouthwatering oven-roasted, slow-cooked baby-back ribs ($22), tender pulled pork ($15), crunchy fried chicken ($15) and fried catfish sandwich ($13). Cash only. Daily 11.30am–1am.

Meatball Shop 84 Stanton St, at Allen St ☎212 982 8895, ⓦthemeatballshop.com; subway F to Second Ave; map p.82. The main event is served in sets of four with bread for $9 – choose your meatball (beef, pork, chicken, veg) and the sauce (tomato, pesto, spicy, parmesan, mushroom). Sun–Thurs 11.30am–2am, Fri & Sat 11.30am–4am.

★**Shopsin's** Stall 16, Essex St Market, 120 Essex St ☎917 907 4506, ⓦshopsins.com; subway F to Delancey St, J, M, Z to Essex St; map p.82. Something of a New York institution, Kenny Shopsin ran his famously idiosyncratic diner in the West Village for years (no mobile phones or parties larger than four), but was forced into this tiny space (two tables and counter top) by high rents. His addictive (and numerous) creations – like peanut-butter-filled pancakes – have a loyal following (most filling plates average $15–24). Cash only. Wed–Sat 9am–2pm, Sun 10am–2pm.

Stanton Social 99 Stanton St, between Ludlow and Orchard sts ☎212 995 0099, ⓦthestantonsocial.com; subway F to Lower East Side-Second Ave; map p.82. Chandeliers, lizard-skin banquettes and retro booths draw a young, cool crowd to this 1940s-inspired restaurant-cum-lounge-bar. The tapas-style small plates here are designed for sharing: try the zesty red-snapper tacos with mango salsa or Thai spiced baby back ribs (sliders $8–11; dishes $14–29). Mon–Thurs 5pm–midnight, Fri 5pm–1am, Sat 11.30am–1am, Sun 11.30am–11pm.

BAKERIES

★**Ceci-Cela** 14 Delancey St, between the Bowery and Chrystie St ☎212 274 9179, ⓦcecicelanyc.com; subway #6 to Spring St; map p.82. Cute French patisserie with a stand-up counter as well as tables in the back. The croissants ($2.20) and *pain au chocolat* ($2.70) are divine, as are the brie baguettes ($3.75). Sun–Thurs 8am–8pm, Fri & Sat 8am–9pm.

Kossar's Bialys 367 Grand St, at Essex St ☎212 473 4810, ⓦ kossars.com; F to Delancey St, J, M, Z to Essex St; map p.82. This generations-old kosher treasure (opened in 1936 and moved here in 1960) serves, bar none, the city's best *bialys* ($1), a flattened savoury dough traditionally topped with onion or garlic; the bagels ($1) aren't far behind. Daily 6am–8pm.

Yonah Schimmel Knish Bakery 137 E Houston St, between Forsyth and Eldridge ☎212 477 2858, ⓦknishery.com; subway F to Lower East Side-Second Ave; map p.82. The fine *knishes* ($3.75–4.75), rounds of vegetable-, cheese- or potato-and-meat-stuffed dough, are baked fresh on the premises at this 1910 store (the chocolate cheese version is legendary), as are the wonderful bagels. Sun–Thurs 9.30am–7pm, Fri & Sat 9am–9pm.

CHINESE

Congee Village 100 Allen St, between Delancey and Broome sts ☎212 941 1818, ⓦcongeevillage restaurants.com; subway F to Delancey St, J, M, Z to Essex St; map p.82. As you exit the rear of the Tenement Museum you'll see this Cantonese restaurant, a shrine to the eponymous fragrant, soupy rice dish served in numerous varieties ($4.95–9.95) and a wide range of other Hong Kong favourites for $10–22. Sun–Thurs 10.30am–12.30am, Fri & Sat 10.30am–1am.

★**Mission Chinese Food** 171 East Broadway ☎212 529 8800, ⓦmcfny.com; subway F to East Broadway; map p.82. Danny Bowien's cultish San Francisco Chinese fusion joint with a menu of small dishes like *char siu* pork cheeks ($13) and rice porridge with trout roe ($16), and large dishes like thrice-cooked bacon ($18) and spicy *mapo* tofu ($16). Mon 5.30–11pm, Tues 5.30pm–midnight, Wed–Sat noon–4pm & 5.30pm–midnight, Sun noon–4pm & 5.30–11pm.

★**Vanessa's Dumpling House** 118a Eldridge St, between Grand and Broome sts ☎212 625 8008, ⓦvanessas.com; subway B, D to Grand St; map p.82. This always-busy Chinese canteen, established by Beijing-native Vanessa Weng in 1999, knocks out various combinations of steamed or fried pork and vegetable dumplings at the bargain price of $1.50 for four. Mon–Sat 10.30am–10.30pm, Sun 10.30am–10pm.

DOMINICAN

Cibao Restaurant 72 Clinton St, at Rivington St ☎212 228 0873; subway F to Delancey St, J, M, Z to Essex St; map p.82. *El Cibao* is the best of a slew of no-frills Dominican restaurants on the Lower East Side. The fare is hearty and inexpensive; the beef, rice and beans (mains $10–12) and huge sandwiches, particularly the Cubano ($6), are bargains. Cash only. Sun–Thurs 7am–2.30am, Fri & Sat 7am–4am, Sun 7am–12.30am.

FRENCH

Dirty French 180 Ludlow St, between Stanton and Houston sts, in Ludlow Hotel ☎212 254 3000, ⓦdirtyfrench.com; subway F to Lower East Side-Second Ave; map p.82. Contemporary French bistro from the team behind *Parm* (see p.286), with cleverly enhanced classics such as duck *à l'orange* made with preserved oranges, and brook trout with sesame and dried apricots (mains $26–39). Mon–Fri 7–11am, noon–3pm & 5.30pm–midnight, Sat 7am–midnight, Sun 7am–3pm & 5.30–11pm.

ITALIAN

★**Trapizzino** 144 Orchard St, at Rivington St ☎212 475 2555, ⓦtrapizzinousa.com; subway F to Delancey St, J, M, Z to Essex St; map p.82. Stefano Callegari's *trapizzino* (fluffy triangles of pizza *bianca* stuffed with popular Roman dishes; $6.50) have made a big splash in Rome since he opened his first shop in 2008, with this his first outpost in the US. Fillings include *pollo alla cacciatora* (chicken, garlic, white wine and rosemary) and *zucca e mandorle* (butternut squash, toasted almonds and pecorino romano). Mon–Thurs 11am–11pm, Fri & Sat 11am–3am, Sun 11am–10pm.

JAPANESE

★**Ivan Ramen** 25 Clinton St, between Stanton and Houston sts ☎646 678 3859, ⓦivanramen.com; subway F to Delancey St, J, M, Z to Essex St; map p.82. Chef Ivan Orkin (who also runs restaurants in Tokyo) helms this popular ramen noodle joint adorned with a huge *papier-mâché* mural. Menu highlights include the sesame noodles ($17), the spicy red chilli ramen ($16) and the steamed pork buns ($10). Sun–Thurs 12.30–10pm, Fri & Sat 12.30–11pm.

22

22

JEWISH

Katz's Deli 205 E Houston St, at Ludlow St ☎ 212 254 2246, ⓦ katzsdelicatessen.com; subway F to Lower East Side-Second Ave; map p.82. Jewish stalwart (opened in 1888), *Katz's* overstuffed pastrami ($21.45) or dry-cured corned beef sandwiches ($20.45) should keep you going for about a week. The egg creams are also delicious ($3.95). Famous faux-gasm scene from *When Harry Met Sally* was shot here. Mon–Wed 8am–10.45pm, Thurs 8am–2.45am, Fri 8am–Sun 10.45pm, open 24hr.

★**Russ & Daughters Café** 127 Orchard St, between Delancey and Rivington sts ☎ 212 475 4880, ⓦ russand daughterscafe.com; subway F, J, M, Z to Delancey St-Essex St; map p.82. The original Manhattan gourmet shop (set up in 1914 to sate the appetites of homesick immigrant Jews with smoked fish) opened this excellent café in 2014, and now sells amazing hand-rolled bagels (smoked salmon from $16), knishes ($8), pickled herring ($9) and classics like sturgeon, eggs and onions ($19). Mon–Fri 10am–10pm, Sat & Sun 8am–10pm.

Sammy's Roumanian Steakhouse 157 Chrystie St, at Delancey St ☎ 212 673 0330; subway B, D to Grand St, Z to Bowery, F to Lower East Side-Second Ave; map p.82. This cramped Jewish steakhouse (there's not much specifically Romanian on the menu these days) offers much more than just dinner, including schmaltzy songs from hilarious curmudgeon Dani Luv, delicious-but-heartburn-inducing food (chopped liver, *schmaltz* aka rendered fat on the mash and massive steaks), and vodka chilled in blocks of ice (bottles can cost up to $125, so beware). "Broilings" (huge meat plates $25.95–46.95) and *prix fixe* menu from $55, but be aware that lots of extras get added to the bill (weekend cover charge is around $5). Sun–Thurs 4–9.30pm, Fri & Sat 4–11pm.

SWEET TREATS

10Below 132 Allen St, between Rivington and Delancey sts ☎ 646 861 2040, ⓦ 10belowicecream.com; F to Delancey St, J, M, Z to Essex St; map p.82. Wildly popular mini-chain specializing in Thai-syle rolled ice cream – servers roll your choice of ingredients (flavours range from cookies and cream to fresh avocado with Himalayan salt) with *crème anglaise* (light custard) on ice-cold metal plates in front of you, a gimmicky and laborious process that results in a silky-smooth treat, with cookie, fruit, and graham cracker toppings (just one size; $7). Sun–Thurs 1–10pm, Fri & Sat 1–11.30pm.

Doughnut Plant 379 Grand St, between Essex and Norfolk sts ☎ 212 505 3700, ⓦ doughnutplant.com; subway F, J, M, Z to Delancey St-Essex St; map p.82. Also in Chelsea Hotel (see p.111). Serious (and seriously delicious) donuts ($2.75–4); be sure to sample the seasonal flavours and glazes, including chestnut cake, pumpkin and matcha green tea. Sun–Thurs 6.30am–8pm, Fri & Sat 6.30am–9pm.

Il Laboratorio del Gelato 188 Ludlow St, at E Houston St ☎ 212 343 9922, ⓦ laboratoriodelgelato.com; subway F to Lower East Side-Second Ave; map p.82. This shrine to cream and sugar (with an espresso bar) serves up around 48 flavours, including basil, lavender and avocado (scoops $4.50–7). Mon–Thurs 7.30am–10pm, Fri 7.30am–midnight, Sat 10am–midnight, Sun 10am–10pm.

Morgenstern's Finest Ice Cream 2 Rivington St, at the Bowery ☎ 212 209 7684, ⓦ morgensternsnyc.com; subway J, Z to Bowery; map p.82. Helmed by Nick Morgenstern, this small shop has a 1950s vibe and some incredibly innovative flavours, from Sichuan chocolate and a jet black "coconut ash", to delicious salted pretzel and salt & pepper pine nut (cups and cones $4.50–8.50). Sun–Thurs 8am–11pm, Fri & Sat 8am–midnight.

Pop Karma 95 Orchard St, between Delancey and Broome sts ☎ 917 675 7450, ⓦ popkarma.com; subway F, J, M, Z to Delancey St-Essex St; map p.82. Artisanal popcorn store, using organic corn and crazy flavours such as "zen cheddar", Mediterranean and porcini. Bags $4.50–10. Mon–Fri 11am–7pm, Sat & Sun 11am–6pm.

★**Sugar Sweet Sunshine** 126 Rivington St, between Essex and Norfolk sts ☎ 212 995 1960, ⓦ sugarsweet sunshine.com; subway F, J, M, Z to Delancey St-Essex St; map p.82. Pudding lovers will be in serious danger at this fabulous bakery, established by two ex-employees of *Magnolia* (see p.298). Choose shots ($3) or cups ($5–7) of banana, choc chip or pumpkin puddings, as well as delectable cupcakes ($2.50) and other treats. Mon–Thurs 8am–10pm, Fri 8am–11pm, Sat 10am–11pm, Sun 10am–7pm.

VEGETARIAN

Dirt Candy 86 Allen St, between Grand and Broome sts ☎ 212 228 7732, ⓦ dirtcandynyc.com; subway F to Delancey St, J, M, Z to Essex St; map p.82. Inventive and beautifully presented vegetarian dishes from lauded chef Amanda Cohen; think Korean fried broccoli ($8), Brussels sprout tacos ($30) and carrot sliders on carrot buns ($13). All dishes can be made vegan. Tues–Fri 5.30–11pm, Sat 11am–3pm & 5.30–11pm, Sun 11am–3pm.

THE EAST VILLAGE

The vast range of culinary options makes dining in this neighbourhood a real pleasure: you can sample dishes at the handful of Polish or Ukrainian restaurants; hit one of the numerous Japanese ramen bars around East 9th Street, aka "Little Tokyo"; try Filipino or Venezuelan food; savour real southern barbecue; or pay homage to cult celebrity chefs such as David Chang and Alex Stupak.

AMERICAN

Crif Dogs 113 St Mark's Place, between First Ave and Ave A ☎ 212 614 2728, ⓦ crifdogs.com; subway #6 to Astor Place; map p.88. Hot-dog aficionados swear by these naturally-smoked, shiny wieners bursting with flavour ($4.50), enjoyed Philly-steak style, smothered in cheese ($6.50), or the Chihuahua, topped with avocado and bacon ($6.50). Sun–Thurs noon–2am, Fri & Sat noon–4am.

★ **Graffiti Food & Wine Bar** 244 E 10th St, between First and Second aves ☎ 212 677 0695, ⓦ graffitinyc .com; subway #6 to Astor Place; map p.88. Pastry chef Jehangir Mehta cooks up a fusion of Chinese, American and Indian flavours in this artsy space, with just four tables and small plates ranging $9–17: pickled ginger scallops and cumin eggplant buns grace the menu. Tues & Sun 5.30–10.30pm, Wed–Sat 5.30–11.45pm.

Lafayette 380 Lafayette St, at Great Jones St ☎ 212 533 3000, ⓦ lafayetteny.com; subway #6 to Bleecker St; map p.88. This huge French brasserie from Andrew Carmellini is a great place to soak up New York's brunch scene, with everything from smoked trout ($30) and *moules frites* ($28) to lemon pancakes ($20) and goat's cheese ravioli ($26). The takeaway pastry counter is also one of the best in the city, with bread, croissants, cookies and tiny cakes. Mon–Wed 8am–10.30pm, Thurs–Sat 8am–11pm, Sun 8am–10pm.

Liquiteria 170 Second Ave, at E 11th St ☎ 212 358 0300, ⓦ liquiteria.com; subway #6 to Astor Place; map p.88. The smoothies here are by far the best in Manhattan (try the "Bulldozer" with peanut butter and vanilla almond milk; $8). There are over thirty combos, and loads of supplement shots. You can also get delicious, healthy breakfasts and lunches such as oatmeal with fresh fruit (from $5.50) or açaí berry bowls ($8–9). Mon–Fri 7am–9pm, Sat & Sun 9am–7pm.

Luke's Lobster 93 E 7th St, between First Ave and Avenue A ☎ 212 387 8487, ⓦ lukeslobster.com; subway #6 to Astor Place; map p.88. Maine lobsters come to the East Village; this small place (just eight stools inside) offers classic lobster rolls ($17), crab rolls ($13), shrimp rolls ($9) and thick chowders ($8). Sun–Thurs 11am–10pm, Fri & Sat 11am–11pm.

Mighty Quinn's Barbeque 103 Second Ave, at E 6th St ☎ 212 677 3733, ⓦ mightyquinnsbbq.com; subway L to Third Ave; map p.88. Texas- and Carolinas-inspired slow-smoked barbecue, with a no-nonsense menu of lip-smacking brisket ($9.40), pulled pork ($8.80) and ribs ($9.95), accompanied by burnt-end baked beans (from $3.25). Sun–Thurs 11.30am–11pm, Fri & Sat 11.30am–midnight.

Prune 54 E 1st St, between First and Second aves ☎ 212 677 6221, ⓦ prunerestaurant.com; subway F to Lower East Side-Second Ave; map p.88. This

Mediterranean-influenced American bistro still delivers one of the city's most exciting dining experiences, serving dishes like sweetbreads wrapped in bacon, wild striped bass with cockles, and ricotta ice cream with salted caramel chunks (dinner mains range $25–33). Mon–Fri 5.30–11pm, Sat & Sun 10am–3.30pm & 5.30–11pm.

Sarita's Mac & Cheese 345 E 12th St, between Second and First aves ☎ 212 358 7912, ⓦ smacnyc.com; subway L to First Ave; map p.88. Indulge your macaroni and cheese cravings at this no-frills joint, with twelve creative varieties on offer, blending cheddar, Gruyère, brie and goat's cheese with herbs and meats. Pick your portion sizes: nosh, major munch or mongo ($6.25–21). Sun–Thurs 11am–11pm, Fri & Sat 11am–midnight.

★ **Saxon & Parole** 316 Bowery, at Bleecker St ☎ 212 254 0350, ⓦ saxonandparole.com; subway #6 to Bleecker St; map p.88. Named in honour of two racehorses kept in stables that once lined this stretch of the Bowery, this modern American grill is decked out in a rustic barn-like style (check the horse blankets on shelves) but it's the food that really impresses: smoked oysters ($23), horseradish-whipped potatoes and whisky jelly with steaks (from $32), washed down with a celery gimlet ($15). The "s'mores" dessert (warm chocolate pudding, graham cracker, lemon marshmallow and whisky-barrel smoke; $12), deserves its own section. Mon–Thurs 6–10pm, Fri 5–11pm, Sat 10am–3.15pm & 5–11pm, Sun 10am–3.15pm & 6–10pm.

★ **Superiority Burger** 430 E 9th St, between Avenue A and First Ave ☎ 212 256 1192, ⓦ superiorityburger .com; subway #6 to Astor Place, L to First Ave; map p.88. This small hole-in-the-wall, with just six seats inside (designed like old-fashioned school desks), has garnered a cult following for its creative vegetarian burgers. The "superiority burger" (made from grains, beans and a little tofu) is a nutty, juicy delight with cheese ($6), while tofu sloppy joe ($7) comes with broccoli salad and nuts. Add an "Arnold Palmer" (iced tea and lemonade) for $3. Wed–Mon 11.30am–10pm.

CHINESE

Han Dynasty 90 Third Ave, between E 7th and St Mark's Place ☎ 212 390 8685, ⓦ handynasty.net; subway L to Third Ave; map p.88. Outpost of Philadelphia-based chef Han Chiang, serving high-quality (and mostly spicy) Sichuan food like *dan dan* noodles ($8.95), beef tendons in chilli oil ($10.95), and dry pepper chicken ($14.95). Sun–Wed 11.30am–10.30pm, Thurs–Sat 11.30am–11pm.

★ **Momofuku Noodle Bar** 171 First Ave, between E 10th and E 11th sts ☎ 212 387 8487, ⓦ momofuku .com; subway #6 to Astor Place; map p.88. Celebrated chef David Chang's first restaurant, where his most simple creations are still the best: silky steamed pork buns, laced

22

22

with hoisin sauce and pickled cucumbers ($13), or steaming bowls of chicken and pork ramen noodles ($15–17). Mon–Thurs noon–4.30pm & 5.30–11pm, Fri noon–4.30pm & 5.30pm–1am, Sat noon–4pm & 5.30pm–1am, Sun noon–4pm & 5.30–11pm.

Tim Ho Wan 85 Fourth Ave, at E 10th St ☎ 212 228 2800, ⓦ timhowanusa.com; subway #6 to Astor Place; map p.88. This cult dim-sum chain from Hong Kong – famed for being the world's cheapest Michelin-starred restaurant – opened here in 2016, and waits of two to three hours for a table (no reservations) are still the norm (put your name down and go do something else – they will message you). It's worth the wait for aficionados as the quality is very high and it's the closest thing to Hong Kong standards (in Manhattan at least). Feast on steamed shrimp dumplings ($4.50), baked buns with barbecue pork ($4.95), and steamed tofu with fish cakes ($4.50). Sun–Thurs 10am–10pm, Fri & Sat 10am–11pm.

COFFEE

Abraço 81 E 7th St, between First and Second aves ⓦ abraconyc.com; subway L to First Ave; map p.88. Café inspired by Spanish and Italian neighbourhood bars that has developed a loyal following for its high-quality coffee, espresso ($2) and pastries (try the cured olive cookie or thyme lemon shortbread; $2–3.50). Tues–Sat 8am–6pm, Sun 9am–6pm.

Mud 307 E 9th St between Second and First aves ☎ 212 228 9074, ⓦ mudnyc.com; subway L to First or Third Ave; map p.88. A local favourite for its intensely strong fair-trade coffee (from $2.75), which is also sold from orange trucks around town (check for one at Astor Place). You can sit for hours at the café tables or in the back garden and enjoy the good brunch and veggie food as well as rocking tunes. Mon–Fri 7.30am–midnight, Sat & Sun 8am–midnight.

FILIPINO

Jeepney 201 First Ave, between E 13th and E 12th sts ☎ 212 533 4121, ⓦ jeepneynyc.com; subway L to First Ave; map p.88. Creative, hip Filipino food from the folks behind lauded *Maharlika* down the avenue; think chicken with peanut butter gravy ($19), *sisig* tacos ($13), an incredible burger ($17) and really special cocktails (the spray of absinthe is a nice touch). Mon–Fri 5–11pm, Sat & Sun 11am–3.30pm & 5–11pm.

INDIAN

Brick Lane Curry House 99 Second Ave, between E 5th and E 6th sts ☎ 212 979 2900, ⓦ bricklanecurryhouse .com; subway #6 to Astor Place; map p.88. One of the best Indian restaurants in Manhattan, thanks to its wide selection of Brit-Indian favourites, including a tasty onion

bhaji, *biryani*, and some fiery *phaal* curries (mains $17–23). The daily lunch buffet is just $11.99 (noon–4pm). Daily noon–11pm.

ITALIAN

★**Artichoke** 321 E 14th St between First and Second aves ☎ 212 228 2004, ⓦ artichokepizza.com; subway L to First Ave, map p.88. Fabulous late-night pizza slices to take away, with just four choices: sumptuous cheese-laden Sicilian ($4.75), Margherita ($5), crab ($5) or the trademark artichoke-spinach, topped with a super-creamy sauce ($5). Cash only. Daily 10am–5am.

Frank 88 Second Ave, between E 5th and E 6th sts ☎ 212 420 0202, ⓦ frankrestaurant.com; subway F to Lower East Side-Second Ave, #6 to Astor Place; map p.88. A tiny neighbourhood favourite (opened by Frank Prisinzano in 1998), where basic, traditional American–Italian dishes like seared salmon ($18.95) and home-made gnocchi ($14.95) are served at communal tables. Cash only. Mon–Fri 10.30am–1am, Sat 10.30am–2am, Sun 10.30am–midnight.

★**Il Posto Accanto** 190 E 2nd St, between aves A and B ☎ 212 228 3562, ⓦ ilpostoaccantonyc.com; subway F to Lower East Side-Second Ave; map p.88. Nab a spot at a high wooden table at this small, intimate wine bar serving a vast array of Italian reds by the glass. You can easily make a meal from the excellent small plates of pasta ($13.50–17), panini ($8.50–10) and the like. Mon–Fri noon–3am, Sat & Sun noon–3.30pm & 5.30pm–3am.

Motorino 349 E 12th St, near First Ave ☎ 212 777 2644, ⓦ motorinopizza.com; subway L to First Ave; map p.88. Another strong claim to serve the best pizza in the city, Mathieu Palombino's mouthwatering creations include the tongue-tingling *stracciatella* pizza (basil, olive oil and sea salt) and the cherry-stone clams masterpiece (pizzas $11–19). Sun–Thurs 11am–midnight, Fri & Sat 11am–1am.

JAPANESE

Curry-Ya 214 E 10th St, between First and Second aves ☎ 866 602 8779, ⓦ nycurry-ya.com; subway #6 to Astor Place; map p.88. Grab a stool at the marble-top bar at this narrow, slick Japanese curry house for its nine types of freshly made, mouthwatering curry, from slightly sweet classic Japanese to organic chicken and seasonal vegetable ($9–16). Daily noon–11pm.

Hasaki 210 E 9th St, at Stuyvesant St ☎ 212 473 3327, ⓦ hasakinyc.com; subway #6 to Astor Place; map p.88. Some of the best sushi in the city is served at this popular but mellow downstairs cubbyhole. Sit at the bar and the chefs will try to tempt you with a variety of improvised dishes not found on the menu (eight pieces and one roll $30). No reservations. Mon & Tues 5.30–11pm, Wed & Thurs noon–3pm & 5.30–11pm, Fri noon–3pm &

TOP 5 PIZZA BY THE SLICE

New Yorkers are passionate about their **pizza**, but that's where agreement on the topic largely ends. There are many strongly held opinions when it comes to defining a good slice, and one man's mozzarella epiphany is often his neighbour's tasteless cardboard triangle. New York-style pizza was pioneered by Italian immigrants in the early 1900s: Gennaro Lombardi's pizzeria (see p.286) opened in 1905 and three of his staff went on to found *Totonno's* (see p.323) in 1924, *John's Pizzeria* (see p.297) in 1929 and *Patsy's* in 1933. Characterized by its wide, thin slices (often eaten folded in half) and thin, hand-tossed crust, aficionados claim that the flavour of New York pizza crust is due to the purity of the city tap water used to make the dough.

Here are some places to sample New York's countless pizza possibilities.

Artichoke East Village. See opposite
Joe's Pizza West Village. See p.297
L&B Spumoni Garden Brooklyn. See p.323
Patsy's Pizzeria East Harlem. See p.316
Prince Street Pizza Nolita. See p.287

22

5.30–11.30pm, Sat 1–4pm & 5.30–11.30pm, Sun 1–4pm & 5.30–11pm.

Ikinari Steak 90 E 10th St, between Third and Fourth aves ☏ 917 388 3546, ⓦ ikinaristeakusa.com; subway #6 to Astor Place; map p.88. This Japanese steakhouse chain is best known for its lack of chairs (instead there are forty standing stations, and just ten table seats) – lunch deals for a 10-ounce (300g) steak with salad, soup and rice are $22, with other cuts priced by the gram (a 200g or 7-ounce sirloin is just $16 for example). Daily 11am–11pm.

★**Ippudo** 65 Fourth Ave, between E 9th and E 10th sts ☏ 212 388 0101, ⓦ ippudony.com; subway #6 to Astor Place; map p.88. The first overseas outpost of Fukuoka-based "ramen king" Shigemi Kawahara, this popular Japanese ramen shop offers steaming bowls of classic *tonkotsu*-style noodles for $16 in booths and at communal wooden tables, as well as tasty pork buns and roast chicken appetizers. Be prepared for a long wait at weekends (no reservations). Mon–Thurs 11am–3.30pm & 5–11.30pm, Fri & Sat 11am–3.30pm & 5–12.30pm, Sun 11am–10.30pm.

Kenka 25 St Mark's Place, between Third and Second aves ☏ 212 254 6363; subway #6 to Astor Place; map p.88. Heart of the *izakaya* scene in the East Village and a real slice of Shinjuku (in Tokyo), popular with Asian students (no English at the entrance, but menus are bilingual). The theme is early twentieth-century Japan; sit on wooden benches and order small plates of Japanese snacks from the huge menu (average $5–6), and from the massive selection of quality sake. Sun–Thurs 6pm–1am, Fri & Sat 6pm–3am.

Otafuku 220 E 9th St, between Second and Third aves ☏ 646 998 3438, ⓦ otafukuny.com; subway #6 to Astor Place; map p.88. Excellent Japanese hole-in-the-wall, serving generous octopus *takoyaki* balls ($7), various types of scrumptious *okonomiyaki* (savoury pancake; $9) and pan-fried noodles ($8.50). Cash only. Sun–Thurs noon–10pm, Fri & Sat noon–11pm.

Robataya NY 231 E 9th St, between Second and Third aves ☏ 212 979 9674, ⓦ robataya-ny.com; subway #6 to Astor Place; map p.88. *The* place to experience *robatayaki*-style cuisine (the sister restaurant is in Roppongi, Tokyo); choose your fresh ingredients first, then watch as the chef cooks them in front of you, before delivering it to your table via a long paddle. Order vegetables ($6–10) and meats from $8–35. Mon–Thurs 6–10.45pm, Fri–Sun noon–3.30pm & 6–10.45pm.

JEWISH

★**Mile End Delicatessen** 53 Bond St, between Lafayette St and the Bowery ☏ 212 529 2990, ⓦ mileenddeli.com; subway #6 to Bleecker St; map p.88. Montréal-inspired Jewish deli specializing in freshly made Jewish comfort food; expect lots of curing, smoking, pickling and baking. Favourites include the smoked meat sandwich ($15) and the chicken & matzo ball soup ($9). Mon 8am–4pm, Tues–Fri 8am–10pm, Sat 10am–10pm, Sun 10am–4pm.

LEBANESE

Mamoun's Falafel 30 St Mark's Place, between Second and Third aves ☏ 646 870 5785, ⓦ mamouns.com; subway #6 to Astor Place; map p.88. This newly expanded joint (with open terrace and tables outside in the summer) is the best place for cheap, wholesome falafel and *baba ganoush* in the city, with filling veggie plates for $6.50 (sandwiches $6.75), kebabs from $12 (plates) and convenient late-night hours. Mon–Wed 11am–2am, Thurs 11am–3am, Fri & Sat 11am–5am, Sun 11am–1am.

MEXICAN

Dos Toros Taqueria 137 Fourth Ave, between 13th and 14th sts ☏ 212 677 7300, ⓦ dostoros.com; subway #4, #5, #6 to Union Square; map p.88. This authentic, reasonably priced Tex-Mex takeaway (with a few benches inside) attracts plenty of students and long queues at

22

lunchtime. Opt for burritos ($8.95–11.95), tacos ($4.50–5.95) or quesadillas ($7.50–9.95) stuffed with carne asada (steak), carnitas (pork) or pollo asado (grilled chicken). Sun & Mon 11.30am–10.30pm, Tues–Sat 11.30am–11pm.

Empellón Al Pastor 132 St Mark's Place, between First Ave and Ave A ☎ 646 833 7039, ⓦ empellon.com/al-pastor; subway L to First Ave; map p.88. Celebrity chef Alex Stupak's welcoming restaurant focuses on just one dish: Mexican-style tacos al pastor ($5) made with spit-roasted pork shoulder, rubbed with chilli and dressed with salsa and pineapple, all served on house-made corn tortillas. Margaritas are $12. Mon–Thurs noon–midnight, Fri noon–2am, Sat 1pm–2am, Sun 1pm–midnight.

Hecho en Dumbo 354 Bowery, between Great Jones and E 4th sts ☎ 212 937 4245, ⓦ hechoendumbo.com; subway #6 to Astor Place; map p.88. This authentic Mexican diner knocks out wonderful small plates ($13–19) and Mexico City contemporary cuisine such as house-cured beef, lamb shank confit and an innovative selection of tacos, sopes and burritos ($14–17). Mon–Thurs 5.30–11pm, Fri 5.30pm–midnight, Sat 11.30am–4pm & 5.30pm–midnight, Sun 11.30am–4pm & 5.30–11pm.

Otto's Tacos 141 Second Ave, between E 9th St and St Mark's Place ☎ 646 678 4018, ⓦ ottostacos.com; subway #6 to Astor Place; map p.88. No-frills, rustic space for delicious southern California-inspired corn tacos stuffed with carne asada (beef; $34), carnitas (pork; $3) and chicken ($3), all perfectly seasoned and accompanied by chips and guacamole (market price), and churros ($3). Sun–Thurs 11am–11pm, Fri & Sat 11am–midnight.

SWEET TREATS

★ Big Gay Ice Cream Shop 125 E 7th St, between First Ave and Avenue A ☎ 212 254 3500, ⓦ biggayicecream.com; subway L to First Ave; map p.88. The utterly addictive ice cream here has cheekily named flavours including the "salty pimp" (vanilla, dulce de leche, sea salt and chocolate dip); and the "gobbler" (pumpkin butter, maple syrup and pie pieces). Speciality cones are $5.75–6.50. Sun–Wed 11am–10pm, Thurs–Sat 11am–midnight.

★ Momofuku Milk Bar 251 E 13th St at Second Ave ☎ 212 254 3500, ⓦ milkbarstore.com; subway L to Third Ave; map p.88. David Chang's tiny takeaway bakery (opposite his Ssäm Bar) sells a host of sweet treats: thick cereal milkshakes ($6.50), crack pie (oat crust and buttery filling; $6) and compost cookies (pretzels, coffee and choc chips; $2.15). Sun–Thurs 9am–midnight, Fri & Sat 9am–1am.

Spot Dessert Bar 13 St Mark's Place, between Second and Third aves ☎ 212 677 5670, ⓦ spotdessertbar.com; subway #6 to Astor Place; map p.88. Celebrated Thai pastry chef Ian Kittichai has concocted some

irresistible treats for this basement café, decked out in a vaguely East Asian rustic style: "tapas" puddings and cakes might come with sesame pear, persimmon or chocolate green tea (all $9.95), while cupcakes and cookies are equally inventive. There's a smaller takeaway branch a few doors down at no. 5. Sun–Wed noon–midnight, Thurs–Sat noon–1am.

Veniero's Pasticceria & Café 342 E 11th St, between First and Second aves ☎ 212 674 7070, ⓦ venieros pastry.com; subway L to First Ave, #6 to Astor Place; map p.88. An East Village bakery and neighbourhood institution since 1894, Veniero's desserts and decor are fabulously over the top. The ricotta cheesecake ($4.50) and cannoli ($4–4.50) are top-notch, and the home-made gelato (one scoop $3) is some of the best in the city. Sun–Thurs 8am–midnight, Fri & Sat 8am–1am.

UKRAINIAN

★ Veselka 144 Second Ave, corner of E 9th St ☎ 212 228 9682, ⓦ veselka.com; subway #6 to Astor Place; map p.88. This always-crowded Ukrainian diner has been an East Village institution since 1954, offering fine home-made hot borscht (and cold in summer) from $4.95, kielbasa sausage ($17.50), veal goulash ($18.50) and pierogi ($8.50 for four). Daily 24hr.

VEGETARIAN

B & H Dairy 127 Second Ave, between E 7th St and St Mark's Place ☎ 212 50 8065; subway #6 to Astor Place; map p.88. A tiny kosher vegetarian luncheonette since the 1950s, serving home-made soups (bowls $5.50), pierogi ($8.50 for four) and absolutely divine challah French toast ($8). You can also create your own juice combinations (carrot-beetroot, for example, from $4.50). Mon–Fri 7am–11.30pm, Sat & Sun 7am–midnight.

VENEZUELAN

Caracas Arepa Bar 91 E 7th St, at First Ave ☎ 212 529 2314, ⓦ caracasarepabar.com; subway #6 to Astor Place; map p.88. Delicious Venezuelan home-made arepas ($9–9.50) served in a tiny cafeteria (it tends to get swamped at the weekend). Choose from various fillings, from cheeses to shredded beef and chorizo. Daily noon–11pm.

VIETNAMESE

Hanoi House 119 St Marks Place, between Avenue A and First Ave ☎ 212 995 5010, ⓦ hanoihousenyc.com; subway L to First Ave; map p.88. Stylish restaurant with sensational Hanoi-style beef pho (noodles) for $14 and charred Brussels sprouts with chilli ($10), plus delicious Sunday brunch items like pork belly baguette (mains from $9–18). Mon 5.30–10pm, Tues–Sat 5.30–11pm, Sun noon–3pm & 5.30–10pm.

THE WEST VILLAGE

Restaurants in the West Village cater to the neighbourhood's many and varied residents – everyone from students to celebrities – so the culinary scene is fairly diverse, from historic Italian coffee shops and pizza joints to farm-to-table American restaurants and elegant sushi spots. You'll find loads of takeaways and places with cheapish prix-fixe meals around New York University; many offer poke bowls (Hawaiian raw fish salad), one of the latest culinary fads. Farther west, dining rooms get snazzier, menus more interesting and prices higher, particularly beyond Seventh Avenue, where there's a preponderance of French and Italian bistros.

AMERICAN

★ Blue Hill 75 Washington Place, between MacDougal and 6th sts ☎ 212 539 1776, ⓦ bluehillfarm.com; subway A, B, C, D, E, F, M to W 4th St; map p.96. One of the better restaurants in the West Village, lauded for Dan Barber's rustic farm-to-table American and New England fare such as Berkshire pig with curried carrots and striped bass with currant, apple and pine nuts, using seasonal upstate ingredients. Don't skip the rich chocolate bread pudding. You get a choice of two fixed-price options only: four courses ($88), or the Farmer's Feast, six courses for $98. Daily 5–11pm.

★ Chumley's 86 Bedford St, between Barrow and Grove sts ☎ 212 675 2081, ⓦ chumleysnewyork.com; subway #1 to Christopher St; map p.96. This classic speakeasy (with unmarked door) has been reborn as a clubby but hip restaurant, with luxurious leather banquettes and ornate wallpaper. The handwritten menu changes daily, but might include huckleberry duck ($34), cod with smoked coconut jus ($36) and the house burger that features a double patty with bone marrow ($27). Mon–Thurs 5.30–10.30pm, Fri & Sat 5.30–11pm.

Corner Bistro 331 W 4th St, at Jane St ☎ 212 242 9502, ⓦ cornerbistrony.com; subway A, C, E, L to 14th St; map p.96. There's been a pub on this spot since at least the 1870s, but this classic dive incarnation dates from 1961 with cavernous cubicles, paper plates and maybe the best burger in town ($10.75). It's a long-standing haunt for West Village literary and artsy types, with a mix of locals and die-hard fans queuing up nightly for excellent and inexpensive food. Mon–Sat 11.30am–4am, Sun noon–4am.

Gotham Bar & Grill 12 E 12th St, between Fifth Ave and University Place ☎ 212 620 4020, ⓦ gothambar andgrill.com; subway L, N, Q, R, #4, #5, #6 to Union Square; map p.96. Generally reckoned to be one of the city's best New American restaurants; if you don't want to splurge on a full meal, at least go for a drink at the bar, where you can watch the beautiful patrons drift in. The seasonal menu features Niman Ranch pork, miso cod, Maine lobster and more (dinner mains range $19–58; three-course set lunch $38). Mon–Thurs noon–2.15pm & 5.30–10pm, Fri noon–2.15pm & 5.30–11pm, Sat 5–11pm, Sun 5–10pm.

★ Mary's Fish Camp 64 Charles St, at W 4th St ☎ 646 486 2185, ⓦ marysfishcamp.com; subway #1 to Christopher St; map p.96. Lobster rolls, bouillabaisse and grilled whole fish adorn the menu at this small, noisy West Village spot. Go early, as they don't accept reservations and the queue lasts into the night. Definitely one of the best seafood spots in the whole city – you can almost smell the salty air. Dinner mains $22–32. Mon–Sat noon–3pm & 6–11pm, Sun noon–4pm.

★ Minetta Tavern 113 MacDougal St, at Minetta Lane ☎ 212 475 3850, ⓦ minettatavernny.com; subway A, B, C, D, E, F, M to W 4th St; map p.96. This classic restaurant from 1937 is loaded with atmosphere, with old photos on the walls and mural-clad dining room beyond the bar. It was revamped in 2008 by the McNally stable, and now serves fine French and New American cuisine; the Black Label Burger ($33) is one of the city's best, while weekend brunch involves delicacies such as roasted bone marrow on baguette ($24) and pan-seared halibut ($42). Excellent service. Mon & Tues 5.30pm–midnight, Wed noon–3pm & 5.30pm–midnight, Thurs & Fri noon–3pm & 5.30pm–1am, Sat 11am–3pm & 5.30pm–1am, Sun 11am–3pm & 5.30pm–midnight.

Murray's Cheese Bar 264 Bleecker St, between Cornelia and Morton sts ☎ 646 476 8882, ⓦ murrays cheesebar.com; subway A, B, C, D, E, F, M to W 4th St; map p.96. Just down the block from the famous cheese shop, sample buffalo cheese curds ($12), classic mac and cheese ($14) and the gut-busting sensation that is Murray's cheeseburger ($17). Mon & Tues 4–10pm, Wed & Thurs 4pm–midnight, Fri noon–midnight, Sat 11am–midnight, Sun 11am–10pm.

Oatmeals 120 W 3rd St, between MacDougal St and Sixth Ave ☎ 646 360 3570, ⓦ oatmealsny.com; subway A, B, C, D, E, F, M to W 4th St; map p.96. Porridge gets the Village treatment in this tiny shop, selling a variety of delicious steel-cut oatmeal in three sizes ($4.25–7.25); sweet morning classics like the peanut butter banana, or a more savoury treat like fig and gorgonzola. Mon–Fri 7am–5pm, Sat & Sun 8am–5pm.

The Spotted Pig 314 W 11th St, at Greenwich St ☎ 212 620 0393, ⓦ thespottedpig.com; subway #1 to Christopher St; map p.96. New York's best gastropub (and a favourite of Kanye West), courtesy of British chef April Bloomfield. The menu is several steps above ordinary bar food – think crispy pig's ear salad with lemon caper dressing ($18) or smoked haddock chowder ($17) – and the wine list is excellent. Mon–Fri noon–2am, Sat & Sun 11am–2am.

22

22

BAGELS

Bantam Bagels 283 Bleecker St, at Seventh Ave ☎ 646 852 6320, ⓦ bantambagels.com; subway #1 to Christopher St; map p.96. It's a bit gimmicky, but these tasty mini stuffed bagel balls (aka Bagel Stuffins) are mouthwateringly good, served chewy and hot with cream cheese fillings such as traditional, cheddar dijon, bacon cheddar and even sweet chocolate chip. Bagels from $1.50. Mon–Fri 7am–3pm, Sat & Sun 9am–3pm.

CAMBODIAN

★ **Num Pang** 28 E 12th St at University Place ☎ 646 791 0439, ⓦ numpangkitchen.com; subway N, Q, R, L, #4, #5, #6 to Union Square; map p.96. Superb Cambodian-style sandwiches served on freshly toasted semolina-flour baguettes with chilli mayo and house-made pickles; try the pulled Duroc pork ($9.95) or peppercorn catfish ($9.95). Mon–Sat 11am–9pm, Sun noon–8pm.

CARIBBEAN

Miss Lily's 132 W Houston St, at Sullivan St ☎ 646 588 5375, ⓦ misslilysnyc.com; subway #1 to Houston St; map p.96. Friendly servers dish out all the favourites at this super-hip Jamaican-style diner – codfish fritters ($10), curry goat ($27) and jerk chicken ($24) – while reggae and ska tracks create a beach-shack vibe. Mon–Wed 11.30am–11.30pm, Thurs & Fri 11.30am–12.30am, Sat 11am–12.30am, Sun 11am–11.30pm.

CHINESE

Boba Guys 11 Waverly Place, at Mercer St ☎ 415 967 2622, ⓦ bobaguys.com; subway #6 to Astor Place; map p.96. This San Francisco-based bubble teashop has a cult following, with NYU students often lining up for its signature milk teas (iced or hot) with added tapioca balls, almond jelly or grass jelly (all made with premium teas and organic milk). Sun–Thurs noon–9pm, Fri & Sat noon–10pm.

Hao Noodle and Tea 401 Sixth Ave, between W 8th St and Waverly Place ☎ 212 633 8900, ⓦ haonoodle.com; subway A, B, C, D, E, F, M to W 4th St; map p.96. Creative and stylish Chinese regional food (with strong Sichuan and Shanghai influences), from the China-based Madam Zhu stable of restaurants (this is their first US venture). The seasonal menus feature items such as tasty Sichuan chicken ($14), wood ear mushrooms ($8) and eight-spice crispy tofu ($8). Mon–Thurs 11.30am–2pm & 5.30–9pm, Fri & Sat noon–3.30pm & 5.30–10.30pm, Sun noon–3.30pm & 5.30–9pm.

★ **Red Farm** 529 Hudson St, between W 10th and Charles sts ☎ 212 792 9700, ⓦ redfarmnyc.com; subway #1 to Christopher St; map p.96. Local and seasonal produce drive this mega-popular contemporary Chinese joint, with playful dim sum creations like the "pac man" shrimp dumplings ($15 for four), and delectable mains such as the crisp-skin smoked chicken ($29). No reservations – go early or be prepared to wait. Mon–Fri 5–11.45pm, Sat 11am–2.30pm & 5–11.45pm, Sun 11am–2.30pm & 5–11pm.

COFFEE

★ **Caffè Reggio** 119 MacDougal St, between Bleecker and W 3rd sts ☎ 212 475 9557, ⓦ caffereggio.com; subway A, B, C, D, E, F, M to W 4th St; map p.96. Historic Village coffee house dating back to 1927, embellished with all sorts of Italian antiques, paintings and sculpture. Tennessee Williams sipped espresso here (now $2.75) and scenes from *Godfather II* were filmed inside. Sun–Thurs 9am–3am, Fri & Sat 9am–4.30am.

Fair Folks & A Goat 96 W Houston St, between LaGuardia Place and Thompson St ☎ 212 420 7900, ⓦ fairfolksandagoat.com; subway C, E to W Spring St; map p.96. Unorthodox café with a memorable name, serving all sorts of coffees, and featuring two large communal tables plus a variety of apparel and household goods – it's $35/month for unlimited beverages (around $3 per drink otherwise). Mon–Thurs 7am–8pm, Fri 7am–9pm, Sat & Sun 8am–8pm.

Toby's Estate Coffee 44 Charles St, at Seventh Ave ☎ 646 590 1924, ⓦ tobysestate.com; subway #1 to Christopher St; map p.96. Also 125 North Sixth St, Williamsburg. One of a new wave of gourmet coffee shops in the West Village (*Toby's* is a small-batch roaster, with beans sourced from Brazil, Colombia and various African nations), with rich lattes and espressos ($3–3.50), and regular classes on coffee tasting. Daily 7am–7pm.

FRENCH

★ **Buvette** 42 Grove St, between Bleecker and Bedford sts ☎ 212 243 9579, ⓦ ilovebuvette.com; subway A, B, C, D, E, F, M to W 4th St; #1 to Christopher St; map p.96. Exquisite but casual and reasonably priced French restaurant, serving the best egg breakfasts in the city, tempting small plates like salted butter and anchovies and beautifully crafted classics like *coq au vin* and *cassoulet* (mains $14–18). Sit in the garden if it's warm enough. No reservations. Mon–Fri 7am–2am, Sat & Sun 8am–2am.

Cornelia Street Café 29 Cornelia St, between Bleecker and W 4th sts ☎ 212 989 9319, ⓦ corneliastreetcafe .com; subway #1 to Christopher St; map p.96. As much American diner as French café, there is no more comfortable restaurant in NYC. The pastas, salads and weekend brunch offerings are great, and the prices aren't bad either (dinner dishes $14–36). Downstairs is a cabaret featuring jazz, poetry and performance art (same hours). Sun–Thurs 10am–midnight, Fri & Sat 10am–1am.

Tartine 253 W 11th St at W 4th St ☎ 212 229 2611, ⓦ tartinecafenyc.com; subway #1 to Christopher St;

map p.96. The French creations are worth lining up for at this tiny Brittany-inspired bistro and bakery; try the warm onion tart ($14), *bouchée à la reine* (chicken pot pie; $20) and the almond croissants ($3). Cash only and BYOB (no corkage fee). Mon–Fri 9am–4pm & 5.30–10.30pm, Sat 10am–4pm & 5.30–10.30pm, Sun 10am–4pm & 5.30–10pm.

ITALIAN

★**Babbo** 110 Waverly Place, between MacDougal St and Sixth Ave ☎212 777 0303, ⓦbabbonyc.com; subway A, B, C, D, E, F, M to W 4th St; #1 to Christopher St; map p.96. Originally a coach house, this Mario Batali establishment is deservedly touted as one of the best Italian restaurants in the city. Try the "mint love-letters" (ravioli) with spicy lamb sausage ($21) or crispy sea bass ($34), or go for one of the excellent tasting menus ($95–99). Reservations are hard to get (you can book up to one month in advance), so just show up early and either eat at the bar or try for one of the tables along the window they save for walk-in customers (they don't take reservations for those). Mon 5.30–11.15pm, Tues–Sat 11.30am–2pm & 5.30–11.15pm, Sun 5–10.45pm.

Carbone 181 Thompson St, at Greenwich St ☎212 428 6000, ⓦcarbonenewyork.com; subway A, C, E to 14th St; map p.96. Fêted homage to New York's classic Italian American diners, this contemporary joint offers lobster ravioli, spaghetti *puttanesca*, a range of fresh fish and meat dishes (such as pork chops and peppers) and Caesar salad tossed with great aplomb, tableside. It's pricey, though, with most mains $28–65 (pastas $23–28). Mon–Fri noon–2pm & 5.30–11.30pm, Sat & Sun 5–11.30pm.

Faicco's 260 Bleecker St, between Morton and Leroy sts ☎212 243 1974; subway A, B, C, D, E, F, M to W 4th St; map p.96. This old-school Italian butcher serves some of the best-value sandwiches in the city – huge rolls of ham, sausage, and chicken cutlet with aged provolone ($14–16). Add a tangy prosciutto ball for $1.75. Tues–Sat 9am–6pm, Sun 9am–2pm.

Joe's Pizza 7 Carmine St, at Sixth Ave ☎212 366 1182, ⓦjoespizzanyc.com; subway A, B, C, D, E, F, M to W 4th St; map p.96. Classic New York pizza to go ($2.75) since 1975 (founder Joe Pozzuoli is from Naples); nothing fancy, just thin-crust slices, with cheese that tastes like cheese and a rich tomato base – add pepperoni for some bite ($3.50). Daily 10am–4am.

John's Pizzeria 278 Bleecker St, between Sixth and Seventh aves ☎212 243 1680, ⓦjohnsbrickovenpizza .com; subway A, B, C, D, E, F, M to W 4th St, #1 to Christopher St; map p.96. True, this is another tourist bottleneck, but the worn-wooden booths, bright neon-red sign and ramshackle floors are dripping with atmosphere. *Lombardi's* graduate John Sasso opened up here in 1929 – his coal-fired brick oven is still knocking

out super-thin crust, sweet tomato sauce and blistered, gooey cheese pizzas ($17–20, no slices; toppings $4; cash only). Be prepared to wait in line for a table. Daily 11.30am–11.30pm.

Kesté Pizza & Vino 271 Bleecker St, between Jones and Cornelia sts ☎212 243 1500, ⓦkestepizzeria .com; subway A, B, C, D, E, F, M to W 4th St; #1 to Christopher St; map p.96. One of the newer pizzerias on the block, stirring things up with its Neapolitan wood-fired oven and perfect pizzas; try the original Mast'nicola (*lardo*, pecorino romano and basil; $10) or lip-smacking Pizza del Papa (butternut squash cream, smoked mozzarella and artichoke; $21). No reservations. Mon–Thurs 11.30am–11pm, Fri & Sat 11.30am–11.30pm, Sun 11.30am–10.30pm.

JAPANESE

Sushi Nakazawa 23 Commerce St, between Bedford St and Seventh Ave ☎212 924 2212, ⓦsushinakazawa .com; subway #1 to Christopher St; map p.96. High-end sushi from Daisuke Nakazawa, former apprentice of Tokyo sushi legend Jiro Ono. His twenty-course *omakase* tasting menus (from $150), paired with sake, are exceptional, with perhaps the freshest *uni* (sea urchin) in the city. Daily 5–10.15pm.

Tomoe Sushi 172 Thompson St, between Bleecker and Houston sts ☎212 777 9346, ⓦtomoesushi.com; subway #1 to Houston St; map p.96. The nightly queues may look daunting, but there's a good reason to join them: this is some of the best, freshest sushi in Manhattan, and it's affordable to boot (ten pieces of sashimi, five pieces of nigiri and half a tuna roll for $35). There are some seasonal dishes (like a soft-shell crab roll) on the menu, but the fresh fish on offer is what draws the crowds. AMEX and cash only. Sun & Mon 5–11pm, Tues–Sat 1–3pm & 5–11pm.

MEXICAN

★**Empellón Taqueria** 230 W 4th St, at W 10th St; ☎212 367 0999, ⓦempellon.com/taqueria; subway A, B, C, D, E, F, M to W 4th St; map p.96. Mexican tacos with creative flair from Alex Stupak; think tacos stuffed with short-rib pastrami ($22 for two) or fish tempura ($16 for two). The Sunday prix-fixe menu is a good deal: $30 for three courses. Even the salsas ($3) come infused with mashed pumpkin seeds and smoked cashews. Mon–Thurs 5.30–11pm, Fri 5.30pm–midnight, Sat 11.45am–midnight, Sun 11.45am–11pm.

MIDDLE EASTERN

Moustache 90 Bedford St, between Grove and Barrow sts ☎212 229 2220, ⓦmoustachepitza.com; subway #1 to Christopher St; map p.96. A small, cheap spot specializing in "pitzas" (pitta bread pizzas with eclectic toppings) for $12–14; also offers great hummus, chickpea

22

22

and spinach salad ($7–14), and bargain lamb ribs ($18). Sun–Thurs noon–11pm, Fri & Sat noon–11.30pm.

SPANISH

Sevilla 62 Charles St, at W 4th St ☎ 212 929 3189, ⓦ sevillarestaurantandbar.com; subway #1 to Christopher St; map p.96. A Village favourite since 1941, *Sevilla* is dark, fragrant (from garlic), and serves good, moderately priced food ($18.75–42). Try the garlic soup, the fried calamari and the large pitchers of strong *sangría*. Mon–Thurs noon–midnight, Fri & Sat noon–1am, Sun 1pm–midnight.

Tertulia 359 Sixth Ave, at Washington Place ☎ 646 559 9909, ⓦ tertulianyc.com; subway A, B, C, D, E, F, M to W 4th St; map p.96. Chef Seamus Mullen's Asturias *sidrería* (cider house)-inspired vision of Spanish cooking thoroughly deserves the plaudits, with a spread of tapas (black and white anchovies with sheep's-milk cheese, or smoked pig cheek with quail egg; $6–14) and small plates to share ($14–32); the crispy Brussels sprouts with pork belly is a masterpiece. Mon–Thurs 11.30am–3pm & 5.30–11pm, Fri 11.30am–3pm & 5.30pm–midnight, Sat 11.30am–3.30pm & 5.30pm–midnight, Sun 11.30am–3.30pm & 5.30–11pm.

SWEET TREATS

Cones 272 Bleecker St, between Seventh Ave and Morton St ☎ 212 414 1795; subway #1 to Christopher St; map p.96. Wonderful *gelati* by two Argentine brothers. Flavours like tiramisu and rich chocolate attract long queues, especially on warm summer nights (scoops from $4.50–6.65). Daily 1–10.45pm.

Dō 432 550 LaGuardia Place, at W 3rd St ☎ 646 892 3600, ⓦ cookiedonyc.com; subway A, B, C, D, E, F, M to

W 4th St; map p.96. Edible cookie-dough? This magical store has developed a cult following (there's often a queue on the other side of the street) for its various unbaked dough concoctions (using pasteurized eggs and heat-treated, ready-to-eat flour; some vegan and gluten-free options), from choc chip and brownie batter to "unicorn" (sugar cookie) and cake batter (scoops $4–9). Tues, Wed & Sun 10am–9pm, Thurs–Sat 10am–10pm.

Magnolia Bakery 401 Bleecker St, at W 11th St ☎ 212 462 2572, ⓦ magnoliabakery.com; subway #1 to Christopher St; map p.96. There are lots of baked goods on offer here, but everyone comes for the heavenly and deservedly famous multicoloured cupcakes (celebrated in both *Sex and the City* and *Saturday Night Live*); $3.50–3.75 each. Queues can stretch around the block. Sun–Thurs 9am–11.30pm, Fri & Sat 9am–12.30am.

Popbar 5 Carmine St, at Sixth Ave ☎ 212 255 4874, ⓦ pop-bar.com; subway A, B, C, D, E, F, M to W 4th St; map p.96. Handcrafted gelato on a stick (4.50), freshly made with natural ingredients such as banana, chocolate, coconut, hazelnut, mint and pistachio, as well as refreshing lemon, mango and peach *sorbettos* (also on a stick), and frozen yogurt versions ($3.75). Sun–Wed noon–11pm, Thurs noon–midnight, Fri & Sat noon–1am.

VEGAN

Peacefood Café 41 E 11th St, between University Place and Broadway ☎ 212 979 2288, ⓦ peacefoodcafe .com; subway N, Q, R, L, #4, #5, #6 to Union Square; map p.96. Vegan kitchen and bakery in hip, contemporary digs. Offers tasty pizzas (mushrooms, roasted sweet peppers, onions and zucchini from $12.95), tempeh avocado sandwiches ($10.75) and fluffy quinoa salads ($11.95). Daily 10am–10pm.

CHELSEA AND THE MEATPACKING DISTRICT

West Chelsea is one of the more vibrant foodie havens in the city; there are excellent Spanish, Italian and New American spots that have sprouted along Ninth and Tenth avenues, and with the advent of the High Line, it's only getting busier. The rest of the neighbourhood has something for everyone, whether it's a retro diner, an old-school steakhouse or wallet-friendly international eats. There are also a number of great places listed in the restaurants section of the "LGBT" chapter.

AMERICAN

Cafeteria 119 Seventh Ave, at W 17th St ☎ 212 414 1717, ⓦ cafeteriagroup.com; subway #1 to 18th St; map p.107. Don't let the name fool you: *Cafeteria* may be open 24 hours and serve great NY sirloin ($32), meatloaf ($20) and macaroni and cheese ($10), but it's nothing like a truck stop. Expect a smart all-white interior, gold-rimmed mirrors and a fashionable clientele. Daily 24hr.

★**Cookshop** 156 Tenth Ave, at W 20th St ☎ 212 924 4440, ⓦ cookshopny.com; subway C, E to 23rd St; map p.107. Part of the Marc Meyer stable, with ever-busy street-side tables and a menu of seasonal, contemporary

American food – dishes change frequently, but might include dayboat sea scallops, grilled rabbit from the Hudson Valley and Vermont lamb shoulder (most $25–32); interesting brunch choices too ($14–21), and excellent vegetarian options. Mon–Fri 8am–11.30pm, Sat 10am–11pm, Sun 10–10pm.

Lobster Place Chelsea Market, 75 Ninth Ave, between 15th and 16th sts ☎ 212 255 5672, ⓦ lobsterplace.com; subway A, C, E to 14th St; map p.107. A serious expansion has given this Chelsea Market fishmonger not just more space but a full-on bar-restaurant addition, the *Cull & Pistol*, which specializes in oysters and whole lobster.

22

They've also ramped up takeaway options, adding oyster po' boys ($11.50) and crab cake sandwiches ($12.50) to their already sterling renditions of chowder, fresh sushi and lobster rolls. Great for a picnic meal on the High Line. Mon–Sat 9.30am–9pm, Sun 10am–8pm.

The Old Homestead 56 Ninth Ave, between W 14th and 15th sts ☎212 242 9040, ⓦtheoldhomestead steakhouse.com; subway A, C, E to 14th St, L to Eighth Ave; map p.107. Steak. Period. But really gorgeous steak, served in an almost comically old-fashioned walnut dining room by waiters in white aprons. Expensive (most cuts are $44–55; a handful of main dishes $25–45), but portions are huge; there's a burger menu at lunch (starting at $19) if you want to keep things modest. Mon–Thurs noon–10.30pm, Fri noon–11.30pm, Sat 1–11.30pm, Sun 1–9.30pm.

Red Cat 227 Tenth Ave, between W 23rd and 24th sts ☎212 242 1122, ⓦtheredcat.com; subway C, E to 23rd St; map p.107. Superb service, a fine American–Mediterranean kitchen and a warm atmosphere all make for a memorable dining experience at *Red Cat*. It's a big local favourite and popular for dates – book ahead. Mains $26–39. Mon–Fri noon–2.30pm & 5–11pm, Sat 11.30am–2.45pm & 5–11pm, Sun 11.30am–2.45pm & 5–10pm.

★**Rocket Pig** 463 W 24th St, between W Ninth and Tenth aves ☎212 645 5660, ⓦrocketpignyc.com; subway C, E to 23rd St; map p.107. They do one thing – well, maybe there are a couple of small diversions, which can all be overlooked – a messy, smoked pork sandwich ($14), whose accoutrements (red onion jam, for one) help make it one of the city's signature sandwiches. Daily 11am–5pm.

BAKERIES

Amy's Bread Chelsea Market, 75 Ninth Ave, between W 15th and W 16th sts ☎212 462 4338, ⓦamysbread .com, subway A, C, E, L to 14th St; map p.107. Also 672 Ninth Ave, between 46th and 47th sts. Launched by ex-*Bouley* pastry chef Amy Scherber (you can find Amy's breads in fine stores citywide). The grilled-cheese sandwiches ($7.95), made with chipotle peppers, are some of the best in the city. Mon–Fri 7am–8pm, Sat 8am–8pm, Sun 8am–7pm.

Billy's Bakery 184 Ninth Ave, between W 21st and W 22nd sts ☎212 647 9956, ⓦbillysbakerynyc.com; subway C, E to 23rd St; map p.107. Opened by a former employee of *Magnolia Bakery*, though the rustic farmhouse interior is far less crowded and the cupcakes cheaper and just as scrumptious (there are a few other locations as well). Other highlights include a tangy Key lime pie. Mon–Thurs 8.30am–11pm, Fri 8.30am–midnight, Sat 9am–midnight, Sun 9am–9pm.

Empire Cake 112 Eighth Ave, between W 15th and W 16th sts ☎212 242 5858, ⓦempirecake.com; subway A, C, E, L to 14th St; map p.107. Exquisite cupcakes, cookies and takes on old-time favourites like snowballs (cake with custard, covered in icing and rolled in coconut flakes). Mon–Wed 8am–10pm, Thurs 8am–11pm, Fri 8am–midnight, Sat 10am–midnight, Sun 11am–10pm.

Sullivan Street Bakery 236 Ninth Ave, between W 24th and W 25th sts ☎212 929 5900, ⓦsullivan streetbakery.com; subway C, E to 23rd St; map p.107. Also 533 W 47th St, between 10th and 11th aves. A lovely array of freshly made crusty breads is on display here, though there are also panini (such as chickpea and cucumber, or goat cheese and roast chicken; $11–13) and, best of all, *pizze* (crisp and cheeseless; $4/slice). Mon–Fri 7am–7pm, Sat & Sun 7.30am–7pm.

ITALIAN

Bottino 246 Tenth Ave, between W 24th and 25th sts ☎212 206 6766, ⓦbottinonyc.com; subway C, E to 23rd St; map p.107. This popular Chelsea restaurant attracts the in-crowd looking for authentic Tuscan food served in a slick, downtown atmosphere. Pastas average $20, meaty main dishes $22–30. Also has a to-go adjunct that's quite crowded at lunchtime. Mon 6–10.30pm, Tues–Sat noon–3.30pm & 6–10.30pm, Sun 5.30–9.30pm.

Co. 230 Ninth Ave, at W 24th St ☎212 243 1105, ⓦco-pane.com; subway C, E to 23rd St; map p.107. Fashionable spot, one of the new wave of pizzerias in town. Start with a sampling of olives ($6) and an escarole salad ($10), then share a few of the oddly shaped pizzas, like mushroom and caramelized onion ($20), meatball ($23) or a classic Margherita ($18). Mon–Fri noon–10pm, Sat & Sun 11am–10pm.

LATIN AMERICAN

Rocking Horse 182 Eighth Ave, between W 19th and 20th sts ☎212 463 9511, ⓦrockinghorsecafe.com; subway C, E to 23rd St, #1 to 18th St; map p.107. Wash down inventive Mexican cuisine (like enchiladas flavoured by pomegranate; $19) with deliciously potent *mojitos* and Margaritas ($12–14) from the bar. Mon–Thurs noon–11pm, Fri noon–midnight, Sat 11am–midnight, Sun 11am–11pm.

SPANISH

El Quijote 226 W 23rd St, between Seventh and Eighth aves ☎212 929 1855, ⓦelquijoterestaurant.com; subway C, E, #1 to 23rd St; map p.107. *El Quijote* has changed very little over its long history (it needed only a minimal makeover when it appeared in the 1996 film *I Shot Andy Warhol*, though the movie was set in 1968). It still serves decent seafood and fried meats (mains around $30), but the bland paella should be avoided; go more for the old-school feel and the atmosphere than anything else. Mon–Thurs & Sun 11.30am–midnight, Fri & Sat 11.30am–1am.

Txikito 240 Ninth Ave, between W 24th and 25th sts ☎ 212 242 4730, ⓦ txikitonyc.com; subway C, E to 23rd St; map p.107. The rough-hewn interior of this Basque tapas-bar-cum-restaurant feels a little like the inside of a wooden ship – albeit one that serves its passengers crispy beef tongue ($16), octopus carpaccio ($16) and an occasional special of suckling pig ($30). The crisp fries with spicy cod roe mayonnaise ($7) should accompany any order. Mon–Thurs 5.30–11pm, Fri & Sat 5.30–11.30pm, Sun 5.30–10.30pm.

UNION SQUARE, GRAMERCY PARK AND THE FLATIRON DISTRICT

These neighbourhoods are heavily trafficked and are prime spots for restaurants. Some of the city's best dining establishments are in this part of town, the finest of which have come to help define New American cuisine – especially as practised by restaurateur Danny Meyer. There are also plenty of places to grab a cheap meal, not to mention superstar chef Mario Batali's **Eataly** (see p.392), which took New York by storm a few years ago and has inspired plenty of imitators. With restaurants, a beer garden and even cooking classes thrown in, this enormous Italian food market is always thronged with visitors.

22

AMERICAN

ABC Kitchen 35 E 18th St, between Park Ave S and Broadway ☎ 212 475 5829, ⓦ abckitchennyc.com; subway L, N, Q, R, W, #4, #5, #6 to 14th St-Union Square; map p.115. Set inside a well-loved, eclectic home decor store, the interior of this upscale New American joint, spearheaded by superstar chef Jean-Georges Vongerichten, has all the whimsy and boho chic of one of ABC's design showrooms. The all-white dining room sets off superb plates like roast carrot and avocado salad ($17) or roasted hake with squash and chilli garlic oil ($34). Top off the meal with a salted caramel sundae ($14). Mon–Wed noon–3pm & 5.30–10.30pm, Thurs noon–3pm & 5.30–11pm, Fri noon–3pm & 5.30–11.30pm, Sat 11am–3pm & 5.30–11.30pm, Sun 11am–3pm & 5.30–10pm.

★**The City Bakery** 3 W 18th St, between Fifth and Sixth aves ☎ 212 366 1414, ⓦ thecitybakery.com; subway L, N, Q, R, W, #4, #5, #6 to 14th St-Union Square; map p.115. A good place to come for a filling lunch, with plenty of healthy options. Try the kale salad with hazelnuts or the idiosyncratic pretzel croissant for heavy snacking; sweet tooths, meanwhile, should not miss out on the hot chocolate complete with home-made marshmallow, so thick you might need a fork. In February, or "hot chocolate month", there's a new, often unusual, flavour available each day. Mon–Fri 7.30am–6pm, Sat 8am–6pm, Sun 9am–6pm.

The Clocktower 5 Madison Ave, at E 24 th St ☎ 212 413 4300, ⓦ theclocktowernyc.com; subway R, W, #6 to 23rd St; map p.115. There's no shortage of atmosphere at this elegant, clubby spot in the Metlife Building. The food isn't shabby either, with a modern British sensibility informing dishes like quail and pigeon pie ($38), Dover sole ($76) and treacle tart (desserts around $15). Mon, Tues & Sun 6.30–10am, 11.30am–3pm & 5.30–10pm, Wed–Sat 6.30–10am, 11.30am–3pm & 5.30–11pm.

Craft 43 E 19th St, between Broadway and Park Ave S ☎ 212 780 0880, ⓦ craftrestaurant.com; subway R, W, #6 to 23rd St; map p.115. The buzz has mostly come and gone at celebrity chef Tom Colicchio's signature restaurant, making this a relatively relaxed place for some of New York's most inventive food. Popular dishes include roast sweetbreads or foie gras (when available), beef short ribs ($43) and tasty, roasted wild mushroom sides ($15–32). Expect to spend well over $100 per person. Mon–Thurs noon–2.30pm & 5.30–10pm, Fri noon–2.30pm & 5.30–11pm, Sat 5.30–11pm, Sun 5.30–10pm.

★**Eisenberg's Sandwich Shop** 174 Fifth Ave, at W 22nd St ☎ 212 675 5096; subway R, W, #6 to 23rd St; map p.115. A colourful luncheonette, this shop has been serving Reubens (hot corned beef and Swiss cheese sandwiches; $12), tuna sandwiches ($7.50), matzoh-ball soup ($4) and old-fashioned fountain sodas at a well-worn counter since 1929. Mon–Fri 6.30am–8pm, Sat 9am–6pm, Sun 9am–5pm.

★**Eleven Madison Park** 11 Madison Ave, between E 24th and E 25th sts ☎ 212 889 0905, ⓦ elevenmadison park.com; subway N, R, #6 to 23rd St; map p.115. Daniel Humm's contemporary American showcase is housed in a gorgeous Art Deco space, with the set menu $295 for roughly ten delectable courses based on primarily seasonal New York state produce (no printed menus; the servers just explain the options); think a fondue bowl made out of squash, with pretzels used to spoon out the cheese, lavender duck or sea urchin with potato cream. Reservations essential. Mon–Wed 5.30–10pm, Thurs 5.30–10.30pm, Fri–Sun noon–1pm & 5.30–10.30pm.

★**Gramercy Tavern** 42 E 20th St, between Broadway and Park Ave S ☎ 212 477 0777, ⓦ gramercytavern .com; subway R, W, #6 to 23rd St; map p.115. The neo-colonial decor, exquisite New American cuisine and perfect service make for a memorable meal. The seasonal tasting menus are well worth the steep prices ($165 for six courses; the three-course prix-fixe is $125), but you can also drop in for a drink and more casual meal in the lively front room (entrées – Brussels sprouts fried rice, meatballs and the like – $29–36). Main room Mon–Thurs 11.45am–2pm & 5.15–9.45pm, Fri 11.45am–2pm & 5.15–10.30pm, Sat 5.15–10.30pm, Sun 5.15–9.45m; Tavern Mon–Thurs & Sun 11.45am–11pm, Fri & Sat 11.45am–midnight.

22

Hill Country Barbecue 30 W 26th St, between Broadway and Sixth Ave ☎ 212 255 4544, ⓦ hillcountry .com; subway R, W, to 28th St, F to 23rd St; map p.115. Some of the most authentic Texas barbecue in the city, with huge servings of moist, fatty brisket and beer-can game hen, as well as peppery sausage brought in from Kreuz Market near Austin. Grab a table, then order your meats (priced by the pound) and sides (such as macaroni and cheese) from the counters. Daily noon–2am, though kitchen closes at 10pm Sun–Wed, 11pm Thurs–Sat.

★ **No. 7 Sub** 1188 Broadway, between W 28th and W 29th sts, in the *Ace Hotel* ☎ 212 532 1680, ⓦ no7sub .com; subway R, W to 28th St; map p.115. Also 1 W 59th St, at Fifth Ave, in Plaza Hotel (see p.273) and 11 Water Street, Dumbo. Part of the dazzling array of food options available at the *Ace Hotel* (see p.272), this sandwich vendor deals up esoteric combinations that aren't done justice by their lists of ingredients (sample: broccoli, lychee *muchim*, fried shallots); they also offer the fillings with grain salads and have a broccoli taco. The menu changes, but you should do well whatever you choose. Mon–Fri 11am–7pm, Sat 11am–4pm.

NoMad 1170 Broadway, at 28th St, in NoMad hotel ☎ 212 796 1500 or ☎ 347 472 5660, ⓦ thenomadhotel .com; subway R, W, to 28th St; map p.115. The dining area in this fashionable hotel rambles through a glassy atrium, dark bar and clubby parlour room. When a triumphal roast chicken for two, stuffed with foie gras, black truffle and brioche ($89), gets carried through, it's reason to pause, wherever you are. Mon–Thurs 7am–10am, noon–2pm & 5.30–10.30pm, Fri 7am–10am, noon–2pm & 5.30–11pm, Sat 11am–2.30pm & 5.30–11pm, Sun 11am–2.30pm & 5.30–10pm.

★ **Shake Shack** Madison Square Park, near E 23rd St and Madison Ave ☎ 212 889 6600, ⓦ shakeshack.com; subway R, W, #6 to 23rd St; map p.115. Plus multiple other locations. Danny Meyer's leafy food kiosk in the centre of Madison Square Park has proved wildly popular since opening in 2004 (there are now offshoots all over town as well as across the country and even abroad), with assorted office workers, tourists and foodies lining up for the perfectly grilled burgers and frozen-custard shakes. You can also buy beer and wine to sip outside, with nearly every item around $7 or less. Daily 11am–10.30pm.

Union Square Café 101 E 19th St, at Park Ave S ☎ 212 243 4020, ⓦ unionsquarecafe.com; subway R, W, #6 to 23rd St; map p.115. After a brief hiatus, Danny Meyer's first and most famous restaurant has resumed producing exquisite New American cuisine with a sideline in practised hospitality – just a few blocks from where it spent its first thirty years. Start off with *fritto misto* ($21) or snap pea salad ($18), move on to pappardelle ($27) or a burger ($28), and save room for dessert. Mon–Thurs 11.45am– 2.30pm & 5.30–10pm, Fri 11.45am–2.30pm &

5.30–11pm, Sat 10am–3pm & 5.30–11pm, Sun 10am–3pm & 5.30–10pm.

ASIAN

★ **15 East** 15 E 15th St, between Fifth Ave and Broadway ☎ 212 647 0015, ⓦ 15eastrestaurant.com; subway L, N, Q, R, #4, #5, #6 to 14th St-Union Square; map p.115. The attention given to both cooked dishes like charcoal-grilled cod ($22) and lobster and *uni* risotto ($34), and the fresh sushi and sashimi (rolls from $6 and up) help elevate this stylish Japanese restaurant to the upper echelons. Mon–Fri noon–1.45pm & 6–10.30pm, Sat noon–1.45pm & 6–11pm.

TsuruTonTan Udon Noodle Brasserie 21 E 16th St, between Union Square West and Fifth Ave ☎ 212 989 1000, ⓦ tsurutontan.com; subway #4, #5, #6, L, N, Q R, W to 14th St-Union Square; map p.115. This outpost of the celebrated Osaka noodle chain has transformed the old *Union Square Café* (see opposite) space, with stylish booths and sleek wood tables. Traditional and more creative bowls of freshly made udon noodles (think cod roe "caviar", curry sauces and truffle cream with crab variations; $16–21) are complemented by a range of tasty small plates such as spicy tuna cones. Mon–Sat 11am–10pm, Sun 11am–9pm.

BAKERIES

★ **Breads Bakery** 18 E 16th St, between Broadway and Fifth Ave ☎ 212 633 2253, ⓦ breadsbakery.com; subway L, N, Q, R, W, #4, #5, #6 to 14th St-Union Square; map p.115. This bakery, by way of Denmark and Israel, is already one of the city's best; you can't go wrong with the sandwiches or quiches, and the breads and *babka* are out of this world; but make sure to top off whatever you get with flaky, melt-in-the-mouth *rugelach* ($2 each). Mon–Fri 6.30am–9pm, Sat 6.30am–8pm, Sun 7.30am–8pm.

COFFEE

Beecher's 900 Broadway, at 20th St ☎ 212 466 3340, ⓦ beechershandmadecheese.com; subway R, W to 19th St; map p.115. A multipurpose food establishment, though centred on their handmade cheeses (some of which are made on site – you can watch the process). There's a café and cheese counter, or you can descend to their cave-like bar-restaurant for more than just a soup or grilled sandwich. Daily 11am–11pm.

Stumptown Coffee Roasters 20 W 29th St, between Broadway and Fifth Ave, in the Ace Hotel (see p.272) ☎ 347 414 7805, ⓦ acehotel.com; subway R, W to 28th St; map p.115. Also 30 W 8th St at Macdougal St; map p.115. At this café of one of the country's most celebrated coffee roasters, you'll have your latte methodically made and can drink it in the attached hotel's columned lobby (also a workspace/bar). Coffees from $4. Mon–Fri 6am–8pm, Sat & Sun 7am–8pm.

ITALIAN

I Trulli Enoteca and Ristorante 124 E 27th St, between Lexington and Park aves ☏212 481 7372, ⓦitrulli.com; subway #6 to 28th St; map p.115. Choose between the lovely restaurant, which features robust dishes like *orecchiette* (ear-shaped pasta) with rabbit *ragù* ($24) and roasted rack of lamb with potato pie ($44), and the wine bar, with its cheeses, cured meats and a handful of fresh pasta dishes. Mon–Thurs noon–3pm & 5.30–10.30pm, Fri noon–3pm & 5.30–11pm, Sat 5–11pm, Sun 3–10pm; wine bar 3pm till late.

★**Maialino** 2 Lexington Ave, in Gramercy Park Hotel ☏212 777 2410, ⓦmaialinonyc.com; subway #6 to 23rd St; map p.115. If a place can be both rustic and refined, Danny Meyer's attractive Roman trattoria, which looks out on Gramercy Park, is it. Much of the focus is on the hog (which gives the place its name) – there's excellent cured *salumi* ($15–22), pasta with *guanciale* ($26) or pork *ragù* ($28), a crispy pig face salad ($25) and roast suckling pig ($58) – but everything's well prepared and desserts are exceptional. Noteworthy patrons: Barack Obama and his wife Michelle dined here when they visited the city in 2014. Reservations essential. Mon–Wed 7.30–10am, noon–2pm & 5.30–10 pm, Thurs 7.30–10am, noon–2pm & 5.30–10.30pm, Fri 7.30–10am, noon–2pm & 5.30–11pm, Sat 10am–2.30pm & 5.30–11pm, Sun 10.30am –2.30pm & 5.30–10.30pm.

MEXICAN

Cosme 35 E 21 st St, between Broadway and Park Ave ☏212 913 9659, ⓦcosmenyc.com; subway #6 to 23rd St; map p.115. The first US outpost for noted Mexican chef Enrique Olvera, *Cosume* gives a modern take on the country's flavors; you might find Brussels sprouts with a green *mole* or a smoky steak tartare, and most plates run $18–29. The celebrated duck *carnitas* ($89) are for sharing. Mon–Thurs noon–2.30pm & 5.30–11pm, Fri noon–2.30pm & 5.30pm–midnight, Sat 11.30am–2.30pm & 5.30pm–midnight, Sun 11.30am–2.30pm & 5.30–11pm.

MIDDLE EASTERN

Turkish Kitchen 386 Third Ave, between 27th and 28th sts ☏212 679 6633, ⓦturkishkitchen.com; subway #6 to 28th St; map p.115. Ruby-red walls and balconies lend a vibrant backdrop to this excellent Turkish restaurant, with dishes such as tender lamb kebabs and *tavuk pirzola* (chicken stuffed with green peppers and creamy cheese) starting at around $18. Mon–Thurs noon–11pm, Fri noon–11.30pm, Sat 5.30–11.30pm, Sun 11am–3pm & 5–10.30pm.

SPANISH AND PORTUGUESE

★**Aldea** 31 W 17th St, between Fifth and Sixth aves ☏212 675 7223, ⓦaldearestaurant.com; subway F, M to 14th St; map p.115. In a cool, relaxed dining room, Portuguese-accented dishes come exquisitely prepared and full of flavour. For this kind of refined seasonal cooking – say, duck confit with crisped duck skin and *chorizo*, or sea-salted cod with smoked mussels and chard – prices are high but not too high (main dishes $27–36) and a four-course prix-fixe ($79) seals the deal. Tues–Thurs 5.30–10pm, Fri & Sat 5.30–11pm.

Casa Mono 52 Irving Place, at E 17th St ☏212 253 2773, ⓦcasamononyc.com; subway L, N, Q, R, W, #4, #5, #6 to 14th St-Union Square; map p.115. This eclectic tapas bar both challenges and enchants the palate with such dishes as burrata with squash ($14) and mussels with cava and *chorizo* sausage ($16). The adjacent and sherry-heavy *Bar Jamón* (see p.336) on 125 E 17th St is open until 2am daily. Daily noon–midnight.

TEASHOPS

Lady Mendl's 56 Irving Place, at E 17th St, in the Inn at Irving Place (see p.278) ☏212 533 4466, ⓦladymendls teasalon.com; subway L, N, Q, R, W, #4, #5, #6 to 14th St-Union Square; map p.115. Classic English high teas are the stock-in-trade of this small inn set in a handsome pair of brownstones. As per tradition, their five-course menus are served in the afternoon, complete with silver service and a tower of sandwiches ($59/person). Reservations necessary. Wed–Fri 1–4pm, Sat & Sun noon–5pm.

22

MIDTOWN EAST

Catering mostly to weekday office crowds, Midtown East overflows with restaurants, food halls and cafés, some nondescript and overpriced, but there are excellent finds as well: a lot of Asian entries plus timeworn favourites such as the *Oyster Bar* in Grand Central Terminal or the classy and refined *Aquavit* and *Modern*.

AMERICAN

'21' Club 21 W 52nd St, between Fifth and Sixth aves ☏212 582 7200, ⓦ21club.com; subway E, M to Fifth Ave-53rd St; map p.124. This is one of New York's most enduring institutions – the city's Old Boys come here to meet and eat. There's a dress code, so wear a jacket and tie. Three-course early dinner prix-fixe menus are $48 in the

Bar Room, which is a pretty good deal, considering some of the more elaborate dishes (roasted monkfish, duck à l'orange – though the simple chicken paillard is most reliable) go for $40 and up on their own. Bar Room Mon–Thurs noon–2.30pm & 5.30–10pm, Fri noon–2.30pm & 5.30–11pm, Sat 5–11pm; upstairs Tues–Sat 5.30–9.30pm.

22

Algonquin Hotel Lobby 59 W 44th St, between Fifth and Sixth aves ☎ 212 840 6800, ⓦ algonquinhotel .com; subway B, D, F, M to 42nd St; map p.124. The archetypal American interpretation of the English drawing room, located in the airy, attractive lobby of the hotel of the same name (see p.272), and reeking of faux nineteenth-century robber-baron splendour. A light menu becomes available late morning, and cocktails are servd until late at night. Daily 11.30am–12.45am.

db Bistro Moderne 55 W 44th St, between Fifth and Sixth aves, in City Club Hotel ☎ 212 391 2400, ⓦ daniel boulud.com; subway B, D, F, M to 42nd St-Bryant Park, #7 to Fifth Ave-Bryant Park; map p.124. Famous chef-owner Daniel Boulud made things more affordable here than his other culinary shrines, though you'll still spend a pretty penny to eat dishes like the signature $35 burger, with foie gras, black truffle and short-rib meat. Mon 7–10am & 11.15am–10pm, Tues–Thurs 7–10am & 11.30am–11pm, Fri 7–10am & 5–11.30pm, Sat 8am–11.30pm, Sun 8am–10pm.

Food Hall at the Plaza 1 W 58th St, Concourse Level of *The Plaza* ☎ 212 986 9260, ⓦ theplazany.com; subway N, Q, R to Fifth Ave-59th St; map p.124. If you're looking for variety in a sumptuous setting, head to the lower level of this venerable hotel, where outlets of *No. 7 Sub* (see p.302), *Luke's Lobster* (see p.291) and *FP Patisserie*, among others, have set up shop; there's also a food hall (daily 11am–10pm) within the food hall, in which celebrity chef Todd English oversees separate spots for raw shellfish, wood-fired pizza and grilled meats. Generally Mon–Sat 11am–9pm, Sun 11am–6pm, but some breakfast places open earliest.

The Modern 9 W 53rd St, inside the Museum of Modern Art ☎ 212 333 1220, ⓦ themodernyyc.com; subway E, M to Fifth Ave-53rd St; map p.124. The highly praised *Modern* appears elegant without trying too hard. Fresh, seasonal ingredients are artfully combined to yield unexpected but wholly delicious dishes. *Chorizo*-crusted codfish with white cocoa-bean purée, and a foie gras tart with cherries are just two of the unlikely options. Set meals start at $158 (considerably less at lunch); the bar room has slightly less expensive dining (spring onion couscous with fried oysters $30, braised duck leg $36). Mon–Sat noon–2pm & 5–10.30pm, bar room also Sun 11.30am–3pm.

★ **Oyster Bar** Lower level, Grand Central Terminal, at E 42nd St and Park Ave ☎ 212 490 6650, ⓦ oysterbarny .com; subway #4, #5, #6, #7 to 42nd St-Grand Central; map p.124. This wonderfully distinctive, century-old place is down in the vaulted dungeons of Grand Central. Midtown office workers who pour in for lunch come to choose from a staggering menu – clam chowder ($6.95), steamed Maine lobster (priced by the pound) and sweet Kumamoto oysters ($3.75 each) top the list. Prices are moderate to expensive; you can eat more cheaply at the counter or just enjoy a chowder and beer while taking in the atmosphere. Mon–Sat 11.30am–9.30pm.

Quality Meats 57 W 58th St, between Fifth and Sixth aves ☎ 212 371 7777, ⓦ qualitymeatsnyc.com; subway F to 57th St, N, R to Fifth Ave; map p.124. The front doors give the impression you're stepping into a meat locker – and you are, in a sense. Top-notch beef (double rib steak $57/person); in contrast to many steakhouses, the appetizers and sides are well done, too. Mon–Wed 11.30am–3pm & 5–10.30pm, Thurs & Fri 11.30am–3pm & 5–11.30pm, Sat 5–11.30pm, Sun 5–10pm, bar open daily till 1am.

Smith and Wollensky 797 Third Ave, at E 49th St ☎ 212 753 1530, ⓦ smithandwollenskynyc.com; subway #6 to 51st St; map p.124. Grand, if clubby, steakhouse, where long-serving waiters wheel out choice cuts of aged beef ($49–59) – New York sirloin and porterhouse are ever popular. If you prefer a more relaxed setting, hit the casual grill around the corner, which serves similar cuts at cheaper prices, plus a giant burger ($19.50). Mon–Fri 11.45am–11pm, Sat & Sun 5–11pm, Wollensky's Grill daily 11.30am–2am.

ASIAN

BCD Tofu House 5 W 32nd St, between Fifth Ave and Broadway ☎ 212 967 1900, ⓦ bcdtofu.com; subway B, D, F, M, N, Q, R, W to 34th St-Herald Square; map p.124. Korean restaurants proliferate on 32nd Street between Fifth and Sixth; this one, one of the neighbourhood's best, specializes in home-made tofu – on its own, in meat dishes, soups and porridges (mains about $17). There's more, though, like *bulgogi* and huge portions of spicy pork belly, meant to share. Daily 24hr.

Hatsuhana 17 E 48th St, between Fifth and Madison aves ☎ 212 355 3345, ⓦ hatsuhana.com; subway #6 to 51st St; map p.124. *Hatsuhana* was one of the first restaurants to introduce sushi to New York many moons ago, and it's still going strong. Despite the spartan decor, this place is not cheap; sushi dinners are $28–45, with *omakase* meals about twice that. Mon–Fri noon–2.30pm & 5.30–10pm, Sat 5–10pm.

Fuku+ 15 W. 56th St, between Fifth and Sixth aves, ⓦ fukuplus.momofuku.com; subway F to 57th St; map p.124. The slightly fancier, or at least cooler looking, version of *Momofuku*'s original fried chicken sandwich offshoot in the East Village, *Fuku+* adds a few twists to its counterpart's more basic equation, like a chicken finger salad, nachos and limited list of cocktails (happy hour, 5–7pm, makes a good time to visit). Mon–Wed & Sun 11.30am–3pm & 5–10pm, Thurs–Sat 11.30am–3pm & 5–11pm.

Hide-Chan Ramen 248 E 52nd St, between Second and Third aves ☎ 212 813 1800, ⓦ hidechanramen.nyc; subway #6 to 51st St; map p.124. Looking for top-notch noodle soups in a sit-down restaurant with a bit more atmosphere than most? *Hide-Chan* does the trick, while also offering one of the better restaurant happy hours around (4.30–6.30pm: $2 pork buns, $2 Sapporos). There's another location at 314 W 53rd St. Mon–Wed 11.30am–11am, Thurs 11.30am–1am, Fri 11.30am–4am, Sat noon–11pm, Sun noon–10pm.

Miss Korea Barbecue 10 W 32 and St ☎ 212 594 4963, ⓦ misskoreabbq.com; subway B, D, F, M, N, Q, R, W to 34th St-Herald Square; map p.124. If you're headed to Manhattan's block-long Koreatown for barbecue, this should be one of your targets. Set over three floors, *Miss Korea* turns out tasty marinated *galbi* (short rib) and other meats on a hot table grill. Daily 24hr.

Szechuan Gourmet 21 W 39th St, between Fifth and Sixth aves ☎ 212 921 0233; subway B, D, F, M to 42nd St-Bryant Park; map p.124. Szechuan cuisine done right, in dishes like spicy *dan dan* noodles ($6.95), braised lamb with chilli ($22.35) and double-cooked pork belly with leeks ($16.45). The lunch specials are a steal. Daily 11.30am–10pm.

BAGELS

Ess-a-Bagel 831 Third Ave, at E 51st St ☎ 212 980 1010, ⓦ ess-a-bagel.com; subway #6 to 51st St; map p.124. Neighbourhood residents swear by this shop, filled with all the lox, whitefish salad and cream cheese you could possibly want. Go early, as the tables fill up quickly. Mon–Fri 6am–9pm, Sat & Sun 6am–5pm.

COFFEE

★**Bluestone Lane** 805 Third Ave, in the atrium of the Meredith Building, at E 50th St ☎ 212 888 8848, ⓦ bluestonelaneny.com; subway #6 to 51st St; map p.124. Slip down the escalator of this skyscraper and you'll discover a tiny Aussie coffee-shop gem. Their signature drink is the "flat white," two espresso shots blended with hot milk that's just short of foamy ($4.75). Pair it with a wholewheat toast topped with smashed avocado, lemon and chilli flakes ($8). There's close to ten other locations in town; this is the original. Mon–Fri 7am–6pm.

Culture Espresso 72 W 38th St, between Fifth and Sixth aves ☎ 212 302 0200, ⓦ cultureespresso.com; subway B, D, F, M, #7 to 42nd St-Bryant Park; map p.124. A bit of an oasis among all the tall office buildings (though it is on the ground floor of one): a comfortable spot for excellent espressos, cappuccinos and the like, as well as incredible cookies and tasty, if small, sandwiches ($8–10). Mon–Fri 7am–7pm, Sat & Sun 8am–7pm.

Lucid Café 311 Lexington Ave, at 38th St ☎ 212 867 3490; subway #4, #5, #6, #7 to 42nd St-Grand Central; map p.124. You'd do well to grab one of the two window seats and enjoy a strong shot of espresso ($3) or a flat white ($4) alongside a buttery croissant at this tiny, charming spot.

Mon–Fri 7am–5pm, Sat 8am–5pm, Sun 8am–3pm.

Perk Kafe 162 E 37th St, between Third and Lexington aves ☎ 212 686 7375, ⓦ perkkafe.com; subway #6 to 51st St; map p.124. Sweet little Murray Hill coffee shop with wood plank walls and tables, lots of exposed brick and its name up in lights behind the counter. Espresso drinks from $3. Mon–Sat 7am–7pm, Sun 8am–7pm.

FOOD HALL

Urbanspace Vanderbilt E 45th Street and Vanderbilt Ave ⓦ urbanspacenyc.com; subway #4, #5, #6, #7 to 42nd St-Grand Central; map p.124. Right outside Grand Central Terminal you'll find this buzzy food hall, which draws a big after-work crowd to its assemblage of gourmet vendors. Among the options are pizza from *Roberta's* (see p.320), ramen from an *Ippudo* (see p.293) offshoot and tasty fried chicken sandwiches from *Delaney Chicken*. There are juice and coffee bars, and plenty of the places sell beer and wine. Mon–Fri 6.30am–9pm, Sat & Sun 9am–5pm.

FRENCH

La Bonne Soupe 48 W 55th St, between Fifth and Sixth aves ☎ 212 586 7650, ⓦ labonnesoupe.com; subway F to 57th St, E, M to Fifth Ave-53rd St; map p.124. This friendly bistro, spread over two levels, makes a good post-museum or pre-Carnegie Hall stop; tasty burgers ($18) and soups ($23 as a meal with bread, salad, dessert and a drink) are highlights of an extensive menu. Daily 11.30am–10.30pm.

★**La Grenouille** 3 E 52nd St, between Fifth and Madison aves ☎ 212 752 1495, ⓦ la-grenouille.com; subway E, M to Fifth Ave-53rd St; map p.124. The haute French cuisine here has melted hearts and tantalized palates since 1962. All the classics (seared foie gras, sautéed frog legs, etc) are done to perfection, the room is welcoming and the service is beyond gracious. Its prix-fixe lunch is $64 though can be ordered à la carte; dinner is $172 without wine; jacket required downstairs. Tues–Sat noon–2.30pm & 5–10.30pm.

ITALIAN

Naples 45 MetLife Building (p.136), 200 Park Ave, at E 45th St ☎ 212 972 7000, ⓦ patinagroup.com; subway #4, #5, #6, #7 to Grand Central-42nd St; map p.124. The Neapolitan pizzas at this place are bursting with flavour (toppings include fennel sausage, roast vegetables and prosciutto di Parma) and come with just the right amount of wood-burning-oven char (individual pizzas $17–19). The to-go counter is the real secret – excellent NY-style slices are just $2 after 2pm. Mon–Fri 7.30am–10pm.

Park Italian Gourmet 60 W 45th St, between Fifth and Sixth aves ☎ 212 382 0589; subway B, D, F, M to 47-50th-Rockefeller Center; map p.124. They may not be reinventing the parmesan wheel here, but *Park Italian*

22

knocks out good-value cold cut sandwiches and a few assorted hot dishes – chicken parm, ziti – that you can enjoy at a formica table or at the park across the street. There's a definite no-nonsense vibe to the place. Mon–Fri 6am–4pm.

22

JEWISH

★ **2nd Avenue Deli** 162 E 33rd St, between Lexington and Third aves ☎ 212 689 9000, ⓦ 2ndavedeli.com; subway #6 to 33rd St; map p.124. This reincarnation of a downtown family-run Jewish institution may no longer be on Second Avenue, but the stuffed cabbage ($13.95), pastrami sandwich ($19.95) and matzoh-ball soup ($8.95) are as tasty as ever. It may seem expensive, but the meaty sandwiches ($14.95–25.95) can often feed two – or at least provide leftovers. Daily 6am–midnight.

MEXICAN

Pampano Taqueria 805 Third Ave, between 49th and 50th sts ☎ 212 751 5257, ⓦ richardsandoval.com; subway #6 to 51st St; map p.124. In a below-street-level atrium of an anonymous office building, this small stand (connected to an upscale Mexican restaurant, whose entrance is on 49th) dishes out small but tasty tacos ($3.25) as well as more filling burritos ($8.75) and home-made guacamole ($2.50, with chips). Find a seat, listen to the waterfall on the wall and the lunchtime piano player, while sitting beneath the skylight – you may forget you're in Midtown. Mon–Fri 11.30am–3pm.

SCANDINAVIAN

★ **Aquavit** 65 E 55th St, between Madison and Park aves ☎ 212 307 7311, ⓦ aquavit.org; subway E, M to Fifth Ave-53rd St; map p.124. Go for a blowout in the main dining room ($98 for three courses, or tasting menu $125–155) or relax over some herring and a variety of the namesake drink in the bar-lounge of this renowned Scandinavian restaurant. Exquisite fish dishes abound – silky gravlax, Arctic char, Spanish mackerel– alongside a few meatier choices, like venison with red beets. Reserve well ahead. Mon–Thurs 11.45am–2.30pm & 5.30–10pm, Fri 11.45am–2.30pm & 5.30–10.30pm, Sat 5.30–10.30pm.

SWEET TREATS

Buttercup Bake Shop 973 Second Ave, between E 51st and E 52nd sts ☎ 212 350 4144, ⓦ buttercupbakeshop .com; subway #6 to 51st St; map p.124. This *Magnolia Bakery* offshoot is similarly known for its 1950s-style comfort sweets, especially the moist cupcakes ($3.25–3.50 each) and banana pudding. Daily 9am–6pm.

La Maison du Chocolat 30 Rockefeller Center, W 49th St between Fifth and Sixth aves and several other locations ☎ 212 265 9404, ⓦ lamaisonduchocolat.com; subway B, D, F, M to 47–50th St-Rockefeller Center; map p.124. The French vibe here is palpable: the original *Maison* is in Paris. The two hot chocolates on the menu (and three iced in summer; all $9.50–11) are so thick you'll need a spoon to eat them, but they're not as sweet as you might expect. Other treats are similarly expensive. Mon–Sat 10am–7pm, Sun noon–6pm.

MIDTOWN WEST

It's safe to say that more overpriced tourist joints exist in Midtown West – especially right around Times Square – than elsewhere in the city. On the other hand, a thriving restaurant scene exists over on Ninth Avenue in Hell's Kitchen– and even further west of that. Elsewhere, Restaurant Row (West 46th St, between Eighth and Ninth aves) is a frequent stopover for theatre-goers seeking a late-night meal, and if you choose carefully, good options can be found closer to the action.

AFGHAN

Ariana Afghan Kebab 787 Ninth Ave, between West 52nd and 53rd sts ☎ 212 262 2323, ⓦ ariananewyork city.com; subway C, E to 50th St; map p.142. A casual neighbourhood restaurant serving inexpensive kebabs (chicken, lamb, fish and beef; $14–18) and vegetarian meals like eggplant curry ($14). Daily noon–11pm.

AMERICAN

The Burger Joint 119 W 56th St, between Sixth and Seventh aves, in Le Parker Meridien ☎ 212 708 7414, ⓦ burgerjointny.com; subway F, N, Q, R to 57th St; map p.142. Though the secret has long been out on this greasy hamburger stand incongruously located in a swish Midtown hotel, it still makes for good fun, good value (around $10 a burger) and, most important, good eating. You might have to wait for a table. Mon–Thurs & Sun

11am–11.30pm, Fri & Sat 11am–midnight.

City Kitchen 700 Eighth Ave, at 44th St ⓦ citykitchen .rownyc.com; subway A, C, E to 42nd St-Port Authority; map p.142. Meandering foodie marketplace tucked just outside of Port Authority. Mind-blowing donuts, *Luke's* lobster rolls, sweet "shaved snow," an *Ippudo* (see p.293) offshoot and more. Sun–Wed 6.30am–9pm, Thurs–Sat 6.30am–11.30pm.

Gloria 401 W 53rd St, at Ninth Ave ☎ 212 956 0709, ⓦ gloria-nyc.com; subway C, E to 50th St; map p.142. Elegant cocktails, natural wines and a novel food approach – a sustainable pescatarian restaurant, no meat anywhere – are *Gloria's* hallmarks. The menu is concise and frequently changing, but might include scallops with sea bean ($18), tile fish with a Béarnaise sauce ($28) and wild mushroom with dashi broth ($17). Tues–Thurs 5.30–10pm, Fri & Sat 5.30–10.30pm.

Gotham West Market 600 Eleventh Ave, between 44th and 45th sts, ⓦgothamwestmarket.com; subway A, C, E to 42nd St-Port Authority; map p.142. Down a bowl of noodles at *Ivan Ramen Slurp Shop*, graze on tapas at *El Colmado* or get ice cream at *Ample Hills*. A handful of other local vendors share the cool space; its location, on the western reaches of Hell's Kitchen, makes it one of the better pit stops for blocks around. There's even a bike rental shop. Hours vary according to vendor, approximately daily 11am–10pm.

Joe Allen 326 W 46th St, between Eighth and Ninth aves ☎212 581 6464, ⓦjoeallenrestaurant.com; subway A, C, E to 42nd St-Port Authority; map p.142. Working to a tried-and-true formula of reliable, modestly priced fare served on white tablecloths in an old-fashioned bar-room atmosphere, *Joe Allen* has long been a favourite of pre- and post-theatre goers. You can't go wrong with a burger ($16), calf's liver ($25) or grilled chicken with potatoes ($25). Mon, Tues & Thurs noon–11.45pm, Wed & Sun 11.30am–11.45pm, Fri noon–midnight, Sat 11.30am–midnight.

ASIAN

★Danji 346 W 52nd St, between Eighth and Ninth aves ☎212 586 2880, ⓦdanjinyc.com; subway C, E to 50th St; map p.142. Sleek and compact, *Danji* serves up modern and tasty Korean small plates. You might want to over-order – some pork sliders ($16) or braised pork belly ($23), maybe whelk salad ($16) – but whatever you do, make sure that the tofu ($12) is on the list: the chef has a way with texture and flavour to make it anything but run of the mill. Mon–Thurs noon–2.30pm & 5pm–midnight, Fri noon–2.30pm & 5pm–1am, Sat 11am–3pm & 5pm–1am, Sun 11am–3pm.

Go! Go! Curry 273 W 38th St, between Seventh and Eighth aves ☎212 730 5555, ⓦgogocurryusa-ny.com; subway A, C, E, #7 to 42nd St-Port Authority, N, Q, R, #1, #2, #3 to Times Square-42nd St; map p.142. Best for lunch or a quick dinner, this quirky hole in the wall slings up delicious and cheap Japanese *katsu* in a thick curry sauce, with all kinds of toppings. It also serves as a temple to former Yankee baseballer Hideki Matsui (who wore #55, hence the opening times). Daily 10.55am–9.55pm.

Larb Ubol 480 Ninth Ave, at 37th St ☎212 564 1822, ⓦlarbubol.com; subway A, C, E to 34th St; map p.142. Tasty northern Thai food from the Isan region, featuring an array of *som tum* (green papaya salad) and *larb* (ground meat salad). Other standouts include the dishes with crispy pork. Lunch specials run from 11.30am to 3.30pm. Mon–Thurs & Sun 11.30am–10.30pm, Fri & Sat 11.30am–11.30pm.

Pure Thai Cookhouse 766 Ninth Ave, between 51st and 52nd sts ☎212 581 0999, ⓦpurethaishophouse .com; subway C, E to 50th St; map p.142. Wok-induced smoke fills the air at this rough-hewn Thai spot, which does

excellent stir-fries and noodles, some a bit more daring than elsewhere (crab and pork dry noodles, $15; chilli turmeric with beef, $14). Mon–Thurs noon–10.30pm, Fri & Sat noon–11.30pm, Sun noon–10.15pm.

Totto Ramen 366 W 52nd St, between Eighth and Ninth aves ☎212 582 0082, ⓦtottoramen.com; subway C, E to 50th St; map p.142. Other locations in Midtown East and Hell's Kitchen. A bit of a surprise on a somewhat desolate block – though the whole area is picking up as a foodie haven – *Totto Ramen* is a narrow spot (with mainly counter seating) to slurp up delicious bowls of pliant noodles and hearty broth, preferably with spicy sesame oil ($11–16; additional toppings extra). Bonus: watch the folks behind the counter periodically apply a blowtorch to colour the *char siu* pork. Mon–Sat noon–4.30pm & 5.30pm–midnight, Sun 4–11pm.

★Yakitori Totto 251 W 55th St (second floor), between Broadway and Eighth Ave ☎212 245 4555, ⓦtottonyc.com; subway A, B, C, D, #1 to 59th St-Columbus Circle, N, Q, R to 57th St or B, D, E to Seventh Ave; map p.142. This popular hideaway is perfect for late-night snacking – though by that time you may miss out on some of the more esoteric grilled skewers (soft knee bone or rare thigh, anyone?). Chicken heart, skirt steak and chicken thigh with spring onions all burst with flavour; a fistful of skewers (most $3–5 each) along with some sides and a cold Sapporo draught make a nice meal. Good set lunches, too. Mon–Thurs 11.30am–2pm & 5.30pm–midnight, Fri 11.30am–2pm & 5.30pm–1am, Sat 5.30pm–1am, Sun 5.30–11pm.

BAKERIES

Little Pie Company 424 W 43rd St, between Ninth and Tenth aves ☎212 736 4780, ⓦlittlepiecompany.com; subway A, C, E to 42nd St-Port Authority; map p.142. True to its name, the *Little Pie Company* serves sweet pies to die for (slices $4.50). The Georgia peach, available only in summer, has earned quite a passionate following, while the sour cream-apple and three-berry varieties are always popular. Mon–Fri 8am–8pm, Sat 10am–8pm, Sun 10am–6pm.

Poseidon Greek Bakery 629 Ninth Ave, between W 44th and W 45th sts ☎212 757 6173; subway A, C, E to 42nd St-Port Authority; map p.142. Known best for the filo dough hand-rolled on the premises and supplied to many of the city's restaurants, *Poseidon* also sells decadent *baklava*, strudel, cookies, spinach-and-meat pies and assorted other sweet Greek pastries. Tues–Sat 9am–7pm.

FRENCH

Aureole One Bryant Park/135 W 42nd St, at Sixth Ave ☎212 319 1660, ⓦcharliepalmer.com; subway B, D, F, M to 42nd St-Bryant Park; map p.142. Unbelievably tasty and inventive French-accented American food. The

22

22

prix-fixe options start at $96 per head, or $125 for the five-course tasting menu. Stop by for the show-stopping desserts (like caramelized pear with almond meringue) or the more affordable lunch special ($43 for three courses). Mon–Fri 11.45am–2.15pm & 5–10pm, Sat 5–10pm.

Chez Napoleon 365 W 50th St, between Eighth and Ninth aves ☎212 265 6980, ⓦcheznapoleon.com; subway C, E to 50th St; map p.142. One of several authentic Gallic restaurants that sprang up in this area during or post-World War II, when it was a hangout for French soldiers. A friendly, family-run bistro, it's stuck in a time warp (in a good way). There's a $35 three-course dinner or you can go for classics like *boeuf bourguignon* ($28) or *sole meunière* ($30). The wines are decent and well priced. Mon–Fri noon–2pm & 5–9.30pm, Sat 5–9.30pm.

★**Le Bernardin** 155 W 51st St, between Sixth and Seventh aves ☎212 554 1515, ⓦle-bernardin.com; subway N, R to 49th St, B, D, E to Seventh Ave, #1 to 50th St; map p.142. The most revered seafood restaurant in the United States, serving incomparable new angles on traditional Brittany fish dishes in elegant surroundings. This is one dinner you'll never forget – marinated Hamachi (yellowtail), sautéed langoustine, crispy bass with *shishito* peppers – especially once the bill arrives ($150 prix fixe; $220 for tasting menu). Mon–Thurs noon–2.30pm & 5.15–10.30pm, Fri noon–2.30pm & 5.15–11pm, Sat 5.15–11pm.

ITALIAN

Becco 355 W 46th St, between Eighth and Ninth aves ☎212 397 7597, ⓦbecco-nyc.com; subway A, C, E, #7 to 42nd St-Port Authority; map p.142. Catering to the pre-theatre crowd, *Becco* is most notable for its $25 Sinfonia di Paste, the all-you-can-eat dinner with a choice of three pasta-and-sauce combinations; there's also a good-value $29 wine menu. Mon noon–3pm & 5–10pm, Tues, Thurs & Fri noon–3pm & 4.30pm–midnight, Wed & Sat 11.30am–3pm & 4pm–midnight, Sun noon–10pm.

Don Antonio by Starita 309 W 50th St, between Eighth and Ninth aves ☎646 719 1043, ⓦdonantonio pizza.com; subway C, E to 50th St; map p.142. The progeny of two celebrated Neapolitan pizza mavens, busy *Don Antonio* showcases a few different styles of pie; its signature, the Montanara Starita ($15), is light, smoky and chewy – and comes by way of the deep fryer and the brick oven. Traditional margaritas ($13) share the menu with items like the pistachio pesto and sausage speciality pie ($25), and filled *pizzes* ($15–19). Mon–Thurs 11.30am–11pm, Fri & Sat 11.30am–11.30pm, Sun 11.30am–10.30pm.

Esca 402 W 43rd St, at Ninth Ave ☎212 564 7272, ⓦesca-nyc.com; subway A, C, E to 42nd St-Port Authority; map p.142. Co-owned by Mario Batali, but more the baby of chef and co-owner Dave Pasternack,

whose passion for fresh fish – and preparations that showcase it – is evident. Lots of *crudo* ($21–24) and whole fish grilled or salt-baked (main dishes $34–44). Mon noon–2.30pm & 5–10.30pm, Tues noon–2.30pm & 4.30–11pm, Wed–Sat noon–2.30pm & 4.30–11.30pm, Sun 4.30–10.30pm.

NY Pizza Suprema 413 Eighth Ave, at W 31st St ☎212 594 8938, ⓦnypizzasuprema.com; subway A, C, E, #1, #2, #3 to 34th St-Penn Station; map p.142. You're not going to do better for a quick, inexpensive bite around Penn Station/Madison Square Garden than this 50-year-old pizza joint. Everything's good, but aim to make an upside-down slice – which subverts the typical order of sauce and cheese – part of your meal. Daily 10.30am–midnight.

LATIN AMERICAN

Churrascaria Plataforma 316 W 49th St, between Eighth and Ninth aves ☎212 245 0505, ⓦplataformaonline.com; subway C, E, #1 to 50th St; map p.142. Meat (the fare of choice) is carried around on swords by waiters in this huge, open Brazilian dining room: they wield succulent slabs of grilled pork, chicken and lots of beef. The $59.95–61.95 prix fixe (your only option) covers all of these various grilled meats and more. Don't miss the addictive *caipirinhas* (Brazil's national cocktail). Mon & Sun noon–10pm, Tues–Thurs noon–11pm, Fri & Sat noon–midnight.

★**Margon** 136 W 46th St, between Sixth and Seventh aves ☎212 354 5013; subway B, D, F, M to 47–50th sts-Rockefeller Center, N, R, W to 49th St; map p.142. This narrow Cuban lunch counter is nearly always packed, but the jostling is worth it; savoury Cuban sandwiches ($9 with rice and beans), garlicky *pernil* (roast pork; Wed special, $11) and, best of all, brightly seasoned octopus salad ($14) top the choices. Mon–Sat 7am–5pm.

MIDDLE EASTERN

★**Gazala's Place** 709 Ninth Ave, between W 48th and W 49th sts; another location at 380 Columbus Ave on the Upper West Side ☎212 245 0709, ⓦgazalasplace .com; subway C, E to 50th St; map p.142. Supposedly the only Druze (a Middle Eastern sect) restaurant in the States – besides the outpost on the UWS – *Gazala's* serves a full lunch and dinner menu but is best known for its *bourekas* (giant savoury pastries stuffed with cheese and other things; around $9). Daily 11am–11pm.

TOP 5 HAUTE CUISINE

Daniel Upper East Side. See p.310
Le Bernardin Midtown West. See p.308
Nobu Downtown See p.281
Per Se Upper West Side. See p.312
Sushi Nakazawa West Village. See p.297

PORTUGUESE

City Sandwich 649 Ninth Ave, between 45th and 46th sts ☎646 684 3943, ⓦcitysandwichnyc.com; subway A, C, E to 42nd St-Port Authority; map p.142. A good lunch option for the area, this Portuguese-Italian sandwich shop places tasty fillings inside impeccable rolls. The Henrique, with a kind of spreadable sausage, is memorable, while the Dave is a roast beef sandwich that's less daring but plenty delicious. Mon–Fri 9am–8.30pm, Sat & Sun 10am–3pm.

RUSSIAN

Russian Tea Room 150 W 57th St, between Sixth and Seventh aves ☎212 581 7100, ⓦrussiantearoomnyc .com; subway F, N, Q, R, W to 57th St; map p.142. In its third incarnation, the restaurant has nowhere near the cachet of the original, but it still pulls folks in – the Stroganoff ($39) and the chicken Kiev ($38) are faves. With appetizers $20–35 and main dishes $38–48, you'll need plenty of dough. Mon–Fri 11.30am–11.30pm, Sat & Sun 11am–11.30pm.

Samovar 256 W 52nd St, between Eighth and Ninth aves ☎212 757 0168, ⓦrussiansamovar.com; subway C, E to 50th St; map p.142. Each dish here is about $10 cheaper than its counterpart at the *Tea Room*, the vodka flows freely and there's live music most nights in this convivial hangout – which also owns the distinction of having been co-founded by the late Russian exile Joseph Brodsky. Daily noon–3am.

22

UPPER EAST SIDE

Upper East Side restaurants mostly exist to serve a discriminating mixture of Park Avenue matrons and young professionals: a mixture of Asian, standard American, Italian and especially posh French restaurants. New Yorkers and visitors alike rarely come up here solely for the food, but since there are so many museums and sights in the neighbourhood you're likely to need a place to eat, at least for lunch. Note that Second Avenue is where you'll find the most diverse scene (branches of *Shake Shack*, *Calexico*, *Mighty Quinn's* and *Luke's Lobster* have opened up around here), though it's a bus ride or fairly stiff walk from Museum Mile.

AMERICAN

★**Cafe Americano** 964 Lexington Ave, between E 70th and E 71st sts ☎646 870 9007, ⓦcafeamericano .com; subway #6 to 68th St; map p.171. Stylish, contemporary all-day restaurant with great breakfast plates (served until 4pm; $12–19) and dinner mains such as poached local monkfish ($32) and Montauk scallops ($36). Daily 8am–11.30pm.

E.A.T. 1064 Madison Ave, between E 80th and E 81st sts (1 block from the Met) ☎212 772 0022, ⓦelizabar .com; subway #6 to 77th St; map p.171. Owned by restaurateur and gourmet grocer Eli Zabar, *E.A.T.* is pricey and crowded (main dishes $24–38) but the food is excellent, notably the soups ($12–14), salads ($16) and sandwich plates ($16–26), which includes the infamous "Tower of Bagel" ($28); the mozzarella, basil and tomato fillings are fresh and heavenly. The takeaway counter and bakery is a bit cheaper. Daily 7am–10pm.

★**Flex Mussels** 174 E 82nd St, between Third and Lexington aves ☎212 717 7772, ⓦflexmussels.com; subway #4, #5, #6 to 86th St; map p.171. Mussels fresh from Prince Edward Island (Canada) take centre stage here, with plates with various sauces ranging $25–28. Also does cornmeal-crusted clam strips ($12). Mon–Thurs 5.30–10pm, Fri 5.30–11pm, Sat 11.30am–11pm, Sun 11.30am–10pm.

Flora Bar 945 Madison Ave, at E 75th St (Met Breuer) ☎646 558 5383, ⓦflorabarnyc.com; subway #6 to 77th St; map p.171. The grand and spacious restaurant at the Met Breuer (p.175) overlooks a tranquil courtyard with trees (garden open in summer), with a menu focused heavily on seafood and vegetables; think shrimp with sea urchin and nori ($18), lobster and crab dumplings ($29) and asparagus, goat cheese and egg tart ($19). Tues–Thurs & Sun 11.30am–3.30pm & 5.30–10pm, Fri & Sat 11.30am–3.30pm & 5.30–11pm.

JG Melon Restaurant 1291 Third Ave, at E 74th St ☎212 650 1310; subway Q to 72nd St; map p.171. One of the few old-school bars on the Upper East Side, but best known for its juicy burgers ($11.25–13.25) and crispy waffle-cut fries. Mon–Thurs 11.30am–2am, Fri & Sat 11.30am–3am, Sun 11.30am–1am.

Neil's Coffee Shop 961 Lexington Ave, at E 70th St ☎212 628 7474; subway #6 to 68th St; map p.171. Classic neighbourhood Greek-owned diner, with gruff service, old bar stools and booths, hearty breakfasts ($7.50–12.75), beer ($5) and cheap coffee ($1.75, with refills). You probably won't spend much more than $10. Popular with Hunter College staff and students. Mon–Fri 6am–8pm, Sat 7am–7pm, Sun 8am–6pm.

★**Penrose** 1590 Second Ave, between E 82nd and E 83rd sts ☎212 203 2751, ⓦpenrosebar.com; subway Q to 86th St; map p.171. This popular gastropub makes an excellent lunch diversion from Museum Mile; highlights include the mighty Pat LaFrieda Penrose burger, worth every morsel at $14, and the beer-battered fish tacos ($5 each). Mon–Fri 11.45am–4am, Sat & Sun 10am–4am.

AUSTRIAN

★**Café Sabarsky** In the Neue Galerie, 1048 Fifth Ave, at E 86th St ☎212 288 0665, ⓦkurtgutenbrunner.com; subway #4, #5, #6 to 86th St; map p.171. Sumptuous

22

decor that harkens back to Old Vienna fills the handsome parlour of the former Vanderbilt mansion. The menu reads like that of an upscale Viennese *kaffeehaus*; it includes superb pastries, like Linzertorte and strudels ($9.50), but also sausages ($20) and goulash ($16). Mon & Wed 9am–6pm, Thurs–Sun 9am–9pm.

BAGELS

Tal Bagels 333 E 86th St, between First and Second aves ☎212 427 6811, ⓦtalbagelsny.com; subway Q to 86th St; map p.171. The bagels ($1.25; cream cheese from $2.95) may be a little too chewy, but the spread selection at this family institution is to die for, especially the smoked whitefish ($9.99). Don't let the queues scare you; they move fast. Daily 5.30am–8pm.

COFFEE

★**Bluestone Lane** 2 E 90th St, at Fifth Ave ☎646 869 7812, ⓦbluestonelaneny.com; subway #4, #5, #6 to 86th St; map p.171. This outpost of the Australian-influenced coffee-shop chain is especially well located in the centre of Museum Mile, with outdoor seating and a dazzling interior that once formed part of the Church of the Heavenly Rest; its brass light fixtures and sandstone archways have featured in architectural magazines. Daily 7.30am–6pm.

FRENCH

Café Boulud 20 E 76th St, between Madison and Fifth aves ☎212 772 2600, ⓦcafeboulud.com/nyc; subway #6 to 77th St; map p.171. The muted but elegant interior of chef Daniel Boulud's second Manhattan restaurant is an exceedingly pleasant place to savour his sublime concoctions (case in point: venison terrine with lingonberry compote). Main dishes $26–46, lunch prix fixe $39–45. Mon–Thurs 7–10am, noon–2.30pm & 5.45–10.30pm, Fri 7–10am, noon–2.30pm & 5.45–11pm, Sat 8–11am, noon–2.30pm & 5.30–11pm, Sun 8–11am, noon–3pm & 5.45–10.30pm.

★**Daniel** 60 E 65th St, between Madison and Park aves ☎212 288 0033, ⓦdanielnyc.com; subway #6 to 68th St; map p.171. Expensive gourmet fare from chef Boulud (again) – think black sea bass in Syrah sauce and "quartet of pig provençale". Prix-fixe (four-course) dinners only from $142 (it's $119 Mon–Thurs till 6pm); there's even an elaborate, seasonal, vegetarian version (seven courses for $234). One of the best French restaurants in New York City (jacket required for men). Mon–Thurs 5.30–10.30pm, Fri & Sat 5–10.30pm.

Maison Kayser 1294 Third Ave, at E 74th St ☎212 744 3100, ⓦmaison-kayser-usa.com; subway Q to 72nd St; map p.171. Parisian boulanger Eric Kayser offers a range of tempting pastries and breads, as well as a sit-down menu of French classics, from quiche Lorraine ($14) and *tartines*

($14–17.50) to fabulous salads ($11–17) and *coq au vin* ($24). Daily 7am–10pm.

GERMAN

Heidelberg 1648 Second Ave, between E 85th and E 86th sts ☎212 628 2332, ⓦheidelberg-nyc.com; subway Q to 86th St; map p.171. The atmosphere here is Mittel-European kitsch, with gingerbread trim and waitresses in Alpine goatherd costumes. The food is the real deal, featuring excellent liver-dumpling soup, *Bauernfrühstück* omelettes, and pancakes, both sweet and potato (dishes range $19.75 to $52.75 for the fondue). And they serve *Weissbier* the right way, too – in two-litre, boot-shaped glasses. Mon 4.30pm–midnight, Tues–Thurs 11am–midnight, Fri & Sat 11am–1am, Sun 11am–midnight.

ITALIAN

Ottomanelli's 86th St Café 1626 York Ave, between E 85th and E 86th sts ☎212 772 0080, ⓦnycotto.com; subway Q to 86th St; map p.171. The Ottomanelli food empire dates back to 1900, and this old-school Italian diner is a real gem, with pizzas ($8.95–11.95), juicy steak burgers ($9.95) and excellent pastas ($13.95–16.95). Daily noon–9.30pm.

JAPANESE

Donguri 309 E 83rd St, between First and Second aves ☎212 737 5656, ⓦdonguriny.com; subway Q to 86th St; map p.171. Sushi lovers won't want to miss this little 24-seat spot featuring some of the best sashimi sets in town (from $28), as well as superb prawn tempura ($25) and various grilled fresh fish, from salmon to sea bass (mains $28–32). Reservations are highly recommended. Tues–Sun 5.30–9.30pm.

Naruto Ramen 1596 Third Ave, between E 89th and E 90th sts ☎212 289 7803, ⓦnarutoramenex.com; subway #4, #5, #6 to 86th St; map p.171. Tiny Japanese noodle shop, cooking up excellent bowls of ramen ($9–11) with pork or miso, and Japanese curry ($10.50). Expect to wait. Cash only. Daily noon–10.45pm.

JEWISH

Pastrami Queen 1125 Lexington Ave, at E 78th St ☎212 734 1500, ⓦpastramiqueen.com; subway #6 to 77th St; map p.171. This friendly diner has been knocking out giant hot pastrami sandwiches ($18) since 1956, as well as corned beef and a host of Jewish kosher classics (matzoh-ball soups) and desserts ($9). Daily 10am–10pm.

Sable's Smoked Fish 1489 Second Ave, between E 77th St and E 78th St ☎212 249 6177, ⓦsablesnyc .com; subway Q to 72nd St; map p.171. Sable's smoked fish sandwiches ($10.99–15.99) are a taste sensation, but they also serve excellent salads ($5–22), beef and turkey sandwiches (from $7.99) and seafood soups (all takeaway only). Mon–Fri 8am–7pm, Sat 7.30am–7pm, Sun 7am–5pm.

MEXICAN

Cascabel Taqueria 1556 Second Ave, at E 81st St ☎ 212 717 7800, ⓦ cascabeltaqueria.com; subway Q to 86th St; map p.171. Funky taco shop offering two fresh corn tacos for $12, with fillings like *chorizo*, fish, shrimp and *carnitas* (plus veggie choices). Also does bigger chicken plates ($22) and delicious *churros* ($6). Great salsas. Sun–Thurs 10am–midnight, Fri & Sat 10am–1am.

Maya 1191 First Ave, between E 64th and E 65th sts ☎ 212 585 1818, ⓦ richardsandoval.com/mayany; subway #6 to 68th St, F, Q to Lexington Ave-63rd St; map p.171. Excellent, high-end Mexican dishes are served in a large, colourful and noisy dining room and adjacent *tequileria* (bar). The rock shrimp *ceviche*, chicken *mole* and grilled dorado fillet make this one of the best Mexican restaurants in the whole city. Main dishes $24–32. Dining room Mon–Wed 5–10pm, Thurs & Fri 5–11pm, Sat 11.30am–4.30pm & 5.30–11pm, Sun 11.30am–4.30pm & 5.30–10pm; bar daily 3pm–midnight.

MIDDLE EASTERN

Beyoglu 1431 Third Ave, at E 81st St ☎ 212 650 0850; subway #4, #5, #6 to 86th St; map p.171. The place to go for mouthwatering meze (the Turkish version of appetizers) for $6–9; the doner kebabs and fish specials are superb as well ($14.50–17). Loud (the second floor is quieter), reasonably priced, and definitely filling. Daily noon–10.30pm.

VEGAN

Candle Café 1307 Third Ave, at E 75th St ☎ 212 472 0970, ⓦ candlecafe.com; subway Q to 72nd St; map p.171. This vegan favourite does its best to dress up all that tofu and seitan, often with surprising results. Salads are a standout, as are the soups and juices from the "farmacy". Moderately priced (main dishes $12–22). Mon–Sat 11.30am–10.30pm, Sun 11.30am–9.30pm.

PERSIAN (IRANIAN)

Persepolis 1407 Second Ave, between E 73th and E 74th sts ☎ 212 535 1100, ⓦ persepolisnewyork.com; subway Q to 72nd St; map p.171. One of the few places in New York for Persian food, this is also one of the best. Aromas of rose, cherry and cardamom fill the dining room (as well as a painting of the owner, a former goalkeeper with Tehran-based soccer team Persepolis F.C.). Main dishes range $16–29. Daily noon–11.30pm.

SWEET TREATS

Glaser's Bake Shop 1670 First Ave, between E 87th and E 88th sts ☎ 212 289 2562; subway Q to 86th St; map p.171. The Glaser family's no-frills bakery has been knocking out New York's beloved black-and-white cookie since opening in 1902 (founders John and Justine Glaser emigrated from Germany), but they also do cakes, donuts and whoopie pies (most items $1.50–5). Cash only. Tues–Fri 7am–7pm, Sat 8am–7pm, Sun 8am–3pm.

Lady M 41 E 78th St, at Madison Ave ☎ 212 452 2222, ⓦ ladym.com; subway #6 to 77th St; map p.171. Posh cake shop with a cult following, known for its *mille crêpes* (twenty layers of paper-thin crêpes and whipped cream; whole cakes $80), checkers cake, strawberry shortcake, Mont Blanc (puréed chestnuts topped with whipped cream) and Japanese-influenced desserts. Mon–Fri 10am–7pm, Sat 11am–7pm, Sun 11am–6pm.

Maison Ladurée 864 Madison Ave, between E 70th and E 71th sts ☎ 646 558 3157, ⓦ laduree.com; subway #6 to 68th St; map p.171. The fad for *macarons* in New York was driven by the likes of this upmarket French bakery, founded in Paris in 1862 (the sweet treats also featured in *Gossip Girl*), with the delicate main event coming in a wide range of flavours – the salted caramel is hard to resist. Expect long queues in the afternoon. Mon–Sat 9am–7pm, Sun 10am–6pm.

Serendipity 3 225 E 60th St, between Second and Third aves ☎ 212 838 3531, ⓦ serendipity3.com; subway N, R, #4, #5, #6 to 59th St; map p.171. Adorned with Tiffany lamps, this long-established café and ice-cream parlour has been a favourite spot for sweet-sixteen parties and first dates since 1954. It serves all sorts of items, from burgers to fresh fish, but is best known for its "frrrozen" hot chocolate ($8.95) and the wealth of ice-cream sundae offerings (from $9.50). Sun–Thurs 11.30am–midnight, Fri & Sat 11.30am–1am.

22

UPPER WEST SIDE AND MORNINGSIDE HEIGHTS

The Upper West Side is family-oriented and residential, with the cuisine on offer tailored to local tastes: generous burger joints, coffee shops and brunch spots, but also an increasing number of ambitious restaurants, especially around Lincoln Center, the Museum of Natural History and Columbia University.

AFRICAN

Awash 947 Amsterdam Ave, between 106th and 107th sts ☎ 212 961 1416, ⓦ awashny.com; subway #1 to 103rd St; map p.184. Also in downtown. Ethiopian expats flock to this brightly coloured restaurant offering sumptuous vegetarian and meat combo platters ($15–21). Dig in with your hands, but lay off the too-sweet honey wine. Daily 12.30–11pm.

22

AMERICAN

Boat Basin Café W 79th St, at the Hudson River with access through Riverside Park ☎ 212 496 5542, ⓦ boatbasincafe.com; subway #1 to 79th St; map p.184. An outdoor restaurant, the *Boat Basin* is only open seasonally. The informal tables are covered in red-and-white-checked cloths, and the food is standard – mostly burgers and sandwiches ($12–16), with the odd outlier – but inexpensive considering the prime location. On weekend afternoons a violin trio adds to the ambience. April–Oct daily noon–11pm, weather permitting.

Boathouse Café Central Park Lake, at W 72nd St entrance ☎ 212 517 2233, ⓦ thecentralparkboathouse .com; subway B, C to 72nd St; map p.151. A peaceful retreat after a day spent museum-hopping on Fifth Avenue. You get great views of the famous Central Park skyline and decent American/Continental cuisine, but at somewhat steep prices – say, branzino with asparagus ($36) and roast pork tenderloin ($36). April–Nov Mon–Fri noon–4pm & 5.30–9.30pm, Sat & Sun 9.30am–4pm & 6–9.30pm.

Dovetail 103 W 77th St ☎ 212 362 3800, ⓦ dovetailnyc .com; subway B, C to 81st St-Museum of Natural History; map p.184. A rare Michelin-starred (and deservedly so) restaurant in this area, with bold, fresh, market-driven dishes like chayote salad with pumpkin seeds, seared halibut with white beans and suckling pig with chanterelles (tasting menu; $145). Special set meal for Sunday "suppa" (prix-fixe; $68); Monday nights are for celebrating vegetables ($68 for three courses plus dessert). Mon–Thurs 5.30–9.45pm, Fri & Sat 5–10.45pm, Sun 5–9.45pm.

Good Enough to Eat 520 Columbus Ave, at 85th St ☎ 212 496 0163, ⓦ goodenoughtoeat.com; subway #1, B, C to 86th St; map p.184. Long-time brunch haunt with lots of cow knick-knacks and sublime, country-style cooking – think corned beef hash ($13), oatmeal pancakes with strawberry butter ($12.50) and club sandwiches filled with freshly roasted turkey ($15.50). Pie for dessert is a must. Aim to come on a weekday, as weekend wait times can be outrageous (around an hour). Mon–Thurs 8am–10.30pm, Fri 8am–11pm, Sat 9am–11pm, Sun 9am–10.30pm.

Gray's Papaya 2090 Broadway, at W 72nd St ☎ 212 799 0243, ⓦ grayspapayanyc.com; subway #1, #2, #3 to 72nd St; map p.184. This popular hot-dog joint is an NYC institution, famous for its long-running "Recession Special": two dogs and a drink for $4.95. No seats; eat at the counter or take it away. Daily 24hr.

★**Jacob's Pickles** 509 Amsterdam Ave, at 85th St ☎ 212 470 5566, ⓦ jacobspickles.com; subway #1, B, C to 86th St; map p.184. Gut-busting Southern food like stacks of pancakes teetering with fried chicken ($15), biscuits slathered in mushroom gravy ($8), mac and cheese ($9) and (of course) superbly tart and tangy pickles. Everything is served up in a fun, noisy, modern dining room with exposed brick and long leather banquettes. Very popular; be prepared to wait thirty minutes or more for a table. Mon–Thurs 10am–2am, Fri 10am–4am, Sat 9am–4am, Sun 9am–2am.

Peacefood cafe 460 Amsterdam Ave, at 82nd St ☎ 212 362 2266, ⓦ peacefoodcafe.com; subway #1 to 79th St, B, C to 81st St; map p.184. A friendly stop to pick up some tasty vegan baked goods, or to linger and make a full meal of it: go for an array of roasted veg ($6.95–12.95), fried seitan panini ($12.95) or cheeseless pizza ($12.95), perhaps washed down with a gingerade ($4). Daily 10am–10pm.

Per Se 10 Columbus Circle (at 60th St), Time Warner Center ☎ 212 823 9335, ⓦ thomaskeller.com; subway A, B, C, D, #1 to 59th St-Columbus Circle; map p.184. The $325 nine-course prix fixe is a series of small plates that seek to transcend the standard dining experience; whimsical ideas along the lines of "Pearls and oysters", which pairs oysters with tapioca and caviar, should give you some idea – and it all works. Menu changes regularly; reservations accepted by phone (or on ⓦ opentable.com) two months prior to the day, and jackets are required for men. Mon–Thurs 5.30–10pm, Fri–Sun 11.30am–1.30pm & 5.30–10pm.

Tom's Restaurant 2880 Broadway, at 112th St ☎ 212 864 6137, ⓦ tomsrestaurant.net; subway #1 to 110th St; map p.184. The greasy-spoon diner – celebrated in song by Suzanne Vega and whose exterior doubled for *Monk's* in *Seinfeld* – is no great shakes food-wise, but the prices almost make up for the quality. Often filled with Columbia University students who come for the great breakfast deals (under $7) on weekday mornings. Mon, Tues & Sun 6.30am–1.30am, Wed 6am–midnight, Thurs–Sat 24hr.

Zabar's Café 2245 Broadway, at W 80th St ☎ 212 787 2000, ⓦ zabars.com; subway #1 to 79th St; map p.184. Adjacent to the famed Upper West Side gourmet shop (see p.393), this small spot is always crowded with locals and tourists. Best for the cheap, freshly prepared bagel-and-lox sandwiches ($8.50), but everything's tasty: scones, panini, sandwiches, soup, coffee, frozen yogurt and smoothies. Mon–Fri 7am–7pm, Sat 7.30am–7pm, Sun 8am–6pm.

ASIAN

Saiguette 935 Columbus Ave, at Duke Ellington Blvd (W 106 St) ☎ 212 866 8886, ⓦ saiguette.com; subway B, C to 103rd St; map p.184. No-frills Vietnamese restaurant serving up aromatic soupy noodles in plastic tubs ($9–11) and fabulous *bánh mì* sandwiches ($8–11) stuffed with lemongrass pork, pickles and spicy mayo. Daily 11.30am–10.30pm.

BAGELS

★**Absolute Bagels** 2788 Broadway, between W 107th and W 108th sts ☎212 932 2052, ⓦabsolutebagels .com; subway #1 to 110th St-Cathedral Parkway; map p.184. This tiny Thai-run shop bakes hot, fresh, chewy bagels that some claim to be the best in the city. Try one with cream cheese and lox ($9) and you might find it hard to disagree. Daily 6am–9pm.

★**Barney Greengrass** 541 Amsterdam Ave, between W 86th and W 87th sts ☎212 724 4707, ⓦbarney greengrass.com; subway #1 to 86th St; map p.184. The "sturgeon king" is an Upper West Side fixture; the deli (and restaurant) have been around seemingly since time began (or at least a hundred years). The smoked-salmon section is a particular treat. Order classic Jewish food like matzoh ball soup ($6), bialys or scrambled eggs with sturgeon ($21) and soak up the no-frills ambience. Cash only. Deli Tues–Sun 8am–6pm; restaurant Tues–Fri 8.30am–4pm, Sat & Sun 8.30am–5pm.

BAKERIES

Bouchon Bakery Ten Columbus Circle, Third Floor, Time Warner Center ☎212 823 9366, ⓦthomaskeller .com; subway A, B, C, D, #1 to 59th St-Columbus Circle; map p.184. Also One Rockefeller Plaza, 49th St, between Fifth and Sixth aves. At this Thomas Keller café, you can get something to go from the counter or sit at a table and stare through the windows onto the corner of Central Park, grazing on a ham-and-cheese sandwich, croissant or decadent pastry. Mon–Sat 8am–9pm, Sun 8am–7pm.

FRENCH

Bar Boulud 1900 Broadway, between 63rd and 64th sts ☎212 595 0303, ⓦbarboulud.com; subway A, B, C, D, #1 to 59th St-Columbus Circle, or #1 to 66th St-Lincoln Center; map p.184. One of superstar chef Daniel Boulud's restaurants; particularly worthwhile are the house-made pâtés ($14), terrines ($14) and charcuterie that comprise the most original part of the menu. There's also an excellent and extensive Rhône wine list. Right next door is the Mediterranean-inspired *Boulud Sud*, another winner. Mon–Thurs 11.30am–2.30pm & 5–11pm, Fri 11.30am–2.30pm & 5pm–midnight, Sat 11am–4pm & 5pm–midnight, Sun 11am–4pm & 5–10pm.

Café Lalo 201 W 83rd St, between Amsterdam Ave and Broadway ☎212 496 6031, ⓦcafelalo.com; subway #1 to 86th St; map p.184. Reminiscent of Paris, down to the cramped tables and inconsistent service. Try the "shirred" eggs (made fluffy with a cappuccino machine) with all sorts of herbs and other add-ins (around $12), or the wonderful Belgian waffles ($14). Great desserts too. Mon–Thurs 8am–2am, Fri 8am–4am, Sat 9am–4am, Sun 9am–2am.

Café Luxembourg 200 W 70th St, between Amsterdam and West End aves ☎212 873 7411, ⓦcafeluxembourg.com; subway #1, #2, #3 to 72nd St; map p.184. Popular Lincoln Center-area bistro that packs in a slightly sniffy crowd to enjoy first-rate, contemporary French food. Main dishes (roasted Arctic char, steak *frites*) run $26–40, while the brasserie menu (sandwiches, salads, burgers, *moules frites*) is a bit cheaper ($12–25). Mon & Tues 8am–11pm, Wed–Fri 8am–midnight, Sat 9am–midnight, Sun 9am–11pm.

Jean-Georges Trump International Hotel, 1 Central Park W, between W 60th and 61st sts, in ☎212 299 3900, ⓦjean-georgesrestaurant.com; subway A, B, C, D, #1 to 59th St-Columbus Circle; map p.184. French food at its finest, crafted by star chef Jean-Georges Vongerichten. The gracious service is a throwback to

22

TOP 5 BAGELS

Though bagels are now an American dietary staple, it's generally accepted that nowhere makes them like New York – go anywhere else in the world (with the notable exception of Montréal), and you'll immediately taste the difference. Theories abound as to the **origin of the modern bagel**. Most likely, it is a derivative of the pretzel, with the word "bagel" coming from the German *biegen*, "to bend." Whatever their birthplace, it is certain that bagels have become a New York institution.

Until the 1950s, bagels were handmade by Eastern European Jewish immigrants in cellars scattered around New York's Lower East Side. Modern-day bagels are softer and have a smaller hole than their ancestors – the hole made them easy to carry on a long stick to hawk on street corners. Their curiously chewy texture is a result of being boiled before they are baked. Bagels are traditionally served with cream cheese and lox (smoked salmon). Below is a list of some of the city's better bagelsmiths.

Absolute Bagels Upper West Side. See p.313

Bagel Pub Park Slope. See p.321

Barney Greengrass Upper West Side. See above

Black Seed Bagels Nolita. See p.286

Ess-A-Bagel Midtown East. See p.305

another, more genteel, era. With meals starting at $138 (tasting menus from $218), it's definitely the place for a special occasion; for the price-conscious, the $58 two-course lunch is a good bet, or adjourn to the front-room *Nougatine* for more reasonable meals in a somewhat casual (but still refined) setting. The wine list includes bottles ranging from $46 all the way to $12,000. Reservations essential. Daily 11.45am–11pm.

22

GREEK

Kefi 505 Columbus Ave St, between W 84th and W 85th sts ☏ 212 873 0200, ⓦ kefirestaurant.com; subway B, C to 86th St; map p.184. Lively and fairly authentic Greek tavern, with bright, contemporary rustic decor and reasonable prices – meze plates from $9 and signature grilled octopus ($16.95) and lamb sausage dumpings ($21.50). Mon–Thurs noon–3pm & 5–10pm, Fri noon–3pm & 5–11pm, Sat 11am–11pm, Sun 11am–10pm.

ITALIAN

Caffè Storico 170 Central Park West, at 77th St ☏ 212 873 3400, ⓦ nyhistory.org/dine; subway B, C to 81st St-Museum of Natural History; map p.184. The on-site dining locale for the New-York Historical Society (see p.190), cheery *Storico* offers serious-minded Italian food; pastas run $16–20, mains (*cioppino*, veal *milanese*) $32–38. Slip in for a coffee or panini during the daytime, or come for the better-priced Sunday brunch ($14–21). Tues–Sun 11am–10pm.

Celeste 502 Amsterdam Ave, between W 84th and W 85th sts ☏ 212 874 4559, ⓦ celestenewyork.com; subway #1 to 86th St; map p.184. Justly popular Italian restaurant specializing in wood-fired pizzas ($11–16), Neapolitan specialities such as deep-fried buffalo-ricotta balls ($8) and Roman-style *carciofi fritti* (artichoke fritters; $7.50). Lined with exposed brick and a sprawling china cabinet, it's sweet and romantic – perfect for a first date. Mon–Fri 5–11.30pm, Sat noon–3pm & 5–11.30pm, Sun noon–3pm & 5–10.30pm.

Gennaro 665 Amsterdam Ave, between W 92nd and 93rd sts ☏ 212 665 5348, ⓦ gennaronyc.com; subway #1, #2, #3 to 96th St; map p.184. A bustling spot for moderately priced favourites like potato gnocchi ($17.50) and mussels with Sicilian couscous ($21), accompanied by

reasonable Italian wines. Save room for dessert. Cash only. Mon–Thurs 5–10.30pm, Fri & Sat 5–11pm.

★**Salumeria Rosi Parmacotto** 283 Amsterdam Ave, between 73rd and 74th sts ☏ 212 877 4801, ⓦ salumeriarosi.com; subway #1, #2, #3 to 72nd St; map p.184. On your left as you enter is a deli counter with a dizzying array of gorgeous cured meats; on your right, the slender dining room, whose mirrored wall and ceiling are partially covered by a food-contoured plaster relief map of Italy. Order lots of small plates: a selection of that *salumi* ($8 each, sampling $20) and some cheeses ($8 each, sampling $18); crisp Brussels sprouts ($13); a pasta or two ($16). For takeaway, the *porchetta calabrese* sandwich ($15) is a no-brainer. Mon–Fri noon–10pm, Sat & Sun 11am–11pm.

LATIN AMERICAN

Calle Ocho 45 W 81st St, between Central Park West and Columbus Ave, in Excelsior Hotel ☏ 212 873 5025, ⓦ calleochonyc.com; subway B, C to 81st St or #1 to 79th St; map p.184. Very tasty Latino fare, including *ceviche* (there's a wide selection priced $14–18) and *chimichurri* steak ($29) with yucca fries, served in an immaculately designed restaurant with a lively lounge. The *mojitos* ($11) are as tasty and potent as any in the city. Mon–Thurs 6–10.30pm, Fri 6–11.30pm, Sat noon–3pm & 5–11.30pm, Sun noon–3pm & 5–10pm.

Flor de Mayo 2651 Broadway, between W 100th and W 101st sts ☏ 212 663 5520, ⓦ flordemayo.com; subway #1 to 103rd St; map p.184. Chinese-Peruvian hybrid with Peruvian specials such as *ceviche* ($14.50) and *lomo saltado* (sliced steak with potatoes and rice; $16), and a vast range of American Chinese classics such as kung po shrimp ($17.25) and chow mein ($14.50). Daily noon–midnight.

MIDDLE EASTERN

Turkuaz 2637 Broadway, at W 100th St ☏ 212 665 9541, ⓦ turkuazrestaurant.com; subway #1, #2, #3 to 96th St; map p.184. Sip a glass of raki in *Turkuaz*'s cavernous dining room and linger over such Turkish delicacies as vine leaves stuffed with grilled salmon cubes ($21.50); there are some vegetarian options too. Bellydancing on weekend nights at 9.30pm. Mon–Thurs noon–11pm, Fri & Sat noon–midnight, Sun 11am–11pm.

HARLEM AND NORTH MANHATTAN

While visitors to Harlem will find plenty of cheap Caribbean and West African restaurants, it would be unthinkable not to try the soul food for which the area is justifiably famous (think ribs or fried chicken and waffles). El Barrio (East Harlem) sees far fewer visitors, but its restaurants are definitely worth a try; Puerto Rican and Latino cuisines dominate. Washington Heights in northern Manhattan is the best place on the island to try authentic Dominican food, and you can often eat like a king for just a few dollars.

AFRICAN

Africa Kine 2267 Powell Blvd, between W 133rd and

134th sts ☏ 212 666 9400, ⓦ africakine.com; subway #2, #3 to 135th St; map p.199. Following the closure of the original space a few years ago, this excellent West African and Senegalese restaurant has been reopened by its Dakar-born owners. Sample the authentic lamb curry, lamb and peanut butter stew, and spicy fish with okra, served with heaps of rice (dinner mains $13–18). Mon–Thurs noon–midnight, Fri–Sun noon–2am.

La Savane 239 W 116th St, between Frederick Douglass and Powell blvds ☎ 646 490 4644; subway A, B, C to 116th St; map p.199. Solid choice for a cheap West African meal, "The Savannah" (it's also a district of Côte d'Ivoire) offers a blend of Ivoirian and Senegalese favourites, from *mafe* (lamb and peanut stew) to tasty grilled fish flavoured with mustard (mains $9–15). Daily noon–1am.

Zoma 2084 Frederick Douglass Blvd, at W 113th St ☎ 212 662 0620, ⓦ zomanyc.com; subway B, C to 116th St; map p.199. One of the sleekest places around, delivering solid Ethiopian food in minimalist digs at low prices. The combination platters are your best bet: the veggie combo goes for $25.60 and is big enough to share. Meat eaters should try the *doro wat*, or long-simmered chicken in spices ($20). Cash and AMEX only. Mon–Fri 5–11pm, Sat & Sun noon–11pm.

AMERICAN/SOUL FOOD

★**Amy Ruth's** 113 W 116th St, between Malcolm X and Powell blvds ☎ 212 280 8779, ⓦ amyruths.com; subway #2, #3 to 116th St; map p.199. The barbecue chicken ($17.50), named in honour of ex-President Obama, is more than enough reason to visit this small, casual family restaurant, but waffle breakfasts ($10.95–17.95) and desserts (think peach cobbler and banana pudding; $7) are equally enticing. Mon 11am–11pm, Tues–Thurs 8.30am–11pm, Fri 8.30am–5.30am, Sat 7.30am–5.30am, Sun 7.30am–11pm.

★**Dinosaur Bar-B-Que** 700 W 125th St, at Twelfth Ave ☎ 212 694 1777, ⓦ dinosaurbarbque.com; subway #1 to 125th St; map p.199. This convivial joint, an outpost of the original (in Syracuse, NY, of all places), is especially known for its pit-smoked chicken wings ($7.95 for six) and pork ribs ($12.50–28.50). Live blues every Sat from 10pm onwards. Mon–Thurs 11.30am–11pm, Fri & Sat 11.30am–midnight, Sun noon–10pm.

The Grange 1635 Amsterdam Ave, at W 141st St ☎ 212 996 2080, ⓦ thegrangebarnyc.com; subway A, B, C, D to 145th St; map p.199. This rustic farm-to-table restaurant, part hip brunch joint, part boozy cocktail bar, has been a big hit up here – expect to wait for a table at weekends (it's close to Alexander Hamilton's "Grange" p.208). The American brunch staples are great value; think eggs with foie gras-slathered hash browns, really thick, mind-bending cuts of bacon, and an amazing duck with sweet potato. Mon–Fri 11.30am–4am, Sat & Sun 10.30am–4am.

Harlem Shake 100 W 124th St, at Malcolm X Blvd ☎ 212 222 8300, ⓦ harlemshakenyc.com; subway #2, #3 to 125th St; map p.199. Classic American diner with 1950s-style counter and stools, street seating and a menu specializing in chilli-cheese dogs ($5.50), burgers (from $7), sweet potato cheesecake ($6) and the eponymous thick shakes ($6–8). Sun–Thurs 8am–11pm, Fri & Sat 8am–2am.

Londel's 2620 Frederick Douglass Blvd, between W 139th and W 140th sts ☎ 212 234 6114, ⓦ londels restaurant.com; subway B, C to 135th St; map p.199. A little soul food, a little Cajun, a little Southern-fried food. This is an attractive, down-home place where you can eat jumbo fried shrimp ($25.95) or more common treats such as Southern fried chicken and waffles ($14.95); either way, follow it up with some sweet-potato pie. Sunday brunch $25.95. Jazz and R&B on Fri and Sat evenings at 8pm, 9pm and 10pm ($5 cover). Tues–Sat 5–11pm, Sun 11am–5pm.

New Leaf Restaurant & Bar 1 Margaret Corbin Drive, Fort Tryon Park ☎ 212 568 5323, ⓦ newleafrestaurant .com; subway A to 190th St; map p.199. An airy, renovated 1930s building with views of Fort Tryon Park, offering fresh American cuisine like burger and fries ($16) and crab cake sandwich ($16), mostly to visitors coming from the nearby Cloisters. Mon noon–3pm, Tues–Thurs noon–4pm & 4.30–8pm, Fri noon–4pm & 4.30–9pm, Sat 11am–3.30pm & 4–9pm, Sun 11am–3.30pm & 5–8pm.

North End Marketplace 4300 Broadway, at W 184th St ⓦ northendnyc.com; subway A to 181st St; map p.199. North Manhattan finally gets in on the food hall action, with this hip place featuring seven kiosks offering sustainable fair-trade *Filtered Coffee*, craft beer at *Mess Hall*, juicy tacos, organic BBQ, burgers and more, with most offerings under $10. Daily 8am–10pm.

★**Red Rooster** 310 Malcolm X Blvd, between W 125th and W 126th sts ☎ 212 792 9001, ⓦ redroosterharlem .com; subway #2, #3 to 125th St; map p.199. Marcus Samuelsson's lauded restaurant offers a sophisticated take on Southern comfort food. Sandwiches are $16–18, while mains such as lamb and sweet potato hash are $24–36 (lunch is cheaper). Leave room for the Red Rooster donuts ($12). Mon–Thurs 11.30am–10.30pm, Fri 11.30am–11.30pm, Sat 10am–11.30pm, Sun 10am–10pm.

Sylvia's Restaurant 328 Malcolm X Blvd, between W 126th and W 127th sts ☎ 212 996 0660, ⓦ sylvias restaurant.com; subway #2, #3 to 125th St; map p.199. Established in 1962, this is the best-known Southern soul food restaurant in Harlem – so famous that Sylvia Woods started her own food line (the matron died in 2012). While the barbecue ribs and fried chicken combo ($21.95) is exceptional and the candied yams ($5) are justly celebrated, *Sylvia's* has become a bit of a tourist trap

22

22

– try to avoid Sundays when tour groups arrive for the Gospel Brunch (11am–2pm). Mon–Sat 8am–10.30pm, Sun 11am–8pm.

CARIBBEAN

Lolo's Seafood Shack 303 W 116th St, between Frederick Douglass Blvd and Manhattan Ave ☎646 649 3356, ⓦlolosseafoodshack.com; subway B, C to 116th St; map p.199. Excellent seafood snack stop, serving Belize-style conch fritters ($10) as well as classic New England treats like shrimp ($10) and snow crab boils ($20) – the shark sandwich ($11) is made with sustainable spiny dogfish. Tues–Sat noon–9.45pm, Sun noon–5pm.

Sister's Cuisine 47 E 124th St, at Madison Ave ☎212 410 3000; subway #4, #5, #6 to 125th St; map p.199. Best Caribbean food in Harlem, offering Trinidadian-style *callaloo* ($4), caramelized-brown stew chicken ($11.50), curry chicken ($11.50) and Guyanese bread pockets ($5) plus Jamaican-style jerk chicken ($10.50) and curry goat ($12.50) – owner Marlyn Lawrie-Rogers hails from Guyana. Tues–Sat 11am–9pm, Sun 11am–8pm.

ITALIAN

Patsy's Pizzeria 2287 First Ave, between E 117th and E 118th sts ☎212 534 9783, ⓦthepatsyspizza.com; subway #6 to 116th St; map p.199. Opened by Pasquale "Patsy" Lancieri in 1933, this is one of the last vestiges of Italian Harlem, churning out paper-thin pizza slices ($1.75; pizzas from $15) from its coal-burning brick oven; Patsy learnt his trade at *Lombardi's* (see p.286), but it was here that he "invented" the pizza slice concept. Cash only. Daily 11am–11pm.

Rao's 455 E 114th St, between First and Pleasant aves ☎212 722 6709, ⓦraosrestaurants.com; subway #6 at 116th St; map p.199. Founded in 1896 and the most authentic Italian (Neapolitan) dining experience in the city. To be honest, you are unlikely to ever eat a meal here (it's only got ten tables "owned" by regulars, and one seating a night), but it's worth soaking up the ambience and live music at the tiny bar – who knows, a table may become available (wearing a suit will help). No menu – the waiters will discuss putting together a meal for you and your group. Cash only (expect to pay $125 per head for a meal with wine), and remember it's "ray-o's". Mon–Fri 7–11pm.

LATIN AMERICAN

El Paso 1643 Lexington Ave at E 104th St ☎212 831 3104, ⓦelpasony.com; subway #6 to 103rd St; map p.199. One of three authentic Mexican restaurants managed by a couple of chefs from Puebla – this is the newest and smartest venue, with fabulous tacos from $8 (for two) and a range of regional Mexican dishes ($18–32) like *carnitas estilo Michoacan* (pork in tequila). Sun–Wed 11am–11pm, Thurs–Sat 11am–midnight.

La Fonda Boricua 169 E 106th St, between Lexington and Third aves ☎212 410 7292, ⓦfonda boricua.com; subway #6 to 103rd St; map p.199. Authentic Puerto Rican diner, where huge plates of rich meat stews, roast pork, rice and beans rarely top $10. Daily 11am–10pm.

Malecón Restaurant 4141 Broadway, between W 175th & W 176th sts ☎212 927 3812, ⓦmalecon restaurants.com; subway A to 175th St; map p.209. This old-school Cuban joint is best known for its glistening spit-roasted chicken ($7–20), but aromatic *asopados* (soupy rice; $19–39), plantains and puddings are just as good. Sun–Thurs 7am–1.30am, Fri & Sat 7am–2am.

Sandy Restaurant 2261 Second Ave at E 116th St ☎212 348 8654, ⓦsandyrestaurant.com; subway #4, #6 to 116th St; map p.199. This is the Dominican heart of East Harlem, where you can feast on fresh rotisserie chicken, garlic-rubbed pork shoulder roast (*pernil*) and tripe soup (*mondongo*). Mains from $5.50 at breakfast to $13–19 for dinner. Daily 7am–10pm.

SWEET TREATS

★Levain Bakery 2167 Frederick Douglass Blvd, between W 116th and W 117th sts ☎646 455 0952, ⓦlevainbakery.com; subway B, C to 116th St; map p.199. Harlem outpost of the Upper West Side favourite, with their raspberry-filled *bomboloncini*, baguettes and massive, chunky cookies centre-stage (try the dark-chocolate peanut butter chip; $4). Mon–Sat 8am–7pm, Sun 9am–7pm.

Make My Cake 121 St Nicholas Ave, at W 116th St ☎212 932 0833, ⓦmakemycake.com; subway #2, #3 to 116th St; map p.199. Generously sized chocolate and red velvet cupcakes ($3.75) lead the offerings at this smart bakery. The shop opened in 1996, but its baking secrets date back to 1940s Mississippi. Mon–Thurs 8am–8pm, Fri 8am–9pm, Sat 9am–9pm, Sun 9am–7pm.

BROOKLYN

Brooklyn has turned into a seriously food-centric borough, with dozens of innovative restaurants cropping up in rapidly changing neighbourhoods like Park Slope, Carroll Gardens, Fort Greene, Williamsburg, Bushwick and further out in Ditmas Park. Restaurants here tend to be more relaxed and cheaper than comparable spots in Manhattan, though there are plenty of places where you can splurge if you want to. International menus flourish in other parts of the borough, from long-established Polish spots in Greenpoint (itself with a trendy scene) to Russian fare in Brighton Beach. You may also want to check out the vendor selection at famed food fair Smorgasburg (see p.392).

DOWNTOWN BROOKLYN

Dekalb Market Hall 445 Albee Square W, at Dekalb Ave ☎929 359 6555, ⓦdekalbmarkethall.com; subway #2,3 to Hoyt St, B, Q, R to Dekalb Ave; map p.218. Located in the basement of a shopping centre, in Brooklyn's industrial heart, this alluring food hall manages to overcome a commercialized setting. Over forty vendors are on hand, including famed *Katz's Deli* (see p.290) and the ice cream of Ample Hills Creamery, but our money is on the more modest stands, like *Pierogi Boys* (potato dumplings; $7) and *Steve's Authentic Key Lime Pies* ($5.50 for an individual tart). Mon–Wed & Sun 11am–9pm, Thurs–Sat 11am–10pm.

Junior's 386 Flatbush Ave Extension, at DeKalb Ave ☎718 852 5257, ⓦjuniorscheesecake.com; subway B, Q, R to DeKalb Ave; map p.218. Lit up like a Vegas casino, *Junior's* offers everything from tuna sandwiches to ribs and a full cocktail bar; servings are mammoth. Known as the city's cheesecake champ, it rests somewhat on its laurels, though it's still good fun, and the desserts are definitely worth digging into. Mon–Thurs & Sun 6.30am–midnight, Fri & Sat 6.30am–1am.

FULTON FERRY DISTRICT AND DUMBO

★**Almondine** 85 Water St, near Main St ☎718 797 5026, ⓦalmondinebakery.com; subway A, C to High St, F to York St; map p.218. Excellent patisserie, run by a former *Le Bernardin* pastry chef with chocolatier Jacques Torres (see below), that churns out all kinds of buttery, flaky treats, as well as crusty baguette sandwiches ($9), soups and quiches. Mon–Sat 7am–7pm, Sun 9am–6pm.

Brooklyn Ice Cream Factory 1 Water St, at the Fulton Ferry pier ☎718 246 3963; subway A, C to High St; map p.218. An old fireboat house contains the perfect reward for the walk across the Brooklyn Bridge: super-rich ice cream with toppings created by the pastry chef at the neighbouring *River Café* (see above). Cash only. Daily noon–10pm.

Grimaldi's 1 Front St, at Old Fulton St ☎718 858 4300, ⓦgrimaldis-pizza.com; subway A, C to Brooklyn Bridge-High St; map p.218. Though this age-old favourite has moved up the street from its original cramped quarters, *Grimaldi's* still draws crowds for its delicious, thin and crispy pizza ($20 for a large marinara) – though thankfully you're less likely to encounter a long queue. Cash only. Mon–Thurs 11.30am–10.45pm, Fri 11.30am–11.45pm, Sat noon–11.45pm, Sun noon–10.45pm.

Jacques Torres Chocolate 66 Water St, Dumbo ☎718 875 1269, ⓦmrchocolate.com, subway A, C to High St or F to York St; map p.218. This French-born chocolatier left highfalutin *Le Cirque* restaurant in 2000 to open his first solo venture; since then, he's expanded to other locations in Soho, Rockefeller Center and elsewhere. Come here for the super-thick hot chocolate ($4) and hand-made creations, from chocolate crunch puffs to champagne truffles ($20 for ten). Takeaway only. Mon–Sat 9am–8pm, Sun 10am–6pm.

Juliana's Pizza 19 Old Fulton St, between Front and Water sts, Dumbo ☎718, 596 6700, ⓦjulianaspizza .com; subway F to York St, A, C to High St; map p.218. Pizza legend Patsy Grimaldi came out of retirement to re-occupy the old location of his famous restaurant (he sold naming rights to the current owners of *Grimaldi's*, next door, in 1998), using the original coal oven to knock out his signature thin pizzas under a new moniker (*Juliana's* is a tribute to his late mother). His near-perfect margheritas are $19–22, while specials are $22–32. Mon–Fri 11.30am–11pm, Sat & Sun 11am–11pm.

River Café 1 Water St, between Furman and Old Fulton sts ☎718 522 5200, ⓦrivercafe.com; subway A, C to Brooklyn Bridge-High St; map p.218. You can get better food for the price (or even much cheaper) in New York, but *River Café* is more about the romantic atmosphere and spectacular views of the Brooklyn Bridge. The prix-fixe dinner, with dishes like foie gras two ways and rack of lamb with house-made *merguez* sausage, costs $130 per person for three courses, and it's $160 for a six-course tasting menu, excluding wine. There's also a prix fixe Sunday brunch ($55). Jackets are required for men at dinner. Mon–Fri 5.30–11pm, Sat & Sun 11.30am–2.30pm & 5.30–11pm.

Superfine 126 Front St, between Jay and Pearl sts ☎718 243 9005, ⓦsuperfine.nyc; subway F to York St; map p.218. *Superfine's* ever-changing menu has a fresh, Mediterranean bent, with big salads (shrimp, calamari), pork chops and pastas ($18–27), while Sunday brunch skews Southwestern: *huevos rancheros* with New Mexican green chillies ($11) is a nod to the chef's roots. The bar is a cool hangout; there's a free pool table too. Tues–Sat 11.30am–3pm & 6–11pm, Sun 11am–3pm & 6–10pm; bar remains open from opening time until 2am weekdays, 4am weekends.

★**Vinegar Hill House** 72 Hudson Ave, between Front and Water sts ☎718 522 1018, ⓦvinegarhillhouse.com; subway F to York St; map p.218. As charming and inviting a restaurant as you'll find, with exposed wood, pressed-tin ceilings, friendly service and a small, well-edited menu of farm-fresh dishes (lamb neck, rabbit leg and the like); there's a hideaway room downstairs, great for a small party, and the sourdough strawberry pancake ($14) at brunch is a singular achievement in the pancake world. Mon–Thurs 6–11pm, Fri 6–11.30pm, Sat 10.30am–3.30pm & 6–11.30pm, Sun 10.30am–3.30pm & 5.30–11pm.

BROOKLYN HEIGHTS

★**Iris Café** 20 Columbia Place, between Joralemon and State sts ☎718 722 7395, ⓦiriscafe.nyc; subway #2, #3, #4, #5 to Borough Hall, R to Court St; map p.218. This wonderful neighbourhood café brews up powerful caffeinated drinks and makes tasty baked goods and unusual sandwiches ($13–15); they've also started full dinner service (mains $14–22). Daily 8am–midnight.

22

22

Noodle Pudding 38 Henry St, at Middagh St ☎ 718 625 3737; subway #2, #3 to Clark St, A, C to High St-Brooklyn Bridge; map p.218. It can get quite busy and the service can be spotty, but this is a great-value Italian in a neighbourhood somewhat lacking in options. The bread with spicy olive oil is addictive, the pastas well executed and the wine ridiculously cheap (if you opt for the quite-drinkable $5/glass, $15/bottle house tipple). Cash only. Tues–Thurs 5.30–10.30pm, Fri & Sat 5.30–11pm, Sun 5–10pm.

WILLIAMSBURG AND GREENPOINT
COFFEE

★**Blue Bottle** 160 Berry St, between N Fourth and N Fifth sts ☎ 718 387 4160, ⓦ bluebottlecoffee.com; subway L to Bedford Ave; map p.225. The original New York outpost (now also in Chelsea and Tribeca, among other locations) of a well-regarded San Francisco roaster. It's a cross between a café and a lab: the java used for iced coffee ($4) dripping in giant bulbous tubes, and a working roastery fills the spacious back. The New Orleans-style cold brew is especially good ($4). Mon–Fri 6.30am–7pm, Sat & Sun 7am–7.30pm.

Café Grumpy 193 Meserole Ave, at Diamond St ☎ 718 349 7623, ⓦ cafegrumpy.com; subway G to Nassau Ave; map p.225. Multiple Manhattan locations. Opened in 2005, this is one of New York's best-known coffee shops, in part because of its starring role in *Girls*, but also for its superb beans, roasted on site. Greenpoint is home to the original location, which has plenty of space and is usually full of locals. Mon–Fri 7am–7.30pm, Sat & Sun 7.30am–7.30pm.

★**Devoción** 69 Grand St, between Wythe and Kent aves ☎ 718 285 6180, ⓦ devocion.com; subway L to Bedford Ave; map p.225. Set in a stunning industrial space with a massive skylight and a "living wall" of plants, this superb café sources coffee beans directly from Colombian farmers and roasts them here on Grand Street, creating a product that's "bean to cup" in just ten days. Mon–Fri 7am–7pm, Sat & Sun 8am–7pm.

Gimme! Coffee 495 Lorimer St, between Grand and Powers sts ☎ 718 388 7771, ⓦ gimmecoffee.com; subway L to Lorimer St, G to Metropolitan Ave; map p.225. This coffee haven is not your typical lounge-about-all-day Williamsburg café, but a bright, narrow spot to pick up a shot of espresso or cup of the house roast to kick-start your next few hours. A refreshing antidote. Daily 7am–7pm.

EATING

Bamonte's 32 Withers St, at Union Ave ☎ 718 384 8831; subway L to Lorimer St, G to Metropolitan Ave; map p.225. Red-sauce restaurants abound in NYC, but this is one of the legends, which has served traditional Italian-American dishes like linguine with clam sauce ($15.50)

since 1900. Mon, Wed & Thurs noon–10pm, Fri & Sat noon–11pm, Sun 1–10pm.

★**DeStefano's Steakhouse** 89 Conselyea St, at ☎ 718 384 2836, ⓦ deesteakhouse.com; subway L to Lorimer St, G to Metropolitan Ave; map p.225. Marked by the special ambience that comes easily to family-run establishments, *DeStefano's* serves incredible steaks ($35–50), chicken cordon bleu ($32) and other meaty classics in a dining room that looks like it was sprung from your nonna's house, complete with fireplace and black-and-white photos. Tues–Thurs 5–9.30pm, Fri & Sat 5–10pm, Sun 5–9.30pm.

Diner 85 Broadway, at Berry St ☎ 718 486 3077, ⓦ dinernyc.com; subway L to Bedford Ave, J, M, Z to Marcy Ave; map p.225. This groovy restaurant in a Pullman diner-car has a tiny, changing menu of American grub (burgers and steaks, roasted chicken and fish, fantastic fries), along with a dozen varieties of champagne. Next door they've opened up the market-cum-restaurant *Marlow and Sons*, which does fresh oysters ($24), chicken-under-a-brick ($30) and elegant cocktails. Mon–Fri 11am–midnight, Sat & Sun 10am–midnight.

Egg 109 N 3rd St, between Bedford Ave and Berry St ☎ 718 302 5151, ⓦ eggrestaurant.com; subway L to Bedford Ave; map p.225. Delicious Southern-style breakfasts, including biscuits and gravy (a scone covered in white gravy; $12.50), though the sandwiches (ham and pimento cheese, $12; duck with eggs, $14) are good choices as well. Mon–Fri 7am–5pm, Sat & Sun 8am–5pm.

Enid's 560 Manhattan Ave ☎ 718 349 3859, ⓦ enids .net; subway G to Nassau Ave; map p.225. As much a bar and daytime hangout as a restaurant, *Enid's* attracts a youthful audience for its loud rock soundtrack, popular brunch and casual sandwich-oriented, Southern-influenced menu (catfish sandwich; $15). Daily 10am–midnight (til 2 or 4am in summer).

Fette Sau 354 Metropolitan Ave, between 4th and Roebling sts ☎ 718 963 3404, ⓦ fettesaubbq.com; subway L to Bedford Ave, G to Metropolitan Ave; map p.225. The industrial-chic vibe (it's in an old garage) of this barbecue specialist seems fitting for the neighbourhood. Order your meat by the pound (beef brisket, pork shoulder or pork belly; $16), tack on a couple of sides (burnt-end baked beans; $5.25) and wash it all down with a microbrew ($6 pints). Mon 5–11pm, Tues–Thurs & Sun noon–11pm, Fri & Sat noon–midnight.

★**Paulie Gee's** 60 Greenpoint Ave, at West St ☎ 347 987 3747, ⓦ pauliegee.com; subway G to Greenpoint Ave; map p.225. In a town with extreme pizza competition, *Paulie Gee's* ranks with the best of the best. The menu is filled with wittily named pies ("Feel Like Bacon Love" etc) and eclectic flavours: the "Cherry Jones" ($18) has gorgonzola, dried cherries and prosciutto di Parma, while the restaurant's signature "Hellboy" ($17) is topped with

22

soppressata and spicy honey. Great vegetarian and vegan options, too. Very popular; get there early to avoid a long wait. Mon–Fri 6–11pm, Sat 5–11pm, Sun 5–10pm.

★ **Peter Luger Steak House** 178 Broadway, at Driggs Ave ☎718 387 7400, ⊛peterluger.com; subway J, M, Z to Marcy Ave; map p.225. Catering to carnivores since 1887, *Peter Luger* may just be the city's finest steakhouse. The service is surly and the decor plain, but the porterhouse steak – the only cut served – is divine (roughly $50/person). Old-school sides like creamed spinach are just a distraction, though don't pass on the bacon starter ($5/slice). At lunchtime, the burger ($14) is a great deal. Cash only; reservations required. Mon–Thurs 11.45am–9.45pm, Fri & Sat 11.45am–10.45pm, Sun 12.45–9.45pm.

★ **Peter Pan Donut** 727 Manhattan Ave, between Norman and Meserole aves ☎718 389 3676, ⊛peterpandonuts.com; subway G to Nassau Ave; map p.225. Totally old-school shop, with swivel stools at a curving formica counter, where you can enjoy airy, delectable crullers and around twenty other donut varieties, including the mouthwatering chocolate cake option. Mon–Fri 4.30am–8pm, Sat 5am–8pm, Sun 5.30am–7pm.

★ **Pies and Thighs** 166 S 4th St, at Driggs Ave ☎347 529 6090, ⊛piesnthighs.com; subway J, M, Z to Marcy Ave; map p.225. This one-time underground institution has found a bright corner location in which to serve its Southern-style food: great chicken biscuits (a scone with a fried chicken filling; $7.50), expertly fried chicken ($14.50 with a side) and a changing rotation of pies (slice $4.50–5.50; favourites include sour cherry and bourbon pecan). Mon–Fri 9am–4pm & 5pm–midnight, Sat & Sun 10am–4pm & 5pm–midnight.

Rye 247 S 1st St, between Roebling and Metropolitan aves ☎718 281 8047, ⊛ryerestaurant.com; subway J, M, Z to Marcy Ave; map p.225. The retro speakeasy feel seems totally natural in this dark wood and pressed-tin setting. The straightforward menu offers the likes of Scotch eggs ($10), meatloaf sandwiches ($18) and ribeye for two (market price) – but there's nothing simple about the expertly and attentively made cocktails. The happy hour special ($5 Old Fashioneds, $5 cheeseburgers) is, quite simply, one of the best deals going. Mon–Thurs 5.30pm–1am (dinner until 11pm), Fri & Sat 5.30pm–2am (dinner until 11.30pm), Sun 11am–1am (dinner until 10.30pm).

Saltie 378 Metropolitan Ave, near Havemeyer St ☎212 387 4777, ⊛saltieny.com; subway L to Lorimer St, G to Metropolitan Ave; map p.225. Tiny shop with a short menu of unusual – and unusually delicious – sandwiches; the Scuttlebutt (with hard-boiled egg, feta, black olives and capers, among other ingredients) is likely the richest vegetarian sandwich you'll ever encounter. Most dishes $11–12. Daily 10am–6pm.

BUSHWICK

Roberta's 261 Moore St ☎718 417 1118, ⊛robertaspizza.com; subway L to Morgan Ave; map p.225. Charmingly ramshackle, this pizza joint draws huge crowds (expect a wait) for killer pies – speck and mushroom ($17) and so on – plus well-executed pastas, salads and entrées, and an extensive drinks menu. It also has a "hidden" restaurant, *Blanca* (☎347 799 2807, ⊛blancanyc.com), which offers a $195 tasting menu for dinner Wed–Sat; reservations a month in advance. Mon–Fri 11am–midnight, Sat & Sun 10am–midnight.

BEDFORD-STUYVESANT

★ **Dough** 448 Lafayette Ave, at Franklin Ave ☎347 533 7544, ⊛doughbrooklyn.com; subway G to Classon Ave; map p.214. Also in Midtown and the Flatiron District. Ridiculously good, enormous donuts ($3), possibly distilled from heaven's own clouds, sold to a zealous queue of patrons from inside a tiny, unassuming storefront. The tangy hibiscus flavour will haunt your dreams, though the *dulce de leche* is no slouch, either. Cash only. Daily 6am–9pm.

Peaches HotHouse 415 Tompkins Ave, at Hancock St ☎718 483 9111, ⊛bcrestaurantgroup.com; subway C to Kingston-Throop aves; map p.214. A more country-fried offshoot of the classic Bed-Stuy brunch spot *Peaches* (just a few blocks away), *Peaches HotHouse* is famed for frying (and spicing!) some of the best chicken in town. The menu boasts Southern staples like blackened catfish ($12) and smoked andouille sausage ($4), served in a small, wood-panelled dining room to a hip clientele. Mon–Fri 11am–11pm, Sat & Sun 10am–11pm.

FORT GREENE AND CLINTON HILL

★ **Emily** 919 Fulton St, between Clinton and Waverly aves ☎347 844 9588, ⊛pizzaloveemily.com; subway C, G to Clinton-Washington Ave; map p.218. Second location in the West Village. A double threat: this modest Brooklyn storefront is famed both for its wood-fired pizzas and gooey burgers alike. The burger (a steep $27) is a magical mix of prime beef, caramelized onion and melted cheddar; pair it with the pepperoni and jalapeño pizza ($21) for entry into foodie heaven. Mon–Fri 5.30–11pm, Sat noon–3pm, 5–11.30pm, Sun noon–3pm, 5–11pm.

Locanda Vini e Olii 129 Gates Ave, at Cambridge Place ☎718 622 9202, ⊛locandany.com; subway C, G to Clinton-Washington aves; map p.218. Gorgeous, inventive Italian food served in a restored pharmacy, all gleaming dark wood and glass. Rabbit terrine, fluffy gnocchi, even beef tongue in parsley sauce may pop up on the menu. Well priced (pasta $15 or so; grilled/roasted meat and fish $22–27) and worth the walk to the far reaches of Fort Greene (aka Clinton Hill). Reservations recommended. Tues–Thurs & Sun 5.30–10.30pm, Fri & Sat 5.30–11.30pm.

Madiba 195 Dekalb Ave, at Carlton Ave ☎ 718 855 9190, ⓦ madibarestaurant.com; subway C to Lafayette Ave, or G to Fulton St; map p.218. Half the fun of this South African restaurant is its ambience – the tin tables come in all sorts of colours, tapestries and art hang wherever you look, and bright paintings of Nelson Mandela rub elbows with soda bottles repurposed as chandeliers. The menu is flavourful and authentic: *bobotie* with curried mince, almonds and yellow rice ($17), oxtail stew ($24) and pumpkin fritters ($7). A neighbourhood institution, the patio positively buzzes in good weather. You might even spy Beyoncé. Mon–Thurs 11am–11pm, Fri & Sat 11am–midnight.

PARK SLOPE AND PROSPECT HEIGHTS
COFFEE

Café Regular 318 11th St, at Fifth Ave ☎ 718 768 4170, ⓦ caferegular.com; subway F, G, R to Fourth Ave-9th St; map p.231. Excellent coffee ($3) and pastries in a tiny, Eurocentric café that feels a little hidden off the main drag. Mon–Fri 7am–7pm, Sat & Sun 8am–7pm.

EATING

Al Di Là 248 Fifth Ave, at Carroll St ☎ 718 783 4565, ⓦ aldilatrattoria.com; subway R to Union St-Fourth Ave; map p.231. Venetian country cooking at its finest at this husband-and-wife-run trattoria. Standouts include beet and ricotta ravioli ($12), a delicate *malfatti* (swiss chard gnocchi; $15), the daily risotto, and braised rabbit with polenta ($29). Early or late, expect at least a 45min wait (they don't take reservations); they've opened up a wine bar around the corner, where you can wait if you like. Mon–Thurs noon–3pm & 6–10.30pm, Fri noon–3pm & 6–11pm, Sat 11am–3.30pm & 5.30–11pm, Sun 11am–3.30pm & 5–10pm.

★ **Ample Hills Creamery** 623 Vanderbilt Ave, at St Mark's Ave ☎ 347 240 3926, ⓦ amplehills.com; subway B, Q to Seventh Ave; map p.231. This ice-cream shop has developed a cult following since its debut here in 2011, with addictive creations such as salted crack caramel (caramel ice cream with chocolate-covered buttered crackers) and "sweet as honey" (honeycomb candy in a sweet cream base). Sun–Thurs noon–11pm, Fri & Sat noon–midnight.

Bagel Hole 400 Seventh Ave, between 12th and 13th sts ☎ 718 788 4014, ⓦ bagelhole.net; subway F, G to Seventh Ave; map p.231. The name works two ways, both to reference the hole in the bagel and that this place is a hole in the wall. That doesn't stop them from churning out cheap crisp-chewy bagels ($1.25 a piece) as good as any in the city. Cash only. Mon–Fri 7am–6pm, Sat 7am–5pm, Sun 7am–4pm.

Bagel Pub 287 9th St, between Fourth and Fifth aves ☎ 718 499 4402, ⓦ bagelpub.com; subway F, G, R to Fourth Ave-9th St; map p.231. Lines snake to the door for

the stellar smoothies and other breakfast offerings at this beloved bagel stalwart. Order the ABC sandwich (avocado, bacon, cheddar and eggs; $7), and aim for a spot in the little garden. Mon–Fri 6am–6pm, Sat & Sun 7am–5pm.

Rose Water 787 Union St, at Sixth Ave ☎ 718 783 3800, ⓦ rosewaterrestaurant.com; subway R to Union St-Fourth Ave; map p.231. Intimate Mediterranean-American bistro, serving stellar seasonal dishes with flavourful accents (say, roast pork loin with bacon and rhubarb; $28), including an excellent-value three-course market-menu dinner for $28. Wonderful brunch too. Mon–Fri 5.30–10pm, Sat & Sun 9.30am–3pm & 5.30–11pm.

Sushi Katsuei 210 7th Ave, at Third St ☎ 718 788 5338, ⓦ sushikatsuei.com; subway F, G to Seventh Ave; map p.231. The sushi chefs here are serious minded and know what they're doing, so put yourself in their hands by ordering the *omakase* ($45 for sushi, $65 to also include sashimi) and enjoy the procession of fresh fish that comes. Mon–Thurs 5–10pm, Fri 4.30–10pm, Sat noon–3pm & 4.30–10pm, Sun noon–3pm & 4.30–9.30pm.

Tom's 782 Washington Ave, at Sterling Place ☎ 718 636 9738; subway #2, #3 to Grand Army Plaza or Eastern Parkway; map p.231. A Brooklyn institution located a few blocks from the Brooklyn Museum, with great pancakes ($7), lots of typical diner favourites and old-fashioned fountain drinks like lime rickeys ($2) and egg creams ($3). Best, though, is an amiable vibe that makes first-timers feel like regulars; expect to wait in line for weekend brunch. Cash only. Mon–Sat 7am–4pm, Sun 8am–4pm.

Wangs 671 Union St, at Fourth Ave ☎ 718 636 6390, ⓦ wangsbk.com; subway R to Union St; map p.231. Tiny hole-in-the-wall (with a few benches outside) knocking out delicious fried chicken, brined in Southeast Asian spices and breaded (half a bird for $14), plus fried Korean-style whole wings (three pieces for $7.50) with hot sauce plus home-made *kimchee* ($4.25) and a variety of sides. Mon–Sat 12.30–11pm, Sun 12.30–10pm.

BOERUM HILL, CARROLL GARDENS AND GOWANUS

Battersby 255 Smith St, between Douglass and Degraw sts ☎ 718 852 8321, ⓦ battersbybrooklyn.com; subway F, G to Carroll St; map p.235. When it opened, this narrow slip of a place set the local foodie world ablaze. There are but a handful of tables, limited reservations (just for the tasting menus; $75, and usually made a month in advance; otherwise, first come, first served) and constantly changing market-driven food. If you get in, consider yourself lucky and let them guide you – dishes may be made up more or less on the spot. Mon–Sat 5.30–11pm, Sun 5.30–10pm.

Buttermilk Channel 524 Court St, at Huntington St ☎ 718 852 8490, ⓦ buttermilkchannelnyc.com; subway F, G to Smith-9th St; map p.235. Beloved

22

22

neighbourhood bistro with a solid menu of upscale creature comforts like linguini with home-made ricotta and summer corn ($19) or fried chicken with cheddar waffles ($25). At breakfast, the pancakes are spectacular. Mon–Wed 5–10pm, Thurs 5–11pm, Fri 5pm–midnight, Sat 10am–3pm & 5pm–midnight, Sun 10am–3pm & 5–10pm.

Café Pedlar 210 Court St, between Warren and Wyckoff sts ☎718 855 7129, ⊛cafepedlar.com; subway F, G to Bergen St; map p.235. Simply but elegantly adorned hangout for excellent coffee and baked goods; hard to get a table or bench spot sometimes, but nearby Cobble Hill Park makes a fine picnic setting. Daily 7am–7pm.

★**Frankies 457 Spuntino** 457 Court St, at Luquer St ☎718 403 0033, ⊛frankiesspuntino.com; subway F, G to Carroll St; map p.235. Co-chefs Frank and Frank revive and refine Italian-American favourites on the south side of Carroll Gardens. Home-made pastas ($16–19) are the way to go, coupled with a fresh salad of seasonal greens and a few crostini; add an order of meatballs ($14) if you think it won't be enough. Enjoy your meal on the breezy garden patio out back. Mon–Thurs & Sun 11am–11pm, Sat & Sun 11am–midnight.

Lucali 575 Henry St, at Carroll St ☎718 858 4086; subway F, G to Carroll St; map p.235. Add this to the list of pizzerias whose devotees claim it as the best in town. Located in a converted old-fashioned candy store, Lucali only serves pies ($24; minimal topping choices, $4 each) and calzones ($10), and it's frequently hard to get a seat, but the product is a knockout. Cash only. Mon & Wed–Sun 6–10pm.

Mile End 97A Hoyt St, between Pacific St and Atlantic Ave ☎718 852 7510, ⊛mileenddeli.com; subway F, G to Bergen St or A, C, G to Hoyt-Schermerhorn St; map p.235. In a short time, this Montréal-style deli has become a fixture, attracting long lunch queues for its poutine (fries with curds and gravy; $8/12) and smoked-meat sandwich: piled on rye bread with a smear of mustard, this is a peppery Canadian version of a Jewish classic ($15). Breakfast and dinner are no slouch, either; they do standards bagels and lox ($13.50) and matzoh-ball soup ($9) proud – not to mention a Sunday-night Chinese set menu ($35). Mon–Wed 8am–4pm & 5–10pm, Thurs & Fri 8am–4pm & 5–11pm, Sat 10am–4pm & 5–11pm, Sun 10am–4pm & 5–10pm.

★**Petite Crevette** 144 Union St, at Hicks St ☎718 855 2632; subway F, G to Carroll St; map p.235. The cosy, casual Petite Crevette employs a rather straightforward approach to fish and seafood: you pick it, they grill or sauté or do whatever to it, you eat every bite (branzino; $25). Crab corn chowder ($8) and soft-shell crabs (when in season) are standouts; alcohol is BYO. Cash only. Daily 11.30am–2.30pm & 6–11pm.

★**Pok Pok NY** 117 Columbia St, at Kane St ☎718 923 9322, ⊛pokpokny.com; map p.235. Portland chef Andy Ricker has set NYC abuzz with his showcase of authentic flavours from northern Thailand (from where he frequently brings back ingredients). While most go crazy over the sticky wings ($15), don't miss out on the pork ribs with mustard greens ($14), seafood crêpe ($16) or spicy eggplant salad ($15). Get a bunch of dishes to share and accompany them with Southeast Asian beers or exotic cocktails (including one with the Thai firewater, Mekhong). No reservations, and it gets crowded; get a drink at his bar, Whiskey Soda (across the street), while you wait. Mon–Fri 5.30–10pm, Sat & Sun noon–10pm.

Prime Meats 465 Court St, at Luquer St ☎718 254 0327, ⊛frankspm.com; subway F, G to Carroll St; map p.235. Frequently packed, this sibling of Frankie's (see above) serves up excellent steaks ($36 or, as a special, a côte de boeuf for two), burgers ($23) and handcrafted sausages in a room that feels decades old. For lunch or brunch, content yourself with biscuits and gravy ($15), mushrooms and eggs with bratwurst ($13) or a hearty sandwich. Mon–Thurs 11am–11pm, Fri 11am–midnight, Sat 8am–midnight, Sun 8am–11pm.

RED HOOK

Baked 359 Van Brunt St, at Dikeman St ☎718 222 0345, ⊛bakednyc.com; subway F, G to Smith-9th St, then bus #61; map p.235. Relaxed neighbourhood café that's justly celebrated for its brownies ($3.50), cakes, muffins, Rice Krispie treats, granola ($6) and marshmallows, all made on the premises but found in cafés and shops throughout the Northeast. Mon–Fri 7am–7pm, Sat & Sun 8am–7pm.

★**Good Fork** 391 Van Brunt St, between Coffey and Van Dyke sts ☎718 643 6636, ⊛goodfork.com; subway F, G to Smith-9th St, then bus #61; map p.235. Though it feels very much a neighbourhood restaurant, this sliver of a place with exposed brick and thrift-store decor turns out terrific food with a focus on local ingredients that's worth travelling for. The changing menu is New American with Asian flourishes, as per the delectable dumplings ($10) and Korean-style grilled skirt steak with kimchee rice and a fried egg ($29). Tues–Fri 5.30–10.30pm, Sat 10am–3pm & 5.30–10.30pm, Sun 10am–3pm & 5.30–10pm.

Hometown Bar-B-Que 454 Van Brunt St, at Reed St ☎347 294 4644, ⊛hometownbarbque.com; subway F, G to Smith-9th St, then bus #61; map p.235. Part of a citywide barbecue insurgence, Hometown does justice to this smoky cuisine. Mix-and-match pulled pork ($11 for half a pound) with brisket ($14 half a pound), and pair with corn bread ($4) and mac and cheese ($4). Counter service only. Tues–Thurs noon–11pm, Fri & Sat noon–midnight, Sun noon–10pm.

★ **Red Hook Lobster Pound** 284 Van Brunt St, between Visitation Place and Verona St ☎718 858 7650, ⓦredhooklobster.com; subway F, G to Smith-9th St, then bus #61; map p.235. The *Pound* does delectable lobster rolls ($25), filled with fresh, plump chunks of lobster meat – the perfect snack on a warm spring or summer day – not to mention lobster mac & cheese ($18) and a number of other treats. They also run a food truck (ⓦtwitter.com/lobstertruckny). Hours change seasonally, but generally April–Nov Tues–Thurs & Sun 11.30am–9pm, Fri & Sat 11.30am–10pm; Dec–March Fri & Sat noon–9pm, Sun noon–8pm.

Steve's Authentic Key Lime Pies Pier 40, 185 Van Dyke St, at Ferris St ☎718 858 5333, ⓦstevesauthentic.com; subway F, G to Smith-9th St, then bus #61; map p.235. Tucked away on the Red Hook waterfront, this beloved shop dishes up some of the tastiest Key Lime pies in the Northeast ($5 for individual tarts). Limited seating. Daily noon–6pm.

DITMAS PARK

Purple Yam 1314 Cortelyou Rd ☎718 940 8188, ⓦpurpleyamnyc.com; subway Q to Cortelyou Rd; map p.214. Husband-and-wife owners (head chef and host too) serve up homestyle Filipino cooking here at friendly prices. The porky *sisig* ($18) and *lechon* ($21) are musts, and the *adobo* ($17) and daily *kimchee* ($5) are not far behind. Finish it off with coconut *buko* pie ($9). Mon–Fri 5.30–10.30pm, Sat 11am–3.30pm & 5.30–11pm, Sun 11am–3.30pm & 5.30–10pm.

MIDWOOD

Di Fara Pizza 1424 Ave J ☎718 258 1367, ⓦdifara.com; subway Q to Ave J; map p.214. It might be hard to fathom a piece of pizza worth $5 (not including toppings; whole pizzas are a much better deal starting at $28) plus what can be up to an hour's wait, but neither of these factors deter people from making the pilgrimage to what the general consensus regards as best slice in the city. Go early. Wed–Sun noon–4.30pm & 6–9pm.

BENSONHURST

★ **L&B Spumoni Gardens** 2725 86th St, at W 12th St ☎718 449 1230, ⓦspumonigardens; subway D to 2th Ave, N to Ave U; map p.214. There is a full-scale dining room with traditional red-sauce Italian at this Bensonhurst standby – which dates back to 1939 – but many folks come to get some Sicilian (read: square) slices of thick, saucy pizza and sit around on the picnic tables outside. Top it off with an Italian ice or *spumoni* (ice cream with candied fruit) and you've got a quintessential Brooklyn experience. Mon–Thurs & Sun 11am–midnight (dining room closes 10.30pm, in winter everything at 10pm), Fri & Sat 11am–1am (dining room closes 11.30pm, in winter everything at 11pm).

CONEY ISLAND

Gargiulo's 2911 W 15th St, between Surf and Mermaid aves ☎718 266 4891, ⓦgargiulos.com; subway D, F, N, Q to Coney Island-Stillwell Ave; map p.214. A gigantic, noisy, century-old family-run Coney Island restaurant famed for its large portions of hearty Neapolitan food. Most pasta dishes are $13–19, while meat and seafood dishes are around $23. Mon, Wed & Thurs noon–10.30pm, Fri & Sat noon–11.30pm, Sun noon–9.30pm.

Nargis Café 2818 Coney Island Ave, at Kathleen Place ☎718 872 7888, ⓦnargiscafe.com; subway B, Q to Sheepshead Bay; map p.214. This unusual gem specializes in Uzbek cuisine in a space richly decorated with Central Asian arts and crafts. The menu includes *bojon* salad (made with eggplant purée and fresh garlic), *plov* (lamb, rice, carrots and chickpeas), *samsa* (steamed meat dumplings) and *lagman* (diced meat, vegetables and noodles). Most mains $6–10. Sun–Wed 11am–11pm, Thurs 11am–midnight, Fri & Sat 11am–1am.

Nathan's 1310 Surf Ave, at Stillwell Ave ☎718 333 2202, ⓦnathansfamous.com; subway D, F, N, Q to Coney Island-Stillwell Ave; map p.214. Right there when you get off the subway, this is the home of the "famous Coney Island hot dog", open since 1916; *Nathan's* even holds a nationally televised annual Hot Dog Eating Contest on July 4. Other dishes served include fresh clams and buffalo wings ($5). Mon–Thurs & Sun 9am–1am, Sat & Sun 9am–2am.

★ **Totonno's Pizzeria Napolitano** 1524 Neptune Ave, between 15th and 16th sts ☎718 372 8606, ⓦtotonnosconeyisland.com; subway D, F, N, Q to Coney Island-Stillwell Ave; map p.214. The coal-oven-fired pizzas at this ancient (circa 1924), no-frills spot inspire devotion among pizza lovers for their sweet, fresh mozzarella and crispy crust. The basic starts at $21; add on toppings from there – you can't really go wrong. No slices; cash only. Thurs–Sun noon–7.30pm.

BRIGHTON BEACH AND SHEEPSHEAD BAY

Randazzo's Clam Bar 2017 Emmons Ave ☎718 615 0010, ⓦrandazzosclambar.com; subway B, Q to Sheepshead Bay, then Voorhees Ave to Ocean Ave, turn right and walk to Emmons Ave, take a left – a 10min walk; map p.214. All kinds of old-school pasta dishes and Italian preparations of fish and seafood (shrimp scampi; $22), along with briny, fresh clams – walk it off afterward along the marina. The family-owned place traces its history back nearly a hundred years, so you know they're doing something right. Mon–Fri 11am–11pm, Sat & Sun 11am–midnight.

Tatiana Grill Café 3145 Brighton 4th St, on the Boardwalk ☎718 646 7630, ⓦtatianagrill.com; subway B, Q to Brighton Beach; map p.214. This Russian

22

mainstay is a long-time boardwalk favourite, with a breezy terrace overlooking the beach. The *borscht* ($5), herring and pork dumplings ($9) are usually good, but this is all about the location and the circa 1970s Eastern bloc atmosphere (replete with surly Russian servers). *Tatiana Restaurant*, a short walk further along, is a little more upscale and more famed for its glitzy nightclub floor shows. Daily 10am–midnight.

QUEENS

The most diverse of all the boroughs, Queens offers some of the city's best opportunities to sample a wealth of foreign flavours, from Bosnian and Greek to Brazilian and Colombian to Szechuan and Thai. Most places listed here are easily accessible by subway.

22

ASTORIA AND LONG ISLAND CITY

Arepas Cafe 33-07 36th Ave, at 33rd St, Astoria ☎718 937 3835, ⓦarepasnyc.com; subway N, Q to 36th Ave; map p.248. A casual, friendly spot for Venezuelan *arepas* ($4.50–7) – a kind of thick corn cake stuffed like a pitta – with everything from shredded beef with plaintain and cheese to saucy shrimp. Mon–Thurs & Sun 11am–10pm, Fri & Sat 11am–midnight.

Casa Enrique 5-48 49th Ave, Long Island City ☎347 448 6040, ⓦhenrinyc.com; subway #7 to Vernon Blvd; map p.246. Michelin-starred Mexican restaurant with gorgeous yet surprisingly affordable takes on classic dishes like *carne asada* ($23), chorizo tacos (two for $10) and chicken slathered in *mole* sauce ($16). There's a lovely enclosed patio, and excellent cocktails and desserts (don't miss the *tres leches* cake; $8). Mon–Fri 5pm–midnight, Sat & Sun 11am–4pm & 5pm–midnight.

Djerdan 34-04 31st Ave, at 34th St, Astoria ☎718 721 2694, ⓦdjerdan.com; subway N, Q to Broadway or 30th Ave; map p.248. Cheap and filling *burek* – savoury meat, spinach or cheese pies, which go for $5 a slice – are the speciality of this simple Balkan eatery, and a tasty alternative to pizza. Try the "special" version, drizzled with garlicky yogurt. Daily 8am–11pm.

Kabab Café 25-12 Steinway St, Astoria ☎718 728 9858; subway N, Q to Astoria Blvd; map p.248. The culinary highlight of Steinway Street's "Little Egypt", this tiny, velvet-swathed den is the domain of Chef Ali, who lavishes patrons with traditional Middle Eastern goodies (smoky *baba ganoush*; lighter-than-air falafel, $5) as well as his own creations – don't miss the honey-glazed duck. Ask the prices of off-the-menu specials if you're on a budget – they can be quite high. Tues–Sun 1–5pm & 6–10pm.

★**Loukoumi Taverna** 45-07 Ditmars Blvd, Astoria ☎718 626 3200, ⓦtoloukoumi.com; subway N, Q to Astoria-Ditmars Blvd; map p.248. A little off the beaten path from Ditmars' famed cluster of Greek restaurants, this casual place remains a local favourite, and worth seeking out. Start your meal with fried saganaki cheese ($10), then move on to a tempting platter of dips and charcoal-grilled octopus ($13.50). Family run, the service is warm and the staff know their stuff. Daily 11am–11pm.

★**M. Wells Dinette** MoMA PS1, 22-25 Jackson Ave, between 46th Rd and 46th Ave, Long Island City ☎718 786 1800, ⓦmagasinwells.com; subway G, #7 to Court Square; E, M to Court Square-Ely; map p.246. Cheekily modelled on a classroom (MoMA PS1's building used to be a school), *M. Wells Dinette* sets itself apart from every school-lunch cafeteria and museum café you may have known. The menu changes, but expect dishes like foie gras and oats, braised tongue with tarragon and other daring, cholesterol-rich exercises (mains around $16). Go with a friend or two, order enough to share and walk it off in the neighbourhood afterwards. Mon & Thurs–Sun noon–6pm.

Mu Ramen 12-09 Jackson Ave, at 47th Rd, Long Island City ☎917 868 8903, ⓦramennyc.wix.com/popup; subway G to 21st St, #7 to Hunters Point; map p.246. Patrons form queues out the door for Mu Ramen's U&I dish (uni and egg roe; market price) and porky ramen with scallions and a soft-boiled egg ($15). The dining room is small and fun, with communal tables and squiggly wooden ribbons covering the ceiling. Mon–Thurs & Sun 5–10pm, Fri–Sat 5–11pm.

Omonia Café 32-20 Broadway, at 33rd St, Astoria ☎718 274 6650, ⓦomoniacafe.com; subway N, Q to Broadway; map p.248. Broadway's liveliest café is still a stronghold for Greek men poring over newspapers during the day, but after dinner the international crowd becomes younger and more lively. Make sure to order a thick wedge of flaky, buttery, sticky-sweet *baklava* ($6), the best of the desserts here. Mon–Thurs 6am–2.30am, Fri 6am–3.30am, Sat 6am–4am, Sun 6am–3am.

The Queens Kickshaw 40-17 Broadway, between Steinway and 41st St, Astoria ☎718 937 4821, ⓦthequeenskickshaw.com; subway E, M to Steinway; map p.248. They specialize in gourmet grilled cheese sandwiches ($9–12), but there's also a full menu for each meal of the day, small-batch beers (and *kombucha* and cider) on draught and a pleasant vibe that makes it a community hangout for coffee lingerers as well. Mon–Thurs 7.30am–midnight, Fri 7.30am–1am, Sat 9am–1am, Sun 9am–midnight.

Sweetleaf 10-93 Jackson Ave, at 49th Ave and 11th St, Long Island City ☎917 832 6726, ⓦsweetleaflic.com; subway #7 to Vernon Blvd-Jackson Ave, G to 21st St; map p.246. With its original pressed-tin details, home-made pastries and caffeinated offerings from cult coffee-roasters, this is a great neighbourhood pit stop – or a prime place to while away a few afternoon hours. Mon–Fri 7am–7pm, Sat & Sun 8am–7pm.

Taverna Kyclades 33-07 Ditmars Blvd, Astoria ☎718 545 8666, ⓦtavernakyclades.com; subway N, Q to Astoria-Ditmars Blvd; map p.248. Friendly, popular Greek *taverna* specializing in seafood. Start with a selection of dips, including the garlic-yogurt-cucumber *tzatziki* ($6.50 on own, $9.95 as part of a trio), then move on to grilled calamari ($15.50) or clams ($11.95). Dessert, a traditional Greek custard, is on the house. Mon–Thurs noon–11pm, Fri & Sat noon–11.30pm, Sun noon–10.30pm.

Tournesol 50-12 Vernon Blvd, Long Island City ☎718 472 4355, ⓦtournesolnyc.com; subway #7 to Vernon Blvd; map p.246. Warm French bistro in Hunters Point, steps from the Vernon Blvd #7 stop and an easy walk from MoMA PS1. Staples like steak frites ($21) and tarragon *escargots* ($9.50) are reliably good, the wine list is small but well chosen, and brunch is very tasty. Mon 5.30–11pm, Tues–Thurs 11.30am–3pm & 5.30–11pm, Fri 11.30am–3pm & 5.30–11.30pm, Sat 11am–3.30pm & 5.30–11.30pm, Sun 11am–3.30pm & 5–10pm.

★**Zenon Taverna** 34-10 31st Ave, between 34 and 35th sts, Astoria ☎718 956 0133, ⓦzenontaverna .com; subway N, Q to 30th Ave, R, M to Steinway St; map p.248. Charred octopus ($19), grilled meatballs ($11) and *taramosalada* ($8) get your meal off on the right foot at this super-friendly Greek-Cypriot tavern; whole grilled bass ($32) or one of the lamb specials ($25–28) keeps it heading in the right direction. Mon–Fri noon–11pm, Sat & Sun 11am–11pm.

JACKSON HEIGHTS, CORONA AND JAMAICA

Benfaremo – The Lemon Ice King of Corona 52-02 108th St, Corona ☎718 699 5133, ⓦthelemonice kingofcorona.com; subway #7 to 111th St – take a left at 108th St, then walk ten blocks; map p.244. Renowned Italian ice-cream purveyor that feels very old school – and has, in fact, been around for seventy years. Lemon is the classic flavour, but there's mango, coconut, even licorice and peanut butter ($1.50 for small); toffee apples are on sale too. Daily 10am–11pm or midnight, depending on crowds and weather.

★**Empanadas Café** 56-27 Van Doren St, at 108th St, Corona ☎718 592 7288, ⓦempanadascafe.com; subway #7 to 111th St – take a left at 108th St, then walk fifteen blocks; map p.244. There's no better place in the city to get a Latin American meat pie than this celebrated café; they're all tasty, especially the beef and cheese, and there's a sweet one that comes with Nutella and sliced bananas. Nothing costs more than $2.50. Daily 7am–10pm.

Jackson Diner 37-47 74th St, between 37th and Roosevelt aves ☎718 672 1232, ⓦjacksondinerny. com; subway E, F, M, R to Roosevelt Ave, #7 to 74th St-Broadway; map p.244. The best-known Jackson Heights Indian restaurant, with outstanding versions of classics like tandoori chicken ($13) and goat curry ($14). Mon–Thurs & Sun noon–10pm, Fri & Sat noon–10.30pm.

La Fusta 80-32 Baxter Ave, Elmhurst ☎718 429 8222, ⓦlafustarestaurant.com; subway #7 to 82nd St-Jackson Heights; map p.244. The longest-running Argentine restaurant in the city, and a welcome alternative to the usual steakhouse experience. The *parillada*'s the thing; go for the mixed grill, a mountain of short ribs, skirt steak, sweetbreads and various sausages, washed down with plenty of Malbec. Mon–Thurs & Sun noon–10.30pm, Fri & Sat noon–11.30pm.

La Pequeña Colombia 83-27 Roosevelt Ave, at 84th St ☎718 478 8700, ⓦpequenacolombia.com; subway #7 to 82nd St-Jackson Heights; map p.244. Literally "Little Colombia", this simple spot doles out inexpensive but filling *empanadas* and *arepas* along with a gut-busting "Mountain Platter" – ground beef and rice with fried egg, pork rind and plantains ($13.95). Try the fruit drinks, such as *maracuya* (passion fruit) or *guanabana* (soursop). Mon–Thurs 10am–midnight, Fri 10am–2am, Sat 9am–2am, Sun 9am–midnight.

Shaheen Sweets 79-14 164th St, Jamaica ☎718 380 4791, ⓦshaheensweets.com; subway E, F Parsons Blvd; map p.244. This famed sweets counter offers treats from the Indian subcontinent like *gulab jamun* ($7), sweet dough balls soaked in syrup, and *kheer* ($7), a type of rice pudding. Mon–Thurs 8am–7pm, Fri 8am–9pm, Sat 9am–9pm, Sun 9am–2pm.

★**Tortilleria Nixtamal** 104–05 47th Ave, between 104th and 108th sts, Corona ☎718 699 2434, ⓦtortillerianixtamal.com; subway #7 to 103rd St-Corona; map p.244. Impeccable tacos – be sure to at least try the *carnitas* ($3.50), *al pastor* and *nopales* (each $4) – as well as platters, tasty *pozole* soup ($6) and *tamales* ($3.50). You can also buy products from the shopfront part of the restaurant (earlier hours than those listed here). Thurs 11am–9pm, Fri & Sat 11am–11pm, Sun 11am–9pm.

FLUSHING

Tai Pan Bakery 37-25 Main St, between 37th and 38th aves ☎718 461 8668; subway #7 to Main St-Flushing; map p.244. Snag a tray and get to work assembling your own Chinese carb feast from among the vast assortment of sweet (pineapple) and savoury (roasted pork) buns, sugary donuts and custard tarts (all around $1.50) in this chaotic and popular spot. There are a few hard-won tables. Daily 7am–8pm.

22

22

Spicy and Tasty 39-07 Prince St ☎718 359 1601; subway #7 to Main St-Flushing; map p.244. Tea-smoked duck ($17) is the signature dish at this Sichuan specialist, regarded by many as the finest in NYC; prepare yourself for plenty of spicy noodle dishes as well. Daily 11am–11pm.

THE ROCKAWAYS

Tacoway Beach 302 Beach 87th St ☎347 213 7466; map p.244. This popular *taqueria* offers a whole other side to New York City (a beachy and relaxed one) and is a reliable stop for good-weather food like fish or chorizo tacos ($4) and sweet fruit juices. Cash only. Daily 11am–8.30pm.

WOODSIDE

SriPraPhai 64-13 39th Ave, Woodside ☎718 899 9599, ⓦsripraphairestaurant.com; subway #7 to 69th St or M, R to 65th St; map p.244. Truly authentic Thai food that puts anything in Manhattan to shame – sweet, sour, (very) spicy and cheap. Try the "drunken" noodles with beef and basil ($10.50) or a whole steamed striped bass with ginger, chilli and lime ($24), along with staples like papaya salad ($9) and hot-and-sour lemongrass soup ($5/$10). An outdoor patio is open in the summer. Cash only. Mon, Tues & Thurs–Sun 11.30am–9.30pm.

THE BRONX

In the Bronx, and for the whole of New York City, Belmont is the place to taste old-school Italian-American "red sauce" cuisine, while City Island's family establishments specialize in freshly caught seafood, best enjoyed on warm summer evenings when the waterside dining is at its most scenic.

SOUTH BRONX

Sam's 596–598 Grand Concourse, at 150th St ☎718 665 5341, ⓦsamssoulfood.com; subway #2, #4, #5 to 149th St-Grand Concourse; map p.256. About a 10min walk from Yankee Stadium, *Sam's* makes for a tasty, cheap pre-game meal, whether you want American soul food or Caribbean standards. There are also DJs and karaoke that add a party atmosphere later at night. Mon 7am–noon, Tues 7am–2am, Wed 7am–midnight, Thurs 7am–2am, Fri & Sat 7am–4am, Sun 7am–midnight (dining room closes earlier than bar).

BEDFORD PARK AND BELMONT

Com Tam Ninh Kieu 2641 Jerome Ave ☎718 365 2680; subway B, D, #4 to Kingsbridge Rd; map p.256. A convenient stop if you're close to the Poe Cottage, Fordham or the Botanical Garden (though Belmont's Little Italy isn't far away either), this small, casual Vietnamese joint has excellent renditions of *pho*, *bun*, *bánh mì* and other inexpensive specialities. Daily 9am–8.30pm.

The Feeding Tree 892 Gerard Ave, at 161st St ☎718 293 5025; subway B, D, #4 to 161st St-Yankee Stadium; map p.256. Spicy jerk shrimp and chicken, curry goat stew and other Jamaican specialities come with rice and beans, mixed vegetables and sweet plantains at this friendly, no-frills fixture near Yankee Stadium (most dishes $7–14). Daily 9am–9pm.

★Mike's Deli 2344 Arthur Ave, between 186th St and Crescent Ave ☎718 295 5033, ⓦarthuravenue.com; subway B, D to Fordham Rd; map p.256. In the back of the Arthur Avenue Retail Market, there's usually a queue of folks waiting for overstuffed Italian sandwiches like eggplant parm or *porchetta* (for a twist, try the "Paula Deen", with prosciutto, spicy *soppressata*, radicchio, fresh mozzarella, sun-dried tomatoes and truffle butter; $9/$12 on roll/hero). Mon–Sat 6am–6pm.

Roberto Restaurant 603 Crescent Ave, between Arthur Ave and Hughes St ☎718 733 9503, ⓦroberto089.com; subway B, D to 182nd-183rd sts; map p.256. Not quite so stuck in a time warp as other Belmont favourites, *Roberto* is renowned for its rich pastas, served with style on giant platters or, sometimes, baked in foil. Chef's specials are usually the way to go; main dishes (most $21–36) are big enough to share. Mon–Thurs noon–2.30pm & 5–10pm, Fri noon–2.30pm & 5–11pm, Sat noon–2.30pm & 4–11pm.

Trattoria Zero Otto Nove 2357 Arthur Ave, between 186th and 187th sts ☎718 242 0899, ⓦ089nyc.com; subway B, D to 182nd-183rd sts; map p.256. In the comfort of an atmospheric, soaring back room, fine brick-oven pizzas ($13–19) and pastas ($12–27) are served up to a crowd that spans generations. Tues–Thurs noon–3pm & 5–10pm, Fri & Sat noon–3pm & 5–11pm, Sun 1–10pm.

CITY ISLAND

Johnny's Reef Restaurant 2 City Island Ave ☎718 885 2086, ⓦjohnnysreefrestaurant.com; subway #6 to Pelham Bay Park, then #Bx29 bus; map p.256. Bustling seasonal joint at the end of the road; eat on a picnic table by the water and watch the gulls fly round. Start with clams on the half-shell ($6 for half-dozen), move on to something steamed or fried – the fried scallops are a good bet ($17) – and pair it with a cold beer. March–Nov: Mon–Thurs & Sun 11am–10pm, Fri & Sat 11am–midnight.

RIVERDALE

Liebman's Deli 552 W 235th St., between Johnson and Oxford aves ☎718 548 4534, ⓦliebmansdeli.com; subway #1 to 238th St; map p.256. One of a very few classic delis left up in these parts, *Liebman's* is an unassuming but worthy destination for thick pastrami sandwiches, *knishes* and kosher hot dogs. Daily 9am–10pm.

STATEN ISLAND

Staten Island is finally catching up with the rest of New York, with the opening of a trendy food hall dubbed MRKTPL in Empire Outlets slated for late 2018, as well as its very own *Shake Shack* (p.302), *Alamo Drafthouse* (p.361), and *Hometown Bar-B-Que* (p.322) all expected the same year. The borough also does Sri Lankan cuisine particularly well, and has its own pizza legend in *Denino's*.

AMERICAN

John's Famous Deli 15 Innis St and Nicholas Ave, Port Richmond ☎718 815 9100; take #S46 bus; map p.265. Justly lauded as producing the best hot roast-beef sandwiches in the state ($8), dripping with onions, mozzarella and gravy. Cash only. Mon–Sat 6am–6pm.

COFFEE

Everything Goes Book Café 208 Bay St ☎718 273 3675, ⓦetgstores.com/bookcafe; SIR to Tompkinsville; map p.265. Alternative café and bookshop, a short walk from the ferry along Bay Street (with internet at $1 for 10min and free wi-fi). Serves hummus wraps ($5.95) and has a huge selection of coffee and teas (from $1.50). Tues–Thurs noon–9pm, Fri & Sat noon–10pm, Sun noon–5pm.

GERMAN

Killmeyer's Old Bavaria Inn 4254 Arthur Kill Rd, at Sharrotts Rd ☎718 984 1202, ⓦkillmeyers.com; take bus #S74; map p.265. A full-tilt German beer garden near the south end of the island, complete with schnitzel, *Sauerbraten* and giant steins of beer, and live oompah music outside on the weekends. Main dishes ($16–24) are large enough to feed two. Mon–Thurs 11.30am–midnight, Fri & Sat 11.30am–2am, Sun noon–midnight.

ITALIAN

Denino's Pizzeria & Tavern 524 Port Richmond Ave, at Hooker Place ☎718 442 9401, ⓦdeninossi.com; take bus #S44; map p.265. A Staten Island favourite since 1937, serving pizza with a slightly thicker, chewier crust than most brick-oven joints in the city (from $15). *Ralph's Famous Italian Ices* (see below) is right across the street, making dessert a no-brainer. Cash only. Daily 11.30am–11pm, Sat & Sun till midnight.

★ **Ralph's Famous Italian Ices** 501 Port Richmond Ave, at Catherine St ☎718 273 3675, ⓦralphsices.com; take #S44 bus; map p.265. In business since 1928, this beloved takeaway place has spawned numerous franchises. Its unusual and wide selection of "water ices", a sweetened frozen dessert made with fruit or other flavourings (such as honeydew, root beer and blueberry; from $2.75), similar to sorbet (not flavoured ice), has won many a heart and tastebud. Cash only. Tends to open during the summer months only – call ahead.

SRI LANKAN

New Asha Sri Lankan Restaurant 322 Victory Blvd, at Cebra Ave ☎718 420 0649; take bus #S48, #S61 or #S66; map p.265. Head here for no-frills paper plates heaped with veggie *roti*, spicy chicken, curries and *idlis*, all for less than $12 (just three tables inside). A favourite of mayor Bill de Blasio. Mon & Wed–Sun 9am–9.30pm.

22

Drinking

New York is packed with an incredible array of watering holes where you're bound to meet friendly locals – and with 24-hour public transport, there's no need to watch the clock. As you'd expect, the city is especially rich in booze history and myth; Abraham Lincoln supped pints at *McSorley's Old Ale House* (see p.334) and Dylan Thomas got wasted (literally) at the *White Horse Tavern* (see p.335). The *21 Club* (see p.303) is where Humphrey Bogart took Lauren Bacall on their first date, and Kerouac and the Beats, Lou Reed, Joe Strummer and a long line of punks, poets and rockers got hammered in the bars of the East and West villages. At the other end of the scale, this is where the Bloody Mary and the Manhattan were invented, and the Cosmopolitan and Martini were perfected.

New York's bar scene is very competitive and so quality of service and drinks is usually very high – you'll find cocktail "mixologists" and real-ale aficionados everywhere. Indeed, New York leads the world when it comes to cocktail innovation, and in recent years the city has also developed a truly local microbrew scene. Options range from student dives and burlesque hotspots to Irish pubs and classy hotel bars like *Bemelmans* (see p.339); and in the summer, enticing boat bars serve drinks and oysters along the Hudson River. All this comes at a price – drinking in New York ain't cheap. Unless it's happy hour, in a basic bar in Manhattan you'll pay around $6–9 for a draught beer or house wine, while at the most fashionable spots, fancy cocktails can start at around $16. Wherever you go, you'll be expected to tip a buck (perhaps more at pricier joints) per drink.

THE FINANCIAL DISTRICT

Stone Street (p.47) morphs into an outdoor beer garden in the summer months, with tables filling the street and its restaurants and Irish pubs serving food and drinks daily, though it still primarily caters to an after-work Wall Street crowd and students chugging "pickle backs" (shot of Jameson's chased with a shot of pickle juice). The Financial District is crammed with Irish-style pubs, and Guinness drinkers are well catered for in this part of the city.

Clinton Hall 90 Washington St, at Rector St ☎ 212 363 6000, ⓦ clintonhallny.com; subway R, W to Rector St; map p.44. All-day bar and beer garden, close to the World Trade Center, with a huge selection of craft ales, twenty different styles of burger, and table tennis. Sun–Wed 11.30am–midnight, Thurs–Sat 11.30am–2am.

23

THE CRAFT BEER REVOLUTION

In the last decade New York City has been undergoing a craft beer brewing renaissance, with generally small breweries knocking out limited batches of hoppy, tasty ales in a variety of styles. Many of these run on-site tasting or "tap" rooms (usually no-frills bars) where you can sample their freshly made beers – some of the best are listed below, but *Brooklyn Brewery* (see p.226) and *Tørst* (see p.341) are also well worth checking out.

Bronx Brewery 856 E 136th St, Port Morris, Bronx ⓦ thebronxbrewery.com; see p.256. Visit the tasting room to sample seasonal pale ales and limited selections of the brewery's barrel-aged beers (it also offers bar snacks like pretzels and cheeses). Wed–Fri 3–9pm, Sat & Sun noon–8pm.

Finback Brewery 7801 77th Ave, Ridgewood, Queens ⓦ finbackbrewery.com; see p.214. This small batch brewer released its first beers in 2014, with their tasting room offering seasonal pours as well as regulars such as Finback IPA. Wed–Fri 5–10pm, Sat 1–10pm, Sun 1–7pm.

Gun Hill Brewing Co 3227 Laconia Ave, Bronx ⓦ gunhillbrewing.com; see p.256. This Bronx brewery boasts an inviting tap room with creative pours ("milk IPAs", brewed with oats, lactose and Mosaic hops) plus tours on Saturday and Sunday afternoons. Mon–Wed 2.30–9pm, Thurs 1–11pm, Fri 1pm–midnight, Sat noon–midnight, Sun noon–10pm.

Other Half Brewing 195 Centre St, Carroll Gardens, Brooklyn ⓦ otherhalfbrewing.com; see p.235. Popular Brooklyn brewer (two blocks from the F, G lines at Smith-9th St station), with a vast array of IPAs and farmhouse ales. Tues–Fri 5–10pm, Sat noon–10pm, Sun noon–8pm.

Rockaway Brewing Co 5-01 46th Ave at 5th St, Long Island City, Queens ⓦ rockawaybrewco.com; see p.246. Queens-based brewer of mellow English ales and chocolatey stouts. Visit their tap room in Long Island City (not Rockaway, despite the name) to fill up. Mon–Wed 5–9pm, Thurs 3–9pm, Fri 3–10pm, Sat noon–10pm, Sun noon–9pm.

SingleCut Beersmiths 19-33 37th St, between 19th and 20th aves, Astoria, Queens ⓦ singlecut beer.com; see p.244. Lager specialist; visit the Tap Room to sip a pint of 19-33 pilsner or hibiscus sour. Wed 6pm–midnight, Thurs & Fri 4pm–midnight, Sat noon–midnight, Sun noon–10pm.

Threes Brewing 333 Douglass St, Gowanus, Brooklyn ⓦ threesbrewing.com; see p.235. This Gowanus-based brewery operates a full bar with 20 of its own beers on tap (German lagers, Belgian farmhouse ales and hoppy American ales) but also wine and other drinks. Mon–Wed 5pm–midnight, Thurs 5pm–2am, Fri 3pm–2am, Sat noon–2am, Sun noon–midnight.

Transmitter Brewing 53-02 11th St, Long Island City, Queens ⓦ transmitterbrewing.com; see p.246. Farmhouse ales from a tiny Queens outfit, with a tasting room located just under the Pulaski Bridge. Fri 4–8pm, Sat noon–8pm, Sun noon–6pm.

NEW YORK DRINKING: THE FINE PRINT

You must be over 21 to buy or consume alcohol in a bar or restaurant in New York, and it's against the law to drink alcohol on the street. Note that many bars insist you **show photo ID** to get in (even if you look well over 21), so make sure you carry some.

23

★**Dead Rabbit** 30 Water St, between Broad St and Coenties Slip ☎646 422 7906, ⓦdeadrabbitnyc.com; subway R, W to Whitehall St; map p.44. Irish-British bar in a gorgeous old space, with a nineteenth-century theme, with a menu of classic cocktails ($16), wine, beer and a vast range of whisky (shots from $10); bar menu features fish and chips, stews and meat pies. Tap Room daily 11am–4am; parlor Mon–Sat 5pm–2am, Sun 5pm–midnight.

★**Jeremy's Alehouse** 228 Front St, at Peck Slip ☎212 964 3537, ⓦjeremysalehouse.com; subway #2, #3, #4, #5, A, C, J, Z to Fulton St; map p.44. Unpretentious neighbourhood bar with bras and ties hanging from the rafters (donated by happy patrons), serving well-priced pints of beer from $5.50 (served in Styrofoam cups) and excellent burgers ($6.95). Happy hour Mon–Fri 4–6pm. The fried clam strips ($10.95) also get rave reviews. Mon–Fri 8am–midnight, Sat 10am–midnight, Sun noon–midnight.

Loopy Doopy Bar Conrad New York, at 102 North End Ave, at Murray St ☎646 769 4250, ⓦconradnewyork .com; subway A, C to Chambers St; map p.44. Stylish roof-top bar from the *Conrad*, offering sensational views of the Hudson River, Statue of Liberty and the harbour, plus innovative drinks such as a prosecco and fresh fruit popsicle/ice lolly ($22; cocktails $18). Sun–Thurs noon–midnight, Fri & Sat noon–1am.

Pier A Harbor House 22 Battery Place ☎212 785 0153, ⓦpiera.com; subway R, W to Whitehall St; map p.44. Set on artfully restored Pier A on the edge of Battery Park, this complex of bars and restaurants includes *Long Hall* and the *Oyster Bar*, the perfect spots for a craft beer ($8), pitchers of sangria ($39) or a plate of oysters while admiring the harbour views; and *Blacktail*, themed around American bars that moved down to Cuba during Prohibition. Mon–Wed 11am–2am, Thurs–Sat 11am–4am, Sun 11am–midnight.

The Porterhouse at Fraunces Tavern 58 Pearl St, between Broad and Water sts ☎212 968 1776, ⓦfrauncestavern.com; subway R, W to Whitehall St; map p.44. Below the Fraunces Tavern Museum lies an outpost of Dublin's Porterhouse Brewing Company – restaurant to the right, and bars to the left. Raise a pint of tangy Oyster Stout or Porterhouse Red ($8) to George Washington, a regular in the 1780s. Happy hour Mon–Fri 4–7pm. Mon & Tues 11am–1am, Wed & Thurs 11am–2am, Fri & Sat 11am–4am, Sun 11am–midnight.

TRIBECA AND SOHO

★**Ear Inn** 326 Spring St, between Washington and Greenwich sts ☎212 226 9060, ⓦearinn.com; subway C, E to Spring St, #1 to Houston St; map p.64. "Ear" as in "Bar" with half the neon "B" blacked out. This historic pub, a stone's throw from the Hudson River, opened in 1890 (the building reputedly dates back to the eighteenth century). Its creaky (and some claim, haunted) interior is as cosy as a Cornish inn, with a good mix of beers on tap, decent cocktails and basic, reasonably priced American food (burgers from $11; cocktails $12). Daily 11.30am–4am.

Fanelli Café 94 Prince St, at Mercer St ☎212 226 9412; subway N, R, W to Prince St; map p.64. Established in 1922 (the building dates from 1853), informal *Fanelli* is a favourite destination of the not-too-hip after-work crowd, with a small dining room at the back (mains $12–16). Daily 10am–2am, Thurs–Sat until 4am.

M1-5 Lounge 52 Walker St, between Church St and Broadway ☎212 965 1701, ⓦm1-5.com; subway N, Q, R, W to Canal St; map p.64. Ultra-hip lounge bar, with a decent range of beers, wines and cocktails to accompany the sleek design and good food. Live music and DJs set the scene. Happy hour (Mon–Wed 4pm–midnight, Thurs & Fri 4–10pm, Sat 1–10pm) beers $4–5. Mon–Wed 4pm–

midnight, Thurs & Fri 4pm–4am, Sat 1pm–4am.

★**Paul's Casablanca** 305 Spring St, between Hudson and Greenwich sts ☎212 620 5220, ⓦpaulscasablanca .com; subway C, E to Spring St; map p.64. Super-hip cocktail bar and model hangout with Moroccan decor, especially packed during Fashion Week (it was opened by Paul Sevigny, actress Chloë's brother). Cocktails are $18, while DJs focus on a different genre every night, from rock to hip-hop (The Smiths are featured on Sunday nights). Look for the *McGovern's Bar* sign. Thurs–Sun 10pm–4am.

★**Pegu Club** 77 W Houston St, at West Broadway ☎212 473 7348, ⓦpeguclub.com; subway B, D, F, M to Broadway-Lafayette St, N, R, W to Prince St; map p.64. One of NYC's most celebrated cocktail lounges, an elegant pioneer that perfected the Gin-Gin Mule (ginger beer with Tanqueray gin, fresh mint and lime juice). Most cocktails $15–17. Sun–Wed 5pm–2am, Thurs–Sat 5pm–4am.

Terroir Tribeca 24 Harrison St, at Greenwich St ☎212 625 9463, ⓦwineisterroir.com; subway #1 to Franklin St; map p.64. Beloved local wine bar, with more than 150 carefully curated bottles on the menu (glasses $11–20), plus eight beers on tap ($8–9) and select grape juices for non-drinkers. There's also a big choice of cheese,

sandwiches and assorted finger foods ($4–8). Mon & Tues 4pm–midnight, Wed–Sat 4pm–1am, Sun 4–11pm.
Toad Hall 57 Grand St, between W Broadway and Wooster St ☎ 212 431 8145; subway A, C, E to Canal St;

map p.64. With a pool table, good service and excellent bar snacks, this dive bar is a little less hip and a little more of a local hangout than some of its neighbours. Daily noon–4am.

CHINATOWN, LITTLE ITALY AND NOLITA

★**Apothéke** 9 Doyers St ☎ 212 406 0400, ⓦ apothekenyc.com; subway J, N, Q, R, W, Z, #6 to Canal St; map p.71. Tucked away in the heart of Chinatown, this cocktail bar feels like an underground, highly exclusive club (no sign out front), with a glamorous clientele enjoying an incredibly creative drinks menu ($16–20; absinthe from $25) while soaking up the vintage apothecary interior (antique medicine bottles, plush banquettes). Try the "Deal Closer" (cucumber, vodka, aged Chinese tea, mint, lime and vanilla). Reservations required after 9pm, and "sophisticated" dress code enforced. Mon–Sat 6.30pm–2am, Sun 8pm–2am.

Baby Grand 161 Lafayette St, between Grand and Howard sts ☎ 212 219 8110, ⓦ babygrandnyc.com; subway N, Q, R, W, #6 to Canal St; map p.71. This tiny but very cute karaoke bar attracts a loyal crowd of regulars (Mon–Wed is quietest) for its excellent, wide-reaching song list ($2 per song) and tasty cocktails. Mon & Tues 6pm–1am, Wed & Thurs 6pm–2am, Fri 6pm–4am, Sat 7pm–4am, Sun 7pm–midnight.

★**Black Lodge** 20 Prince St, between Mott and Elizabeth sts ☎ 646 248 3855, ⓦ theblacklodgenyc .com; subway N, R, W to Prince St; map p.71. Subterranean cocktail bar that becomes more like a club as the night goes on, with DJs spinning a crowd-pleasing mix of tunes every night. Cocktails from $14, wine by the glass from $12. Tues–Sat 8pm–4am.

★**Goldbar** 389 Broome St, at Mulberry St ☎ 212 274 1568, ⓦ goldbarnewyork.com; #6 to Spring St; map

p.71. Exclusive lounge bar with a lavish gold theme (vaulted ceiling with gold leaf and crystal chandeliers, and walls stacked with gold-painted skulls), make this one of New York's most iconic nightspots; enjoy innovative cocktails ($18) and small plates while DJs spin house and hip-hop. Thurs–Sun 11am–4am.

Mulberry Street Bar 176 Mulberry St, between Broome and Grand sts ☎ 212 226 9345, ⓦ mulberry streetbar.com; subway J, Z to Bowery, #6 to Canal St; map p.71. Though it looks like a back-room hangout from *The Sopranos*, this is actually a friendly local bar and restaurant open to all (plenty of Mob movies have been filmed here). The wooden bar, tile floor and pressed-tin roof have barely changed since it opened in 1908. Pints from $6; happy hour Mon–Fri 5–7pm. Sun–Thurs noon–3am, Fri & Sat noon–4am.

Pulquería 11 Doyers St ☎ 212 227 3099, ⓦ pulqueria nyc.com; subway J, N, Q, R, W, Z, #6 to Canal St; map p.71. *Apothéke*'s sister bar with an upscale Mexican theme, specializing in margaritas ($15), micheladas ($12) and tacos ($16–18). Happy hour Tues–Fri 6–9pm (cocktails $10). Tues–Thurs 6pm–midnight, Fri & Sat 6pm–2am.

Sweet & Vicious 5 Spring St, between Bowery and Elizabeth St ☎ 212 334 7915, ⓦ sweetandviciousnyc .com; subway J, Z to Bowery; map p.71. The epitome of rustic chic, with exposed brick, lots of wood and antique chandeliers. The back garden is just as cosy as the inside bar. Happy hour daily 2–7pm. Daily 2pm–4am.

23

LOWER EAST SIDE

Back Room 102 Norfolk St, between Delancey and Rivington sts ☎ 212 228 5098, ⓦ backroomnyc.com; subway F to Delancey St, J, M, Z to Essex St; map p.82. With a hidden, back-alley entrance, this former speakeasy was reputedly once a haunt of gangster Meyer Lansky; cocktails are still served in teacups (pricey at $14). To find it, walk down the metal steps and through to the back of the building. Live jazz Mon at 9pm. Sun & Mon 7.30pm–2am, Tues–Thurs 7.30pm–3am, Fri & Sat 7.30pm–4am.

★**Bar Goto** 245 Eldridge St, between Stanton and E Houston sts ☎ 212 475 4411, ⓦ bargoto.com; subway F to Second Ave; map p.82. Elegant Japanese-inspired bar from *Pegu Club* alum Kenta Goto, offering craft cocktails ($13–15) and Japanese bar food (think *okonomiyaki* and octopus in plum vinegar). Tues–Thurs & Sun 5pm–midnight, Fri & Sat 5pm–2am.

Barrio Chino 253 Broome St, at Orchard St ☎ 212 228

6710, ⓦ barriochinonyc.com; subway B, D to Canal St; map p.82. Don't be confused by the Chinese lanterns or drink umbrellas – the speciality here is tequila, and there are a dozen brands to choose from. Shots are served with a traditional *sangría* chaser, made from a blend of tomato, orange and lime juices. Cocktails $11–16. Mon–Thurs & Sun 11.30am–1am, Fri 11.30am–2am, Sat 10am–2am, Sun 10am–1am.

TOP 5 OLD NEW YORK PUBS

Ear Inn Tribeca. See opposite
Fanelli Café Soho. See opposite
McSorley's Old Ale House East Village. See p.334
Pete's Tavern Gramercy Park. See p.338
Subway Inn Upper East Side. See p.340

Copper & Oak 157 Allen St, between Stanton and Rivington sts ☎212 460 5545, ⓦcopperandoak.com; subway F to Delancey St, J, M, Z to Essex St; map p.82. This whiskey bar occupies a narrow but spectacular space, with backlit walls made from bourbon barrels and lined with bottles. Also serves other dark spirits (brandy, tequila, rum; shots from $7), to a soundtrack of 1980s tunes. Tues–Sat 5pm–1am, Sun 2–10pm.

The Delancey 168 Delancey St, at Clinton St ☎212 254 9920, ⓦthedelancey.com; subway F to Delancey St, J, M, Z to Essex St; map p.82. Williamsburg hipsters meet Lower East Side chic at this bar and rock club, with a rooftop lounge in summer. Things can get frisky in the basement, which pulsates with live music. Drinks from $11 (shots $15; minimum $30 for credit card); pizza ($10) and panini ($12) also served. Daily 5pm–4am.

★**Forgetmenot** 138 Division St, between Ludlow and Orchard sts ☎646 707 3195, ⓦforgtmenotnyc.com; subway F to East Broadway; map p.82. This quirky bar and restaurant smothered with bumper stickers, graffiti and 1980s memorabilia is a favourite local hangout that also serves tasty pub food. Try the spicy watermelon margarita ($11). Mon–Fri noon–midnight, Sat & Sun noon–1am.

Libation 137 Ludlow St, between Stanton and Rivington sts ☎866 216 1263, ⓦlibationnyc.com; subway F to Delancey St, J, M, Z to Essex St; map p.82. A sexy lounge spanning two floors. It's a bit eclectic, with buckets of beer for $96 (12 bottles), an American-style tapas menu and DJs spinning '80s, hip-hop and everything

in between. Tues–Thurs 5pm–1am, Fri 5pm–4am, Sat noon–7pm & 9pm–4am, Sun 1pm–midnight.

Magician 118 Rivington St, between Essex and Norfolk sts ☎212 673 7881; subway F to Delancey St, J, M, Z to Essex St; map p.82. Generally quiet during the week, the brightly lit back room with large round tables is usually packed at the weekends, when the jukebox throws out plenty of 1980s indie music. Cash only. Daily 5pm–4am.

Max Fish 120 Orchard St, between Delancey and Rivington sts ☎212 529 3959, ⓦmaxfish.com; subway F to Delancey St, J, M, Z to Essex St; map p.82. This Lower East Side institution reopened in new digs in 2014, a high-ceilinged space with pool table in the back, artsy decor and wall-to-wall hipsters (drinks from $7). Daily 5.30pm–4am.

Wassail 162 Orchard St, between Stanton and Rivington sts ☎646 918 6835, ⓦwassailnyc.com; subway F to Delancey St; map p.82. Small plates vegetarian restaurant but best known as being New York's only cider bar, with a vast range of fermented apple tipples ($6–11) from around the globe (plus cider cocktails $10–13). Tues–Thurs 5pm–midnight, Fri 5pm–2am, Sat 4pm–1am.

Whiskey Ward 121 Essex St, between Delancey and Rivington sts ☎212 477 2998, ⓦthewhiskeyward .com; subway F to Delancey St; map p.82. Easy-going old-style saloon with huge menu of Scotch whisky and bourbon (with plenty from micro distilleries; shots from $9), plus free peanuts all night. Mon–Sat 5pm–4am, Sun 6pm–4am.

THE EAST VILLAGE

7B 108 Ave B, at E 7th St ☎212 473 8840; subway L to First Ave; map p.88. Opened as a Polish catering hall in 1935 ("Vazac's"), and also known as the *Horseshoe Bar*, this quintessential East Village hangout has often been used as the sleazy set in films and commercials (most recently featuring in the *Jessica Jones* TV series). It features deliberately zany bartenders, cheap pitchers of beer (under $20) and one of the best punk and rock 'n' roll jukeboxes in the East Village. Daily noon–4am.

Angel's Share 8 Stuyvesant St, between E 9th St and Third Ave ☎212 777 5415; subway #6 to Astor Place; map p.88. This serene, candlelit haven is a great date spot, kept deliberately romantic by the entry rules – parties larger than four will not be admitted. The cocktails ($15–16) are reputed to be some of the best in the city. Can be hard to find: walk into the Village Yokocho complex, up the stairs to the *Gyu-ya* restaurant and look for the unmarked door on the left. Sun–Wed 6pm–1.30am, Thurs 6pm–2am, Fri & Sat 6pm–2.30am.

Bar Veloce 175 Second Ave, between E 11th and E 12th sts ☎212 260 3200, ⓦbarveloce.com; subway L to Third Ave; map p.88. Stylish Italian wine bar fit for the Mod Squad, with excellent hors d'oeuvres and a fine wine

list (by the glass from $14). Mon–Thurs 5pm–2am, Fri & Sat 3pm–3am, Sun 3pm–2am.

★**Bua** 122 St Mark's Place, between First Ave and Ave A ☎212 979 6276, ⓦbuabar.com; subway L to First Ave; map p.88. Popular bar with great happy hour (Mon–Fri 3–8pm, Sat & Sun noon–5pm) draught beers ($5–7) and cocktails ($8), plus a front that opens up onto the street in summer, with wooden booths outside. Mon–Fri 3pm–4am, Sat & Sun noon–4am.

Burp Castle 41 E 7th St, between Second and Third aves ☎212 982 4756, ⓦburpcastlenyc.wordpress.com; subway #6 to Astor Place; map p.88. Delightfully weird Belgian beer bar: Bruegel-style murals adorn the walls and you are encouraged to speak in tones below a whisper. Oh, and there are over 550 different types of beer (12 on tap, from $7). Mon–Fri 5pm–4am, Sat & Sun 4pm–4am.

Cozy Café Hookah Lounge 43 E 1st St, between First and Second aves ☎212 475 0177, ⓦcozycafenyc.com; subway F to Lower East Side-Second Ave; map p.88. Comfortable sofas and soft pillows make this subterranean Middle Eastern hookah bar all the more relaxing. Belly dancers Fri & Sat nights. Cash only, with drinks from $10. Daily 4pm–4am.

BOOZE AND BIVALVES – THE HUDSON BOAT BARS

Though Manhattan's Hudson River shoreline is lined by parks rather than docks these days, you can get a taster of the city's salty past at a series of converted boat bars – the perfect places to enjoy a plate of oysters washed down with a drink or two on a summer's day (or evening).

Grand Banks Pier 25, N Moore St (Tribeca) ☎ 212 960 3390 ⓦ grandbanks.org; map p.64. This stylish 1942 wooden schooner (the *Sherman Zwicker*) was converted into a bar and restaurant in 2014. There's a decent spread of seafood and Atlantic oysters ($3–4 each) as well as cocktails ($15–16), draught craft beers ($10) and wine (by the glass $13–17). There are no reservations, so get there early. As a joint venture with the not-for-profit Maritime Foundation, a share of the earnings goes to support local maritime conservation, education and preservation. Mon & Tues 3pm–midnight, Wed–Fri noon–midnight, Sat & Sun 11am–midnight.

North River Lobster Co Pier 81, W 41st St, at Twelfth Ave (Midtown West) ☎ 212 630 8831, ⓦ northriverlobsterco.com; map p.142. This boat actually sails up and down the river while serving food and drinks – sailings last around 45min. It's meant to be a casual lobster shack-style experience (no table service, just place your order at the bar), but with a spectacular view of Midtown. No reservations so arrive early (it's $10 to sail). Cocktails $15, beer $8–9, wine $8–12 (by the glass). May–Sept Mon & Wed 4–9pm, Thurs–Sun noon–9pm; sailings Mon & Wed–Sun 5pm & 7pm (Thurs–Sun extra sailings 1pm & 3pm).

Pier 66 Maritime Pier 66 at W 26th St, at Twelfth Ave (Chelsea) ☎ 212 989 6363, ⓦ pier66maritime .com; map p.107. This former railroad barge offers riverside drinking and dining, plus access to the historic lightship *Frying Pan* salvaged from the bottom of Chesapeake Bay – you can explore the shell-encrusted interior. Drinks here are a bit cheaper than the other boat bars ($12–13 cocktails, $8–11 wine, $7 for beer). The far end of the barge often doubles as space for live acts. May–Oct noon–midnight.

23

d.b.a. 41 First Ave, between E 2nd and E 3rd sts ☎ 212 475 5097; subway F to Lower East Side-Second Ave; map p.88. A beer-lover's paradise with a vague New Orleans theme, *d.b.a.* has at least sixty bottled beers, fifteen brews on tap, $5 pickle backs and an authentic hand pump. Garden seating is available in summer. Daily noon–4am.

★ **Death & Co** 433 E 6th St, between First Ave and Ave A ☎ 212 388 0882, ⓦ deathandcompany.com; subway L to First Ave; map p.88. Justly celebrated cocktail bar with a stylish speakeasy theme (bartenders in bow ties and braces) and a huge menu of lavish drinks, from "Cloud Nine" (absinthe, rum, egg white and apple eau de vie; $23) to "Clockwork Orange" (gin, vermouth, Mandarine Napoléon cognac and Mirabelle plum; $16). Sun–Thurs 6pm–2am, Fri & Sat 6pm–3am.

Decibel 240 E 9th St, between Second and Third aves ☎ 212 979 2733, ⓦ sakebardecibel.com; subway #6 to Astor Place; map p.88. A rocking atmosphere (with good tunes) pervades this beautifully decorated underground sake bar with lots of graffiti. The inevitable wait for a wooden table will be worth it, guaranteed, though as be prepared for grouchy service. Sake bottles from $65, beers from $5. Mon–Sat 6pm–2.50am, Sun 6pm–12.50am.

★ **Ghost Donkey** 4 Bleecker St, between the Bowery and Elizabeth St ☎ 212 254 0350, ⓦ ghostdonkey.com; subway #6 to Bleecker St; map p.88. Tequila and mezcal bar, with a menu of fun, Mexican-themed cocktails ($12–15) and a giant ceramic donkey on the back wall. Nachos and other Mexican bar snacks served (cinnamon churros $9). Daily 5pm–2am.

Grassroots Tavern 20 St Mark's Place, between Second and Third aves ☎ 212 475 9443; subway #6 to Astor Place; map p.88. This wonderful, roomy underground dive in the historic Daniel LeRoy House (built in 1832) has dirt-cheap beers (from $3), $1 bowls of popcorn, an extended happy hour and at least three of the manager's pets roaming around at all hours of the day or night. Cash only. Daily 4pm–4am.

Hi Fi 169 Ave A, between E 10th and E 11th sts ☎ 212 420 8392, ⓦ thehifibar.com; subway L to Third Ave; map p.88. This venerable bar and live music venue (Green Day's Billie Joe Armstrong was a regular in 2000) has one room featuring the famed digital jukebox with over four thousand albums, and the other hosting bands, comedians and literary events. Great-looking hipster boys and girls pack this place, drinking hard pretty much every night of the week. Cocktails $13, plus "shot and a beer" deals from just $6. Mon–Thurs 4pm–4am, Fri–Sun 3pm–4am.

KGB Bar 85 E 4th St, at Second Ave ☎ 212 505 3360, ⓦ kgbbar.com; subway F to Lower East Side-Second Ave; #6 to Astor Place; map p.88. On the second floor, this dimly lit bar is set in what was the Ukrainian Labor Home (a club for Ukrainian socialists) in the 1950s. Better known now for its marquee literary readings and the Kraine Theater in the basement (see p.356). Cocktails from $12, wine by the glass from $10 and mixed drinks from $8. Daily 7pm–4am.

Manitoba's 99 Ave B, between E 6th and E 7th sts ☎ 212 982 2511, ⓦ manitobas.com; subway L to First

23

Ave, #6 to Astor Place; map p.88. Run by Dick Manitoba, lead singer of the punk group The Dictators, the kicking jukebox and rough-and-tumble vibe at this spot make it a favourite among East Villagers who really just like to drink. Daily 3pm–4am.

McSorley's Old Ale House 15 E 7th St, between Second and Third aves ☎ 212 473 9148, ⓦ mcsorleysoldale house.nyc; subway #6 to Astor Place; map p.88. Yes, it's often full of tourists and NYU students, but this sawdust-strewn bar opened in 1854 – it's the oldest pub in NYC. Today, it only pours its own ale (brewed by Pabst) – light or dark (you get two small glasses with every order; $5.50). Try the turkey sandwich with raw onion (add mustard); it's one of the best bar snacks in the city ($6). Cash only. Mon–Sat 11am–1am, Sun 1pm–1am.

Pouring Ribbons 225 Ave B, between 13th and 14th sts ☎ 917 656 6788, ⓦ pouringribbons.com; subway L to 1st Ave; map p.88. The somewhat strict door policy – which limits patrons inside and does at least guarantee you

a seat – is worth braving to sip expertly made cocktails (from $15) from a cool second-floor perch. Tasty snacks provided by Beecher's (see p.302). Daily 6pm–2am.

★ **Proletariat** 102 St Mark's Place, between Ave A and First Ave ☎ 212 777 2017, ⓦ proletariatny.com; subway #6 to Astor Place; map p.88. Small, boutique alehouse (just twelve bar stools), serving all sorts of rare and unusual brews from a rotating list of eleven draught – drinks are pricier (top brands $9–18) than the average around here, but aficionados will appreciate the selection. Daily 5pm–2am.

Third Man 116 Ave C, at E 8th St ☎ 212 598 1040, ⓦ thethirdmannyc.com; subway L to First Ave, #6 to Astor Place; map p.88. This homage to Orson Welles' 1949 masterpiece looks the part, with stylish, dimly lit digs and cocktails with names like "Expecting Fall" and "Aphrodite's Kiss" ($13). Sun–Wed 7pm–2am, Thurs & Fri 7pm–4am.

The Wayland 700 E 9th St at Ave C ☎ 212 777 7022; subway L to First Ave, #6 to Astor Place; map p.88.

NYC AND THE NFL – BARS WITH FOOTBALL FAN CLUBS

Virtually every NFL (American football) team has an informal supporters club in New York, as well as a favourite pub where fans gather to watch games September to February. If you can't get to see a live game (p.395), the noisy, boisterous atmosphere in the bars listed below can more than compensate, with a taste of the supporters' hometown thrown in. Note that baseball fans from the same city as the NFL teams below tend to watch MLB games at the same pubs April to October.

Chicago Bears Expats from the Windy City congregate at *Overlook*, 225 E 44th St (☎ 212 682 7266, ⓦ overlooknyc.com) on game days, which features a roof-deck with two giant screens, thirty TVs in the main bar and Chicago-style hot dogs and other themed food.

Dallas Cowboys A little bit of Dallas comes alive in New York when Texas transplants cheer on the Cowboys at *Stone Creek*, 140 E 27th St (☎ 212 532 1037, ⓦ stonecreeknyc .com), with cheap buckets of Texas-made Shiner beers.

Green Bay Packers *The Kettle of Fish* (see opposite) gets crammed with Packers fans and all things Wisconsin on game days – Usinger bratwurst, free cheeses and summer sausage snacks. Listen to fans chant classics such as "I Love My Green Bay Packers" and "The Bears Still Suck".

Miami Dolphins The base of "Dolfans NYC" is *Slattery's Midtown Pub*, 8 E 36th St (☎ 212 683 6444, ⓦ slatterysmidtownpub.com), featuring a specially-crafted Dolphins-inspired menu and DJ Tropic spinning South Beach-inspired tunes during commercials.

New England Patriots *Professor Thom's* at

219 Second Ave (☎ 212 260 9480, ⓦ professorthoms.com) is essentially the anti-New York bar; it attracts hordes of rowdy Boston-sports fans and is festooned with Boston memorabilia, a sign proclaiming "Behind Enemy Lines Since 2005", and (allegedly) the college jersey of Tom Brady, the quarterback every New Yorker loves to hate. Lots of New England craft beers on tap. It's also the Red Sox homebase in NYC.

Oakland Raiders The "Silver & Black Empire Raider Nation" assembles at *Peter Dillon's Pub* (☎ 212 213 3998, ⓦ peterdillons.com), an Irish bar at 130 E 40th St. Even if you're not a fan, the electric atmosphere on game days is worth experiencing, with an exuberant SoCal crowd and several well-known super fans leading the chants.

San Francisco 49ers Fans of Bay Area and west-coast sports (including baseball's Giants and basketball's Golden State Warriors, as well as the 49ers) meet at *Finnerty's* (☎ 212 677 2655, ⓦ finnertysnyc .com), 221 Second Ave, another Irish pub that serves Californian craft beers such as Bear Republic, Sierra Nevada, 21st Amendment, Mission IPA and Eel River.

Another rustic-chic cocktail bar on Avenue C, with some dazzling blends and creations from apple-pie moonshine with apple-spice bitters ($13), to Fernet Branca and home-made citrus-infused cola on tap ($7). Snack on chicken liver and bacon on toast ($10) while you sip. Mon–Fri 4pm–4am, Sat & Sun 11am–4am.

★**Zum Schneider** 107 Ave C, at E 7th St ☎212 598

1098, ⊚zumschneider.com; subway #6 to Astor Place; map p.88. A German beerhall (and indoor garden) with a mega-list of brews ($4–8) and *Wursts* ($19) from the Fatherland. It can be a bit packed with frat-boy types; in the early evening, though, the old-world vibe is sublime. Cash only. Mon–Thurs 5pm–2am, Fri 4pm–4am, Sat 1pm–4am, Sun 1pm–midnight.

THE WEST VILLAGE

★**55 Bar** 55 Christopher St, between Sixth and Seventh aves ☎212 929 9883, ⊚55bar.com; subway #1 to Christopher St; map p.96. A gem of an underground dive-bar that's been around since 1919, with a great jukebox, congenial clientele and live jazz and blues music seven nights a week (including guitarist Mike Stern and Dave Binney). Cover $10 plus two drink minimum per set. Cash only. Daily 2pm–4am.

★**124 Old Rabbit Club** 124 MacDougal St, at Minetta Lane ☎212 691 8845; subway A, B, C, D, E, F, M to W 4th St; map p.96. Best re-creation of a speakeasy in the Village, with over seventy beers (from $6) to choose from, a cosy, cavern-like space and decent bar food. To get in, walk down the steps to the black door and press the buzzer. Cash only. Sun–Thurs 6pm–2am, Fri & Sat 6pm–4am.

Amélie 22 W 8th St, between Fifth Ave and MacDougal St ☎212 533 2962, ⊚ameliewinebar.com; subway A, B, C, D, E, F, M to W 4th St; map p.96. Modern French-themed wine bar, with vintage theatre seats in the up-front lounge, a lacquered red bar and quieter tables at the back (wine by the glass $8–18). Mon 5pm–midnight, Tues–Thurs 11.30am–4pm & 5pm–midnight, Fri & Sat 11.30am–4pm & 5pm–2am, Sun 11am–4pm.

Blind Tiger Ale House 281 Bleecker St, at Jones St; ☎212 462 4682, ⊚blindtigeralehouse.com; subway A, B, C, D, E, F, M to W 4th St, #1 to Christopher St; map p.96. This wood-panelled pub is the home of serious ale connoisseurs, with 28 rotating draughts (primarily US microbrews such as Sixpoint and Smuttynose, from $7), a couple of casks and loads of bottled beers – they also serve decent bar food. The prime location means it tends to get packed. Daily 11.30am–4am.

Fat Cat 75 Christopher St, between Seventh Ave and Bleecker St ☎212 675 6056, ⊚fatcatmusic.org; subway #1 to Christopher St; map p.96. This lively pub is an NYU favourite, with diverse live music (from jazz and African to classical and rock; $3 cover), pool and table tennis, plus a huge stash of board games (games $6/hr per person). Most drinks $6–7. Mon–Thurs 2pm–5am, Fri–Sun noon–5am.

Houston Hall 222 W Houston St, at Varick St ☎212 675 9323, ⊚houstonhallny.com; subway #1 to Houston St; map p.96. This huge beer hall, housed in a converted garage, offers a vast selection of craft beers from Shmaltz Brewing in upstate New York, plus excellent bar food.

Happy hour (all day Mon, plus Tues–Fri 4–7pm) wine and beer is $6 (pints are otherwise $9.50; wine $12.50). Mon & Tues 4pm–1am, Wed 4pm–2am, Thurs noon–2am, Fri & Sat noon–3am, Sun noon–1am.

Jane Ballroom 113 Jane St, between Washington and West sts, in Jane Hotel ☎212 924 6700, ⊚thejanenyc .com; subway A, C, E to 14th St; map p.96. Gorgeous hotel bar that morphs into a club, with opulent furnishings that make it look like a stately home (with a disco ball). Head up to the balcony for the best celebrity-watching. Getting in is a bit easier than it used to be (the door policy is notoriously discriminatory), but aim to arrive before 11pm (all-male groups can forget it, though). Cocktails from $12. Mon, Tues & Sun 5pm–2am, Wed–Sat 5pm–4am.

Kettle of Fish 59 Christopher St, at Seventh Ave ☎212 414 2278, ⊚kettleoffishnyc.com; subway #1 to Christopher St; map p.96. This basement bar (until 1996 it was the legendary writer's hangout Lion's Head) offers plenty of real ales (including Sixpoint, from $6), no-nonsense staff and a mix of Green Bay Packers fans (opposite), tourists and students. The original on MacDougal St was a legendary Beat hangout (the famous old sign was moved here). Daily 3pm–4am.

Orient Express 325 W 11th St, between Greenwich and Washington sts ☎212 691 8845, ⊚orientexpress nyc.com; subway #1 to Christopher St; map p.96. This classy, old-fashioned cocktail bar is a tribute to the famous train, with beechwood panelling, faux train windows and a long list of creative drinks – the Agatha V (Nolet's Gin and lemon with house-made grapefruit-thyme soda; $14) is a winner. Sun–Wed 5pm–1am, Thurs 5pm–2am, Fri & Sat 3pm–3am.

Rusty Knot 425 West St, at W 11th St ☎212 645 5668, ⊚cargocollective.com/therustyknot; subway #1 to Christopher St; map p.96. Popular neighbourhood dive bar, with an eclectic, slightly kitsch nautical theme, pool table and free jukebox. Happy hour (Mon–Fri 4–7pm) is two for one, but the pretzel dogs are good anytime. It's a popular gay hangout on Sunday nights. Cocktails $11–13, beer $6–8, wine $7. Mon–Fri 4pm–4am, Sat & Sun 2pm–4am.

White Horse Tavern 567 Hudson St, at W 11th St ☎212 243 9260, ⊚whitehorsetavern1880.com; subway #1 to Christopher St; map p.96. A Greenwich

23

Village institution, which opened in 1880: Dylan Thomas supped his last here before being carted off to the hospital with alcohol poisoning (check out his portrait and plaque inside), while Norman Mailer and Hunter S. Thompson were also regulars. Draft beers from $7, wine $6–8. Cash only. Sun–Thurs 11am–2am, Fri & Sat 11am–4am.

CHELSEA AND THE MEATPACKING DISTRICT

★ Bar B 84 Seventh Ave, between W 15th and W 16th sts ☎ 212 229 1888, ⊕ barbnyc.com; subway #1, #2, #3 to 14th St; map p.107. Tiny, fantastic, standing-room-only tapas spot serving superb food like octopus salad with capers ($10) and gorgonzola bruschetta ($5). There's a rather spellbinding ceiling made of cork, and a hip and happy crowd. Daily noon–midnight.

Bathtub Gin 132 Ninth Ave (inside Stone Street Coffee), between W 18th and W 19th sts ☎ 646 559 1671, ⊕ bathtubginnyc.com; subway A, C, E, L to 14th St; map p.107. Hidden inside *Stone Street Coffee*, this dark and enchanting, Prohibition-styled boîte is a fun place to get into the speakeasy trend. The menu features cocktails from the 1920s; expect plenty of gin and cheeky names, such as the "kilted gardener" and "fanciful musings" (both $16). It's quite small so reservations are recommended, especially on nights with live jazz or burlesque. Mon–Wed & Sun 5pm–2am, Thurs–Sat 5pm–4am.

El Quinto Pino 401 W 24th St at Ninth Ave ☎ 212 206 6900, ⊕ elquintopinonyc.com; subway C, E to 23rd St; map p.107. There are relatively few seats in this elegant tapas bar, so come early to nibble on tahini-devilled eggs ($6) and a remarkable sea-urchin sandwich ($16), paired with a good selection of Spanish wines. Mon–Thurs 5.30pm–11.30pm, Fri 5.30pm–midnight, Sat 11.30am–midnight, Sun 11.30am–10.30pm.

Peter McManus Café 152 Seventh Ave, at 19th St ☎ 212 929 9691; subway #1 to 18th St; map p.107. Unlike many Irish pubs in the city, this is the real deal, moving to this location in 1936 and appearing in episodes of *Seinfeld* and *Law & Order*. The worn oak bar adds character, along with the tasty in-house McManus Ale ($6) and two old-style telephone booths inside. Mon–Sat 11am–4am, Sun noon–4am.

Smithfield Hall 138 W 25th St, between Sixth and Seventh aves ☎ 212 929 9677, ⊕ smithfieldnyc.com; subway #1 to 23rd St; map p.107. One of Manhattan's best spots for watching soccer, with decent craft beer on tap. Many of the world's top clubs have ardent fan groups that show up regularly here for games; FC Barcelona players and Sir Alex Ferguson have all stopped by for drinks. Mon–Fri 11am–2am, Sat 8am–2am, Sun 10am–midnight.

Tía Pol 205 Tenth Ave, between 22nd and 23rd sts ☎ 212 675 8805, ⊕ tiapol.com; subway C, E to 23rd St; map p.107. This popular tapas bar frequently fills up its narrow space – consider coming early if you want to miss the crowds. You can graze on bar snacks like *croquetas* ($4/$8) and fried chickpeas ($4) or construct a meal with heartier plates like octopus salad ($14) and shrimp *al ajillo* ($12); wash it all back with the easy-drinking house-made *sangría* ($9 glass). Mon 5.30–11pm, Tues–Thurs noon–11pm, Fri noon–midnight, Sat 11am–midnight, Sun 11am–10.30pm.

Wilfie & Nell 228 W 4th St, at W 10th St ☎ 212 242 2990, ⊕ wilfieandnell.com; subway #1 to Christopher St; map p.96. Welcoming bar offering cocktails ($12–14), including an indulgent Pimms Cup, and locally sourced food (from burgers to cottage pie). Mon–Thurs 4pm–4am, Fri 3pm–4am, Sat & Sun 11am–4am.

UNION SQUARE, GRAMERCY PARK AND THE FLATIRON DISTRICT

230 Fifth 230 Fifth Ave, at E 27th St ☎ 212 725 4300, ⊕ 230-fifth.com; subway N, R, #6 to 23rd St; map p.115. Slightly corny lounge bar, with unbelievable views of the Empire State Building and Midtown, and the biggest roof garden in the city (14,000 square feet) – blankets handed out to drinkers and special heaters mean that the roof is open even in winter. Drinks and snacks are reasonably priced for this type of experience (Martinis from $14, hot apple cider $12), and there is no cover. Note the dress code (no sneakers/trainers; shirts for men). Mon–Fri 4pm–4am, Sat 10am–4am, Sun 10am–midnight.

Bar Jamón 125 E 17th St, at Irving Place ☎ 212 253 2773, ⊕ barjamonnyc.com; subway L, N, Q, R, #4, #5, #6 to 14th Street-Union Square; map p.115. A superb place to sip on sherry and nosh on Spanish tapas (most between $6 and $13). Be forewarned, though: there are only fourteen stools. Mon–Fri 5pm–2am, Sat & Sun noon–2am.

The Flatiron Room 37 W 26th St, between Broadway and Sixth Ave ☎ 212 725 3860, ⊕ theflatironroom.com; subway R, W to 28th St; map p.115. If you're a whiskey lover (or just in the mood for a classy drink – cocktails $15), look no further than this vaunted jazz haunt with lit-up liquor cabinets, leather banquettes, a red-curtained stage and one of the biggest whiskey menus in the east. Reservations recommended. Mon–Fri 4pm–2am, Sat 5pm–2am, Sun 5pm–midnight.

★ Molly's 287 Third Ave between E 22nd and E 23rd sts ☎ 212 889 3361, ⊕ mollysshebeen.com; subway #6 to 23rd St; map p.115. While the city veers from throwback cocktails and nouveaux speakeasies to local microbrew palaces, the friendly bartenders at *Molly's* are content to

pour some of the best pints of Guinness around ($8) – sawdust floor included. Daily 11am–4am.

Old Town Bar 45 E 18th St, between Broadway and Park Ave S ☎ 212 529 6732, ⓦ oldtownbar.com; subway L, N, Q, R, #4, #5, #6 to 14th St-Union Square; map p.115. This atmospheric bar is popular with the after-work crowd. Opened in 1892, much of the creaking interior is original, including the rickety dumbwaiter and fine mahogany bar. A beer will set you back $6–8. Mon–Fri 11.30am–11.30pm, Sat noon–11.30pm, Sun noon–10pm.

Pete's Tavern 129 E 18th St, at Irving Place ☎ 212 473 7676, ⓦ petestavern.com; subway L, N, Q, R, #4, #5, #6 to 14th St-Union Square; map p.115. Open since 1864, this former speakeasy now trades unashamedly on its

history, which has included such illustrious patrons as O. Henry and Ludwig Bemelmans. The etched gaslights, rosewood bar and dark wooden booths are all original to the property. Wines by the glass $9–11. Daily 11am–2.30am.

★**Raines Law Room** 48 W 17th St, between Fifth and Sixth aves ☎ 212 213 1350, ⓦ raineslaw.room; subway F, M to 14th St; map p.115. Second location at 24 E 39th St. A true speakeasy, with zero pretension and all the fun of knowing a shared secret. Hidden in what looks like a regular townhouse (it's unmarked), ring the doorbell to check in with the host (wait times are shorter than you'd expect). Once inside, sip a Manhattan on a velvet couch and ogle the cheeky wallpaper. Cocktails $15. Reservations recommended. Mon–Thurs 5pm–2am, Fri & Sat 5pm–3am, Sun 7pm–1am.

23 MIDTOWN EAST

The Campbell 15 Vanderbilt Ave, between 42nd and 43rd sts, in Grand Central Terminal ☎ 212 297 1781, ⓦ thecampbellnyc.com; subway #4, #5, #6, #7 to 42nd St-Grand Central; map p.124. Once the office space of businessman John W. Campbell, who oversaw the construction of Grand Central, this majestic space – built to look like a Florentine palace – was sealed up for years. Now, after a snappy refit, it's one of New York's most distinctive cocktail bars (vodka spritz, $18). Get there early; it's a popular spot. Daily noon–2am.

King Cole Bar & Salon 2 E 55th St, between Fifth and Madison aves, in St Regis hotel ☎ 212 339 6857, ⓦ stregisnewyork.com; subway E, M to Fifth Ave-53rd St; map p.124. The reputed birthplace of the Bloody Mary has been refurbished and reborn as a bar-restaurant meant to evoke a 1920s jazz lounge. Fortunately, the grand Maxfield Parrish mural remains in its proper spot, right above the bar. Ask about the secret in the painting while sipping on a cocktail (Grey Goose martini, $24) and sampling the refined menu (grilled lamb with grapes, $26). Mon–Sat 11.30am–1am, Sun noon–midnight.

Middle Branch 154 E 33rd St, between Lexington and Third aves ☎ 212 213 1350; subway #6 to 33rd St; map p.124. Also *Little Branch*, in the West Village at 22 Seventh Ave S. Classy but very approachable Murray Hill retreat serving up ravishing cocktails ($16) packed with hand-chopped ice, a strong tipple of booze and fresh fruit infusions. The bar has two storeys, though the ground floor

is standing room only. Daily 5pm–2am.

P.J. Clarke's 915 Third Ave, at E 55th St ☎ 212 317 1616, ⓦ pjclarkes.com; subway #6 to 51st St, E, M to Lexington Ave-53rd St; map p.124. Friendly bartenders serve from a decent array of wine (fifteen by the glass) and a moderate selection of beer at *P.J. Clarke's*, one of the city's most famous watering holes. The bar is casual, though there is a pricey restaurant (known for its burgers; $18) out back as well as a clandestine, members-only restaurant, *Sidecar* (though membership is free). Daily 11.30am–3am.

Rattle N Hum 14 E 33rd St, between Madison and Fifth aves ☎ 212 481 1586, ⓦ rattlenhumbarnyc.com; subway B, D, F, N, Q, R to 34th St, #6 to 33rd St; map p.124. With forty-odd beers on draught ($8–10) and a few times that in bottles, this long, busy bar is a prime destination for craft-brew lovers. Daily 11am–2am.

Salvation Taco 145 E 39th St, between Lexington and Third aves, in Pod 39 hotel ☎ 212 865 5800, ⓦ salvationtaco.com; subway #4, #5, #6, #7 to 42nd St-Grand Central; map p.124. Hard to know what to label it – café, restaurant, gastrocantina – but *Salvation Taco*, in all its garishly hued, folk-art aesthetic glory, is best treated as a bar where you can get some intriguing south-of-the-border-influenced snacks. Indonesian beef tacos with ginger ($17), chorizo in puff pastry ($9) and lamb on *roti* "taco" ($15) pair up with similarly daring cocktails (most around $14). The rooftop is a gem in summer. Mon & Sun 7am–midnight, Tues–Sat 7am–2am.

MIDTOWN WEST

Ardesia 510 W 52nd St, between Tenth and Eleventh aves ☎ 212 247 9191, ⓦ ardesia-ny.com; subway C, E to 50th St; map p.142. A sleek but comfortable Hell's Kitchen wine bar with a bold snack menu (home-made pretzels, quail-egg toast, burrata with bacon jam) and diverse selection of vintages, about 25 or so of which are available by the glass (most $11–15). Mon–Wed 4pm–midnight, Thurs & Fri 4pm–2am, Sat 2pm–2am, Sun 2–11pm.

Hellcat Annie's 637 Tenth Ave, at W 45th ☎ 212 586 2707, ⓦ hellcatannies.com subway A, C, E to 42nd St-Port Authority; map p.142. They take their beer seriously at this Hell's Kitchen favourite – aside from cocktails, there are only craft brews on offer, most on tap. Fridays, you can "crush the craft" – pours from the keg of the day are only $5. Daily noon–4am.

★**Jimmy's Corner** 140 W 44th St, between Broadway

DRINKS WITH A VIEW

230 Fifth Union Square. See p.336
The Ides at the Wythe Hotel Williamsburg. See p.276
Pier A Harbor House Financial District. See p.330

Press Lounge Midtown West. See below
Roof Garden Café, The Met Upper East Side. See below

---

and Sixth Ave ☎ 212 221 9510; subway B, D, F, M to 42nd St-Bryant Park, N, Q, R, #1, #2, #3 to Times Square-42nd St; map p.142. The walls of this long, narrow corridor of a bar, owned by ex-fighter/trainer Jimmy Glenn, are a virtual boxing hall of fame. You'd be hard pressed to find a more colourful dive anywhere in the city – or a better jazz/R&B jukebox. Great prices, too – drinks start from $4. Mon–Fri 11.30am–4am, Sat noon–4am, Sun 3pm–4am.

★**Kashkaval** 852 Ninth Ave, between W 55th and W 56th sts ☎ 212 245 1758, ⓦ kashkavalgarden.com; subway A, B, D, #1 to 59th St-Columbus Circle; map p.142. Tucked in the back of a cheese shop, this cosy wine bar serves up tasty bites, including excellent cheese and meat plates, cold meze (the stuffed peppadews are good; $7) and an array of fondues ($14/person). Mon–Thurs noon–2am, Fri noon–3am, Sat 11am–3am, Sun 11am–midnight.

Press Lounge 16th floor, 653 Eleventh Ave at W 48th St, in Ink48 Hotel ☎ 212 757 2224, ⓦ thepresslounge .com; subway C, E to 50th St; map p.142. Spacious rooftop bar with a gasp-inducing panorama of midtown Manhattan and the Hudson River, which you can soak up while sipping a seasonal cocktail ($20). Over-21s only, and "casual elegant" dress code enforced. Mon & Tues 4pm–1am, Wed 4pm–2am, Thurs–Sat 4pm–3am, Sun 4pm–midnight.

★**Rudy's** 627 Ninth Ave, between W 44th and W 45th sts ☎ 646 707 0890, ⓦ rudysbarnyc.com; subway A, C, E to 42nd St-Port Authority; map p.142. One of New York's cheapest, friendliest and liveliest bars, a favourite with local actors and musicians. *Rudy's* offers free hot dogs, a backyard that's great in summer and some of the cheapest pitchers of beer in the city ($8–18). Mon–Sat 8am–4am, Sun noon–4am.

Rum House 228 W 47th St, between Broadway and Eighth Ave, in Hotel Edison ☎ 646 490 6924, ⓦ edison rumhouse.com; subway N, Q, R to 49th St, map p.142. Kitted out in a retro style, this is a fun live jazz bar in the heart of the Theater District. Barkeeps here are experts at their craft, and quick to pour a perfect pint or mix a lemony martini ($14). Daily noon–4am.

Russian Vodka Room 265 W 52nd St, between Broadway and Eighth Ave ☎ 212 307 5835, ⓦ russian vodkaroom.com; subway C, E, #1 to 50th St, N, R to 49th St; map p.142. They serve more than fifty different types of vodka here, as well as their own fruit-flavoured and sublime ginger-infused concoctions ($7); there's also caviar and plenty of small plate choices (herring, pâté and the like). Under the dim lighting, office workers mingle with Russian and Eastern European expats; don't ask for a mixer with your shot, unless you want to attract a stare or a laugh. Mon–Thurs & Sun 4pm–2am, Fri & Sat 4pm–4am.

UPPER EAST SIDE

★**Balcony Lounge & Roof Garden Bar** Metropolitan Museum of Art, 1000 Fifth Ave, at E 82nd St ☎ 212 535 7710, ⓦ metmuseum.org; subway #4, #5, #6 to 86th St; map p.171. It's hard to imagine a more romantic spot to sip a glass of wine and kick off the evening, whether in the *Roof Garden Bar*, which has some of the best views in the city, or in the *Balcony Lounge* overlooking the Great Hall. Beers $9–10, wines by the glass from $13. Roof Garden Bar: mid-April to mid–Oct Sun–Thurs 11am–4.30pm, Fri & Sat 11am–8.15pm; Balcony Lounge: Sun–Thurs 10am–5pm, Fri & Sat 10am–8pm.

Bar Pléiades 20 E 76th St, between Fifth and Madison aves, in The Surrey ☎ 212 772 2600, ⓦ barpleiades .com; subway #6 to 77th St; map p.171. This stylish Art Deco hotel bar is chef Daniel Boulud's homage to Chanel, with black-and-white lacquered surfaces, quilted walls and leather banquettes; cocktails ($18–20) and pricey canapés

from *Café Boulud* ($9–28). Live jazz Fri 9pm–midnight. Sun–Thurs noon–midnight, Fri & Sat noon–1am.

★**Bemelmans Bar** 35 E 76th St, at Madison Ave, in Carlyle Hotel ☎ 212 744 1600, ⓦ rosewoodhotels.com /en/carlyle; subway #6 to 77th St; map p.171. This hotel bar oozes old-school New York class, with Ludwig Bemelmans' exuberant murals plastered all around, live piano, white-jacketed waiters and an opulent gold-leaf ceiling (martinis from $21). Live jazz after 9pm, with cover charge ($35 for a table, $15 at the bar). Sun & Mon noon–12.30am, Tues–Thurs noon–1am, Fri & Sat noon–1.30am.

★**Earl's Beer & Cheese** 1259 Park Ave, at E 97th St ☎ 212 289 1581, ⓦ earlsny.com; subway #6 to 96th St; map p.171. Right up on the edge of East Harlem, this tiny bar boasts cool tunes, great food (lots of cheesy things) and a non-frat clientele – draught beers change daily from a

23

roster of excellent microbrews. Sun–Thurs 11am–midnight, Fri & Sat 11am–2am.

The Jeffrey 311 E 60th St, at the Queensboro Bridge Exit ☎ 212 355 2337, ⊛ thejeffreynyc.com; subway N, R, W to Lexington Av-59th St; map p.171. Espresso bar, craft beers, cocktails and bar snacks in one no-frills space under the Queensboro Bridge ramp, with coffee supplied by *Café Grumpy* (p.318) and a wide range of quality

microbrews on tap ($6–10). Daily 6am–2am.

Subway Inn 1140 Second Ave, at E 60th St ☎ 212 223 8929; subway N, R, W to Lexington Ave-59th St; map p.171. This neighbourhood dive-bar survived across from Bloomingdale's from 1937 to 2015, but this location (with the original neon sign and *Atomic Wings* in the back) is still perfect for a no-frills, late-afternoon beer ($6). Mon–Fri 11am–4am, Sat & Sun noon–4am.

UPPER WEST SIDE

Dead Poet 450 Amsterdam Ave, between W 81st and W 82nd sts ☎ 212 595 5670, ⊛ thedeadpoet.com; subway #1 to 79th St; map p.184. You may be waxing poetic and then dropping dead if you stay for the duration of this sweet little bar's happy hour, usually involving $4–5 pints or $5 Bloody Marys and running all weekend – there's some sort of special drink deal every day of the week. The back room has armchairs and books, and there's a full dinner menu. Daily noon–4am.

Dublin House 225 W 79th St, between Broadway and Amsterdam Ave ☎ 212 874 9528, ⊛ dublinhousenyc .com; subway #1 to 79th St; map p.184. Beneath the cool

neon sign, this lively, sometimes overcrowded Upper West Side Irish pub is the place to go before or after a gig at the Beacon Theatre. A beer will set you back around $7. Daily 9am–4am.

E's Bar 511 Amsterdam Ave, between W 84th and W 85th sts ☎ 212 877 0961, ⊛ e-barnyc.com; subway #1 to 86th St; map p.184. Beloved neighbourhood bar with excellent burgers ($5 at happy hour), darts, a huge selection of board games and cosy booths upstairs. Happy hour deals run Mon–Fri 5–7pm. Mon–Wed 5pm–midnight, Thurs 4pm–midnight, Fri 4pm–2am, Sat 11am–2am, Sun 11am–midnight.

HARLEM

★**67 Orange Street** 2082 Frederick Douglass Blvd at W 113th St ☎ 212 662 2030, ⊛ 67orangestreet.com; subway A, B, C to Cathedral Parkway; map p.199. Justly popular cocktail bar, with a long list of drinks ($14–15), friendly clientele, tasty snacks (like lobster mac and cheese) and a stylish speakeasy theme. Mon & Tues 5pm–midnight, Wed & Thurs 5pm–2am, Fri 5pm–4am, Sat 6pm–4am, Sun 6pm–midnight.

Bier International 2099 Frederick Douglass Blvd, at W 113th St ☎ 212 280 0944, ⊛ bierinternational.com; subway B, C, #2, #3 to 116th St; map p.199. Harlem's first beer garden is a fine effort, with eighteen top-notch draughts ($5–9) and over thirty bottled beers ($7–12) on offer, and plenty of space to enjoy those summer evenings. Mon–Wed 4pm–1am, Tues–Fri 4pm–2am, Sat 11.30am–2am, Sun noon–1am.

Camaradas El Barrio 2241 First Ave, at E 115th St ☎ 212 348 2703; subway #6 to 116th St; map p.199. Smart redbrick local bar in the heart of Spanish Harlem, with great Puerto Rican food and bottled beers from all

over Latin America; expect the salsa to get louder as the night progresses. Sometimes charges $5 cover for live acts, and usually cash only. Beers $6–8, mojitos $11. Sun–Tues 3pm–1am, Wed–Fri 3pm–2am, Sat 3pm–3am.

★**Ginny's Supper Club** 310 Malcolm X Blvd, between W 125th and W 126th sts ☎ 212 421 3821, ⊛ ginnyssupperclub.com; subway #2, #3 to 125th St; map p.199. Stylish bar and jazz venue (under *Red Rooster*), with live sets accompanied by punchy house cocktails ($12–15) and excellent soul food plates ($16). Thurs 6pm–midnight, Fri & Sat 6pm–3am, Sun 10.30am–2pm.

Harlem Tavern 2153 Frederick Douglass Blvd, at W 116th St ☎ 212 866 4500, ⊛ harlemtavern.com; subway B, C, #2, #3 to 116th St; map p.199. Restaurant, bar and enticing beer garden (excellent seasonal beer selection), with live jazz and weekend brunches (set price $15.95). Mon–Thurs noon–midnight, Fri noon–1am, Sat 11am–1am, Sun 11am–midnight.

BROOKLYN

BROOKLYN HEIGHTS

Floyd 131 Atlantic Ave, between Clinton and Henry sts ☎ 718 858 5810, ⊛ floydny.com; subway F, G to Bergen St, R to Court St, #2, #3, #4, #5 to Borough Hall; map p.218. Decked out with antique couches and comfy leather chairs, the main draws here are the cheap draught beers ($6), popular indoor bocce court and televised English Premier League games. Mon–Thurs 5pm–4am, Fri

4pm–4am, Sat & Sun noon to 4am.

★**Montero's Bar & Grill** 73 Atlantic Ave, at Hicks St ☎ 646 729 4129; subway F, G to Bergen St, R to Court St, #2, #3, #4, #5 to Borough Hall; map p.218. Old-timey joint with a nautical theme (dating to 1945, it used to be a sailors' hangout); there's a pool table, decent-priced drinks (PBR, $3), great karaoke on Thursdays and Fridays and an incredibly friendly bartender. Cash only. Daily 2pm–4am.

23

FORT GREENE AND CLINTON HILL

Habana Outpost 757 Fulton St, at S Portland Ave ☎ 718 858 9500, ⊛ habanaoutpost.com; subway C to Lafayette Ave, G to Fulton St; map p.218. The seasonal branch of an ever-popular Nolita institution, the patio of *Habana Outpost* twinkles with tealights and, in summer, a jubilant crowd gathers to sip frozen margaritas ($10) and share quesadillas ($6–9) with cheese-slathered ears of corn ($4). Sunday movie nights are justly popular. Mid-April to Oct daily 11am–midnight.

Mayflower 132 Greene Ave, at Waverly Ave ☎ 718 576 3584, ⊛ aitarestaurant.com; subway C, G to Clinton-Washington Ave; map p.218. Teensy, enchanting locals' hideaway outfitted with just one long, wall-hugging banquette and dotted with candlelit bistro tables. Mon–Thurs 7pm–2am, Fri & Sat 7pm–3am, Sun 6am–1am.

WILLIAMSBURG AND GREENPOINT

Allswell 124 Bedford Ave, at N 10th St ☎ 347 799 2743, ⊛ allswellnyc.com; subway L to Bedford Ave; map p.225. A bright, cheerful gastropub from an alum of the *Spotted Pig* (see p.295), this brunch favourite (eggs Benedict, $16) in the heart of Williamsburg is also great for a drink, especially during the daily happy hour (4–7pm). Mon–Thurs noon–midnight, Fri & Sat 10am–2am, Sun 10am–11pm.

Barcade 388 Union Ave, between Powers and Ainslie sts ☎ 718 302 6464, ⊛ barcadebrooklyn.com; subway L to Lorimer St, G to Metropolitan Ave; map p.225. This former metalwork shop is crammed with old-fashioned arcade games (think Donkey Kong), each of which takes the original 25 cents per game. The beers are good, too, with an excellent choice of 25 brews on tap ($6). There are other locations in the East Village and Chelsea. Mon–Thurs 4pm–4am, Fri 2pm–4am, Sat & Sun noon–4am.

The Commodore 366 Metropolitan Ave, at Havemeyer St ☎ 718 218 7632; subway L to Lorimer St, G to Metropolitan Ave; map p.225. Straight out of Williamsburg central casting: a retro-style rec-room vibe, better-than-expected bar food (fried chicken, grilled cheese and *poblano* sandwich, sautéed kale), inexpensive cocktails and pitchers ($10-18), a hip, young crowd, a few old video games… and somehow it all works perfectly. Mon–Thurs 4pm–midnight, Fri 4pm–1am, Sat & Sun 11am–4am; kitchen closes 11 or 11.30pm.

★**Pete's Candy Store** 709 Lorimer St, between Frost and Richardson sts ☎ 718 302 3770, ⊛ petescandystore .com; subway L to Lorimer St, G to Metropolitan Ave; map p.225. This terrific little spot was once a real candy store. There's free live music every night, a reading series, Scrabble and Bingo nights, pub quizzes and some well-poured cocktails ($11). Mon–Wed 5pm–2am, Thurs 5pm–4am, Fri 4pm–4am, Sat 3.30pm–4am, Sun 3.30pm–2am.

Radegast Hall and Biergarten 113 N 3rd St, at Berry St ☎ 718 963 3973, ⊛ radegasthall.com; subway L to Bedford Ave; map p.225. This spacious, wooden, Austro-Hungarian beer hall serves steins of foamy German brews (from $7). The dining room does great food and is popular with families, while the beer garden attracts serious boozers. Mon–Thurs noon–2am, Fri noon–3am, Sat 11am–3am, Sun 11am–2am.

★**Tørst** 615 Manhattan Ave, between Nassau and Driggs aves ☎ 718 389 6034, ⊛ torstnyc.com; subway G to Nassau Ave; map p.225. A shiny new temple for beer drinkers, *Tørst* boasts reclaimed wood and a sleek marble bar, behind which 21 draughts sit hooked up to the "flux capacitor", which allows bartenders to monitor and adjust the gas and carbonation without descending to the kegs below. The results: flawless draughts, available in 8oz or 14oz pours. Settle in and sample a few; it may be a while before you want to leave. Sun–Thurs noon–midnight, Fri & Sat noon–2am.

BUSHWICK

Featherweight 135 Graham Ave, at Johnson Ave ☎ 347 763 0872, ⊛ featherweightbk.com; subway L to Montrose Ave; map p.225. Entered by the lit-up photograph of a boxer that serves as its welcome mat, this low-key speakeasy muddles, pours and shakes some of New York's best cocktails ($12). Mon–Thurs 7pm–2am, Fri & Sat 7pm–3am, Sun 2pm–2am.

BEDFORD-STUYVESANT

Doris 1088 Fulton St, at Claver Place; subway C, S to Franklin Ave; map p.214. Heavenly in warm weather, *Doris* has a snug, whitewashed interior and a spacious candlelit patio with fig plants and potted palms. There's a small grilled cheese-type menu ($6–10), and frequent DJs spinning good vinyl. Mon–Thurs & Sun 5pm–2am, Fri & Sat 5pm–4am.

Tip-Top Bar & Grill 432 Franklin Ave, between Madison St and Putnam Ave; subway C, S to Franklin Ave; map p.214. A true dive (rather than a hipster dive), this long-time haunt, decorated with family photos and Obama memorabilia, has been charming patrons for over forty years. Cocktails will set you back about $7, while Aunt Sally's Kitchen's deep-fried chicken and chips is $9. The jukebox is superb. Mon–Fri 5pm–4am, Sat 2pm–4am.

23

TOP 5 BROOKLYN BAR GAMES

Bocce (like boules) at Floyd See opposite
Karaoke at Montero's Bar & Grill See opposite
Shuffleboard at Royal Palms See p.342
Trivia at Pete's Candy Store See above
Video games at Barcade See above

23

PARK SLOPE AND GOWANUS

Blueprint 196 Fifth Ave, between Union and Sackett sts ☎718 622 6644, ⓦblueprintbrooklyn.com; subway R to Union St; map p.231. Upscale lounge bar specializing in artfully crafted cocktails ($13), plus seasonal small plates (such as baby octopus and roasted beets). Fresh juices, syrups and bitters are prepared in-house. Mon–Thurs 4pm–2am, Fri 4pm–4am, Sat 3pm–4am, Sun 3pm–1am.

Dram Shop 339 Ninth St, between Fifth and Sixth aves ☎718 788 1444, ⓦdramshopbrooklyn.com; subway F, G, R to Fourth Ave-Ninth St; map p.231. Popular spot for a few generations of drinkers and sports watchers, who fill up the wooden booths and, in good weather, tiny outdoor area. The double-patty burger (with fries, $12) is addictive, and, perhaps best of all, there's a shuffleboard table under the twin TVs. Mon–Thurs 3pm–4am, Fri 2pm–4am, Sat & Sun noon–4am.

Freddy's Bar 627 Fifth Ave, between 17th and 18th sts ☎718 768 0131, ⓦfreddysbar.com; subway R to Prospect Ave; map p.231. After being pushed out of Prospect Heights thanks to the Atlantic Yards project, this vaunted hangout has been transplanted to the South Slope – its divey soul (and colourful decor) intact; live music, or some kind of performance, most nights. Draft beer $5. Daily noon–4am.

Owl Farm 297 9th St, between Fourth and Fifth aves ☎718 499 4988, ⓦtheowlfarm.com; subway F, G, R to Fourth Ave-9th St; map p.231. Cosy pub with exposed-brick interiors, pinball machines and a vast range of craft beers and ciders (some thirty on tap) from $4. It also sells a rotating selection of unique distilled beers (liquor derived from beer). Mon–Fri 2pm–4am, Sat & Sun 12.30pm–4am.

★Royal Palms Shuffleboard Club 514 Union St, between Third Ave and Nevins St ☎347 223 4410, ⓦroyalpalmsshuffle.com; subway R to Union St; map p.231. Shuffleboard has come to Brooklyn at this hip and spacious retro-style venue, with courts rented for $40/hr and food trucks parked on the premises. The decor is 1940s-era Florida – think black-and-white-striped booths and flamingo wallpaper in the bathroom. Mon–Thurs 6pm–2am, Fri 6pm–2am, Sat noon–2am, Sun noon–10pm.

Union Hall 702 Union St, at Fifth Ave ☎718 638 4400, ⓦunionhallny.com; subway R to Union St-Fourth Ave; map p.231. Vast bar, restaurant (poutine, $9) and live music venue, with a library-like interior of bookshelves, fireplaces and sofas near the bar, and two wildly popular bocce courts (arrive early to get a game). The basement hosts bands three or four times a week – check out the website for the schedule. Mon–Fri 4pm–4am, Sat & Sun 1pm–4am.

BOERUM HILL, COBBLE HILL AND CARROLL GARDENS

★Black Mountain Wine House 415 Union St, at Hoyt St ☎718 522 4340; subway F, G to Carroll St; map p.235. Great date spot, but fun under any circumstances, *Black Mountain* offers shared plates like crostini with white beans and ricotta ($11) and a superior wine list in a setting that feels very New England-chic, complete with crackling fireplace. Daily 3pm–midnight.

Brooklyn Inn 148 Hoyt St, at Bergen St ☎718 522 2525; subway F, G to Bergen St, A, C, G to Hoyt-Schermerhorn; map p.235. Locals – and their dogs – gather at this convivial favourite with high ceilings, a whittled wood bar imported from Germany in the 1870s and friendly staff. Great place for a daytime buzz (beer around $6) or shooting pool in the back room. Cash only. Mon–Thurs 4pm–4am, Fri 3pm–4am, Sat & Sun 2pm–4am.

Brooklyn Social 335 Smith St, between President and Carroll sts ☎718 858 7758, ⓦbrooklynsocialbar.com; subway F, G to Carroll St; map p.235. Longtime cocktail haunt (it gets its name from an old Italian "social club" that used to convene here) with dimly lit corners and no sign on the door. Great for a date (cocktails $12). Cash only. Mon–Thurs & Sun 5pm–2am, Fri & Sat 5pm–4am.

Clover Club 210 Smith St, between Butler and Baltic sts ☎718 855 7939, ⓦcloverclubny.com; subway F, G to Bergen St; map p.235. Painstakingly constructed cocktails ($13), served in an old-timey atmosphere of pressed tin ceilings, leather-topped stools and burgundy banquettes. Mon–Thurs 4pm–2am, Fri 4pm–4am, Sat 10.30am–4am, Sun 10.30am–1am.

Gowanus Yacht Club 323 Smith St, at President St ☎718 246 1321; subway F, G to Carroll St; map p.235. There's not much to it – some beat-up benches, hot dogs and cheap beer ($3–6) – and yet, many Brooklyn residents would put *Gowanus Yacht Club* at the top of their favourite bars list. Outdoor seating only, and a squished but happy "gang's-all-here" vibe. Cash only. May–Oct Mon–Fri 3pm–midnight, Sat & Sun 2pm–midnight.

RED HOOK

Fort Defiance 365 Van Brunt St, at Dikeman St ☎347 453 6672, ⓦfortdefiancebrooklyn.com; subway F, G to Smith-9th sts; map p.235. It bills itself as a "café-bar" and does offer restaurant-like full meals (eg mushroom risotto, $20), but what *Fort Defiance* does best is make lovingly prepared cocktails (though the well-curated wine list and strong coffee rate highly too), which honour storied classics from famous bars. Mon–Fri 10am–midnight (closes 3pm Tues), Sat & Sun 9am–midnight.

★Sunny's 253 Conover St, between Reed and Beard sts ☎718 625 8211, ⓦsunnysredhook.com; subway F, G to Smith-9th sts; map p.235. This neighbourhood stalwart had a hiccup after Hurricane Sandy, but it's back and just as welcoming as ever. The beer comes in bottles, the (free) music goes till late and the decor and vibe are pretty much unlike anywhere else. Mon & Tues 4pm–2am, Wed–Fri 4pm–4am, Sat 11am–4am, Sun 11am–midnight.

QUEENS

ASTORIA

Bohemian Hall and Beer Garden 29-19 24th Ave, between 29th and 31st sts ☎718 274 4925, ⓦbohemianhall.com; subway N, Q to Astoria Blvd; map p.248. This hundred-year-old Czech bar is the real deal, catering to old-timers and serving a good selection of pilsners, among other offerings. Out back there's a large beer garden with picnic tables, trees, free-flowing pitchers ($18), burgers ($12) and sausages ($9), and a bandstand for polka groups. Great fun in good weather, and worth the trip. Mon–Thurs 5pm–1am, Fri 5pm–3am, Sat noon–3am, Sun noon–midnight.

Cronin & Phelan's 38-14 Broadway, between 38th and Steinway sts ☎718 545 8999, ⓦcronin andphelans.com; subway E, M, R to Steinway St; map p.248. Boisterous locals' watering hole with cheap pub fare – enormous portions of shepherd's pie ($12.95), veggie burger with fries ($9), roast turkey with cranberries ($14.95) – plus an outdoor area and the odd open-mic night. Mon–Sat 8am–4am, Sun 11am–4am.

LONG ISLAND CITY

Domaine Wine Bar 50-04 Vernon Blvd, at 50th Ave ☎718 784 2350, ⓦdomainewinebar.com; subway #7 to Vernon Blvd-Jackson Ave, E, M, #7 to Court Square, G to 21st St; map p.246. Forty sublime wines by the glass (around $11), low, antique lighting and a menu of tempting cheese plates ($14) set the scene for a romantic rendezvous or a great night unwinding with friends. Daily 5pm–1am.

Dutch Kills 27-24 Jackson Ave, at Queens St ☎718 383 2724, ⓦdutchkillsbar.com; subway E, M, R to Queens Plaza; map p.246. Cocktail bar with a speakeasy theme (look for the "Bar" sign) from renowned mixologist Richard Boccato, with wooden booths and iconic drinks made for $13 – a good deal compared to similar spots across the East River. Daily 5pm–2am.

L.I.C. Bar 45-58 Vernon Blvd, at 46th Ave ☎718 786 5400, ⓦlicbar.com; subway #7 to Vernon Blvd-Jackson Ave, E, M, #7 to Court Square, G to 21st St; map p.246. A friendly, atmospheric place for a beer ($4–10), burger and some free live music (Mon, Wed, Sat & Sun); hunker down at the old wooden bar or in the pleasant outdoor garden. Mon–Fri 4pm–4am, Sat 1pm–4am, Sun 1pm–midnight.

THE BRONX

Yankee Tavern 72 E 161st St, at Gerard Ave ☎718 292 6130; subway B, D, #4 to 161st St-Yankee Stadium; map p.256. Since 1923, this has been the "original sports bar". Everyone wears their pinstripes on their sleeves in this dive, and Yankees employees come to blow off steam (or celebrate). Beers around $8. Hours vary, but generally daily 10am–2am.

STATEN ISLAND

Jade Island 2845 Richmond Ave, between Independence and Yukon aves ☎718 761 8080, ⓦjadeislandstaten .com; bus #S44, #S61; map p.265. Staten Island's sole tiki bar (cum Chinese restaurant) offers bamboo booths, blowfish lamps, rum cocktails in coconuts and girls in hula skirts. And you wanted to head straight back to Manhattan. Mon–Thurs 11.30am–11pm, Fri 11.30am–midnight, Sat 12.30pm–midnight, Sun 12.30pm–11pm.

Liedy's Shore Inn 748 Richmond Terrace, between Clinton and Lafayette aves ☎718 447 9240; bus #S40; map p.265. Staten Island's oldest pub was opened in 1905 by German immigrant Jacob Liedy (his great-grandson Larry Leidy now runs it) – once popular with sailors, today it's convenient to Snug Harbor and retains a no-nonsense local bar vibe. Drinks $6. Sun–Thurs 11.30am–10pm, Fri & Sat 11.30am–midnight.

23

Nightlife

As the city that never sleeps, New York is a global nightlife hotspot. Even confirmed early birds should try to stay out late at least a few times during their stay, as the city's legendary energy is most obvious when most other cities have bedded down for the night. Since the early 2000s, New York's rock scene has been fuelled by bands from the East Village, the Lower East Side and Williamsburg in Brooklyn, while the city continues to set the standard in jazz, especially in Harlem. Hip-hop also remains a vital part of the musical scene in New York – Mos Def, Nas, 50 Cent and Jay-Z are all based here, along with up-and-coming rappers such as A$AP Rocky (and the A$AP Mob), French Montana, Joey Bada$$ (and Pro Era) and Azealia Banks.

Whatever you're planning to do after dark, remember to **carry ID** at all times to prove you're over 21 – you're likely to be asked by every doorman. Note that some venues do not even allow under-21s to enter, let alone drink – call to check if you're concerned. Note also that although **smoking is illegal** at most clubs, you'll soon realize that in practice this is only sporadically enforced (despite regular police crackdowns).

The sections that follow provide accounts of the pick of the city's venues, but it's a good idea to get up-to-date info once you hit the ground.

ESSENTIALS

Listings *Time Out New York* (free every Wed) is pretty reliable. Otherwise, the *Village Voice* website (ⓦ villagevoice.com) or check out ⓦ nycgo.com.

Tickets For most of the large venues, tickets are sold through Ticketmaster (ⓦ ticketmaster.com). For many mid-size and small venues, try Ticketweb (ⓦ ticketweb.com).

LIVE MUSIC

New York has a vibrant **live music** scene, though most places are eclectic when it comes to genres; the same place can feature rock, hip-hop, folk and Latin music on different nights, and only jazz has a truly separate club culture (see p.349). New York's **rock scene** has leant heavily toward garage and pop/indie rock in the last decade, with newer, more eclectic bands like Parquet Courts, Holy Hail, Sleigh Bells and Yeasayer adding to an established roster that includes Vampire Weekend, Interpol, The Strokes and the Yeah Yeah Yeahs. As for **venues**, rising rents have forced many smaller and medium-sized places to close or decamp to Brooklyn (especially Williamsburg) and New Jersey. Most of the best performance spaces are still in Manhattan, though; there's a large cluster of exceptionally good venues in the East Village and Lower East Side.

LARGE VENUES

★ **Barclays Center** 620 Atlantic Ave, at Flatbush Ave, Brooklyn ☎ 917 618 6100, ⓦ barclayscenter.com; subway B, D, N, Q, R, #2, #3, #4, #5 to Atlantic Ave; map p.218. Brooklyn's big stage hosts NBA team the Nets (see p.397) and major sports events, but is also gaining a rep for mega concerts from the likes of Jay-Z, Beyonce, Rihanna and Kendrick Lamar.

★ **Hammerstein Ballroom** 311 W 34th St, between Eighth and Ninth aves ☎ 212 564 4882, ⓦ mceventsnyc .com/hammerstein-ballroom; subway A, C, E to 34th St; map p.142. This grand 1906 building has seen many incarnations: it's been an opera house, a vaudeville hall and a Masonic temple, and it now hosts meetings, galas and live indie and rock bands. Capacity is 3500, but the sound system and acoustics are of high enough quality that most seats are pretty good. Tickets $50 and up.

Madison Square Garden Seventh Ave, at W 32nd St ☎ 212 465 6741, ⓦ thegarden.com; subway A, C, E, #1, #2, #3 to 34th St; map p.142. New York's principal big stage, the Garden hosts not only hockey and basketball games but also a good portion of the stadium rock and pop acts that visit the city. Seating capacity is 20,000-plus, so the arena's not exactly the most soulful place to see a band – but for big names, it's the handiest option.

Radio City Music Hall 1260 Sixth Ave, at W 50th St ☎ 212 247 4777, ⓦ radiocity.com; subway B, D, F, M to 47-50th St; map p.124. Not the prime venue it once was; it occasionally hosts a terrific concert, but for the most part its schedule is clogged with cutesy tribute shows, schlocky musicals and, of course, the "Christmas Spectacular". The acoustics are flawless and the building itself does have a great sense of occasion (see p.128) – it seems to inspire the artists who play here to put on a memorable show.

MID-SIZE AND SMALL VENUES
SOHO

City Winery 155 Varick St, at Vandam St ☎ 212 608 0555, ⓦ citywinery.com; subway #1 to Houston St, C, E to Spring St; map p.64. Offers a fine roster of rock, folk and

24

NEW YORK BURLESQUE

In the last ten years burlesque shows and clubs have gained a cult following in New York, with fêted local performers such as Sugar Shack Burlesque, Ruby Solitaire (ⓦ rubysolitaire.com) and Calamity Chang (ⓦ calamitychang.com). Sometimes dubbed "neo-burlesque", performances can include anything from classic striptease and campy comedy acts to variety shows and extravagant mini-dramas. Though rarely suitable for children and usually involving nudity in some form, acts are more focused on the wildly exaggerated performance than just stripping. Most shows take place in various venues across the Lower East Side and East Village such as the **Slipper Room**, 167 Orchard St (ⓦ slipperroom.com). Check ⓦ timeout.com/newyork for the latest listings.

NEW YORK LIVE MUSIC FESTIVALS

New York hosts numerous live music festivals in virtually all genres throughout the year, with many concerts falling under the River to River Festival, SummerStage and Celebrate Brooklyn umbrellas (see p.407). Jazz fans should also check out the Charlie Parker Jazz Festival (see p.407) and Washington Square Music Festival (see p.358).

Winter Jazzfest Jan; Ⓦwinterjazzfest.com. High-quality mid-winter jazz festival, held over four days in around ten venues with over one hundred acts.

Brooklyn Folk Festival Late April; Ⓦbrooklyn folkfest.com. American and world folk music festival, with concerts held at St Ann's Church at 157 Montague St, between Clinton and Henry streets in Brooklyn Heights.

Blue Note Jazz Festival Early June; Ⓦbluenote jazzfestival.com. New York's premier jazz festival since 2010, with some of the world's best musicians and singers performing at locations such as *B.B. King Blues Club* (see p.350) and the *Blue Note Jazz Club* itself (see p.350).

Governors Ball Music Festival Early June; Ⓦgovernorsballmusicfestival.com. NYC's premier multi-stage summer concert festival, held over three days on Randall's Island, has featured acts as diverse as the Black Keys, Drake and Kate Tempest. Single day passes from $105.

Northside Festival Brooklyn June; ☎718 596 3462, Ⓦnorthsidefestival.com. Hundreds of primarily Brooklyn-based bands performing over four days at various venues in Williamsburg and Greenpoint, centred on McCarren Park (there's also a film component to the festival).

Summer Jam June; ☎212 229 9797, Ⓦhot97.com/summerjam. Annual hip-hop/R&B show hosted by NYC radio station Hot 97 (the event is usually held at MetLife Stadium in New Jersey). Think Kendrick Lamar, Chris Brown, Trey Songz and Big Sean. Tickets from $70.

Seeger Fest Late July; Ⓦseegerfest.org. Free events and concerts in New York and the Hudson Valley to commemorate the lives of revered folk musician Pete Seeger and his wife, Toshi Seeger.

Electric Zoo Labor Day weekend (Sept); ☎347 263 7376, Ⓦelectriczoofestival.com. The Northeast's largest electronic music festival, held on Randall's Island, attracting the likes of David Guetta, Candyland and Zeds Dead. Three-day admission from $199.

---

roots music performers on its stage; also has full dinner service (food is OK, nothing special) and wine is actually made on the premises. Most tickets $15–55. Mon–Thurs & Sun 11.30am–3.30pm & 5pm–midnight, Fri 11.30am–3.30pm & 5pm–2am, Sat 5pm–2am.

LOWER EAST SIDE

★**Arlene's Grocery** 95 Stanton St, between Ludlow and Orchard sts ☎212 473 9831, Ⓦarlenesgrocery.net; subway F to Lower East Side-Second Ave; map p.82. An intimate, erstwhile bodega (hence the name) that hosts nightly gigs by local, reliably good indie bands. Go on Mon nights (free) after 10pm for punk and heavy-metal karaoke, when you can sing along with a live band. Tues–Thurs & Sun admission $8, Fri & Sat $10. Daily 6pm–4am.

★**Bowery Ballroom** 6 Delancey St, at Bowery ☎212 533 2111, Ⓦboweryballroom.com; subway J, Z to Bowery, B, D to Grand St; map p.82. No attitude, great acoustics and even better views have earned this venue praise from both fans and bands. Major labels test their up-and-comers here, so it's a great place to catch the Next Big Thing of any genre. Most shows cost $15–35. Daily from 7pm.

Mercury Lounge 217 E Houston St, at Essex St ☎212 260 7400, Ⓦmercuryloungenyc.com; subway F to Lower East Side-Second Ave; map p.82. Mainstay featuring a mix of local, national and international rock and pop acts. It's

owned by the same crew as the *Bowery Ballroom*, and is similarly used by major labels (The Strokes started out here in 2000). Tickets usually $8–20. Daily shows from 7pm.

Pianos 158 Ludlow St, between Stanton and Rivington sts ☎212 505 3733, Ⓦpianosnyc.com; subway F to Delancey St, J, M, Z to Essex St; map p.82. There's no admission charge to get in the door at this converted piano factory (hence the name), but to get into the tiny back room – where the music is – you'll need to fork out extra at the weekend ($8–10). The sound system's a standout, and the endless roster of mostly rock bands (expect four choices nightly) means the place is usually packed. Drink prices are somewhat high, and the queue to get in habitually long. Daily 2pm–4am (live music daily at 8pm).

Rockwood Music Hall 196 Allen St, between Houston and Stanton sts ☎212 477 4155, Ⓦrockwoodmusichall.com; subway F to Lower East Side-Second Ave; map p.82. Seven nights of live music draw hordes of locals to this tiny space. Though there are no bad seats, it's a good idea to come early – it's often packed. Most tickets $10–15. Mon–Fri 6pm–4am, Sat & Sun 3pm–4am.

EAST VILLAGE

Joe's Pub 425 Lafayette St, between Astor Place and 4th St ☎212 539 8778, Ⓦpublictheater.org/Joes-Pub-at-The-Public; subway #6 to Astor Place, N, R, W to 8th

St; map p.88. The hipper, late-night arm of the Public Theater (p.355), and one of the sharpest and most popular music venues in the city – this is where Amy Winehouse and Adele made their US headlining concert debuts. Tickets usually from $15, with a $12 food/two-drink minimum. Check website for show times.

Otto's Shrunken Head 538 E 14th St, between aves A and B ☎212 228 2240, ⓦottosshrunkenhead.com; subway L to First Ave; map p.88. This East Village joint is hard to pigeonhole; a Tiki bar that hosts live indie and punk rock bands, as well as some of the most popular club nights on the island. Usually no admission charge. Mon–Fri noon–4am, Sat & Sun 4pm–4am.

Sidewalk Café 94 Ave A, at E 6th St ☎ 212 473 7373, ⓦsidewalkny.com; subway L to First Ave; map p.88. Mainstay of the East Village scene since 1985, serving up mean burgers and live folk, pop, rock and indie most nights of the week. Monday is open-mic night, with Tuesdays devoted to slam poetry. Usually no admission charge, with two-item minimum. Mon–Thurs & Sun 11am–1am, Fri & Sat 11am–4am.

WEST VILLAGE

The Bitter End 147 Bleecker St, between LaGuardia Place and Thompson St ☎212 673 7030, ⓦbitterend .com; subway A, B, C, D, E, F, M to W 4th St; map p.96. Young MOR bands in an intimate club setting, mostly folky rockers in the Dylan mould since 1961, though Lady Gaga got started here in 2007. A catalogue of the famous people who've played the club is posted by the door – it's a pretty long list. Admission is usually $8–15, but some gigs are free; there's a two-drink minimum. Daily 7pm–1am, Mon, Fri & Sat until 4am.

★**(Le) Poisson Rouge** 158 Bleecker St, at Thompson St ☎212 505 3474, ⓦlpr.com; subway A, B, C, D, E, F, M to W 4th St; map p.96. Mix of live rock, folk, pop and electronica at 7pm ($10–25), with dance parties most weekends (Fri & Sat; often free, otherwise $15–20). Daily 5pm–2am, Fri & Sat until 4am.

SOB's (Sounds of Brazil) 204 Varick St, at W Houston ☎212 243 4940, ⓦsobs.com; subway #1 to Houston St; map p.96. Premier place to hear hip-hop, Brazilian, West Indian, Caribbean and world music acts in Manhattan. Vibrant and danceable, with a high quality of music. Shows most nights; ticket prices vary according to the performer. Mon–Thurs hours vary depending on shows, Fri 5pm–4am, Sat 6.30pm–4am, Sun noon–4pm.

★**Village Underground** 130 W 3rd St, at Sixth Ave ☎212 777 7745, ⓦthevillageunderground.com; subway A, B, C, D, E, F, M to W 4th St; map p.96. Tiny basement performance space that is one of the most intimate and innovative clubs around. Monday is jam-session night, the house band (playing vintage rock and R&B, funk and reggae) holds court Wednesday through

Friday, while Tuesday & Saturday are club nights (all from 8.30pm). Sunday is open-mic night. Admission $10–15.

GRAMERCY PARK

Irving Plaza 17 Irving Place, at E 15th St ☎212 777 6800, ⓦvenue.irvingplaza.com; subway L, N, Q, R, W #4, #5, #6 to Union Square; map p.115. Once home to Off-Broadway musicals (hence the dangling chandeliers and blood-red interior), *Irving Plaza* now features an impressive array of rock, electronic and techno acts. The main room has wildly divergent acoustics; stand towards the back on the ground floor for the truest mix of sound. Tickets usually range $35–85. See website for show times.

CHELSEA

High Line Ballroom 431 W 16th St, between Ninth and Tenth aves ☎212 414 5994, ⓦhighlineballroom .com; subway A, C, E to 14th St; map p.107. One of the newer venues, with table seating available (full dinner if you like) for shows – acts run from indie rock to hip-hop, reggae and big band (most tickets $20–50). There are DJ sets too. $10 minimum for table seating during shows. Daily 6pm–late.

MIDTOWN

Iridium 1650 Broadway, at W 51st St ☎212 582 2121, ⓦtheiridium.com; subway #1 to 50th St; map p.142. Jazz but also blues, rock and folk performed seven nights a week amid Surrealist decor described as "Dolly meets Disney". The late godfather of electric guitar, Les Paul, regularly played here from 1996 to 2009. Admission $25–45, $15 food and drink minimum. Daily 8pm–midnight.

UPPER WEST SIDE

Postcrypt Coffeehouse 2098 Broadway, at W 116th St, in the basement of St Paul's Chapel ⓦblogs.cuit .columbia.edu/postcrypt; subway #1 to 116th St; map p.184. Venerable Columbia University student-run folk venue, with hardly any seating but free music and cheap drinks; only 35 people can legally fit inside, making for exceptionally intimate shows. Fri & Sat 8pm–midnight when the university's in session.

COLUMBIA STREET WATERFRONT DISTRICT (BROOKLYN)

Jalopy Theatre & School of Music 315 Columbia St, at Woodhull St ☎718 395 3214, ⓦjalopy.biz; subway F, G to Carroll St; map p.235. If you want to hear bluegrass, folk or the occasional hard-to-classify musician in a relaxed setting, this tiny instrument shop/venue will be just the ticket. Lessons and workshops as well. Most shows $10–40. Tues–Fri 2pm–2am, Sat & Sun noon–2am.

24

LATIN AND BALLROOM DANCE NIGHTS AND VENUES

Baila Wednesdays at Solas 232 E 9th St, between Second and Third aves; subway #6 to Astor Place. Mambo and salsa dancing to DJs 9pm–1am (classes 7–8pm; $7), with $7 admission. See ⓦsalsanewyork .com for a full list of weekly salsa events.

Fridays at SOB's (see p.347). Lessons followed by live salsa bands from 8pm on Fridays, featuring not only Latin greats but newer acts as well. Admission $10–15. Fri from 5pm.

Milonga Falucho 499 Grand St, Williamsburg ☎718 782 9477, ⓦcafeargentinony.com; subway G to Metropolitan Ave. Fabulous tango party every Monday at *Café Argentino* (7.30–11.45pm), beginning with a tango class 7.30–8.30pm. Admission $10, or $15 with class. For other tango events, visit ⓦnewyork tango.com.

Salsa Salsa Tumbao at Yayo's 36 Fifth Ave, between Dean and Bergen sts, Brooklyn ☎718 622 8922, ⓦyayoslatincuisine.com; subway #2, #3, #4, #5 to Atlantic Ave. This Puerto Rican restaurant hosts a big party every Thursday 8pm to 12.30am, with DJs

spinning salsa, chachacha, bachata and merengue. Admission $7, or $10 if live band playing. Free salsa class led by Salsa Salsa Dance Studio 8–8.30pm.

Salsamania Saturdays DanceSport 22 W 34th St, between Fifth and Sixth aves ☎347 522 6320, ⓦdancesport.com; subway B, F, D, M, N, Q to 34th St-Herald Square; map p.142. Huge salsa party every second and fourth Saturday of every month (admission from $15), with a separate bachata dancefloor (bachata classes at 7pm, salsa classes at 8pm). Second and fourth Sat of the month 7pm–4am.

Samba New York ☎917 684 9447, ⓦsamba newyork.com. Centre for Brazilian samba culture in New York, offering shows and classes in drumming and dancing. Check the website for class times and events.

Swing 46 349 W 46th St, between Eighth and Ninth aves ☎212 262 9554, ⓦswing46.com; subway A, C, E to 42nd St; map p.142. Jazz and supper club offering live swing bands and dance lessons (1hr). Admission $15–20 (includes lesson). Daily 5pm–1am (lessons at 9pm).

24

WILLIAMSBURG AND GREENPOINT

Baby's All Right 146 Broadway, at Bedford Ave ☎718 599 5800, ⓦbabysallright.com; subway J, M, Z to Marcy Ave; map p.225. Bar, restaurant and live venue with the cool name, with live acts every night (from indie rock to hip-hop) – get tickets on-line, as shows often sell out. Most tickets $10–15 (or free). Mon–Fri 6pm–4am, Sat & Sun noon–4am.

★**Brooklyn Bowl** 61 Wythe Ave, between 11th and 12th sts ☎718 963 3369, ⓦbrooklynbowl.com; subway L to Bedford Ave; map p.225. A converted warehouse with live concerts, DJ sets, karaoke, food by the Blue Ribbon group and ... oh yeah, the purported main attraction: bowling (see p.400). Shows usually $5–20, with the odd big name a lot more. Mon–Thurs 6pm–2am, Fri 6pm–4am, Sat noon–4am, Sun noon–2am.

Knitting Factory 361 Metropolitan Ave, at Havemeyer St ☎347 529 6696, ⓦbk.knittingfactory.com; subway L to Bedford Ave, G, L to Metropolitan Ave; map p.225. This intimate showcase for indie rock and underground hip-hop has a loyal following and books quality acts. Most tickets $10–20. Daily shows start from 5pm to 9pm.

★**Music Hall of Williamsburg** 66 N 6th St, between Wythe and Kent aves ☎718 486 5400, ⓦmusichallof williamsburg.com; subway L to Bedford Ave; map p.225. A large performance space with excellent acoustics, set in an old factory. One of Brooklyn's really great venues and another in the *Bowery Ballroom* stable – expect the same kind of acts. Tickets free–$40. Daily shows start

between 6pm and 8pm.

★**Saint Vitus** 1120 Manhattan Ave, at Clay St ⓦsaintvitusbar.com; subway G to Greenpoint Ave; map p.225. Tucked away at the top end of Greenpoint, this is *the* place for metal bands and their fans. Black walls, black mahogany bar, red candles, pickle-backs (a shot of Jameson's and a shot of pickle juice) and a solitary Iron Maiden poster – you get the picture. Take a cab; the G train is a hassle at night. Mon–Thurs & Sun 6pm–2am, Fri & Sat 6pm–4am.

Warsaw 261 Driggs Ave, between Eckford and Leonard sts ☎212 777 6800, ⓦwarsawconcerts.com; subway G to Nassau Ave; map p.225. Brooklyn's legendary *Warsaw at the Polish Home* (a converted social club) offers a no-frills atmosphere with punk (and sometimes hip-hop) served up with *pierogis* (cheap plates of Polish dumplings). Cash only. Tues–Sun 6pm–2am.

GOWANUS

The Bell House 149 7th St, between Second and Third aves ☎718 643 6510, ⓦthebellhouseny.com; subway F, M, G, R to Fourth Ave-9th St; map p.235. A converted printing house provides the setting for indie band performances and wacky events – cook-offs, Burt Reynolds film celebrations and so on. The front-room bar is a pleasantly spacious place to drink, with happy-hour specials. Shows usually $15–30. Daily 5pm–4am.

Littlefield 622 Degraw St, between Third and Fourth aves ☎718 855 3388, ⓦlittlefieldnyc.com; subway R to

Union St; map p.235. Housed in an old warehouse, this art and performance space hosts a diverse line-up of bands from indie rock and hip-hop to jazz and reggae, as well as art exhibitions, literary events and film screenings. Wed–Sun 8pm–2am.

Rock Shop 249 Fourth Ave, between President and Carroll sts ☏718 230 5740, ⓦtherockshopny.com; subway R to Union St; map p.231. Brooklyn rock club featuring primarily up-and-coming bands, with a full bar and restaurant upstairs. Mon–Thurs 5pm–2am, Fri 4pm–4am, Sat noon–4am, Sun noon–1am.

JAZZ AND BLUES

Jazz in New York has seen a major resurgence since the 1990s. You'll find the best clubs in the **West Village** and especially **Harlem**, where a host of small, intimate venues showcase a variety of local talent, from Hammond-organ players to Afro-beat performers. Note that **Woody Allen** (with The Eddy Davis New Orleans Jazz Band) still plays jazz clarinet at *Café Carlyle* (see p.350), though this has turned into a bit of a tourist circus. To find out **who else is playing**, check the usual sources, notably the *Village Voice* (ⓦ villagevoice.com) and *Time Out New York* (ⓦ timeout.com/newyork); other good jazz rags are the monthlies *Hothouse* (ⓦ hothousejazz.com), a free magazine available at venues and hotels, and *DownBeat* (ⓦ downbeat.com). **Price** policies vary from club to club; the major places that attract famous performers charge a hefty admission charge ($20–50) and a minimum for food and drinks. Smaller venues (especially in Harlem) come cheaper; some have neither admission fee nor minimum drink charge.

HARLEM JAZZ VENUES

★American Legion Post (Col. Charles Young #398) 248 W 132nd St, between Powell and Frederick Douglass blvds ☏212 283 9701; subway #2, #3 to W 135th St; map p.199. This veterans' club hosts one of the best deals in Harlem, the free Sunday-evening jam sessions that run 7pm–midnight; the headliner is Seleno Clarke on his classic Hammond B3 organ, but the home-cooked meals and cheap drinks are also worth sampling. You have to sign in at the door. Jazz nights also Wed, Thurs and every other Sat 8pm–midnight.

★Bill's Place 148 W 133rd St, between Malcolm X and Powell blvds ☏212 281 0777, ⓦbillsplaceharlem.com; subway #2, #3 to 135th St; map p.199. Showcase for local star saxophonist Bill Saxton, hosted in an old speakeasy on what was Jungle Alley; he performs Fridays and Saturdays only, at 8pm and 10pm (doors open 7.30pm; admission $20; no alcohol sold).

Cotton Club 656 W 125th St, at Twelfth Ave ☏212 663 7980, ⓦcottonclub-newyork.com; subway #1 to 125th St; map p.199. No relation to the famous original (this version opened in 1977), it packs in the tourists nonetheless with the Cotton Club All Stars knocking out swing, blues and jazz classics. Saturday- and Thursday-night shows (with buffet) are $56.50, while the Saturday and Sunday Gospel brunch is $43.50. Monday is swing dance night ($25; food extra) while Friday is Latin night

($20). Mon 8pm–midnight, Thurs 8pm–midnight, Fri 9pm–2am, Sat noon–6pm & 9pm–midnight, Sun noon–6pm.

Minton's 206 W 118th St, between St Nicholas Ave and Powell Blvd ☏212 243 2222, ⓦmintonsharlem.com; subway B, C, #2, #3 to 116th St; map p.199. The birthplace of bebop has been reopened as a jazz supper club, and though it's not the same without Dizzy, Bird and Thelonius Monk, the atmosphere remains (look for the famous mural behind the bandstand) and there's also weekend jazz brunches (there are limited spots at the bar if you are not eating). Admission $10 Fri & Sat night. Wed & Thurs 6–10pm, Fri 6–11pm, Sat noon–3pm & 6–11pm, Sun noon–3pm & 6–10pm.

Showman's 375 W 125th St, at Morningside Ave ☏212 864 8941; subway A, B, C, D to 125th St; map p.199. This small, long-established blues, jazz and gospel-music haunt (since 1942) is often packed – it also features a real Hammond B3 organ. Jazz shows Wed & Thurs 8.30pm, 10pm, 11.30pm, Fri & Sat 9.30pm, 11.30pm, 1.30am; two-drink minimum ($14) but no admission charge. Wed–Sat 1pm–4am.

★Shrine 2271 Powell Blvd, between W 133rd and W 134th sts ☏212 690 7807, ⓦshrinenyc.com; subway B, #2, #3 to 135th St; map p.199. Named for Fela Kuti's legendary joint in Lagos, Nigeria, this cosy bar and performance space features African decor and walls lined

24

PARLOR JAZZ AT MARJORIE ELIOT'S

Something of a rite of passage for local jazz fans, every Sunday (3.30–6pm; free), a jazz concert has taken place in the parlour of legendary singer Marjorie Eliot's home at 555 Edgecombe Ave (at W 160th St; buzz Apt #3F; map p.209). Marjorie started the concerts in her living room in 1992, as a way to cope with the premature death of her son Phil. Just buzz-in and join the small crowd sitting in front of Marjorie's piano (go early to get a good seat); halfway through you get served apple juice and cookies.

with album sleeves. The focus here is on world music, but it's mostly jazz, with the Sunday sessions (from 5pm) the most fun. Shows start at 6pm most other nights, and there's flavoursome Israeli and West Africa-inspired food from the owners. Daily 4pm–4am.

WEST VILLAGE JAZZ VENUES

Bar Next Door 129 MacDougal St, between W 3rd and W 4th sts ☎212 529 5945, ⊚lalanternacaffe.com; subway A, B, C, D, E, F, M to W 4th St; map p.96. Great underground venue, with live sets. Free or admission $12 per set. Mon–Thurs & Sun 6pm–2am, Fri & Sat 6pm–3am.

Blue Note 131 W 3rd St, between Sixth Ave and MacDougal St ☎212 475 8592, ⊚bluenote.net; subway A, B, C, D, E, F, M to W 4th St, #1 to Christopher St; map p.96. Open since 1981 (and unrelated to the record label), this jazz institution regularly hosts top international performers, with the likes of Sarah Vaughan, Dizzy Gillespie and Oscar Peterson appearing in past years. Tickets usually range $10–45, plus $5 food or beverage minimum per person. Daily 6pm–1am, Fri & Sat until 3am.

Smalls Jazz Club 183 W 10th St, at W 4th St ☎212 252 5091, ⊚smallsjazzclub.com; subway #1 to Christopher St; map p.96. This cosy jazz dive is all about the music, with an impressive roster of visiting artists and a cool audio archive online – listen to the performers first to decide which night to visit. Admission $20. Mon–Fri 7pm–3.30am, Sat & Sun 4pm–3.30pm.

Village Vanguard 178 Seventh Ave, between Perry and W 11th sts ☎212 255 4037, ⊚villagevanguard .com; subway #1, #2, #3 to 14th St; map p.96. An NYC jazz landmark since 1935 (Sonny Rollins' *A Night at the Village Vanguard* was recorded here in 1957), with a regular diet of big names. Admission $30 per set, plus a one-drink minimum (no food). Daily 7.30pm–1am.

Zinc Bar 82 W 3rd St, between Thompson and Sullivan sts ☎212 477 8337, ⊚zincbar.com; subway A, B, C, D, E, F, M to W 4th St; map p.96. Great jazz venue with strong drinks and a loyal bunch of regulars. The blackboard above the entrance announces the evening's featured band. Hosts both new talent and established greats, with an emphasis on Latin American rhythms. Admission $10–20 with a one-drink minimum (two at the tables). Mon–Fri 6pm–2.30am, Sat & Sun 6pm–3am.

OTHER JAZZ VENUES

★**Birdland** 315 W 44th St, at Ninth Ave ☎212 581 3080, ⊚birdlandjazz.com; subway A, C, E to 42nd St; map p.142. Not the original place where Charlie Parker played, but nonetheless an established supper club that hosts some big names. Sets nightly at 8.30pm and 11pm.

Music charge of $25–50; at a table, you'll need to spend a minimum of $10 or more on food or drink. Daily 5pm–1am.

Café Carlyle 35 E 76th St, at Madison Ave, in Carlyle Hotel ☎212 744 1600, ⊚rosewoodhotels.com/en/ Carlyle; subway #6 to 77th St; map p.171. Woody Allen plays clarinet here with the Eddy Davis New Orleans Jazz Band most Mon nights Jan–June at 8.45pm (admission: general seating $165; bar seating $120 plus $25 drink/food minimum); add on dinner and this is essentially a very expensive way to see Allen up close, along with hordes of camera-wielding fans (photos are allowed). Mon–Sat 6.30pm–midnight.

Jazz at Lincoln Center Frederick P. Rose Hall, 33 W 60th St (use the JAZZ elevators on the ground floor of The Shops at Columbus Circle) ☎212 258 9800, ⊚jazz.org; subway #1, A, B, C, D to 59th St; map p.184. There are several different spaces at this venue (which is not at the Lincoln Center, despite the name), but the 140-seat *Dizzy's Club Coca-Cola* has the best shows, panoramic views and a speakeasy-style atmosphere – the food is great also. Admission varies, usually $20–35 (Mon) and $30–45 (Tues–Sun). Daily 6pm–1am, Fri & Sat until 2.30am.

Smoke 2751 Broadway, at W 106th St ☎212 864 6662, ⊚smokejazz.com; subway #1 to 103rd St; map p.184. This Upper West Side joint is a real neighbourhood treat, with plush couches, lavish chandeliers and a retro feel. Sets start at 8pm, 10pm and 11.30pm. Tickets usually $35–45 at weekends (Fri & Sat), $9 other nights. Mon–Sat 5.30pm–3am, Sun 11am–3am.

BLUES

B.B. King Blues Club & Grill 237 W 42nd St, between Seventh and Eighth aves ☎212 997 4144, ⊚bbking blues.com; subway #1, #2, #3, N, Q, R, W to Times Square-42nd St; map p.142. Yes, this is an unashamedly tourist experience, but adjust your expectations accordingly and it can be good fun: some big names in rock and blues play here (most shows 8pm and 10.30pm; $12–30, plus $10 food/drink minimum), and the Harlem Gospel Choir buffet brunch ($44 in advance, $47 at the door) on Sundays (12.30–2.30pm) is always entertaining. Daily 11am–1am.

★**Terra Blues** 149 Bleecker St, between Thompson St and LaGuardia Place ☎212 777 7776, ⊚terrablues .com; subway A, C, E to 42nd St; map p.96. The last remaining, exclusively blues club in the city offers acoustic blues from 7pm (Sat 6pm) and electric blues after 10pm, seven nights a week for $10–20 admission; all the big national names play here, and there's an excellent house band. No food. Mon–Thurs & Sun 6.30pm–2.30am, Fri 6.30pm–3.30am, Sat 6pm–3.30am.

24

NIGHTCLUBS

After a difficult decade, New York's club and party scene seems to be gaining strength, with the opening of new venues in Brooklyn and the arrival of Ibiza outpost *Space* (🌐 spaceibizany.com) bringing a new range of options for clubbers (though rival Pacha NYC closed in 2015). Yet the old adage remains true: the average New York nightclub lasts just eighteen months. You'll find the action spread out across the city, with the Lower East Side, Tribeca, the East and West villages and Brooklyn offering as many venues as the Meatpacking District, once the city's premier, if slightly overrated, nightlife hub. The really cutting-edge club nights are organized by outfits that tend to move around, such as **Blackmarket Membership** (📧 blkmarketrsvp@gmail.com; $20–30)) and the Victorian- and Rococo-themed events of **Dances of Vice** (🌐 dancesofvice.com). It's important to check up-to-date info with magazines like *Time Out New York*.

bOb Bar 235 Eldridge St, between Houston and Stanton sts ☎212 529 1807, 🌐 bobbarnyc.com; subway F to Lower East Side-Second Ave; map p.82. This cosy bar turns into one of the best dance parties in town after midnight, with DJ Church spinning a mix of hip-hop, reggae and R&B. Admission $5 after 10pm. Wed–Sat 7pm–4am, Sun 7pm–2am.

Bossa Nova Civic Club 1271 Myrtle St, at Hart St, Bushwick (Brooklyn) 🌐 bossanovacivicclub.com; subway M to Central Ave; map p.214. Cosy club for electronic dance music fans (mostly techno and some house), with a cool, tropical theme. Admission $10–30. Mon–Sat 5pm–4am, Sun 5pm–midnight.

★**Cielo** 18 Little W 12th St, between Washington St and Ninth Ave ☎212 645 5700, 🌐 cieloclub.com; subway L to Eighth Ave, A, C, E to 14th St; map p.96. Expect velvet rope-burn at this super-exclusive see-and-be-seen place: there's only room for 250 people. "Toca Tuesdays" features classic hip-hop, funk and soul, while "Roots NYC" on Wednesdays features classic house from the likes of DJ Louie Vega. Best sound system in the city. Admission $20–25. Mon & Wed–Sat 10pm–4am.

Good Room 98 Meserole Ave, at Manhattan Ave, Greenpoint (Brooklyn) ☎718 349 2373, 🌐 goodroombk.com; subway G to Nassau Ave; map p.225.

Down-to-earth drinking and dancing, hipster DJs (including popular locals Justin Strauss and Lloydski), big sound system and a fairly relaxed door policy. Admission $10–20. Wed–Sat 10pm–4am.

Le Bain The Standard, 848 Washington St, at W 13th St ☎212 645 7600, 🌐 standardhotels.com; subway A, C, E, L to 14th St/8th Ave; map p.107. This penthouse lounge bar and disco atop the trendy *Standard* can be pretentious, but if you're looking for glamour this is your spot. In summer, the rooftop deck features an infamous hot tub right on the dancefloor (which plays mainly techno and house). Dress up – it's tough to get in ("admission is determined at entrance"). Admission $10–30. Tues–Fri 10pm–4am, Sat 2pm–4am, Sun 2pm–3am.

Marquee 289 Tenth Ave, at W 27th St ☎646 473 0202, 🌐 marqueeny.com; subway C, E to 23rd St; map p.107. New York's long-standing "models and bottles" club regularly attracts celebs (from Bono to the Olson twins), with bottles of spirits $350 and up, but the roster of EDM DJs here is what really attracts the crowds, and it's not as hard to get in as you might think (buy tickets in advance and arrive before midnight). Admission $15–50. Wed, Fri & Sat 11pm–4am.

★**Output** 78 Wythe Ave, at N 12th St, Williamsburg (Brooklyn) 🌐 outputclub.com; subway L to Bedford

24

BOWL, SPIN AND PARTY

Even **bowling** has been turned into a glamorous, club-like experience in New York, where you're more likely to see high heels and cocktails than bowling shoes and Budweiser. If **table tennis** is more your thing, head to *SPiN*, Susan Sarandon's ping-pong club.

Bowlmor Lanes Times Square, 222 W 44th St, between Seventh and Eighth aves ☎212 680 0012, 🌐 bowlmor.com; subway A, C, E to 42nd St; map p.142. Offers seven plush, themed lounges in addition to fifty lanes. Bowl a few sets or just enjoy the cocktails and food cooked up by celebrity chef David Burke. Check the dress code online before visiting. Mon–Thurs 2pm–midnight, Fri noon–3am, Sat 11am–3am, Sun 11am–midnight.

Lucky Strike Lanes 624–660 W 42nd St, at Twelfth Ave ☎646 829 0170, 🌐 bowlluckystrike.com; subway A, C, E to 42nd St; map p.142. This

Hollywood-based operation has a similar bar/bowl combo, with lane-side food service, lounges and addictive mini-burgers. Also has a dress code. Mon–Wed & Sun noon–midnight, Thurs noon–1am, Fri & Sat noon–2am.

SPiN 48 E 23rd St, near Park Ave ☎212 982 8802, 🌐 newyork.wearespin.com; subway N, R, W, #6 to 23rd St. Table-tennis club (walk-in rates $19/30min before 6pm, $29 after 6pm), but with live music, events, DJs, booze and a hipster crowd. Sarandon often pops in. Mon–Thurs 11am–midnight, Fri & Sat 11am–2am, Sun 11am–8pm.

TOP CLUB NIGHTS

In addition to the clubs reviewed in this section, New York hosts some innovative club nights in some unusual places – many events take place only a few times a year, organizers often rotate venues and there's always something new going on. Check *Time Out New York* on arrival for the latest; at the time of writing these nights guaranteed good times.

718 Sessions w dannykrivit.net. Legendary monthly dance night from Danny Krivit (soul and house classics) and Angel Moraes. Check the website for venues and times. Sun around 6pm–midnight ($12–20).

The Bunker ☎ 718 384 4586, w thebunkerny.com. Major club night twice a month at various venues around Brooklyn, including *Trans Pecos* (in Ridgewood) and *Good Room* (p.351), with iconic DJs (electronica/techno dominates), 8hr sets and no guest list. Advance purchase required ($10–20). Club nights 10pm–5am.

Mister Saturday Night & Mister Sunday w mistersaturdaynight.com. Parties featuring resident DJs Eamon Harkin and Justin Carter; venues vary, but their Mister Sunday outdoor party takes place at *Nowadays*, 56-06 Cooper Ave, Ridgewood, Queens (May–Oct Sun 3–9pm; $15–20).

NY Night Train Soul Clap & Dance-Off w newyorknighttrain.com/soulclap. Wild 1960s soul all-nighter from DJ Jonathan Toubin, with a $100 dance contest in the middle. Admission just $7, usually in various Brooklyn locations. 10.30pm–4am (check website for dates).

One Step Beyond at the Rose Center Central Park West at W 79th St ☎ 212 769 5200, w amnh.org/plan-your-visit/one-step-beyond; subway B, C to 81st St; map p.184. Monthly dance parties at the American Museum of Natural History's trippy space centre (advance tickets $25; $30 at the door). Fri 9pm–1am.

Tiki Disco w tikidisco.com; map p.214. DJs Eli Escobar, Andy Pry and Lloydski typically hold their popular "Tiki" funky disco parties at *The Well*, 272 Meserole St in Bushwick (Brooklyn) every other Sun 2–10pm. Admission usually $10–15.

Warm Up at MoMA PS1 22-25 Jackson Ave, at 46th Ave, Long Island City ☎ 718 784 2084, w moma.org; subway #7 to 45th Rd-Court Square, E, M to 23rd St-Ely Ave. Outdoor music series that runs over ten Saturdays July to early Sept, featuring top live acts and DJs. Tickets $18–22. Club days 3–9pm.

Ave; map p.225. The "official club of Williamsburg" opened with much fanfare in 2013, with a smallish, industrial warehouse space, big sound system and a focus on dancing, not posing. The new home of legendary club night "Deep Space" with DJ François K (most Wednesdays). Admission $10–30. Wed–Sat 10pm–6am.

Pyramid Club 101 Ave A, between E 6th and 7th sts ☎ 212 228 4888, w thepyramidclub.com; subway L to First Ave, #6 to Astor Place; map p.88. This small club has been an East Village standby for years, but it's the insanely popular 1980s dance parties (admission $6) that are not to be missed. Thurs–Sat 8pm–4am.

Rumpus Room 249 Eldridge St, at Houston St ☎ 212 777 5153, w rumpusroomnyc.com; subway F to Lower East Side-Second Ave; map p.82. The former digs of iconic Sapphire Lounge remains a popular student hangout, thanks to Smiths Night on Sundays, and dance parties through the week. Usually no admission charge. Daily 9pm–4am.

Schimanski 54 N 11th St, between Wythe and Kent aves, Williamsburg (Brooklyn) ☎ 347 223 4732, w schimanskinyc.com; subway L to Bedford Ave; map p.225. Cutting-edge club showcasing all forms of underground dance music (though techno predominates). Admission $20–30, though often free before midnight. Tues–Sat 6pm–4am (club nights Fri & Sat).

Webster Hall 125 E 11th St, between Third and Fourth aves ☎ 212 353 1600, w websterhall.com; subway N, Q, R, W, L, #4, #5, #6 to Union Square; map p.88. Four floors, a hip, young crowd and big electro mash-ups (Fri & Sat) make this a solid bet for a good night out. Admission $15–30. Club nights Thurs–Sat 10pm–4am.

METROPOLITAN OPERA HOUSE

Performing arts and film

The range of New York's cultural offerings is astounding. "Broadway" has long been a universal byword for theatre and musicals – pioneered here by the Gershwin brothers, Irving Berlin, Cole Porter and Rodgers and Hammerstein, and kept alive today by blockbusters such as *Hamilton*. Off-Broadway theatre (and even Off-Off Broadway) is just as dynamic, while the comedy scene attracts big names to iconic clubs such as *Caroline's* and *Comic Strip Live*. Founded back in 1880 and now at the Lincoln Center, the Met Opera is one of the greatest companies in the world. The New York City Ballet is similarly fêted, while the American Ballet Theatre and dance companies established by such luminaries as Paul Taylor, Alvin Ailey and Martha Graham are also world-class. The silver screen is just as important, with events such as the Tribeca Film Festival and a thriving arthouse and revival scene.

25

ESSENTIALS

INFORMATION

Listings The most useful sources are the clear and comprehensive listings in the free *Time Out New York* magazine (Ⓦtimeout.com/newyork), Ⓦnypress.com and the "Voice Choices" section of Ⓦvillagevoice.com. Fancier events are usually touted in *New York* magazine's "Agenda" section (Ⓦnymag.com), "Goings On About Town" in *The New Yorker* (Ⓦnewyorker.com), and the Friday "Weekend" and Sunday "Arts and Leisure" sections of *The New York Times* (Ⓦnytimes.com). Information on arts events, Broadway shows and local theatre listings is available at Ⓦnycgo.com, Ⓦbroadway.com and Ⓦoffbroadway.com.

Prices Prices for live performances vary wildly: expect to shell out $150 or so for orchestra seats at the hottest Broadway shows, while Shakespeare is performed for free in Central Park every summer. Off-Broadway's best seats are cheaper than those on Broadway but can still be high ranging, from $30 all the way up to $100. Off-Off-Broadway tickets should rarely set you back more than $25.

TICKET AGENCIES

When buying tickets, always ask where your seats are located, as once you get to the theatre and find yourself in the last row of the balcony, it's too late (for most seating plans, check Ⓦplaybill.com).

TKTS booths Duffy Square (Times Square), located under the red steps at Broadway and W 47th St; South Street Seaport at the corner of Front and John sts (near the rear of 199 Water St); Lincoln Center (in the David Rubenstein Atrium at 61 W 62nd St); 1 Metro Tech Center, Brooklyn ☎212 912 9770, Ⓦtdf.org. Offers cut-rate, day-of-performance tickets for many Broadway and Off-Broadway shows. Expect to pay half the face value, plus a $4.50 service charge. Broadway booth: Mon, Thurs & Fri 3–8pm, Tues 2–8pm, Wed & Sat 10am–2pm (for matinees) & 3–8pm, Sun 11am–7pm; South Street Seaport booth: Mon–Sat 11am–6pm, Sun 11am–4pm; Lincoln Center: Tues–Sat noon–7pm; Metro Tech Center: Tues–Sat 11am–6pm.

Telecharge ☎800 432 7250 or ☎212 239 6200, Ⓦtelecharge.com.

Ticket Central Playwrights Horizons theater, 416 W 42nd St, between Ninth and Tenth aves ☎212 279 4200 or ☎564 1235, Ⓦticketcentral.com or Ⓦplaywrights horizons.org. Sells tickets to many Off-Broadway theatres. Expect a $5–7 surcharge per ticket. Daily noon–8pm.

Ticketmaster ☎800 745 3000, Ⓦticketmaster.com.

THEATRE

Theatre venues in the city are referred to as being "Broadway", "Off-Broadway" or "Off-Off-Broadway". These groupings don't necessarily mean a theatre's address is physically on or off Broadway; instead they tend to represent a descending order of ticket prices, production polish, elegance and comfort – as well as seating capacity. The majority of **Broadway** theatres are located in the blocks just east or west of Broadway (the avenue) between 41st and 53rd streets (see p.146); if you're hitting any of those, it's the show, rather than the venue, that will dictate interest and attendance. Less glitzy is **Off-Broadway**, the best place to discover new talent and adventurous new American drama and musicals (most venues for which seat between 100 and 500). **Off-Off-Broadway** is the fringe of New York's theatre world; venues (often fewer than 100 seats) aren't bound by union regulations to use professional actors, and shows range from shoestring productions of the classics to outrageous performance art. Quality varies from execrable to electrifying; frankly, there's a lot more of the former than the latter, so use weekly reviews as your guide.

OFF-BROADWAY

Astor Place Theatre (Blue Man Group) 434 Lafayette St, at Astor Place ☎212 254 4371, Ⓦblueman.com; subway #6 to Astor Place, N, R, W to 8th St-NYU. Located in historic Colonnade Row, this theatre has been the home of the comically absurd but very popular performance artists Blue Man Group since 1991, with shows on most days. Tickets range $52–103.

Barrow Street Theatre 27 Barrow St, at Seventh Ave S ☎212 243 6262, Ⓦbarrowstreettheatre.com; subway

---

THEATRE FESTIVALS AND EVENTS

New York is home to some of the world's best theatre festivals, especially in the summer. If you're visiting in August, check out the highly regarded New York International Fringe Festival (see p.407). Shakespeare in the Park (June–Aug) is an experience not to be missed (see box, p.157), while Shakespeare in the Parking Lot (see p.356) offers a tongue-in-cheek alternative. The other major summer theatre events are the Lincoln Center Festival (see p.358) and New York Musical Theatre Festival in July (Ⓦnymf.org). The Downtown Urban Arts Festival in May (Ⓦduafnyc .com) and Midtown International Theatre Festivals (Ⓦmidtownfestival.org) in July/August (MITF Summer) and October (MITF Fall) nurture new and up-and-coming talent.

A, B, C, D, E, F, M to W 4th St, #1 to Christopher St. This small theatre inside the landmark Greenwich House (which opened as a nonprofit community centre in 1902) is operated by producers Scott Morfee and Tom Wirtshafter, known for generating artistically excellent but commercially viable productions.

★**Brooklyn Academy of Music** 30 Lafayette Ave, Brooklyn ☎718 636 4100, ⓦbam.org; subway B, D, N, Q, R, #2, #3, #4, #5 to Atlantic Ave-Barclays Center. Despite its name, Brooklyn Academy of Music (usually referred to as BAM) regularly presents high-quality theatrical productions on its three stages, often touring international shows starring big names such as Cate Blanchett. Not so much Off-Broadway as Off-Manhattan, and well worth the trip.

★**Cherry Lane Theatre** 38 Commerce St, between Bedford and Barrow sts ☎212 989 2020, ⓦcherry lanetheatre.org; subway #1 to Christopher St-Sheridan Square. A historic Village spot, this was once a farm silo until Edna St. Vincent Millay and the Provincetown Players converted the structure into a theatre in 1924. There's a main stage and the smaller Studio Theatre, good places to see the odd revival and new works by up-and-comers.

Lincoln Center Broadway, at W 65th St ☎212 362 7600, ⓦlct.org; subway #1 to 66th St. Lincoln Center holds venues for all manner of audiences and dramatic productions on its campus. The Vivian Beaumont Theater qualifies technically as a Broadway theatre, though it and the Mitzi E. Newhouse Theater are great places to see stimulating new work by playwrights like Tom Stoppard and John Guare; the modern Claire Tow Theater (opened in 2012), meanwhile, focuses on relative unknowns.

Linda Gross Theater (Atlantic Theater Company) 336 W 20th St, at Eighth Ave ☎212 645 8015, ⓦatlantictheater.org; subway C, E to 23rd St, #1 to 18th St. As you'd expect from a theatre company founded by David Mamet and William H. Macy, this atmospheric place (the renovated 1871 St Peter's Church Parish House) is known for accessible, intelligent productions of modern dramatic classics, with works by everyone from Harold Pinter to Martin McDonagh. The ATC also runs Atlantic Stage 2, at 330 W 16th St.

Lucille Lortel Theatre 121 Christopher St, between Bleecker and Hudson sts ☎212 352 3101, ⓦlortel.org; subway #1 to Christopher St-Sheridan Square. Built in 1926 and operating since 1955 as New York's premiere Off-Broadway theatre, the Lortel has hosted several different companies, most recently contemporary specialists MCC Theater (ⓦmcctheater.org). *The Threepenny Opera* and *Buried Child* made their Off-Broadway debuts here.

New World Stages 340 W 50th St, between Eighth and Ninth aves ☎212 239 6200, ⓦnewworldstages.com; subway C, E to 50th St. Five stages with good sightlines, ranging in size from 199 to 499 seats and operated by the

Shubert Organization. Several productions that debuted here have grown into small-scale hits (most recently *The Imbible: A Spirited History of Drinking*, playing since 2014 and including three free cocktails).

★**New York City Center** 131 W 55th St, between Sixth and Seventh aves ☎212 581 1212, ⓦnycity center.org; subway B, D, E to Seventh Ave, F to 57th St, N, Q, R, W to 57th St-Seventh Ave. This gorgeous Moorish Revival theatre, built in 1923, is best known for its Encores! series. These readings and studio performances usually run for one weekend only, and are designed to revive long-forgotten or overlooked musicals, from Rodgers and Hart to modern dance. It's also home to the Alvin Ailey American Dance Theater (p.359) and Manhattan Theatre Club (ⓦmanhattan theatreclub.com), which deals in serious new theatre featuring major American actors. Many productions eventually transfer to Broadway.

Orpheum Theatre (Stomp) 126 Second Ave, between E 7th St and St Mark's Place ☎212 477 2477, ⓦstomponline.com; subway #6 to Astor Place. One of the East Village's biggest (and oldest) theatres, once known for hosting David Mamet and other influential new voices, but since 1994 as the home of the percussion group Stomp. Wheelchair-accessible. Shows (1hr 45min) Tues–Sun, with tickets ranging $48–100.

Playwrights Horizons 416 W 42nd St, at Ninth Ave ☎212 279 4200, ⓦplaywrightshorizons.org; subway A, C, E, #7 to 42nd St-Port Authority; N, Q, R, S, W, #1, #2, #3 to Times Square-42nd St. This well-respected drama-centric space is located right by Times Square, though its mission remains the same as it was when it was founded in a YMCA in 1971 – championing works by undiscovered playwrights. They also get top-line actors.

★**The Public Theater** 425 Lafayette St, between Astor Place and E 4th St ☎212 539 8500, ⓦpublic theater.org; subway #6 to Astor Place. Founded by Broadway legend Joe Papp as the Shakespeare Workshop in 1954, The Public Theater is the city's primary presenter of the Bard's plays. In the summer, it produces the free Shakespeare in the Park series at the open-air Delacorte Theater in Central Park (see p.156). For most of the year, though, this major Off-Broadway institution (housed in the artfully renovated Astor Library, which dates back to 1881) delivers thought-provoking and challenging productions from new, mostly American writers.

Signature Center 480 W 42nd St, between Ninth and Tenth aves ☎212 244 7529, ⓦsignaturetheatre.org; subway A, C, E to 42nd St-Port Authority, N, Q, R, S, W, #1, #2, #3, #7 to Times Square-42nd St. The Gehry-designed Signature Center, unveiled in 2012, showcases works on its three stages in conjunction with the Signature Theatre Company; playwrights-in-residence for the group have included Tony Kushner and Athol Fugard.

Westside Theatre 407 W 43rd St, between Ninth and Tenth aves ☎212 315 2244, ⓦwestsidetheatre.com; subway A, C, E to 42nd St-Port Authority. Two small theatres (in a former church built in 1890), especially known for its productions by Eve Ensler (*The Vagina Monologues* premiered here in 1996) and for the Off-Broadway run of *Love, Loss, and What I Wore* by Nora and Delia Ephron.

OFF-OFF-BROADWAY AND PERFORMANCE-ART SPACES

Dixon Place 161A Chrystie St, between Rivington and Delancey sts ☎212 219 0736, ⓦdixonplace.org; subway B, D to Grand St, F to Second Ave, J to Bowery. Very popular small venue dedicated to experimental theatre, dance and literary readings.

★**The Drilling CompaNY** 236 W 78th St, at Broadway ☎212 873 9050, ⓦdrillingcompany.org; subway B, C to 81st St. Small company with a mission to develop work by emerging American playwrights, but best known for producing the summer-long Shakespeare in the Parking Lot series of free performances at the Clemente parking lot on Norfolk Street between Delancey and Rivington, and sometimes in Bryant Park (ⓦshakespeareintheparkinglot.com).

The Flea 20 Thomas St, between Broadway and Church St ☎212 226 2407, ⓦtheflea.org; subway #1, #2, #3 to Chambers St. Cutting-edge drama space founded in 1996 by Jim Simpson, Sigourney Weaver's husband. The programme stretches from performance art and drama to acrobatics. Though many of the actors here are not professionals, the quality of the resident volunteer acting company (known as "The Bats"; supposedly one of the founders said you'd have to be "bats to work Off-Off Broadway") remains impressively high.

Here 145 Sixth Ave, at Spring St ☎212 352 3101, ⓦhere.org; subway C, E to Spring St. A very open-minded, intriguing organization with two theatres, supporting experimental fare from both new artists and established performers. Puppetry and multimedia performance art are special strengths.

Kraine Theater 85 E 4th St, between Second Ave and the Bowery ☎212 777 6088, ⓦhorsetrade.info; subway F to Second Ave. This 99-seat East Village theatre is home to several residential companies (notably the Horse Trade Theater Group) and is mostly known for presenting unusual comedies and burlesque. Another plus for this budget space is the tiered seating. It's in the basement of the same building as artsy *KGB* (see p.364).

★**La MaMa** 74a E 4th St, at Second Ave ☎212 475 7710, ⓦlamama.org; subway F to Second Ave. The mother of all Off-Off venues, founded in 1961. A real gem with three different auditoria, La MaMa is known for politically and sexually charged material as well as visiting dance troupes from overseas. For raw amateur performances, check out The Galleria space a few blocks away at 47 Great Jones St.

New York Theatre Workshop 79 E 4th St, at Second Ave ☎212 460 5475, ⓦnytw.org; subway F to Second Ave. An eminent experimental workshop that often chooses cult hit shows and has presented plays by Tony Kushner, Susan Sontag and Paul Rudnick; best known these days as the place the global musical mega-hit *Rent* was first shown to the public.

Performance Space 122 150 First Ave, at E 9th St ☎212 477 5829, ⓦps122.org; subway #6 to Astor Place, L to First Ave, F to Second Ave. A converted school in the East Village that is perennially popular for its jam-packed schedule of revolutionary performance art, dance, one-person shows and wintertime COIL Festival in its two theatres.

Performing Garage 33 Wooster St, at Grand St ☎212 966 9796, ⓦtheperforminggarage.org; subway A, C, E to Canal St. The Wooster Group (early members include Willem Dafoe and the late Spalding Gray) performs regularly in this Soho space (ⓦthewoostergroup.org). Tickets are like gold dust, but the effort to find them is worth it.

★**St Ann's Warehouse** 45 Water St (Brooklyn Bridge Park), Dumbo, Brooklyn ☎718 254 8779, ⓦstannswarehouse.org; subway A, C to High St, F to York St. Housed in an atmospheric tobacco warehouse from the 1860s, St Ann's is consistently impressive for both drama and music – there are Broadway try-outs and major stars (Mark Rylance has performed here a couple of times)

FOR THE CITY THAT DOESN'T SLEEP: SLEEP NO MORE

One of the most innovative theatre productions to come out of New York in recent years is **Sleep No More** (530 W 27th St, between Tenth and Eleventh aves ☎866 811 4111, ⓦmckittrickhotel.com; tickets $109.50, book in advance), the masterwork of British company **Punchdrunk**. Set in a fictional turn-of-the-twentieth-century hotel (the "McKittrick") – albeit one that houses a graveyard and asylum, among other spaces – this enveloping performance, loosely based on *Macbeth*, sends viewers betwixt and between actors who dance, fight, embrace and swoon with passion, but rarely speak. There is plenty of audience interaction, and you are encouraged to sleuth around unattended – afterwards, when comparing notes with your friends, you'll be amazed by how individualized your experience was.

as well as big-name musicians looking for a more intimate venue.

Theater for the New City 155 First Ave, at E 10th St ☏ 212 254 1109, ⓦ theaterforthenewcity.net; subway #6 to Astor Place; L to First Ave, F to Second Ave. This indie performance collective (based inside the former First Avenue Retail Market since 1986), is best known for producing Sam Shepard's Pulitzer Prize-winning *Buried Child* in 1978. It's still churning out fine drama through its emerging-playwrights programme. TNC also performs outdoors for free at a variety of venues throughout the summer and hosts the Lower East Side Festival of the Arts at the end of May.

Tribeca Performing Arts Center 199 Chambers St, at Greenwich St ☏ 212 220 1460, ⓦ tribecapac.org; subway #1, #2, #3 to Chambers St. TriPac, as it's known, is owned by Manhattan Community College, a fact reflected in its programming: mostly high-end local theatre and dance groups, plus kids' workshops and multicultural events. It's also known for fine jazz performances.

CLASSICAL MUSIC AND OPERA

New Yorkers take their classical music and opera seriously. Long queues form for anything popular, many concerts sell out, and summer evenings can see a quarter of a million people turning up in Central Park for free performances by the **New York Philharmonic**. Tickets can be somewhat easier to come by for performances by the city's top-notch chamber-music ensembles. When it comes to **opera**, the Met dominates the New York scene, regularly attracting the world's greatest performers and most lavish sets.

OPERA VENUES

Juilliard School 60 Lincoln Center Plaza, at W 65th St ☏ 212 799 5000, ⓦ juilliard.edu; subway #1 to 66th St. Located right next door to the Met (see below), Juilliard students often perform under the direction of a famous conductor, usually for low ticket prices.

Metropolitan Opera 30 Lincoln Center Plaza, Columbus Ave, at W 64th St ☏ 212 362 6000, ⓦ metoperafamily.org; subway #1 to 66th St. More popularly known as the Met, New York's premier opera venue is home to the world-renowned Metropolitan Opera Company from Sept/early Oct to late April/early May. Tickets are expensive (up to $300) and can be well-nigh impossible to snag for well-known operas, though 175 standing-room tickets go on sale at 10am on day of performance ($20–30) at the box office or the website, and "rush-tickets" for orchestra seats ($25) on the website only (these are the remaining unsold seats – popular shows will have sold out long before, meaning rush-tickets are unlikely to become available); buyers are limited to two tickets to one performance every seven days. Tickets go on sale for evening performances Mon–Fri at noon, for matinees four hours before curtain, and for Sat evenings at 2pm.

CONCERT HALLS

92nd Street Y Kaufmann Concert Hall 1395 Lexington Ave, at E 92nd St ☏ 212 415 5740, ⓦ 92y.org; subway #4, #5, #6 to 86th St, #6 to 96th St. This 85-year-old, wood-panelled space is especially welcoming since performers are usually available to chat or mingle with the audience after shows. Great line-up of chamber music and solo events.

Alice Tully Hall Lincoln Center, 1941 Broadway, at W 65th St ☏ 212 671 4050 or ☏ 212 875 5788, ⓦ lincolncenter.org; subway #1 to 66th St. A smaller Lincoln Center hall for the top chamber orchestras, string quartets and instrumentalists (it's home to the Chamber Music

Society). The weekend chamber series is deservedly popular, though the crowd is composed almost exclusively of the 65-and-over set. Tickets for performances vary greatly, but mostly run in the $30–70 range.

★ **Bargemusic** Fulton Ferry Landing, Brooklyn ☏ 718 624 4924, ⓦ bargemusic.org; subway A, C to High St, F to York St. Chamber music in a wonderful river setting on a converted coffee barge below the Brooklyn Bridge. Tickets are usually $40–45, $20–25 for full-time students. Fri & Sat (sometimes Thurs too) 8pm, Sun 4pm (concerts 1hr–1hr 30min).

Brooklyn Academy of Music 30 Lafayette Ave, Brooklyn ☏ 718 636 4100, ⓦ bam.org; subway #2, #3, #4, #5, N, R to Atlantic Ave-Barclays Center. The BAM Howard Gilman Opera House is the perennial home of Philip Glass operatic premieres and Laurie Anderson performances. It also hosts a number of contemporary imports from European and Chinese companies, often with a large modern-dance component.

Carnegie Hall 154 W 57th St, at Seventh Ave ☏ 212 247 7800, ⓦ carnegiehall.org; subway N, Q, R, W to 57th St-Seventh Ave. The greatest names from all schools of music have performed here, from Tchaikovsky (who conducted the hall's inaugural concert in 1891) to Toscanini to Gershwin to Billie Holiday to, um, Lady Gaga. The stunning acoustics – said to be the best in the world – still lure big-time performers at sky-high prices. Check the website for up-to-date admission rates and schedules.

David Geffen Hall 10 Lincoln Center Plaza, Broadway and W 65th St ☏ 212 875 5030, ⓦ lincolncenter.org or ⓦ nyphil.org; subway #1 to 66th St. The permanent home of the New York Philharmonic, with most ticket prices $45–150. The open rehearsals (9.45am on the first day of new concert weeks, usually Wed or Thurs) are a great bargain; tickets are $20. It also hosts the very popular, annual Mostly Mozart Festival in Aug.

25

FREE SUMMER CONCERT SERIES

It's easy to think of fusty old churches (though those can add a bit of character to a performance) or glittering concert halls (with their attendant high-priced seats) as the places to go to hear serious-minded music. Perhaps true for the most part, but in summertime, a number of free outdoor events provide a salve for those opera or philharmonic fans looking to avoid paying an arm and a leg – and an easy introduction for those interested in seeing what all the fuss is about.

Bryant Park ☎212 768 4242, ⓦbryantpark.org. Home to free Broadway and Off-Broadway musical performances during the summer (weekly at lunchtime; check schedules), as well as Fall Festival with music and dance.

Celebrate Brooklyn May–Aug; ☎718 855 7882, ⓦbricartsmedia.org. See p.407.

Lincoln Center Out-of-Doors ☎212 875 5108, ⓦlcoutofdoors.org. Hosts an eclectic selection of daily free performances of music and dance events on the Lincoln Center plaza from late July to Aug, featuring everything from techno and disco to classical and Randy Newman.

New York Philharmonic's Concerts in the Park

☎212 875 5709, ⓦnyphil.org. A series of concerts and fireworks displays that turns up all over the city and the outer boroughs in June. Similarly, there's the Met Opera Summer Recital Series, held in parks (☎212 362 6000, ⓦmetopera.org) in late June.

River to River Festival Late June; ⓦlmcc.net/program/river-to-river. See p.407.

SummerStage June–Aug; ☎212 360 2777, ⓦcityparksfoundation.org/summerstage. See box, p.157.

Washington Square Music Festival ☎212 252 3621, ⓦwashingtonsquaremusicfestival.org. This series has run since 1953, and it consists of chamber orchestra pieces and occasional jazz performances outdoors every Tues at 8pm from late June to July.

Lehman Center for the Performing Arts 250 Bedford Park Blvd, Bronx ☎718 960 8833, ⓦlehmancenter.org; subway D, #4 to Bedford Park. First-class concert hall that puts on an array of performances: modern ballet, gospel, funk, oldies and major international names.

Merkin Concert Hall 129 W 67th St, at Broadway ☎212 501 3330, ⓦmerkinconcerthall.org; subway #1 to 66th St. This intimate and adventurous venue in the Kaufman Music Center is a great place to hear music of any kind: classical, jazz, Broadway, kid-friendly, etc. Hosts the wintertime Ecstatic Music Festival.

★**Symphony Space** 2537 Broadway, at W 95th St ☎212 864 5400, ⓦsymphonyspace.org; subway #1, #2, #3 to 96th St. The Symphony Space has a varied

performance schedule, from "ground-breaking, style-crashing" new classical to jazz and even the odd rock event. **Town Hall** 123 W 43rd St, between Sixth Ave and Broadway ☎212 840 2824, ⓦthetownhall.org; subway B, D, F, M to 42nd St-Bryant Park, N, R, Q, W, #1, #2, #3, #7 to Times Square-42nd St. This Midtown hall has an unusual history: it was designed by Stanford White (the mastermind of the original Madison Square Garden) for suffragettes in 1921 as a protest-friendly space. One of the egalitarian innovations in the design was the omission of any box seats in order to provide better acoustics and sightlines from every seat in the house. As for programming, it's got an eclectic policy – from Broadway celebrations and folk singers to Cole Porter tributes and whirling dervishes.

DANCE

Dance – especially experimental or avant-garde performance – is quite popular in New York. The city has five major **ballet companies**, dozens of **modern troupes** and untold thousands of **soloists**; all performances are listed in broadly the same periodicals and websites as music and theatre, though you might also want to pick up *Dance Magazine* (ⓦdancemagazine.com) for a closer look. The official dance season runs April–June and Sept–Jan. The following list takes in major dance venues in the city, though a lot of the smaller, more esoteric companies and solo dancers also perform at spaces like Dixon Place (see p.356) and PS122 (see p.356).

92nd Street Y Harkness Dance Center 1395 Lexington Ave, at E 92nd St ☎212 415 5552, ⓦ92y.org; subway #4, #5, #6 to 86th St, #6 to 96th St. Hosts a variety of performances, including a "Fridays at noon" series (tickets for which are $10 in advance, $15 on the door) and the Harkness Dance Festival (usually Feb–March), showcasing emerging talent.

Brooklyn Academy of Music 30 Lafayette St, Brooklyn ☎718 636 4100, ⓦbam.org; subway B, D, N, Q, R, #2, #3, #4, #5 to Atlantic Ave-Barclays Center. America's oldest performing-arts academy is still one of the busiest and most daring dance producers in New York. In the autumn, BAM's Next Wave festival features the hottest international attractions in avant-garde dance and music, and each spring since 1977 it has hosted the annual Dance Africa Festival (May), America's largest showcase for African and African American dance and culture.

★ **Damrosch Park** Lincoln Center, W 62nd St between Columbus and Amsterdam aves ☎ 212 875 5766, ⓦ lincolncenter.org and ⓦ midsummernightswing .org; subway #1 to 66th St. A delightful open-air venue for the enormously popular Midsummer Night Swing, where each night you can learn a different dance style en masse (everything from polka to rockabilly) and watch a performance – all for $17. Tickets go on sale in Damrosch Park at 5.30pm the night of the show (or pick them up earlier at David Geffen Hall; see p.357); the season runs June–July. Lessons begin at 6.30pm, music and dance sets run 7.30–8.30pm & 9–10pm.

Danspace Project St Mark's Church-in-the-Bowery, 131 E 10th St, at Second Ave ☎ 212 674 8112 or ☎ 866 811 4111, ⓦ danspaceproject.org; subway #6 to Astor Place. Experimental contemporary dance, with a season running Sept–June, in one of the more distinctive performance spaces around – an airy church that dates back more than 200 years (see p.91).

David H. Koch Theater 20 Lincoln Center Plaza, W 65th St, at Columbus Ave ☎ 212 870 5570, ⓦ lincolncenter .org; subway #1 to 66th St. Lincoln Center is home to the revered New York City Ballet (ⓦ nycballet.com), founded in 1948 by legendary choreographer George Balanchine. Seasonal productions Jan & Feb, April & May, Sept & Oct, plus *The Nutcracker* in December. It also hosts the annual three-week New York season (March) of the Paul Taylor Dance Company (ⓦ ptamd.org).

Joyce Theater 175 Eighth Ave, at W 19th St ☎ 212 691 9740, ⓦ joyce.org; subway #1 to 18th St, C, E to 23rd St. The Joyce is one of the best-known downtown dance venues, hosting short seasons by a wide variety of acclaimed dance troupes such as Pilobolus, the Parsons Dance Company and Savion Glover's.

Juilliard Dance Division 60 Lincoln Center Plaza, W 65th St at Broadway ☎ 212 799 5000, ⓦ juilliard.edu; subway #1 to 66th St. The dance division of the Juilliard School often holds free workshop performances (some fifteen public ones a year, at the Peter Jay Sharp Theater on Lincoln Center's campus), and each spring six students work with six composers to present a Composers and Choreographers concert.

Metropolitan Opera House 30 Lincoln Center Plaza, 65th St at Columbus Ave ☎ 212 362 6000, ⓦ metopera .org; subway #1 to 66th St. Home of the renowned American Ballet Theater (ⓦ abt.org) and Misty Copeland (the company's first African American female principal dancer), who perform at the Opera House from mid-May into July. Prices for ballet at the Met range from as little as $22 up to $375 for the best seats at special performances (usually more like $220 tops); standing-room tickets go on sale at 10am on the morning of the performance ($20–35).

New York City Center 131 W 55th St, at Seventh Ave ☎ 212 581 1212, ⓦ nycitycenter.org; subway B, D, E to Seventh Ave, N, Q, R, W to 57th St-Seventh Ave, F to 57th St-Sixth Ave. This large, Midtown venue hosts some of the most important troupes in modern dance, including the Alvin Ailey American Dance Theater (ⓦ alvinailey.org); there's Sept–Oct's Fall for Dance Festival as well.

New York Live Arts 219 W 19th St, at Seventh Ave ☎ 212 924 0077, ⓦ newyorklivearts.org; subway #1 to 18th St. Home to the Bill T. Jones/Arnie Zane Dance Company, New York Live Arts has a mid-size main stage and some smaller studios that host movement-based performances from numerous troupes throughout the year.

CABARET AND COMEDY

New York is one of America's **comedy** capitals. Visit at any time and its major clubs will feature artists you'll recognize from television and film. Most mainstream clubs have shows every night, with two or more on weekends; it's usual to be charged a cover plus a two-drink minimum fee, and you usually need to be over 18 or 21 to enter. There are still a couple of top **cabaret** venues in New York, though for the city's **burlesque** scene, see the Nightlife section (see box, p.345).

COMEDY CLUBS

Carolines on Broadway 1626 Broadway, at W 49th St (Times Square) ☎ 212 757 4100, ⓦ carolines.com; subway #1 to 50th St, N, R, W to 49th St. *Carolines* books some of the best stand-up acts in town; this is where most of the biggest names perform. Also has a "supper lounge", *Comedy Nation*, downstairs. Entry starts at $16.50–30, with tickets for popular performers from around $45 (plus two-drink minimum). Daily shows from 7.30pm.

Comedy Cellar 117 MacDougal St, at Bleecker St ☎ 212 254 3480, ⓦ comedycellar.com; subway A, B, C, D, E, F, M to W 4th St. Open since 1982, this popular Greenwich Village comedy club is a good late-night hangout, with a second stage around the corner at the *Village Underground* (see p.347). Tickets $12–24 plus two-item minimum (drink or food). Shows Mon–Thurs 7.45pm, 9.30pm & 11.30pm, Fri & Sat 7pm, 8.45pm, 10.30pm & 12.15am, Sun 8pm, 9.45pm & 11.30pm.

Comic Strip Live 1568 Second Ave, between E 81st and E 82nd sts ☎ 212 861 9386, ⓦ comicstriplive.com; subway #4, #5, #6 to 86th St. Famed showcase for stand-up comics and young singers going for the big time since 1975. Cover $15–20 plus two-drink minimum. Shows daily from 8pm.

Dangerfield's 1118 First Ave, at E 61st St ☎ 212 593 1650, ⓦ dangerfields.com; subway #4, #5, #6, N, R, W

25

TV STUDIOS

If you want to experience American TV up close, you can pick up free tickets to be the "live audience" at numerous shows taped in New York. For most shows you must be at least 16, sometimes 17 or 18, to be in the audience; if you're underage or travelling with children, call ahead. Most tickets are available through ⓦ 1iota.com.

MORNING SHOWS

Good Morning America ⓦ gma.yahoo.com. Show up at the Broadway entrance (at 44th St, Times Square) around 6.45am or earlier for a shot at the best view of the ABC show (through the studio windows) and possible interaction with hosts like George Stephanopoulos (and celebrity guests). No advance tickets required. Mon–Fri 7–9am.

Today Show There's no way to get advance tickets; just show up at 49th St, between Fifth and Sixth aves (Rockefeller Plaza), as early as possible (6.30am on a non-concert day) to join the other tourists with their goofy signs. Unlike the rest of the morning shows, which run until 9am, NBC's *Today* (with Matt Lauer and Savannah Guthrie) ends at 11am. Some of their free Friday concerts (May–Sept) are mobbed by fans – Harry Styles, Ed Sheeran, Coldplay and Iggy Azalea attracted thousands who camped out for several days. Check the website for the concert schedule (ⓦ today.com). Mon–Fri 7–11am.

The View ☎ 212 456 7000, ⓦ abc.go.com/shows/the-view. ABC talk show hosted by Whoopi Goldberg, Joy Behar, Paula Faris, Sara Haines, Jedediah Bila and Sunny Hostin at ABC Television Studios, 57 W 66th St. You have to request tickets online, but these are usually a little easier to get (over-16s only). You can also show up at the studios at 9.30am for standby tickets. Note the dress code here (no solid white or black clothing, no shorts, no T-shirts, no sleeveless tops or hats). Mon–Thurs 9.30–11am.

LATE-NIGHT SHOWS

The Daily Show with Trevor Noah 733 11th Ave, at W 52nd St ☎ 212 586 2477, ⓦ cc.com/shows/the-daily-show-with-trevor-noah. The satirical Comedy Central news show formerly hosted by Jon Stewart (with a fanatical following) was inherited by relative unknown South African comedian Trevor Noah in 2015; tickets to this show are traditionally very hard to secure. There's no point in showing up for standby tickets; try the website above and follow the instructions. Over-18s only. Mon–Thurs 6–7.30pm (sometimes later); check-in from 4.30pm.

Full Frontal with Samantha Bee CBS Broadcast Center, 528 W 57th St (between Tenth and Eleventh aves) ⓦ samanthabee.com. This *Daily Show* alumna made a big splash in 2017, hammering President Trump on her own weekly comedy show. Visit the website for ticket information. Over-18s only. Wed 5.45pm.

Last Week Tonight with John Oliver CBS Broadcast Center, 530 W 57th St (between Tenth and Eleventh aves). The Brit comedian has been wildly successful stateside, with tickets to his seasonal HBO news satire show hard to get (see ⓦ lastweektickets.com). Over-18s only. Sun 6.15–7.30pm.

Late Night with Seth Meyers 30 Rockefeller Plaza ☎ 212 664 3056, ⓦ nbc.com/late-night-with-seth-meyers. Former SNL comedian Seth Meyers took Fallon's old job in 2014. Advance tickets are offered via the website but Meyers is extremely popular. Standby tickets are handed out under the NBC marquee on 49th St at 9am on the day of the show. Tickets to the monologue rehearsal are handed out in The Shop at NBC Studios (30 Rockefeller Plaza) every day at 11.30am (the show tapes on the second floor). Mon–Thurs 6.30–7.45pm (check-in by 5pm).

Late Show with Stephen Colbert 1697 Broadway, between W 53rd and W 54th sts ☎ 212 247 6497, ⓦ cbs.com/shows/the-late-show-with-stephen-colbert. The late-night comedian took over from the legendary David Letterman in 2015, choosing to keep the CBS show at the Ed Sullivan Theatre. You can reserve tickets in advance through the website or try your luck with standby tickets at 1697 Broadway. Get in line no later than 15min prior to the 3.15pm cut-off time. The show remains wildly popular. Over-18s only. Mon–Wed at 4.30pm, Thurs at 3.30pm & 6pm (1–2hr).

Saturday Night Live 30 Rockefeller Plaza ☎ 212 664 3056, ⓦ nbc.com/saturday-night-live. It's tough to get tickets in advance to the iconic NBC comedy show that launched the careers of Chevy Chase, Bill Murray, Eddie Murphy, Mike Myers, Adam Sandler, Will Ferrell, Tina Fey and many others; for each upcoming season (usually Oct–May), you must send an email, in Aug only, to ✉ snltickets@nbcuni.com – include all contact information. If selected by lottery, you'll get two tickets assigned randomly (you cannot fix the date). Alternatively, standby tickets are distributed at 7am on the 48th St side of 30 Rockefeller Plaza on Sat morning (some weeks are reruns; call ahead). You can opt for either the 8pm dress rehearsal or the 11.30pm live taping. Sat 11.30pm–1am.

The Tonight Show with Jimmy Fallon 30 Rockefeller Plaza ☎ 212 664 3056, ⓦ nbc.com/the-tonight-show. After years in Leno's Los Angeles, NBC's *The Tonight Show* moved back to New York City in 2014 to rave reviews. Get advance tickets at the website – you'll have to be quick as it's almost always sold out. The show is taped in Studio 6B, 30 Rockefeller Plaza. Over-16s only. Mon–Fri 5–6.30pm.

to Lexington Ave/59th St. Vegas-style new-talent showcase founded in 1969 by the late Rodney Dangerfield, making it among the oldest – if not *the* oldest – continually running comedy club in the States. Cover $20 plus two-drink minimum, though big discounts available online (tickets usually $5). Shows Mon & Thurs–Sun 8.30pm, Fri & Sat 8.30pm & 10.30pm.

Gotham Comedy Club 208 W 23rd St, between Seventh and Eighth aves ☎212 367 9000, ⊛gothamcomedyclub.com; subway C, E, #1 to 23rd St. A swanky comedy venue in Chelsea, highly respected by New York media types and those who scout up-and-coming comics. Most tickets from $10–25 plus two-drink minimum. Shows daily from 7pm or 8pm.

Stand-Up New York 236 W 78th St, at Broadway ☎212 595 0850, ⊛standupny.com; subway #1 to 79th St. Upper West Side all-ages forum for established comics, many of whom have appeared on late-night TV shows; also has nights for up-and-comers. Cover $15–20 plus two-drink minimum – you're required to arrive 30min before showtime, so call or check the website for the night's schedule before arriving. Shows daily from 8pm.

★**Upright Citizens Brigade Theatre** 307 W 26th St, between Eighth and Ninth aves ☎212 366 9176, ⊛ucbtheatre.com; subway C, E to 23rd St, #1 to 28th St. Consistently hilarious sketch-based and improv comedy, seven nights a week. You can sometimes catch *Saturday Night Live* cast members (or ex-members) in the ensemble. Second location in East Village, 153 E 3rd St at Ave A. Tickets $5–10, though some late-night free shows too. Shows daily from 7pm or 8pm.

CABARET

Don't Tell Mama 343 W 46th St, at Ninth Ave ☎212 757 0788, ⊛donttellmamanyc.com; subway A, C, E to 42nd St-Port Authority. Lively and convivial Midtown West restaurant, piano bar and cabaret established in 1982, featuring rising stars and singing waitresses. Tickets usually $10–25 plus two-drink minimum. Mon, Tues & Thurs 4–11pm, Wed 11.30am–11pm, Fri 4pm–midnight, Sat & Sun 11.30am–midnight (shows from 7pm Mon–Fri, 3pm Sat & Sun).

Duplex 61 Christopher St, at Seventh Ave ☎212 255 5438, ⊛theduplex.com; subway #1 to Christopher St. West Village cabaret popular with a boisterous, gay-friendly crowd since 1950. Barbra Streisand and Lea Delaria have both performed here, and Off-Off-Broadway shows like *Nunsense* played here in their infancy. Has a rowdy piano bar downstairs and a cabaret room upstairs. Cover free to $25 plus two-drink minimum. Daily 4pm–4am.

FILM

Despite rising costs that put a normal ticket in Manhattan at $16–17, New York is a movie-lover's dream. There are plenty of state-of-the-art **cinemas** all over the city; most are charmless multiscreen complexes, but they also have the advantages of superb sound, luxurious seating and perfect sightlines. For **listings** (see p.28), your best bets are *Time Out New York*, *New York* magazine or the *Village Voice*; otherwise check ⊛fandango.com or ⊛moviefone.com. We've highlighted our pick of New York's best cinemas below, divided into those showing first-run mainstream and indie fare, and the venues that specialize in revivals and more obscure and experimental flicks, though the list is by no means exhaustive.

FIRST-RUN MOVIES

★**Alamo Drafthouse** 445 Albee Square West, between Fulton and Willoughby sts, Brooklyn ☎718 513 2547, ⊛drafthouse.com; subway #2, #3 to Hoyt St. The latest chain to offer dinner and booze (craft beer, wine) with your movie opened in Downtown Brooklyn in 2016, shows all the just-released movies ($15.10). Extra bonus – there's zero tolerance for talking, texting and any phone use whatsoever.

AMC Empire 25 234 W 42nd St, at Eighth Ave ☎212 398 2597, ⊛amctheatres.com; subway A, C, E to 42nd St-Port Authority, N, Q, R, W, #1, #2, #3, #7 to Times Square-42nd St. One of the few skyscraper multiplexes: 25 screens, all with stadium seating, soaring upward. Usually crowded on weekends, it offers a decent mix of mainstream and indie films.

AMC Loews Lincoln Square 13 & IMAX 1998 Broadway, at 68th St ☎212 336 5020, ⊛amctheatres .com; subway #1 to 66th St. More and more mainstream films are being converted to IMAX technology and are being re-released on the huge screens here in high resolution just months after their original theatrical debuts. Worth checking out for sci-fi spectaculars, if nothing else. Oh, and the venue has twelve other first-run theatres besides, though it's often bedlam.

BAM Rose Cinemas 30 Lafayette Ave, at Ashland Place, Brooklyn ☎718 636 4133, ⊛bam.org/#Film; subway C to Lafayette Ave, G to Fulton St, B, D, N, R, Q, #2, #3, #4, #5 to Atlantic Ave-Barclays Center. There are four screens at BAM's film site. The programme is mostly one or two current films mixed with a couple of classics or rarities; the year-round BAMcinématek series usually offers the most interesting choices.

iPic Fulton Market 11 Fulton St, at Front St ☎212 776 8272, ⊛ipictheaters.com; subway #2, #3 to Fulton St. Luxury cinema in the South Street Seaport District, offering gourmet dishes, snacks and cocktails delivered to your plush leather seats ($16 to $28 for VIP seats).

Regal Battery Park Stadium 11 102 North End Ave ☎212 945 4370, ⊛regmovies.com; subway #1, #2, #3

25

to Chambers St. One great reason to visit: its out-of-the-way location makes this possibly the quietest multiplex around.

INDIES AND FOREIGN

Angelika Film Center 18 W Houston St, at Mercer St ☎ 212 995 2570, ⓦ angelikafilmcenter.com; subway B, D, F, M to Broadway-Lafayette. Six-screen arthouse venue with a rather overhyped reputation – screens are tiny, floors are hardly sloped and the subway tends to rumble by at inopportune moments, rattling the subterranean rooms. Still, it's one of the few surviving venues for smaller films in the city. Tickets $15.

Cinema Village 22 E 12th St, between University and Fifth aves ☎ 212 924 3363, ⓦ cinemavillage.com; subway L, N, Q, R, W, #4, #5, #6 to 14th St-Union Square. Open since 1963 with three screens (and limited seating), still showing indie flicks and numerous documentaries. Tickets $12.

IFC Center 323 Sixth Ave, at W 3rd St ☎ 212 924 7771, ⓦ ifccenter.com; subway A, B, C, D, E, F, M to W 4th St. An independent with five screens, showing new indies, foreign and documentaries, and popular (weekend) midnight shows. Features a much larger screen and a

---

FILM FESTIVALS

There always seems to be some **film festival** or other running in New York. The granddaddy of them all, the **New York Film Festival** (see p.409), starts at the end of September and runs for two weeks at the Lincoln Center, while the **Tribeca Film Festival** (see p.406) runs in April. It's well worth catching either if you're in town, though tickets for the most popular films can sell out very quickly. If you're determined to see something, watch the reviews in *The New York Times* each morning – when movies are panned, there's usually a cluster of people trying to sell off their tickets outside the cinema that night.

For info on the larger film festivals, see the Parades and festivals chapter (p.404); below is a list of some of the smaller, but still worthwhile, festivals and seasonal screenings.

New York Jewish Film Festival at Lincoln Center ⓦ nyjff.org; Jan.

New York International Children's Film Festival ⓦ gkids.com; March, though screenings on weekend mornings year-round.

Harlem International Film Festival ⓦ harlemfilmfestival.org; May.

New York African Film Festival ⓦ africanfilmny .org; May.

New York Indian Film Festival ⓦ iaac.us; May.

New York Polish Film Festival ⓦ nypff.com; May.

Soho International Film Festival ⓦ sohofilmfest .com; June.

Brooklyn Film Festival ⓦ brooklynfilmfestival .org; June.

Lower East Side Film Festival ⓦ lesfilmfestival .com; June.

Human Rights Watch International Film Festival ⓦ ff.hrw.org; June.

TromaDance Film Festival ⓦ tromadance.com; June. Free screenings of cutting-edge indie movies at the Paper Box, 17 Meadow St, Williamsburg (Brooklyn).

Bryant Park Summer Film Festival ⓦ bryantpark .org; late June–late Aug. Each Mon night (5–11pm) picnickers watch old Hollywood classics like *Breakfast at Tiffany's* on the lush lawn of Bryant Park. Get there very early and bring a blanket. Free.

Asian American International Film Festival ⓦ asiancinevision.org; July–Aug.

Hudson RiverFlicks ⓦ hudsonriverpark.org; July–Aug, Wed. Free screenings of box-office hits and cult crowd-pleasers at Pier 61/62 at Chelsea Piers. "Hudson Riverkids" offers more family-friendly programming at Pier 25 in Tribeca and Pier 62 in Chelsea (usually Mon & Thurs).

Socrates Sculpture Garden Outdoor Cinema ⓦ socratessculpturepark.org; July–Aug. Free screenings of classics every Wed starting at 7pm in Long Island City, Queens.

Coney Island Film Festival ⓦ coneyisland filmfestival.com; Sept.

Manhattan Short Film Festival ⓦ manhattan short.com; Sept–Oct.

NewFest: The New York LGBT Film Festival ⓦ newfest.org; Oct.

New York Independent Film Festival ⓦ nycindieff.com; Oct.

Margaret Mead Film Festival ⓦ amnh.org; Oct or Nov. Anthropological films at the Museum of Natural History (see p.190).

New York City Short Film Festival ⓦ nycshorts .com; Nov.

Big Apple Film Festival ⓦ bigapplefilmfestival .com; Nov. Showcases movies from the New York City independent film community.

NYC Horror Film Festival ⓦ nychorrorfest.com; Nov.

Williamsburg Independent Film Festival ⓦ willfilm.org; Nov.

better sound system than you'll find at most other arthouses. Tickets $15.

Lincoln Plaza Cinema 1886 Broadway, at 62nd St ☎ 212 757 2280, ⊛ lincolnplazacinema.com; subway A, B, C, D, #1 to 59th St-Columbus Circle. This six-screen cinema is as close as the Upper West Side gets to an arthouse venue. While it plays an occasional smaller mainstream Hollywood picture, it's known for acclaimed foreign and independent films. Tickets $15.

★**Nitehawk Cinema** 136 Metropolitan Ave, between Wythe Ave and Berry St, Williamsburg ☎ 718 782 8370, ⊛ nitehawkcinema.com; subway L to Bedford Ave. The popular dine-in cinema chain opened this outpost in Brooklyn in 2011, pairing first-run (and classic) films with tableside food and drinks service – usually not just-released movies, however. Tickets just $12.

Paris Theatre 4 W 58th St, at Fifth Ave ☎ 212 688 3800, ⊛ theparistheatre.com; subway F to 57th St, N, Q, R, W to 59th St/Fifth Ave. An old-fashioned cinema opening in 1948 (there's even a balcony), that specializes in foreign films as well as well-reviewed mainstream fare. Manhattan's sole-surviving single-screen cinema. Tickets $15.50.

The Quad 34 W 13th St, between Fifth and Sixth aves ☎ 212 255 2243, ⊛ quadcinema.com; subway F, L, M to 14th St, L, N, R, W, #4, #5, #6 to 14th St-Union Square. Shows a selection of indie movies – including numerous gay-themed flicks – that can be quite hard to find anywhere else. Tickets $15.

REVIVALS

Anthology Film Archives 32 Second Ave, at E 2nd St ☎ 212 505 5181, ⊛ anthologyfilmarchives.org; subway F to Second Ave. A bastion of experimental film-making. Programmes of mind-bending abstraction, East Village grunge flicks and auteur retrospectives all rub shoulders here. Tickets $11.

★**Film Forum** 209 W Houston St, between Sixth and Seventh aves ☎ 212 727 8110, ⊛ filmforum.org; subway #1 to Houston St, A, B, C, D, E, F, M to W 4th St. The cosy three-screen Film Forum has an eccentric but famously popular programme of new independent movies, documentaries and foreign films, as well as a repertory programme specializing in silent comedy, camp classics and cult directors. All in all, one of the best alternative spaces in town. Tickets $14.

Museum of Modern Art 11 W 53rd St, at Fifth Ave ☎ 212 708 9400, ⊛ moma.org; subway E, M to Fifth Ave/53rd St. MoMA (see p.129) is famous among local cinephiles for its vast collection of films, exquisite programming and regular audience of cantankerous senior citizens. The movies themselves range from Hollywood screwball comedies to hand-painted Super 8. Tickets $12.

Museum of the Moving Image 36-01 35th Ave, at 36th St, Astoria, Queens ☎ 718 777 6888, ⊛ movingimage.us; subway N, W to 36th Ave, G, R to 36th St. The AMMI is usually well worth a trip out to Queens, either for the pictures – which are often serious director retrospectives and silent films, with a strong emphasis on cinematographers – or for the cinema museum itself (see p.246). Tickets $15.

Symphony Space 2537 Broadway, at 95th St ☎ 212 864 5400, ⊛ symphonyspace.org; subway #1, #2, #3 to 96th St. A varied and often surprising programme of festivals (including one for shorts), special directors' series and weekend double features. Tickets $14.

★**Walter Reade Theater** Lincoln Center, 165 W 65th St, at Broadway ☎ 212 875 5601, ⊛ filmlinc.com; subway #1 to 66th St. Programmed by the Film Society of Lincoln Center, the Walter Reade is simply the best place in town to see great films. This beautiful, modern theatre has perfect sightlines, a huge screen and impeccable acoustics. The emphasis is on foreign films and the great auteurs; it's also home to many of the city's festivals, including the New York Film Festival (see p.409). Tickets $14.

LITERARY EVENTS AND READINGS

New York has long been viewed as a literary hotspot (authors such as Martin Amis, Paul Auster, Peter Carey, Don DeLillo, Jennifer Egan, Jonathan Franzen, Nicole Krauss, Salman Rushdie, Téa Obreht and Tom Wolfe all reside here), and the city's proliferation of competitive bookstores (see p.388) means that you can see someone performing wordy wonders any night of the week. For more on **literary festivals** and **Project Shaw**, see the Parades and festivals chapter (see p.404).

★**92nd Street Y Unterberg Poetry Center** 1395 Lexington Ave, at E 92nd St ☎ 212 415 5760, ⊛ 92y.org/poetry; subway #4, #5, #6 to 86th St, #6 to 96th St. Quite simply the definitive place to hear all your Booker, Pulitzer and Nobel prize-winning favourites, as well as many other exciting new talents. Name almost any American literary great – from Tennessee Williams to Langston Hughes – and they've probably appeared here.

Barnes & Noble ⊛ barnesandnoble.com. The city's

numerous B&Ns host a surprisingly diverse range of readings almost every night of the week. The Union Square branch generally gets the highest-profile authors and events, though the Tribeca and Fifth Ave outposts compete too.

Half King 505 W 23rd St, between Tenth and Eleventh aves ☎ 212 462 4300, ⊛ thehalfking.com; subway C, E to 23rd St. Popular bar owned by a cadre of writers and others; it's not surprising, then, that most Monday nights

25

TOP SPOTS FOR POETRY

Poetry and story slamming is a literary version of freestyle rapping, in which performers take turns presenting stories and poems (often mostly or entirely improvised) on stage. At their best, slams can be thrilling, raw and very funny, not to mention competitive – many feature a judges' panel.

Bowery Poetry 308 Bowery, between Houston and Bleecker sts ☎ 212 614 0505, ⓦ bowerypoetry.com; subway F to Second Ave, #6 to Bleecker St. For most of the week, this spot is *Duane Park*, an upscale burlesque club, but Sunday (from noon) and Monday (from 6pm), poetry takes centre stage; the founder, Bob Holman, used to run *Nuyorican* (see below). Tickets free–$15.

Brooklyn Poets Reading Series ⓦ brooklynpoets .org. Free bimonthly readings by three poets at select venues in Brooklyn, with a summer stop on Governors Island.

Franklin Park Reading Series 618 St John's Place, between Franklin and Classon sts, Crown Heights, Brooklyn ⓦ franklinparkbrooklyn.com. Free readings from emerging and established fiction writers, memoirists, poets and storytellers. Every second Mon of each month 8–10pm.

The Moth ⓦ themoth.org. Offbeat literary company that's known for its story slams – open-mic nights

where amateurs vie for a 5min on-stage storytelling spot. They move around at venues such as the Village's *Bitter End*, Brooklyn's *Bell House* (see p.348), and *Housing Works Bookstore Café* (see p.388). There's also the yearly Moth Ball (Nov) in aid of charity.

★**Nuyorican Poets Café** 236 E 3rd St, between aves B and C ☎ 212 780 9386, ⓦ nuyorican.org; subway F to Second Ave. Known for its poetry slams, Alphabet City's *Nuyorican* remains one of the most vibrant performance spaces in town. There are also theatre and film-script readings. Tickets $10–25. Daily 6pm–midnight.

The Poetry Project at St Mark's Church 131 E 10th St, at Second Ave ☎ 212 674 0910, ⓦ poetryproject.org; subway L to Third Ave, #6 to Astor Place. Founded in 1966 by Paul Blackburn and friends (and hosting the likes of Allen Ginsberg, Patti Smith and many others), with poetry readings three nights a week. Tickets $8. Mon, Wed & Fri 8pm–midnight.

are devoted to free readings by a big-name contemporary author. On other occasions there's an intriguing programme centred on great magazine writing read by a group of journalists. Check the calendar on the website for schedules.

KGB 85 E 4th St, at Second Ave ☎ 212 505 3360, ⓦ kgbbar.com; subway F to Second Ave, #6 to Astor Place. Grubby but welcoming little bar that hosts free readings pretty much every night; expect to see top names and well-known local writers. Check the website for up-to-date schedules (most readings start at 7pm). The building also houses the Kraine Theater (see opposite).

Strand Bookstore 828 Broadway, at E 12th St ☎ 212 473 1452, ⓦ strandbooks.com; subway N, R, Q, L, W, #4, #5, #6 to Union Square; map p.88. New York's iconic secondhand bookshop offers readings, talks and literary panels most days of the week. Mon–Sat 9.30am–10.30pm, Sun 11am–10.30pm.

★**Symphony Space** 2537 Broadway, at 95th St ☎ 212 864 5400, ⓦ symphonyspace.org; subway #1, #2, #3 to 96th St. The highly acclaimed Selected Shorts series, in which actors read the short fiction of a variety of authors (everyone from James Joyce to David Sedaris), usually packs the Symphony Space theatre (Wed 7.30pm).

LGBT PRIDE MARCH

LGBT New York

There are few places in America – indeed in the world – where gay culture thrives as it does in New York City. Open gays and lesbians are mainstream here – so much so that the city is one of the few places where Republican administrations avidly court LGBT votes. That acceptance makes it easy to find shops, bars, clubs, media, entertainment, social services and much more dedicated to the sizeable gay, lesbian, bisexual and transgender population. And all of the city comes together for major events like Pride Week in late June (Pride Month), which takes in a rally, street fairs, outdoor films, innumerable parties and the legendary (if commercialized and sweltering) LGBT Pride March (see p.406).

26

The largely liberal orientation of city politics has been generally beneficial to the LGBT community since the 1969 riots at the *Stonewall Inn* marked the onset of the gay-rights movement (see box, p.104); the state – with major vocal elements from the city – has helped lead the recent charge toward **marriage equality**. The New York Court of Appeals initially ruled gay marriage illegal in 2006; two years later, Governor David Paterson issued a directive that required state agencies to recognize same-sex marriages officiated elsewhere as valid in New York. He followed that with legislation to legalize such marriage in the city, which the State Assembly passed but the Senate voted down in late 2009. Paterson's successor, Andrew Cuomo, a strong supporter of the cause, was able to mount a successful drive for its passage in 2011 (and three-time mayor, Michael Bloomberg, was an outspoken proponent); helped by a few key Republican votes, the State Senate voiced its approval two days before the Pride Parade in June. The US Supreme Court's June 2013 decision in favour of marriage equality was greeted with jubilation outside the *Stonewall Inn* (see p.368) and elsewhere.

A strong gay presence still lingers in the vicinity of Christopher Street in the West Village, but it's in the Chelsea **neighbourhood** (especially Eighth Ave between 14th and 23rd sts) that gay male socializing is most ubiquitous and open. Other neighbourhoods with a strong gay and lesbian presence are Hell's Kitchen (particularly Ninth Ave between 46th and 53rd sts), Morningside Heights (Columbia University's college town), Queens' Astoria and Brooklyn's Bushwick and East Williamsburg.

ESSENTIALS

LISTINGS

Several free weekly newspapers and magazines serve New York's LGBT community: *Gay City News* (ⓦgaycitynews .nyc) and *GO* (for women; trans-friendly; ⓦgomag.com). You'll find these at the resource centres noted below, at newspaper dispensers on street corners, bars, cafés, and occasionally at newsstands, where national mags such as *Out* and *Metrosource* are available. The listings in ⓦgayletter.com and *Time Out New York* magazine (ⓦtimeout.com/newyork/lgbt) are also very helpful.

ONLINE DATING

NYC singles live by dating apps. If you're a man looking to meet someone while here, try Grindr (ⓦgrindr.com), Scruff (ⓦscruff.com), or GROWLr (ⓦgrowlrapp.com), or, for the ladies, Her (ⓦweareher.com).

RESOURCES

New York City has a wealth of resource centres serving the gay community – arguably the best and most historic collection of LGBT organizations in the world.

The Audre Lorde Project 147 W 24th St, 3rd floor, Manhattan ☎212 463 0342, and 85 S Oxford St, Brooklyn ☎718 596 0342, ⓦalp.org. Community centre for LGBT people of colour, focused on the New York City area.

Callen-Lorde Community Health Center 356 W 18th St, between Eighth and Ninth aves ☎212 271 7200, ⓦcallen-lorde.org. Named for two luminaries – a poet and an AIDS activist – *Callen-Lorde* is an excellent

sliding-scale health clinic that is welcoming to all, with a focus on the LGBT community. Primary care, STD testing, dentistry, a pharmacy and more.

Gay Men's Health Crisis (GMHC) 446 W 33rd St, between Ninth and Tenth aves ☎212 367 1000, ⓦgmhc.org. Despite the name, this incredible organization – the oldest and largest not-for-profit AIDS organization in the world – provides testing, information and referrals to everyone: gay, straight and transgender.

The Lesbian, Gay, Bisexual & Transgender Community Center 208 W 13th St, west of Seventh Ave ☎212 620 7310, ⓦgaycenter.org. The Center houses well over a hundred groups and organizations, sponsors workshops, parties, movie nights, guest speakers, readings, youth services, programmes for parents and lots more.

SAGE: Services and Advocacy for LGBT Elders 305 Seventh Ave, at 27th St, 15th floor ☎212 741 2247, ⓦsageusa.org. Employment programmes, legal resources, healthcare assistance and events for gay seniors. On weekdays, the group maintains a drop-in centre at the LGBT Center, 208 W 13th St (see above), and has additional locations in Harlem, the Bronx, Brooklyn and Staten Island.

Sylvia Rivera Law Project 127 W 24th St, between Sixth and Seventh aves, 5th floor ☎212 337 8550, ⓦsrlp.org. Performs advocacy for and offers free legal services to members of the transgender community.

Trans Justice Funding Project ⓦtransjustice fundingproject.org. Based in Brooklyn, Trans Justice is a grassroots fundraising organization that offers grants to groups which empower trans communities.

ACCOMMODATION

As well as the hotels reviewed below, check out *Chelsea Pines Inn* (p.271). In New York and elsewhere, Purple Roofs (ⓦpurpleroofs.com) is a great online locator for gay-friendly accommodation.

Colonial House Inn 318 W 22nd St, between Eighth and Ninth aves ☎212 243 9669, ⓦcolonialhouseinn.com; subway C, E to 23rd St; map p.107. You won't mind that this B&B is a little worn around the edges – its attractive design and contributions to the GMHC (see opposite) make for a feel-good experience. Only the deluxe rooms include en-suite bathrooms, while some have refrigerators, fireplaces and sleep five. Continental breakfast included. <u>$190</u>

Incentra Village House 32 Eighth Ave, between W 12th and Jane sts ☎212 206 0007, ⓦincentravillage.com; subway A, C, E to 14th St, L to Eighth Ave; map p.96. Located on a lovely residential block, this townhouse pair has a dozen Early American-styled studios, some with kitchenettes, and one guest room has access to a private garden. Three-night minimum stay at weekends. <u>$259</u>

The Out NYC 510 W 42nd St, between Tenth and Eleventh aves ☎212 947 2999, ⓦtheoutnyc.com; subway A, C, E to 42nd St-Port Authority; map p.142. A breath of fresh air on an uninspiring stretch of Midtown, this sprawling contemporary hotel boasts a range of youthful amenities like bamboo gardens with ping pong, a sunroom with dual hot tubs and pet-friendly suites with dog houses. Guest rooms are modern and plush; the "quads" are set up with curtained bunk beds, fun for a weekend with friends. There's a great spa and gym, too. <u>$350</u>

EATING

New York restaurants are, on the whole, exceptionally gay-friendly. The places below are useful if you're looking to patronize an establishment where the tables are filled with LGBT diners.

Cafeteria 119 Seventh Ave, at W 17th St ☎212 414 1717, ⓦcafeteriagroup.com; subway #1 to 18th St; map p.107. See p.298.

Cowgirl 519 Hudson St, at W 10th St ☎212 633 1133, ⓦcowgirlnyc.com; subway #1 to Christopher St; map p.96. Genial, woman-owned restaurant with a Western theme. It's big on burger-and-bbq offerings ($12–23), and hosts a sometimes lively bar scene among the kitschy decor. Mon–Thurs 8am–11pm, Fri 8am–midnight, Sat 10am–midnight, Sun 10am–11pm; bar until 2am Fri & Sat.

Elmo 156 Seventh Ave, between W 19th and 20th sts ☎212 337 8000, ⓦelmorestaurant.com; subway #1 to 18th St; map p.107. American classics like tomato soup ($8) with grilled cheese ($9) and fried chicken with mashed potatoes ($19) are dolled up and served here amid striped banquettes and design details that conjure Art Deco Miami. It's renowned for brunch, and there's a fun bar and outdoor seating, too. Mon–Fri 11am–midnight, Sat & Sun 10am–midnight.

★ **Empanada Mama** 763 Ninth Ave, between W 51st and 52nd sts ☎212 698 9008, ⓦempmamanyc.com; subway C, E to 50th St; map p.142. Tempting snack shop that pulls in patrons around the clock for its wheat and corn patties stuffed with spicy meats, cheeses, veggies or sweets like chocolate and bananas. Great proximity to Hell's Kitchen's gay bars. Open 24hr.

Rocking Horse 182 Eighth Ave, between W 19th and 20th sts ☎212 463 9511, ⓦrockinghorsecafe.com; subway C, E to 23rd St, #1 to 18th St; map p.107. See p.300.

Vynl 756 Ninth Ave, at W 51st St ☎212 974 2003, ⓦvynl-nyc.com; subway C, E to 50th St; map p.142. Campy diner where the tables are encrusted with mosaics of pop stars and walls are chock-a-block with disco balls and old 45s. Don't miss the Michael Jackson- and Beyoncé-themed bathrooms, with tunes to match. Mon & Tues 11am–11pm, Wed–Fri 11am–midnight, Sat 9.30am–1am, Sun 9.30am–11pm.

DRINKING

Gay men's bars cover the spectrum from relaxed pubs to hard-hitting clubs full of glamour and attitude. Most of the more-established places are in Greenwich Village and Chelsea, with the newer spots popping up in Hell's Kitchen, particularly on Ninth Avenue between 46th and 53rd streets. Williamsburg in Brooklyn and the West Village are the centres of the lesbian bar scene, with additional spots in Chelsea and along Hudson Street in the West Village.

MAINLY FOR MEN

Atlas Social Club 753 Ninth Ave, between 50th and 51st sts ☎212 262 8527; subway C, E to 50th St; map p.142. A Hell's Kitchen mainstay, this low-key pub gets noisy come nightfall and has a cool, retro boxing theme, complete with gloves and vintage magazine spreads. Daily 4pm–4am.

Barracuda 275 W 22nd St, between Seventh and Eighth aves ☎212 645 8613; subway C, E, #1 to 23rd St; map p.107. A favourite spot in New York's gay scene, and pretty laidback for Chelsea. Daily two-for-one happy hour (4–9pm), crazy drag shows, karaoke nights. Daily 4pm–4am.

26

26

The Boiler Room 86 E 4th St, between First and Second aves ☎ 212 254 7536; subway F to Second Ave; map p.88. Longtime local bar with a pool table and great tunes on the jukebox. While it's a fun hangout (mostly gay but with some lesbian presence), don't expect much atmosphere; it's got the look of a retiree's garage during the summer. Daily 4pm–4am.

Boxers 742 Ninth Ave, at 50th St ☎ 212 951 1518; subway C, E to 50th St; map p.142. Bartended by beautiful men in boxers (hence the name), this spacious haunt, loosely a sports bar, boasts a gorgeous rooftop patio in summer. There's another branch at 37 W 20th St, between Fifth and Sixth aves. Mon–Wed 4pm–2am, Thurs & Fri 4pm–4am, Sat 1pm–4am, Sun 1pm–2am.

Brandy's Piano Bar 235 E 84th St, between Second and Third aves ☎ 212 744 4949, ⓦ brandyspianobar .com; subway #4, #5, #6 to 86th St; map p.171. Handsome uptown cabaret/piano bar with a crazy, mixed and generally mature clientele. Definitely worth a visit; note there's a two-drink minimum during the nightly sets (which start at 9.30pm). Daily 4pm–3.30am.

The Cock 29 Second Ave, between E 1st and 2nd sts, ⓦ thecockbar.com; subway F to Second Ave; map p.88. Scuzzy, dark, divey and legendary, this cruise-fest is a glimmer of Old New York. Expect scantily clad dancers and men looking for action. Cash only; generally a $15 admission. Mon 11pm–4am, Tues–Sat & Sun 6pm–4am.

The Eagle NYC 554 W 28th St, between Tenth and Eleventh aves ☎ 646 473 1866, ⓦ eaglenyc.com; subway C, E to 23rd St, #1 to 28th St; map p.107. The place for leather-bar fans, with a super-cool industrial feel and bi-level, multi-room layout, plus an open roof terrace that's inevitably the most packed part of the bar. Dress code some nights. Mon–Sat 10pm–4am, Sun 4pm–4am.

★Flaming Saddles 793 Ninth Ave, between 52nd and 53rd sts ☎ 212 713 0481, ⓦ flamingsaddles.com; subway C, E to 50th St; map p.142. Friendly Hell's Kitchen hangout with a Texas twist – one of the owners is a former Coyote Ugly choreographer, and the Saddles' employees frequently line-dance on the bar. Be sure to try the Frito pie (chilli, mustard, onions, sour cream and melted cheddar served in a bag of corn chips; $7). Cash only. Mon–Fri 3pm–4am, Sat & Sun noon–4am.

GYM 167 Eighth Ave, between 18th and 19th sts ☎ 212 337 2439, ⓦ gymsportsbar.com; subway A, C, E, L to 14th St-Eighth Ave, #1 to 18th St; map p.107. Casual, friendly, non-sceney hangout with large-screen TVs, video games, a pool table and smokers' patio. A sports bar that's rare in that you can actually watch a game. Mon–Thurs 4pm–2am, Fri 4pm–4am, Sat 1pm–4am, Sun 1pm–2am.

Hombres 85-28 37th Ave, between 85th and 86th sts, Jackson Heights ☎ 718 930 0886, ⓦ hombreslounge .com; subway #7 to 82nd St-Jackson Heights; map

p.244. Latin-leaning spot well out in Queens, but draws a crowd for happy hours and late-night DJ parties. Daily 5pm–4am.

Julius 159 W 10th St, at Waverly Place ☎ 212 243 1928, ⓦ juliusbarny.com; subway #1 to Christopher St-Sheridan Square; A, B, C, D, E, F, M to W 4th St; map p.96. Its claim to being the oldest gay bar in the city gives it distinction; its divey feel, inexpensive burgers and lack of attitude give you the reasons to go. Mon–Sat 11am–4am, Sun noon–3am.

★Marie's Crisis 59 Grove St, between Seventh Ave S and Bleecker St; subway #1 to Christopher St-Sheridan Square; map p.96. Well-known cabaret/piano bar popular with tourists and locals, straights and gays alike. Features nightly old-time singing sessions. Often packed, always fun. Mon–Sat 4pm–3am, Sun 4pm–midnight.

Rockbar 185 Christopher St, between Washington St and the West Side Hwy ☎ 212 675 1864, ⓦ rockbarnyc .com; subway #1 to Christopher St-Sheridan Square, A, B, C, D, E, F, M to W 4th St; map p.96. If it's a bear scene you seek, be sure to pop into this West Village pub, particularly on Sundays starting at 4.30pm. The rest of the week you'll still find a friendly crowd, with trivia on Tuesday nights and karaoke on Thursdays. Mon–Thurs 4pm–2am, Fri 4pm–4am, Sat & Sun 2pm–4am.

Stonewall Inn 53 Christopher St, between Waverly Place and Seventh Ave S ☎ 212 488 2705, ⓦ thestone wallinnnyc.com; subway #1 to Christopher St-Sheridan Square, A, B, C, D, E, F, M to W 4th St; map p.96. Yes, *that* Stonewall, site of the seminal 1969 riot, mostly refurbished and flying the pride flag like they own it – which, one could say, they do. Bingo, DJs, drag variety shows, male dancers and lesbian nights; call or check the website to see what's on. Daily 2pm–4am.

Therapy 348 W 52nd St, between Eighth and Ninth aves ☎ 212 397 1700, ⓦ therapy-nyc.com; subway C, E to 50th St; map p.142. Sleek bi-level bar/lounge geared to Midtowners and the post-work drinking crowd. DJ sets, drag shows and theme nights make up the weekly calendar; wash down bar snacks while imbibing signature cocktails that keep up the psychological motif like the Freudian Sip (citron vodka, lemonade and fresh ginger) and the Psychotic Episode (suffice to say it includes banana liqueur). Mon–Thurs & Sun 5pm–2am, Fri & Sat 5pm–4am.

MAINLY FOR WOMEN

★Cubbyhole 281 W 12th St, at W 4th St ☎ 212 243 9041, ⓦ cubbyholebar.com; subway A, C, E, L to 14th St-Eighth Ave; map p.96. This small, kitschy West Village bar is worn-in and welcoming, and feels like it's been here forever (really just twenty or so years). An essential stop-off. Mon–Fri 4pm–4am, Sat & Sun 2pm–4am.

Ginger's 363 Fifth Ave, between 5th and 6th sts, Park Slope, Brooklyn ☎ 718 788 0924, ⓦ gingersbarbklyn

.com; subway F, G, R to Fourth Ave-9th St; map p.231. Dark, laidback, longstanding Park Slope joint with a pool table, outdoor space, dance and karaoke nights and plenty of convivial company. Mon–Fri 5pm–4am, Sat & Sun 2pm–4am.

Henrietta Hudson 438 Hudson St, at Morton St ☎212 924 3347, ⓦhenriettahudson.com; subway #1 to Houston St or Christopher St-Sheridan Square; map p.96. Relaxed in the afternoon but brimming by night, especially on weekends, this is the top lesbian place in Manhattan. Weekly theme nights – karaoke, game night, DJs, etc. Daily 4pm–4am.

MIXED

Metropolitan 559 Lorimer St, at Metropolitan Ave, Brooklyn ☎718 599 4444, ⓦmetropolitanbarny.com; subway L to Lorimer St, G to Metropolitan Ave; map

p.225. Hipster hangout without (much) attitude helps it attract all types. Hosts wild dance parties every Saturday night. In warm weather, its patio is a lovely place to be. Daily 3pm–4am.

Nowhere 322 E 14th St, between First and Second aves ☎212 477 4744, ⓦnowherebarnyc.com; subway L to First Ave or Third Ave; map p.88. Relaxed East Village bar, dark and on the divey side, with good dance tunes and DJs, pool tables and a friendly clientele comprising people of all stripes. Daily 3pm–4am.

Phoenix 447 E 13th St, between Ave A and First Ave ☎212 477 9979, ⓦphoenixbarnyc.com; subway L to First Ave; map p.88. This laidback East Village pub is much loved by the so-not-scene boys who live there, and other LGBT crew who just want reasonably priced drinks and a fun crowd; things heat up for its popular Friday-night party. Daily 3pm–4am.

26

NIGHTLIFE

Gay and lesbian club nights in New York can be some of the most outrageous in the world; however, they can change time, venue and level of hipness with speed. Check *Time Out New York* magazine (ⓦtimeout.com/newyork/lgbt), *Next Magazine* (ⓦnextmagazine.com) and *GO* (ⓦgomag.com) for up-to-date info.

Big Apple Ranch 25 W 31st St, 4th floor, between Fifth Ave and Broadway ☎212 807 0802, ⓦbigappleranch.com; subway N, Q, R to 34th St-Herald Square; map p.107. Not a club per se, but a bi-monthly country-and-western dance party, complete with lessons in two-step and line dancing. Admission $15. It's held on second and fourth Saturdays. Lessons 8pm, 9pm–12.30am open dancing.

Industry 355 W 52nd St, between Eighth and Ninth aves ☎646 476 2747, ⓦindustry-bar.com; subway C, E to 50th St; map p.142. Cavernous Hell's Kitchen hotspot whose dancefloor is perennially packed with pretty young

things finding their groove under spinning mirrorballs. Drag shows are held on weeknights, but weekends have the best scene. Cash only. Daily 4pm–4am.

The Monster 80 Grove St, at Sheridan Square ☎212 924 3558, ⓦmonsterbarnyc.com; subway #1 to Christopher St; map p.96. Large, campy bar with drag cabaret, piano and downstairs dancefloor. Very popular, especially with tourists, yet has a strong "neighbourhood" feel. Every night brings something else, from amateur and professional go-go boys to Latin grooves and a Sunday tea dance. Usually no admission charge, but $6–10 when there is one. Mon–Fri 4pm–4am, Sat & Sun 2pm–4am.

ARTS AND CULTURE

For theatre, check out *Dixon Place* (see p.356), *Joe's Pub* (see p.346), and La MaMa (see p.356) in Chapter 25, "Performing arts and film."

Center for LGBTQ Studies CUNY Graduate Center, 365 Fifth Ave, between 34th and 35th sts ☎212 817 1955, ⓦgc.cuny.edu. Fascinating talks and seminars featuring academic luminaries. Particular attention is paid to international, transgender and disability studies.

Lesbian Herstory Archives 484 14th St, between Eighth Ave and Prospect Park West, Park Slope,

Brooklyn ☎718 768 3953, ⓦlesbianherstoryarchives.org. Original materials on lesbian life, mostly throughout the twentieth century. Old-school and inspiring. Open a few days a week on a variable schedule, so call ahead or visit the website for times.

Leslie-Lohman Museum of Gay and Lesbian Art 26 Wooster St, between Grand and Canal sts ☎212 431

POPCORN WITH HEDDA LETTUCE

Every Thursday at Chelsea Bow Tie Cinema (7pm; $10), the convivial Hedda Lettuce takes the stage to introduce fun films like *Roman Holiday* or *Desperately Seeking Susan*. It's a relaxed way to ease into the weekend, and a great local tradition. 260 W 23rd St, between Seventh and Eighth aves, ⓦbowtiecinemas.com; subway C, E, #1 to 23rd St.

26

2609, ⓦleslielohman.org. The Lohman maintains an archive and permanent collection of LGBT art, with galleries open to the public during shows. Free. Tues–Sun noon–6pm, Thurs till 8pm.

LGBT Community Center National History Archive/ The Pat Parker–Vito Russo Center Library LGBT Community Center (see p.366) ☎212 620 7310, ⓦgaycenter.org. Terrific, interesting archive of gay life in America, and a lending library with 12,000 titles. Archive drop-in hours Thurs 4–8pm; library Tues–Thurs 6–9pm, Fri & Sat 1–4pm.

MIX (New York Queer Experimental Film Festival) ☎212 742 8880, ⓦmixnyc.org. This celebrated annual festival, which takes place in February, offers politically radical and technically avant-garde films.

NewFest ⓦnewfest.org. This not-to-be-missed annual film festival has kicked off Pride Month in June and been held in October; check the website first. Expect celebrities, outrageous parties and an interesting array of flicks.

New York City Gay Men's Chorus ☎212 344 1777, ⓦnycgmc.org. Wildly popular gay men's choral group (with over 250 members) that has sung with Jesse Tyler Ferguson (of *Modern Family* fame) and other big names at major venues like Carnegie Hall. Call or check website for concert schedule and membership information.

WOW Café Theatre 59-61 E 4th St, 4th floor, between Bowery and Second Ave ☎917 725 1482, ⓦwowcafe .org; subway R to 8th St, #6 to Astor Place; map p.88. Smart, cutting-edge theatre collective with works produced, acted and directed by women and transgender people. Encourages participation for those interested in all aspects of theatre creation; no experience required.

SHOPS

If you're looking for books, clothes or something to spice up the after-hours, you should be able to find it at one of these specialized spots. The West Village and Chelsea have the greatest concentration of gay-oriented stores.

★**Babeland** 94 Rivington St, between Orchard and Ludlow sts ☎212 375 1701, ⓦbabeland.com; subway F to Delancey St; map p.82. Also 43 Mercer St, between Grand and Broome sts, and in Brooklyn at 462 Bergen St, between Fifth and Sixth Aves. Superlative, sophisticated feminist sex-toy store, perhaps the best in the nation. Sex workshops fill up quickly. Mon–Wed & Sun noon–10pm, Thurs–Sat noon–11pm.

★**Bluestockings** 172 Allen St, between Stanton and Rivington sts ☎212 777 6028, ⓦbluestockings.com; subway F to Second Ave or Delancey St; map p.82. Lefty bookstore that functions as an informal centre for the LGBT community and is staffed by volunteers. Hosts near-nightly readings, performances, meetings and screenings. Daily 11am–11pm.

Bureau of General Services–Queer Division Room 210, 108 W 13th St, west of Seventh Ave ☎212 620 7310, ⓦbgsqd.com. Set inside The Center (see p.366), the Bureau is an excellent indie bookstore that doubles as a performance space with workshops, readings, films, book club meetings and more. Tues–Sun 1–7pm.

Housing Works Thrift Shop 143 W 17th St, between Sixth and Seventh aves ☎718 838 5050, ⓦhousing works.org; subway #1 to 18th St; map p.107. Multiple other locations. See p.382.

The Leather Man 111 Christopher St, between Bleecker and Hudson sts ☎212 243 5339, ⓦthe leatherman.com; subway #1 to Christopher St-Sheridan Square, A, B, C, D, E, F, M to W 4th St; map p.96. Landmark shop, dating to 1965, that's filled to the gills with neoprene, spandex and leather toys, clothes and fetish wear. Many items are custom-made on the premises. Daily noon–8pm.

Nasty Pig 259 W 19th St, between Seventh and Eighth aves ☎212 691 6067, ⓦnastypig.com; subway #1 to 18th St; map p.107. Casual and sporty clothing and fetish store with a friendly attitude. Mon–Sat noon–8pm, Sun 1–8pm.

Pleasure Chest 156 Seventh Ave S, between Perry and Charles sts ☎212 242 2158, ⓦthepleasurechest.com, subway #1 to Christopher St-Sheridan Square, A, B, C, D, E, F, M to W 4th St; map p.96. Also 1150 Second Ave, between E 60th and 61st sts ☎212 355 6909. Established in 1971, this approachable sex shop has a knowledgeable staff and light-hearted workshops (free) that give Babeland's classes (see above) a run for their money. Mon–Wed 10am–10pm, Thurs–Sat 10am–midnight.

Commercial galleries

Art, especially contemporary art, is huge in New York. The city is arguably the
nexus of the international art world, with hundreds of dealers and more than
six hundred galleries, major auction houses such as Sotheby's and Christie's
and numerous high-profile art schools and colleges. Though several other
cities claim to have more innovative scenes – the 1950s and 1960s were
really New York's creative heyday – plenty of artists continue to live here,
from classical realist Jacob Collins and "relational" artists Maurizio Cattelan
and Liam Gillick to well-known figures such as Maya Lin. New York is also the
home of modern graffiti, with street artists such as Ellis Gallagher, Cern and
Swoon leading the current scene.

Even if you have no intention of buying, many of the high-profile galleries are well worth a visit. **Chelsea** boasts the most venues (around three hundred), while galleries on the **Lower East Side** and in **Chinatown** are arguably the city's most cutting-edge. Some of the most vibrant galleries are to be found outside Manhattan, however, especially in **Dumbo** and **Bushwick** (in Brooklyn).

Listed below are some of the more interesting exhibition spaces in Manhattan and elsewhere. Openings – usually free and easily identified by crowds of people swilling wine from plastic cups – are excellent times to view work, eavesdrop on art-world gossip and snag free food.

INFORMATION

Admission to galleries is almost always free. Check ⓦartsy.net, ⓦartdealers.org or the weekly *Time Out New York* (ⓦtimeout.com/newyork/art) and ⓦartsy.net for openings and listings of the major commercial galleries.

TRIBECA AND SOHO

27

Apex Art 291 Church St, between White and Walker sts ☎212 431 5270, ⓦapexart.org; subway N, Q, R to Canal St, #1 to Franklin St. A nonprofit exhibition space that invites dealers, artists, writers, critics and international art organizations to act as curators and mount idea-based shows, along with lectures and associated events. Tues–Sat 11am–6pm.

Art Projects International 434 Greenwich St, at Vestry St ☎212 343 2599, ⓦartprojects.com; subway #1 to Canal St. Highly respected for showing leading contemporary artists from Asia, this gallery's engaging exhibits are mostly in print and have featured artists like Zheng Xuewu, Gwenn Thomas and Richard Tsao. Tues–Sat 11am–6pm.

★**Artists Space** 55 Walker St, between Broadway and Church St ☎212 226 3970, ⓦartistsspace.org; subway A, C, E, N, R, Q to Canal St. One of the most respected alternative spaces, with frequently changing theme-based exhibits, film screenings, videos, installations and events. In over thirty years of existence, Artists Space has presented the work of thousands of emerging artists. Daily 10am–6pm.

★**Center for Italian Modern Art** 421 Broome St, 4th floor, between Crosby and Lafayette sts ☎646 370 3596, ⓦitalianmodernart.org; subway #6 to Spring St, R, W at Prince St. Nonprofit that beautifully realizes its vision: to spark a conversation between contemporary,

touring works with the permanent collection of twentieth-century Italian art. Visits kick off with complimentary espresso and group sizes are deliberately kept small (below fifteen), with discussion and quiet contemplation equally welcome. Reservations required; $10 admission (free for students with ID). Fri & Sat 11am, 1pm, 3pm & 5pm; closed July–Sept.

★**The Drawing Center** 35 Wooster St, between Grand and Broome sts ☎212 219 2166, ⓦdrawingcenter.org; subway A, C, E, N, R, Q to Canal St. Presents shows of contemporary and historical works on paper, from emerging artists to the sketches of the Great Masters. Charges admission of $5 (free Thurs 6–8pm). Wed–Sun noon–6pm, Thurs until 8pm.

★**Elizabeth Street Gallery** 209 Elizabeth St, between Prince and Spring sts ☎212 941 4800, ⓦelizabethstreetgallery.com; subway #6 to Spring St. This intriguing gallery specializes in antiques, sculpture and decorative objects, but the real highlight is the building itself – an 1850s New York City firehouse – and the adjacent garden, studded with romantic sculptures like a Florentine park. Mon–Fri noon–7pm, Sat noon–6pm.

HERE 145 Sixth Ave (enter on Dominick St) ☎212 352 3101, ⓦhere.org; subway C to Spring St. Eclectic experimental art space, with a comfy lobby café and a range of multimedia galleries hosting new works by the likes of Karinne Keithley and Tina Satter. Opening times vary.

DROP-IN DRAWING CLASSES AT SPRING STUDIO

Established in 1992 by artist and inimitable spirit Minerva Durham, **Spring Studio** (293 Broome St, between Forsyth and Eldridge sts ☎212 226 7240, ⓦspringstudiosoho.com; subway B, D to Grand St, F to Delancey St; classes daily; check website for scheduling; $20 per session) is one of the great vestiges of Old New York, offering life drawing lessons in a unique environment. Do not attend a life drawing class here if you are unable to distance yourself from your mobile phone, plan on being late or are uncomfortable with silence. Do drop in if you miss (or are curious about) the pre-internet age, want to work with a fascinating mix of fellow students (many have attended Minerva's classes for over a decade) and want a brilliant octogenarian teacher. Beginners are encouraged and sessions are small; first-come, first-served (walk-ins only).

Team Gallery 83 Grand St, at Greene St ☎ 212 279 9219, 🌐 teamgal.com; subway A, C, E, N, R, Q to Canal St. Beautiful, voyeuristic and cutting-edge work by artists such as Tracey Emin and Genesis P-Orridge, and web artist Cory Arcangel, is shown here. Tues–Sat 10am–6pm.

CHINATOWN AND THE LOWER EAST SIDE

★**47 Canal** 291 Grand St, at Eldridge St ☎ 646 415 7712, 🌐 47canal.us; subway B, D to Grand St. Hip, non-commercial artist-run space for very experimental projects (including a tiled room with an exterior wall that once leaked olive oil) and work from the likes of Michele Abeles and Josh Kline. Wed–Sun noon–6pm.

Front Room 48 Hester St, between Ludlow and Essex sts ☎ 718 782 2556, 🌐 frontroomles.com; subway F to East Broadway, B, D to Grand St. Relocated in 2017 from Williamsburg, this is one of the neighbourhood's best galleries and also a popular performance-art space. Wed–Sun 1–6pm.

Frosch & Portmann 53 Stanton St, between Eldridge and Forsyth sts ☎ 646 266 5994, 🌐 froschportmann .com; subway F to Second Ave. Extremely hip gallery curated by Swiss owners Eva Frosch and H.P. Portmann, offering a line-up of young contemporary artists who tend to produce surreal or abstract work. Wed–Sun noon–6pm.

Pierogi 155 Suffolk St, between Stanton and E Houston sts ☎ 646 429 9073, 🌐 pierogi2000.com; subway F to Delancey St, J, M, Z to Essex St. Formerly housed in a Williamsburg workshop, this gallery mounts fascinating installations of various kinds. It is noted in the art world for its travelling "flatfiles", a collection of folders containing the work of seven hundred or so artists, stored clinically and provocatively in sliding metal cabinets. Tues–Sat 11am–6pm.

Salon 94 Bowery 243 Bowery, at Stanton St ☎ 212 979 0001, 🌐 salon94.com; subway J, Z to Bowery, F to Second Ave. Fashionable downtown branch of Upper East Side's Salon 94 (12 E 94th St), with a 20ft screen beaming video art onto the street, and works from David Benjamin Sherry, Marilyn Minter, Lorna Simpson and Huma Bhabha. Tues–Sat 11am–6pm, Sun 1–6pm.

Sperone Westwater 257 Bowery, between Houston and Stanton sts ☎ 212 999 7337, 🌐 speronewestwater .com; subway F to Second Ave. Founded in Soho in 1975, Sperone Westwater moved to this new Norman Foster-designed building in 2010 and is overseen by art-world maven Angela Westwater. Expect a wide range of artists in all media, with a particular dedication to Arte Povera artists and Bruce Nauman. Tues–Sat 10am–6pm.

Tibor de Nagy 15 Rivington St, between Bowery and Chrystie St ☎ 212 262 5050, 🌐 tibordenagy.com; subway #6 to Spring St, F to Second Ave. Established in 1950 to further "the love of looking", Tibor de Nagy quickly grew into an Abstract Expressionist powerhouse, discovering and forging connections between poets and painters such as Frank O'Hara, Helen Frankenthaler and Jane Freilicher. Its bright pieces and superb exhibits remain just as compelling today. Tues–Sat 10am–6pm.

27

THE WEST VILLAGE

White Columns 320 W 13th St, entrance on Horatio St, between Hudson and W 4th sts ☎ 212 924 4212, 🌐 whitecolumns.org; subway A, C, E to 14th St. White Columns focuses on emerging artists, and is considered very influential. Check out the fascinating, ever-changing group shows. Tues–Sat noon–6pm.

CHELSEA

303 Gallery 555 W 21 St, at Eleventh Ave ☎ 212 255 1121, 🌐 303gallery.com; subway C, E to 23rd St. 303 Gallery was founded by Lisa Spellman and shows works in a comprehensive range of media by fairly well-established contemporary artists. Moved into these new Norman Foster-designed premises in 2016. Tues–Sat 10am–6pm.

★**David Zwirner** 537 W 20th St, between Tenth and Eleventh aves; also 519, 525 and 533 W 19th St ☎ 212 727 2070, 🌐 davidzwirner.com; subway C, E to 23rd St. High-quality shows from major players such as Richard Serra, Lisa Yuskavage and Yayoi Kusama. Tues–Sat 10am–6pm.

Edward Thorp Gallery 210 Eleventh Ave, 6th floor, between W 24th and W 25th sts ☎ 212 691 6565, 🌐 edwardthorpgallery.com; subway C, E to 23rd St. Mainstream contemporary American, South American and European painting and sculpture. Highlights of their roster include painter Matthew Blackwell and sculptor Deborah Butterfield. July Tues–Fri 11am–5pm; Aug by appointment only; Sept–June Tues–Sat 11am–6pm.

★**Gagosian Gallery** 555 W 24th St, between Tenth and Eleventh aves ☎ 212 741 1111, 🌐 gagosian.com; subway C, E to 23rd St. A stalwart fixture on the New York scene, the Gagosian features both modern and contemporary works, including pieces by artists such as Damien Hirst, David Salle, Eric Fischl and Richard Serra, and photographer Alec Soth. There's also a branch uptown, at 980 Madison Ave. Tues–Sat 10am–6pm.

Gladstone Gallery 515 W 24th St, between Tenth and Eleventh aves ☎ 212 206 7606, 🌐 gladstonegallery .com; subway C, E to 23rd St. Paintings, sculpture and photography by hot contemporary artists like Matthew

Barney and Rosemarie Trockel. Tues–Sat 10am–6pm.

Greene Naftali Gallery 508 W 26th St, between Tenth and Eleventh aves ☎212 463 7770, ⓦgreenenaftali gallery.com; subway C, E to 23rd St. A wide-open, airy gallery noted for its top-notch large group shows and conceptual installations. Very cool stuff. Tues–Sat 10am–6pm.

Hauser & Wirth 548 W 22nd St, between Tenth and Eleventh aves ☎212 790 3900, ⓦhauserwirth.com; subway C, E to 23rd St. Major gallery representing emerging and established contemporary artists, in a new, purpose-built premises that includes a bar/café spectacularly crafted from salvaged materials. Mon–Fri 10am–6pm.

Lehmann Maupin 536 W 22nd St, between Tenth and Eleventh aves ☎212 255 2923, ⓦlehmannmaupin .com; subway C, E to 23rd St. Shows a range of established international and American contemporary artists working in a variety of media, among them Tracey Emin, Juergen Teller and Gilbert & George. Also showcases a wide range of new talent. Tues–Sat 10am–6pm.

Luhring Augustine 531 W 24th St, between Tenth and Eleventh aves ☎212 206 9100, ⓦluhringaugustine .com; subway C, E to 23rd St; second location at 25 Knickerbocker Ave, Bushwick. Thought-provoking shows by contemporary artists (Pipilotti Rist, Rachel Whiteread and Zarina Hashmi, to name a few) – this is one of New York's big-gun galleries. Tues–Sat 10am–6pm.

Marianne Boesky Gallery 509 W 24th St, between Tenth and Eleventh aves ☎212 680 9889, ⓦboeskygallery.com; subway C, E to 23rd St. Highly regarded gallery hosted by longtime dealer Boesky, credited with discovering Takashi Murakami, Yoshitomo Nara and Lisa Yuskavage, as well as representing Frank Stella. Tues–Sat 10am–6pm.

Mary Boone Gallery 541 W 24th St, between Tenth and Eleventh aves ☎212 752 2929, ⓦmaryboone gallery.com; subway C, E to 23rd St. An extension of Boone's uptown gallery 745 Fifth Ave (see opposite), this Chelsea space has facilities for large-scale works and installations by the up-and-coming darlings of the art world. At least a couple of the artists nurtured by Boone – David Salle and Julian Schnabel – have achieved superstar status. Tues–Sat 10am–6pm.

Matthew Marks Gallery 522 W 22nd St ☎212 243 0200, ⓦmatthewmarks.com; subway C, E to 23rd St. The centrepiece of Chelsea's art scene, Matthew Marks shows pieces by such well-known minimalist and abstract artists as Cy Twombly and Ellsworth Kelly. Also has nearby branches at 523 W 24th St and 526 W 22nd St. Tues–Sat 10am–6pm.

★**Pace Gallery** 510 W 25th St, between Madison and Park aves ☎212 255 4044, ⓦthepacegallery.com; subway #4, #5, #6 to 59th St. This celebrated gallery exhibits works by most of the great modern American and European artists, from Picasso and Calder to Noguchi and

27

NEW YORK STREET ART

Street art flourishes among the concrete corners and gritty sidewalks of New York. What originated in the 1960s and '70s as gorgeous (if illicit) subway graffiti morphed into the murals and tags of the '80s, a movement headed by now-legendary artists Jean-Michel Basquiat, Keith Haring (whose *Crack is Wack* mural is still on view; see box, p.201) and Futura 2000. Nowadays, though the messages are no less personal or politicized, street art has become more widely accepted as an art form, and many of its long-time masters have received private commissions for their public works. Below are some favourite locations for street art in the city.

Bushwick Collective Intersection of St Nicholas Ave and Troutman St (Bushwick, Brooklyn). Bushwick is famed for its murals, and you'll find a stunning collection of them here at this crossroads, with a line-up including the chromatic melding of Dasic Fernández and Beau Stanton's intricate "cathedral".

Coney Island Art Walls 3050 Stillwell Ave, Coney Island, Brooklyn. May–Sept only. Just steps from the beach and boardwalk, this collection of 35 murals makes for a fantastic summer pilgrimage. Past highlights have included graffiti legend Lady Pink, the moustachioed whimsy of Kashink and international duo Yok & Sheryo.

JMZ Walls Myrtle Ave, at Broadway, Brooklyn. This ongoing project, curated by Alberto Mejia, organizes numerous stellar murals alongside the J, M, Z subway stations on the Bed-Stuy/Bushwick border. Artists to look out for include Claw Money, Fumero and rap devotee Jay Shells. You can also pop into the garden at Gallery Bar (1056 Broadway), which features several mural installations to enjoy alongside your beer and wings.

Little Italy Mulberry St, north of Canal St. Along Little Italy's main drag you'll find the fruits of the L.I.S.A. Project (short for "Little Italy Street Art"), a nonprofit that has been successfully pioneering a Manhattan mural arts district. Here you'll see pieces by Shepard Fairey (famed for his Obama "Hope" poster), Hanksy and an exultant, nebula-like work by Miishab, next to The Church of the Most Precious Blood (109 Mulberry St).

Rothko. Also has a good collection of prints and African art. Other locations at 537 W 24th St (☎ 212 421 3292) and 32 E 57th St (☎ 212 421 3292) specialize in edgier works and large installations. Tues–Sat 10am–6pm (all galleries).

Paula Cooper Gallery 521 & 534 W 21st St, between Tenth and Eleventh aves ☎ 212 255 1105, ⓦ paula coopergallery.com; subway C, E to 23rd St. An influential gallery that shows a wide range of contemporary painting, sculpture, drawings, prints and photographs, particularly minimalist and conceptual works, and even has a recording label, Dog w/a Bone. Tues–Sat 10am–6pm.

Sikkema Jenkins & Co 530 W 22nd St, between Tenth and Eleventh aves ☎ 212 929 2262, ⓦ sikkemajenkinsco .com; subway C, E to 23rd St. This somewhat controversial space often features exhibits with a political slant. Recent exhibitors have included Erin Shirreff, working in video, sculpture and photography. Tues–Sat 10am–6pm.

Tanya Bonakdar 521 W 21st St, between Tenth and Eleventh aves ☎ 212 414 4144, ⓦ tanyabonakdar gallery.com; subway C, E to 23rd St. An art-world heavy-hitter, Bonakdar's capacious walls have been fronted by the likes of sculptor and chromatic master Olafur Eliasson as well as minimalist painter Rita Lundqvist. Tues–Sat 10am–6pm.

WEST 57TH STREET AND AROUND

Marlborough Gallery 40 W 57th St, between Fifth and Sixth aves ☎ 212 541 4900, ⓦ marlboroughgallery .com; subway F to 57th St, N, R to Fifth Ave-59th St. Specializing in famous American and European names, with sister galleries in Chelsea, London, Monaco and Madrid. The original London gallery was founded in 1947 to help foster artistic talents such as Henry Moore and Philip Guston. Mon–Sat 10am–5.30pm.

Mary Boone Gallery 745 Fifth Ave, between 58th and 57th sts, 4th floor ☎ 212 752 2929, ⓦ maryboone gallery.com; subway F to 57th St, N, R to Fifth Ave-59th St. Mary Boone was Leo Castelli's protégée, and her gallery specializes in installations, paintings and works by up-and-coming European and American artists, as well as established artists already involved with the gallery. There's now also an interesting branch in Chelsea (see opposite). Tues–Fri 10am–6pm, Sat 10am–5pm.

27

DUMBO AND FORT GREENE

BRIC Arts 647 Fulton St at Rockwell Place, Fort Greene ☎ 718 875 4047, ⓦ bricartsmedia.org; subway #2, #3, #4, #5 to Nevins St. This mixed-media, not-for-profit exhibition space in the former Strand Theater building features work by Brooklyn-based contemporary artists. Tues & Thurs 10am–8pm, Wed & Fri–Sun 10am–6pm.

Smack Mellon Gallery 92 Plymouth St, at Washington St, Dumbo ☎ 718 834 8761, ⓦ smackmellon.org; subway F to York St, A, C to High St. An interesting space that displays multidisciplinary, high-tech work by artists who have for the most part flown under the radar of art critics and spectators. Wed–Sun noon–6pm.

UrbanGlass 647 Fulton St at Rockwell Place, Fort Greene ☎ 718 625 3685, ⓦ urbanglass.org; subway F, G to Fourth Ave. Small but amazing glass gallery attached to the studio of the same name. Wed, Thurs & Sun noon–6pm, Fri & Sat noon–7pm.

WILLIAMSBURG

WAH (Williamsburg Art and Historical) Center 135 Broadway, between Bedford and Driggs aves ☎ 718 486 6012, ⓦ wahcenter.net; subway J, M, Z to Marcy Ave. Beautiful, fascinating multimedia arts centre, with a focus on painting and sculpture. Thurs–Sun noon–6pm.

BUSHWICK

Art 3 Gallery 109 Ingraham St, between Knickerbocker and Porter aves ☎ 646 331 3162, ⓦ art-3gallery.com; subway L to Morgan Ave. This compelling mixed-media gallery has helped to solidify Bushwick's reputation as the city's coolest new art space. Expect contemporary works like Dan Bainbridge's fabric-and-wire *Bestiary*, or painter Claudia Baez's vivid, softly swooping lines. Wed–Sat noon–6pm, Sun 1–5pm.

★**ArtHelix** 289 Meserole St, between Bogart and Waterbury sts ☎ 718 782 2863, ⓦ arthelix.com; subway L to Montrose or Morgan Ave. In the heart of the Bushwick scene, ArtHelix is a multidisciplinary gallery that runs the gamut – shows could take place over a barbecue, or inside, along elegantly curated white-brick walls. It doubles as the home of SHIM, an art service connecting artists to galleries (and vice versa). Sat & Sun noon–6pm.

SIGNAL 260 Johnson Ave, between Bushwick Ave and White St ☎ 347 746 8457, ⓦ ssiiggnnaall.com; subway L to Montrose or Morgan Ave. SIGNAL excels at spotting talented up-and-comers, and its space – a renovated warehouse – makes a superb canvas for viewing emerging artists. Sat & Sun 1–6pm.

BERGDORF GOODMAN

Shopping

New York City is an endless celebration of style. The flagship capital of the world, if you follow a particular brand, you'll most likely find the best representation of it here. In between all the big names, you'll uncover dozens of quirky local boutiques, secondhand stores and bazaars. The city also houses some of America's most famous department stores – Bloomingdale's and Macy's among them – as well as a roster of gourmet grocers and specialist book shops. Finally, enticing markets – green, flea and craft – are scattered throughout the five boroughs. In terms of which neighbourhoods sell what, as a general rule, smaller boutiques and more inexpensive shops live downtown, department stores are in Midtown, and designer labels make their home on Fifth and Madison avenues, hugging Central Park.

TAX FREE

As with basically everything in New York City, shopping leans towards the pricier side of the spectrum. In addition to the price on the tag, an 8.875 percent sales tax is added to every purchase. There is one cheerful exception to this rule, however: clothing and footwear sales under $110 are exempt from taxes. That's money, honey.

DEPARTMENT STORES

Barneys, Bergdorf Goodman and Saks Fifth Avenue are among the world's most famous (and most beautiful) **department stores** – each of their buildings is a landmark in itself. Many of these stores offer **in-house discount cards** for foreign visitors; be sure to enquire at the information desk.

Barneys New York 660 Madison Ave, at E 61st St ☎ 212 826 8900, ⓦ barneys.com; subway N, R to Fifth Ave-59th St; map p.124. Barneys is considered the trendiest New York department store, and shows no sign of weakening. It's a temple to designer fashion, and the best big shop for edgy labels and of-the-moment wares. Bag lovers note: it is also the only department store in the world to house a vintage Hermès shop. Mon–Fri 10am–8pm, Sat 10am–7pm, Sun 11am–7pm.

Bergdorf Goodman 754 and 745 Fifth Ave, at E 58th St ☎ 212 753 7300, ⓦ bergdorfgoodman.com; subway F to 57th St, N, R to Fifth Ave-59th St; map p.124. This venerable department store caters to the city's wealthiest shoppers. Haute-couture designers and salons fill both buildings, one for men, one for women, though it's the fairer sex that gets to shop within the former Vanderbilt mansion on the east side of Fifth. During lunch hour, it's speculated that the maître'd makes $500 in tips seating guests at *BG Restaurant*, which has stunning views of Central Park – patrons want to see that view, and be seen seeing the view. Mon–Sat 10am–8pm, Sun 11am–7pm.

Bloomingdale's Lexington Ave and E 59th St (officially 1000 Third Ave) ☎ 212 705 2000, ⓦ bloomingdales .com; subway N, R, #4, #5, #6 to Lexington Ave-59th St;

28

SHOPPING BY NEIGHBOURHOOD: A NEW YORK INDEX

In a nutshell: if you want elegance, head uptown, for style, down. Still, there are sections of the city distinguished by certain tones and known for varying specialities – "I Heart NY"T-shirts, fresh flowers and designer labels, to name a few.

Canal Street Particularly between Church and Centre sts (Chinatown); subway N, Q, R to Canal St. Head here for every "I Heart NY" object imaginable, cheap produce and souvenir trinkets. It's mayhem – thronged with crowds – but still a lively and quintessential New York experience.

Flower Market W 28th St between Sixth and Seventh avenues (Chelsea); subway N, R to 28th St. If you're in a wooing state, impress your honey by heading to the source – florists come from all over town to pick up their goods directly from this slice of heaven in east Chelsea (see p.107).

Grand Central 89 E 42nd St, between Lexington and Park Ave (Midtown East); subway #4, #5, #6, #7 to Grand Central-42nd St. In recent years, Grand Central (see p.134) has become nearly as well known for its shopping merits as it is for transport; the fact that it's a gorgeous city landmark doesn't hurt the browsing experience, either. There's an excellent food market with delights like Li-Lac (see p.393) and Murray's Cheese Shop (see p.392), an Apple Store (see p.390), great book and stationery vendors, a gourmet food court and more.

Madison and Fifth avenues Particularly between E 56th and E 80th sts (Upper East Side); subway N, R to Fifth Ave-59th St, #4, #5, #6 to Lexington Ave-59th St. The ultimate designer pilgrimage, these distinguished avenues are known the world over for their grace and top-tier labels. Here, you'll find Tiffany's (see p.384) and Bergdorf's (see above), in addition to numerous venerable flagships (see box, p.379).

Sixth Avenue Between 18th and 22nd sts (Flatiron District); subway F, M to 23rd St. This efficient stretch boasts "get it done" shops and discount vendors like Marshall's, The Container Store, Michaels (see p.382), Harmon Face Values (see p.385) and everyone's favourite cheapo supermarket, Trader Joe's.

Soho Bound by Houston, Crosby, Canal and Sixth Ave; subway #6 to Spring St, N, R to Prince St. Manhattan's prime clothes-shopping neighbourhood, centring on Broadway and Spring St. You'll find heavy hitters like Uniqlo (see p.381), H&M (see p.380), Topshop (see p.381) and nearly every other chain and boutique you can think of, all housed in lovely cast-iron buildings. Aim to visit on a weekday – it gets unbearably mobbed on weekends – and do try to drift onto the more atmospheric and often cobblestoned side streets, such as Wooster and Greene.

HOLIDAY WINDOW-SHOPPING

December is one of New York's most visited months, and with good reason: the city becomes a dazzling parade of holiday traditions, performances and embellishments. The corner of Fifth Ave and West 58th St offers the best in retail holiday spirit: here, store windows offer jaw-dropping displays of theatrical skill and design one-upmanship. **Bergdorf's** (see p.377), is the undisputed king of windows, but you'll also find Bulgari and Tiffany & Co. (see p.384). Barneys (see p.377), a few blocks north, also deserves a nod. Continuing south on Fifth Avenue, you'll find great decorations all the way down to Lord & Taylor (between W 38th and W 39th sts). Be sure to make a stop to see **Rockefeller Center**'s world-famous Christmas tree; this block, with Saks Fifth Avenue (see below), at E 50th St, is another winter wonderland. Other notable holiday traditions include shopping the fairs in decked-out Grand Central Station and the **Angel Tree** at the Metropolitan Museum.

map p.124. Out-of-towners flock here for its famed "classiness", though local power-shoppers are more likely to view it as a bit of a has-been. It does still have the atmosphere of a large, bustling bazaar, packed with concessionaires offering perfumes and designer clothes. Be sure to pop by the *Forty Carrots* café for a sampling of its famous frozen yogurt (the mesmerizingly tangy "plain" flavour is best). Mon–Wed & Sat 10am–8.30pm, Fri & Sat 10am–10pm, Sun 11am–7pm.

Macy's 151 W 34th St, on Broadway at Herald Square ☎212 695 4400 or ☎800 289 6229, ⓦmacys.com; subway B, D, F, M, N, Q, R to 34th St-Herald Square; map p.142. With two buildings, two million square feet of floor space and ten floors (four for women's garments alone), Macy's is the second-largest department store in the world (only Shinsegae, in Korea, is larger). As much a city attraction as it is a shop, Macy's is famed for holiday extravaganzas such as its flower show in early April (when showrooms come alive with elaborate floral sculptures), the humongous-balloon-filled Thanksgiving Day Parade and winter visits from Santa, with window displays to match. If you're not American, head to the visitor centre to receive a ten-percent discount card (bring your passport). Mon–Sat 10am–10pm, Sun 11am–9pm.

Saks Fifth Avenue 611 Fifth Ave, at E 50th St ☎212 753 4000, ⓦsaksfifthavenue.com; subway E, M to Fifth Ave-53rd St, B, D, F, M to 47–50th St-Rockefeller Center; map p.124. Opened in 1924, Saks retains an elegant, gracious style, yet has been updated to carry the merchandise of all the big designers. Saks goes all out during the holidays – in December, its displays match the grandeur of St Patrick's Cathedral, across the street. Mon–Sat 10am–8.30pm, Sun 11am–7pm.

DISCOUNT DEPARTMENT STORES

★ **Century 21** 21 Dey St, between Broadway and Church St ☎212 227 9092, ⓦc21stores.com; subway R to Cortlandt St or Rector St, #1 to Rector St, #4, #5 to Fulton St; map p.44. The king of designer discount department stores, where all the showrooms send their samples to be sold at the end of the season, usually at forty to sixty percent off retail prices – the richest pickings are in January and July. A limited number of dressing rooms, so buy what you want and return whatever doesn't fit. Mon–Wed 7.45am–9pm, Thurs & Fri 7.45am–9.30pm, Sat 10am–9pm, Sun 11am–8pm.

Nordstrom Rack 60 E 14th St, at Broadway ☎212 220 2080, ⓦnordstromrack.com; subway N, R, Q, L, #4, #5, #6 to Union Square; map p.115. Unlike many other discount clothing stores, which sell knock-offs sewn overseas, Nordstrom Rack has original pieces at discount rates. The menswear department is particularly well stocked. If you're lucky you'll snag treasures for a steal – such as a Burberry trench coat – that you couldn't find anywhere else. Mon–Sat 10am–10pm, Sun 11am–8pm.

CLOTHING

New York is one of the major nerve centres of the global fashion industry, and you'll find outposts for just about every major designer, with prices significantly lower than in European cities. The city's clothing stores are supplemented by a host of accessory specialists, with vendors dedicated to everything from jewellery and designer shades to bespoke luggage and the perfect suede boots.

NEW YORK DESIGNERS

Alexander Wang 103 Grand St, between Greene and Mercer sts ☎212 977 9683, ⓦalexanderwang.com; subway N, Q, R to Canal St; #6 to Spring St; map p.64. This avant-garde American designer has grown up to become an international brand, recognized for his very successful fashion collaborations with houses both high (Balenciaga) and fast (H&M). Mon–Sat 11am–7pm, Sun noon–6pm.

Diane von Fürstenberg (DVF) 874 Washington St, at W 14th St ☎646 486 4800, ⓦdvf.com; subway A, C, E, L to Eighth Ave; map p.107. Belgian-born, ex-German

28

princess who is now an NYC fashion powerhouse, best known for her iconic knitted-jersey wrap dress, sparkling party dresses and glittering clutches. Mon–Sat 11am–7pm, Sun 11am–6pm.

John Varvatos 122 Spring St, at Greene St ☎212 965 0700, ⓦjohnvarvatos.com; subway N, R to Prince St, #6 to Spring St; map p.64. Also at 315 Bowery, in the old CBGB space. Boxy though flattering casual wear and suits, plus the American designer's highly successful line of leather Converse trainers. Mon–Sat 11am–7pm, Sun noon–6pm.

★**Marc Jacobs** 163 Mercer St, between Houston and Prince sts ☎212 343 1490, ⓦmarcjacobs.com; subway N, R to Prince St; map p.64. Marc Jacobs rules the New York fashion world like a Cosmopolitan-sipping colossus. Style mavens from all walks of life come here to blow the nest egg on his latest "it" bag or pair of boots. Mon–Sat 11am–7pm, Sun noon–6pm.

Michael Kors 384 Bleecker St, at Perry St ☎212 242 0700, ⓦmichaelkors.com; subway #1 to Christopher St; map p.96. Classic American sportswear for women. Kors, a Long Island native, boosted his career by starring with Heidi Klum on *Project Runway*. Mon–Sat 10am–7pm, Sun 11am–6pm.

Morgane Le Fay 980 Madison Ave, between E 76th and E 77th sts ☎212 879 9700, ⓦmorganelefay.com; subway #6 to 77th St; map p.171. Ethereal, sombre-hued,

nearly frilly dresses that look like they'd be right at home on a heroine in a fairytale – but one about a wolf or a witch, not a prince missing his date. Mon–Sat 10am–6pm, Sun noon–5pm.

Proenza Schouler 822 Madison Ave, between E 68th and E 69th sts ☎212 585 3200, ⓦproenzaschouler.com; subway #6 to 68th St-Hunter College; map p.171. New York darlings Jack McCollough and Lazaro Hernandez (the label is named for their mothers) took off – and haven't showed any sign of slowing – when Barneys bought their college thesis back in 2002. This, their flagship, showcases Proenza's punky yet graceful style amid potted cacti and concrete walls. Mon–Thurs 11.30am–7pm, Fri & Sat 11am–7.30pm, Sun noon–6pm.

Supreme 274 Lafayette St, between Houston and Prince sts ☎212 966 7799, ⓦsupremenewyork.com; subway N, R to Prince St; map p.64. Founded here in 1994, Supreme is at the forefront of the luxury streetwear movement, selling clothing and equipment for die-hard skateboarders, hip-hop and modern punk fans. Mon–Thurs 11.30am–7pm, Fri & Sat 11am–7.30pm, Sun noon–6pm.

RETAIL TRENDSETTERS

Creatures of Comfort 205 Mulberry St, between Broadway and Kenmare sts ☎212 925 1005, ⓦcreaturesofcomfort.us; subway #6 to Spring St;

28

DESIGNER LABELS

Like museums filled with clothing instead of canvases, Manhattan's **designer stores** are experiences in themselves, worth visiting even if they're outside your budget. You'll find the most elegant outposts on the Upper East Side, but there are often additional, handsome gems in the Soho vicinity.

agnès b 1063 Madison Ave, between E 80th and E 81st sts ☎212 570 9333, ⓦusa.agnesb.com

Alexander McQueen 747 Madison Ave, between E 64th and E 65th sts ☎212 645 1797, ⓦalexander mcqueen.com

Balenciaga 148 Mercer St, between Prince and W Houston sts ☎212 206 0872, ⓦbalenciaga.com

Burberry 9 E 57th St, between Madison and Fifth aves ☎212 407 7100, ⓦus.burberry.com

Céline 870 Madison Ave, at E 71st St ☎212 535 3703, ⓦceline.com

Chanel 737 Madison Ave, at E 64th St ☎212 535 5505, ⓦchanel.com

Chloé 850 Madison Ave, at E 70th St ☎212 717 8220, ⓦchloe.com

Christian Dior 21 E 57th St, at Madison Ave ☎212 931 2950, ⓦdior.com

Comme des Garçons 520 W 22nd St, at Tenth Ave ☎212 604 9200, ⓦcomme-des-garcons.com

Dolce & Gabbana 717 Fifth Ave, at E 56th St ☎212

897 9653, ⓦdolcegabbana.com

Giorgio Armani 717 Fifth Ave, at E 56th St ☎212 209 3500, ⓦarmani.com

Gucci 725 Fifth Ave, at 56th St ☎212 826 2600, ⓦgucci.com

Lanvin 815 Madison Ave, between E 68th and E 69th sts ☎646 439 0380, ⓦlanvin.com

Marni 161 Mercer St, between Houston and Prince sts ☎212 343 3912, ⓦmarni.com

Miu Miu 11 E 57th St, between Fifth and Madison aves ☎212 641 2980, ⓦmiumiu.com

Prada 575 Broadway, at Prince St ☎212 334 8888, ⓦprada.com

Saint Laurent 3 E 57th St, at Fifth Ave ☎212 980 2970, ⓦysl.com

Stella McCartney 112 Greene St, between Prince and Spring sts ☎212 255 1556, ⓦstellamccartney .com

Versace 647 Fifth Ave, at E 52nd St ☎212 317 0224, ⓦversace.com map p.64. Appealing to a younger generation of fashion-savvy women, this high-end boutique offers beautifully presented wares – think suede boots by Acne Studios, colourful eyewear by Thierry Lasry and exquisite Japanese soaps on ropes – from its sunny, high-ceilinged Soho digs. Mon–Sat 11am–7pm, Sun noon–6pm.

Dover Street Market 160 Lexington Ave, between E 30th and E 31st sts ☎646 837 7750, ⓦdoverstreet market.com; subway #6 to 33rd St; map p.124. The mothership of retail trendsetters, a plain exterior hides this hyper-trendy Comme des Garçons "department store", seven whimsically designed floors that take their fashion very seriously. There's an arty café just inside the entrance, if you need to revive after rifling through all those racks. Mon–Sat 11am–7pm, Sun noon–6pm.

Maryam Nassir Zadeh 123 Norfolk St, at Rivington St ☎212 673 6405, ⓦmnzstore.com; subway F to Delancey St, J, M, Z to Essex St; map p.82. Indie clothes designer with great instincts and a cult following for her chic, lounge-y daywear and bright suede flats. Daily 11am–7pm.

Opening Ceremony 35 Howard St, between Broadway and Cosby St ☎212 219 2688, ⓦopeningceremony.us; subway J, N, Q, R, Z, #6 to Canal St; map p.71. Wildly popular boutique that has expanded to manufacture its own line and includes outposts in Tokyo and LA. The shop is four vibrantly decorated storeys, and filled to the rafters with colourful, edgy designs. Mon–Sat 11am–8pm, Sun noon–7pm.

BOUTIQUES

Intermix 1003 Madison Ave, at E 77th St ☎212 249 7858, ⓦintermixonline.com; subway #6 to 77th St; map p.171. Also 125 Fifth Ave, at E 20th St ☎212 533 9720; and 98 Prince St, between Mercer and Greene sts ☎212 966 5303. A flat-out fun place to shop, with a wide assortment of brands both high and low, and an admittedly confusing merchandise layout – they're called "intermix" for a reason. Mon–Thurs 10am–7.30pm, Fri & Sat 10am–8pm, Sun noon–7pm.

Jeffrey 449 W 14th St, between Ninth and Tenth aves ☎212 206 1272, ⓦjeffreynewyork.com; subway A, C, E to 14th St; map p.107. This all-white emporium is set in the heart of the cutting-edge Meatpacking District, with offerings from trend-setting lines like Louboutin and Thakoon. Very pricey, but a cool, surprisingly friendly spot to pop into. Mon–Wed & Fri 10am–8pm, Thurs 10am–9pm, Sat 10am–7pm, Sun 12.30–6pm.

Kirna Zabête 477 Broome St, between Wooster and Greene sts ☎212 941 9656, ⓦkirnazabete.com; subway N, R to Canal St; map p.64. One of the best of the downtown boutiques, this concept store stocks hand-picked highlights from designers such as Jason Wu, Phillip Lim and Proenza Schouler. Mon–Sat 11am–7pm, Sun noon–6pm.

Yumi Kim 105 Stanton St, at Ludlow St ☎212 420 5919, ⓦyumikim.com; subway F to Delancey St, J, M, Z to Essex St; map p.82. Also 1331 Third Ave, between E 76th and E 77th sts. Downtown-chic clothing by New York–based Kim Phan, whose silk printed dresses, vintage style and flirty prints have been a big hit since launching in 2004 (everything is 100 percent silk). Daily noon–7.30pm.

FLAGSHIPS

Abercrombie & Fitch 720 Fifth Ave, at W 56th St ☎212 306 0936, ⓦabercrombie.com; subway F to 57th St, N, Q, R to Fifth Ave-59th St; map p.124. Incredibly popular casualware brand, targeted at young adults – prepare for long queues of shoppers outside the store (prices here are often half the price of its UK outposts). Infamous for having bare-chested male models at the door. Mon–Sat 10am–8pm, Sun 11am–6pm.

Adidas 610 Broadway, between W Houston and Bleecker sts ☎212 529 0081, ⓦadidas.com; subway B, D, F, M to Broadway-Lafayette, #6 to Bleecker St; map p.64. Multi-storey temple dedicated to the triple-striped sneakers and gear famously celebrated by Run DMC. Some vintage stuff, but for old-school styles, you're better off at the Originals Store (136 Wooster St). Mon–Sat 10am–9pm, Sun 11am–8pm.

Forever 21 1540 Broadway, between W 45th and W 46th sts ☎212 302 0594, ⓦforever21.com; map p.142. The old Virgin Records space is now a behemoth teenage magnet, a sprawling space with floors of fashion, bumping tunes and display cases dedicated to various New York neighbourhoods – and it's open till 2am. Daily 8am–2am.

H&M 435 Seventh Ave, at W 34th St ☎855 466 7467, ⓦhm.com; map p.142. With four floors, 63,000 square feet and everything from trendy dresses to homeware, maternity and shoes, H&M's Herald Square juggernaut fulfils every need you could have for this affordable Swedish superpower and then some. Mon–Thurs 9am–10pm, Fri & Sat 9am–11pm, Sun 10am–9pm.

J. Crew 91 Fifth Ave, between E 16th and E 17th sts ☎212 255 4848, ⓦjcrew.com; map p.115. With a thumbs-up from Michelle Obama, this classic daywear brand, filled with cashmere, linen, stripes and bright colours, is enjoying a resurgence. Its flagship location stocks everything from womenswear, men's suits, stylish shoes and kids' clothing; plus it boasts a well-loved bridal department. Mon–Sat 10am–8pm, Sun 11am–7pm.

Niketown 6 E 57th St, at Fifth Ave ☎212 891 6453, ⓦnike.com; subway N, R to Fifth Ave-59th St; map p.124. Five-floor sports-shoe temple at the ready to outfit your entire family with athletic wear and bouncy sneakers. Mon–Sat 10am–8pm, Sun 11am–8pm.

Polo Ralph Lauren 711 Fifth Ave, between E 55th and E 56th sts ☎646 774 3900, ⓦralphlauren.com; subway E, M to Fifth Ave-53rd St, F to 57th St; map p.124. The master of all things preppy: buy a blazer at this distinguished shop

28

and try to get a seat at *Polo Bar* – reservations here are notoriously elusive. Daily 10am–9pm.

Topshop 478 Broadway, at Broome St ☎ 212 966 9555, ⓦ us.topshop.com; subway N, R to Prince St, #6 to Spring St; map p.64. Brits may be mildly amused, but America's first Topshop attracted round-the-block queues when it opened in 2009 (Top Girl herself Kate Moss cut the ribbon). Regular collaborations with of-the-moment designers and affordable prices keep the punters coming back. Mon–Sat 10am–9pm, Sun 11am–8pm.

★ **Uniqlo** 666 Fifth Ave, at 53rd St ☎ 877 486 4756, ⓦ uniqlo.com; subway E, M to 5th Ave-53rd St, F to 57th St; map p.124. Some of the best jeans in New York City, and ridiculously priced – one pair will set you back about $40 (or less), with free, same-day alterations. Original to Japan, this is the world's largest Uniqlo store, a wonderland of affordably priced button-downs, sherbet-coloured cashmere, fun socks, kids' gear, men's clothing and (in season) outerwear. Mon–Sat 10am–9pm, Sun 11am–8pm.

VINTAGE AND THRIFT

★ **Amarcord** 223 Bedford Ave, between N 4th and N 5th sts, Williamsburg ☎ 718 963 4001, ⓦ amarcord vintagefashion.com; subway L to Bedford Ave; map p.225. This place is a real find. The owners make regular trips through their home country of Italy in search of discarded Dior, Gucci, Yves Saint Laurent and so forth from the 1940s onward. Things aren't too expensive, especially considering all the pieces are in mint condition. Daily noon–8pm.

Antoinette 119 Grand St, between Berry St and Wythe Ave, Williamsburg ☎ 718 387 8664, ⓦ antoinette brooklyn.com; subway L to Bedford Ave; map p.225. Slim, inviting shop with effervescent staff, wide plank floors and a beautifully curated selection of vintage clothes. Named after the owner's fashion-industry mum, and inspired by her vast vintage collection, the store also

carries new clothing and wares made by Brooklyn designers. Mon–Sat noon–7pm, Sun noon–6pm.

AuH2O 84 E 7th St, between First and Second aves ☎ 212 466 0844, ⓦ auh2o.com; subway #6 to Astor Place, L to First Ave; map p.88. Excellent thrift store with a devoted following and a small but carefully chosen selection of items, most under $25. They also regularly put out a $10 and $5 rack. A gem. Daily noon–8pm.

★ **Awoke Vintage** 132 N 5th St, between Bedford Ave and Berry St, Williamsburg ☎ 718 387 3130, ⓦ awokevintage.com; subway L to Bedford Ave; map p.225. The name fits at this happy shop – bright clothes, white walls and an enthusiastic staff make for a little pocket of sunshine amidst Williamsburg's fashionable fray. The owner has a great eye; you won't leave disappointed. Good prices, too. Daily 10am–9pm.

Beacon's Closet 74 Guernsey St, between Berry St and Wythe Ave, Greenpoint, Brooklyn ☎ 718 486 0816, ⓦ beaconscloset.com; subway G to Nassau Ave; map p.225. Also 10 W 13th St, between Fifth and Sixth aves, West Village. Vast 5500-square-foot used-clothing paradise, with both modern fashions and vintage attire. Mon–Fri 11am–9pm, Sat & Sun 11am–8pm.

Buffalo Exchange 332 E 11th St, at Second Ave ☎ 212 260 9340, ⓦ buffaloexchange.com; subway L to First Ave; map p.88. Plus several other locations. US clothes exchange that started in Arizona in the 1970s; bring in your former threads for a trade-in or cash on the spot. Fancy jeans and fairly high-quality men's and women's clothes grace the store. Mon–Sat 11am–8pm, Sun noon–7pm.

Domsey Express 431 Broadway, at Hewes St, Williamsburg ☎ 718 384 6000; subway J, M to Hewes St; map p.225. This five-storey thrift store sells everything from boutique pieces to boot-camp salvage. Plan to rifle ruthlessly; most of the offerings here are workaday basics from brands like Old Navy. Mon–Fri 9am–6pm, Sat

28

DENIM DOCTORS, SHOE SAVIOURS AND HANDBAG HOSPITALS

It may be a great place to shop, but New York wears on your clothes – with all the walking and gritty sidewalks, shoes in particular take a beating. The following shops are dedicated to keeping your goods in tip-top shape.

Artbag 1130 Madison Ave, at 84th St ☎ 212 744 2720, ⓦ artbag.com. If your favourite bag suffers a tear or stain, head to this landmark Upper East Side shop, established over eighty years ago (long enough to know its way around a crocodile clutch), which specializes in repairing vintage items. Pricey. Mon–Fri 9.30am–5pm, Sat 10am–4pm.

Denim Therapy 555 Eighth Ave (Suite 910), at W 38th St ☎ 347 935 0089, ⓦ denimtherapy.com. As if by magic, this specialist shop can make holes and rips disappear from your jeans; additional services include

zipper replacement, hemline adjustment and monogramming. Mon & Tues 10am–7pm, Fri 10am–6pm.

★ **Pavlos Shoe Repair** 125 E 88th St, between Lexington and Park aves ☎ 212 876 8569. In a city chock-a-block with excellent cobblers, Pavlos stands out as the best of the best. It's so esteemed in the community that Parsons professors send their design students here to study the art of shoemaking. Cash only. Mon–Fri 7.30am–6pm, Sat 8am–5pm.

SAVAGE BEAUTY: NEW YORK STYLE

The joy of New York style is its wanton expressionism. Residents here are competitive, and they like to look their best, priding themselves on wearing what is different and exciting – whether that preference is to teeter in Louboutins or bicycle in bright *huaraches*.

Manhattan is rich with fashion history, much of it celebrated in film and popular culture. The effervescent Holly Golightly, who epitomized the city's fascination with casual-meets-formal, wore ankle-length Givenchy while gazing at Tiffany's and eating breakfast from a paper bag. In the 1980s, Madonna sped around town in *Desperately Seeking Susan* wearing crop tops, lace, bright red lipstick and punk rock bedazzlement – the city has never looked better. Possibly the best example of resident appreciation for clothing-meets-culture, however, was **Alexander McQueen**'s show, "Savage Beauty", at the Metropolitan Museum. Displaying the fashion designer's vast collection of work, "Beauty" garnered historic attendance and rave reviews; enthusiasts waited as long as four hours to view galleries, and on its final day, the Met remained open until midnight for the first time in its 140-year history.

11am–5.30pm, Sun 10am–7pm.

★**Edith Machinist** 104 Rivington St, at Ludlow St ☎212 979 9992; subway F to Delancey St, J, M, Z to Essex St; map p.82. Extremely popular with the trendy vintage set, this used-clothing emporium holds some amazing finds (particularly shoes) along its well-curated racks and displays. Mon, Fri & Sun noon–6pm, Tues–Thurs & Sat noon–7pm.

Gabay's Outlet 195 Avenue A, between E 12th and E 13th sts ☎212 254 3180, ⓦgabaysoutlet.com; subway L to First Ave; map p.88. An East Village store crammed with good deals on labels like Prada, Chanel and Saint Laurent. Excellent handbag selection and (surprisingly) designer furniture, too. Mon–Wed & Sun 11am–7pm, Thurs–Sat 11am–8pm.

Housing Works Thrift Shop 143 W 17th St, between Sixth and Seventh aves ☎718 838 5050, ⓦhousingworks .org; subway #1 to 18th St; map p.107. Plus several other locations. Upscale thrift stores where you can find secondhand designer pieces in very good condition. All proceeds benefit Housing Works, an AIDS charity. Mon–Fri 10am–7pm, Sat 10am–6pm, Sun noon–5pm.

INA 15 Bleecker St, at Elizabeth St ☎212 228 8511, ⓦinanyc.com; subway B, D, F, M to Broadway-Lafayette, N, R to Prince St, #6 to Bleecker St; map p.88. Long-standing designer-consignment shop well stocked with barely worn pieces by top-tier designers. Mon–Sat noon–8pm, Sun noon–7pm.

Michael's Consignment 1041 Madison Ave, at 79th St ☎212 737 7273, ⓦmichaelsconsignment.com; subway #6 to 77th St; map p.171. Consignment stores on the Upper East Side are one of the world's best-kept secrets for vintage, and Michael's – going strong since 1954 – is foremost on that list. You'll find the top of the line here: Missoni, Chloé, Louboutin and more. Mon–Sat 10am–6.30pm (Thurs till 8pm), Sun noon–6pm (closed Sun July & Aug).

Resurrection 45 Great Jones St, between Lafayette St and Bowery ☎212 625 1374, ⓦresurrectionvintage .com; subway B, D, F, M to Broadway-Lafayette, N, R to

Prince St, #6 to Bleecker St; map p.71. The best high-end place for vintage clothing in the city, with first-class Pucci and Halston classics from the '60s to the '80s. The prices are high, but it's worth visiting just to check out the Versace gowns and python Dior jackets. Mon–Sat 11am–7pm.

Screaming Mimi's 240 W 14th St, between Seventh and Eighth aves ☎212 677 6464, ⓦscreamingmimis .com; subway A, C, E, L to Eighth Ave; map p.88. One of the most well-established lower-end secondhand stores in Manhattan. All sorts of vintage offerings, including costumes, bags, shoes and housewares, at reasonable prices. Mon–Sat noon–8pm, Sun 1–7pm.

Tokio 7 83 E 7th St, between First and Second aves ☎212 353 8443, ⓦtokio7.net; subway #6 to Astor Place; map p.88. Attractive secondhand and vintage designer consignment items; known for its flashy, eccentric selection – think plenty of Gaultier, Moschino and McQueen – rather than basic black. Daily noon–8pm.

What Comes Around Goes Around 351 W Broadway, between Broome and Grand sts ☎212 343 1225, ⓦwhatgoesaroundnyc.com; subway A, C, E to Canal St; map p.64. Established and well-loved downtown vintage store. Popular with magazine stylists borrowing pieces for shoots. Mon–Sat 11am–8pm, Sun noon–7pm.

LINGERIE

Agent Provocateur 133 Mercer St, at Prince St ☎212 965 0229, ⓦagentprovocateur.com; subway N, R to Prince St; map p.64. New York outpost of the saucy, sexy, luxury lingerie line, co-owned by Joe Corré, son of avant-garde designer Vivienne Westwood. Think frills, bows and lashings of lace. Mon–Sat 11am–7pm, Sun noon–6pm.

Town Shop 2270 Broadway, between 81st and 82nd sts ☎212 595 6600, ⓦtownshop.com; subway #1 to 79th St; map p.184. Upper West Side undergarment institution that has been sizing and fitting women for over a century. Go once and you'll be hooked for life. Mon–Fri 10am–7pm, Sat 9.30am–6pm, Sun 11am–6pm.

ACCESSORIES

Flight 001 96 Greenwich Ave, at W 12th St ☎ 212 989 0001, ⓦ flight001.com; subway A, C, E to 14th St; map p.96. The best place for luggage in the city, from Hideo to Rimoma, plus a stylish selection of travel accessories (alarm clocks, adapters, speciality mini-toiletries) and books. Mon–Sat 11am–8pm, Sun noon–6pm.

★ **J.J. Hat Center** 310 Fifth Ave, between W 31st and W 32nd sts ☎ 212 239 4368, ⓦ jjhatcenter.com; subway #6 to 33rd St, N, R to 28th St; map p.115. Boaters, bebops, porkpies, bogarts, straw weaves – even just the names sound fun at this classic millinery, established in 1911 and offering great service and customized hats ever since. Mon–Fri 10am–7pm, Sat 10am–6pm.

Meg Cohen Design 59 Thompson St, between Spring and Broome sts ☎ 212 966 3733, ⓦ megcohendesign .com; subway C, E to Spring St; map p.64. Sweet Soho boutique, with a superb collection of high-quality yet fairly priced cashmere scarves, hats and gloves. Mon–Fri 10am–7pm, Sat 10am–6pm, Sun 11am–6pm.

Moscot 108 Orchard St, at Delancey St ☎ 212 477 3796, ⓦ moscot.com; subway F to Delancey St, J, M, Z to Essex St; map p.82. Charming eyewear stalwart (established in 1915) that has moved seamlessly with the times. Its frames are favoured by everyone, from hipsters to grandparents, socialites and bookworms. Mon–Fri 10am–7pm, Sat

10am–6pm, Sun 11am–6pm.

Rain or Shine Umbrellas 45 E 45th St, between Madison and Vanderbilt aves ☎ 212 741 9650, ⓦ rainorshine.com; subway #4, #5, #6, #7 to Grand Central-42nd St; map p.124. Old-timey shop carrying every type of umbrella under the sun (or thundercloud). Plenty of beautiful luxury brands, including numerous imports, but there are also great finds in the $40 range. Mon–Wed & Fri 10am–6.30pm, Thurs 10am–7pm, Sat 10am–6pm, Sun only when it's raining.

Warby Parker 161 Sixth Ave, between Vandam and Spring sts ☎ 646 517 5223, ⓦ warbyparker.com; subway C, E to Spring St; map p.64. Also at 121 Greene St. Every cool cat in town (well, everyone with less than 20/20 vision) owns a pair of Warby Parker frames. The brand originated here in 2010; pop into this space, its headquarters, to see the magic happen or to browse its pale-wood boutique, full of reasonably priced shades and scrips. Bonus: for each pair of glasses sold, one is donated to a person in need. Daily 10am–6pm.

★ **Yestadt Millinery** ⓦ yestadtmillinery.com. Beloved by the fashion industry, local artisan Molly Yestadt creates incredible hats – be it a dressy number for the Kentucky Derby, a perfect, unfrilly lace wedding veil, or a lush cashmere cap to spice up your winterwear. There is currently no bricks-and-mortar shop; check the website for order details.

28

JEWELLERY

Few stores anywhere can claim the iconic status of Tiffany & Co, but there are many other exceptional jewellers in New York. If stones are your thing, be sure to pay a visit to the hectic stalls in Diamond Row (see box below).

Annex Markets W 25th St, between Broadway and Sixth Ave ☎ 212 243 5343, ⓦ annexmarkets.com; subway F, N, R, #1, #6 to 23rd St; map p.107. Also Hell's

Kitchen market at W 39th St and Ninth Ave; subway A, C, E, to Port Authority-42nd St; map p.142. Two alfresco, weekend-only fairs, one uptown, one a few short blocks

---

THE DIAMOND DISTRICT

Marked by quasi-bejewelled lampposts, the strip of **47th Street between Fifth and Sixth avenues** is known as the Diamond District. At street level are dozens of retail shops and more than twenty specialist marts known as "exchanges" – combined, they sell more fine jewellery than any other area in the world. There are separate dealers for different gems, gold and silver – even dealers who will string your beads for you, appraisers and "findings" stores where you can pick up the basic makings of do-it-yourself jewellery, like chains and earring posts. Some jewellers trade only among themselves; some sell retail; and others do business by appointment only. Most shops are open Monday to Saturday 10am to 5.30pm, though a few close on Friday afternoon and Saturday for religious reasons, and the standard vacation time is from the end of June to the second week in July.

It is very important that you shop armed with some information. Research what you are looking for and be as clear as possible. If at all feasible, it's best to go to someone who has been specifically recommended. For a listing of all the district's vendors, shopping tips and the "Buyers Bill of Rights", visit ⓦ diamonddistrict.org.

If you want to get your jewellery graded or appraised, try the Gemological Institute of America at 50 W 47th St, unit 400 (Mon–Thurs 8am–6pm, Fri 8am–5pm; ☎ 800 366 8519, ⓦ gia.edu), or the Universal Gemological Laboratory at 71 W 47th St, suite 1002 (☎ 212 921 3324, ⓦ uglinc.com).

from the Flatiron Building. There's a superb array of vintage wares, but the best treasure is the jewellery selection. See p.387.

★**Ted Meuhling** 52 White St, at Broadway ☎ 212 431 3825, ⊕ tedmeuhling.com; subway J, N, Q, R, Z, #6 to Canal St; map p.64. Occasionally called upon to moonlight as a curator for the Cooper-Hewitt Museum, Ted Meuhling is a design superstar who flies under the radar. His jewellery, presented here in a narrow, earthy space, is a mix of delicate gold pieces paired with pops of turquoise and chalcedony. Tues–Sat noon–6pm.

Tiffany & Co 727 Fifth Ave, at E 57th St, subway N, R to Fifth Ave-59th St ☎ 212 755 8000, ⊕ tiffany.com; map p.124. Even if you're just window-shopping, Tiffany's is worth a visit, its soothing green marble and weathered wood interior best described by Truman Capote's fictional Holly Golightly: "It calms me down right away… nothing very bad could happen to you there." Mon–Sat 10am–7pm, Sun noon–6pm.

COSMETICS

All department stores stock the main brands of **beauty products** – as does Century 21 (see p.378), often at a heavy discount, but if you're looking for hard-to-find cosmetics lines, these are the best options.

★**Aedes de Venustas** 7 Greenwich Ave, between W 10th and Christopher sts ☎ 212 206 8674, ⊕ aedes .com; subway A, B, C, D, E, F, M to W 4th St, #1 to Christopher St; map p.96. Enchanting fragrance purveyor, housed in a slender shop that's filled with ornate, gilded furniture, chandeliers and enormous flower arrangements. You'll find plenty of international offerings and perfume rarities; best of all, they'll wrap your purchase in fresh blooms. Mon–Sat noon–8pm, Sun 1–7pm.

Aesop 232 Elizabeth St, between Prince and E Houston sts ☎ 212 431 4411, ⊕ aesop.com; subway N, R to Prince St, #6 to Spring St; map p.71. Plus several other locations. The current darling of the skincare industry, Aussie-borne Aesop crafts lush, all-natural products such as bergamot face wash and geranium leaf body scrub. The store is spare but inviting, with a big farm sink, slate walls and cherrywood shelves. Daily 11am–8pm.

★**C.O. Bigelow Chemists** 414 Sixth Ave, between W

BEST SPAS FOR STEAMING, SOOTHING AND REJUVENATING

New York is crammed with all sorts of spas and steam baths in which to escape the hectic streets outside, from rooms caked in sea salt to Japanese-style retreats. These are some of the best places to relax for a few hours.

Aire Ancient Baths 88 Franklin St, between Church St and Franklin Place ☎ 212 374 3777, ⊕ ancient bathsnyc.com. Originating in Spain, but based on the Roman bath tradition, this shrine to soaking has three candlelit pools of varying temperatures, jacuzzi tubs and a steam room. It's $80 for 90min access to all facilities; massages and aromatherapy are available as extras. Occasional live flamenco music adds to the romantic ambience. Daily 9am–11pm.

Bliss 568 Broadway, 2/F, between Houston and Prince sts ☎ 212 965 8599, ⊕ blissworld.com. Also two locations in Midtown. Top-notch spa, now an international brand, with massage, facial, nail and wax services. There's a bevy of beauty potions to purchase, including the spa's own popular lotions and the full line of Crème de la Mer skin products. Daily 9am–9pm.

Mermaid Spa 3703 Mermaid Ave, Brooklyn ☎ 347 462 2166, ⊕ seagatebaths.com. Best Russian baths in the city; just $45/visit. Note that you'll have to schlep out to Coney Island, however. Daily 8am–midnight.

Moonflower 8 E 41st St, 3/F, between Madison and Fifth aves ☎ 212 683 8729, ⊕ moonflowerspa.com. Tranquil, affordable Japanese spa offering up some of

the city's best facials (great for deep-tissue massages, too). Mon & Wed–Fri 11am–9pm, Sat & Sun 11am–8pm.

Ohm 260 Fifth Ave, 5/F, between W 28th and W 29th sts ☎ 212 845 9812, ⊕ ohmspa.com. Tasteful yet unfrilly decor makes this excellent day-spa an appealing option for both men and women. Try the 30-30 massage and facial package ($169). Mon–Fri 10am–8.30pm, Sat 10am–7.30pm, Sun 11am–6.30pm.

The Spa at Mandarin Oriental 80 Columbus Circle, between Broadway and Columbus Ave ☎ 212 805 8880, ⊕ mandarinoriental.com. Ultra-luxurious spa in the *Mandarin Oriental* hotel; treatments start at $225, but you'll feel like royalty. Daily 9am–9pm.

Spa Castle 131-10 Eleventh Ave, College Point, Queens ☎ 718 939 6300, ⊕ spacastleusa.com. Also 115 E 57th St, Midtown. With five storeys, four pools, numerous restaurants and a "valley" of saunas (one is lined with gold, another with polished jade), Spa Castle is a pleasure-dome dedicated to leisure and rejuvenation. It's way up in Queens, but worth the effort (the Manhattan venue is smaller and less fun). Weekend day-pass $50, weekday $40. Daily 6am–midnight.

28

8th and W 9th sts ☎ 212 533 2700, ⓦ bigelowchemists
.com; subway A, B, C, D, E, F, M to W 4th St, #1 to
Christopher St; map p.96. Established in 1882, C.O.
Bigelow is one of the oldest pharmacies in the country –
and that's exactly how it looks, with the original Victorian
shopfittings still in place. Specializing in lesser-known and
European beauty brands, this is the place to come for
beauty and cosmetic items that you can't find elsewhere in
the city. Mon–Fri 7.30am–9pm, Sat 8.30am–7pm, Sun
8.30am–5.30pm.

Harmon Face Values 675 Sixth Ave, between W 21st
St and W 22nd St ☎ 212 243 3501, ⓦ harmondiscount
.com; subway F, M to 23rd St; map p.107. Sleek discount
shop, offering cut-rate prices on every type of beauty
product imaginable, and overseen by a friendly, helpful
staff. Basically, it's a total Manhattan anomaly, well worth
popping into. Mon–Sat 10am–9pm, Sun 10am–7pm.

Kiehl's 109 Third Ave, between E 13th and E 14th sts
☎ 212 677 3171, ⓦ kiehls.com; subway L to Third Ave,
N, R, Q, L, #4, #5, #6 to Union Square; map p.88.
Decorated with aviation and motorcycle memorabilia, this
150-year-old pharmacy sells its own range of natural-
ingredient-based classic creams, oils and so on. Known for
giving out plenty of samples to customers, whether you're
buying or not. Lots of celebs swear by this stuff, especially
the patented Crème de Corps body lotion. Mon–Sat
10am–9pm, Sun 11am–7pm.

MAC Cosmetics 506 Broadway, between Spring and
Broome sts ☎ 212 334 4641, ⓦ maccosmetics.com;
subway #6 to Spring St; map p.64. Also 689 Fifth Ave,
Times Square, and several other locations. MAC is
known for both its high-quality, non-animal-tested

cosmetics and its HIV/AIDS fundraising (pick up a Viva Glam
lipstick to donate). Home of the famed Ruby Woo lipstick,
popular with models and celebs. Mon–Sat 10am–9pm,
Sun 11am–8pm.

MiN New York Apothecary & Atelier 117 Crosby St,
between Houston and Prince sts ☎ 212 206 6366,
ⓦ min.com; subway N, R to Prince St, #6 to Spring St;
map p.64. Stylish boutique offering a range of niche
brands, fragrances and beauty products for both men and
women. Mon & Sun noon–6pm, Tues–Sat 11am–7pm.

Ricky's 590 Broadway, between Houston and Prince sts
☎ 212 226 5552, ⓦ rickysnyc.com; subway N, R to
Prince St; map p.64. Plus several other locations. New
York's haven for the overdone, the brash and the OTT (think
drag favourites and plenty of lurid wigs). Stocks cool
brands like Urban Decay and Tony & Tina as well as a house
line of products. Mon–Sat 10am–9pm, Sun 11am–8pm.

Sephora 555 Broadway, between Prince and Spring sts
☎ 212 625 1309, ⓦ sephora.com; subway N, R to Prince
St, #6 to Spring St; map p.64. Plus several locations
downtown. A cosmetics wonderland where the perfumes,
make-up and body-care products are systematically
organized and everything is at the ready for sampling and
dabbing on your friends. Mon–Sat 10am–9pm, Sun
11am–8pm.

★**Zitomer** 969 Madison Ave, at E 76th St ☎ 212 737
5560, ⓦ zitomer.com; subway #6 to 77th St; map
p.171. A venerable pharmacy that has transformed itself
into a full-blown mini-department store, Zitomer serves
the beauty and cosmetic needs of the Fifth Ave gentry.
Stocked to the gills with every brand and item imaginable.
Mon–Fri 9am–8pm, Sat 9am–7pm, Sun 10am–6pm.

28

SHOES

In addition to vending plenty of upscale heels, New York is the sneaker capital of the world, and it's great fun browsing
Niketown (see p.380), the Adidas flagship (see p.380), or one of the high-end boutiques devoted to exclusive trainers.
Barneys and Bloomingdale's are both known for their selection of fancy footwear, while the greatest concentration of
bargain shoe shops is in the Village on West 8th Street, between University Place and Sixth Avenue, and on Broadway
below West 8th Street.

John Fluevog 250 Mulberry St, at Prince St ☎ 212 431
4484, ⓦ fluevog.com; subway N, R to Prince St; map
p.71. Innovative designs for a walk about town – most
styles are casual but quirky, with buckles or brightly

coloured detailing. Mon–Sat 11am–8pm, Sun
noon–7pm.

Jutta Neumann 355 E 4th St, between aves C and D
☎ 212 982 7048, ⓦ juttaneumann-newyork.com;

SAMPLE SALES

At the beginning of each fashion season, designers' and manufacturers' showrooms are full of
leftover merchandise. These pieces are removed via informal **sample sales**, held throughout
the year. You'll always save at least fifty percent (and up to ninety!) off the retail price, though
you may not be able to try on the clothes and you can never return them. Always take plenty
of cash with you; some sales will not accept credit cards. The best way to find out what sales
are coming up is to check the current issues of *Time Out New York* (see p.29) and *New York*
magazine (see p.29), or follow the Twitter feeds of your favourite designers.

subway F to Second Ave-Lower East Side; map p.88. Her custom-designed, super-comfy sandals are all the rage downtown, and she also sells popular leather handbags. Mon–Fri noon–7pm, Sat 1–6pm.

Kith 644 Broadway, at Bleecker St ☎ 646 648 6285, ⓦ kithnyc.com; subway B, D, F, M to Broadway-Lafayette, #6 to Bleecker St; map p.64. Also 233 Flatbush Ave in Brooklyn. Posh sneakers (including the shop's own brand), loungewear and backpacks displayed in a gorgeous, arty space of wood plank floors, neon lights and a ceiling covered with *papier-mâché* high-tops. Mon–Sat 10am–9pm, Sun 11am–8pm.

Louboutin 967 Madison Ave, between E 75th and E 76th St ☎ 212 396 1884, ⓦ us.christianlouboutin.com; subway #6 to 77th St; map p.171. The new Blahnik, this French superstar has set the high-heel world ablaze with its arresting red-soled designs. A small shop, but with a great selection (including men's) and impeccable service.

Mon–Sat 10am–6pm.

Manolo Blahnik 31 W 54th St, at Fifth Ave ☎ 212 582 3007, ⓦ manoloblahnik.com; subway E, M to Fifth Ave-53rd St; map p.124. Skyrocketing to fame thanks to Carrie Bradshaw's fondness for them in *Sex and the City,* this Spanish designer's strappy stilettos remain as popular as ever. Mon–Fri 10.30am–6pm, Sat 10.30am–5.30pm, Sun noon–5pm.

★ **Moulded Shoe** 10 E 39th St, between Madison and Fifth aves ☎ 212 683 9389, ⓦ mouldedshoeny.com; subway #4, #5, #6, #7 to Grand Central-42nd St; map p.124. Men flock all the way from Paris and Milan to this family-run shop, a craftsman of customized shoes since the 1940s. They're famed for the coveted "Alden modified last", produced in dress styles ranging from wing tips to medallion caps. Mon–Fri 9.30am–6pm, Sat 10am–5pm (closed Sat in July & Aug).

NEW YORK NOVELTY

Manhattan is home to hundreds of unique, obscure and just plain crazy independent stores, though these are increasingly being pushed to the outer boroughs. Details of specialist book and comic stores (see p.389) and record stores (see p.390) appear later in the chapter.

28

Brooklyn Superhero Supply Co. 372 Fifth Ave, between Fifth and Sixth sts, Park Slope ☎ 718 499 9884, ⓦ superherosupplies.com; subway F, G, R to Fourth Ave; map p.231. At this kids' favourite that doubles as a laudable non-profit, you can buy everything a cartoon crime fighter needs, toss your friends into the "de-villainizer", test the air flow of different capes and pick up an "evil blob containment capsule" for the subway ride home. Daily 11am–5pm.

Exit 9 51 Ave A, between E 3rd and E 4th sts ☎ 212 228 0145, ⓦ shopexit9.com; subway F to Lower East Side-Second Ave; map p.88. Also 127 Smith St, Brooklyn. Kooky emporium of kitsch, stocking soaps, bags, cards and various other offbeat goodies – great for last-minute gifts. Mon–Fri 11am–7.30pm, Sat 11am–8pm, Sun noon–7pm.

Obscura Antiques and Oddities 207 Ave A, between E 12th and E 13th sts ☎ 212 505 9251, ⓦ obscuraantiques .com; subway L to First Ave; map p.88. This spooky East Village classic specializes in antiques, rare taxidermy and strange, freaky artefacts – owners Mike Zohn and Evan Michelson even have a show on the Discovery Channel

(*Oddities*). Daily noon–8pm.

Posteritati 239 Centre St, between Broome and Grand sts ☎ 212 226 2207, ⓦ posteritati.com; subway #6 to Spring St; map p.71. Over nine thousand movie posters, ranging from classics like *20,000 Leagues Under the Sea* and *Goldfinger* to modern blockbusters like *Avatar.* Tues–Sat 11am–7pm.

Toy Tokyo Shop 91 Second Ave, between E 5th and E 6th sts ☎ 212 673 5424, ⓦ toytokyo.com; subway #6 to Astor Place; map p.88. Dizzying ensemble of Asian toys and cult memorabilia, mostly from Japan: action figures, vintage robots, roto-plastic figures and wind-ups. Mon–Thurs & Sun 1–9pm, Fri & Sat 12.30–9.30pm.

The Uncommons 230 Thompson St, between E 5th and E 6th sts ☎ 646 543 9215, ⓦ uncommonsnyc.com; subway A, B, C, D, E, F, M to W 4th St; map p.96. Get your nerd on at this enjoyable little board-game café with craft beer and wine, great coffee, snacks and an enormous selection of diversions (over seven hundred, rented for $5/ person). Mon–Thurs 8.30am–midnight, Fri & Sat 8.30am–1am, Sun 8.30am–11pm.

ARTS AND CRAFTS

Beads of Paradise 16 E 17th St, between Broadway and Fifth Ave ☎ 212 620 0642, ⓦ beadsofparadisenyc .com; subway N, R, Q, L, #4, #5, #6 to Union Square; map p.115. Beads originating from all corners of the globe (Africa and Southeast Asia are specialities), arranged here in dazzling chromatic and textural schemes. Great for gifts, but they also do lessons and workshops, and can help

re-string necklaces in need. Mon–Sat 11am–7.30pm, Sun noon–6.30pm.

Brooklyn Women's Exchange 55 Pierrepont St, between Henry and Hicks sts, Brooklyn Heights ☎ 718 624 3435, ⓦ brooklyn-womens-exchange.org; subway #2, #3 to Clark St; map p.218. A crafts co-operative that dates back more than 150 years, the Exchange offers lots of handmade toys, clothes, bedding and jewellery. Tues–Fri 11am–6pm, Sat & Sun 11am–5pm.

★ **Casey Rubber Stamps** 322 E 11th St, between First and Second aves ☎ 917 669 4151, ⓦ caseyrubberstamps .com; subway #6 to Astor Place, L to First Ave; map p.88. Teensy, characterful *Casey's* overflows with kooky stamps depicting everything under the sun: from birds and Victoriana to stringed instruments and stacks of skeleton bones. All the stamps are made in-house, and they can even craft you a customized one – great for take-home gifts or party invitations. Mon 2–8pm, Tues–Sat 1–8pm, Sun 2.30–7pm.

CW Pencil Enterprise 100 Forsyth St, between Grand and Broome sts ☎ 917 734 8117, ⓦ cwpencils.com; subway B, D to Grand St, F to Delancey St; map p.82. Enchanting little shop that's a love letter to the world's humblest writing instrument: the pencil. Heart-shaped, jasmine-scented, the classic No. 2 and even the elusive Blackwing 602 – favoured by Nabokov, Steinbeck and Quincy Jones – the gang is all here and elegantly displayed alongside erasers, notebooks and cases. Check website for hours.

La Sirena 27 E 3rd St, between the Bowery and Second Ave ☎ 212 780 9113, ⓦ lasirenanyc.com; subway #6 to Bleecker St, F to Second Ave; map p.88. Mexican folk-art store selling pieces direct from Mexico, everything from museum-quality items to brilliantly coloured, traditional marketplace merchandise like serapes, sombreros and religious icons. Daily noon–7pm.

Michaels 675 Sixth Ave, between W 21st St and W 22nd St ☎ 646 259 3911, ⓦ michaels.com; subway F, M to 23rd St; map p.107. If you have even a remote interest in crafts, a visit to this enormous flagship is a must-do while touring New York City. Fabric markers, poster frames, stencils, glitter, holiday decor and basically anything else your creative little heart desires, ready for the picking. Mon–Sat 9am–10pm, Sun 10am–8pm.

Purl Soho 459 Broome St, between Greene and Mercer sts ☎ 212 780 9113, ⓦ purlsoho.com; subway J, N, Q, Z to Canal St, #6 to Spring St; map p.64. Knitter's paradise, with an exceptional selection of plush skeins, in a huge spectrum of colours and materials. Great notions too, like bias tape and hard-to-find zippers. Pricey. Mon–Fri noon–7pm, Sat & Sun noon–6pm.

Soho Art Materials 7 Wooster St, between Canal and Grand sts ☎ 212 431 3938, ⓦ sohoartmaterials.com; subway A, C, E, N, Q, R, W to Canal St; map p.64. Carries all manner of paints and brushes, printmaking supplies and drawing materials (charcoal to pastels), along with portfolios in which to carry the finished products. Mon–Sat 10am–7pm, Sun noon–5pm.

28

FLORISTS

Miho Kosuda 310 E 44th St, between First and Second aves ☎ 212 922 9122; subway #4, #5, #6, #7 to 42nd St-Grand Central; map p.124. Manhattan's most esteemed master of flower arrangements, a bouquet sent from Miho is like an engagement ring by Harry Winston – the crème de la crème. Extremely expensive; expect to pay $300. Mon–Fri 10am–6pm.

★ **Saffron** 31 Hanson Place, between Saint Felix and Fort Greene Place, Fort Greene ☎ 718 852 6053, ⓦ saffron-brooklyn.com; subway B, D, N, Q, R, #2, #3, #4, #5 to Atlantic Ave; map p.218. In a little unassuming storefront off a main Brooklyn drag, husband-and-wife team Kana and Tetsuji, both artists, create stunning bouquets of unusual blooms, many imported from Japan. Very fairly priced. Mon, Wed, Thurs & Fri noon–8pm, Sat 11am–7pm, Sun 11am–5pm.

FLEA MARKETS AND CRAFT FAIRS

New York **flea markets** are good hunting grounds for vintage and outrageous clothes, collectibles, jewellery and crafts; there's also any number of odd places – car parks, playgrounds or maybe just an extra-wide bit of pavement – where people set up to sell their wares, especially in spring and summer, as well as weekly street fairs. Note also that in December you'll find major Christmas gift and **craft markets** at Union Square (ⓦ urbanspacenyc.org) and Bryant Park (ⓦ bryantpark.org).

Annex Markets W 25th St, between Broadway and Sixth Ave ☎ 212 243 5343, ⓦ annexmarkets.com; subway F, N, R, #1, #6 to 23rd St; map p.107. Also Hell's Kitchen market at W 39th St and Ninth Ave; subway A, C, E, to Port Authority-42nd St; map p.107. Two year-round weekend-only markets, with hundreds of vendors who peddle all sorts of old knick-knacks, the city's best collection of antique jewellery, art, toys, furniture and more. Chelsea: Sat & Sun 6.30am–6pm; Hell's Kitchen: Sat & Sun 9am–5pm.

Brooklyn Flea 100 Sixth Ave, between Watts and Grand sts, Soho; 80 Pearl St, at Front St, Dumbo, ⓦ brooklynflea.com; subway #1, A, C, E to Canal St; F to York St; map p.64 & p.218. The "flea" epithet is a bit of a misnomer, as this is as much a high-quality arts and crafts fair as it is a secondhand bazaar, with eighty stalls and superb artisan food thrown in. The Sunday Dumbo fair takes place outside, under a beautiful archway of the Manhattan Bridge. Smorgasburg (see p.392) is a food and drink spin-off. April–Oct only. Soho: Sat & Sun 10am–6pm; Dumbo: Sun 10am–6pm.

Hester Street Fair Hester and Essex sts ⓦ hesterstreetfair.com; subway F to East Broadway;

map p.82. Hip flea and craft market best known for its gourmet food stalls, including *La Sonrisa empanadas*, *Macaron Parlor, La Newyorkina* popsicles and *Luke's Lobster*. April–Oct Sat 11am–6pm.

BOOKS

New York is a paradise for book lovers. Despite the challenge of Amazon.com and the internet in general, there are still more independent **booksellers** here than in most other parts of America. Quick literary fixes can be easily taken care of, too – superstores like Barnes & Noble (ⓦ barnesandnoble.com) also have a presence in New York.

GENERAL INTEREST AND NEW BOOKS

★**Bookbook** 266 Bleecker St, between Sixth and Seventh aves ☎ 212 807 8655, ⓦ bookbooknyc.com; subway #1 to Christopher Place; map p.96. The old Biography Bookshop was reincarnated here in 2010, with an appealing roster of recent and backlist fiction, children's books, travel, history, drama, cookbooks, art and fashion titles. Mon–Thurs & Sun 11am–10pm, Fri & Sat 11am–11pm.

★**Book Culture** 2915 Broadway at W 114th St ☎ 646 403 3000, ⓦ bookculture.com; subway #1 to Cathedral Parkway-110th St; map p.184. The newer main shop of the largest independent bookstore in the city (the first Book Culture, now mostly academic-oriented, remains at 536 W 112th St) boasts a fine selection of literary (especially international) fiction, children's books and much more. Mon–Fri 9am–11pm, Sat 10am–11pm, Sun 10am–10pm.

McNally Jackson 52 Prince St, between Mulberry and Lafayette sts ☎ 212 274 1160, ⓦ mcnallyjackson.com; subway N, R to Prince St; map p.71. This Canadian book chain has gained a foothold in the heart of Manhattan with its prime Soho location. Great service, and the staff here are friendly, too. Mon–Sat 10am–10pm, Sun 10am–9pm.

Powerhouse Arena 28 Adams St, between Water and Front sts, Dumbo ☎ 718 666 3049, ⓦ powerhousearena .com; subway F to York St; map p.218. With a stunning setting beside the Brooklyn and Manhattan bridges, this spacious loft offers a stellar browsing experience and draws a fun scene for book signings and its other (frequent) events. Mon–Sat 11am–7pm, Sun 11am–6pm.

Shakespeare & Co. 939 Lexington Ave, between E 68th and E 69th sts ☎ 212 570 0201, ⓦ shakeandco .com; #6 train to 68th St; map p.171. New and used books, both paper and hardcover. Great for fiction and psychology. Mon–Fri 7.30am–8pm, Sat 9am–7pm, Sun 9am–6pm.

★**Three Lives & Company** 154 W 10th St, at Waverly Place ☎ 212 741 2069, ⓦ threelives.com; subway A, B, C, D, E, F, M to W 4th St, #1 to Christopher St; map p.96. Excellent literary shop that has an especially good selection of works by and for women, as well as general titles. There's a superb reading series in the fall, which has previously hosted the likes of Maya Angelou and Peter Carey. Mon & Tues noon–8pm, Wed–Sat 11am–8.30pm, Sun noon–7pm.

WORD 126 Franklin St, at Milton St, Greenpoint ☎ 718 383 0096, ⓦ wordbookstores.com; subway G to Greenpoint Ave; map p.225. Beloved Brooklyn indie store, with a beautifully curated range of paperback fiction (especially classics), cookbooks, cute cards and stationery and a full roster of literary events. Daily 10am–9pm.

SECONDHAND BOOKS

Argosy Bookstore 116 E 59th St, at Park Ave ☎ 212 753 4455, ⓦ argosybooks.com; subway #4, #5, #6 to 59th St-Lexington Ave; map p.124. Open since 1925 and unbeatable for rarities, Argosy also sells clearance books and titles of all kinds, though the shop's reputation means you may find mainstream works cheaper elsewhere. Mon–Fri 10am–6pm; Sept to mid-May also Sat 10am–5pm.

Book Thug Nation 100 N 3rd St, between Berry St and Wythe Ave, Williamsburg ⓦ bookthugnation.com; subway L to Bedford Ave; map p.225. Serious used bookstore and event space in Williamsburg; the main focus is literary fiction (with one of the best used sections in the city), film and philosophy. Daily noon–8pm.

★**Housing Works Bookstore Café** 126 Crosby St, between Houston and Prince sts ☎ 212 334 3324, ⓦ housingworks.org; subway B, D, F, M to Broadway-Lafayette, N, R to Prince St, #6 to Bleecker St; map p.64. Excellent selection of very cheap and secondhand books. With a small espresso and snack bar and comfy chairs, it's a great place to spend an afternoon. Proceeds benefit its AIDS charity. Mon–Fri 9am–9pm, Sat & Sun 10am–5pm.

Spoonbill & Sugartown 218 Bedford Ave, between N 5th and N 4th sts, Williamsburg ☎ 718 387 7322, ⓦ spoonbillbooks.com; subway L to Bedford Ave; map p.225. Specializing in used, rare and new books on contemporary art, architecture, art history and various design fields. Daily 10am–10pm.

★**Strand Bookstore** 828 Broadway, at E 12th St ☎ 212 473 1452, ⓦ strandbooks.com; subway #4, #5, #6, N, R, Q, L to Union Square; map p.88. Yes, it's hot and crowded, and the staff seem to resent working here, but with "18 miles of books" and a stock of more than 2.5 million titles, this is the largest discount book operation in the city, and a New York landmark. There are recent review copies and new books for half-price in the basement; older books go for anything from 50¢. Mon–Sat 9.30am–10.30pm, Sun 11am–10.30pm.

28

SPECIAL-INTEREST BOOKSTORES

ART AND ARCHITECTURE

There are also excellent bookstores at the Met (see p.158), MoMA (see p.129) and New Museum of Contemporary Art (see p.79).

MoMA Design Store 81 Spring St, at Crosby St ☎646 613 1367, ⓦmomastore.org; subway N, R to Prince St, #6 to Bleecker St; map p.64. Contemporary art books galore. You could spend an afternoon browsing the oversized titles and lush collections of works. Mon–Sat 10am–8pm, Sun 11am–7pm.

Unoppressive, Non-Imperialist Bargain Books 34 Carmine St, between Bleecker and Bedford sts ☎212 229 0079, ⓦunoppressivebooks.blogspot.com; subway A, B, C, D, E, F, M to W 4th St, #1 to Houston St; map p.96. Arty overstock among a hotchpotch of travel guides, biographies, children's pop-up books and spiritual titles. Mon–Thurs & Sun 11am–10pm, Fri & Sat 11am–midnight.

COMICS AND SCI-FI

Forbidden Planet 832 Broadway, at E 13th St ☎212 473 1576, ⓦfpnyc.com; subway #4, #5, #6, L, N, R, Q to 14th St-Union Square; map p.88. Science fiction, fantasy, horror fiction, graphic novels and comics. Great for its large backlist of indie and underground comics, they also hawk T-shirts and the latest sci-fi toys and collectibles. Mon & Tues 9am–10pm, Wed 8am–midnight, Thurs–Sat 9am–midnight, Sun 10am–10pm.

JHU Comic Books 32 E 32nd St, between Madison and Park aves ☎212 268 7088, ⓦjhucomicbooks.com; subway #6 to 28th St; map p.124. Offers mainstream issues from the big leagues (DC, Marvel) as well as graphic novels, manga, small pressings and collectibles. Authors, illustrators and comic-related media types (Neil Gaiman, Mr Tarantino, Guillermo Del Toro) often stop by to discuss their work. Staff are knowledgeable and happy to assist. Mon, Tues, Sat & Sun noon–9pm, Wed–Fri 9am–11pm.

St Mark's Comics 11 St Mark's Place, between Second and Third aves ☎212 598 9439, ⓦstmarkscomics.com; subway #6 to Astor Place; map p.88. Pilgrimage site for comic, manga and graphic-novel fans from all over the world, with plenty of rare memorabilia (T-shirts, action figures) to enhance their huge stock of printed material. Mon & Tues 10am–11pm, Wed 9am–1am, Thurs–Sat 10am–1am, Sun 11am–11pm.

CRIME AND MYSTERY

★**The Mysterious Bookshop** 58 Warren St, at West Broadway ☎212 587 1011, ⓦmysteriousbookshop .com; subway #1, #2, #3, A, C to Chambers St; map p.64. The founder of this store started the Mysterious Press (now owned by Warner Books). The shop sells mysteries of every kind, from classic detectives to just-published titles, and also trades in some first editions and "Sherlockiana". Mon–Sat 11am–7pm.

FOREIGN LANGUAGE

J. Levine Books & Judaica 5 W 30th St, between Fifth Ave and Broadway ☎212 695 6888, ⓦlevinejudaica .com; subway R, N to 28th St; map p.115. The best selection of Bibles, Torahs and Jewish texts in the city – a huge range of books in English. Mon–Wed 9am–6pm, Thurs 9am–7pm, Fri 9am–2pm, Sun noon–5pm; closed Sun in July.

★**Kinokuniya Bookstore** 1073 Sixth Ave, between W 40th and W 41st sts ☎212 869 1700, ⓦkinokuniya .com; subway B, D, F, M to 42nd St-Bryant Park; map p.142. With three well-stocked floors, this is the largest Japanese bookstore in New York. Lots of titles in English as well as manga, stationery, origami, plushies and much more – there's even a café with green tea lattes, bento boxes and mouthwatering desserts. Mon–Sat 10am–8pm, Sun 11am–7.30pm.

Rizzoli 1133 Broadway, at W 26th St ☎212 759 2424, ⓦrizzolibookstore.com; subway N, R to 28th St; map p.115. Manhattan branch of the prestigious Italian bookstore chain and publisher. They specialize in European publications, and have a good selection of foreign newspapers and magazines along with art books of all sorts. Mon–Fri 10.30am–8pm, Sat 11am–7.30pm, Sun 11am–6pm.

TRAVEL AND MAPS

Idlewild Books 170 Seventh Ave S, between Perry St and Waverly Place ☎212 414 8888, ⓦidlewildbooks .com; subway #1, #2, #3 to 14th St; map p.96. Travel book and world literature specialist, just the place to inspire your next trip; also carries a wide selection of books in French and Spanish. Mon–Thurs noon–8pm, Fri–Sun noon–6pm.

The Old Print Shop 150 Lexington Ave, between E 29th and E 30th sts ☎212 683 3951, ⓦoldprintshop .com; subway #6 to 28th St; map p.115. The place to find a great old map of a New York neighbourhood, a first-edition art book or a print from an old *Harper's Weekly*. June–Aug Mon–Thurs 9am–5pm, Fri 9am–4pm; Sept–May Tues–Fri 9am–5pm, Sat 9am–4pm.

POLITICAL

Bluestockings 172 Allen St, between Stanton and Rivington sts ☎212 777 6028, ⓦbluestockings.com; subway F to Second Ave-Lower East Side; map p.82. New and used titles on LGBT and gender studies, capitalism, the prison system and other left-leaning subjects. Cosy, well-stocked, collective-style store in what was once a dilapidated flophouse; nice Fairtrade café and frequent readings. Daily 11am–11pm.

28

CULINARY

★**Kitchen Arts & Letters** 1435 Lexington Ave, between E 93th and E 94th sts ☎212 876 5550, ⊚kitchenartsandletters.com; subway #6 to 96th St; map p.171. Excellent selection of cookbooks and titles on food and wine; run by a former culinary editor and his encyclopedic staff. Lots of out-of-print works and rare finds. Mon 1–6pm, Tues–Fri 10am–6.30pm, Sat 11am–6pm (closed Sat July & Aug).

THEATRE

Drama Bookshop 250 W 40th St, between Seventh and Eighth aves ☎212 944 0595, ⊚dramabookshop.com; subway A, C, E to 42nd St; map p.142. Established in 1917, this venerable emporium sells theatre books, scripts and publications on all manner of drama-related subjects. Mon–Sat 11am–7pm, Thurs till 8pm, Sun noon–6pm.

BOOK ARTS

Center for Book Arts 28 W 27th St, in between Broadway and Sixth Ave, 3rd floor ☎212 481 0295, ⊚centerforbookarts.org; subway N, R to 28th St; map p.107. Not so much a bookstore as a space dedicated to the art of bookmaking. Hosts regular readings and workshops – fascinating stuff. Mon–Fri 11am–6pm, Sat 10am–5pm.

MUSIC

The age of **music stores** is fading fast. Nevertheless, a few excellent independent record stores survive in the East and West villages and, increasingly, in Brooklyn. For classical and opera music, the gift shop at Lincoln Center (see p.186) is also a great resource.

Academy Records 12 W 18th St, between Fifth and Sixth aves ☎212 242 3000, ⊚academy-records.com; subway F, M to 14th St; map p.115. Used, rare and/or hard-to-find CDs and LPs (especially classical, rock and jazz) are the Academy's forte. Serious operaphiles, they know which is the recording of the title you are looking for. Mon–Wed & Sun 11am–7pm, Thurs–Sat 11am–8pm.

Downtown Music Gallery 13 Monroe St, between Catherine and Market sts ☎212 473 0043, ⊚downtown musicgallery.com; subway F to East Broadway; map p.71. New York's most comprehensive selection of avant-garde jazz, contemporary classical, progressive rock and related styles, on used CD, LP and DVD. Daily noon–6pm.

Generation Records 210 Thompson St, between Bleecker and W 3rd sts ☎212 254 1100, ⊚generation records.com; subway A, B, C, D, E, F, M to W 4th St; map p.96. The focus here is on hardcore, metal and punk with some indie. New CDs and vinyl upstairs, used goodies downstairs. It also gets many of the imports the others don't have, plus fine bootlegs. Mon–Thurs & Sun noon–9pm, Fri & Sat noon–10pm.

Halcyon 74 Wythe Ave, at N 12th St, Williamsburg ☎718 360 0992, ⊚halcyontheshop.com; subway L to Bedford Ave and G to Nassau Ave; map p.225. A trusted source for electronic music, but covers everything from disco to reggae and rock. Mon–Fri 2–8pm, Sat & Sun noon–8pm.

House of Oldies 35 Carmine St, between Bleecker St and Bedford St ☎212 243 0500, ⊚houseofoldies.com; subway A, B, C, D, E, F, M to W 4th St, #1 to Houston St; map p.96. Just what the name says – oldies but goldies of all kinds from the 1950s to the 1970s. Vinyl only. Pricey. Tues–Sat 10am–5pm.

★**Jazz Record Center** 236 W 26th St, Room 804, between Seventh and Eighth aves ☎212 675 4480, ⊚jazzrecordcenter.com; subway #1 to 28th St, C, E to 23rd St; map p.107. The place to come for rare or out-of-print jazz LPs from the dawn of recording through the bebop revolution, avant-jazz and beyond. They also have rare books, videos and memorabilia. Mon–Sat 10am–6pm.

★**Permanent Records** 159 20th St, between Third and Fourth aves, South Slope ☎718 383 4083, ⊚permanentrecords.info; subway R to Prospect Ave; map p.231. Friendly little shop stocking new and used LPs, CDs, DVDs, singles and 12 inches in all genres – you'll find some classics in the $1 section. Wed–Sat noon–7pm.

Record Grouch 986 Manhattan Ave, between Huron and India sts, Greenpoint ☎718 389 0122; subway G to Greenpoint Ave; map p.225. A Greenpoint gem and a must for all vinyl aficionados: they buy, sell or trade records in all genres, for reasonable prices. And yes, owner Doug Pressman can be a bit of a grouch; it's part of the appeal. Daily noon–8pm.

ELECTRONIC AND VIDEO EQUIPMENT

Buying **electronic and video equipment** in New York can be a good deal, especially if you are visiting from Europe, where such merchandise is more expensive; make sure that appliances are compatible with your home country before handing over the cash.

Apple Store 103 Prince St, at Greene St ☎212 226 3126, ⊚apple.com; subway N, R to Prince St; map p.64. Also 767 Fifth Ave; map p.124 and several other locations. The original Apple store in Manhattan gets extremely crowded,

28

but the latest in laptops, iPads, iPhones and iPods are all here for as cheap as you'll find them anywhere – you can also play with the newest models. Head upstairs for technical support at the genius bar or sit in on one of the many tutorials in the theatre. The Fifth Ave location is open 24hr. Mon–Sat 9am–9pm, Sun 10am–8pm.

B&H Photo Video 420 Ninth Ave, between W 33rd and W 34th sts ☎212 444 6615 or ☎800 606 6969, ⓦbhphotovideo.com; subway A, C, E to 34th St; map p.142. For film, cameras and speciality equipment; knowledgeable sales staff will take the time to guide you through a buying decision. Excellent used-goods section upstairs. Mon–Thurs 9am–7pm, Fri 9am–2pm, Sun 10am–6pm; closed Jewish holidays.

Leica Store Soho 460 West Broadway, between Houston and Prince sts ☎212 475 7799, ⓦleica-camera.com; subway C to Spring St; map p.64. Stylish showcase for the German camera-maker, with artsy photographic exhibits and special-edition cameras enhancing the usual selection of products. Mon–Fri 10am–6pm, Sat & Sun 11am–7pm.

Microsoft Store Time Warner Center, 10 Columbus Circle ☎855 270 6581, ⓦmicrosoftstore.com; subway A, B, C, D, #1 to 59th St-Columbus Circle; map p.184. Shrine dedicated to all the best Microsoft products, including the popular Surface, Windows 10 and Windows 10 PCs, the Lumia phone and Xbox. Mon–Sat 10am–9pm, Sun 11am–7pm.

FOOD AND DRINK

Food is a New York obsession – hence the proliferation of gourmet groceries and speciality markets across the city. For general snacking and late-night munchies, there's usually a 24-hour corner shop (known as a "bodega") within a few blocks' walk of anywhere. Note that New York State's liquor-licensing laws mean that supermarkets and bodegas can only sell beer, and wine and spirits are only available in liquor stores. In either place, you'll need to be 21 to buy (expect to be asked to show ID).

Aji Ichiban 37 Mott St, between Mosco and Pell sts; ☎212 233 7650; subway J, N, Q, Z, #6 to Canal St; map p.71. Snug Hong Kong confectionery shop packed with candy jars, cured meats, preserved fruits (the dried guava is incredible) and rare but tasty snacks like sesame codsticks. Lots of free samples. Daily 10am–8pm.

Alleva Dairy 188 Grand St, at Mulberry St ☎212 226 7990, ⓦallevadairy.com; subway J, Z, #6 to Canal St; map p.71. Oldest Italian *formaggiaio* (cheesemonger) and grocery in America. Makes its own smoked mozzarella, provolone and ricotta. Daily 9am–7pm.

Barney Greengrass 541 Amsterdam Ave, between W 86th and W 87th sts ☎212 724 4707, ⓦbarneygreengrass.com; subway #1 to 86th St; map p.184. "The Sturgeon King" is an Upper West Side smoked-fish institution, trading since 1908. You can sit down, or take your brunch makings to go and eat in Central Park. Cash only. Tues–Sun 8am–6pm.

Chelsea Market 75 Ninth Ave, between W 15th and W 16th sts ☎212 652 2110, ⓦchelseamarket.com; subway A, C, E to 14th St; map p.107. A complex of eighteen former industrial buildings, among them the old Nabisco Cookie Factory. A true smorgasbord of stores, including Amy's Bread (see p.300), Bowery Kitchen Supply, Fat Witch Bakery, Morimoto, Lobster Place (see p.298), Manhattan Fruit Exchange and Very Fresh Noodles. Grab your fare to-go and head up to the High Line, which has an entrance at the Market's western entrance. Mon–Sat 7am–9pm, Sun 8am–8pm.

D'Amico Coffee 309 Court St, between Sackett and Degraw sts, Carroll Gardens ☎718 875 5403, ⓦdamicocoffeeroasters.com; subway F, G to Carroll St; map p.235. Old-school coffee purveyors (since 1948), with a small seating area in the back where you can sip espresso and listen to the long-time regulars hold court. Mon–Fri 7am–7pm, Sat 7am–6pm, Sun 9am–3pm.

Di Palo's Fine Foods 200 Grand St, at Mott St ☎212 226 1033, ⓦdipaloselects.com; subway B, D to Grand St; map p.71. Charming and authoritative family-run business since 1925 that sells some of the city's best ricotta, along with a fine selection of aged balsamic vinegars, oils and home-made pastas. Mon–Sat 9am–6.30pm, Sun 9am–4pm.

28

GREENMARKETS

Several days each week, long before sunrise, hundreds of farmers from Long Island, the Hudson Valley and parts of Pennsylvania and New Jersey set out in trucks to transport their fresh-picked bounty to New York City, where they are joined by bakers, cheesemakers and other artisans at **greenmarkets**. These are run by the city authorities, roughly one to four days a week, and are busiest from June to September.

To find the greenmarket nearest to you, call ☎212 788 7476 or visit ⓦgrownyc.org; the largest and most popular is held in Union Square, at E 17th Street and Broadway, year-round on Monday, Wednesday, Friday and Saturday from 8am to 6pm.

East Village Cheese Store 80 E 7th St, between First and Second aves ☎ 212 477 2601; subway F to Second Ave, #6 to Astor Place; map p.88. The city's most affordable source for cheese; its front-of-the-store bins sell pungent blocks and wedges of the stuff starting at just $1. Daily 8.30am–6.30pm.

Eataly 200 Fifth Ave, at W 23rd St ☎ 212 229 2560, ⓦ eatalyny.com; subway #6, F, N, R to 23rd St; map p.115. This wildly popular Mario Batali venture is part Italian café/restaurant complex, part food market, with an incredible range of wine, cheese, meat, breads and seafood, sourced locally or flown in from Italy. Market daily 9am–11pm.

Essex Street Market 120 Essex St, between Rivington and Delancey sts ☎ 212 388 0449, ⓦ essexstreetmarket .com; subway F to Delancey St, J, M, Z to Essex St; map p.82. Here, a Latin American fruit plaza, Saxelby Cheesemongers, a Swedish snack shop and vegan Japanese fare all live under one roof, reflecting the many stripes of the Lower East Side. Mon–Sat 8am–7pm, Sun 10am–6pm.

Ideal Cheese 942 First Ave, between E 51st and E 52nd sts ☎ 212 688 7579, ⓦ idealcheese.com; subway #6 to 51st St, subway E, M to Lexington Ave-53rd St; map p.124. Tucked away in the eastern hinterlands of Midtown – but well worth a visit – *Ideal Cheese* delivers the same knockout level of knowledge, care and product as *Murray's* (see below), but without the accompanying crowds. In business for over sixty years. Mon–Sat 8.30am–6pm.

★**Kalustyan's** 123 Lexington Ave, between E 28th and E 29th sts ☎ 212 685 3451, ⓦ kalustyans.com; subway #6 to 28th St; map p.124. Aromatic spice shop with a focus on Southeast Asian flavours, but really, nearly any curry, nut, hot sauce or international mix imaginable will be found on its absurdly well-stocked shelves. Be sure to sample the authentic cuisine upstairs in the tiny, cheap café – try the *mujadara* sandwich, packed with lentils, tomatoes and tahini ($5). Mon–Sat 10am–8pm, Sun 11am–7pm.

Ladurée 864 Madison Ave, between E 70th and E 71st sts ☎ 646 558 3157, ⓦ laduree.com; subway #6 to 68th St; map p.171. Also 398 W Broadway, Soho. *Macarons* – the world's most famous sweet of the moment – presented by formal salespeople in a shop that looks like a gilded jewellery box. Mon–Sat 9am–7pm, Sun 10am–6pm.

Moore Street Market 110 Moore St, at Humboldt St, East Williamsburg ☎ 718 384 1371, ⓦ nycedc.com; subway L to Montrose Ave, J, M to Flushing Ave; map p.225. Dubbed "La Marketa", this indoor market has been serving Brooklyn's Latino community (and its appreciators) for over seventy years. Excellent *pasteles* (*tamales* made with *masa*), stews and banana fritters. Mon–Thurs 8am–6pm, Fri & Sat 8am–7pm, Sun 10am–5pm.

★**Murray's Cheese Shop** 254 Bleecker St, at Cornelia St ☎ 212 243 3289, ⓦ murrayscheese.com; subway A, B, C, D, E, F, M to W 4th St, #1 to Christopher St; map p.96. There's another location in Grand Central. More than three hundred fresh cheeses and excellent panini sandwiches, all served by a knowledgeable staff. Mon–Sat 8am–9pm, Sun 9am–8pm.

Porto Rico Importing Company 201 Bleecker St, between Sixth Ave and MacDougal St ☎ 212 477 5421, ⓦ portorico.com; subway A, B, C, D, E, F, M to W 4th St; map p.96. Plus several other locations. An astounding 110 coffees (their speciality) and 140 types of tea on offer. The house blends are almost as good as many of the more expensive varieties. Mon–Fri 8am–9pm, Sat 9am–9pm, Sun noon–7pm.

★**Sahadi's** 187 Atlantic Ave, between Clinton and Court sts, Brooklyn Heights ☎ 718 624 4550, ⓦ sahadis .com; subway #4, #5 to Borough Hall; map p.218. Established in 1948, this fully stocked Middle Eastern grocery store sells everything from Iranian pistachios to creamy home-made hummus. Grab a number and fill up on dried mango, chocolate, olives, flours and a rainbow of spices sold by the pound. Very reasonably priced. Mon–Sat 9am–7pm.

Smorgasburg 90 Kent Ave, at N 7th St, Williamsburg (Sat); subway L to Bedford Ave; map p.225; Prospect Park (Sun), East Drive at Lincoln Rd, South Slope; subway Q to Prospect Park or F, G to 15th St; map p.231; ⓦ smorgasburg.com. From April to October, these two scenic parks brim with more than a hundred gourmet food vendors. Thronged by locals and visitors alike, it has grown to become a signature New York experience. Highlights include John's Juice, pasta donuts (for real) from Pop Pasta, baked *empanadas* by Bolivian Llama Party, Best Buds burritos, scallion pancake wraps by Outer Borough and the technicolour Filipino desserts served up at Ube Kitchen. Tips for Saturday visits: arrive early to avoid obscene queues and don't come on a super-hot day (there's limited shade and seating). For both events, be sure to arm yourself with plenty of cash (most vendors won't take cards). Williamsburg: Sat 11am–6pm; Prospect Park (Park Slope): Sun 11am–6pm.

Titan Foods 25–56 31st St, between Astoria Blvd and 30th Ave, Queens ☎ 718 626 7771, ⓦ titanfood.com; subway N, Q to Astoria Blvd; map p.248. Olympic-sized store for comestible Greek goods, including imported feta cheese, yogurt and stuffed vine leaves. Mon–Sat 8am–9pm, Sun 9am–8pm.

Warehouse Wines and Spirits 735 Broadway, between W 8th St and Waverly Place ☎ 212 982 7770, ⓦ warehousewinesandspirits.com; subway #6 to Astor Place; map p.88. The top place to get a buzz for your buck, with a wide selection and frequent reductions on popular lines: cava and prosecco for $5–7, decent reds and whites for under $10. Mon–Thurs 9am–8.45pm, Fri & Sat 9am–9.45pm, Sun noon–8.45pm.

28

WESTPFAL HENRY & CO: KNIFE BUFFS

If you need to sharpen knives, scissors, or pretty much anything with an edge, pop into **Westpfal Henry & Co.** (115 W 25th St, between Sixth and Seventh aves ☎212 563 5990, ⓦnysharpeningservice.com; subway F, M to 23rd St, N, R to 28th St, Mon–Fri 9.30am–6pm). Established in 1874, this revered establishment knows its way around all kinds of blades – serious foodies come here, as well as fashion designers and barbers. A throwback in time, staff are exceedingly charming and great care is put into the work.

Zabar's 2245 Broadway, at W 80th St ☎212 787 2000, ⓦzabars.com; subway #1 to 79th St; map p.184. Zabar's is still the city's pre-eminent gourmet shop. Choose from an astonishing variety of cheeses, olives, meats, salads, freshly baked breads and croissants and prepared dishes. Upstairs, shop for shiny kitchen and household implements. Mon–Fri 8am–7.30pm, Sat 8am–8pm, Sun 9am–6pm.

SWEET TREATS

Dylan's Candy Bar 1011 Third Ave, at E 60th St ☎646 735 0078, ⓦdylanscandybar.com; subway N, Q, R, #4, #5, #6 to Lexington Ave-59th St; map p.171. Dylan Lauren's iconic New York sweet store, with giant multicoloured lolly pops, chocolate fountain, Belgian hot chocolate and all sorts of old-fashioned candy. Expensive but fun. Mon–Thurs 10am–9pm, Fri & Sat 10am–11pm, Sun 11am–9pm.

★**Economy Candy** 108 Rivington St, between Essex and Ludlow sts ☎212 254 832, ⓦeconomycandy.com; subway F to Delancey St, J, M, Z to Essex St; map p.82. A sweet shop on the Lower East Side, selling mountains of nostalgic candies (think Lemonheads, Milk Duds and Double Bubble), chocs, nuts and dried fruit at low prices.

Mon & Sat 10am–6pm, Tues–Fri & Sun 9am–6pm.

Li-Lac 40 Eighth Ave at Jane St ☎212 924 2280, ⓦli-lacchocolates.com; subway A, C, E, L, #1, #2, #3 to 14th St; map p.96. Multiple locations, including Grand Central. Li-Lac's delicious chocolates have been handmade since 1923. One of the city's best treats for those with a sweet tooth – try the fresh fudge or hand-moulded Lady Liberties and Empire States. Mon–Sat 11am–8pm, Sun 11am–7pm.

M&M's World 1600 Broadway, at W 48th St ☎212 295 3850, ⓦmmsworld.com; map p.142. Yes, a multistorey emporium dedicated solely to M&Ms – check out the candy wall on the second floor, packed with thousands of milk, peanut and speciality chocolate dots. You can even get your photograph imprinted onto the sweets. Daily 9am–midnight.

Mast Brothers Chocolate 111 N 3rd St, Williamsburg ☎718 388 2625, ⓦmastbrothers.com; subway L to Bedford Ave; map p.225. Once you've tried the handmade artisan chocolate here, you'll be utterly hooked; the delicate dark chocolate with almonds and sea salt is a mind-bending treat. Quality comes at a price – it's around $10 a bar. Daily 9am–8pm.

SPORTS

New York has plenty of sporting-goods outlets – from cookie-cutter chain stores and mom-and-pop cycle shops to multistorey sneaker pleasure-domes (see p.380). Visit them for merchandise or just to tap into a wealth of information about sports activities in and around the city.

Ciel Bicycle 360 E 65th St, between First and Second aves ☎212 288 0996, ⓦcielbikes.com; N, R, #4, #5, #6 to Lexington Ave-59th St; map p.171. Six blocks from Central Park, this friendly bike shop rents wheels for $30/day (helmet included). If you're in the market to buy, Ciel specializes in Birias but has a vast selection of quality offerings. Mon–Fri 10am–7pm, Sat 10am–6pm, Sun 11am–5pm.

Mason's Tennis Mart 56 E 53rd St, at Park Ave ☎212 755 5805, ⓦmasonstennis.com; subway E, M to Fifth Ave-53rd St; map p.124. New York's last remaining tennis speciality store – they let you try out all rackets. Mon–Fri 10am–7pm, Sat 10am–6pm, Sun noon–6pm.

NBA Store 545 Fifth Ave, between W 44th and W 45th sts ☎212 457 3120, ⓦnba.com/nycstore; subway #7 to 5th Ave, B, D, F, M to 42nd St; map p.124. New York's shrine to basketball, a vast space selling merchandise for all the NBA teams, not just the much-maligned NY Knicks.

Mon–Fri 10am–8pm, Sat 10am–9pm, Sun 11am–7pm.

Paragon Sports 867 Broadway, between E 17th and E 18th sts ☎212 255 8889, ⓦparagonsports.com; subway N, R, Q, L, #4, #5, #6 to Union Square; map p.115. Established in 1908, this Union Square landmark is like a department store for sports, offering everything under the sun from hiking equipment and sneakers to baseball bats and scuba gear. Mon–Fri 10am–8.30pm, Sat 10am–8pm, Sun 11am–7pm.

Yankees Clubhouse Shop 245 W 42nd St, between Seventh and Eighth aves ☎212 768 9779, ⓦnewyork.yankees.mlb.com; subway #1, #2, #3, #7, N, R, Q, S to Times Square-42nd St; map p.124. Multiple locations. In case you want that celebrated "NY" logo on your clothing, this emporium has all things related to the legendary baseball team (2009 World Series winners). Mon–Sat 9am–midnight, Sun 10am–10pm.

28

Sports and outdoor activities

If measured by sheer number of teams and the coverage devoted to them, New York ranks as the number-one sports city in America. TV stations broadcast most regular-season games and all post-season games in the big four American team sports – baseball, football, basketball and ice hockey – and soccer is gaining plenty of traction too. Baseball is a vital part of New York culture; even tepid sports fans have some allegiance to either the Yankees or the Mets. Tickets can on occasion be hard to find (for certain games, impossible) and most don't come cheap. Still, nothing compares to the chill (or heat) of the arena, the vibrant green of the outfield grass, the anticipation that comes from pre-game introductions and the camaraderie of a home-field crowd.

Many participatory activities in the city are either free or fairly affordable and take place in all kinds of weather. New Yorkers are passionate about jogging – there are plenty of places to take a scenic run – and you can swim at local pools or borough beaches. However, even with the help of the Parks Department (☎311, ⓦnycgovparks.org) it can be hard to find facilities for some sports (like tennis), especially if you are not a city resident. To this end, many locals spend $50–100 (or more) a month to be members of private health clubs; you can sometimes get a free trial week or a discounted month at one of the major ones (the YMCAs, New York Sports Clubs, Crunch, etc).

29

SPECTATOR SPORTS

For most sporting events, **tickets** can be booked ahead with a credit card through Ticketmaster (☎1 800 745 3000, or ☎1 866 448 7849, ⓦticketmaster.com) and collected at the gate or electronically, though it's cheaper – and of course riskier for popular events – to try to pick up tickets on the night of the event, at the venue. You can also call or go to the stadium's box office and buy advance tickets. Numerous internet brokers sell secondary tickets (tickets that are resold by agencies or individuals); prices are set according to supply and demand, so can be cheaper or substantially more. Among your choices are ⓦtickpick.com, ⓦstubhub.com and ⓦseatgeek.com. Alternatively, wacth the game at a sports bar (see box, p.334).

VENUES

Barclays Center 620 Atlantic Ave at Flatbush, Downtown Brooklyn ☎917 618 6700, ⓦbarclayscenter .com; subway B, D, N, Q, R, #2, #3, #4, #5 to Atlantic Ave-Barclays Center, C to Lafayette Ave, G to Fulton St. The Brooklyn behemoth debuted in Sept 2012 and plays host to basketball's Nets and hockey's Islanders (though that latter honour may change soon). Box office Mon–Fri noon–6pm, Sat noon–4pm.

Citi Field 126th St and Roosevelt Ave, Willets Point, Queens ☎718 507 8499, ⓦmlb.com/mets; subway #7 to Mets-Willets Point. The home of the New York Mets takes its cues from old-fashioned stadiums like Ebbets Field, former stomping ground of the departed Brooklyn Dodgers; the Mets Hall of Fame and Museum is just outside the rotunda. Box office Mon–Fri 9am–5.30pm (including off season), Sat 10am–2pm, later on game days.

Madison Square Garden Seventh Ave, between 31st and 33rd sts ☎212 465 6741, ⓦthegarden.com; subway A, C, E, #1, #2, #3 to 34th St-Penn Station. Hockey's Rangers and basketball's Knicks are the primary tenants of this famous arena, which even has extra seating on suspended bridges high above the action (see p.143). Box office Mon–Sat 10am–6pm.

MetLife Stadium Off routes 3, 17 and New Jersey Turnpike exit 16W, East Rutherford, New Jersey ☎201 559 1300, ⓦmetlifestadium.com. The Jets and the Giants play at MetLife Stadium, which hosts more NFL games than any other venue. Occasional international soccer games are held here too, especially in summer. Regular buses from Port Authority Bus Terminal on 42nd St and Eighth Ave. Box office Mon–Fri 11am–5pm.

Prudential Center 165 Mulberry St, between Edison Place and Lafayette St, Newark, New Jersey ☎973 757 6000 or ☎973 757 6600, ⓦprucenter.com. The home of the New Jersey Devils is just two blocks from Newark Penn Station, easily accessible by NJ Transit, Amtrak and PATH trains from Manhattan. Box office Mon–Fri 11am–6pm.

Yankee Stadium 161st St and River Ave, South Bronx ☎718 293 4300, ⓦmlb.com/yankees; subway B, D, #4 to 161st St. Yankee Stadium is right next door to where the old one was; get to the game early and visit Monument Park, where all the Yankee greats are memorialized. In 2015 the newest MLS team, New York City FC, began calling the stadium its home pitch (and will continue to, until a purpose-built venue is constructed for them). Box office Mon–Fri 9am–5pm, Sat 10am–4pm, later on game days.

BASEBALL

The two Major League Baseball (MLB) teams – **New York Mets** (which compete in the East Division of the National League) and **New York Yankees** (East Division of the American League) – play for what seems the better part of the year; try to make time for a game if your visit coincides with a homestand by either. Pre-season games take place in Florida from late Feb to late March, with the regular season (in New York) beginning right after and running through Sept; Oct is playoff time. The organizations also have minor-league squads that play in small area stadiums – a more intimate way to enjoy the sport.

NEW YORK YANKEES

Reciting the achievements of the Yankees (also known as "The Bronx Bombers") over the decades can get tedious. They are the team with the most World Series titles (27 up to the end of 2016) and they have been in the playoffs more than half of the past ninety seasons: an almost-unheard-of success rate for major-league sports. Their main rivals are the Boston Red Sox; bitter feelings can be traced back to 1920, when former Red Sox star pitcher Babe Ruth was traded to the Yankees. If you can get a ticket to see a game between the two, or a "Subway Series" tilt, when the

29

LOCAL BASEBALL HISTORY

In the early 1840s, the **New York Knickerbocker Club** played "base ball" near Madison Square in Manhattan, before moving to Elysian Fields, across the Hudson River in Hoboken, New Jersey. There, on June 26, 1846, they laid down the basic rules (the "Knickerbocker Rules") of the game of baseball, as it is played to this day. For half the twentieth century, New York was home to three Major League Baseball (MLB) teams: the **New York Giants** and the **Brooklyn Dodgers**, who represented the National League, and the **New York Yankees**, who represented the American League. Additionally, in the years before MLB was integrated, the Negro League had several notable teams based in the city. The almost-decade between 1947 and 1956 was the golden age of baseball in New York, with a Yankees team first led by Joe DiMaggio, then by Mickey Mantle, steamrolling their opponents, and barrier-breaking heroes (not to mention great players) like Jackie Robinson and Roy Campanella playing for the Dodgers. This period ended abruptly in 1957, when the Giants and Dodgers bolted to California at the end of the season – though the city has mostly forgotten the Giants, old-time Brooklyn residents are still scarred by the loss of the Dodgers. New York was bereft of a National League franchise until the Mets arrived at the Polo Grounds in 1962, moving two years later to Shea Stadium and, most recently (on the same site as Shea), to Citi Field, in Flushing, Queens.

Bombers face their cross-town adversaries, the Mets, in June interleague play, you won't be disappointed. Tickets start around $20, before fees, for the bleachers (stands) and can exceed $300 for the best seats (see p.395).

NEW YORK METS

The Mets have often been regarded as the ugly bridesmaids – or, perhaps more optimistically, the loveable losers – of the city; their last championship, in 1986 (one of two in their fifty-year-plus history), feels awfully long ago. The fact that the team's ownership has been overly cautious in spending for new talent in recent years makes it seem even more distant. Still, they have some exciting young pitchers, plenty of die-hard fans, an attractive stadium, Citi Field, to showcase the team and rather affordable tickets: prices can start as low as $14 and go up to $180 (see p.395), before fees.

MINOR-LEAGUE BASEBALL

Attending a minor-league baseball game is great fun. Not only do you get the chance to see up-and-coming players compete with those hanging on for one last shot at The Show, but the crowds are smaller, the seats are better, tickets much cheaper – and there are some fun-spirited theme nights as well. The season for the local teams is a short one, running from June to September.
Brooklyn Cyclones ☏ 718 449 8497, ⊛ brooklyn cyclones.com. After a 43-year absence, baseball returned to Brooklyn in 2001 in the form of the Cyclones, an affiliate of the Mets that play in the same New York–Penn League as the Staten Island Yankees. The beautiful, seafront stadium (MCU Park) is at the former Steeplechase Park in Coney Island. Another reason to go: wacky promotional nights. Tickets $10–17.
Staten Island Yankees ☏ 718 720 9265, ⊛ siyanks .com. The franchise debuted in 1999: they play in the Class A New York–Penn League (June–early Sept). Catch them at

the Richmond County Bank Ballpark at St George, within a two-minute walk of the Staten Island ferry terminal. Tickets $12–17.

AMERICAN FOOTBALL

The National Football League (NFL) regular season stretches from September till the end of December, with playoffs and the Super Bowl running throughout January and usually into February. New York's teams are the Jets and the Giants; both play at MetLife Stadium, which is, in fact, not in New York at all – it's part of the Meadowlands Sports Complex in New Jersey. Tickets for both teams are always officially sold out well in advance, but you can often pick up tickets (legally) from secondary-broker websites such as ⊛ stubhub.com (see p.397).

NEW YORK GIANTS

The Giants have a long and proud history dating back to the 1920s, having won eight NFL titles (including four Super Bowl championships), most recently in 2012. Due to the long waiting list for season tickets, the Giants (☏ 201 935 8222, ⊛ giants.com) actually encourage current ticket-holders to sell their unused seats to people further down on the list; you have to join the waiting list (by mail) to have a shot at these tickets. Tickets at MetLife Stadium start at $100 (see p.395), though average prices go well past that.

NEW YORK JETS

Founded in 1960 as part of the upstart American Football League, the Jets (☏ 973 549 4600, ⊛ newyorkjets.com), originally known as the Titans, share MetLife Stadium with the Giants. They've endured a lot of difficult times (really, most of their existence) and are still trying to get back to their first Super Bowl since 1969, when they beat the heavily favoured Baltimore Colts 16–7. Secondary websites offer the best deals on tickets, but they'll still usually be quite pricey (see p.395).

PROFESSIONAL BASKETBALL

The National Basketball Association (NBA) regular season begins in November and runs till the end of April. The two professional teams in the New York area are the New York Knicks (Knickerbockers), who play at Madison Square Garden, and the Brooklyn Nets, whose venue is the Barclays Center. There is also a women's professional team in New York, the WBNA Liberty; tickets to see them play are easier to come by.

NEW YORK KNICKS

It hasn't been easy being a Knicks (⊛ nba.com/knicks) fan in the new millennium, even though the venerable franchise is one of the most recognizable in any sport. Madison Square Garden – despite recent renovations – is one of the less attractive stadiums in North America; their last championship win was way back in 1973; the team has had losing records in thirteen of the past sixteen seasons, as of 2016–17; and after all that, tickets are virtually impossible to come by – and astronomically expensive when procured. The team continues in a state of turbulence, having cycled through coaches at a high rate the past few years; these days, they're pinning their hopes on young international star Kristaps Porzingis. Expect list prices to start around $80, with an average closer to $130.

BROOKLYN NETS

The Nets (⊛ nba.com/nets) began life in 1967 as the New Jersey Americans. Led by legendary Julius Erving ("Dr J"), they won two championships (1974 and 1976) playing on Long Island before joining the NBA. With a resurgence in the early 2000s, they (back again in New Jersey) made the finals twice in a row, and made a celebrated move to Brooklyn in

2012. Since the transition, the team has generally been in the doldrums, and Nets tickets are easier to come by than for the Knicks — though they would be regardless of their success. Their popular black and white logo was designed by hip-hop star Jay Z (briefly a part owner of the club). Tickets at the Barclays Center (see p.395) usually start around $45, but can generally be had for less.

NEW YORK LIBERTY

The Women's National Basketball Association (WNBA) season opens when the NBA season ends and runs through the summer to its playoffs in Sept. The league jumped off in 1997, with the New York team, the Liberty, finishing as runners-up for the title; despite making the playoffs almost every year and appearing in four finals, the Liberty have yet to win the championship. Games are at Madison Square Garden, and prices are low compared with those for the Knicks. You can usually get a ticket; call ☎ 212 465 6073, go to ⊛ liberty.wnba.com, or pick some up at Madison Square Garden (see p.395). Ticket prices: $40–225.

COLLEGE BASKETBALL

The college basketball season begins in November and ends with "March Madness", in which conference tournaments are followed by a 68-team competition to select a national champion. The NCAA (National Collegiate Athletic Association) Tournament may be the most exciting, eagerly anticipated sporting event in the US. Madison Square Garden (see p.395) provides the setting for pre-season tournaments and the semifinals and finals of the National Invitation Tournament, which takes the best of the rest that don't make it to the NCAA Tournament. Metropolitan-area colleges pursuing hoop dreams include

---

FIVE NEW YORK SPORTS LEGENDS

It's impossible to set criteria by which to choose the five most legendary New York sports figures. With sincere apologies to Derek Jeter, Yogi, The Mick (they can't all be Yankees, can they?) and a whole host of others (John McEnroe, Tom Seaver, every member of the 1955 Brooklyn Dodgers), here's a starter list to get the ball rolling, so to speak.

Joe DiMaggio (1914–99) Yankees Hall of Fame centerfielder whose career was highlighted by his untouchable 56-game hitting streak in 1941. Nicknames: The Yankee Clipper, Joltin' Joe.

Walt Frazier (born 1945) Current Knicks television announcer was their star point-guard for their titles in 1970 and 1973; worth catching on the small screen for his zany fashion sense and zanier use of language. Nickname: Clyde.

Mark Messier (born 1961) The longtime (Canadian-born) Edmonton Oiler was the captain, best player and emotional leader of the Rangers' hockey team when they won their only Stanley Cup of the last seventy years, in 1994. Nicknames: The Moose, The Messiah.

Joe Namath (born 1943) Not the best quarterback of all time, but the one with the most swagger and style; guaranteed the Jets' victory in Super Bowl III (their only one), then backed it up on the field. Nicknames: Broadway Joe, Joe Willie.

George Herman "Babe" Ruth (1895–1948) Came to the Yankees from the Red Sox in one of the most lopsided deals in history; went on to hold the all-time home-run title for around forty years and the single-season record nearly as long. The greatest baseballer of all time? Nicknames: The Babe, The Bambino, The Sultan of Swat.

29

STREET BASKETBALL

Free of the image-building and marketing that makes the NBA so superficial, and the by-the-books officiating of the NCAA, **street basketball** presents the game in its purest form. New York City is the capital of playground hoops, with a host of asphalt legends: Lew Alcindor (Kareem Abdul-Jabbar), Wilt Chamberlain, Julius Erving and Stephon Marbury are a few who have made it to the pros, though others who never made the transition, like Earl "The Goat" Manigault, were said to be just as skilled. *Hoops Nation* by Chris Ballard is an invaluable (if, by now, somewhat dated) guide to basketball courts in the five boroughs (and across the nation) and a useful primer in the etiquette of pickup ball; the courts in **Rucker Park** (155th St and Eighth Ave in Harlem) are the most celebrated, though the **West 4th Street** courts (at Sixth Ave) are likely more convenient to stop by for a look. Scout out the next NBA superstar – or watch for current ones dropping by for an off-season tune-up.

NYU (Manhattan; ⊚ gonyuathletics.com), Columbia (Manhattan; ⊚ gocolumbialions.com), St John's (Queens; ⊚ redstormsports.com), Fordham (Bronx; ⊚ fordham sports.com), Wagner (Staten Island; ⊚ wagnerathletics .com), St Francis (Brooklyn; ⊚ sfuathletics.com) and Long Island (Brooklyn; ⊚ liuathletics.com) universities; it's easy enough to get tickets for games on any of the university athletics websites.

ICE HOCKEY

There are two professional hockey teams in New York: the Rangers, who play at Madison Square Garden, and the Islanders, who have moved from Nassau Coliseum on Long Island to Barclays Center in Brooklyn. In addition, the New Jersey Devils play out at the Prudential Center in Newark. All three compete in the Atlantic Division of the Eastern Conference of the National Hockey League (NHL). The season lasts throughout the winter and into early spring, when the playoffs take place.

NEW YORK RANGERS

One of the six original NHL teams, the Rangers (☎ 212 465 6000, ⊚ rangers.nhl.com) were founded in 1926 and won the Stanley Cup – awarded to the winner of the playoffs – three times in the following fifteen years. According to hockey lore, giddy from their 1940 playoff-finals victory over the Toronto Maple Leafs, the Madison Square Garden owners paid off their $3 million mortgage and celebrated by burning the deed in Lord Stanley's cup – an act of desecration that provoked a curse. The Rangers then had a 54-year championship drought that ended in 1994; in 2014 they returned to (and lost in) the finals and nearly made them again in 2015. Tickets at Madison Square Garden (see p.395) are pricey; expect to pay $80–370.

NEW YORK ISLANDERS

Founded in 1972, the Islanders (☎ 1 800 882 4753, ⊚ islanders.nhl.com) were fortunate enough to string together their four Stanley Cups in consecutive years (1980–83) and thus qualify as a bona fide hockey dynasty.

Since then, however, it's been mostly downhill. They've played in Brooklyn's Barclays Center (see p.395) since the beginning of the 2015–16 season, though rumours abound they'll head back out to Long Island some point in the near future; tickets run $40 to $200.

NEW JERSEY DEVILS

The nomadic New Jersey Devils franchise (⊚ devils.nhl.com) was founded in 1974 as the Kansas City Scouts and moved to New Jersey (after a brief stint as the Colorado Rockies in Denver) in 1982. A succession of mediocre seasons was interrupted when the Devils beat the heavily favoured Detroit Red Wings in four straight games to win the 1995 Stanley Cup. They regained the Cup in 2003; since then, the team has frequently put together strong seasons but been disappointing in the playoffs – and has gone through an almost revolving door of coaches. Tickets are $25–325 and are available at the Prudential Center (see p.395).

SOCCER

The game of **soccer** (European football) continues to grow in popularity in America, thanks in part to World Cup results and the importing of some international (if usually aged) stars to the professional league, which has been expanding and increasing its exposure. Though soccer coverage is not as extensive in the US as it is abroad, it's not too hard to catch on TV and in sports bars (see box, p.334), and interest has only grown with the prominence of the US men's and women's national teams and a new professional club in town. The Major League Soccer season runs from April to Nov.

NEW YORK CITY FC

New York City FC (☎ 1 855 776 9232, ⊚ nycfc.com) debuted in spring 2015; co-owned by the New York Yankees and Manchester City, of the English Premier League, the club is calling Yankee Stadium its home until it gets its own digs (many sites have been rumoured but nothing is in the works). The talent is top heavy, with young winger Jack Harrison and international stars David Villa and Andrea Pirlo leading the way. Ticket prices: $20–100.

29

NEW YORK RED BULLS

The New York Red Bulls (☎1 877 727 6223, ⓦnewyork redbulls.com), one of the more successful MLS sides in recent years, play at the purpose-built Red Bull Arena in Harrison, New Jersey. Their best-known player is Bradley Wright-Phillips, who has led the league in goals multiple times over the past few seasons. Ticket prices: $20–90.

NEW YORK COSMOS

The New York Cosmos (☎1 212 369 7000, ⓦnewyork cosmos.com) play in the NASL, US soccer's second-tier league. The best part about seeing them is an excuse to watch the sport right by the Coney Island boardwalk; they play in MCU Park, home of the Brooklyn Cyclones (see p.396). Ticket prices: $15–40.

HORSE RACING

Aqueduct 110-00 Rockaway Blvd, South Ozone Park, Queens ☎718 641 4700, ⓦnyra.com/aqueduct; subway A to Aqueduct North Conduit Ave or Aqueduct Racetrack. This spot in Queens has racing from late Oct to April. It's also allied with a casino, Resort Worlds Casino New York City (ⓦrwnewyork.com), a slot-machine, roulette and baccarat heaven. Racetrack admission is free; valet parking at the casino entrance costs $10 weekdays, $20 weekends (there's also general parking for $7).

Belmont 2150 Hempstead Turnpike, Elmont ☎516 488 6000, ⓦnyra.com/belmont. Elmont, Long Island, is

home to the Belmont Stakes (held in June), one of the three American races in which 3-year-olds compete for the Triple Crown. Belmont is open late April to July and Sept to Oct; admission is $5 (more for the Belmont Stakes; ⓦbelmontstakes.com), general parking is free.

TENNIS

US Open Championship The top US tennis event of the year; held late Aug/early Sept at the National Tennis Center in Flushing Meadows–Corona Park, in Queens. Tickets go on sale the first week or two of June at the Billie Jean King National Tennis Center's box office (☎718 760 6363, ⓦusopen.org; Mon–Fri 9am–5pm), though advance tickets go on sale to USTA members and AmEx card members earlier; you can also use Ticketmaster (☎1 800 745 3000 or ☎1 866 673 6849, ⓦticketmaster.com). There are different tickets for day-sessions – grounds only, which don't include access to the main stadium; and ones that give you assigned seats in one of the three biggest courts – and they range in price, starting at $60 but going up much higher. Evening tickets are just for Arthur Ashe Stadium and generally start around $65. Though big-name matches are frequently saved for the main stadium in the evening, you can get very close to the action at the outer courts during the day. If events are sold out, keep trying up to the day of the event because corporate tickets are often returned. Qualifying matches and practise rounds are free; there's also a kids' day.

ACTIVITIES

BOATING

Chelsea Piers ☎212 336 6777 or ☎212 627 1825, ⓦsail-nyc.com. Join the crew of the *Adirondack* and *Imagine*, two beautiful wooden schooners, which sail from

Pier 62. During the 2hr tour of lower New York Harbor, passengers can take the wheel, help hoist the sails or just enjoy the surroundings; there's also *The Manhattan*, a yacht that sails from here. Sightseeing, jazz and sunset cruises are

---

ESCAPE TO THE BEACH

New York's **beaches** aren't worth a trip to the city in and of themselves, but they can be a cool summer escape from the heat of the street. Most are only a MetroCard ride away.

Brighton Beach Brooklyn; subway B, Q to Brighton Beach. Technically the same stretch as Coney Island Beach, but less crowded and populated mainly by the local Russian community. Stop on Brighton Beach Ave at one of the many Russian supermarkets to get picnic supplies.

Coney Island Beach Brooklyn; subway B, D, F, Q to Coney Island-Stillwell Ave. One of the city's most popular bathing spots, jam-packed on summer weekends. The Atlantic here is only moderately dirty, and there's a good, reliable onshore breeze.

Jacob Riis Park Queens; subway #2, #5 to Flatbush Ave, then #Q35 bus, or A to Rockaway Park, then #Q35 or #Q22. Good sandy stretches and very pristine,

though Hurricane Sandy in Oct 2012 hit it hard (the 1930s Art Deco bathhouse, however, still stands).

Orchard Beach The Bronx; subway #6 to Pelham Bay Park, then bus #Bx5 or #Bx12 to Orchard Beach. This man-made beach is a wide, crescent-shaped strand, fronted by a decaying pavilion and lots of volleyball and basketball courts.

Rockaway Beach Queens; subway A, C to any stop along the beach, or NYC Ferry to Rockaway Beach. This seven-mile strip has historically been the best for surf – so good that the Ramones wrote a song about it. A few hip nearby openings, like that of the Rockaway Beach Surf Club, *Rockaway Beach Bakery* pizza and the Off Season boutique, have brought a revived buzz to the beach.

JAMMERS AND GOOGLIES

There are a lot of small-time organized sports that competitors take plenty seriously, even if they don't attract the attention that the major teams and sports do. Going to watch can be fun, not to mention inexpensive and accessible.

Gotham Girls Roller Derby ☎ 888 830 2253, ⓦ gothamgirlsrollerderby.com. Four borough teams (Brooklyn Bombshells, Queens of Pain, Manhattan Mayhem and the Bronx Gridlock) compete against one another in this fast-paced, bruising skate-fest; tickets are around $25 and take place in venues around the city.

Commonwealth Cricket League ⓦ usacricketers .com. The biggest cricket league in the city plays in the newly renovated fields of Van Cortlandt Park's parade grounds (see p.261).

---

available throughout the week; check the website for schedule and prices (a basic 1.5hr yacht sightseeing sail is $46; 2hr schooner trip is $52–62).

Downtown Boathouse Hudson River Pier 26, 72nd St and Pier 96 (Clinton Cove) at 56th St ⓦ downtown boathouse.org. Free kayaks and canoes can be rented May–Oct at weekends (9am–5pm at Pier 26, 10am–6pm at Pier 96, 10am–5pm at 56th St); also available on weekdays at Pier 26 mid-June to mid-Sept (5–7.30pm) and Pier 96 June–Aug (5.30–7.30pm). A similar kayak programme is run from Brooklyn Bridge Park (see p.219) and in Long Island City (see p.243).

Loeb Boathouse East Side of Central Park, between 74th and 75th sts ☎ 212 517 2233, ⓦ thecentral parkboathouse.com. Rowboats for rent April–Nov (daily 10am–dusk). Rates are $15 for the first hour, $4 per additional 15min, plus $20 deposit. A gondola costs $45 per 30min.

Seaport Museum South Street Seaport ☎ 212 748 8786, ⓦ southstreetseaportmuseum.org. A number of historic ships are docked at the Seaport Museum harbour; though many are somewhat endangered and either being repaired or in need of repair, the 125-year-old *Pioneer* schooner runs public sails beginning in May (until Oct). $32

BOWLING

Brooklyn Bowl 61 Wythe Ave, between 11th and 12th sts, Williamsburg, Brooklyn ☎ 718 963 3369, ⓦ brooklynbowl.com; subway L to Bedford Ave. As much a nightspot (see p.348) as a bowling alley, located in a renovated industrial warehouse; upscale bar food by the Blue Ribbon group and lots of borough-brewed beers too. Lanes $25/30min, shoe rental $4.95. Mon–Fri 6pm–2am (sometimes later on Fri), Sat noon–4am, Sun noon–2am.

Frames 550 Ninth Ave at 40th St, second floor in Port Authority ☎ 212 268 6909, ⓦ framesnyc.com; subway A, C, E to 42nd St-Port Authority, or N, Q, R, #1, #2, #3, #7 to Times Square-42nd St. For an unlikely bowling setting in a fashionable place, look no further than this full-service, modern alley in Port Authority Bus Terminal (see p.144). Mon–Sat $7 per game per person before 5pm, $12 evenings; Sun $12; shoe rental $7. Mon–Thurs noon–11pm, Fri noon–2am, Sat 11am–2am, Sun 11am–11pm.

CYCLING

New York has more than 100 miles of cycle paths; those in Central Park, Riverside Park, Hudson River Park and the East River Promenade are among the nicest. Three sources do an excellent job of providing specific cycling routes and maps, laws and regulations, and other relevant info: the bike-advocacy organization Transportation Alternatives (☎ 212 629 8080, ⓦ transalt.org), which has some good maps; the New York City Department of City Planning (ⓦ nyc.gov), which has a wealth of information available as part of their BND (Bicycle Network Development) project; and ⓦ nycbikemaps.com, with extensive bike maps for all five boroughs, information on cycling events and links to other relevant sites. A popular bike share programme, instituted by former mayor Mike Bloomberg, has made bike transport much more accessible for New Yorkers and visitors (see p.28). By law, you must wear a helmet when riding your bike on the street. Most bike stores rent bicycles by the day or hour. Refer to websites such as ⓦ bike.nyc and ⓦ bikenyc.org.

USEFUL CONTACTS

Bicycle Habitat 244 Lafayette St ☎ 212 431 3315, ⓦ bicyclehabitat.com; subway B, D, F, M to Broadway-Lafayette, N, R to Prince St, #6 to Spring St. Known for an excellent repair service, they also offer rentals, tune-ups and advice; other locations in Chelsea and Brooklyn's Park Slope and Prospect Heights. Mon–Wed & Sat 10am–7pm, Thurs & Fri 10am–8pm, Sun 10am–6pm.

Citi Bike ☎ 855 245 3311, ⓦ citibikenyc.com. This ever-expanding initiative involves renting bikes from the thousands locked up at various locations around the city. You can either be a member ($163/year) and use a bike free of charge for short rides (45min; longer spells incur extra charges), unlocking it with your personalized key, or you can just get day ($12) or three-day passes ($24), which will give you a code to access the bike (30min maximum for each ride). Bikes can be returned to any station – check the

29

website for a map of kiosks with available bikes and parking slots.

Five Borough Bike Club ☎ 347 688 2925, ⓦ 5bbc.org. This club organizes rides throughout the year, including ones to Montauk, Long Island, and Bear Mountain, north of the city.

New York Cycle Club ⓦ nycc.org. A two-thousand-member club that offers many different rides every weekend and some weekdays.

FISHING

Sometimes the amount of concrete in New York can make you forget that the city is actually surrounded by water, much of it teeming with fish. If you're looking to get out on the water, it's best to hit City Island (see p.261). Call the New York State Department of Health's Environmental Health Information line (☎ 1 800 458 1158) for the latest tips on clean water and to find out if you should toss your catch in the frying pan or back into the current.

Big City Fishing Pier 25 (N Moore St), Pier 63 (W 23rd St), Pier 84 (W 44th St) ☎ 212 627 2020, ⓦ hudson riverpark.org. Hudson River Park Trust runs this free summer programme, July and Aug (weather permitting), on different days: Mon at 5pm on Pier 25 and 63, and Sun at 11am on piers 25 and 84. The trust provides free fishing rods, reels and bait (as well as instruction) on a first-come, first-served basis, with a 30min limit when others are waiting. Common species caught include American eel, striped bass, black sea bass, fluke and snapper – all fish are returned to the river at the end of the day.

GOLF

Manhattan has no public golf courses but has a year-round, four-level driving range at Chelsea Piers (☎ 212 336 6400). These outer borough spots are subject to low, mostly standardized prices; full information is available at

ⓦ nycgovparks.org, ⓦ americangolf.com, ⓦ golfnyc.com and ⓦ nycteetimes.com. The fee for eighteen holes can vary a bit, but reckon on weekdays before noon being around $41, $32 thereafter; weekend rates are $51 before noon, $40 thereafter. Non-residents must pay an additional fee of $8–11. The biggest issue you'll face is pace of play; it's frequently slow, with six-hour rounds possible.

Dyker Beach Golf Course 86th St and Seventh Ave, Dyker Heights, Brooklyn ☎ 718 836 9722; subway R to 86th St. Noted for its striking views of the Verrazano-Narrows Bridge, Dyker is also one of the more convenient local courses, just a few blocks from the subway.

La Tourette 1001 Richmond Hill Rd, Staten Island ☎ 718 351 1889. An excellent place to play a round; very well kept, and with a driving range.

Van Cortlandt Park Golf Course Van Cortlandt Park S and Bailey Ave, Bronx ☎ 718 543 4595; subway #1 to Van Cortlandt Park or #4 to Woodlawn. The oldest eighteen-hole public golf course in the country.

HEALTH AND FITNESS: POOLS, GYMS AND BATHS

You can join one of the city's recreation centres (ⓦ nycgovparks.org) for $100–150 per year (ages 18–54), $25 (seniors) or free (under 18); paying a six-month pro-rated fee is also an option. All have gym facilities; some hold fitness and other classes, and most have an indoor and/or outdoor pool.

New York Spa Castle 131-10 Eleventh Ave, College Point, Queens ☎ 718 939 6300, ⓦ spacastleusa.com/ny; subway #7 to Main St-Flushing, then walk to shuttle bus at Union St and 39th Ave. If the Russian baths (see p.92) are too old-school for you, hit this modern spot in Queens for saunas, massages and even an outdoor pool (open in winter, too). Towels, soap and uniforms are provided, but you'll need to bring a swimsuit and beach towel for the pool.

FIVE MINI-GOLF COURSES

If it seems too much trouble to play a round of eighteen on the links, consider the fun – and family-friendly – alternative of a game of mini-golf.

Flushing Meadows Golf Center Flushing Meadows–Corona Park (mid-May to Sept daily 8am–midnight, Oct to mid-May daily 9am–5.30pm ; $9.25, under 13 $7.25; ☎ 718 271 8182).

Governors Island Summer only (Sat & Sun 10am–6pm; free), part of the Figment Art Festival held here each year.

Pier 25 Hudson River Park, Tribeca (mid-April to mid-May & mid-Sept to mid–Oct daily 11am–7pm, mid-May to mid-Sept 10am–10pm, mid-Oct to mid-April open on seasonal days; $6, under 14 $5; ☎ 347 756 5813, ⓦ manhattanyouth.org).

Randall's Island Golf Center 1 Randall's Island (Mon–Fri 9am–9pm, Sat & Sun 8am–7pm; $9, under 13 $7; ☎ 212 427 5689, ⓦ randallsislandgolfcenter.com).

Rocket Park Mini Golf New York Hall of Science, Flushing Meadows–Corona Park (April–Oct Mon–Fri 9.30am–5pm, Sat & Sun 10am–6pm; Nov Mon–Fri 9.30am–4pm, Sat & Sun 10am–4pm; $6, ages 2–17 $5, note that museum admission, $16/$13, is required to enter; ☎ 718 699 0005, ⓦ nysci.org).

29

Weekdays $40, weekends $50. Daily 8am–midnight, though some areas have more limited hours.

Riverbank State Park ⓦ 145th St and Riverside Drive ☏ 212 694 3600. Beautiful facility built on top of a waste refinery in Harlem. Tennis courts, an outdoor track, an ice-skating rink (Nov–March; $5; skate rental $6) and several indoor facilities including a roller-skating rink ($1.50; skate rental $6) and Olympic-sized swimming pool ($2, seniors and ages 5–15 $1). Park admission is free. Daily 6am–11pm.

Russian & Turkish Baths 268 E 10th St between First Ave and Ave A ☏ 212 674 9250, ⓦ russianturkishbaths .com. A neighbourhood landmark, and highly recommended (see p.92).

HORSERIDING

Jamaica Bay Riding Academy 7000 Shore Parkway, Brooklyn ☏ 718 531 8949, ⓦ horsebackride.com; subway B, D, Q to Sheepshead Bay then 5min taxi ride. Trail riding, both Western and English, around the eerie landscape of Jamaica Bay. $47 for a guided 40min ride; lessons $80–98/hr. Roughly 10am–5pm, till 8pm Tues & Thurs.

Kensington Stables 51 Caton Place at E 8th St, Prospect Park, Brooklyn ☏ 718 972 4588, ⓦ kensington stables.com; subway F to Fort Hamilton Pkwy. Horses and classes available for rides along Prospect Park's 3.5-mile bridle path for $42/hr (extra fee for a ground person for kids under 11). Private lessons are $42/30min, $68/hr. Daily 10am–sunset.

ICE-SKATING

New York's freezing winter weather makes for good ice-skating, and there are plenty of parks in which to do it. Just don't try it on any old pond or lake: the ice can be deceptively thin.

Lasker Rink 110th St, Central Park ☏ 917 492 3856, ⓦ laskerrink.com. This lesser-known ice rink is at the northern end of Central Park and is used as a pool in summer. Much cheaper ($8, under 12 $4, skate rental $7) but less accessible than the Wollman Rink. Nov–March hoursvary,butusuallyMon–Thurs10am–4pm,Fri10am–5pm & 6–11pm, Sat 1–11pm, Sun 12.30–4.30pm.

LeFrak Center at Lakeside Southeast corner of Prospect Park ☏ 718 426 0010, ⓦ lakesidebrooklyn .com. A newish development ($6 weekdays, $9 weekends, skate rental $6), the rink has seasonal ice-skating, and roller-skating in the summer.

Rink at Rockefeller Center Between 49th and 50th sts, off Fifth Ave ☏ 212 332 7654, ⓦ rinkatrockcenter .com; subway B, D, F, M to 47–50th St-Rockefeller Center. It's a quintessential New York scene, lovely to look at but with long queues and high-ish prices ($32 in the weeks around Christmas, $25 otherwise, under 11 $15, rentals $12). Oct to mid-April daily 8.30am–midnight (with half-hour breaks every two hours).

Sky Rink Pier 61 ☏ 212 336 6100, ⓦ chelseapiers.com; subway C, E to 23rd St. Ice-skate year-round at this indoor rink at Chelsea Piers ($11, rentals $6). Mon 1.30–5pm, Tues & Thurs 3–5pm, Fri 1.30–5.20pm, Sat & Sun 1–3.50pm.

Winter Village at Bryant Park ☏ 917 438 5166, ⓦ wintervillage.org; subway B, D, F, M, #7 to 42nd St-Bryant Park. Skate in a busy, scenic and (just) slightly less touristy spot than Rockefeller Center (free, rental $20). Nov–Feb daily 8am–10pm.

Wollman Rink 62nd St, Central Park ☏ 212 439 6900, ⓦ wollmanskatingrink.com. Lovely rink ($12 Mon–Thurs, $19 Fri–Sun; under 12 $6, rentals $9), where you can skate against the backdrop of the lower Central Park skyline – incredibly impressive at night. Nov–March Mon & Tues 10am–2.30pm, Wed &

NEW YORK CITY MARATHON

Every year on the first Sunday in November – save 2012, when Hurricane Sandy forced the event's cancellation – nearly fifty thousand runners line up to run (or walk or wheelchair) the **New York City Marathon** (ⓦ nycmarathon.org). Along with the competitors come the fans: on average, two million people turn out each year to watch the runners try to complete the 26.2-mile course, which starts in Staten Island, crosses the Verrazano-Narrows Bridge and passes through all the other boroughs before ending in Central Park.

If you are a **runner**, you can try to take part, but beware: the competition is fierce before the race even starts. Not everyone who submits the necessary entry forms is chosen to participate; race veterans (who have run fifteen or more New York marathons), qualified New York Road Runners (NYRR; ⓦ nyrr.org), members who have completed at least nine official races during the calendar year, and those who have applied and been rejected for the last three NYC marathons receive guaranteed entry, which can also be (completely legitimately) procured for you by a travel agent in your home country. The **application window is in January and February**, with a draw soon after (check ⓦ tcsnycmarathon.org for exact dates); and you must be at least 18 years old on race day. Running for charity is a guaranteed way to enter; see the website for details.

Thurs 10am–10pm, Fri & Sat 10am–11pm, Sun 10am–9pm.

JOGGING AND RUNNING

Jogging is still very much the number-one fitness pursuit in the city. The most popular venues are Central Park, Prospect Park, Hudson River Park and the Battery City Esplanade. A favourite circuit in Central Park is the recently renovated 1.5-mile loop around the reservoir; just make sure you jog in the right direction along with everyone else: counterclockwise. For company on your runs, contact the New York Road Runners (☎212 860 4455, ⓦnyrr.org; Mon–Fri 9am–7.30pm, Sat 9am–2pm), who sponsor many races and fun runs every year.

TENNIS

Playing tennis There's not a great deal of court space in New York, so finding an affordable one can be tough. For information on all city courts, including those in Central Park (☎212 360 8133 for permits, ☎212 280 0205 for reservations; best to reserve ahead), go to ⓦnyc.gov/parks; the ones at Prospect Park are also nice (open year-round, with a bubble cover in winter; ☎718 436 2500 for reservations). Most city parks require a permit to play, which runs $100 for the year (seniors $20, under 18 $10), though you can buy one-off single sessions for $15; the courts are open April–Nov. Hudson River Park has three courts that are free to all and work on a first-come, first-served basis (West St between Canal and Houston), or practise in the footsteps of the greats at the Billie Jean King National Tennis Center (ⓦusta.com).

POOL AND PING PONG

Along with bars and nightclubs, a good option for an evening in Manhattan is to play pool or ping pong. You can frequently find dive bars with pool tables; ping pong requires a bit more searching – although in addition to a few dedicated clubs, some outdoor places also have tables for public use, like Bryant Park, where it's free (see p.126).
Fat Cat 75 Christopher St, at Seventh Ave ☎212 675 6056, ⓦfatcatmusic.org; subway #1 to Christopher St-Sheridan Square. A somewhat dingy, fun subterranean space with ping pong, pool tables and other gaming options, not to mention free live music that runs till very late. Tables $6/hr per person Mon–Thurs & Sun, $7/hr per person Fri & Sat. Mon–Thurs 2pm–5am, Fri–Sun noon–5am.
SPiN New York 48 E 23rd St, between Madison and Park aves ☎212 982 8802, ⓦnewyork.wearespin.com; subway R, #6 to 23rd St. A sprawling ping pong centre with sixteen tables, restaurant and plenty of star power – actress Susan Sarandon is a co-owner; it's as much a social and nightlife space as anything (see box, p.351). Tables weekdays $19/30min before 5pm and after 10pm,

TOP 5 SPACES FOR ACTIVE TYPES

29

Note that these are a selective and subjective list of (mainly) outdoor highlights at each park.
Central Park For running, biking, paddling and tennis. See p.150
Chelsea Piers For hockey, rock climbing and volleyball. See p.399
Hudson River Park For boating, biking and skateboarding. See p.104
Prospect Park For Frisbee, hiking and horseriding. See p.230
Van Cortlandt Park For cricket, cross-country running and fishing. See p.261

$29/30min 5–10pm and on weekends (50 percent less for members). Mon & Tues 11am–midnight, Wed 11am–1am, Thurs–Sat 11am–2am, Sun 11am–10pm.

YOGA

New York is a great place to try yoga for the first time, with classes offered throughout the day at scores of locations. You'll find all difficulty levels and numerous styles; like much of the Western world, the ancient practice has a large following in fitness clubs, where it tends to be regarded as just another gym class (with aerobic hybrids like Yogalates), though there are plenty of traditional forms like *jivamukti*, and classes where breathing is more important than flexibility and strength. Yoga studios will also be able to tell you where to practise martial arts and Pilates. If you intend to take a number of sessions, you may want to purchase a New York Yoga PassBook, an excellent deal at $95 for hundreds of free visits and classes at workshops throughout the city and suburbs (☎212 808 0765, ⓦhealth-fitness.org/newyork_yoga). From spring till fall, many outdoor classes are free; check *Time Out New York* magazine or websites such as ⓦyogacitynyc.com for listings. A few reliable spots include:
Iyengar Yoga 150 W 22nd St, 2nd floor, between Sixth and Seventh aves ☎212 691 9642, ⓦiyengarnyc.org; subway F, M, #1 to 23rd St. Dedicated to the practices of the late BKS Iyengar, this studio allows drop-ins for classes ($25 for nonmembers). There's also a studio near Barclays Center in Brooklyn. Classes 8am–7.30pm, earlier some nights.
Yoga Vida 99 University Place, at E 12th St; also 666 Broadway ☎212 675 6056, ⓦyogavida.com; subway L, N, Q, R, #4, #5, #6 to 14th St-Union Square. Modest prices (from $20 for a one-off class to $160 monthly unlimited pass) make this *vinyasa*-oriented studio, which has a few beginner classes every day, a local favourite. Classes usually 6am–9pm.

HALLOWEEN PARADE, THE WEST VILLAGE

Parades, festivals and events

As one of the world's most multicultural cities, it's no surprise that New York City overflows with festivals – whatever their official reason for existing, they are generally just an excuse for music, food and dance. Almost every large ethnic group in the city – from the Irish to the Puerto Ricans – holds an annual get-together, often using Fifth Avenue as the main drag; in general, it is a big mistake to drive, take a taxi or ride the buses anywhere near these. In addition, the city also hosts numerous annual special events, everything from America's oldest dog show to the New York City Marathon. Turn to the Performing arts and film chapter (see p.353) for more on film festivals.

FESTIVAL CALENDAR

JANUARY

New York Jewish Film Festival Mid- to late Jan ☎212 496 3809, ⓦnyjff.org. Screenings of complex, provocative Jewish films with an international bent, as well as some rare oldies. Most films are shown at Lincoln Center's Walter Reade Theater. Tickets usually $14–15.

Lunar (Chinese) New Year Usually Jan or Feb ⓦexplorechinatown.com. A noisy, joyful occasion celebrated for two weeks along and around Mott St in Chinatown, as well as in Sunset Park in Brooklyn and Flushing in Queens. Most events free.

Restaurant Week Late Jan to mid-Feb; also late July to mid-Aug ☎212 484 1200, ⓦnycgo.com/restaurant-week. Actually for about two weeks, you can get prix-fixe three-course lunches at some of the city's finest establishments for around $29, or three-course dinners for $42. This can be quite a saving though the limited menus don't always show off the cuisine at its best, and you must reserve months in advance for the most desirable places.

Winter Antiques Show Late Jan ☎718 292 7392, ⓦwinterantiquesshow.com. Foremost American antiques show takes over the Park Avenue Armory, 643 Park Ave at E 67th St, for one week. $25/day.

Outsider Art Fair Late Jan ☎212 777 5218, ⓦoutsiderartfair.com. Leading dealers of outsider, primitive, visionary and intuitive art exhibit their collections; Metropolitan Pavilion, 125 W 18th St. From $20/day.

FEBRUARY

Empire State Building Run-Up Early Feb ☎212 860 4445, ⓦnycruns.com. Organized by NYCRUNS, contenders race up the 1576 steps of this city landmark. Registration for hopeful runners opens in Dec ($125; it's free to watch).

Westminster Kennel Club Dog Show Mid-Feb ☎212 213 3165, ⓦwestminsterkennelclub.org. Second only to the Kentucky Derby as the oldest continuous sporting event in the country (dating back to 1877), this show at Madison Square Garden welcomes 2500 canines competing for best in breed, along with legions of fanatic dog-lovers. Tickets $40–65/day.

MARCH

St Patrick's Day Parade March 17 ☎212 484 1222, ⓦsaintpatricksdayparade.com. Based on an impromptu march through the Manhattan streets by Irish militiamen on St Patrick's Day in 1762, this parade is a draw for every Irish band and organization in the US (and often Ireland itself), and it's impressive for the sheer mobs of people – no cars or floats are allowed. Starting around 11am at St Patrick's Cathedral on Fifth Ave and 44th St (following 8.30am Mass), it heads uptown to 86th St.

Greek Independence Day Parade Late March ☎718 204 6500, ⓦhellenicsocieties.org. Not as long or as boozy as St Pat's, a more patriotic nod to the old country (and the Greek Revolution of 1821) from floats of pseudo-classically dressed Hellenes. When Independence Day (March 25) falls in the Orthodox Lent, the parade is shifted to April or May. It usually kicks off from 60th St and Fifth Ave and runs up to 79th St.

New Directors, New Films Late March ☎212 875 5638, ⓦfilmlinc.org. Lincoln Center and MoMA present this two-week series, one of the city's best, but rarely surrounded by hype. Films range from the next indie hits to obscure, never-to-be-seen-again works of genius, and the majority of the film-makers are from other countries. Tickets ($16) go on sale several weeks before the beginning of the festival, and films with a lot of buzz will sell out.

APRIL

Affordable Art Fair Early April & mid-Sept ☎212 255 2003, ⓦaffordableartfair.com/newyork/. Don't let the name fool you – four days of quality art sales for which everything is priced less than $10,000 (half costs under $5000, and lots under $1500), held at the Metropolitan Pavilion, 125 W 18th St – but for $18 a day, it's the best contemporary art museum in the world.

Easter Parade Easter Sun ☎212 360 8111, ⓦnycgo.com. Evoking the old fashion parade on the city's most stylish avenue, hundreds of people promenade up Fifth Ave, from 49th to 57th sts (10am–4pm) in elaborate, flower-bedecked Easter bonnets. These days, it's more like Halloween, with

30

STREET FAIRS

In various sections of the city on weekend afternoons in the spring, summer and fall, **street fairs** close a stretch of several blocks to traffic to offer pedestrians T-shirts, curios and gut-busting snacks like sausage sandwiches and fried dough. Unfortunately, once you've seen one, you've seen them all, as the vendors are rarely neighbourhood-specific. You'll find the most local flavour at September's raucously tacky **Feast of San Gennaro** (see p.408).

Street fairs are usually listed on ⓦnycstreetfairs.com or in *Time Out New York* and neighbourhood newspapers. Smaller **block parties**, sponsored by community groups rather than business organizations, are more intimate affairs, generally with one side street closed to cars, kids performing, politicos popping in to shake hands and everyone taking part in a huge pot-luck meal. They're typically not advertised, however, so consider yourself lucky to stumble upon one.

30

people using it as an excuse to dress up in wacky costumes.

New York Antiquarian Book Fair Early April ☎212 944 8291, ⓦnyantiquarianbookfair.com. Sellers of rare books, letters, drawings, etc, exhibit at the Park Avenue Armory over four days. Get free appraisals of up to five items on "Discovery Day" (Sun). Admission $25/day.

Tribeca Film Festival Late April to early May ☎212 941 400, ⓦtribecafilm.com. This glitzy two-week fest presents an admirable mix of soon-to-be-blockbusters and indie work, including shorts and international films. Purchase tickets ($12 matinees; $21 after 5.30pm and all day Sat & Sun) well in advance.

MAY

Sakura Matsuri (Cherry Blossom Festival) Early May ☎718 623 7200, ⓦbbg.org. Music, art, dance, traditional fashion and sword-fighting demonstrations celebrate Japanese culture and the brief, sublime blossoming of the Brooklyn Botanic Garden's (see p.233) two hundred cherry trees. Free with garden admission ($15).

Five Boro Bike Tour First Sun in May ☎212 932 2453, ⓦbike.nyc. Cars are banished from the route of this forty-mile charity ride through all five boroughs, and some 32,000 cyclists take to the streets. It's $100 to take part (and free to watch).

New York Indian Film Festival Early May ☎212 594 3685, ⓦiaac.us. Screenings of films focusing on the Indian (South Asian) diaspora. Various locations, with tickets from $15.

Ukrainian Festival Mid-May ☎212 674 1615, ⓦbrama .com/stgeorge. This weekend festival (sponsored by St George Church) sees East 7th St – between Second and Third aves – filled with marvellous Ukrainian costumes, folk music and dance, plus foods and traditional crafts such as egg-painting. Most events are free.

Celebrate Israel Parade Late May or early June ☎212 245 8200, ⓦcelebrateisraelny.org. Since 1964 this celebration of Israeli independence attempts to display unity within New York's ideologically and religiously diverse Jewish community. On Fifth Ave, between 57th and 79th streets, rain or shine.

JUNE

Museum Mile Festival First Tues evening ☎212 606 2296, ⓦmuseummilefestival.org. On Fifth Ave from E 82nd to E 105th sts. Nine museums, including the Museum of the City of New York, the Cooper Hewitt, the Guggenheim, the Neue Galerie and the Met, are open free 6–9pm, and the street is closed down for a massive block party.

American Crafts Festival Early June ☎973 746 0091, ⓦcraftsatlincoln.org. Over two weekends in June, entertainment and food accompany four hundred juried displays at Lincoln Center. Free admission.

National Puerto Rican Day Parade Second Sun ☎718 401 0404, ⓦnprdpinc.org. The largest of several buoyant Puerto Rican celebrations in the city: seven hours of bands, flag-waving and baton-twirling from 44th to 86th sts on Fifth Ave, with an estimated two million people in attendance.

Mermaid Parade First Sat on or around June 21 ☎718 372 5159, ⓦconeyisland.com. At this outstanding event, participants dress like mermaids, fish and other sea creatures, and saunter through Coney Island, led by assorted offbeat celebs. A Mermaid Ball with burlesque entertainment follows.

Pride Week Third or fourth week of June ☎212 807 7433, ⓦnycpride.org. The world's biggest LGBT Pride event kicks off with a rally in Bryant Park and ends with a march down Fifth Ave, a street fair in Greenwich Village and a huge last-night dance.

Dyke March Fourth Sat ☎212 479 8520, ⓦdyke marchnyc.org. This technically illegal march (the organizers never apply for the necessary permit) rallies a diverse group of lesbian and bisexual women, from youngsters to topless grannies, at Bryant Park, to protest discrimination.

Washington Square Music Festival June ☎212 252

TOP 5 NEW YORK TRADE SHOWS

New York plays host to major expos, trade shows and conventions almost every week of the year – the following are some of the best.

International Artexpo NY Early April ☎641 472 2257, ⓦartexponewyork.com. The world's largest fine-art trade show, usually held on Pier 94, 711 Twelfth Ave. Tickets $20.

International Fashion Jewelry & Accessory Show Early May ☎212 563 1800, ⓦifjag.com. Major expo for all things glittery, usually held at the *Stewart Hotel*, 371 Seventh Ave, at W 31st St.

New York Comic Con Early Oct ⓦnewyork comiccon.com. The largest pop-culture event (and geek fest) on the East Coast. Bring your light saber.

Jacob K. Javits Convention Center, 655 W 34th St. Single-day tickets $45–50.

NY Art Book Fair Late Sept ⓦnyartbookfair.com. World's premier event for artists' books, catalogues, monographs, periodicals and 'zines, with over 350 booksellers; usually held at MoMA PS1, Long Island City, Queens (see p.245). Free admission.

NY NOW End Jan, and Aug ☎212 204 1060, ⓦnynow.com. "Home, lifestyle and handmade" trade shows, held at the Jacob K. Javits Convention Center, 655 W 34th St. Entry $25–60 (trade only).

SUMMER OUTDOOR FUN

Summer arts programmes are pleasant treats for those who stay in the city through the muggiest months. As most of these shows are free or at least very cheap, they're swarmed with fun-seeking New Yorkers – plan on arriving very early to stake out a picnic spot on the grass, and book tickets ahead when possible.

Blues BBQ Festival Aug ☎212 627 2020, ⓦhudsonriverpark.org. Best blues bands from across the country combine with best city BBQ restaurants for a fabulous summer day on the river. Pier 97 at W 57th St (Midtown West). Free.

Bryant Park Summer Film Festival Late June to late Aug ☎212 512 700, ⓦbryantpark.org. See p.362.

Celebrate Brooklyn May–Aug ☎718 855 7882, ⓦbricartsmedia.org. One of New York's longest-running free music series, at the bandstand in Prospect Park and Brooklyn Bridge Park; great Latin performances, among others.

Lincoln Center Out-of-Doors Late July to early Aug ☎212 875 5108, ⓦlcoutofdoors.org. See p.358.

Midsummer Night Swing Late June to early July ☎212 875 5766, ⓦmidsummernightswing.org. In Lincoln Center's Damrosch Park, W 62nd St at Amsterdam Ave, Tuesday to Saturday evenings, learn a different dance en masse each night to the rhythm of live swing, mambo, merengue, samba or country. Lessons at 6.30pm, music and dancing at 7.30pm. Tickets from $17.

New York Philharmonic's Concerts in the Park Late June ☎212 875 5709, ⓦnyphil.org. See p.358.

River to River Festival Late June ⓦlmcc.net/program/river-to-river. Big-name performers in pop, world music and dance take to the stage in Battery Park, the World Financial Center and elsewhere in Lower Manhattan. Free.

Rooftop Films May–Aug ☎718 417 7362, ⓦrooftopfilms.com. Set on factory roofs and in public parks in Brooklyn and Manhattan, this movie series offers nifty backdrops for watching hip indie shorts. Tickets $15.

Shakespeare in the Park June–Aug ☎212 539 8500, ⓦpublictheater.org. See p.157.

SummerStage June–Aug; ☎212 360 2777, ⓦcityparksfoundation.org/summerstage. See p.157.

30

3621, ⓦwashingtonsquaremusicfestival.org. Since 1953, a series of classical, jazz and big-band concerts, every Tues at 8pm, at this outdoor venue (rain space is usually St Joseph's Church, 371 Sixth Ave). Free.

JULY

Independence Day July 4 ☎212 494 4495. The massive firework display – above either the East or Hudson river – is visible from all over Manhattan, but the best places to view it are along the waterfront (and Brooklyn or Jersey depending on which river is being used), from about 9pm.

Restaurant Week Late July to early Aug. See p.405.

Festa del Giglio Mid-July ☎718 384 0223, ⓦolmcfeast.com. Since 1903, Havemeyer St between N 8th and N 11th sts in Williamsburg is taken over by this twelve-day Italian Catholic street festival ("Giglio" means lily), which culminates around July 16, the feast day of Our Lady of Mount Carmel, with a procession of a giant wooden boat and a figure of St Paulinus on an 85ft tower.

New York Antique Jewelry & Watch Show Late July ⓦusantiqueshows.com. Huge consumer and dealer antique fair over four days, specializing in vintage jewellery and watches at the Metropolitan Pavilion, 125 W 18th St (between Fifth and Sixth aves); admission $20/day.

Mostly Mozart Late July to late Aug ☎212 875 5766, ⓦmostlymozart.org. More than forty concerts and Mozart-themed events at Lincoln Center, in the longest-running indoor summer festival in the US. Most tickets range $35–85.

AUGUST

Hong Kong Dragon Boat Festival First weekend in Aug ☎718 767 1776, ⓦhkdbf-ny.org. Flushing Meadows–Corona Park is the site of this highly competitive race of 38ft-long sculls; live entertainment, an arts and crafts market and a dumpling-eating contest round out the weekend. Free.

Charlie Parker Jazz Festival Third week ⓦcityparksfoundation.org. Weekend festival of jazz celebrating the legacy of Charlie Parker, who spent the last years of his life in the East Village. Free concerts at Tompkins Square Park and in Harlem.

Harlem Week All month ☎212 862 8473, ⓦharlemweek.com. What began as a week-long festival around Harlem Day (a huge Sunday block party on W 135th St, between Fifth and St Nicholas aves) has stretched into a month of African, Caribbean and Latin performances, lectures and parties; some events in July, Sept and Oct, too.

New York International Fringe Festival Mid- to late Aug ☎212 279 4488, ⓦfringenyc.org. With more than two hundred companies performing at various downtown venues, this cutting-edge series has been one of the biggest for performance art, theatre, dance, puppetry and more. The festival skipped 2017 pending a format review – at the time of research future plans were unknown.

SEPTEMBER

West Indian-American Day Parade and Carnival Labor Day ☎718 467 1797, ⓦwiadcarnival.org.

30

LITERARY FESTIVALS

Bloomsday on Broadway Mid-June ⓦsymphony space.org. A one-day celebration of James Joyce's *Ulysses*, at Symphony Space, 2537 Broadway at W 95th St. Tickets from $26.

Brooklyn Book Festival Mid-Sept ⓦ brooklynbook festival.org. The largest free literary event in New York, presenting an array of literary stars.

A Christmas Carol Marathon Late Dec ⓦhousing works.org. Marathon-style reading of Charles Dickens' seasonal classic, *A Christmas Carol*, usually at the *Housing Works Bookstore Café* (p.388).

Little Red Lighthouse Festival Late Sept or early Oct ⓦnycgovparks.org. Special guest reading of Hildegarde Swift's children's classic, *The Little Red Lighthouse*, in Fort Washington Park. Free.

Moby Dick Marathon Mid-Nov ⓦmelvillesociety .org. Marathon-style reading of Herman Melville's American classic, *Moby Dick*, over three days in book stores across the city (Melville was born here in 1819). Free.

New York Book Festival Late June ⓦnewyork bookfestival.com. Open-air book competition and fair held in front of the Naumburg Bandshell in Central Park, with book sales, literary readings and live music. Most events free.

Pen America World Voices Festival Early May ⓦ worldvoices.pen.org. Founded after 9/11 by Salman Rushdie, Esther Allen and Michael Roberts, this international lit festival features challenging discussions on topical issues all over the city. Tickets from $10.

Project Shaw One Monday every month ⓦgingold group.org. Ongoing reading series from the Gingold Theatrical Group, held every month (7pm on a Monday) at Symphony Space (see p.358), where guest speakers read works by George Bernard Shaw and the writers who inspired him; tickets ($30) go fast.

Pynchon In Public Day Early May ⓦpynchonin publicpodcast.com. Various events to celebrate the novelist Thomas Pynchon's birthday, May 8.

Brooklyn's largest parade, modelled after the carnivals of Trinidad and Tobago, features music, food, dance, floats with enormous sound systems and scores of steel-drum bands – not to mention more than a million attendees.

Feast of San Gennaro Ten days in mid-Sept ☎212 226 6427, ⓦsangennaro.org. Since 1927, this festival has celebrated the patron saint of Naples (aka St Januarius) along Mulberry St and its environs in Little Italy, with a cannoli-eating contest, midway games and tasty things to eat. In three parades (the largest is Sept 19, the saint's day), a San Gennaro statue is carried through the streets with donations pinned to his cloak.

German-American Steuben Parade Third Sat ☎347 263 7376, ⓦgermanparadenyc.org. A celebration of German-American traditions that began in Queens, and now runs from 64th St to 86th St (once the heart of German Yorkville) in Manhattan, starting at noon.

African American Day Parade Late Sept ☎212 384 3080, ⓦafricanamericandayparade.org. Drum lines,

step-dancers, politicians, the Boys Choir of Harlem and other participants march through Harlem from W 111th St and Adam Clayton Powell Jr Blvd to W 136th St, in the largest black parade in America.

New York Burlesque Festival Late Sept ⓦthe newyorkburlesquefestival.com. Since 2003 this annual four-day event has spotlighted New York's booming modern burlesque scene, with performers from all over the world at various venues throughout Manhattan and Brooklyn. Most tickets range $15–35.

Atlantic Antic Late Sept ☎718 875 8993, ⓦatlanticave.org. Massive, chaotic and incredibly entertaining street festival of food, art, music, shopping and festivities in the heart of Brooklyn (one mile of Atlantic Ave from Hicks St to Fourth Ave). Noon–6pm (free).

New York City Wine & Food Festival Late Sept to mid-Oct ⓦnycwineandfoodfestival.com. The Food Network and *Food & Wine* magazine team up to present the city's biggest food festival, with big-name television and

THE BROADWAY BOMB

One of Manhattan's greatest spectacles is also technically illegal. Since 2002, the **Broadway Bomb** has been an 8.5-mile skateboard race down Broadway from 116th Street to the *Charging Bull* statue at Bowling Green. Some two thousand skaters dodge trucks and taxis in what is dubbed, accurately, as "the most dangerous longboard race in the world" (the race's slogan used to be "You Could Die"). Watching the skaters thrash towards the bull at the end of the race is a thrilling, if bizarre, experience – check skate shops to find out when the next event takes place (it's usually October). In 2012 the NYPD stepped up its attempts to stop the Bomb, arresting participants and erecting barriers on the streets; however, the 2016 event attracted virtually no police attention, which means it's likely to continue for some time.

MACY'S PARADE INFLATION EVE

See Mickey Mouse and the other characters being inflated the night before **Macy's Thanksgiving Day Parade**. It's not as crowded as on parade day, and you can wander around the feet of these giants and experience something not broadcast to every home in America. The huge nylon balloons are set up on West 77th and West 81st streets between Central Park West and Columbus Avenue at the American Museum of Natural History.

cookbook personalities giving talks and demonstrations, and Meatpacking District restaurants hosting specially priced dinners. Tickets are expensive (from $95–250), but the proceeds go to charity.

New York Film Festival Late Sept to mid-Oct 📞 212 875 5600, 🌐 filmlinc.com. One of the world's leading film festivals unreels at Lincoln Center; tickets ($20–25) can be hard to come by, as anticipated art hits debut here.

OCTOBER

Pulaski Day Parade First Sun 🌐 pulaskiparade.org. Held on Fifth Ave (29th to 53rd sts from 12.30pm) since 1937 for the celebration of Polish heritage, beginning with Mass at St Patrick's Cathedral – it's named after the famous Polish general who fought for America in the Revolutionary War (he was killed in Charleston in 1779).

New Yorker Festival Early Oct 🌐 festival.newyorker .com. Literary, music and film celebrities hobnob on stage with *New Yorker* editors, writers and cartoonists at this three-day festival, held at venues throughout the city. Tickets sell out quickly; sign up online for the Festival Wire to get advance notification of events by email.

Columbus Day Parade Second Mon 📞 212 249 9923, 🌐 columbuscitizensfd.org. On Fifth Ave between 49th and 79th streets, 35,000 marchers commemorate Italian-American heritage and the day America was put on the map. Parallel events celebrate the heritage of Native Americans and other indigenous peoples.

Village Halloween Parade Oct 31 🌐 halloween-nyc .com. In America's largest Halloween celebration, starting at 7pm on Sixth Ave at Spring St and making its way up to W 23rd, you'll see spectacular costumes, giant puppets, bands and any other bizarre stuff New Yorkers can muster. Get there early for a good viewing spot; marchers (anyone in costume is eligible) line up at 6.30pm. (A tamer children's parade usually takes place earlier that day in Washington Square Park.)

NOVEMBER

New York City Marathon First Sun 📞 212 423 2249, 🌐 tcsnycmarathon.org. Over 50,000 runners from all over the world assemble for this high-spirited 26.2-mile run on city pavements through the five boroughs. One of the best places to watch is Central Park South, almost at the finish line. Entry fees range $255–358, with general participants chosen by lottery.

Veterans Day Parade ("America's Parade") Nov 11 📞 212 693 1476, 🌐 americasparade.org. The United War Veterans sponsor this annual event on Fifth Ave from 26th to 52nd sts. Opening ceremony at 10am (Eternal Light Monument, Fifth Avenue at 24th St, next to Madison Square Park); salute and parade at 11.25am.

Macy's Thanksgiving Day Parade Thanksgiving Day 📞 212 494 4495, 🌐 macys.com/social/parade. A made-for-TV extravaganza, with big corporate floats, dozens of marching bands and Santa Claus's first appearance of the season. Some two million spectators watch it along Central Park West from W 77th St to Columbus Circle, and along Broadway down to Herald Square, 9am–noon.

Rockefeller Center Christmas Tree Lighting Late Nov 📞 212 632 3975, 🌐 rockefellercenter.com. Switching on the lights on the enormous tree in front of the ice rink begins the holiday season, in a glowing moment sure to warm even the most Grinch-like heart. The crowds, however, can be oppressive.

African Diaspora Film Festival Late Nov to early Dec 📞 212 864 1760, 🌐 nyadff.org. Films from throughout the world, by and about people of African descent, are shown at several Manhattan venues. Tickets from $13.

DECEMBER

Hanukkah Celebrations Usually mid-Dec. During the eight nights of this Jewish feast, a menorah-lighting ceremony takes place at Brooklyn's Grand Army Plaza (📞 718 778 6000), and the world's largest menorah is illuminated on Fifth Ave near Central Park (📞 212 736 8400).

SantaCon Mid-Dec 🌐 santacon.nyc. Wildly popular, nonsensical Santa Claus "convention", where folks dressed in Santa costume go on a huge bar crawl around the city. It's a bit like a giant student booze-up – it's fun if you join in, but it can be extremely annoying if you don't.

Kwanzaa Dec 26–Jan 1 📞 212 568 1645, 🌐 official kwanzaawebsite.org. Celebrations city-wide honouring African American heritage (the festival was established in the US in the 1960s), including a storytelling show by the African Folk Heritage Circle in Harlem (free).

New Year's Eve in Times Square Dec 31 📞 212 768 1560, 🌐 timessquarenyc.org. Several hundred thousand revellers party in the cold and well-guarded streets – a crowd-management nightmare, so take the subway and get where you're going early.

30

AMERICAN MUSEUM OF NATURAL HISTORY

Kids' New York

New York is a wonderful place to bring children. Obvious attractions like museums, theatres, skyscrapers, ferry rides and the city's numerous parks will certainly thrill them, but a visit with kids may also give you reason to appreciate simpler pleasures, from watching street entertainers to introducing youngsters to strange foods and fascinating neighbourhoods. The city is full of high-calibre free events aimed at children, especially in the summer: puppet shows, cultural celebrations, park festivals and storytelling hours at local bookstores are all excellent ways to entertain. Many museums and theatres also feature specific children's programmes. What follows are details of some attractions especially appealing to kids, but it's not exhaustive; you'll find plenty else sprinkled throughout the Guide.

ESSENTIALS

Getting around Once in the city, your main problem won't be finding things to do with your kids but transporting them; subways are the fastest way to get around and are perfectly safe – as a bonus, children under 44 inches (112cm) ride free on the subway and buses when accompanied by an adult. Though some natives navigate the streets and subway stairs with pushchairs, most prefer to keep infants conveniently contained in a backpack or front carrier. Indeed, many attractions do not accommodate pushchairs, though some will keep yours temporarily while you visit – call ahead for details.

Listings To find out what's available when you're in town, check listings in *Time Out New York* magazine (and the extra-specialized *TONY Kids*), the *Village Voice*, *New York* magazine and *The New York Times*; websites such as ⓦ mommypoppins.com and ⓦ achildgrows.com are also valuable resources. A solid directory of family-oriented events all around the city is available through NYC & Company, the marketing and tourism bureau, which has a a couple of kiosks throughout the city (hours vary; ⓦ nycgo .com).

MUSEUMS

You could spend an entire holiday just checking out the city's many museums, almost all of which contain something fascinating for kids. The following is a brief overview of the ones that tend to evoke special enthusiasm. Take particular note of any kids' programmes at the museums; MoMA, for example, has a family weekend deal where you can sign up for a free tour with your child (10am, in Education Building next door; see p.129) and stay on to explore the museum for free once the hands-on lesson is over. See the appropriate Guide chapters for more details on these and other museums.

31

American Museum of Natural History and the Rose Center for Earth and Space Central Park West, between 77th and 81st sts ☏ 212 769 5100, ⓦ amnh .org; subway B, C to 81st St-Museum of Natural History. One of the best museums of its kind, this enormous complex is filled with bones, taxidermy animals and other natural objects (more than thirty million in all). Your first stop should be the Fossil Halls on the Fourth Floor, where you'll find towering dinosaur skeletons. Elsewhere, a full-scale herd of elephants dominates the Akeley Hall of African Mammals; a 94ft-long blue whale hangs over the Milstein Hall of Ocean Life; the Hall of Biodiversity re-creates a Central African rainforest; and the seasonal Butterfly Conservatory is a sure bet for younger children. Just across from the Hall of Biodiversity, the Rose Center for Earth and Space features two high-tech theatres and the Cosmic Pathway, an evolutionary timeline. Daily 10am–5.45pm, Rose Center until 8.45pm on first Fri of month; IMAX shows every hour on the half-hour daily 10.30am–4.30pm. Suggested donation $22, ages 2–12 $12.50 (includes the Rose Center). Special exhibits and IMAX additional charge; combination packages available.

Brooklyn Children's Museum 145 Brooklyn Ave, at St Mark's Ave ☏ 718 735 4400, ⓦ brooklynkids.org; subway #3 to Kingston Ave. Founded in 1899, this was the world's first museum designed specifically for children. It's full of authentic ethnological, historical and technological artefacts with which kids can play (or pretend to shop or make pizza), plus live animals and a "Totally Tots" play area for smaller children. Tues, Wed & Fri–Sun 10am–5pm, Thurs 10am–6pm. $11, free Thurs 2–6pm.

Children's Museum of Manhattan 212 W 83rd St, between Broadway and Amsterdam Ave ☏ 212 721 1233, ⓦ cmom.org; subway #1 to 86th St. This participatory museum, founded in 1937, has five floors of imaginative, rotating displays. Tues–Fri & Sun 10am–5pm, Sat 10am–7pm, first Fri of month until 8pm. $14, free first Fri 5–8pm.

Children's Museum of the Arts 103 Charlton St, between Hudson and Greenwich sts ☏ 212 274 0986, ⓦ cmany.org; subway C, E to Spring St, #1 to Houston St. At this gallery, children are encouraged to look at different types of art and then create their own with paints, paper, clay, fabric and other simple media. Holiday special events are particularly interesting – African mask-making for Kwanzaa, for example. Admission includes various dance, movie and music programmes at weekends; the museum also runs a free summer programme on Governors Island. Mon & Wed noon–5pm, Thurs & Fri noon–6pm, Sat & Sun 10am–5pm. $12, pay what you wish Thurs 4–6pm.

DiMenna Children's History Museum 170 Central Park West, at 77th St ☏ 212 873 3400, ⓦ nyhistory.org/ childrens-museum; subway B, C to 81st St-Museum of Natural History. This small basement museum within the New-York Historical Society has a library and handful of

---

FIVE CULTURAL THINGS TO DO WITH KIDS

BAMKids programs p.415
Bargemusic (free Saturdays for kids) p.357
Broadway matinees p.354
Film series at Museum of the Moving Image p.412
Grand Central Terminal tours p.134

themed stations about the history of kids. Tues–Thurs & Sat 10am–6pm, Fri 10am–8pm, Sun 11am–5pm. $20, ages 5–13 $6, pay what you wish Fri 6–8pm.

Houdini Museum of New York Fantasma Magic Shop, 3rd Floor, 421 Seventh Ave, at 33rd St ☎ 212 244 3633, ⓦ houdinimuseumny.org; subway A, C, E, #1, #2, #3 to 34th St-Penn Station. It might be a bit of an overstatement to rate this a museum, but most of the floor space at the magic shop is given over to Houdini memorabilia: straitjackets, cuffs, vintage advertisements and pictures, among various tricks of the trade. Mon–Fri 10am–6pm, Sat & Sun 10am–5pm. Free.

Intrepid Sea, Air & Space Museum Pier 86, W 46th St, at Twelfth Ave ☎ 212 245 0072, ⓦ intrepidmuseum .org; subway A, C, E to 42nd St-Port Authority. Even non-military-minded kids will be impressed by the massive scale of this aircraft-carrier-cum-museum – not to mention the huge collection of aeroplanes and helicopters. The site includes a 15,000-square-foot space for hands-on learning, in which children can climb a cargo net, experience (via computer) life on a ship and (for older kids or adults) simulate aircraft launches; kids can also marvel at the *Enterprise* space shuttle. One unusual programme involves the possibility of sleeping over on the ship: Operation Slumber takes place on Saturdays for groups of kids 7–17 years old (there is adult supervision; $120 per person). April–Oct Mon–Fri 10am–5pm, Sat & Sun 10am–6pm; Nov–March daily 10am–5pm. $33, ages 5–12 $24, ages 4 and under free.

Museum of the Moving Image 36-01 35th Ave, between 36th and 37th sts, Astoria, Queens ☎ 718 777 6888, ⓦ movingimage.us; subway M, R to Steinway St or N, W to 36th Ave-31st St. The largest collection of film-related ephemera in the States is housed in this museum, which features plenty of interactivity: kids can pose in front of the camera, try some film animation and, if all else fails, play classic video games on the cheap. Wed & Thurs 10.30am–2pm, Fri 10.30am–8pm, Sat & Sun 11.30am–7pm. $15, ages 3–17 $7, free Fri 4–8pm.

National Museum of Mathematics 11 E 26th St, between Fifth and Madison aves ☎ 212 542 0566, ⓦ momath.org; subway R, W, #6 to 23rd St or 28th St. MoMath – as it's sometimes known – has some engaging

interactive exhibits that will keep kids' minds and bodies occupied for a couple of hours; check out the Human Tree and Robot Swarm in particular. Daily 10am–5pm. $15, 12 and under $9.

New York City Fire Museum 278 Spring St, between Hudson and Varick sts ☎ 212 691 1303, ⓦ nycfire museum.org; subway C, E to Spring St, #1 to Houston St. A sure hit with the preschool crowd, this space pays pleasing homage to New York City's firefighters. On display are fire engines from yesteryear (horse-drawn and steam-powered), helmets, dog-eared photos and a host of motley objects on three floors of a former fire station; a 9/11 memorial is on hand as well. Daily 10am–5pm. Suggested donation $8, 12 and under $5.

New York Hall of Science 47-01 111th St, at 46th Ave, Flushing Meadows–Corona Park, Queens ☎ 718 699 0005, ⓦ nysci.org; subway #7 to 111th St. Housed in a cylindrical tower built for the 1964–65 World's Fair, this is one of the top science museums in the country. A highlight is the giant, outdoor Science Playground (open April–Dec; an additional $5), where kids can clamber around as they learn about scientific principles. Located in Queens, the Hall of Science makes for a good day-trip combined with a visit to any of the attractions in Flushing Meadows–Corona Park: Queens Zoo, Queens Museum or the park itself. April–Aug Mon–Fri 9.30am–5pm, Sat & Sun 10am–6pm; Sept–March same hours except closed Mon. $16, kids $13, free Sept–June Fri 2–5pm & Sun 10–11am.

New York Transit Museum Old subway entrance at Schermerhorn St and Boerum Place, Brooklyn ☎ 718 694 1600, ⓦ mta.info/mta/museum; subway #2, #3, #4, #5 to Borough Hall, A, C, F, R to Jay St-MetroTech. Housed in an abandoned 1930s subway station, this museum offers more than a hundred years of transportation memorabilia, including old subway cars and buses dating back to the turn of the twentieth century. Frequent activities for kids include underground tours, workshops and an annual bus festival (part of the popular Atlantic Antic) – all best for younger school kids, of which there are usually plenty running around. The museum has an annexe at Grand Central in Manhattan. Tues–Fri 10am–4pm, Sat & Sun 11am–5pm. $10, ages 2–17 $5. Also: Transit Museum Gallery and Store at Grand Central Terminal, open daily. Free.

Queens County Farm Museum 73-50 Little Neck Pkwy, Queens ☎ 718 347 3276, ⓦ queensfarm.org; subway E, F to Kew Gardens, then bus #Q46 to Little Neck Pkwy. Just barely within the city limits is this working farm whose history goes back more than 300 years. Kids will enjoy feeding the livestock and seeing some of the agricultural machinery on show. Daily 10am–5pm. Free except for special events (like fall's Queens County Festival).

South Street Seaport Museum 12 Fulton St ☎ 212 748 8600, ⓦ southstreetseaportmuseum.org; subway

---

TOP 5 PLAYGROUNDS

Heckscher Playground Central Park. See p.150

Imagination Playground South Street Seaport. See p.56

Pier 6 Brooklyn Bridge Park. See p.411

Pier 51 Hudson River Park. See p.63

Science Playground New York Hall of Science. See p.250

#2, #3, #4, #5 to Fulton St, A, C, J to Broadway-Nassau. South Street Seaport's dock is home to a small fleet of historic ships: you can look round the *Ambrose* and *Peking* (weather permitting) at Pier 16, and boat rides are available on the *Pioneer* (usually Wed–Sun May–Oct, but check website; $32, ages 2–11 $28). The museum's holdings, in galleries across a few warehouses, may seem staid in comparison to the boats – at least as far as kids' attention goes. Bowne Print Shops daily 11am–7pm, Street of Ships and visitor centre Wed–Sun 11am–5pm.

Lobby free, tickets that include boats $12.

Staten Island Children's Museum Snug Harbor Cultural Center, 1000 Richmond Terrace, Staten Island ☎ 718 273 2060, ⓦ sichildrensmuseum.org; bus #S40 from Ferry Terminal. Expect, among other things, giant chess sets, a small-scale playhouse, a great exhibit about bugs that includes a human-size anthill and an outdoor play area on the water where kids can sail boats and learn about oysters. Tues–Fri 11am–5pm, Sat & Sun 10am–5pm. $8, free Wed 3–5pm.

SIGHTS AND ENTERTAINMENT

Non-museum sights mostly comprise the various parks and gardens that help make New York a greener city than some might imagine. There's plenty of ongoing progress in that area, too: the Brooklyn waterfront between Dumbo and the Heights has undergone massive kid-friendly redevelopment, and similar things have taken place along Manhattan's west side.

31

Bronx Zoo Bronx River Parkway at Fordham Rd ☎ 718 367 1010, ⓦ bronxzoo.org; subway #2, #5 to East Tremont Ave. The largest urban zoo in America, with thrilling permanent exhibits – check out Wild Asia by monorail (May–Oct only; $6), the lush rainforest of JungleWorld and the Congo Gorilla Forest. Kids can watch penguins being fed, get close to Siberian tigers or ride a giant bug on an insect-themed carousel. Highly recommended, particularly in spring, when many baby animals are born. April–Oct Mon–Fri 10am–5pm, Sat & Sun 10am–5.30pm; Nov–March daily 10am–4.30pm. $23.95, ages 3–12 $16.95; pay what you wish on Wed; some exhibits have additional fees.

Brooklyn Botanic Garden 900 Washington Ave ☎ 718 623 7200, ⓦ bbg.org; subway #2, #3 to Eastern Parkway, #4, #5 to Franklin Ave. This gorgeous landscape behind the Brooklyn Museum of Art is very child-friendly, with giant carp in the ponds and ducks to chase around. Kids will enjoy the City Farmers and Discovery Garden programmes, and parents can drop in for flower-arranging classes (dried and silk), garden tutorials and *t'ai chi*

sessions. Families crowd the place for seasonal events like late April's Cherry Blossom Festival. March–Oct Tues–Fri 8am–6pm, Sat & Sun 10am–6pm; Nov–Feb Tues–Fri 8am–4.30pm, Sat & Sun 10am–4.30pm. $15, 11 and under free; March–Oct free Tues & Sat before noon, Nov–Feb free Mon–Fri.

Brooklyn Bridge Park ⓦ brooklynbridgepark.org. A number of piers along the once-downtrodden waterfront by Dumbo and Brooklyn Heights have been refashioned for family fun. The main prize for kids is Pier 6, at the end of Atlantic Avenue, where giant slides, an enormous sandbox, various climbing contraptions and, best of all, a waterpark for hot summer days, rule the roost; there's a pop-up pool and skating area at Pier 2, play spaces at piers 1 and 5 and other highlights along the way. Some choice food vendors and great views make it good for adults too.

New York Aquarium Surf Ave, at W 8th St, Coney Island, Brooklyn ☎ 718 265 3474, ⓦ nyaquarium.com; subway F, Q to W 8th St-New York Aquarium. Although it dates to 1896, the aquarium has very modern looking exhibits dedicated to rays, eels and other underwater

---

CENTRAL PARK

Year-round, Central Park provides sure-fire entertainment for children; in the summer, it becomes one giant playground. The following are merely a few of the highlights; turn to Chapter 12 (see p.150) for detailed information on these and other sights.

The Carousel Mid-park at 64th St. For $3, children can take a (surprisingly fast) spin on the country's largest hand-carved horses.

Central Park Zoo Fifth Ave, at 64th St. A small but enjoyable spot, with sea lions, penguins, monkeys and the Tisch Children's Zoo.

Hans Christian Andersen statue East side at 72nd St, just west of the boat pond. June–Sept Sat 11am–noon. A sixty-year tradition of hosting storytelling sessions.

Loeb Boathouse East side at 72nd St. Rent a rowboat on the Central Park lake and enjoy the views, or take a gondola ride in the evening.

Swedish Cottage Marionette Theatre West side at 79th St. Home to puppet shows throughout the week.

Wollman Rink East side at 62nd St. Ice-skating during the winter; in the summer it's Victorian Gardens, an old-fashioned amusement park.

FIVE FUN RIDES

Cyclone See p.240
Jane's Carousel See p.219
Roosevelt Island Tram See p.181
Staten Island Ferry See p.37
The Wonder Wheel See p.240

animals. Open-air sea otter and penguin feedings are held several times daily. It's right by the famous Coney Island boardwalk and amusement parks: older children and teens will find it a good spot to people-watch or enjoy the thrill of riding some of the old and new contraptions. June–Aug Mon–Fri 10am–6pm, Sat & Sun 10am–7pm; Sept, Oct,

April & May Mon–Fri 10am–4.30pm, Sat & Sun 10am–5.30pm; Nov–March daily 10am–4.30pm. $11.95.

New York Botanical Garden 2900 Southern Blvd, at Fordham Road and Bronx River Parkway, Bronx (across from the Bronx Zoo) ☎718 817 8700, ⓦnybg.org; subway B, D, #4 to Bedford Park. One of America's foremost public gardens, with an enormous conservatory showcasing a rainforest and other types of ecosystems, plus the 12-acre Everett Children's Adventure Garden, which includes a maze and various hands-on science lessons. Tues–Sun 10am–6pm, closes 5pm most of Jan & Feb. All-garden pass $23–28, ages 2–12 $10–12, grounds-only $15, ages 2–12 $4.

31 ## SHOPS

Apple Store 767 Fifth Ave, between 58th and 59th sts ☎212 336 1440, ⓦapple.com; subway N, Q, R to Fifth Ave-59th St, F to 57th St; map p.124 (plus multiple other locations). The Apple Store teems with gadget-loving kids, looking for the latest technology in cool shopping surroundings. The one on Fifth Ave, where you descend down a giant glass cube (though at time of writing it had been temporarily removed), might be the coolest of the nine locations in town. Daily 24hr.

Bank Street Bookstore 2780 Broadway, at W 107th St ☎212 678 1654, ⓦbankstreetbooks.com; subway #1 to 110th St; map p.184. This children's bookstore moved a few blocks south from its longtime location, but still stocks the wide array of literature and games that helped establish its reputation. Frequent events and puppet shows, plus daily story hours. Mon–Wed 9am–7pm, Thurs & Fri 9am–8pm, Sat & Sun 10am–7pm.

Books of Wonder 18 W 18th St, between Fifth and Sixth aves ☎212 989 3270, ⓦbooksofwonder.com; subway F, M to 14th St, #1 to 18th St; map p.115. Showpiece kids' bookstore, with a great Oz section, story hour Saturday at 11am and Sunday at 11.30am, and frequent author appearances. Mon–Sat 10am–7pm, Sun 11am–6pm.

Brooklyn Strategist 333 Court St, between Union and Sackett sts, Carroll Gardens, Brooklyn ☎718 576 3035, ⓦthebrooklynstrategist.com; subway F, G to Carroll St; map p.235. There is a handful of gaming stores in the city; this one doubles as a community centre and place to meet like-minded foes for cards, strategic games and plenty else. Mon & Sun 11am–8pm, Tues–Sat 11am–11pm.

Brooklyn Superhero Supply Co. 372 Fifth Ave, between 5th and 6th sts, Park Slope, Brooklyn ☎718 499 9884, ⓦsuperherosupplies.com; subway F, G, R to Fourth Ave; map p.231. Want a unique souvenir for your young one? This Dave Eggers brainchild has everything an aspiring superhero will need, from jars of antimatter and omnipotence to capes. Money goes to a nonprofit

organization dedicated to creative writing and education for kids – which takes place behind a hidden door at the back. Daily 11am–5pm.

Lego Store 200 Fifth Ave, at 23rd St ☎212 255 3217, ⓦlego.com; subway R, W to 23rd St; map p.115. Also at 620 Fifth Ave, at W 50th St ☎212 245 5973; subway B, D, F, M to 47–50th St-Rockefeller Center. The Flatiron District Lego store has a section devoted to Lego models that depict the neighbourhood's history; those are in the so-called Lego Lounge, where kids can also build their own inventions. The Rockefeller Center store is famed for its giant displays, florid murals and Lego models of New York. Mon–Sat 10am–8pm, Sun 11am–6pm (Rock Center till 7pm).

Midtown Comics 200 W 40th St, at Seventh Ave; two other locations in the city ☎212 302 8192, ⓦmidtowncomics.com; subway N, Q, R, W, #1, #2, #3 to Times Square-42nd St; map p.142. Vintage action figures and other collectibles abound, but its walls and shelves full of comics and character books that make this a true teenager's dream. Mon–Sat 8am–midnight, Sun noon–8pm.

Red Caboose 23 W 45th St, between Fifth and Sixth aves, lower level ☎212 575 0155, ⓦtheredcaboose .com; subway B, D, F, M, #7 to 42nd St-Bryant Park; map p.124. A unique, cluttered subterranean shop specializing in models, particularly trains, and various die-cast

TOP 5 CHILD-FRIENDLY RESTAURANTS

Dinosaur Bar-B-Que Harlem. See p.315
John's Pizzeria West Village. See p.297
L&B Spumoni Gardens Brooklyn. See p.323
Peking Duck House Chinatown. See p.285
Shake Shack Madison Square Park (and elsewhere). See p.302

NEW YORK WITH TEENS

For many teenagers, the sights and sounds of New York (paired with a little well-placed downtime) will be fascinating enough, particularly if they have certain obsessions.

Art MoMA (see p.129) has something called Art Undergrounds, aka free teen nights with pizza and films on Friday, along with other dedicated events and workshops for kids.

Fashion Wander to the Fashion Institute of Technology, which has a free museum (see p.112), or go for a free make-up consultation at Sephora, 555 Broadway in Soho (plus fourteen other city locations).

Games Head to Washington Square Park (see p.95) or Bryant Park to see – or join – chess players in action.

Music Hush Birthplace of Hip Hop Tours (see p.30) introduce people to what made the Bronx the epicentre of hip-hop street culture – though youngsters may also want to check out sites in Brooklyn, like Adam Yauch Park in Brooklyn Heights and Biggie Smalls' apartment on the Clinton Hill–Bed-Stuy border; Hush also runs tours of Brooklyn.

Sports Pier 62 on Chelsea's waterfront boasts a skate park, part of Hudson River Park (not Chelsea Piers), open from 8am until sunset.

transportation toys. Mon–Fri 11am–7pm, Sat 11am–5pm.

Space Kiddets 26 E 22nd St, between Park Ave and Broadway ☎212 420 9878, ⓦspacekiddets.com; subway R, W, #6 to 23rd St; map p.115. Show your baby's musical taste with a CBGB onesie or a Van Halen T-shirt from this funky clothes shop that stocks infant to pre-teen sizes; vintage toys can be found at the shop around the block (46 E 21st St). Mon, Tues, Fri & Sat 10.30am–6pm, Wed & Thurs 10.30am–7pm, Sun 11am–5pm.

Tannen's Magic Studio 45 W 34th St, Suite 608, between Fifth and Sixth aves ☎212 929 4500, ⓦtannensmagic.corecommerce.com; subway B, D, F, M, N, Q, R, W to 34th St-Herald Square; map p.124. Your kids will never forget a visit to the largest magic shop in the world (and oldest in the city), with nearly eight thousand props, tricks and magic sets. The staff generally consists of magicians who can show you a trick or two. Mon–Fri 11am–6pm, Sat & Sun 10am–4pm.

THEATRE, CIRCUSES AND OTHER ENTERTAINMENT

BAMkids Brooklyn Academy of Music, 30 Lafayette Ave ☎718 636 4100, ⓦbam.org. This series presents public performances for families on weekends as well as some that run a bit longer, along with the international BAMkids Film Festival (usually early Feb).

Big Apple Circus Damrosch Park, Lincoln Center ☎212 257 2330, ⓦbigapplecircus.org. Small circus that performs late in the year (around late Oct) in a tent next to the Metropolitan Opera House. Tickets $20–65.

New Victory Theater 209 W 42nd St, at Broadway ☎646 223 3010, ⓦnewvictory.org. The city's first theatre for families, located in a grand old renovated Times Square space, presents a rich mix of theatre, music, dance, storytelling, film and puppetry, in addition to pre- and post-performance workshops. Affordable shows (most tickets $15–40) run 1–2hr, and some are quite popular. In keeping with the cultural calendar that much of the city runs on, the theatre is dark (no performances) during the summer.

Puppetworks 338 Sixth Ave, at Fourth St, Park Slope, Brooklyn ☎718 965 3391, ⓦpuppetworks.org; subway F, G to Seventh Ave. Founded back in 1980, the nonprofit Puppetworks puts on child-friendly shows – frequently adapted from familiar fairy tales – in an intimate setting; tickets usually around $10.

Streb Laboratory for Action Mechanics (S.L.A.M.) 51 N 1st St, Williamsburg, Brooklyn ☎718 384 6491, ⓦstreb.org. MacArthur-grant-winning choreographer Elizabeth Streb has developed a dynamic, physical dance style she calls Pop Action – go for one of the company's inspiring performances in its Brooklyn warehouse, or sign kids up for the week-long S.L.A.M. Summer Camps in July. The space also offers trampoline work, trapeze fun and basic tumbling; most classes are Tues–Thurs though it's open all week.

KING KONG

Contexts

History

To Europe she was America, to America she was the gateway of the earth. But to tell the story of New York would be to write a social history of the world.   H.G. Wells

Early days and colonial rule

Long before the arrival of European settlers, several Native American tribes inhabited New York; the **Lenni Lenape** tribe – part of the **Algonquin** nation – was the largest and most populous in the area that is now New York City. Although descendants of the Algonquins and other tribes still live on Long Island's Shinnecock reservation, the appearance of Europeans in the sixteenth century essentially destroyed their settled existence.

Giovanni da Verrazano was the first explorer to discover Manhattan. An Italian in the service of French king Francis I, he had set out to find the Pacific's legendary Northwest Passage, but like his countryman Christopher Columbus, had been blown off-course into what would become New York Harbor in 1524. Verrazano returned to France to woo the court with tales of fertile lands and friendly natives, but it was nearly a century before the powers of Europe were tempted to follow him.

In 1609 **Henry Hudson**, an Englishman employed by the **Dutch East India Company**, landed at Manhattan, sailing his ship, the *Half-Moone*, upriver as far as Albany. Hudson found that the route did not lead to the Northwest Passage, which he, too, had been commissioned to discover – but in charting its course for the first time he gave his name to the mighty river. Returning home, Hudson was persuaded to embark on another expedition, this time under the British flag. He arrived in Hudson Bay in the dead of winter, the temperature below freezing and his mutinous crew doubting his ability as a navigator; he, his son and several loyal sailors were set adrift in a small boat on the icy waters where, presumably, they froze to death.

British fears that they had lost the upper hand in the newly discovered land proved justified when the Dutch established a trading post at the most northerly point on the river that Hudson had reached, **Fort Nassau**, and quickly seized the commercial advantage. In 1624, four years after the Pilgrims had sailed to Massachusetts, thirty families left Holland to become New York's first European settlers, most sailing up to Fort Nassau. But a handful – eight families in all – stayed behind on a small island they called Nut Island because of the many walnut trees there: today's Governors Island. The community slowly grew as more settlers arrived, and the little island became crowded; the **settlement of Manhattan**, taken from the Lenape word *Manna-Hata* meaning "Island of the Hills", began when families from Governors Island moved across the water.

The Dutch gave this new outpost the name **New Amsterdam**, and in 1626 the Dutch West India Company sent over **Peter Minuit** to govern the small community. Among his first, and certainly more politically adroit, moves was to buy the whole of Manhattan Island from the Native Americans for trinkets worth sixty guilders (the equivalent of $24, at least according to a nineteenth-century historian); whether the Native Americans from whom Minuit "bought" the land had the same concept of permanent ownership as the Dutch is another matter altogether.

1609	1624	1626	1664
English explorer Henry Hudson, working for the Dutch, sails past Manhattan upriver as far as Albany	Dutch colony established on Governors Island	Peter Minuit arrives as governor, moves the Dutch settlement to Manhattan, which is named New Amsterdam	Revolt against Gov. Peter Stuyvesant's rule coincides with surrender to British naval troops, who rename the colony New York

As the colony slowly grew, a string of governors succeeded Minuit, the most famous of them **Peter Stuyvesant** or "Peg Leg Pete", a seasoned colonialist from the Dutch West Indies who'd lost his leg in a scrape with the Spanish. Under his leadership New Amsterdam doubled in size, population and fortifications, with an encircling wall (today's **Wall Street** follows its course) and a rough-hewn fort on what is now the site of the Customs House built to protect the settlement from the encroaching British. Stuyvesant also built himself a farm (*bouwerij* in Dutch) nearby, giving Manhattan's Bowery district its name.

Meanwhile, the **British** were steadily and stealthily building up their presence to the north. They asserted that all of America's east coast, from New England to Virginia, was theirs, and in 1664 Colonel Richard Nicholls was sent to claim the lands around the Hudson for King Charles II. To reinforce his sovereignty, Charles sent along four warships and enough troops to land on Nut and Long islands. Angered by Stuyvesant's increasingly dictatorial leadership and the high taxes levied by the Dutch West India Company, the Dutch settlers refused to defend the colony against the British. Captain Nicholls' men took New Amsterdam, renamed it **New York** in honour of Charles II's brother, the Duke of York, and started what was to be a hundred-odd years of British rule, a period interrupted only briefly in 1673 when the Dutch again gained, then lost, power in the region.

Revolution

By the 1750s the city had reached a population of sixteen thousand, spread roughly as far north as Chambers Street. As the community grew, it also operated increasingly independently of the British, but England reasserted control in 1763, when France conceded sovereignty over most of explored North America. Within a year the British had riled colonists by imposing punitive taxes and requisitioning private dwellings and inns. Skirmishes between British soldiers and the insurrectionist **Sons of Liberty** culminated in January 1770 with the fatal stabbing of a colonist in New York City.

New York did not play a large role in the **War of Independence**, due to several decisive defeats in the autumn of 1776, first in Brooklyn in the vicinity of Prospect Park, then in Westchester County (the Bronx), with the British pushing the Americans ever northward. Though the Patriots were under the command of George Washington himself, the campaign was a disaster, ending with the routing of three thousand American troops at Fort Washington and the occupation of the city by the British for the remainder of the war.

Lord Cornwallis's **surrender** to the Americans in October 1783 marked the end of the Revolutionary War, and a month later New York was finally liberated. Washington – an infinitely sharper commander than he was in the early days of the conflict – was there to celebrate, riding in triumphal procession down Canal Street and saying farewell to his officers at **Fraunces Tavern**, a facsimile of which stands at the end of Pearl Street. Soon after, New York became the fledgling nation's capital, and, on April 30, 1789, Washington its first president. The seat of the federal government was transferred to the District of Columbia a year later.

1776	1789	1792	1825
British naval vessels arrive to capture New York after the Declaration of Independence	George Washington takes oath as America's first president on Wall Street	Buttonwood Agreement, signed by 24 stockbrokers on Wall Street, signals beginning of New York Stock Exchange	Opening of the Erie Canal makes New York a major shipping port

Immigration and civil war

In 1790 the first official census of Manhattan numbered the population around 33,000. Business and trade were steadily increasing, with the forerunner of the New York Stock Exchange created under a buttonwood tree on Wall Street in the early 1800s and ferry services established between New York and Albany, and between Brooklyn and Manhattan.

In 1825, the completion of the **Erie Canal** (running from the Hudson River across the state to the Great Lakes) opened up internal trade and increased demand for cheap labour. The first waves of **immigrants**, mainly **Irish** and **German**, began to arrive in the mid-nineteenth century, the former forced out by famine, the latter by the failed revolutions of 1848–49. Though traders grew wealthy, the city could not handle the arrival of so many people all at once: epidemics of yellow fever and cholera were common, exacerbated by poor water supplies, unsanitary conditions and the poverty of most of the newcomers, not least in the Lower East Side where two of the largest communities – **Italians** and **Eastern Europeans** (many of them Jewish) – shared one of the most notorious slum areas of its day.

When the **Civil War** broke out in 1861, New York sided with the Union (North) against the Confederates (South). While the city saw little hand-to-hand fighting, it was fertile ground for much of the liberal thinking that had informed the war. In 1863, an unjust **conscription law** provoked the draft riots, with impoverished New Yorkers (especially Irish immigrants) burning buildings, looting shops and lynching African Americans; more than a thousand people were killed.

The late nineteenth century

After the Civil War, New York began to assume the mantle as the wealthiest and most influential city in the nation by dint of its skilled immigrant workers, distribution networks and financial resources. Broadway developed into the main thoroughfare, with grand hotels, restaurants and shops catering to the rich; newspaper editors **William Cullen Bryant** and **Horace Greeley** founded the *Evening Post* and the *Tribune*, respectively; and the city became a magnet for intellectuals, with **Washington Irving** and **James Fenimore Cooper** among notable residents. **Cornelius Vanderbilt** controlled a vast shipping and railroad empire from here, and **J.P. Morgan**, the banking genius, was instrumental in organizing financial mergers, creating the nation's first major corporations.

The latter part of the nineteenth century was in many ways the city's golden age: elevated railways (**Els**) sprang up to transport people quickly and cheaply around the city; **Thomas Edison** lit the streets with his new electric light bulb, powered by the nation's first commercial power plant, on Pearl Street; and in 1883, the **Brooklyn Bridge** was unveiled. In 1898, New York City – formerly just Manhattan – assumed its current size by officially incorporating Brooklyn, Staten Island, Queens and the part of Westchester County known as the Bronx. All this expansion stimulated the city's cultural growth. **Walt Whitman** eulogized the city in his poems, and **Henry James** recorded its manners and mores in novels like *Washington Square*. Along Fifth Avenue, **Richard Morris Hunt** built palaces for the wealthy robber-barons who had plundered Europe's collections of fine art – collections that would eventually find their way into the newly opened **Metropolitan Museum**.

1830–50	1835	1856–71	1858
First wave of mass immigration, principally German and Irish. The Lower East Side developed	Great Fire of New York destroys most buildings on the southern tip of Manhattan around Wall Street	The city is ruled by a corrupt group of politicians known as Tammany Hall, headed by William "Boss" Tweed	First Chinese immigrants arrive in what would become Manhattan's Chinatown

Expansion at the turn of the twentieth century

In 1898, boosted by the first wave of Asian immigrants, New York's population topped three million for the first time, making it the largest city in the world. Nearly half its residents were foreign-born, with **Ellis Island**, the depot that processed arrivals, handling two thousand people a day. Many immigrants worked in sweatshops for the city's growing, notoriously exploitative, garment industry. Although workers began to strike for better pay and conditions, it took the **Triangle Shirtwaist Factory** fire (see box, p.98) to rouse public and civic conscience; within months the state passed 56 factory-reform measures, and unionization spread through the city.

On the upside of New York's capitalist expansion, the early 1900s saw some of the city's wealth delving into adventurous new architecture. In Soho classical facades were mass-produced from **cast iron**, and the **Flatiron Building** of 1902 announced the arrival of what was to become the city's trademark – the skyscraper (while a series of tall buildings had been constructed along Park Row in the 1890s, most of them were eventually demolished). **Stephen Crane**, **Theodore Dreiser** and **Edith Wharton** all wrote stories about the city, and in 1913 the **Armory Exhibition** of paintings by Picasso, Duchamp and others caused a sensation. Skyscrapers pushed ever higher, and in 1913 a building that many consider the *ne plus ultra* of the genre, downtown's **Woolworth Building**, was completed. **Grand Central Terminal** also opened that year, celebrating New York as the gateway to the continent.

The war years and the Depression: 1914–45

As New York benefited from the trade and commerce generated by World War I, there was – perhaps surprisingly – little conflict between the various European communities crammed into the city, and few attacks on Germans.

Prohibition was passed in 1920 in an attempt to sober up the nation, but New York paid little heed. Under the helm of **Mayor Jimmy Walker**, who was quoted as saying, "No civilized man goes to bed the same day he wakes up", the city entered the Jazz Age. Writers as diverse as **Damon Runyon**, **F. Scott Fitzgerald** and **Ernest Hemingway** portrayed the excitement of the times, and musicians such as **George Gershwin** and **Benny Goodman** packed nightclubs with their new sound. Bootleg liquor ran freely in speakeasies all over town. The **Harlem Renaissance** soared to prominence, propelled by writers like **Langston Hughes** and **Zora Neale Hurston**, and music from **Duke Ellington**, **Cab Calloway** and **Billie Holiday**.

The **Wall Street Crash** of 1929 brought the party to an abrupt end. On October 24, known as "**Black Tuesday**", sixteen million shares were traded in a panicked sell-off; five days later, the New York Stock Exchange collapsed, losing $125 million ($1.5 billion in today's dollars). Millions lost their savings; banks, businesses and industries shut their doors. By 1932 approximately one in four New Yorkers was out of work, and shantytowns, known as "Hoovervilles" (after then-President Hoover, widely blamed for the Depression), had sprung up in Central Park to house the jobless and homeless.

The 1930s were a mixed bag in the city. The decade that began with the Great Depression also saw a number of architectural landmarks built (see box opposite) as well as – with the help of the Works Progress Administration (WPA) – New York's largest pool, in Astoria Park, Queens. In 1939–40, Queens hosted the **World's Fair**, in

1886	1898	Early 20th century	1920s
The Statue of Liberty, a gift from the French people to America, is unveiled	The outer boroughs of Brooklyn, Queens, the Bronx and Staten Island are incorporated into New York City	The first skyscrapers built, including the Flatiron Building (1902) and the Woolworth Building (1913)	Despite Prohibition, economic confidence brings Jazz Age and Harlem Renaissance

DEPRESSION-ERA NEW YORK

As the city – and country – sank into the Great Depression , some advances were nevertheless made. During this period three of New York's most beautiful skyscrapers were built: the **Chrysler Building** in 1930, the **Empire State** in 1931 (though it stood near-empty for years) and in 1932 the **Rockefeller Center**. Still, this impressive spate of construction was of little immediate help to those in Hooverville, Harlem or other depressed parts of the city. It fell to **Fiorello La Guardia**, Jimmy Walker's successor, to run the crisis-strewn city. He did so with stringent taxation, anticorruption and social-spending programmes that won him public approval. Simultaneously, President Roosevelt's **New Deal** supplied funds for roads, housing and parks, the latter undertaken by controversial Parks Commissioner **Robert Moses**. Under La Guardia and Moses, the most extensive public-housing programme in the country was undertaken; the Triborough, Whitestone and Henry Hudson bridges were completed; fifty miles of new expressway and five thousand acres of new parks were designed and built; and, in 1939, the airport in Queens that still bears the legendary mayor's name was opened.

Flushing Meadows–Corona Park; the year-long event focused largely on technology and the future. The country's entry into **World War II** in 1941 saw New York take on a top-secret role: the **Manhattan Project**, wherein scientists at Columbia University performed the experiments crucial to the creation of the first atomic weapon.

The postwar years to the 1960s

After World War II, New York regained its top-dog status in the fields of finance, art and communications, both in the US and the world, its intellectual and creative community swollen by European refugees. The city was the obvious choice as the permanent home of the **United Nations Organization**: lured by Rockefeller-donated land on the east side of Manhattan, the UN started construction in 1947; the Secretariat building in the complex introduced the glass curtain wall to Manhattan.

But even as the city, like the rest of the country, experienced a postwar boom, uniquely urban pressures were building. Immigrants from Puerto Rico and elsewhere in Latin America once more crammed East Harlem, the Lower East Side and other poor neighbourhoods, as did blacks from poor rural areas. Racial disturbances and riots started flaring up in what had for two hundred years been one of the more liberal of American cities. One response to the problem was a general exodus of the white middle classes – the **Great White Flight** as the media labelled it – out of New York. Between 1950 and 1970 more than a million families left the city. Things went from bad to worse during the 1960s with **race riots** in Harlem and Bedford-Stuyvesant in Brooklyn.

The **World's Fair** of 1964, again in Flushing Meadows, was a white elephant to boost the city's international profile, but on the streets the calls for civil liberties for blacks and withdrawal from Vietnam were, if anything, stronger than in most of the rest of the country. What few new buildings went up during this period seemed wilfully to destroy much of the best of earlier traditions. In particular, the eyesore that is **Madison Square Garden**, built over the old **Pennsylvania Station**, is still lamented as one of the city's worst architectural blunders; however, the **Verrazano-Narrows Bridge**, which linked Brooklyn to Staten Island, was an elegant, minimalist engineering addition.

1939	**Late 1940s to 1950s**	**1950**	**1965**
Jazz legend Charlie Parker moves to New York, where he helps create bebop	The East Village becomes home to the Beat poets – Jack Kerouac, Allen Ginsberg and William Burroughs	United Nations established in New York	Malcolm X is assassinated at Washington Heights' Audubon Ballroom

The 1970s and 1980s

Manhattan reached **crisis point** in 1975 as companies, along with their employees, began leaving the city, lured by cheap land and low taxes in the suburbs. Even after municipal securities were sold, New York ran up a debt of millions of dollars. Essential services, long shaky due to underfunding, were ready to collapse. Ironically, the mayor who oversaw this fiasco, **Abraham Beame**, was an accountant.

Three things saved the city: the **Municipal Assistance Corporation**, which was formed to borrow the money the city could no longer get its hands on; the 1977 election of **Edward I. Koch** as mayor, a man whose tough talking helped reassure jumpy corporations; and, in a roundabout way, the plummeting of the dollar on the world currency market following the rise of oil prices in the 1970s. This last factor, combined with cheap transatlantic airfares, brought European tourists into the city en masse for the first time.

The city's slow reversal of fortunes coincided with the completion of two face-saving building projects: the former **World Trade Center** was a gesture of confidence by the Port Authority of New York and New Jersey, which financed it; and the 1977 construction of the **Citicorp** (now Citigroup) **Center** added modernity and prestige to its environs on Lexington Avenue. Meanwhile, the raucous nightlife scene that started in the mid-1970s was best exemplified by hotspot **Studio 54**, where drugs and illicit sex were the main events off the dancefloor.

The real-estate and stock markets boomed during the 1980s, ushering in another era of Big Money. A spate of construction gave the city more eye-catching, though not necessarily well-loved, architecture, notably **Battery Park City**, and master builder **Donald Trump** provided glitzy housing for the super-wealthy. The stock market dip in 1987 started yet another downturn, and Koch's popularity waned. In 1989, he lost the Democratic mayoral nomination to **David Dinkins**, a 61-year-old black ex-marine who went on to beat Republican Rudolph Giuliani, a hard-nosed US attorney, in a tightly contested election. Even before the votes were counted, though, pundits forecasted that the city was beyond any mayoral healing. New York slipped, hard and fast, into a **massive recession**: in 1989 the city's budget deficit ran at $500 million. Of the 92 companies that had made the city their base in 1980, only 53 remained, the others having moved to cheaper pastures; and one in four New Yorkers was officially classed as poor – a figure unequalled since the Depression. By the end of 1990, the budget deficit was $1.5 billion.

The 1990s: the Giuliani years

Throughout 1991 the effects of these financial problems on the city's ordinary people became more and more apparent: homelessness increased; some public schools became no-go zones with armed police and metal detectors at the gates; and a garbage-workers' strike left piles of rubbish rotting on the streets. In 1993 New York, traditionally a Democratic city, elected **Rudolph Giuliani** – the city's first Republican mayor in 28 years.

The voters were rewarded: Giuliani's first term ushered in a dramatic upswing in New York's prosperity. Remarkable decreases in crime and a revitalized economy helped spur the tourism industry to some of its best years ever. Giuliani emerged as a very proactive mayor and one quite happy to take credit for making the streets safer and city bureaucracy leaner. While he made enemies among progressives for gutting rent

1969	1972	1977	1979
The Stonewall Riots in Greenwich Village inaugurate the gay-rights movement	World Trade Center Towers are built, dramatically altering the New York skyline	New York City Blackout (25hr): city suffers looting and civil unrest	The first hip-hop record, *Rapper's Delight*, released by The Sugarhill Gang (actually from New Jersey)

stabilization laws and providing massive tax breaks to corporations for moving to or remaining in the city (even as he reduced payments to the poor), Giuliani was handily re-elected to a second term in 1997. The city's economy continued to grow, and a series of civic improvements, including the cleaning up of Times Square, the renovation of Grand Central Terminal and the influx of chain stores into Harlem, ensued. Several high-profile incidents involving shocking allegations of **police brutality** marred Giuliani's second term, but these issues would all be superseded by events that would shake not just the city but the whole country – and cause the locals to lean on Giuliani once more.

9/11

As if the dot-com bust in the spring of 2001 weren't hobbling enough, New York City was hit by the worst terrorist attack of the modern era on **September 11, 2001** (see box, box, p.49). The story is now horribly familiar: two hijacked planes crashed into the Twin Towers of the World Trade Center, killing thousands. Over the next nine months, workers carted off 1.5 million tonnes of steel and debris, and by March 2002 the site was clear, well ahead of schedule (some would later ask if the job was perhaps done too quickly: several thousand Ground Zero workers continue to have chronic breathing problems as a result of not wearing ventilators and not following other environmental precautions at the site). So assured was his guidance throughout the ordeal that if Rudolph Giuliani had been able to run for mayor again, he most certainly would have won in a landslide. The law at the time, however, precluded him from running for a third term – he set his sights on the presidency instead – and so on January 1, 2002, businessman **Michael Bloomberg** replaced him as mayor.

The Bloomberg era

Though he had no prior political experience, Bloomberg, also a Republican (at least in name – as it's New York City, he not surprisingly has liberal views on same-sex marriage, gun control and a variety of other social issues), proved himself an able leader, using his corporate know-how to shore up the city's shaky finances and reorganize the school system. One of the mayor's most controversial acts was to follow California's lead and **ban smoking** in bars, clubs and all restaurants in 2003. Bar owners, naturally, fought the move, but it turned out to be good for business. In 2005 Bloomberg won re-election to a second term, during which he signed a law banning "trans-fats" in New York restaurants, unveiled a plan to replace the city's thirteen thousand taxicabs with hybrid vehicles (though it later got tripped up in the court system), and proposed a congestion pricing scheme to reduce traffic in Manhattan similar to the one in London.

In autumn 2007 the economy began to slump once more, as Wall Street registered heavy losses connected to the subprime mortgage crisis. The following year was a tough one for the city and some of its political figures. On Wall Street, investment banking giant **Bear Stearns** hit rock bottom and was bought out by JPMorgan, and later in the year **Lehman Brothers** declared bankruptcy. The real-estate market finally began to cave in and numerous construction projects were put on hold due to lack of funds. The 2008 presidential election season ended up as a disappointment for both Giuliani and

1987	1989	1993	2001
Black Monday: the stock exchange crashes and the Dow Jones index plunges 508 points in one day	David Dinkins becomes first black mayor of New York City, defeating Ed Koch and Rudolph Giuliani	Rudolph Giuliani is elected mayor – the city's first Republican mayor in 28 years	Twin Towers are destroyed in September 11 terrorist attacks; entrepreneur Michael Bloomberg succeeds Giuliani

the state's junior senator, **Hillary Rodham Clinton**, who lost their bids for the Republican and Democratic nominations, respectively (though Clinton became Secretary of State under President Barack Obama). Meanwhile, Bloomberg pushed a change through the city council to allow him to stand for a third stint in the autumn of 2009; he won a closer-than-expected vote over Comptroller William Thompson.

The following year the economy finally began to rebound, a spate of new hotels opened and construction sped up both on the buildings around the World Trade Center site and on the long-awaited arena in Brooklyn's Atlantic Yards; meanwhile, the High Line and Hudson River Park developments helped spur revitalization on Manhattan's west side. Bloomberg presided over some difficult times, facing criticism for each event – one of the largest snowstorms in city history just after Christmas 2010; some unpopular (and, eventually, failed) appointments to high positions in the Department of Education; the protest movement known as Occupy Wall Street, which began in Zuccotti Park in late 2011 and brought attention to the economic disparity between finance titans and the working class; and, in October 2012, Hurricane Sandy (see box, p.253). The last of these shook the city like nothing since 9/11, disrupting subway lines, washing away shoreline houses and creating the need for heavy rebuilding in neighbourhoods from the Financial District (namely around South Street Seaport) to Far Rockaway. Meanwhile, a citywide bike-sharing plan – which almost immediately became the nation's largest such enterprise, with more than 40,000 members signed up within a month – was established; the long-debated Second Avenue subway line picked up speed in its construction; and the fight over Bloomberg's soda ban (an attempt to eradicate the sale of sugary drinks over sixteen ounces, overturned by the Manhattan Supreme Court) raged on.

The city today

The 2013 race to succeed Bloomberg as mayor saw what was largely regarded as an uninspiring field run; emerging late from the pack to win the Democratic primary and the mayoral election was progressive Bill de Blasio, who ran in part on a platform promising to address racial and economic inequality in the city. It was not smooth sailing early on, as he ruffled feathers by bringing back William Bratton as police commissioner, the man who had helped institute the "broken windows" theory of policing – focusing on cracking down on minor crimes to deter major ones – under Giuliani. He then ticked off police by appearing to side with protestors after an unarmed African American man, Eric Garner, was killed in an encounter with a few cops in a Staten Island park. Despite this, the city seems on an upward swing, with the opening of One World Trade Center and its sky-high observatory, the relocation of the Whitney Museum at the foot of the High Line and the continued reclamation of the city's waterfront. The mayor looks set to win another term, despite many folks being dissatisfied with his performance (and that of various public services, like the MTA).

To almost everyone's astonishment, reality TV star – and New Yorker – Donald Trump won the 2016 presidential elections. Since then, the city has become a site for frequent protests, with the area around Midtown's Trump Tower always buzzing with security.

2006	**2008**	**2012**	**2014**	**2017**
7 World Trade Center finished, first in WTC rebuilding	US mortgage crisis hits Wall Street: Lehman Brothers goes bankrupt; several other merchant banks are sold	Hurricane Sandy makes landfall in New York City on October 29	One World Trade Center becomes the western hemisphere's tallest building	The Second Avenue Subway line opens and ferry service expands

Books

Since the number of books about or set in New York is so vast, what follows is necessarily selective – use it as a place to begin further sleuthing. Most of the books listed are currently in print, but those that aren't should be available on websites such as ⓦabebooks.co.uk or ⓦamazon.co.uk.

ESSAYS, MEMOIRS AND NARRATIVE NONFICTION

Josh Alan Friedman *Tales of Times Square*. Expanded in 2007, the book chronicles activities on and around the square between 1978 and 1984, pornography's golden age, documenting a culture under siege by impresarios, pimps and 25-cent thrills.

William Grimes *Appetite City: A Culinary History of New York*. The former *New York Times* restaurant critic engagingly traces the rise of the city's restaurants from way stations and early taverns to the glamour of today's celebrity-driven institutions.

Pete Hamill *Downtown: My Manhattan*. Former *Post* (and *Daily News*) editor Hamill is an authentic city voice. This isn't just his memoir of the island, though; it skilfully takes in centuries of New York characters and vanished settings along the way.

Phillip Lopate (ed) *Writing New York*. A massive literary anthology of both fiction and nonfiction writings on the city, with selections by authors from Washington Irving to Tom Wolfe.

Federico García Lorca *Poet in New York*. The Andalusian poet and dramatist spent nine months in the city around the time of the 1929 Wall Street Crash. This collection of over thirty poems reveals his feelings on loneliness, greed, corruption, racism and mistreatment of the poor.

★**Joseph Mitchell** *Up in the Old Hotel*. Mitchell's collected *New Yorker* essays are works of sober, if manipulative, genius, definitively chronicling NYC characters and situations with a reporter's precision and near-perfect style.

Jan Morris *Manhattan '45*. Morris's best piece of writing on Manhattan, reconstructing New York as it greeted returning GIs in 1945. Effortlessly written, fascinatingly anecdotal and marvellously warm about the city.

Georges Perec and Robert Bober *Ellis Island*. A brilliant, moving, original account of the "island of tears": part history, part meditation and part interviews. Some of the stories are heartbreaking (between 1892 and 1924 there were 3000 suicides on the island); the pictures even more so.

Suze Rotolo *A Freewheelin' Time: A Memoir of Greenwich Village in the Sixties*. Bob Dylan's formative years in the Village are recounted by his smart and sensitive girlfriend of four years, Suze Rotolo, who also talks about her own artistic pursuits and her family's devotion to communism.

Patti Smith *Just Kids*. The story of Smith's relationship with photographer Robert Mapplethorpe, as they and a cast of artists and musicians hang out in the *Chelsea Hotel* and generally define the art-punk ethos of 1970s New York City.

James Wolcott *Lucking Out*. Wolcott made connections to become a writer at the *Village Voice* (he eventually became a major critic for *Vanity Fair*), and he portrays the highs and lows of being young and new in the city in the 1970s with candour and wit.

HISTORY, POLITICS AND SOCIETY

Tyler Anbider *City of Dreams*. This history is just the ticket if you're looking for background on how New York became the locus for immigrant success stories.

★**Herbert Asbury** *The Gangs of New York*. First published in 1928, this fascinating telling of the seamier side of New York is essential reading. Full of historical detail, anecdotes and character sketches of crooks, the book describes New York mischief in all its incarnations and locales.

Edwin G. Burrows and Mike Wallace *Gotham: A History of New York City to 1898*. Enormous and encyclopedic in its detail, this is a serious history of the development of New York, with chapters on everything from its role in the Revolution to reform movements to its racial make-up in the 1820s.

★**Robert A. Caro** *The Power Broker: Robert Moses and the Fall of New York*. Despite its imposing length, this brilliant and searing critique of New York City's most powerful twentieth-century figure is one of the most important books ever written about the city and its environs. Caro's book brings to light the megalomania and manipulation responsible for the creation of the nation's largest urban infrastructure.

George Chauncey *Gay New York: The Making of the Gay Male World 1890–1940*. Definitive, revealing account of the city's gay subculture.

William B. Helmreich *The New York Nobody Knows: Walking 6,000 Miles in the City*. The fascinating observations of a man who traversed every block in New York over the course of years (and multiple pairs of shoes). While not a guide, it will give you a real feel for the city's neighbourhoods and its people.

Irving Howe *World of Our Fathers: The Journey of the East European Jews to America and the Life They Found and Made.* The title more or less says it all. If you're looking for a narrative about how Jewish immigrant experience played out in New York City's Lower East Side, you'll find a stirring and sweeping account of it right here.

Kenneth T. Jackson (ed) *The Encyclopedia of New York.* Massive, engrossing and utterly comprehensive guide to just about everything in the city. Did you know that Truman Capote's real name was Truman Streckfus Persons?

Roger Kahn *The Boys of Summer.* This account of the 1950s Brooklyn Dodgers by a beat writer who covered them is considered one of the classic baseball reads.

David Levering Lewis *When Harlem Was in Vogue.* Much-needed account of the Harlem Renaissance, a brief flowering of the arts in the 1920s and 1930s that was suffocated by the dual forces of the Depression and racism.

★**Jonathan Mahler** *Ladies and Gentlemen, the Bronx Is Burning: 1977, Baseball, Politics, and the Battle for the Soul of a City.* Incredible portrait of the city as it was in the late 1970s, weaving together Yankee Reggie Jackson's conflicts with manager Billy Martin, the duel between Mario Cuomo and Ed Koch, the birth of punk rock, the hunt for serial killer Son of Sam, the blackout and looting and more.

Legs McNeil and Gillian McCain *Please Kill Me.* An oral history of punk music in New York, artfully constructed by juxtaposing snippets of interviews as if the various protagonists (artists, financiers, impresarios) were in a conversation. Sometimes hilarious, often quite bleak.

Dan Okrent *Great Fortune: The Epic of Rockefeller Center.* Everything you ever wanted to know about the construction of one of New York's cultural and architectural high-water marks: fascinating stories of the Rockefeller family, the designers, the art commissioned (and, in one case, removed) and much more.

★**Luc Sante** *Low Life: Lures and Snares of Old New York.* This chronicle of the city's seamy side between 1840 and 1919 is a pioneering work. Full of outrageous details usually left out of conventional history, it reconstructs the day-to-day life of the urban poor, criminals and prostitutes with shocking clarity.

Russell Shorto *The Island at the Centre of the World.* Before New York was New York it was New Amsterdam; Shorto delivers a much-needed and highly readable account of this largely forgotten chapter in the city's history, using newly researched Dutch sources. Shorto's central thesis – that it was the freedom-loving and multicultural Dutch city that laid the roots of modern New York – is highly compelling.

Gay Talese *Fame and Obscurity.* Talese deftly presents interviews with New York City's famous (Sinatra, DiMaggio, etc) and its obscure (bums, chauffeurs, etc), offering not only a window into the heart of NYC, but that of human existence.

Jennifer Toth *The Mole People.* A creepy sociological study of the people who live below NYC streets, in the dark reaches of the subway tunnel system. You may never again ride the subway without your face plastered to the window looking for signs of human life.

ART, ARCHITECTURE AND PHOTOGRAPHY

Lorraine Diehl *The Late Great Pennsylvania Station.* The anatomy of a travesty. How could a railroad palace, modelled after the Baths of Caracalla in Rome, stand for only fifty years before being destroyed? The pictures alone warrant the price.

Horst Hamann *New York Vertical.* This beautiful book pays homage to the New York skyscraper, and is filled with dazzling black-and-white vertical shots of Manhattan, accompanied by witty quotes from famous and obscure folk.

★**Jane Jacobs** *The Death and Life of Great American Cities.* Landmark 1961 screed authored by Robert Moses' nemesis, and railing against urban over-planning.

David McCullough *Great Bridge: The Epic Story of the Building of the Brooklyn Bridge.* The story of the father-and-son Roebling team who fought the laws of gravity, sharp-toothed competitors and corrupt politicians to build a bridge that has withstood the test of time and become one of NYC's most noted landmarks.

Jed Perl *New Art City.* A thoughtful look at the artists (some household names, like de Kooning; some less so, like Hans Hoffman) who defined the 1940s, 50s and 60s of the New York scene – and how New York helped define them.

Jacob Riis *How the Other Half Lives.* Photojournalism reporting on life in the Lower East Side at the end of the nineteenth century. Its original publication in 1890 awakened many to the plight of New York's poor.

Stern, Mellins and Fishman/Stern, Gilmartin and Massengale/Stern, Gilmartin and Mellins/Stern, Mellins and Fishman/Stern, Fishman and Tilove *New York 1880/1900/1930/1960/2000.* These five exhaustive tomes contain all you'll ever want or need to know about architecture and the organization of the city.

★**N. White, E. Willensky and F. Leadon** (eds) *AIA Guide to New York.* The definitive contemporary guide to the city's architecture – witty, immensely informative and opinionated – and useful as an on-site reference; look for the 2010 edition, which is the latest.

OTHER GUIDES

Richard Alleman *The Movie Lover's Guide to New York.* More than two hundred listings of corners of the city with cinematic associations: TV and film locations, stars' childhood homes and final resting places, and more.

Interestingly written, painstakingly researched.

★ **Federal Writers' Project** The WPA Guide to New York City. Originally written in 1939 and subsequently reissued, this detailed guide offers a fascinating look at life in New York City when the Dodgers played at Ebbetts Field, a trolley ride cost five cents and a room at the Plaza was $7.50. A surprising amount of description remains apt.

Eric Sanderson Mannahatta. Get this for the illustrations, charts and maps if nothing else: it's a geographic, ecological history of the city that is bound to give you new perspectives on what Manhattan was before becoming such a densely populated island.

FICTION

Julia Alvarez How the Garcia Girls Lost Their Accents. Four Latina sisters are uprooted from their privileged life in the Dominican Republic to the Bronx in this compelling look at the modern immigrant experience.

Paul Auster The New York Trilogy: City of Glass, Ghosts and The Locked Room. Three Borgesian investigations into the mystery, madness and murders of contemporary NYC.

★ **James Baldwin** Another Country. Baldwin's best-known novel, tracking the feverish search for meaningful relationships among a group of 1960s New York bohemians.

Lawrence Block When the Sacred Ginmill Closes. It's tough to choose between Block's perfectly pitched Matthew Scudder suspense novels, all set in the city; this might be the most compelling, with Hell's Kitchen, Downtown Manhattan and far-flung parts of Brooklyn expertly woven into a dark mystery.

Truman Capote Breakfast at Tiffany's. Far sadder and racier than the movie, this novel is a rhapsody to New York in the early 1940s, tracking the dissolute youthful residents of an uptown apartment building and their movements about town.

Caleb Carr The Alienist. This 1896-set thriller evokes old New York to perfection. The heavy-handed psychobabble grates at times, but the storyline (the pursuit of one of the first serial killers) is still involving. Best for its descriptions of New York as well as saliva-inducing details of meals at long-gone restaurants.

Michael Chabon The Amazing Adventures of Kavalier and Clay. A wartime fantasy of Jewish youths in Brooklyn and their fascination with all forms of escapism – magic, radio and, most important, comic strips.

Teju Cole Open City. This heralded debut novel has a young Nigerian immigrant in the role of narrator and walker in the city; he meets many other immigrants, thinks about death, philosophy and classical music, and brings modern Manhattan to life.

Reed Farrel Coleman Walking the Perfect Square. Coleman's mysteries contain one of the genre's great (relatively) unknown creations: Brooklyn detective-cum-wine-store-operator Moe Prager, a very flawed protagonist. This, the first, flashes back between the late Seventies and late Nineties; the plot is involving enough but, most importantly, sets the scene for Prager's emotional development.

Stephen Crane Maggie: A Girl of the Streets. An 1893 melodrama about a girl growing up in a Lower East Side slum. Although luridly over-described, its ground-breaking naturalism brought deserved acclaim to Red Badge of Courage author Crane; the fictional counterpart to Riis's work.

Don DeLillo Underworld. Following the fate of the baseball hit out of the park to win the 1951 pennant for the New York Giants, DeLillo's sprawling novel offers a counterhistory of twentieth-century America. His luminous prose is spellbinding even when the story feels faintly ridiculous.

Jennifer Egan A Visit from the Goon Squad. Egan's Pulitzer Prize-winning "novel" – really, a series of loosely connected short stories that jump around in time and space – bristles with energy, imagination and musical reference; many take place in or around New York, including one in a disquieting version of the city's future.

★ **Ralph Ellison** Invisible Man. The definitive, if sometimes long-winded, novel of what it's like to be black and American, using Harlem and the 1950s race riots as a backdrop.

★ **Paula Fox** Desperate Characters. A depressing, engrossing drama about a faded marriage in 1960s Brooklyn, this slim book is exquisitely crafted and brilliantly observed.

Oscar Hijuelos Our House in the Last World. A warmly evocative novel of a Cuban immigrant's life in New York from before the war to the present day.

Chester Himes The Crazy Kill. Himes wrote violent, fast-moving and funny thrillers set in Harlem; this and Cotton Goes to Harlem are among the best.

Henry James Washington Square. Skilful and engrossing examination of the mores and strict social expectations of genteel New York society in the late nineteenth century.

Sue Kaufman Diary of a Mad Housewife. This is a classic dissection of 1960s New York, satirically chronicling the antics of a group of social climbers along with the disintegration of a marriage.

Ben Lerner 10:04. This meta-novel about writing a novel, both of which take their title from a crucial time in the plot of Back to the Future, brings all kinds of local institutions to life (Brooklyn Bridge, the High Line, the Met) while engaging the reader in the inner workings of the writer-narrator's mind.

★ **Jonathan Lethem** Motherless Brooklyn. Brooklyn author sets this quirky suspense novel in Cobble Hill and its environs, where a Tourette's sufferer tries to track down his boss's killer. See also his subsequent The Fortress of Solitude, which treats childhood and gentrification with great wit and sensitivity, or *Chronic City*, a kind of send-up of Manhattan.

Colum McCann *Let the Great World Spin*. Though set in the 1970s, its touchstone of Philippe Petit's tightrope walk across the new towers of the World Trade Center – then zooming to the ordinary lives of the people below – makes it clear that the effects of 9/11 are the true social subject of this involving novel.

Alice McDermott *Charming Billy*. Billy is a poetry-loving drunkard from Queens, looking to bring his Irish love over to New York City. National Book Award winner.

Jay McInerney *Bright Lights, Big City*. A trendy, "voice of a generation" book when it came out in the 1980s, it made first-time novelist McInerney a household name. The story follows a struggling New York writer in his job as a fact-checker at an important literary magazine (a thinly disguised *New Yorker*), and from one cocaine-sozzled nightclub to another. Still amusing.

Emma McLaughlin and Nicola Kraus *The Nanny Diaries: A Novel*. A delicious and nimble comic novel, culled from the authors' own experiences nannying for the wealthy families of the Upper East Side; later made into an entertaining film with Scarlett Johansson.

Joseph O'Neill *Netherland*. Bringing together threads about friendship, marriage, cricket, the immigrant experience and 9/11, this literary novel, if at times overwritten, ranks as one of the more important and memorable New York stories of the past decade.

Dorothy Parker *Complete Stories*. Parker's tales are, at times, surprisingly moving, depicting New York in all its glories, excesses and pretensions with perfect, searing wit.

★**Richard Price** *Lush Life*. With perfect pitch for the language of the streets, Richard Price tells the sprawling story of the murder of a bartender on today's Lower East Side, a place where struggling writers, old Jewish immigrants, drug dealers, cops and club kids uneasily coexist.

Judith Rossner *Looking for Mr Goodbar*. A disquieting book, tracing the life – and eventual demise – of a female teacher in search of love in volatile and permissive 1970s New York.

Henry Roth *Call It Sleep*. Roth's novel traces the awakening of a small immigrant child to the realities of life among the slums of the Jewish Lower East Side. Read more for the evocations of childhood than the social comment.

Paul Rudnick *Social Disease*. Hilarious, often incredible send-up of Manhattan night owls. Very New York, very funny.

J.D. Salinger *The Catcher in the Rye*. Salinger's gripping novel of adolescence, following Holden Caulfield's sardonic journey of discovery through the streets of New York. A classic.

Hubert Selby, Jr *Last Exit to Brooklyn*. When first published in Britain in 1966, this novel was tried on charges of obscenity. Even now it's a disturbing read, evoking the sex, immorality, drugs and violence of Brooklyn in the 1960s with fearsome clarity.

Betty Smith *A Tree Grows in Brooklyn*. A classic, and rightly so – a courageous Irish girl learns about family, life and sex against a vivid prewar Brooklyn backdrop. Totally absorbing.

Rex Stout *The Doorbell Rang*. Stout's Nero Wolfe is perhaps the most intrinsically "New York" of all the literary detectives based in the city, a larger-than-life character who, with the help of his dashing assistant, Archie Goodwin, solves crimes from the comfort of his sumptuous Midtown brownstone. Wonderfully evocative of the city in the 1940s and 1950s.

Donna Tartt *The Goldfinch*. This Pulitzer Prize winner touches on terrorism, art, counterfeiting and drugs while following the peregrinations of a would-be orphan in NYC (and beyond). Don't look for the title painting in the Metropolitan Museum of Art, by the way (it's actually in a museum in the Hague).

Colm Tóibín *Brooklyn*. Another immigrant story, this time via Ireland to 1950s Brooklyn; a methodical, literary work that rewards your patience and persistence.

Lara Vapnyar *Still Here*. A novel about a group of young Russian emigres looking to make it in NYC, *Still Here* combines a currency (political and digital age) with equal measures of wit and woe.

Jess Walter *The Zero*. This dark, hallucinatory and probing satire, set just after 9/11, may set your head spinning like that of its protagonist – who endures memory loss, a self-inflicted gunshot wound and an unusual mission that he has no idea why he's on.

Lauren Weisberger *The Devil Wears Prada*. A satirical snapshot of New York's cut-throat magazine world, this *roman à clef* from *Vogue* editor Anna Wintour's former assistant is pleasant enough, but the film version with Meryl Streep is even better.

★**Edith Wharton** *Age of Innocence*. A withering, deftly drawn picture of New York high society at the turn of the twentieth century and how rigid social convention keeps two sensitive, ill-fated lovers apart. See also Wharton's astounding *House of Mirth* and her classic stories *Old New York*.

Don Winslow *The Force*. A master of gritty detective storytelling leavened with ample wit, Winslow tackles race, police tactics and the brotherhood of the badge in this modern epic, largely set on the streets of Harlem.

Tom Wolfe *Bonfire of the Vanities*. Set all around New York City, this sprawling novel skewers 1980s status-mongers to great effect.

New York on film

With its skyline and rugged facades, its mean streets and swanky avenues, its electric energy and edgy attitude, New York City is a natural-born movie star; indeed, it's probably been the most filmed city on Earth, home to noir, gangster flicks, sappy romances and low-budget indie movies in equal measure. What follows is a selection not just of the best New York movies but the most New York of New York movies – movies that capture the city's atmosphere, pulse and style.

NEW YORK STORIES

Basquiat (Julian Schnabel, 1996). Haunting portrait of the artist as a young (doomed) man, rising from spray-painting graffiti and living in a box in a Lower East Side park to taking the New York art world by storm in the early 1980s. David Bowie plays a sensitive Andy Warhol.

The Cruise (Bennett Miller, 1998). A documentary portrait of a true New York eccentric, Timothy "Speed" Levitch, a Dostoyevskian character with a baroque flair for language and an encyclopedic knowledge of local history, who takes puzzled tourists on guided "cruises" around the city, on which he rails against the tyranny of the grid plan and rhapsodizes about "the lascivious voyeurism of the tour bus".

Man on Wire (James Marsh, 2008). This documentary on Philippe Petit's astounding tightrope walk between the Twin Towers in 1974 is illuminating both about the feat and the character of the man behind it.

Pollock (Ed Harris, 2000). From a cramped Manhattan apartment to the barren nature of the Hamptons, abstract artist Jackson Pollock drips on canvases and battles his wife (Oscar-winner Marcia Gay Harden), fame and drink. Harris is powerful in the title role.

Unmade Beds (Nicholas Barker, 1998). This poignant, occasionally hilarious and beautifully stylized documentary about four single New Yorkers looking for love in the personal columns, visualizes the city as one endless Edward Hopper painting.

TWENTY-FIRST-CENTURY NEW YORK

The 25th Hour (Spike Lee, 2002). Lee stacks his film (based on an excellent first novel by David Benioff) with an impressive cast, headed by Ed Norton as a drug dealer on the last day before he goes to prison, ricocheting round between friends and lovers. Bleak but gripping.

Birdman (Alejandro González Iñárritu, 2014). Something between comedy and drama about a onetime star actor (Michael Keaton), who portrayed a movie superhero (a wink at his turn as Batman), coming to grips with his past while trying to open a play on Broadway.

The Devil Wears Prada (David Frankel, 2006). A delicious turn by Meryl Streep as an Anna Wintour-clone propels this story of a young woman who arrives in the city with high journalistic ambitions but can only find work at a glamorous fashion magazine (a thinly disguised *Vogue*); based on a popular novel (see opposite).

It's Kind of a Funny Story (Anna Boden and Ryan Fleck, 2010). Frequently cited as a modern-day *One Flew Over the Cuckoo's Nest*, this has a much lighter touch, following the travails of a depressed Brooklyn high-school student who checks himself into a psychiatric ward.

NEW YORK HISTORY

The Age of Innocence (Martin Scorsese, 1993). The upper echelons of New York society in the 1870s brought gloriously to life. Though Scorsese restricts most of the action to drawing rooms and ballrooms, look out for the breathtaking matte shot of a then-undeveloped Upper East Side.

The Crowd (King Vidor, 1928). "You've got to be good in that town if you want to beat the crowd." A young couple try to make it in the big city but are swallowed up and spat out by the capitalist machine. A bleak vision of New York in the 1920s, and one of the great silent films.

The Last Days of Disco (Whit Stillman, 1998). About the most unlikely setting for Stillman's brand of square WASPy talkfests would be the bombastic glittery bacchanals that were *Studio 54* in its late-1970s heyday, which is what makes this far more enjoyable than the same season's overly literal and melodramatic *54* (Mark Christopher, 1998).

Radio Days (Woody Allen, 1987). Woody contrasts reminiscences of his loud, vulgar family in 1940s Rockaway with reveries of the golden days of radio and the glamour of Times Square.

COMEDY

Annie Hall (Woody Allen, 1977). Oscar-winning autobiographical comic romance, which flits from reminiscences of Alvy Singer's childhood living beneath the Coney Island Cyclone to life and love in uptown Manhattan, is a valentine both to ex-lover co-star Diane Keaton and to the city. Simultaneously clever, bourgeois and very winning.

Elf (Jon Favreau, 2003). A Will Ferrell vehicle with an actual heart, in which a young orphan mistakenly gets carried off to the North Pole, is brought up as an elf, then goes as an adult to Manhattan to find his real father. Dad (James Caan) works in the Empire State Building; the romantic interest (Zooey Deschanel) works at Gimbel's; and the climactic scenes take place in and around Central Park.

Ghostbusters (Ivan Reitman, 1984). Plenty of NYC locales are featured in this comedy, which stars Bill Murray, Dan Aykroyd and Harold Ramis as three slime-fighting parapsychologists, looking to save Sigourney Weaver – and the city – from ghosts, ghouls and a marshmallow giant.

Moonstruck (Norman Jewison, 1987). Cher has never been as radiant as in this Brooklyn-set romance, as she falls for a soulful baker – the brother of her fiancé. The opera scene should make you want to dress up for a night at Lincoln Center, at the least.

The Out-of-Towners (Arthur Hiller, 1969). If you have any problems getting into town from the airport take solace from the fact that they can be nothing compared to those endured by Jack Lemmon and Sandy Dennis – for whom everything that can go wrong does go wrong – in Neil Simon's frantic comedy.

So This Is New York (Richard Fleischer, 1948). A bomb on its initial release, this rarely shown but edgy and innovative comedy plants three Midwesterners among the sharpies and operators of 1930s New York. The voiceover by star Henry Morgan (an Indiana salesman thoroughly unimpressed by the big city) is sublimely sarcastic.

The Squid and the Whale (Noah Baumbach, 2005). A

TEN NEW YORK CLASSICS

Breakfast at Tiffany's (Blake Edwards, 1961). The most charming and cherished of New York movie romances, starring Audrey Hepburn as party girl Holly Golightly. Hepburn and George Peppard run up and down each other's fire escapes and skip along Fifth Avenue, taking in the New York Public Library and that jewellery store.

Do the Right Thing (Spike Lee, 1989). Set over 24 hours on the hottest day of the year in Brooklyn's Bed-Stuy – a day on which the melting pot reaches boiling point – Spike Lee's colourful, stylish masterpiece moves from comedy to tragedy to compose an epic song of New York.

The Godfather Part II (Francis Ford Coppola, 1974). Flashing back to the early life of Vito Corleone, Coppola's great sequel re-created the Italian immigrant experience at the turn of the twentieth century, portraying Corleone quarantined at Ellis Island and growing up tough on the meticulously re-created streets of Little Italy.

King Kong (Merian C. Cooper and Ernest B. Schoedsack, 1933). *King Kong* paints a vivid picture of Depression-era Manhattan, and gives us the city's most indelible movie image: King Kong straddling the Empire State Building and swatting at passing planes.

Manhattan (Woody Allen, 1979). This black-and-white masterpiece, one of the truly great eulogies to the city, details the self-absorptions, lifestyles and romances of middle-class intellectuals, to the tune of a Gershwin soundtrack.

On the Town (Gene Kelly and Stanley Donen, 1949). Three sailors get 24 hours' shore leave in NYC and fight over whether to see the sights or chase the girls. Starring Gene Kelly, Frank Sinatra and Ann Miller, this was the first musical taken out of the studios and onto the streets. Smart, cynical and satirical with a bunch of terrific numbers.

On the Waterfront (Elia Kazan, 1954). Few images of New York are as unforgettable as Marlon Brando's rooftop pigeon coop at dawn and those misty views of the New York Harbor (actually shot just over the river in Hoboken), in this unforgettable story of long-suffering longshoremen and union racketeering.

Shadows (John Cassavetes, 1960). Cassavetes' debut film is a New York movie *par excellence*: a New Wave melody about jazz musicians, young love and racial prejudice, shot with bebop verve and jazzy passion in Central Park, Greenwich Village and even the MoMA sculpture garden.

Sweet Smell of Success (Alexander Mackendrick, 1957). Broadway as a nest of vipers. Gossip columnist Burt Lancaster and sleazy press-agent Tony Curtis star in this snappy, cynical study of showbiz corruption. Shot on location and mostly at night, in steely black and white.

Taxi Driver (Martin Scorsese, 1976). A long night's journey into day by the great chronicler of the city's dark side. Scorsese's New York is hallucinatorily seductive and thoroughly repellent in this superbly unsettling study of obsessive outsider Travis Bickle (Robert de Niro).

sometimes uncomfortable but quite funny and resonant coming-of-age story in Park Slope, Brooklyn; the title refers to an exhibit in the Ocean Life section of the American Museum of Natural History.

Trainwreck (Judd Apatow, 2015). Amy Schumer stars in a romantic comedy for our edgier times; it's notable for some good acting by basketball superstar LeBron James and the love it shows to Staten Island, à la 1988's *Working Girl*.

DRAMA AND ACTION

After Hours (Martin Scorsese, 1985). Yuppie computer programmer Griffin Dunne inadvertently ends up on a night-long odyssey into the Hades of downtown New York, a journey that goes from bad to worse to awful as he encounters every kook south of 14th Street. Amazing footage of pre-gentrified Soho.

American Psycho (Mary Harron, 2000). This stylized adaptation of the Bret Easton Ellis novel succeeds largely due to Christian Bale, pulling off some blacker-than-black comedy in his role as a securities trader consumed by designer labels, the ladder of success and Huey Lewis lyrics.

Deux hommes dans Manhattan (Jean-Pierre Melville, 1958). Translated as "Two Men in Manhattan", Melville's film works as a road movie set within the city: a journalist and a photographer set off to investigate what happened to a missing UN diplomat. The scenes of a bebop-style New York at night are lovingly rendered.

The French Connection (William Friedkin, 1971). Plenty of heady Brooklyn atmosphere in this sensational Oscar-winning cop thriller starring Gene Hackman, whose classic car-and-subway chase takes place under the Bensonhurst Elevated Railroad.

The Lost Weekend (Billy Wilder, 1945). Alcoholic Ray Milland is left alone in the city with no money and a desperate thirst. The film's most famous scene is his long trek up Third Avenue (shot on location) trying to hawk his typewriter to buy booze, only to find all the pawn shops closed for Yom Kippur.

Mean Streets (Martin Scorsese, 1973). Scorsese's brilliant breakthrough film breathlessly follows small-time hood Harvey Keitel and his volatile buddy Robert de Niro around a

vividly portrayed Little Italy before reaching its violent climax.

Midnight Cowboy (John Schlesinger, 1969). The odd love story between Jon Voight's bumpkin hustler and Dustin Hoffman's touching urban creep Ratso Rizzo plays out against both the seediest and swankiest of New York locations. The only X-rated film to receive an Oscar for Best Picture.

Prince of the City (Sidney Lumet, 1981). Lumet was a die-hard New York director, and this is his New York epic. A corrupt narcotics detective turns federal informer to assuage his guilt.

Rosemary's Baby (Roman Polanski, 1968). Mia Farrow and John Cassavetes move into their dream New York apartment and think they have problems with nosy neighbours – but that's just until Farrow gets pregnant and hell, literally, breaks loose. Arguably the most terrifying film ever set in the city.

Superfly (Gordon Parks Jr, 1972). Propelled by its ecstatic Curtis Mayfield score, this blaxploitation classic about one smooth-looking drug dealer's ultimate score is best seen today for its mind-boggling fashion excess and almost documentary-like look at the Harlem bars, streets, clubs and diners of thirty-odd years ago.

The Taking of Pelham One Two Three (Joseph Sargent, 1974). Just when you thought it was safe to get back on the subway, a gang of mercenary hoods hijacks a train on its way through Midtown and threatens to start killing one passenger per minute if their million-dollar ransom is not paid within the hour.

The Warriors (Walter Hill, 1979). A ragtag but determined band of youths from Coney Island spend a hard night trying to get back home after a gang summit uptown goes awry. A cult classic.

MUSICALS

42nd Street (Lloyd Bacon, 1933). One of the best films ever made about Broadway – though the film rarely ventures outside the theatre. Starring Ruby Keeler as the young chorus girl who has to replace the ailing leading lady: she goes on stage an unknown and, well, you know the rest.

A Great Day in Harlem (Jean Bach, 1994). A unique jazz documentary that spins many tales around the famous Art Kane photograph for which the cream of New York's jazz world assemble on the steps of a Harlem brownstone one August morning in 1958. Using home-movie footage of the event and present-day interviews, Bach creates a wonderful portrait of a golden age.

Guys and Dolls (Joseph L. Mankiewicz, 1955). The great Broadway musical shot entirely on soundstages and giving as unlikely a picture of Times Square hoodlums (all

colourfully suited sweetie-pies) as was ever seen. And a singing and dancing Marlon Brando to boot.

Saturday Night Fever (John Badham, 1977). What everybody remembers is the tacky glamour of flared white pantsuits and mirror-balled discos, but *Saturday Night Fever* is actually a touching and believable portrayal of working-class youth in the 1970s, Italian-American Brooklyn and the road to Manhattan.

West Side Story (Robert Wise and Jerome Robbins, 1961). Sex, singing and Shakespeare in a hyper-cinematic Oscar-winning musical (via Broadway) about rival street gangs.

Wild Style (Charlie Ahearn, 1983). To learn about graffiti, breakdancing and early hip-hop in the South Bronx, check out this pioneering movie. It's not a documentary nor quite a musical but does star artist Lee Quinones and numerous DJs and MCs.

Small print and index

A ROUGH GUIDE TO ROUGH GUIDES

Published in 1982, the first Rough Guide – to Greece – was a student scheme that became a publishing phenomenon. Mark Ellingham, a recent graduate in English from Bristol University, had been travelling in Greece the previous summer and couldn't find the right guidebook. With a small group of friends he wrote his own guide, combining a contemporary, journalistic style with a thoroughly practical approach to travellers' needs.

The immediate success of the book spawned a series that rapidly covered dozens of destinations. And, in addition to impecunious backpackers, Rough Guides soon acquired a much broader readership that relished the guides' wit and inquisitiveness as much as their enthusiastic, critical approach and value-for-money ethos. These days, Rough Guides include recommendations from budget to luxury and cover more than 120 destinations around the globe, from Amsterdam to Zanzibar, all regularly updated by our team of roaming writers.

Browse all our latest guides, read inspirational features and book your trip at **roughguides.com**.

Rough Guide credits

Editor: Emma Gibbs and Ann-Marie Shaw
Layout: Pradeep Thapliyal
Cartography: Swati Handoo
Picture editor: Aude Vauconsant
Proofreader: Diane Margolis
Managing editor: Keith Drew
Assistant editor: Payal Sharotri

Production: Jimmy Lao
Cover photo research: Mark Thomas
Editorial assistant: Aimee White
Senior DTP coordinator: Dan May
Programme manager: Gareth Lowe
Publishing director: Georgina Dee

Publishing information

This sixteenth edition published February 2018 by
Rough Guides Ltd,
80 Strand, London WC2R 0RL
11, Community Centre, Panchsheel Park,
New Delhi 110017, India
Distributed by Penguin Random House
Penguin Books Ltd, 80 Strand, London WC2R 0RL
Penguin Group (USA), 345 Hudson Street, NY 10014, USA
Penguin Group (Australia), 250 Camberwell Road,
Camberwell, Victoria 3124, Australia
Penguin Group (NZ), 67 Apollo Drive, Mairangi Bay,
Auckland 1310, New Zealand
Penguin Group (South Africa), Block D, Rosebank Office
Park, 181 Jan Smuts Avenue, Parktown North, Gauteng,
South Africa 2193
Rough Guides is represented in Canada by DK Canada, 320
Front Street West, Suite 1400, Toronto, Ontario M5V 3B6
Printed in Singapore
© Rough Guides, 2018
Maps © Rough Guides

A catalogue record for this book is available from the
British Library
ISBN: 978-0-24130-633-8
The publishers and authors have done their best to
ensure the accuracy and currency of all the information
in **The Rough Guide to New York City**, however, they
can accept no responsibility for any loss, injury, or
inconvenience sustained by any traveller as a result of
information or advice contained in the guide.
1 3 5 7 9 8 6 4 2

MIX
Paper from
responsible sources
FSC
www.fsc.org
FSC™ C018179

Help us update

We've gone to a lot of effort to ensure that the sixteenth
edition of **The Rough Guide to New York City** is accurate
and up-to-date. However, things change – places get
"discovered", opening hours are notoriously fickle,
restaurants and rooms raise prices or lower standards. If
you feel we've got it wrong or left something out, we'd like
to know, and if you can remember the address, the price,
the hours, the phone number, so much the better.

Please send your comments with the subject line
"**Rough Guide New York City Update**" to mail@
uk.roughguides.com. We'll credit all contributions and
send a copy of the next edition (or any other Rough Guide
if you prefer) for the very best emails.

ABOUT THE AUTHORS

Sarah Hull has been a contributor to Rough Guides since 2005, writing about New England, Canada, Miami and the American South. She has spent the last ten years in New York City searching for the elusive fifteen-minute route from Brooklyn to the Upper East Side, and counts the Cloisters and the Brooklyn Botanic Garden as some of her favorite places on earth. When she's not on the road, she's in New York Supreme Court reporting on corporate shenanigans and celebrity lawsuits.

Stephen Keeling has lived in New York City since 2006. He worked as a financial journalist and editor for seven years before writing his first travel book and has written several titles for Rough Guides, including guides to the USA, California, Puerto Rico, New England, Florida and Canada.

Andrew Rosenberg is a copy editor and sometime writer. He lives in Brooklyn with his wife, Melanie; son, Jules; and cats, Caesar and Louise. Feel free to send book comments to ❸nycroughguide @gmail.com.

Acknowledgements

Sarah Hull would like to thank Andrew Rosenberg for taking a chance on me all those years ago, and Stephen Keeling for being the best kind of friend: wise, sympathetic and hilarious. Emma Gibbs and Annie Shaw were wonderfully kind and terrific editors. Julio Espada, world-class designer and style inspiration, offered indispensable advice and one-liners for the Shopping chapter. Bonnie Rychlak and Amanda Hurn were Gallery chapter gamechangers – a million thanks to these two powerhouses. I would like to dedicate my work this round to my great aunt Priscilla Morgan, New Yorker nonpareil.

Readers' updates

Thanks to all the readers who have taken the time to write in with comments and suggestions (and apologies if we've inadvertently omitted or misspelt anyone's name):

Hugh Bayley; Marie Carpenter; Devin Carrieiro; Maria Correia; Yvette Cruz; Bree Evans; Florian Fahrbach; Jason Grisales; Rachel Hoffman; Alison Hunt; Ed Hutchings; Andrea Janes; Carla Jiminez; Amanda Karlsson; Claire Laporte; Matt Lindley; Leonie Groot Lipman; Cody Nailor; Dennis Piunno; Chuck Post; Adolf Przemek; Kate Rapacchi; Michael Richardson; Jamie Soltis; Polly Trottenberg; Amy Uytingco; Hally Wolhandler.

Photo credits

All photos © Rough Guides, except the following:
(Key: t-top; c-centre; b-bottom; l-left; r-right)

1 AWL Images: SIME/Estock
2 4Corners: Maurizio Rellini
4 Getty Images: Siegfried Layda
7 Getty Images: Rachel Lewis (b); Michael Yamashita (t)
9 Alamy Stock Photo: Danita Delimont
10 Getty Images: Marvin E Newman
11 Corbis: Benjamin Beytekin (br). **Getty Images:** Pete Seaward (t);
12 Getty Images: Mitchell Funk
13 Alamy Stock Photo: Randy Duchaine (b); Richard Green (c). **Corbis:** Icon SMI/Rich Graessle (t).
14 Getty Images: Brad Barket (b); Jorg Greuel (t).
15 Alamy Stock Photo: Arcaid Images (tr); Randy Duchaine (tl). **Axiom Photographic Agency:** Katja Neinemann (b)
16 Alamy Stock Photo: Ed Rooney (t). **Corbis:** Jon Hicks (c). **Getty Images:** Gavin Hellier (b)
17 Alamy Stock Photo: Rudy Sulgan (b). **Getty Images:** Travelstock44/Juergen Held (t). Pablo Enriquez: Pablo Enriquez (c)
18 Alamy Stock Photo: Randy Duchaine
19 Getty Images: The Image Bank/Zack Seckler
36 Getty Images: Harald Sund
55 Corbis: Chris Melzer (br). **Getty Images:** Stan Honda (bl); Herald Sund (tl); Camille Tokerud (tr)
62 Corbis: Patrick Batchelder
69 Alamy Stock Photo: Richard Green
77 Alamy Stock Phot: Randy Duchaine (b); Richard Levine (t)
80 Getty Images: Andrew Burton
86 Getty Images: Hemis
94 SuperStock: Hemis
101 Alamy Stock Photo: Len Holsborg (t). **SuperStock:** age fotostock/Andria Patino (b)

105 Alamy Stock Photo: Robert K. Chin
113 Getty Images: Ellen Stagg
119 Getty Images: Michael Marquand
122 Getty Images: Berthold Trenkel
135 Getty Images: Siegfried Layda (t)
140 Alamy Stock Photo: Ed Rooney
150 Getty Images: Piotr Powietrzynski
158 Corbis: Massimo Borchi
169 Getty Images: Christian Kober
179 Alamy Stock Photo: Sandra Baker (t). **Getty Images:** Mitchell Funk (b)
197 Alamy Stock Photo: Ambient Images
213 Alamy Stock Photo: Randy Duchaine
227 Alamy Stock Photo: Peter Horree (t)
242 Alamy Stock Photo: Pegaz
254 Getty Images: Luca Trovato
263 Alamy Stock Photo: Ambient Images
279 Alamy Stock Photo: Jenny Acheson
299 Getty Images: Frank Whitney (br)
319 Alamy Stock Photo: Danita Delimont (br); Ted Pink (bl). **Getty Images:** Corbis Documentary / Owen Franken (tr)
328 Alamy Stock Photo: Stan Tess
344 Getty Images: Cory Schwartz
353 Alamy Stock Photo: Sandra Baker
365 Getty Images: Stan Honda
371 Alamy Stock Photo: Alex Segre
376 Getty Images: Larry Busacca
394 Robert Harding Picture Library: Frank Fell
404 Getty Images: Mario Tama
410 Corbis: Jon Hicks
416 Getty Images: John Kobal Foundation

Cover: *Empire State Building* **AWL Images:** Alan Copson

Index

Maps are marked in grey

T

TEST YOUR KNOWLEDGE WITH OUR ROUGH GUIDES TRAVEL QUIZ

1 Denim, the pencil, the stethoscope and the hot-air balloon were all invented in which country?

a. Italy
b. France
c. Germany
d. Switzerland

2 What is the currency of Vietnam?

a. Dong
b. Yuan
c. Baht
d. Kip

3 In which city would you find the Majorelle Garden?

a. Marseille
b. Marrakesh
c. Tunis
d. Malaga

4 What is the busiest airport in the world?

a. London Heathrow
b. Tokyo International
c. Chicago O'Hare
d. Hartsfield-Jackson Atlanta International

5 Which of these countries does not have the equator running through it?

a. Brazil
b. Tanzania
c. Indonesia
d. Colombia

6 Which country has the most UNESCO World Heritage Sites?

a. Mexico
b. France
c. Italy
d. India

7 What is the principal religion of Japan?

a. Confucianism
b. Buddhism
c. Jainism
d. Shinto

8 Every July in Sonkajärvi, central Finland, contestants gather for the World Championships of which sport?

a. Zorbing
b. Wife-carrying
c. Chess-boxing
d. Extreme ironing

9 What colour are post boxes in Germany?

a. Red
b. Green
c. Blue
d. Yellow

10 For three days each April during Songkran festival in Thailand, people take to the streets to throw what at each other?

a. Water
b. Oranges
c. Tomatoes
d. Underwear

For more quizzes, competitions and inspirational features go to **roughguides.com**

Map index

Listings key

Accommodation

Eating

Drinking/nightlife/bar/clubs/ live music venues/lgbt bar

Shopping

City plan

The **city plan** on the pages that follow is divided as shown:

Map symbols

♦	Point of interest
ⓘ	Information office
✉	Post office
✚	Hospital
🅿	Parking
@	Internet access
Ⓜ	Subway station
✈	Airport
⛴	Boat
🏊	Swimming pool
⛳	Golf course
🗼	Lighthouse
🏛	Monument
⌣	Bridge
✡	Synagogue
🛕	Buddhist temple
🕌	Mosque
	Church
	Motorway
	Main road
	Minor road
⊫⊐⊏	Tunnel
- - - -	Path
	Wall
	Ferry
	Railway
•–•–•	Cable car
⬯	Stadium
	Building
	Park
	Beach
⊞⊞	Cemetery
	International boundary
	State boundary
– – –	Chapter boundary
	Subway line

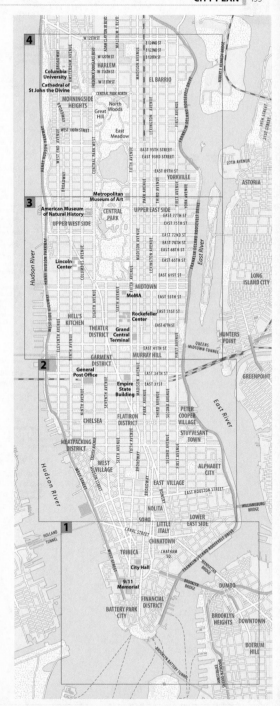

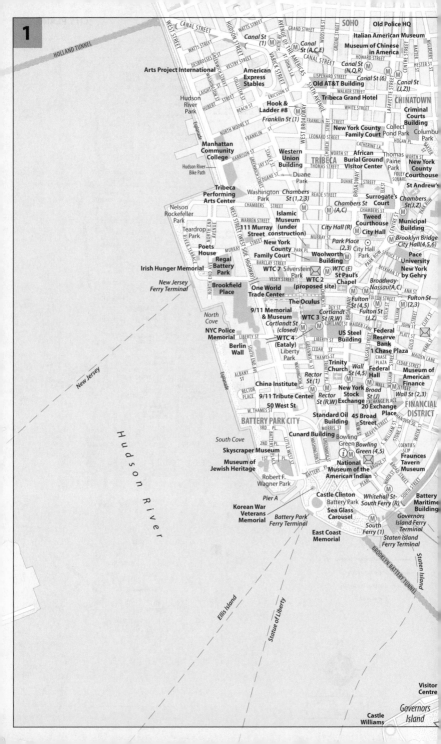

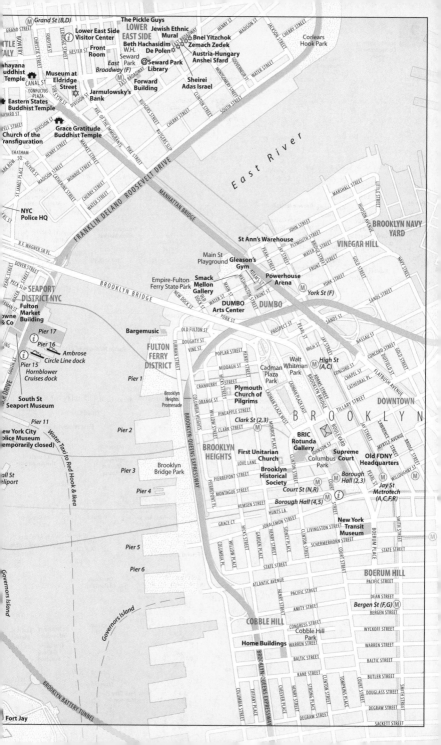

Jacob Javits Convention Center

GARMENT DISTRICT

Morgan Library & Museum

WEST 37TH STREET
WEST 37TH STREET

WEST 36TH STREET

34th St–Hudson Yards (7) Ⓜ

WEST 35TH STREET
WEST 35TH STREET

WEST 34TH STREET

Macy's ⓘ HERALD SQ.

34th St Herald Sq (B,D,F,M,N,Q,R,W) Ⓜ

Empire State Building

34th St-Penn Station (A,C,E) Ⓜ

34th St-Penn Station Ⓜ (1,2,3)

WEST 34TH STREET

WEST 33RD STREET

KOREATOWN

WEST 33RD STREET

General Post Office

Madison Square Garden

Penn Station

WEST 32ND STREET

GREELEY SQ.

BROADWAY

WEST 31ST STREET

WEST 31ST STREET

Church of the Transfiguration

High Line

WEST 30TH STREET

WEST 30TH STREET

Marble Collegiate Church

WEST 29TH STREET

SEVENTH AVENUE

WEST 29TH STREET

SIXTH AVENUE

Museum of Sex

CHELSEA GALLERY DISTRICT

WEST 28TH STREET

Chelsea Park

28th St (1) Ⓜ

28th St (R,W) Ⓜ

WEST 27TH STREET

WEST 28TH STREET

NOMAD

National Museum of Mathematics

Pier 66

Edward Thorp

WEST 26TH STREET

FIT Museum

WEST 26TH STREET

FLOWER MARKET

West 25th St Market

State Supreme Court

Gladstone Gallery

Greene Naftali

WEST 25TH STREET

WEST 25TH STREET

Eataly

Madison Square Park

Mary Boone Gallery

The Pace Gallery

Gagosian

Marianne Boesky Gallery

WEST 24TH STREET

Antiques Garage Flea Market

WEST 24TH STREET

Edith Wharton Birthplace

23rd St (R,W) Ⓜ

200 Eleventh Avenue

Luhring Augustine HL 23

London Terrace

The Chelsea Hotel

23rd St (C,E) Ⓜ

WEST 23RD STREET

23rd St (F,M) Ⓜ

23rd St (1) Ⓜ

WEST 22ND STREET

Flatiron Building

Chelsea Waterside Park

Lehmann Maupin

Sikkema Jenkins & Co

CHELSEA HISTORIC DISTRICT

One Madison Park

Pier 62

Hauser & Wirth

303 Gallery

General Theological Seminary

CHELSEA

WEST 21ST STREET

FLATIRON DISTRICT

WEST 21ST STREET

180 Tenth Avenue

Cushman Row

Oldest House in Chelsea

WEST 20TH STREET

WEST 20TH STREET

901 Bzroadway

Pier 61

100 Eleventh Avenue

WEST 19TH STREET

FIFTH AVENUE

Chelsea Piers

IAC Building

NINTH AVENUE

Joyce Theater

WEST 19TH STREET

BROADWAY

Pier 60

WEST 18TH STREET

18th St (1) Ⓜ

WEST 18TH STREET

SIXTH AVENUE

Pier 59

WEST 17TH STREET

Rubin Museum of Art

WEST 17TH STREET

Decker Building

TENTH AVENUE

Chelsea Market

WEST 16TH STREET

WEST 16TH STREET

WEST 15TH STREET

WEST 15TH STREET

Tibet House

MEATPACKING DISTRICT

Apple Store

WEST 14TH STREET

14th St (A,C,E,L) Ⓜ

Soho House

LGBT Community Center

14th St (1,2,3) Ⓜ

6th Av-14th St (F,L,M) Ⓜ

The Standard Hotel

WEST 13TH STREET

LITTLE WEST 12TH STREET

WEST 13TH STREET

Quad Cinema

Forbes Galleries

High Line

White Columns Gallery

GREENWICH AVENUE

WEST 12TH STREET

First Presbyterian Church

Whitney Museum of American Art

GANSEVOORT STREET

WAVERLY PLACE

WEST 11TH STREET

no.18

PATCHIN PLACE

EIGHTH AVENUE

WEST 4TH STREET

Church of the Ascension

HORATIO STREET

ABINGDON SQ.

Jefferson Market Courthouse

WEST 10TH STREET

JANE STREET

HUDSON STREET

GREENWICH STREET

WEST VILLAGE

WEST 9TH STREET

Pier 51

WEST 12TH STREET

BLEECKER STREET

WEST 8TH STREET

BETHUNE STREET

Carrie's Stoop

SEVENTH AVENUE

WASHINGTON SQ. NORTH

WEST 13TH STREET

Charles St Synagogue

STONEWALL PLACE

WASHINGTON PLACE

WASHINGTON STREET

BANK STREET

Christopher St-Sheridan Square (1) Ⓜ

SHERIDAN SQ.

W. WASHINGTON PLACE

Washington Square Park

WASHINGTON SQ. W.

WASHINGTON SQ. E.

PERRY STREET

W. 4TH STREET

W 4th St-Washington Sq (A,B,C,D,E,F,M) Ⓜ

Lucille Lortel Theatre

Washington Sq New York University

CHARLES STREET

WEST 3RD STREET

Friend's House

GROVE STREET

COMMERCE STREET

BARROW STREET

BEDFORD STREET

MINETTA LA.

Pier 46

GROVE COURT

St Luke's-in-the-Fields

Our Lady of Pompeii

BLEECKER STREET

WEST 10TH STREET

Jimmy Walker House

CHRISTOPHER STREET

BARROW STREET

James J. Walker Park

HUDSON STREET

WEST HOUSTON STREET

LA GUARDIA PLACE

Christopher Street Pier (Pier 45)

MORTON STREET

Hudson River Park

SIXTH AVENUE

Houston St (1) Ⓜ

LEROY STREET

St Anthony of Padua

Louis K. Meisel

VARICK STREET

CLARKSON STREET

Old SoHo Gallery Building

PRINCE STREET

MACDOUGAL STREET

KING STREET

WEST HOUSTON STREET

SULLIVAN STREET

THOMPSON STREET

WEST BROADWAY

Pier 40

CHARLTON STREET

Spring St (C,E) Ⓜ

SPRING STREET

VANDAM STREET

Trump Soho

no.116

Hudson River

New York City Fire Museum

DOMINICK STREET

BROOME STREET

WATTS STREET

WEST SIDE HIGHWAY

Hudson River Bike Path

Hudson River Greenway

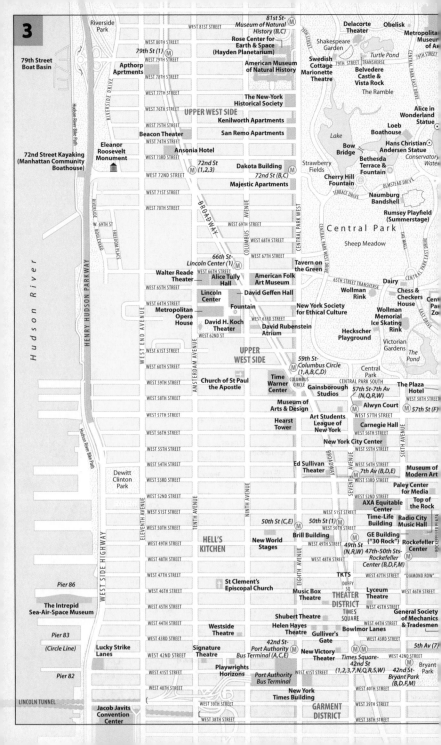

4

125th St (A,B,C,D)

House of Hoops
WEST 125TH STREET
Apollo Theater
Blumstein's
Theresa Towers
Magic Theatres
WEST 124TH STREET
Studio Museum
(i)
125th St (2,3)

WEST 123RD STREET

no. 133-143

St Martin's Church

SEMINARY ROW
WEST 122ND ST

General Grant National Memorial (Grant's Tomb)

Riverside Church

Hale House
WEST 121ST STREET
Mount Olivet Church

WEST 120TH STREET

Columbia University

W. 119TH ST
WEST 119TH STREET

Mount Morris Park Historic District

Barnard College

W. 118TH ST
WEST 118TH STREET

HARLEM

St Paul's Chapel

WEST 117TH STREET

116th St Columbia University(1)

Low Memorial Library

Morningside Park

116th St (B,C)

116th St (2,3)

W. 116TH ST

WEST 116TH STREET

(LITTLE SENEGAL)

Masjid Malcolm Shabazz

WEST 115TH ST

First Corinthian Baptist Church

WEST 115TH STREET

MIST Harle

WEST 115TH STREET

WEST 114TH STREET

WEST 114TH STREET

Malcolm Shabazz Harlem Market

WEST 113TH STREET

WEST 113TH STREET

Cathedral Parkway (110th St)(1)

WEST 111TH STREET

WEST 112TH STREET

WEST 112TH STREET

Cathedral of St John the Divine

Cathedral Parkway (110th St)(B,C)

WEST 111TH STREET

WEST 110TH STREET

CENTRAL PARK NORTH

Charles A. Dana Discovery Center

WEST 109TH STREET

Nicholas Roerich Museum

WEST 108TH STREET

MORNINGSIDE HEIGHTS

Harlem Meer

Blockhouse

Riverside Park

WEST 107TH STREET

Lasker Pool & Rink

River Mansion

WEST 106TH STREET

DUKE ELLINGTON BOULEVARD

Duke Ellington Monument

NY Buddhist Church

WEST 105TH STREET

Great Hill

Conservatory Garden

Riverside Study Center

WEST 104TH STREET

103rd St (1)

103rd St (B,C)

W. 103RD ST

The Loch

The Pool

WEST 103RD STREET

Fireman's Memorial

W. 102ND ST

WEST 102ND STREET

WEST 101ST STREET

W. 101ST ST

WEST 100TH STREET

WEST 100TH STREET

North Meadow

WEST 99TH STREET

East Meadow

WEST 98TH STREET

North Meadow Recreation Center

WEST 97TH STREET

96th St (1,2,3)

96th St (B,C)

97TH ST

97TH STREET TRANSVERSE

97TH ST

WEST 96TH STREET

Joan of Arc Monument

WEST 95TH STREET

Symphony Space

WEST 94TH STREET

WEST 93RD STREET

Tennis Courts

WEST 92ND STREET

WEST 91ST STREET

The Reservoir

WEST 90TH STREET

Main Entrance for Reservoir Track & NY Road Runners Club Booth

WEST 89TH STREET

Soldiers & Sailors Monument

WEST 88TH STREET

UPPER WEST SIDE

WEST 87TH STREET

86th St (1)

86th St (B,C)

WEST 86TH STREET

WEST 86TH STREET

86TH STREET TRANSVERSE

WEST 85TH STREET

Central Park

WEST 84TH STREET

WEST 83RD STREET

Children's Museum of Manhattan

Great Lawn

Riverside Park

WEST 82ND STREET

Metropolitan Museum of Art

Hudson River

RIVERSIDE DRIVE WEST

BROADWAY

AMSTERDAM AVENUE

MORNINGSIDE AVENUE

MORNINGSIDE DRIVE

FREDERICK DOUGLASS BLVD (EIGHTH AVENUE)

ADAM CLAYTON JR BLVD

ST NICHOLAS AVENUE

(SEVENTH AVENUE)

MALCOLM X BLVD

LENOX AVENUE

CLAREMONT AVENUE

RIVERSIDE DRIVE

MANHATTAN AVENUE

WEST END AVENUE

AMSTERDAM AVENUE

COLUMBUS AVENUE

CENTRAL PARK WEST

CENTRAL PARK WEST DRIVE

CENTRAL PARK EAST DRIVE

HENRY HUDSON PARKWAY

RIVERSIDE DRIVE

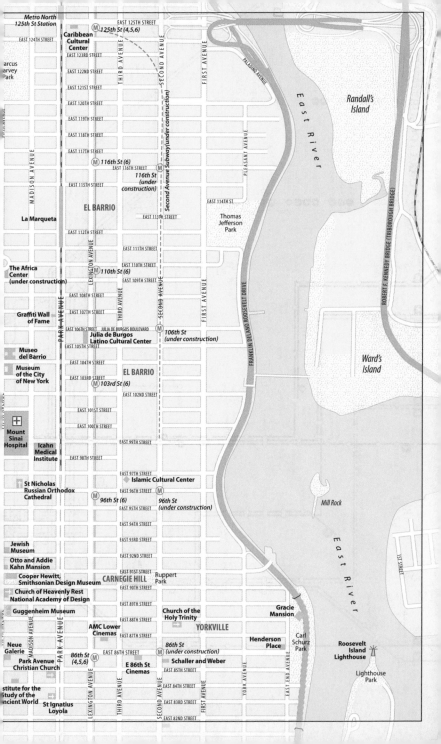

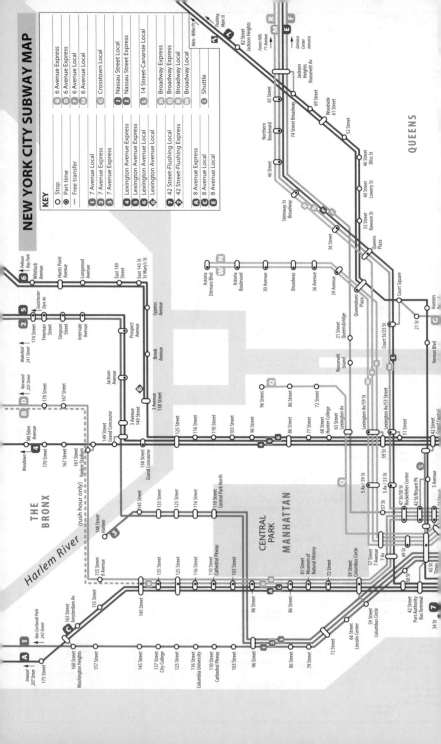

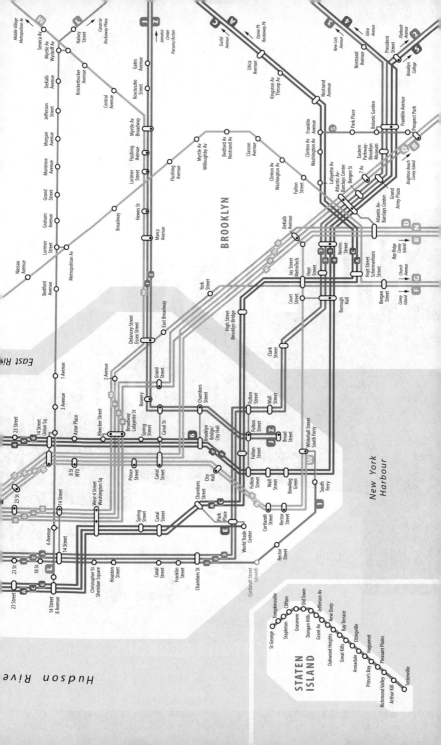

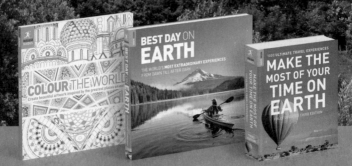